Society in Action

Society in Action: Introduction to Sociology
Second Edition

William F. Kenkel
University of Kentucky

HARPER & ROW, PUBLISHERS, New York
Cambridge, Hagerstown, Philadelphia, San Francisco,
London, Mexico City, São Paulo, Sydney

1817

Photo credits: Facing page 1, Malave, Stock, Boston; 5, Joel Gordon; 7, Anspach, EPA; 10 (top), Burnett, DeWys; 10 (bottom), DeWys; 11, © George W. Gardner; 12, Fishman, DeWys; 19 (top), Siteman, Stock, Boston; 19 (bottom), Bernheim, Woodfin Camp; 22, Lejeune, Stock, Boston; 31, Charles Gatewood; 37, Martens, Nancy Palmer; 42, Vannucci, DeWys; 44, Wolinsky, Stock, Boston; 48, DeWys; 53, UPI; 62, Charles Gatewood; 67, Kirschenbaum, Stock, Boston; 69, Marjorie Pickens; 79, Charles Gatewood; 81, Kessler, Stock, Boston; 84 (top left), © Wood, Taurus; 84 (top right), © Gordon, Taurus; 84 (bottom), Kroll, Taurus; 101, DeWys; 107, Balzer, Stock, Boston; 112 (top), Alexander, Stock, Boston; 112 (bottom), Kirschenbaum, Stock, Boston; 115, Wolinsky, Stock, Boston; 117, Charles Gatewood; 121, Herwig, Stock, Boston; 123, Alper, Stock, Boston; 126, Berndt, Stock, Boston; 131, Hopker, Woodfin Camp; 134, Menzel, Stock, Boston; 140, Marjorie Pickens; 141, Hamlin, Stock, Boston; 142, Marjorie Pickens; 145, Hopker, Woodfin Camp; 150, Herbert, DeWys; 155, Southwick, Stock, Boston; 160, Marjorie Pickens; 164, Kroll, Taurus; 165, Wolinsky, Stock, Boston; 167, Running, Stock, Boston; 169, Gross, Stock, Boston; 175, Wannemacher, Taurus; 180, Franken, Stock, Boston; 181, Malave, Stock, Boston; 187, Marjorie Pickens; 195, Raynor, DeWys; 197, Mayer, Woodfin Camp; 199, Newman, Woodfin Camp; 203, DeWys; 208, © George Gardner; 220, Zeiberg, Taurus; 225, Franken, Stock, Boston; 229, Charles Gatewood; 231, Kirschenbaum, Stock, Boston; 238, Holland, Stock, Boston; 244, Tracy Ecclesine; 247, Charles Gatewood; 251, Franken, Stock, Boston; 258, Menzel, Stock, Boston; 263, Simon, Stock, Boston; 266, Antman, Stock, Boston; 269, Baldwin, DeWys; 273, Jane Hamilton-Merritt; 274, Newman, Woodfin Camp; 279, © George Gardner; 282, Charles Gatewood; 285, Jane Hamilton-Merritt; 286, Menzel, Stock, Boston; 288, © George Gardner; 295, Czarnecki, Nancy Palmer; 299, Bernheim, Woodfin Camp; 308, Holland, Stock, Boston; 312, Bernheim, Woodfin Camp; 316, Zeiberg, Taurus; 318, 321, 326, Charles Gatewood; 327, Franken, Stock, Boston; 333, Lejeune, Stock, Boston; 335, Armstrong, Rapho/Photo Researchers; 342, Anderson, Woodfin Camp; 344, Johnson, DeWys; 354, Herwig, Stock, Boston; 353, Laycock, Photo Researchers; 360, Charles Gatewood; 367, Collidge, Taurus; 371, Charles Gatewood; 377, Gary Brunleve, Enterprize Photo; 378, Wolinsky, Stock, Boston; 379, Charles Gatewood; 381, UPI; 383, Kroll, Taurus; 384, Evans/Contact, DeWys; 393, Joel Gordon; 394, Bellerose, Stock, Boston; 400 Brody, Stock, Boston; 405, Lawrence, Stock, Boston; 409, Bernheim, Woodfin Camp; 425, Bellerose, Stock, Boston; 417, Taurus; 421, Charles Gatewood; 427, Gazdar, Woodfin Camp; 429, Franken, Stock, Boston; 435, DeWys; 447, Hansen, Stock, Boston; 451, DeWys; 454, UPI; 457, Whitaker, DeWys; 463, Kroll, Taurus; 465, DeWys; 467, Skobe, DeWys; 469, Herwig, Stock, Boston; 475, Bonnell, DeWys; 487, 494, Charles Gatewood; 478, Mast, DeWys; 501, Anderson, Woodfin Camp; 498, 507, Charles Gatewood; 513, © Marjorie Pickens, courtesy AICPA; 519, DeWys; 523, Heron, Woodfin Camp; 524, Hammid, Rapho/Photo Researchers; 527, UPI; 530, 537, Charles Gatewood; 542, © Marjorie Pickens; 543, Kroll, Taurus; 547, © George Gardner; 548, 550, Charles Gatewood; 554, © Joel Gordon

Sponsoring Editor: Alan Spiegel
Developmental Editor: Jackie Estrada
Project Editor: H. Detgen
Designer: Emily Harste
Production Manager: Jeanie Berke
Photo Researcher: Myra Schachne
Compositor: Ruttle, Shaw & Wetherill, Inc.
Printer and Binder: Halliday Lithograph Corporation
Art Studio: J & R Technical Services Inc.
Cover Photo: Newman, Woodfin Camp

Society in Action: Introduction to Sociology, Second Edition

Copyright © 1980 by Harper & Row, Publishers, Inc.

All rights reserved. Printed in the United States of America. No part of this book may be used or reproduced in any manner whatsoever without written permission except in the case of brief quotations embodied in critical articles and reviews. For information address Harper & Row, Publishers, Inc., 10 East 53rd Street, New York, N.Y. 10022.

Library of Congress Cataloging in Publication Data

Kenkel, William F
    Society in action.

    Bibliography: p.
    Includes indexes.
    1. Sociology. I. Title.
HM51.K377   1980   301   79-9267
ISBN 0-06-384486-9

Contents

Preface xv

PART ONE
UNDERSTANDING SOCIOLOGY

1 The Sociological Point of View 4

The Focus of Sociology 6

BOX 1.1 THE SOCIAL FACTS OF WIFE ABUSE 8

   The Study of Social Characteristics 10
   Sociology: The Study of What Is 12
   A Definition of Sociology 13
The Origins of Sociology 13
   Auguste Comte 14
   Herbert Spencer 14
   Karl Marx 15
   Emile Durkheim 16
   Max Weber 17
Models in Contemporary Sociology 18
   The Structural-Functional Model: How Society Holds Together 18
   The Conflict Model: Society in Strife 21
   The Need for Different Models 22
Why Study Sociology? 23

BOX 1.2 WHAT DOES IT ALL MEAN? THE SYMBOLIC INTERACTION MODEL 24

2 Sociology as a Science: Goals and Methods 30

Elements of Scientific Research 33
Theory: The Generalizing Tool 35
   Scientific Theories 35
   Sociological Theories—Predictions and Limitations 36
Concepts and Hypotheses 38

Collecting Data 39
>   BOX 2.1   PUTTING A THEORY TO THE TEST: SHOPLIFTING 40
>   Sampling: Some Represent All 42
>   Research by Observation 43
>   BOX 2.2   THE ETHICS OF PARTICIPANT OBSERVATION 44

Analyzing Data: Finding the Meaning in Facts 47
>   Measures of Central Tendency 47
>   Correlations 48
>   Interpreting Findings 50

Report of the Research 52
Making Predictions 54
Value Judgments, Scientific Neutrality, and Social Responsibility 55
>   BOX 2.3   SHOULD ANY SOCIAL ISSUES BE OFF-LIMITS TO THE SOCIOLOGIST? 56

PART TWO
UNDERSTANDING SOCIAL ORGANIZATION   63

3 Culture 66

Why Culture? 68
>   BOX 3.1   LANGUAGE AND CULTURE 70

The Meaning of Culture 72
>   Ethnocentrism 73
>   Sharing Cultural Alternatives 74
>   Culture: Material and Nonmaterial 74

Functions of Culture 75
>   Ensuring Physical Survival 75
>   BOX 3.2   CAUTION: CULTURE IS AN ABSTRACTION 76
>   Maintaining Group Living 77
>   Meeting Psychological Needs 78

Why a Spectrum of Cultures? 80
>   Geographic Environment 80
>   Race and Culture 82
>   BOX 3.3   DO ANIMALS HAVE CULTURE? 82
>   Human Inventiveness in Meeting Needs 83

The Evolution of Human Cultures 87
>   Technology and Change 87
>   BOX 3.4   THE TASADAY: THE STONE AGE AS THE GARDEN OF EDEN 88
>   A Classification of Human Societies 89

Processes of Cultural Change 91
>   Adding Cultural Elements 92
>   Loss and Redefinition of Cultural Elements 95

4 Socialization 100

BOX 4.1 THE WOLF-GIRLS OF INDIA 102

The Raw Materials for Socialization: Heredity versus Environment 104
The Socialization Process 105
    Cultural Factors in Socialization 107
    Agents of Socialization 109

BOX 4.2 CHILDHOOD SOCIALIZATION IN COMMUNIST CUBA 110

    Methods of Socialization 116
The Self: A Social Creation 118
    The Looking-Glass Self 118
    The Social Steps to the Self 119
Socialization in Adult Life 122

BOX 4.3 JOIN THE SERVICE AND BECOME A MAN 124

5 Positions and Roles in Society 130

The Social System and Its Parts 133
    The Network of Positions 134
    Roles and Role Analysis 135
How Roles Promote Group Stability 136

BOX 5.1 THE GAME OF GUARD AND PRISONER 136

How Roles Change 138
How Roles Are Learned 139
    Learning by Instruction and Observation 139
    Learning by Playing a Reciprocal Role 141
    Learning Through Generalization and Imagination 142
Role Failure: Kinds and Causes 143
    Role Discrepancy 143
    Role Conflict 144

BOX 5.2 ROLE CONFLICT ON THE JOB 146

    Role Strain 148
    Inadequate Role Preparation 148
    Discontinuity in Socialization 149

6 Human Groups 154

Primary Groups 157
    Primary Group Relationships 157

BOX 6.1 SOCIAL OSTRACISM OF JAPANESE GANGSTERS 158

    The Importance of Primary Groups 160
Secondary Groups 162

BOX 6.2 THE NEW CULTS AND THE SEARCH FOR PRIMARY RELATIONSHIPS 162

Group Size 163

viii CONTENTS

    Formal versus Informal Groups 166
    Leadership in Groups 166
    Extragroup Linkage 168
Voluntary Associations 168
    Functions of Voluntary Associations 169

BOX 6.3 SELF-HELP GROUPS 170

    Organizational Needs of Voluntary Associations 173
    Extent of Participation 174
Bureaucracies 174
    Characteristics of Bureaucracy 175
    Problems with Bureaucracies 178
Community and Society 180
Institutions 182

7 The Sociology of Sex Roles 186

Biology and Sex Roles 188
    Anatomical Differences 189
    Hormonal Differences 189
    Hereditary Differences 190
Culture and Sex Roles 191

BOX 7.1 NONVERBAL BEHAVIOR AND SEX-ROLE STEREOTYPES 192

Sex Roles in History 194
Sex Roles in Other Societies 196
    The Soviet Union 196
    The Israeli Kibbutz 198
Sex Roles in the United States 201
    Inequality in Education 201
    Inequality in Occupations 202

BOX 7.2 WOMEN MINERS CAN DIG IT, TOO 204

    Inequality in Earnings 206
    Inequality in Political Power 207
    Inequality in the Home 207
    Why Inequalities? 208
Sex-Role Socialization 211
    The Role of the Schools 211
    The Role of the Mass Media 213
    Growing Up Female 213
Consequences of Sex-Role Stereotyping 214
    Consequences for Society 214
    Consequences for Women 215
    Consequences for Men 216
The Future of Sex Roles 217

BOX 7.3 WOMEN'S LIBERATION AS MEN'S LIBERATION 218

8 Stratification and Mobility 224

The Origins of Inequalities 227
Basic Stratification Concepts 228
    Class, Stratum, Rank 228
    Social Mobility versus Social Rigidity 230
Differential Rewards in the United States 231
    Income Inequalities 232
    Prestige Inequalities 235
The Importance of Social Class 239
    Social Class and Life Chances 240

BOX 8.1 TO WHICH SOCIAL CLASS DO YOU BELONG? 240

    Social Class and Lifestyle 244
Social Mobility 248
    Types of Social Mobility 248
    Technological Change and Social Mobility 249
    Fertility Differentials and Vertical Mobility 249
    Extent of Occupational Mobility 250
Is Social Stratification Necessary? 251

BOX 8.2 EVERYONE HERE IS EQUAL 252

PART THREE
UNDERSTANDING SOCIAL INSTITUTIONS 259

9 The Family 262

Biological Roots of the Family 264
What Is a Family? 265
Marriage: Universal but Varied 267
Functions of the Family 269
    Producing Children 270
    Socializing Children 272

BOX 9.1 THE "FAMILY" IN THE ISRAELI KIBBUTZ 274

    Ascribing Status 275
    Controlling Sexual Behavior 276

BOX 9.2 ARE PARENTS SEXUAL BEINGS? 276

    Meeting the Need for Love 281
    Meeting the Need for Clothes, Food, and Shelter 284
The Future of the Family 288
    Divorce 289
    Cohabitation 290
    Restructuring Marriage 290
    Economic Stress 290

10 Religion and Society 294

The Evolution of Religion 297
Magic, Religion, and Science 298
    Magic and Religion: How Do They Differ? 299
    Science and Religion: Competition and Co-existence 301
The Nature of Religion 303
    Ultimate Meanings 303
    Beliefs 305

BOX 10.1 INDIA'S SACRED COW 306

    Ritual 307
Functions of Religion 309
    Social Functions 309
    Personal Functions 437

BOX 10.2 CULTISM IN THE EXTREME: THE PEOPLES TEMPLE 314

Religion in the United States 317
    Separation of Church and State 317
    Pluralism and Ecumenism 319
    How Religious Are Americans? 321
    The Future of Religion in the United States 323

BOX 10.3 RELIGION AND SOCIAL CLASS 324

11 Education and Society 332

The Functions of Education 334
    Transmission of Knowledge 335
    Equality of Opportunity 336
    Creation of New Knowledge 337
    Placement 338
    Other Educational Functions 339

BOX 11.1 HIGH SCHOOLS AS PRISONS 340

Education in the United States 341
Major Issues in American Education 345
    Problems Concerning the Transmission of Knowledge 345

BOX 11.2 BACK TO THE FUNDAMENTALS 350

    Problems with Equality of Opportunity 351
    Problems with the Custodial Function 358
    Problems with Control of the Schools 360
    Disenchantment with the Schools 363
Education and the Two Chief Sociological Models 364

BOX 11.3 CAN'T READ, JOHNNY? SO SUE THE TEACHER 364

12 Government and Economy: Distributing Goods and Power 370

Evolution of the Political-Economic Institution 373
    The Rise of the Nation-State 374
    The Rise of Mass Society 374
The Economic Institution 375
    Economic Production 375

BOX 12.1 A NATION OF CONSUMERS 376

    Economic Consumption 379
The Institution of Government 380
    Maintaining Sovereignty 381
    Regulating the Economy 383
    Participating in the Economy 384
    Administering the Government 387
Major Political Systems 387
    Totalitarianism 387
    Constitutional Democracy 389
Power and Politics 390
    Dimensions of Power 390
    Power Elite versus Pluralism 391
    People Power 392

BOX 12.2 POLITICAL SOCIALIZATION 394

    A Balanced View of Power 395

PART FOUR
UNDERSTANDING CONFLICT AND CHANGE 401

13 Social and Cultural Change 404

Theories of Social Change 407
    Cyclical Theory 407
    Evolutionary Theory 408
    Structural-Functional Theory 410
    Conflict Theory 410
Social Movements: People as Agents of Change 411

BOX 13.1 THE CROWD AS AN AGENT OF SOCIAL CHANGE 412

    Types of Social Movements 414
    The Natural History of Social Movements 416

BOX 13.2 BIOGRAPHY OF A SOCIAL MOVEMENT: THE ANTIRAPE MOVEMENT 418

    The Results of Social Movements 420
Dealing with Social Change 421

BOX 13.3 SOCIAL CHANGE AND THE IRISH TINKERS 422

    Stages in the Adoption Process 424
    Change and Social Values 427
Change and the Future 428

14 Social Demography 434

The Goals of Social Demography 436
Gathering Demographic Data 438
    Census Data 438
    Registration Data 440
    Surveys and Special Studies 441
Analyzing Demographic Data 441
    Population Pyramids 441
    Dependency Ratios 443
Fertility 444
    Fertility Statistics 444
    Social Factors Affecting Fertility 447
Mortality 451
    Infant Mortality Rates 452

BOX 14.1 MEN, WOMEN, AND DEATH 452

    Life Expectancy 454
Migration 455
    Immigration 455
    Internal Migration 456
World Population Growth 458
    Was Malthus Right? 459
    Population Growth in Western Societies 460
    Population Growth in Developing Countries 462

BOX 14.2 VALUES AND FERTILITY: THE HUTTERITES 462

Population Growth in the United States 465
    Optimum versus Maximum Population Size 466
    Maintaining Replacement Level Fertility 468
    Adjusting to a Stationary Population 469

15 The City 474

The Origin of Cities 476
    World Urbanization Trends 477
    Urbanism in the United States 479
Urban Ecology: The City as a System 483
Slums and Ghettos 486
    Slums: Hells with an Escape Hatch 487
    Ghettos: Hells with No Way Out 488

BOX 15.1 WILL THE FOLKS WHO BROUGHT YOU ACUPUNCTURE BRING YOU CRIME-FREE CITIES? 488

BOX 15.2 YOUNG PROFESSIONALS DISCOVER THE INNER CITY 492

Suburbs 493
    The Myth of Suburbia 494
    The Facts of Suburbia 495
    The Push-Pull of Cities and Suburbs 496

BOX 15.3 LIVING PATTERNS: DAYDREAMS VERSUS FACTS 496

    Social Characteristics of the Suburbs 498
Planning our Urban Future 500
    Urban Planning: The Major Challenge 500
    Planning versus Other Values: The Inescapable Compromises? 501

16 Minority Group Relations 506

Minority Groups 508
What Is Race? 509
    The Origin of Races 510
    Are There Racial Differences in Intelligence? 512
Majority-Minority Relations 514
    Prejudice 514
    Discrimination 514
    Racism 515

BOX 16.1 REVERSE DISCRIMINATION: THE BAKKE CASE 516

    Treatment of Minorities 518
Trends Among Minority Groups in the United States 522
    Indian Americans 522
    Mexican Americans 523
    Puerto Rican Americans 525
    Japanese Americans 525
    American Jews 527
    Blacks 528

BOX 16.2 PIOUS RACISM 528

17 Deviancy 536

Types of Deviancy 539
    The Deviant as Criminal 539
    The Deviant as Mentally Ill 540

BOX 17.1 THE FAT PERSON AS TRIPLE DEVIANT 540

    The Deviant as Social Dropout 543
Social Theories of Deviancy 544
    The Anomie Theory 544
    Deviant Subculture Theory 546
    Labeling Theory 547
    Needed: Integration of the Three Theories 549
Major Forms of Deviancy in the United States 549

Drug Abuse 549
Homosexuality 553
Crime and Juvenile Delinquency 557

BOX 17.2 FEAR OF CRIME 560

White Collar Crime: Crime by "Noncriminals" 563

Glossary 567
Bibliography 577

INDEXES
Name Index 589
Subject Index 593

Preface

The overriding concern in the writing of the first edition of this text was to produce a book that would help students learn sociology. It was hoped that students would come to see the sense in, appreciate, and even become fond of what C. Wright Mills called the "sociological imagination"—that unique way of looking at reality that is sociological. The book was designed to help students understand the basic concepts of sociology, which is necessary before they can use the sociological imagination, and learn of sociological findings that make the imagination come alive. For instructors, the book was meant to be a tool that would assist them in that sometimes difficult, sometimes frustrating, but always potentially rewarding task of teaching sociology. These were the hopes and challenges of the first edition.

The challenges of the first edition have taken on new dimensions as a result of my own growth and the reactions of students, instructors, and reviewers. The same primary goal has been retained, but the challenge was accepted to improve the text in every way possible. Accordingly, a careful, painstaking review was made of everything in the text—the organization of the chapters; the pedagogical aids, such as chapter openers and summaries; the methods of presentation, including charts, graphs, and pictures; the basic concepts presented; and the style and level of the writing itself. As a result, there is much that is new in this second edition.

One important change made for this edition is the emphasis on evolutionary theory. The general concept of the role of technology in sociocultural change is introduced early, in Chapter 3. In later chapters the approach is developed for specific areas, as I deal, for example, with the evolution of the family, of social stratification, of sex-role differentiation, of religion, and of the economic institution. The evolutionary thread that winds through the text serves to integrate the material and to keep the focus of the text on human societies as a whole.

Reactions to the first edition showed me that I was on the right track in concluding that a balance was needed between contemporary relevancy and historical and geographical breadth. The former has been addressed by an updating of all of the statistical materials and by the inclusion of recent studies from the literature. Then, too, there are boxed inserts on contemporary matters, such as the antirape movement, the fat person as deviant, and the Peoples Temple cult. The question of breadth has been dealt with through the use of more cross-cultural references and studies. At times, major sections of a chapter are devoted to cross-cultural emphases, such as the experiences of the Soviet Union and the Israeli kibbutzim with regard to sex roles and the position of women or, on a lesser scale, deviancy among the Mbuti Pygmies and the Sardinians. There are boxed inserts dealing with cross-cultural matters, such as government day care in Cuba and Japanese gangsters, which should help students to see that the focus of the book is on sociology and not merely on American sociology in the 1980s.

Chapter 7, "The Sociology of Sex Roles," is new to this edition. Most of us see the area of sex roles as important, interesting, and relevant to the concerns of today's students. Treated sociologically, the topic loses none of its importance and interest but provides an excellent way to apply sociological concepts, to illustrate sociological methodology, and perhaps to test sociological objectivity. The chapter is not a polemical appendage to please instructors or to interest students but is integrated with the rest of the text. Concepts such as status, role differentiation, socialization, resocialization, and ethnocentrism come alive. Students will learn that discrimination can be measured and not just deplored; in the process they will learn what kind of and how much discrimination against women is going on in American society and elsewhere in the areas of education, occupations, earnings, politics, and the home.

As was mentioned, no aspect of the book was spared when it came to revisions necessary for enhancing it as a tool for teaching and learning sociology. Most of the boxed inserts are new, and all of them are better integrated into the chapters. Part and chapter openers have been rewritten to provide students with an overview of what is to come, and the new chapter summaries help them to review the material that has been covered. Key sociological terms are listed at the end of the chapter in which they are first used. The glossary at the end of the book contains definitions of all the key terms. In this way, the definitions are readily available, but the student need not feel that the most important part of each chapter is the learning of definitions.

There is no way to teach sociology without presenting data, but there are a variety of ways in which data can be presented. In this edition, greater use has been made of charts and graphs, which, I feel, have been artfully prepared. The textual matter accompanying each graph highlights for the student what the graph shows. Great care has been taken in selecting the photographs, always with the student foremost in mind. Pictures have been used liberally in each chapter to illustrate a point, to show how a sociological principle can be applied, or to direct the student's attention to an everyday occurrence that has sociological relevance.

The arrangement of the text benefits from the reactions of many instructors, although, of course, there is a healthy diversity of opinion on the ordering of topics in the introductory course. In Part One, not only is the sociological perspective described at length, but a brief history of the discipline and the chief sociological models in current use are given. The hope is to give the student an appreciation of the healthy divergencies in the field rather than to propogandize for a particular model. New to this edition is attention to the symbolic interaction model. In Chapter 2, the scientific characteristics of sociology and research methodology are thoroughly described. Inclusion of case studies and participant observation methods reinforce the theme that there is no single, correct approach to sociological study.

The aim of Part Two remains that of treating the basic concepts necessary for understanding social organization in such a way as to clarify for students the world of their own experience. The completely reworked chapter "Human Groups" (Chapter 6) and the new chapter "The Sociology of Sex Roles" (Chapter 7) appear in this part. The effort to make the student's own world understandable while illuminating sociological concepts is continued through Part Three, on social institutions, and Part Four, on change and conflict in societies. At no time, however, is the sociologist's analytical concern abandoned for a "social problems" approach—even on such topics as sex roles, ethnic relations, urban life, and deviancy.

Considerable effort has gone into the new supplemental materials that accompany the text. The Instructor's Manual has a section, for each chapter in the text, on ideas for lectures and classroom discussion. Some of these suggestions require little advance preparation on the part of the instructor. Another major section of the manual contains essay test questions that, of course, also can be used in the classroom to stimulate classroom discussion. A separate Test Bank with multiple-choice questions is available. The goal of the Study Guide is to help students learn the material in the text. It explains how each chapter is broken down into smaller learning components, reviews the major concepts in each component, and provides a postcheck that requires students to phrase answers in their own words.

I have benefited immensely from the constructive criticism of those who reviewed the manuscript at earlier stages. The text has profited from the insights of Joan Huber, University of Illinois at Urbana-Champaign; Charlotte G. O'Kelly, Providence College; Martha Loustaunau, New Mexico State University; Ellen Nason Rosengarten, Sinclair Community College; and Gregory Staat, Emporia State University.

My many colleagues, who sent comments on the first edition, also deserve my thanks; and I trust that each will read this personally and understand why he or she could not be listed by name. Marlene Pettit typed the drafts and revisions of the manuscript. I have thanked her for her skill and for her extreme cooperativeness, but my appreciation must be shared with a larger audience.

Jackie Estrada, the developmental editor, has been intimately involved with the revision since its inception. She has seen it through a number of drafts and has prepared some of the boxed inserts. Her major contributions have been to style and clarity, and they are evident, especially to me, on every page of the text.

William F. Kenkel

Society in Action

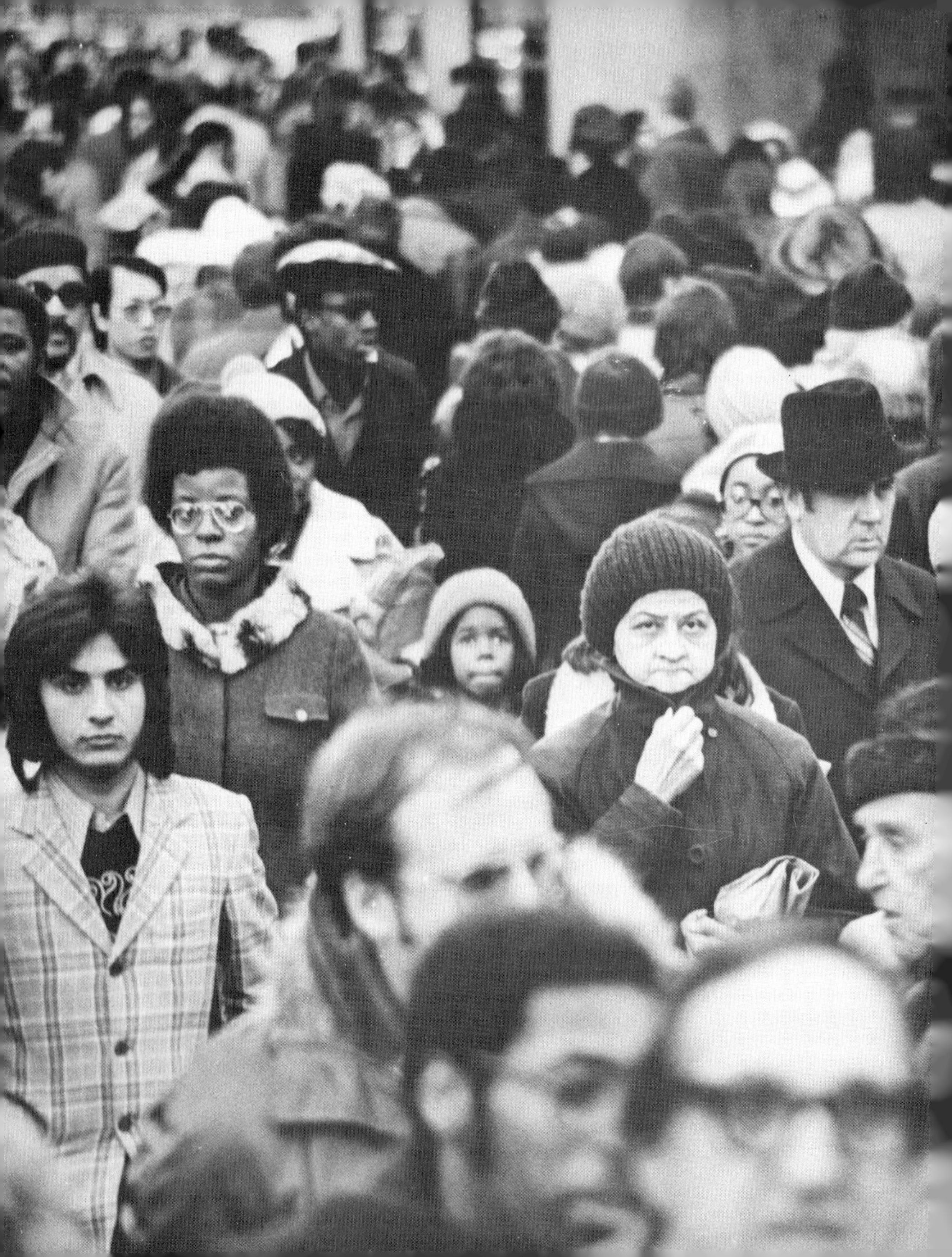

Part One

Understanding Sociology

Have you ever stood on a street corner in a large city and just watched the people go by? By their dress, you might have imagined that some were on their way to their offices, shopping, or looking for a place to eat. You might have thought about all the other lives that would be touched by these people. Those going to their offices would be interacting with supervisors and secretaries making phone calls to people across town or across the country; the people out shopping would be going home to their families or to a roommate and might greet or talk with dozens of people before the day was over; those looking for a place to eat would eventually be interacting with waitresses and cashiers.

By simply standing on a street corner for a few minutes, then, you can begin to sense how people's actions affect and are affected by those of others. All their activities somehow fit together, and this interaction enables the work of the city to get done and people to get the food and goods they need. But this is an example of just one city in our large society. The more you think about it, the more your curiosity may be aroused. So many people doing so many things, but their lives seem to intermesh. What holds society together, and how does it work?

Many of the earliest records are in the form of answers rather than questions. The tendency to keep the questions and the thoughts about them to oneself but to make the answer public was a rather common human trait until only a few centuries ago. Nevertheless, if we go back to about the fifth century B.C. in classical Greece, we find that a few people recorded their questions or tried to formulate ways of measuring the reliability of their answers. That is, there were people who became aware that appearances can be deceiving and that a method of asking and answering questions is essential for getting at the truth of whatever is being investigated. They no longer accepted imaginative answers, myths, and parables at face value.

Unfortunately, despite a few glimmerings here and there (about one in every five centuries that we know of), some 2000 years had to pass before, in the sixteenth century, the intuitions of the Greek philosophers began to be refined into the set of assumptions and rules that today we call the scientific method. Like our knowledge of the world, our ways of acquiring that knowledge have undergone a constant, gradual refinement. Not only did the instruments of science improve, but so did the rules that govern the scientist's ways of working and of judging the value of the results.

Success bred success, and from the seventeenth to the nineteenth century the number of scientists grew immensely, as did the scope of their investigations. More than once it was declared that science had finally solved every mystery of the physical world. Although such boasts were short-lived, they do show the confidence that was placed in science and the satisfaction many felt about the work that it had done.

Those who had now come to be called scientists had, for all previous centuries, been called natural philosophers, for their methods had been much like those of other philosophers (the moral philosophers, metaphysicians, political theorists, and so on). Usually, in fact, the same people felt capable of pursuing knowledge in all of these fields of inquiry (Aristotle, the man who was known for tens of centuries simply as "the Philosopher," is usually also considered the father of most sciences).

While the natural philosophers were perfecting their methods and evolving into scientists, it was rare for anyone to confuse human beings with atoms, stars, or living biological cells. The methods of studying these objects were not applied to people, and the study of societies and of men and women continued to be a mixture of logic, ethical rule-laying, and myths about our origins and nature. What is and what should be were considered inseparable. The one man who proposed to tell his prince about the realities of political power, Machiavelli, saw his name become synonymous with cynicism and evil.

Not until the nineteenth century did anyone seriously propose to study people and society by the same methods that had yielded so much knowledge of the physical world. Those who did were moved to do so partly by the unsettled conditions of the advanced societies of their day; for the social, economic, and political consequences of the Industrial Revolution were enormously troubling. So Auguste Comte, and soon after him, a growing number of others, divorced themselves from social philosophy and pursued social science.

Each of the social sciences adapts the general methods and assumptions of science to its own field of study. The particular insight of sociologists, and the one they seek to refine and expand in detail by the use of the scientific method, is that human beings are social animals. Although sociologists do not deny the fact that each of us is an individual, they are well aware that each of us is also a member of various social groupings, and that our beliefs, values, and patterns of behavior are the products of our membership in groups and our interactions with other people.

Sociologists maintain that studying the individual as an individual is like studying that person in an artificial vacuum. You may find this confusing at first, for don't you experience yourself as an individual? Aren't your joys, your fears, your frustrations your own, to be shared with others only by the effort of communication? That much is true, but it is only part of the truth. For example, suicide is surely the ultimate individual act to which a person can be driven by no less than extreme despair, physical pain, personal loneliness, or insanity. Yet Emile Durkheim's classic sociological study, Suicide, demonstrated that social factors play an important role in suicide rates.

But like any science, sociology includes a variety of other processes as well, without which data collecting—by whatever methods—would be useless. Without the fundamental premise that the world shows order and regularity in its workings, no science could have developed. For, each science is basically a collection of interrelated methods of confirming such regularity and finding the laws by which it operates. To do this, physical and social scientists form concepts, make and confirm generalizations, and from these create theories, which in turn are the bases for hypotheses to be tested by the methods of research.

True, scientific investigation begins and ends with observation of the perceptible world, but without these mental activities there can be no true observation. Consider the myth that Isaac Newton discovered the law of gravity when a falling apple landed on his head. Now ask yourself: If Newton wasn't the first to be sitting under a tree when an apple fell, why was he the first to see a law of universal scope in the fall of that humble object?

So the two chapters that follow should give you the perspectives and methods you'll need as you begin to try to solve the puzzle of society. The first chapter will familiarize you with sociology, the second with the scientific method and its use by sociologists.

There are many approaches to the study of human behavior. The biologist, for example, examines the physiological bases of behavior, while the psychologist explores the mental and emotional causes of behavior. The sociologist, however, looks beyond individual behavior to the group or society in which the behavior occurs. Divorce and unemployment, for example, can be viewed as personal problems, but the sociologist looks for the roots of these problems in the system of marriage itself and in the economic system endorsed by our society. From the sociological point of view, knowledge of the groups to which people belong is fundamental to an understanding of their behavior. Thus, the focus of sociological study is on social characteristics and social groups.

The scientific study of human behavior in groups did not just emerge suddenly. Indeed, the origins of sociology can be traced to the writings of social philosophers in the nineteenth century. Because the discipline is relatively young, sociologists are still exploring several different approaches to the study of human interaction. Some sociologists use the structural-functional model, which compares society to a living organism; others use the conflict model, which considers clashes of interest groups as a basic feature of society; and still others take what is useful from several models of society. To get a feel for the field of sociology, one must know something about the sociological approach to understanding human behavior, about the origins of the discipline, and about the current frameworks or models used by sociologists. These are, therefore, the main topics that will be dealt with in this introductory chapter.

1
The Sociological Point of View

It has been said, "Man is the only animal that blushes . . . or needs to." Perhaps this is so. It has also been said that humans are the only animals that drink when they are not thirsty and that make love in every season. Again, perhaps this is so. Actually, there are many more important traits that make humans unique and set them apart from the rest of the animal kingdom. It all depends on which slice of reality you choose to examine—with which aspect of humanness you deal. The human's highly developed brain, upright posture, and opposable thumb clearly distinguish this animal from all others. Equally important, these physical characteristics as well as mental and emotional processes can be studied in a scientific way; and we can learn how such characteristics and processes affect overt individual behavior. For every aspect of our biological and psychological being, there is a science or a discipline of study. Because the human being is also a social animal, there is a science that studies this aspect of human existence—the science of sociology.

We are social animals in many ways. To become fully human, we need the nurturance of other human beings. Studies of children reared in isolation demonstrate that, although one can survive physically with a bare minimum of interaction, children raised away from social contact lack almost all the traits we call "human" (Davis, 1947). The only reason we have personalities is that we have interacted with other persons. Human beings have a deep, powerful interest in other human beings: we seek acceptance in ongoing human groups or establish new groupings if none exist to meet our needs; we derive satisfaction from interacting with others; we desire companionship and response from others in our groups. To be sure, we also band together to destroy people or to express our hate for them, but even in such instances our social nature is apparent.

THE FOCUS OF SOCIOLOGY

To understand the behavior of individuals, the sociologist looks beyond the specific behavior (Mills, 1959). For example, although a couple with serious marital difficulties may view their problem as personal, it is a fact that, in the United States, more than one out of three marriages end in divorce. This figure suggests that there are serious problems with the institutions of marriage and the family. Thus, even though a marriage counselor may be able to help a husband and wife adjust to their situation, and in this sense, deal with their personal problems, the sociologist would approach the issue of divorce in quite another way. From the sociologist's point of view, an important question may have to do with how the role of the woman makes her subordinate to her husband. Is the wife's inferior status in a marriage compatible with our country's expressed values of equality and democracy? Has the role she is expected to play been made obsolete by social and technological developments? In short, do society's expectations of how a wife should feel and behave make divorce almost inevitable?

The sociologist would also examine how the family has declined as an educator and as a provider for the economic needs of husband, wife, and children, and how many married couples are ill-prepared for marriage and burdened with glamorized, romantic myths. Thus, the sociologist would state the problem and search for its explanations in the institution of marriage, not in a series of individual crises to be dealt with by the unhappy couples.

The problem of unemployment further illustrates the sociological perspective. A man or a woman who cannot find work has a personal problem, and so does his or her family. To solve this problem, the job skills of the man or the woman could be matched with available employment opportunities. But when unemployment is widespread, there is no such personal solution. Recurring slumps in the economy, the automation of factories, and the changing nature of work, which renders some skills and abilities obsolete, are social factors in unemployment that individual ingenuity cannot change. In the same way, an individual has little power to change a system that puts down women, blacks, and other groups or that creates urban sprawl or international wars. An individual may search for ways to adjust to his or her personal situation, but the sociologist looks into the broader issues and into the institutions in society in order to explain specific conditions. (For another example of this approach, see Box 1.1.)

The causes of racial problems lie not so much in individual personalities but in the society which for years has systematically practiced discrimination.

BOX 1.1
THE SOCIAL FACTS OF WIFE ABUSE

What makes a man beat a woman—a woman he has solemnly promised to love, cherish, and protect for a lifetime? This is the sort of question a psychologist might ask and pursue, but perhaps it is the wrong question for a sociologist, since it implies that the major cause of the problem is to be found in the personalities of the individual wife beaters. As we have noted in this chapter, sociologists look beyond the behavior of individuals to the social factors that might be related to the behavior in question. What social facts can help explain why each year over three million women are severely beaten by their husbands?

One important social fact is the social definition of wife beating. Is it really defined as deviant? Wife beating is commonly thought of as a family affair, something to be settled between husband and wife. Studies have shown that bystanders are more willing to intervene when they see a man beating another man than when they see a man beating a woman (Borofsky, Stollak, and Meese, 1971). In the latter case, it is assumed that the woman is the man's wife and that what he does to her is his business. Other types of assault are considered criminal deviance; but wife assault is not always considered as such.

The social definition of wife beating as a private affair—almost a husband's right—affects how wife beating is dealt with by the police and the courts. Police officers called to the home by neighbors don't always take the matter seriously and often try to get the couple to calm down and settle the matter peacefully. Some officers actively discourage the wife from pressing charges against her husband. They may ask her what she did to provoke the attack, or they may suggest that if she makes trouble for her husband the next beating may be worse. They may point out that bringing charges against the husband will involve legal costs and lengthy court appearances, with no guarantee of conviction. It _is_ true that convictions for wife beating have been difficult to obtain. The attack often occurs at night and in the home, so that there are no witnesses—only medical evidence in the form of bruises and marks on the wife's body.

Another social fact that affects the incidence of wife beating is the prevalence of violence in our society. The battered-child syndrome has finally come into the open, and we are now aware that millions of children have been severely beaten, maimed, and even killed by their own parents. What is more, husbands are beaten by their wives. The number of husbands who are victims of spouse abuse is not nearly as large as the number of wives who are victims, but because men are supposed to be the stronger, more dominant sex, most husbands are too embarrassed to report such incidents when they do occur. The sociologist Suzanne Steinmetz (1977) holds that the most unreported crime is not wife beating but husband beating. Millions of Americans have grown up in violent homes: as children, either they were severely beaten themselves, or they witnessed their fathers beating their mothers or vice versa. The experience of violence in the family is thought to produce more violence in the next generation.

What about the victims of wife beating, the battered wives? Instead of blaming the victim by asking what kind of weird, possibly masochistic, women stay with husbands who beat them, sociologists look to society and to the dependent role that is assigned to many women. It has been found that many battered wives married quite young and have not developed the skills or received the education they need to make it economically feasible to leave a violent home. Even women with marketable skills who have been at home rearing children for a number of years are dismayed to discover that it is difficult for a woman to get a good job and that the annual income of female workers is only about two-thirds that of male workers. Many wives would find it difficult to support themselves alone, much less any dependent children. To add to her difficulties, the battered wife who does leave her husband may find that she is ineligible for welfare because she "voluntarily" left the home. Unable to support themselves and their children, many battered wives thus remain with their husbands and can only hope that future beatings will not be too bad.

Identifying the social factors associated with wife beating does not mean that nothing can or should be done to change the behavior of the wife beater. Most such men are in serious need of counseling or treatment. On an immediate basis, however, recognizing the social factors associated with wife abuse helps us to develop remedies for the problem. For example, some cities have established shelters where the battered wife and her children can find refuge. In recognition of the economic plight of the battered wife, some states have made it easier to obtain an inexpensive divorce if it seems that there is no hope for the marriage. In some cities rigorous training has been provided for policemen to sensitize them to the problem of the battered wife, so that they will take her and her needs seriously. Of course, these are only stop-gap measures. Closer to the root of the problem are the economic discrimination against women and their role in society in general—factors that keep so many wives dependent on their husbands.

You may think of death as a personal, private act. Yet culture teaches us the meaning of death and there are numerous social expectations concerning how we should handle the dead and how we should react to death.

The Study of Social Characteristics

From what we have said, it should be clear that sociology concentrates on the group basis of human behavior. Although groups obviously are made up of individuals, the fundamental unit of the sociologist's analysis is not the individual but the group. To understand human behavior, the sociologist studies the family, criminal gangs, societies, religious organizations, cities, rural communities, and many other groupings, both large and small. In seeking to explain the behavior of individuals in groups, the sociologist concen-

THE SOCIOLOGICAL
POINT OF VIEW

trates on the **social characteristics** shared by the individuals. It is not always easy, however, to distinguish between individual characteristics and social characteristics. For example, age is an individual trait, but society also treats age as a category, and on the basis of age, gives or withholds privileges, such as driving a car or signing a contract.

The way in which sociologists can use social characteristics to explain human behavior can be illustrated by a look at the birth rate in the United States (see Chapter 14). Birth can be viewed as a biological matter, for obviously, if sperm and ovum never meet, there can be no conception and no birth. Yet, we have known for some time that education, race, and rural or urban residence are also related to the birth rate. In the United States, college-educated women have fewer than half as many children as women who did not go to high school—a rather striking difference. Black women have more children than white women, and rural women have more children than urban women. The differences in family size in a society can thus be understood by learning what social characteristics are linked with family size. Thus, anyone seeking to lower the birth rate of a society would have to find ways of changing the behavior not of individuals but of large groups of people.

The people in this middle-class suburb have similar incomes and work at the same kinds of jobs. The social characteristic of middle class is also related to voting behavior, recreational preferences, educational values, and many other things.

Sociology: The Study of What Is

It will become clear later in this chapter and in Chapter 2 that sociology, as a social science, conforms to the general definition of a science. And as such, sociology is a descriptive, not a normative, discipline: it is concerned with what is, not with what should be. Although sociologists study different groups' values and ideas of right and wrong, they do not advocate one system of beliefs over another. However, sociological knowledge can be used normatively by others. For instance, in the chapter on social demography, we present information on our past, present, and probable future national birth rates. The organization Zero Population Growth (ZPG) drew heavily on such information and reached the normative position that our birth rate is too high and should be reduced, so that the population will not continue to grow. As a citizen, a sociologist may well be in sympathy with the goals of ZPG; but as a sociologist, he or she would not recommend the adoption of

The aim of the sociologist is to study human behavior in groups, not to approve or disapprove of it.

a particular value position. As we shall discuss in Chap[ ]
all sociologists adopt this value-free stance.

A Definition of Sociology

At this point you should have some idea about how sociologists view the social world and human behavior within it. Although understanding the point of view of sociology is more important than defining the field, some definition of it may help you keep in mind its chief features as you study its concerns and methods throughout this book.

Sociology is the study of interaction among people and of the way this interaction affects human behavior. People are interacting whenever they respond to the actions of other people and whenever their actions produce responses from others. A greeting is interaction, for in it, one person is acknowledging the other's presence and his or her acknowledgment receives a return greeting. A formal meeting is interaction, and so is a mugging, a casual conversation, a gesture, or a kiss. Even posture, the tightening of muscles, or other manifestations of "body language" can be interaction if these actions are either a response to or affect the behavior of another (Fast, 1971). The essence of interaction is that the spoken words, gestures, writings, or other acts of one person influence another person in some way.

The study of human interaction and how it has affected human groups and societies has fascinated scholars and scientists for a long time. To give you some sense of the origin and development of this interest, let us turn to a brief account of the history of sociology.

THE ORIGINS OF SOCIOLOGY

Sociology is as old as the efforts of humans to understand themselves and society. In ancient times many rulers and thinkers observed human behavior and speculated about its effects on society. Often, they drew up codes of laws to be followed by all for the good of society. Examples of such laws are the commandments of Moses and the code of Hammurabi, which was written over 4000 years ago. The 282 laws in this code dealt with the treatment of children, property rights, husband-wife relations, and other matters affecting the welfare of society. In *The Republic,* written in the fourth century B.C., Plato planned an ideal society, describing in great detail his ideas about the proper organization of the government, the economy, education, and the family. Many philosophers, religious leaders, and kings have spoken—often brilliantly—on the human condition, the ills of society, and the promotion of harmonious social relationships. All who have tried to understand the behavior of their fellow human beings can be thought of as forerunners of sociology. Their speculations, however, were a far cry from the daring idea that came into prominence in the nineteenth century—the idea that society could be studied by the scientific method—which was the true beginning of sociology. The man who put forth the idea of a science of society was Auguste Comte.

Auguste Comte

The Frenchman Auguste Comte (1798–1857) is often called "the father of sociology," for not only did he develop an elaborate system for the scientific study of society, but he called this discipline "sociology." In many important ways, his writings, which appeared between 1830 and 1854, provided the foundation of the discipline. Comte divided all of human history into three great stages: the theological, the metaphysical, and the positive. During the first, or theological, stage, people used theology to explain everything that occurred, and they believed that all phenomena were "produced by the immediate action of supernatural beings" (Comte, 1853). In the second, or metaphysical, stage, abstract principles of peoples' own creation, such as the idea of "goodness," were thought of as ultimate causes. During the final, or positive, stage "the mind has given over the vain search after Absolute notions, the origin and destination of the universe, the causes of phenomena, and applies itself to the study of their laws" (Comte, p. 2). **Positivism,** Comte's system of thinking, stresses the existence of invariable laws and the need for observation, experimentation, and comparison to discover and interpret the causes of events.

Thus, the idea that society should be studied scientifically was expressed well over a hundred years ago. Comte was mainly concerned with social order, or *social statics,* as he called it, which he saw as the forces that held the parts of society together and governed the relationships of one part to the other. But he also sought laws of *social dynamics,* or social change, thinking these laws would explain the progression of society to an ideal state.

Comte's dual interest in social order and social change is still the core of modern sociology, which deals with social order by describing the regularity in social interaction that tends to keep human groups together. Unlike Comte, however, modern sociologists view change and conflict as normal processes of ongoing groups rather than as necessary steps in the progress of society toward an unchanging utopia.

Herbert Spencer

Herbert Spencer (1820–1903) was a wealthy, straight-laced English gentleman. He employed numerous secretaries to collect facts on human behavior from all over the world, while he was content to remain in his library and write an elaborate theory of society. Like Comte, Spencer was a *positivist,* and also like Comte, he believed that the scientific study of society would solve humanity's social problems and maladjustments.

He stated that sociology is "the study of evolution in its most complex form (Spencer, 1873). He believed in the existence of a "natural law" (a law operating unyieldingly through the processes of nature) that would guide societies through progressively higher stages and lead eventually to "the survival of the fittest" (a phrase borrowed by Darwin). In keeping with his ideas on social evolution, Spencer opposed aiding the poor and the dependent, for to do so would interfere with the process of natural selection. And he was against free education, holding that those who truly wanted to learn would find a way to do so.

Spencer's individualistic ideas on the survival of the fittest were adopted by a few early American sociologists but were generally not well accepted. Yet, his strong conviction that the scientific method could be applied with great benefit to the study of society was readily accepted by many early sociologists. Modern sociologists recognize that societies undergo fundamental changes as they move from the hunting and gathering stage, through an agricultural stage, to an industrial stage (see Chapter 3). The changes are seen as a result of an increase in human knowledge of and ability to deal with the environment. Thus, Spencer's theory that societies are governed by natural laws of social evolution has, for the most part, been abandoned.

Karl Marx

While Spencer used an evolutionary model of social development to support his conservative, laissez-faire political arguments, Karl Marx (1818–1883) focused on conflict within society in order to buttress his political theories of the extreme left. According to Marx's model, each stage of civilization contains within itself "the seeds of its own destruction." Each must be followed inevitably by the next, higher stage. But, because in each stage there is resistance to the coming of the new, in order to achieve each new step in the evolutionary process, revolution is necessary.

Marx was an *economic determinist*. He explained history, society, and social change as functions of the economic relationships between people and between groups. Marx defined groups basically by their economic characteristics—that is, according to whether or not they owned the means of production (factories, machines, investment capital). He saw the capitalistic system as plagued with injustices and "internal contradictions" and felt that a struggle between the workers and the capitalists—that is, between those who did not own the means of production and those who did—was inevitable. Because the system resisted change, Marx believed that only a major revolution could bring about a classless society.

Modern sociologists are indebted to Marx for his focus on conflict within society. Although his ideas on resistance to social change are generally considered extreme and seem to be discredited by history, they are nevertheless a useful reminder that change is not always orderly and that people and groups often find it difficult to accept and adjust to social change.

Emile Durkheim

Another early social theorist, the Frenchman Emile Durkheim (1858–1917), also developed an evolutionary model of society. Durkheim focused on the division of labor—the degree of specialization within a society. According to Durkheim, societies can be arranged on a scale ranging from those with very little specialization to those with a great deal of specialization. In smaller communities with little division of labor, people are held together by the strong bonds of their personal, intimate groups, such as the family and the church. Durkheim called this type of social cohesion **mechanical solidarity.** In larger societies with greater division of labor, social cohesion rests on the formal contracts and common interests that bind persons to one another. Durkheim called this form of social cohesion **organic solidarity.**

Other sociologists have typed human societies in ways similar to Durkheim's, suggesting that by describing the different kinds of bonds between people Durkheim was getting at a basic feature of human groups. You will note the similarity, too, between Durkheim's notion of mechanical solidarity and the concept of *primary group*, which will be discussed in Chapter 6. Primary groups are characterized by intimate, personal, and usually face-to-face relations among members, whereas in secondary groups people are bound by more formal ties. Although contemporary sociologists do not accept Durkheim's notion of evolution as a fixed, unchangeable course of movement from one type of society to another, they do accept as fundamental the change in societies from primary, personal relations to impersonal, secondary ones (see Becker, 1950; Redfield, 1941).

Durkheim's study of suicide, published in 1897, is considered the first scientific study in sociology. In this work Durkheim sought to discover whether the degree to which people are integrated into cohesive groups is related to suicide rates. According to his theory, people who have strong emotional ties to an enduring group, such as the family or the Church, should, as a *category*, have a lower suicide rate than those without such ties. Durkheim collected statistics on suicide from many European countries for many years. The results of his study showed that single people had a higher rate of suicide than did married people.

Earlier, we discussed how sociologists use social characteristics to explain human behavior. You can see how, in his study of suicide, Durkheim was the first to set forth this idea and also the first to demonstrate the validity of the sociological approach. He did not try to explain individual acts of suicide in terms of mental illness or emotional stress or imbalance; rather, he studied how the *rate* of suicide varied among different *categories* of people. This method of study is an excellent example of the sociological perspective.

Max Weber

The German sociologist Max Weber (1864–1920) received his academic training in economics and law. He taught at the University of Heidelberg, but because of severe ill health, he dropped out of academic work for eighteen years. Because he was independently wealthy, Weber used this time for travel and scholarly research.

Weber's contributions to sociology were enormous. Many of his important ideas on the nature of sociology are contained in writings that deal with concrete problems. He did not formulate a grand scheme of society as did Comte, Spencer, and Marx, but instead he wrote widely on such social topics as religion, economics, bureaucracy, the city, and social history. (In Chapter 8 we will deal with Weber's ideas on power and social class.)

One of Weber's most important studies is *The Protestant Ethic and the Spirit of Capitalism* (1958). His methods and logic in this work are as fascinating as his findings. The data that he collected, indicating that the Protestant areas of Germany were wealthier than the Catholic sections, suggested to Weber that there was a relationship between the economic and religious systems of society. Capitalism, as Weber saw it, is a system of profit-making enterprises that are all bound together. Mature capitalism, the rise of which he sought to explain, is more than just profit-making: it is a rational activity that stresses order and discipline. Success in profit-making is seen as an indication that the organization is functioning smoothly and efficiently.

In the Calvinist form of Protestantism, salvation was thought to be predetermined; that is, a person was born already saved by God or damned to an eternity in Hell. But Calvinists also believed that one's worldly success was a sign that one was chosen. Calvinism stressed that people should work hard at their worldly callings and should practice self-discipline. To work hard and to achieve worldly success were thus important elements in Calvinist doctrine.

Weber noted that the kind of behavior promoted by the religious doctrines of Calvinism closely fitted the behavior needed for the success of mature capitalism. As he saw it, if general economic conditions are ripe for the development of mature capitalism, the Protestant ethic will stimulate its emergence. Not content to rest his case with the study of Western societies, Weber studied the economic systems and religions of India and China. These studies led him to conclude that economic conditions cannot in themselves guarantee the development of capitalism; another ingredient is necessary—an ethical, or moral, system that promotes behavior conducive to capitalistic success. Weber's study is not merely of historical interest. A recent research article compared the occupational histories of 161 fathers and sons and found that Protestant men tend toward greater occupational and educational achievement than do Catholic men (Crowley and Ballweg, 1971).

Max Weber's definition of sociology as "a science which attempts the interpretive understanding of social action in order thereby to arrive at a causal explanation of its course and effects" is close to our definition of sociology as the study of social interaction. Note, too, that Weber held sociology to be a science and that he saw sociology's mission as the explanation, not merely the description, of human behavior. Many modern sociologists share these ideas.

MODELS IN CONTEMPORARY SOCIOLOGY

Sociology is a young science. As the field has developed, the ideas and theories of the early founders have not always been useful for explaining the conditions and problems of human society. For example, the evolutionary model, with its assumption that all societies progress through immutable stages of growth toward some kind of utopia, does not square with the known facts. Ancient China, once more advanced than many other cultures, later slowed down in its development and was surpassed by European civilizations. The many primitive tribes studied by anthropologists show a variety of change patterns, proving that they grow in different ways and at different rates. Thus, the early assumptions about rules of social progress have been abandoned and new ways of studying the social world have been developed. Today, different models of society guide research and determine what aspects of social reality the researcher will study.

A **model** is a set of integrated assumptions about some system we wish to understand. Sociological models are used to explain the ordered set of assumptions the researcher uses to understand human interaction and its results. The two most common sociological models are the structural-functional model and the conflict model.

The Structural-Functional Model: How Society Holds Together

The **structural-functional model** implicitly compares society to a living organism (see Parsons, 1951, 1949; Merton, 1957). Just as your body has its digestive, circulatory, and reproductive systems, a society has interacting systems, which are called *structures*. The family system, the religious system, the educational system, and the political system are the major structures of society.

How a structure contributes to the survival and well-being of the total society is its *function*. Structural-functional analysts thus examine the total society in order to determine how the structures that make up the whole af-

Structural-functionalism focuses on what keeps society running smoothly. Every society has a system, with rules and customs, for distributing goods to its people.

fect that society. In Chapter 9, for example, we analyze the functions of the family—we look at the consequences that different aspects of this institution have for the survival of society and the solution of social problems. An obvious function of the family is to care for dependent infants and to train and educate children so that they will become acceptable adult members of the society. If any society is to endure, this function must be performed in one way or another. Here, again, the sociological point of view is clear. Although a man or a woman may like to rear children and may get married to make this possible, the sociologist is less concerned with personal satisfactions and motivations than with the social functions served by child-rearing.

Structural-functional analysis yields insights into the workings of human society in many ways. It can reveal how the various structures work together to keep the society in operation—for example, how the family and the school share the task of child-rearing. Structural-functional analysis also shows that social customs are more than merely interesting practices with no relation to the whole of society. For example, although the custom we call "dating" may be something that people do because it is fun, it has a functional importance within the larger institutions of marriage and the family as well. In our society we expect that a husband and wife will like each other and get along well together. Dating serves this expectation by allowing a man and a woman to test their compatibility before committing themselves to marriage. Dating, therefore, is not an isolated social custom but is a functional part of the mate-selection process. In some other cultures, marriages are arranged by parents with the expectation that love and personal attraction will come after the union. In such cultures there is no need for a couple to test their compatibility before marriage, and the custom of dating does not exist.

The structural-functional model also allows us to compare different societies as well as different stages in the same society, which are related points. In studies of different societies, structural-functionalists may discover various structures that perform the same social functions. For example, they may find that in one society children are reared by more specialized persons than their parents, such as in day-care centers. They would then explore how performing the function in this way fits in with other group values, such as an emphasis on communal values. They could also compare how, at different points in the history of a given society, the same structure performed different functions. For example, at one time the family structure might have performed the function of caring for the elderly as well as for the young, whereas at present it cares only for the young.

The structural-functional model is not without its critics. One criticism is that the model is an oversimplified view of social reality. Something may be called functional simply because it seems to work. For example, the pre-Civil War institution of slavery could be labeled as either functional or highly dysfunctional. As a means of producing goods, slavery was functional. But, can any system that virtually tears the country apart and degrades human beings be called functional? The system was actually harmful to the Southern economy, in that cheap labor retarded the development of improved agricultural practices and nonagricultural pursuits. And, of course, the social problems left in the wake of slavery have been with us for more than a century.

Another criticism of structural-functionalism is that it has a conservative bias. By focusing on how certain practices keep society running, it is easy to conclude, critics say, that such practices are therefore good. Slavery can be used to illustrate this point, but so can our current economic system: by concentrating on how the society works to produce and distribute goods, the problems of unemployment, poverty, and great differences in income, all of which are also part of the system, can be ignored. Because structural-functionalism stops the motions of society at a given time and examines how various structures contribute to the society at that time, the model tends to emphasize stability rather than change, even though it does not assume that society is unchanging.

The severest criticism of structural-functionalism is that it does not give a true picture of social reality. Proponents of the conflict model claim that it is a serious misconception to view society as being in a state of equilibrium with all of its parts contributing to the harmonious balance of the whole. While this overstates the functionalist position, the idea that conflict, and not order, is the dominant social condition is worth considering.

The Conflict Model: Society in Strife

When conflict theorists look at society, they see group struggling against group and clashes of interest everywhere. Karl Marx, as we have seen, was an early conflict theorist. His theory of the inevitable struggle between the workers and those who own the means of production (the capitalists) is an early example of the **conflict model** of social interaction.

No single capitalist today owns a modern factory system. Nevertheless, one group, the board of directors, manages the system, while another group, the laborers, works for a wage. At times there are strikes, and between times there are many negotiations between workers and managers, threats of strikes, and the establishment of numerous rules and regulations specifying the rights and obligations of each party. These expressions of disagreement are important to the conflict theorist. Yet, because the system is in operation most of the time, it is reasonable to ask what holds it together. The conflict theorist sees the order that exists as being a result of one group's ability to control the other (see Coser, 1956; Dahrendorf, 1959; Gouldner, 1970; Horowitz, 1964).

Clashes of interest and the unequal distribution of power are two of the main concepts studied by the conflict theorist. Labor unions, associations of manufacturers, lobbies, and pressure groups are vivid proof of differences of

The groups and issues change, but scenes like this are common. They illustrate the point of conflict theory that society is characterized by clashes of interest and group struggling against group

interests within society, but many less organized groups differ with one another over who should get what share of its goods and social privileges. Clearly, power—that is, the ability of persons or groups to get their own way, even when opposed—is unequally distributed in society; some people have more "clout" than others. Thus, society can be divided into those who have power and those who do not, with the "haves" seeking to retain power and the "have nots" seeking to obtain it.

Conflict and power struggles are easy to find in modern American society. Riots in cities and prisons are frequently coupled with demands by the dissenters, a clear indication that one group wants more control over its life and living conditions. Consumer groups are formed to secure truth in advertising and to obtain redress from shoddy manufacturing. Environmentalists clash with energy interests over such matters as the Alaskan pipeline. Antiabortionists vie with those who favor legal abortion on demand. School boards clash with parents over what should be taught and who should decide the issues. The list could go on and on. In every nook and cranny of society we find group pitted against group in an unending struggle to determine which shall have the power to achieve its goals at some other group's expense. Although not always violent or noisy, conflict must be considered a part of social reality.

The Need for Different Models

Modern sociologists are not disturbed by the different models employed in the study of social interaction. The discipline is not at the stage where a single, all-encompassing model can guide sociologists in each of their studies. As we build toward such a stage, each existing model can act as a corrective or cleansing mechanism for others. Overemphasis on what holds society together and what promotes stability is corrected by focus on conflict and change. Overemphasis on the structure of groups, which in a sense ignores the individual, is balanced by other approaches, such as the *humanistic* (Lee, 1973) and *symbolic interaction* (Blumer, 1969) models. (The **symbolic interaction model** and its application to the understanding of violent crime are discussed in Box 1.2.)

If sociologists differ among themselves about which model yields the most valid knowledge of social interaction, it is both understandable and desirable that such differences exist in a young discipline. As the sociologist Morris Cohen (1931) put it, "Science means the rigorous weighing of all evidence, including a full consideration of all possible theories" (p. 347).

Eclecticism is the selection of elements from various models rather than the strict adherence to a single model. It has an obvious advantage in a field that studies broad, complex phenomena but that has not yet developed stable, incontestably proven theories. Different sociologists can approach their studies from different viewpoints, thus adding a variety of dimensions to our knowledge of human interaction. A single model is neat and precise, but if certain kinds of studies cannot be performed because they do not fit the model, valuable knowledge can be lost. Eclecticism can be confusing if one is prematurely concerned with what is the best model, but not if one views it as a necessary stage in the development of a comprehensive theory.

The approach followed in this book is eclectic, but it places more emphasis on structural-functionalism than on other models. However, some issues are better handled by other models. In Chapter 11, for example, we start off with a structural-functional approach to the educational institution, analyzing how this institution fits in with the rest of the social order. But to deal with such issues as who should control the schools, the conflict model is more appropriate. The modern American city could scarcely be handled without reference to conflict, nor could the subject of minority group relations. Throughout this book the various models are not labeled when they are used; rather, elements of each simply are applied to each issue, concept, or topic being discussed.

WHY STUDY SOCIOLOGY?

Anyone who has felt intellectual curiosity about the world can understand the sociologist's motivation. Sociologists are simply men and women who are curious about how people interact with one another and form themselves into enduring groups and societies. They are interested in people and have decided to study them in a scientific way.

The sociologist's laboratory is wherever people are gathered. The sociologist is not really concerned with *who* these people are or *why* they are gathered together, but only with *how* they interact with one another. Every kind of human interaction between every kind of human being is interesting to sociologists, because they have questions about human behavior that press for answers. Sociologists seek to learn as much as they can about human interaction and to impart this knowledge to others, because they feel this is the most relevant way in which to spend their lives.

As a student, what will you get from the study of sociology? Will you learn anything that will be useful to you? We could dodge the question by saying that it all depends on how much you put into your studies. But how much you put into studying sociology depends, in part, on what you think

---

**BOX 1.2
WHAT DOES IT ALL MEAN?
THE SYMBOLIC INTERACTION MODEL**

What is the deeper meaning that stems from the simple action of a man opening a door for a woman? Does this symbolize his feeling that women are weak and need to be protected? What meaning can be found in the interaction between a doctor and a patient as she attempts to explain to him the need for exploratory surgery? She may not use the word "cancer," but by the tone of her voice and by urging her patient to schedule the operation immediately, she can convey a definite meaning.

These are the kinds of questions and answers of interest to those sociologists who base their research in the symbolic interaction model. The structural-functional model focuses on the total of society and analyzes the consequences of broad societal institutions. The conflict model looks at clashes of interest between and among major segments of society. In contrast, the symbolic interaction model starts at the bottom and focuses on the interaction between individuals. Symbolic interactionists emphasize that it is individuals, not groups or structures, that interact. Through the day-to-day interaction of people, human bonds are created, linkages are extended, and culture is developed and transmitted.

Symbolic interaction refers to the interaction between people through the use of symbols. A symbol is something that stands for something else. The primary symbols used by humans are words, but gestures, facial expressions, groans, and the like are also symbols. Neither words nor other symbols have meaning in and of themselves; the only meaning they have is given to them by their user. Through symbols, meaning can be conveyed from one person to another.

In their attempts to understand how the interaction of people creates meaning and defines situations for them, symbolic interactionists often study minute aspects of everyday life. In a recent study, Lonnie H. Athens

you will get out of it. Chiefly, what you should get out of an exploration of sociology is an understanding of the sociological point of view—that sometimes frustrating, but always exciting, way in which sociologists view reality. The study of sociology should contribute to your ability to examine human behavior objectively and to appreciate the need to get information that is as complete as possible. The sociologist seeks, as the courtroom oath puts it, the truth, the whole truth, and nothing but the truth.

Surely, all reasonable people believe that it is good to see things without bias or prejudice. Or do they? At times, sociology is unpopular precisely because its findings conflict with what people would like to believe. Sociologists are not really cantankerous people with a sadistic streak, but they do seek the truth—and the truth can be quite disturbing.

(1977) looked at violent crime from a symbolic interactionist point of view. Athens conducted in-depth interviews with 58 persons convicted of such crimes as assault and homicide. Each actor—that is, violent crimnal—described, in detail, what happened in the situation in which he committed the violent crime and what went through his mind.

One pattern that emerged in these descriptions was that the actor defined the situation as one in which the victim was attempting to frustrate his or her attempted action. For example, a victim's actions were interpreted as meaning that he or she was trying to prevent a theft or was going to call the police. From the actor's point of view, the attempt to block his or her plans was a bad thing to do. Finally, the actor related his or her interpretation of the situation and his or her definition of the victim's actions and concluded that physical violence was the most appropriate way to deal with the situation. Thus, the actor can be seen as a goal-directed person who, because of the meaning ascribed to the actions of the victim, commits a violent act. This study allows us to understand what might otherwise be called "senseless" or "impulsive" violent crimes.

It is not difficult to appreciate the symbolic interactionist point of view. After all, if we do not understand the meanings that are conveyed when people communicate with words and other symbols, we miss the essential features of the interaction. One criticism of the symbolic interaction model, however, is that it fails to deal with the broad social forces that affect human behavior. The study of violent crime, for example, does not deal with the different rates of such crimes in various sections of the city or with the different backgrounds of criminals. What the symbolic interaction approach does allow us to do is understand what actually goes on when a violent crime is committed.

Sociological studies have shown, for example, that it is quite common on college campuses for unmarried couples to live together. Many middle-aged and older people find this practice to be a disturbing and serious threat to their cherished values. Even more threatening is the sociologist's discovery that couples living together are happy and that they find in their relationship trust, companionship, and involvement with another person, and not just a simple opportunity for sexual satisfaction (Lyness, Lipetz, and Davis, 1972; Thorman, 1973). It would be more comforting to believe that such couples are a handful of sexually depraved neurotics who soon recognize the error of their ways, come to their senses, and opt for conventional marriage. It may be more comforting, but to the best of our knowledge, it is not true.

We should not conclude from this example that sociologists study only controversial behaviors and interactions. As we have shown, sociologists study *all* human group behavior. And what sociologists have discovered about human interaction and human societies will be found throughout this book. We will consider information dealing with such matters as births, income, education, crime, and church attendance. But one course in sociology cannot provide you with all the findings of sociological research. Your introductory study of sociology should direct you to the sources of reasonably accurate information on human interaction. Perhaps you will want to seek out such information, and in doing so, you will better equip yourself to understand your society and to do your part in solving its problems.

Sociology is often required in the training programs for a number of professions or occupations, such as teaching, social work, city planning, nursing, and law. The sociological approach to understanding human behavior is considered valuable for those who, in the course of their occupation, need to work closely with other people. All of us, of course, deal with other people, so the insights of sociology into human interaction, human groups, and society in general really have broad applications. The study of sociology is also part of general education. That is, the study of sociology develops the human intellect by providing new information, new understandings of human interaction, and new interpretations of human behavior. Such knowledge, when added to that acquired in other fields, contributes to one's being an educated person. From the earliest social philosophers to the sociologists in a modern university, those who have knowledge of human interaction have sought to dispel ignorance and to teach the truth as they see it.

From this brief history of sociology we can see that human beings have been investigating and speculating on society for centuries but that sociology itself is only about a century old. What creates this sharp distinction between social speculation and evaluation on the one hand and sociology on the other is the use of the scientific method in analyzing society. The scientific outlook and its method of research are the fundamental traits of any social science, and the sociologist employs these traits to study ... and groups. How this is done is the topic of the next cha...

SUMMARY

1. **Sociology** is the study of interaction among people and ... way this interaction affects human behavior. It goes beyond the behavior of individuals and focuses on the group basis of human behavior.

2. Although philosophers have been interested in human interaction for centuries, the science of sociology did not appear until about 100 years ago, with the writings of Auguste Comte. Comte was the first to develop a system for the scientific study of society. He divided all of human history into three stages: the theological, the metaphysical, and the positive. Comte was interested in both *social statics* (forces that hold society together) and *social dynamics* (social change).

3. Like Comte, Herbert Spencer was a positivist. He saw society as evolving through progressively higher stages, guided by "natural law," and resulting in "survival of the fittest."

4. According to Karl Marx, societies evolve by passing through successive stages that each carry their own "seeds of destruction." At each stage, it takes revolution to resolve conflict and advance society to the next stage. Marx saw capitalistic society as a struggle between those who owned the means of production and those who did not. In Marx's view, the final stage in societal evolution would be a classless society.

5. Emile Durkheim saw society evolving from one in which there is little division of labor and great emotional ties to the group to one in which there is great division of labor and social ties are more formal and impersonal. Durkheim's study of suicide in relation to social ties is considered the first scientific study in sociology.

6. Max Weber did not have a grand theory of sociology, but he did do some pioneering research in the field. For example, he found a major relationship between the Protestant ethic and the capitalist economic system. Weber not only discovered relationships in society but tried to explain them.

7. Sociological **models** are sets of assumptions researchers use to understand human interaction and its results. Two major models used in sociology are the structural-functional model and the conflict model.

8. According to the **structural-functional model,** society is made up of major structures that contribute to the survival and well-being of the total society. This model has been criticized for offering an oversimplified view of reality and for having a conservative bias.

9. According to the **conflict model,** society is made up of groups with unequal power that are constantly in conflict. Order exists because the groups in power are able to control those groups that are not.

10. Sociology is a young science, and there is room for many approaches and models. The eclectic approach is to select elements from various models and to look at each issue from various viewpoints without being biased by adherence to a single model.

11. Sociologists seek the truth about human interaction, which sometimes makes them unpopular, for they often find things that people would rather leave hidden.

KEY TERMS

Note: Definitions of all key terms can be found in the Glossary at the end of the book.

conflict model
eclecticism
mechanical solidarity
model
organic solidarity
positivism
social characteristics
sociology
structural-functional model
symbolic interaction model

SUGGESTED READINGS

Aron, Raymond. *Main Currents in Sociological Thought.* 2 vols. Garden City, N.Y.: Doubleday, 1970.
An excellent secondary source on the major classical theorists.

Berger, Peter L. *Invitation to Sociology: A Humanistic Perspective.* Garden City, N.Y.: Doubleday, 1963.
Provides a humanistic sociological perspective for understanding the relationship of humans to social institutions and to society in general.

Bottomore, T. B. *Sociology: A Guide to Problems and Literature.* New York: Random House, 1972.
The author begins by defining the scope of sociology, then integrates major theoretical perspectives, and finally shows how these perspectives can be used to understand social problems.

Faris, Robert E., ed. *Handbook of Modern Sociology.* Chicago: Rand McNally, 1964.
A wide range of essays covering the various theoretical positions of the main schools of sociological thought.

Gouldner, Alvin W. *The Coming Crisis of Western Sociology.* New York: Basic Books, 1970.
Essentially a critical review of the development and present stance of modern sociology. Gouldner concludes by calling for a "reflexive sociology."

Hinkle, Roscoe C., and Gisela Hinkle. *The Development of Modern Sociology.* New York: Random House, 1954.
   The authors trace the development of American sociology from 1905 to 1954, focusing primarily on the influence of classical European sociology on American sociology.

Mills, C. Wright. *The Sociological Imagination.* New York: Oxford University Press, 1959.
   Mills criticizes bureaucratic, or "establishment," sociology and calls for a sociology that takes into account the effects of both history and social institutions on people.

Nisbet, Robert. *The Sociological Tradition.* New York: Basic Books, 1967.
   The author integrates the classical social theorists around five conceptual areas: community, authority, status, the sacred, and alienation.

Stein, Maurice, and Arthur Vidich, eds. *Sociology on Trial.* Englewood Cliffs, N.J.: Prentice-Hall, 1963.
   A collection of essays dealing with problems that have plagued the discipline of sociology, including value neutrality, bureaucratic sociology, and historical sociology.

Wallace, Walter L., ed. *Sociological Theory: An Introduction.* Chicago: Aldine, 1969.
   A collection of articles about the major conceptual approaches in sociology. There are several especially good articles comparing the structural-functional model to the conflict model.

All sciences, the social as well as the natural, are based on the firm assumption that the world reflects order and predictability. It is further assumed that this order can be discovered. A sequence of steps, called the scientific method, has been developed to help discover the order in the universe, and in this chapter, we will explore those steps. The method begins with a theory which gives some order to what has already been discovered and what one expects to discover. Then, we look for instances in which the theory holds true, as well as for those in which it doesn't hold true. The tools used for this in the natural sciences include such instruments as microscopes and telescopes; the tools used by sociologists include sample surveys, interviews, questionnaires, census reports, and careful observations of people interacting. Whatever tools are used, the purpose is to discover what is really going on and how the results square with the theory being tested. Some people find the methods used in sociological studies as fascinating as the findings of those studies.

2
Sociology as a Science: Goals and Methods

It is difficult to imagine living in an unpredictable world in which all features and events in the environment—and human behavior, as well—occur haphazardly. Fortunately, we can predict that night will give way to day, that the oceans will keep their water, and that our clocks will continue to run forward. We do not know with absolute certainty that these things will happen, but our knowledge allows us to predict that they probably will. This predictability is inseparable from the notion of regularity, or order, in the universe. The fundamental assumption of science is that there is such order in the universe. All scientists believe that no event occurs by chance and that no elements of the universe are arranged haphazardly. Only if there is order in the universe can the scientific goals of understanding and the ability to predict phenomena be achieved.

We do not know when, in the dim past, humans first began to sense order in their surroundings. No doubt humans were aware, early in their evolution, of the regularity of periods of dark and light, of the inflexible sequence of the seasons, and of the growth cycle of their own and other species. But we will never know which food gatherer, faintly sensing a regularity in nature, first mentally classified fruits as edible and inedible, or which ancient shepherd, pondering the night skies, first speculated that there were system and harmony up there.

Almost everyone knows enough about human behavior to predict many types of social interaction. No one knows, with certainty, what will occur tomorrow between student and teacher, clerk and shopper, or doctor and patient, but we can predict with a good deal of accuracy these and other patterns of social interaction.

Prediction is both an application of knowledge and a test of our knowledge or understanding. That is, if an event is correctly predicted before it happens, the principle that yielded the prediction will be confirmed. If the event does not occur as predicted, then it will be accepted that, for some reason, the general principle does not apply to the specific event.

We should note here that the scientific meaning of the term "understanding" is a more rigorous application of what the word usually means in the everyday world. We understand the behavior of a close friend in a particular situation because we have been able to apply our knowledge—our past familiarity with his or her personality and temperament—to the particular facts. From our general knowledge about our friend—for our notion of his or her personality is a generalization built from our own observations and/or reports from other friends—we are able to explain why our friend behaved as he or she did.

The scientific meaning of understanding is not fundamentally different from the above example. From careful observation of particulars, the scientist builds generalizations that can serve to explain later happenings and that can be tested by those happenings as well. Each generalization is tested by how well it fits the particulars and by how accurately it predicts each new occurrence. The sociologist believes that human interaction and the formation and maintenance of groups are governed by *principles*—that is, generalizations. The scientific task of the sociologist is to discover these principles and to explain how they work and how they relate to one another. All of the many principles in sociology are tentative: new knowledge could cause them to be qualified, or even discarded.

In this chapter we will be exploring the ways in which sociologists acquire knowledge about human interaction and how they develop theories and discover principles to account for the facts that are found. The entire process involved is referred to as *scientific research*.

ELEMENTS OF SCIENTIFIC RESEARCH

To understand a phenomenon we must gather and assemble information about it—we must do research. The basic elements of research are the same for all sciences—whether the exact, the natural, or the social sciences (see Miller, 1970). The simplified scheme in Figure 2.1 shows the flow from one element of the scientific method to another (Wallace, 1971). Let us run through this scheme quickly and then examine each part in detail.

Good research begins and ends with **theory,** at the top of the figure. Every science has sets of systematically related propositions. These propositions are the theories of science. A simple illustration of a proposition can be taken from family sociology: "The greater the conflict between parents, the greater the inconsistency in the parents' treatment of a child; the greater the inconsistency in child-rearing, the poorer will be the personality development of the child." Knowing these propositions, a researcher may want to test whether marital conflict is related to juvenile delinquency. It would appear from the theory that such conflict could affect the child's behavior, for it is related to poor child-rearing and poor personality development of the child. Thus, after choosing a research problem, researchers must choose an appropriate theory. Sociologists are guided in the selection of a theory by their knowledge of the field. That is, they know which theories deal with the particular area of human interaction they wish to research, and they know which theories have been used in similar research. Following the selection of a theory, sociologists would then go through the process of **deduction.** Reasoning from the general theory, they state a relationship they expect to find in a particular situation (in other words, they predict). This predicted relationship is called the **hypothesis.**

Next, the hypothesis must be tested to see whether it is true. Hypotheses are tested by **observation,** which may consist of watching, counting, weighing, asking questions, and so on, depending on what is being observed.

FIGURE 2.1 Diagram Showing the Flow of Elements in the Research Process

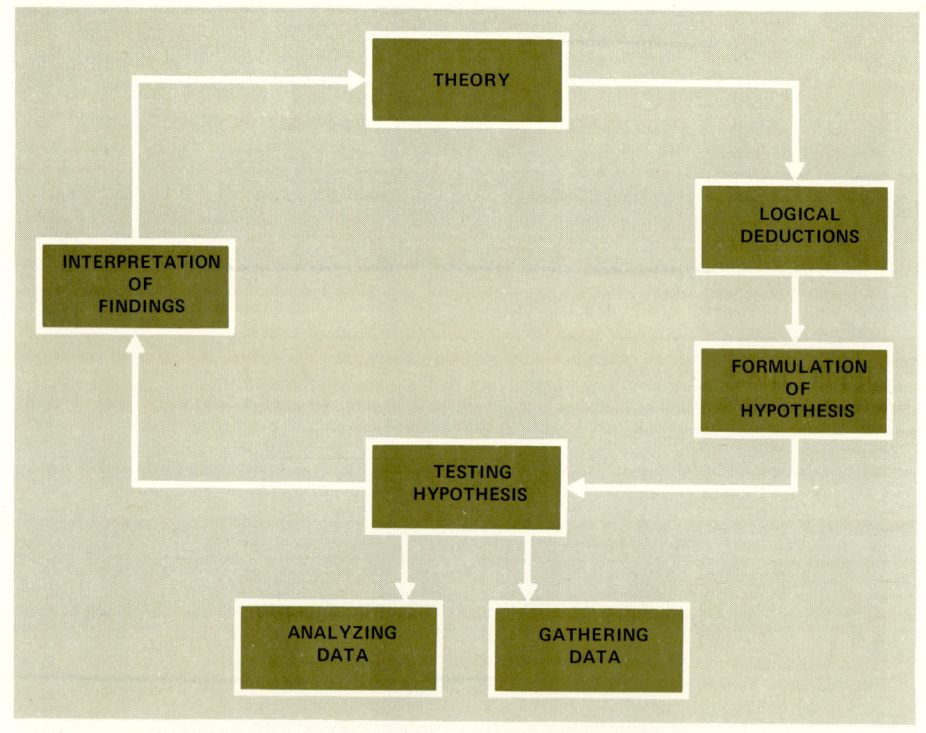

Sociologists do research by applying an already established theory to a specific problem. Following this procedure of deduction, hypothesis formulation, and hypothesis testing, they arrive at a result that either confirms the original theory or suggests ways in which the theory should be modified.

Source: Adapted and modified from Walter L. Wallace, *The Logic of Science in Sociology* (Chicago: Aldine, 1971), p. 18.

Researchers must first be satisfied that they have observed the phenomenon (juvenile delinquency, marital conflict, or whatever is being studied) adequately. Then, if what is observed squares with what they expected to find, they accept the hypothesis; if it does not, they reject it.

In either case, it is important that researchers relate their conclusions back to the original theory. If the results of a particular set of observations support the general theory, they provide further evidence that the theory has good predictive validity. If the results don't support the theory, this, too, provides valuable information. It indicates that the theory must be modified or replaced by another theory that can account for the facts. Beginning with a fuller explanation of theory, we will now take a closer look at the various elements of the research process.

THEORY: THE GENERALIZING TOOL

In popular speech, the word "theory" is often used simply to mean speculation or conjecture; for example, "My theory is that he was stoned when he had the accident." The scientist does not use theory in this sense. A scientific theory is a systematic statement of propositions or ideas that are logically related and give general explanations of phenomena and relationships among phenomena. A theory enables us to understand, explain, and predict situations or events that are more specific than the relationships contained in the theory. It also provides us with an order into which we can fit observations or newly discovered facts. Let us look at a couple of well-known theories to show what we mean.

Scientific Theories

Charles Darwin's theory of evolution, despite its weaknesses, is a good illustration of the way in which a theory can be used. From Darwin's general theory of evolution by random mutation and natural selection, it would follow that, among fish that migrated from open waters to cave waters, those having mutated in ways most compatible with life in a cave would survive and reproduce their kind. Small eyes are less likely to be injured than large ones, so eventually (according to Darwin's theory), fish with no eyes should evolve in the cave species. This is exactly what is found in Mammoth Cave and similar places (Barr, 1968). When tied to a theory, the cave fish's blindness takes on meaning and is not just a random bit of information.

When the principles of gravitational theory were applied to the orbits of the known planets, the astronomer Percival Lowell concluded that there was a planet in our solar system that had not yet been discovered. Unless the theory was wrong, something in space was exerting the pull that gave Uranus its irregular movement. In 1905, using theory, Lowell proved mathematically that another planet did exist, and he even fixed the planet's approximate location. It was not until 1930 that this planet, Pluto, was first sighted. Thus, gravitational theory provided both an explanation for the behavior of the known planets and a correct prediction about a new phenomenon. Moreover, Lowell's predictions, based on theory, alerted other astronomers to look for a planet in an area they had previously presumed to be empty.

On the other hand, a theory that does not explain the known facts must be modified. If repeated tests show that it cannot explain events, it must be replaced by one that does. In the 1800s physicists sought to explain how light waves travel. The knowledge of the time led them to believe that light needs a medium, or substance, in which to travel. They thus developed the theory that an invisible substance, called "ether," fills all space and provides the medium through which light travels. An experiment designed to measure the relative motion of the earth and ether was conducted by the physicists Albert Michelson and Edward Morley in 1897. The results of that experiment found no support for the ether theory. Later, the theories developed by Albert Einstein provided an explanation for the movement of light. Thus, the ether theory, which could not explain the events it was supposed to explain, was replaced by a theory that could.

Sociological Theories—Predictions and Limitations

As a young science, sociology has yet to develop theories like those of Darwin, Lowell, and Einstein. Nonetheless, sociological theories work in basically the same way. For example, in 1945, the sociologists Kingsley Davis and Wilbert Moore presented a theory to explain how social stratification (class systems) relates to the rest of the social order. Beginning with the need to fill different positions in a society and the unequal distribution of talent in any society, their theory proposed that a system attaching more rewards to some positions than to others is universally necessary. Although this theory requires some modification, we can deduce from it that in a utopian community established on the principle of uniform rewards, it would be difficult to get people to accept jobs that are more demanding or that require considerable training. With its important jobs unfilled, the community would fail to survive.

Now, what if we were to find a society providing uniform rewards that manages to get its positions filled and is surviving? Because such a finding would be contrary to what our theory predicts, we would examine the society closely to understand how it operates. Perhaps the society is a religious group, and one of its religious beliefs is that some people will work harder than others or will undergo long years of training while others will not, but everyone will get the same rewards. The original theory would have to be modified to exclude this presumably unique case. But the theory would still be presumed to hold true generally.

Perhaps in another society, such as the Israeli communal farms, called *kibbutzim*, we might discover that the society operates without a system of differential rewards but is not a complete society, for it depends on other groups for medical services and technical assistance of various sorts (Spiro, 1956). These social tasks, according to the original theory, would be difficult to accomplish without a system of unequal rewards. Although the results of observing this community basically support the theory, it would be necessary to refine the theory still further, so that it would apply only to completely self-sufficient societies.

Any science needs the generalizing activity we call *theorizing* in order to make sense out of accumulated facts and predict new events. For example, if a sociologist were to consult with a group that had fairly complete plans for a unique, classless society, she could say, in effect, that although there has never been a society exactly like the one proposed, her theory predicts that the group will have some problems to overcome if it is to survive.

The beggar is asking for money. According to exchange theory, the giver of alms should get something out of the act. What are the giver's rewards?

We should bear in mind that the theories of sociology are neither as well developed nor as well tested as those of the older sciences. Sometimes sociologists have no good theoretical basis for predicting a certain kind of human behavior, or they predict behavior incorrectly because the existing theory is an inadequate guide for prediction.

According to **exchange theory**, for example, persons who interact are guided by the principle of seeking the most favorable cost-benefit ratio; that is, when given a choice between two relationships, a person is likely to choose the one that promises to yield greater rewards or satisfactions. As the family sociologist and theorist William Goode has suggested, exchange theory can be used to predict whether women with one child will remarry sooner after divorce than those with several children (Goode, Hopkins, and McClure, 1971). From our knowledge of exchange theory, we would probably predict that women with several children would be less of a bargain in the marriage market and would, thus, take longer to remarry than women with only one child. The data suggest exactly the opposite, however: women with more children remarry more quickly. Exchange theory can still provide the explanation for this. Women with several children, who are in greater need of financial help and often more desirous of a father figure in the home, probably work harder at finding a husband than do women with only one child. The mother of several children must convince a potential husband that she will provide rewards that will be greater than the costs of taking on a family. If she does so, she is a bargain in the husband's eyes. The original deduction from exchange theory—that women with fewer children are more of a bargain—is not entirely wrong. What it fails to take into account, however, is that the costs of additional children can be offset by many other types of rewards, such as greater attentiveness to the husband's needs and higher responsiveness to his feelings and desires.

CONCEPTS AND HYPOTHESES

From our observations of, say, many tables, each of us has built up an idea of "table." This idea includes only what is common to all tables—such as a flat surface and supporting legs—and not all the variations among tables—such as color and size. We can communicate about the concept "table" knowing that it does not refer to any specific item in its class—that is, to any specific table. A **concept** is a generalized way of summarizing a large number of experiences we have had with a particular object or idea. Every science has developed concepts: physics has the concepts of mass, volume, velocity, and so on; zoology has the concepts of organism, living and nonliving, and so on.

A sociological concept is a generalized idea about human interactions, conditions, states, or characteristics or about the products of human interaction. It is a shorthand method of summarizing observations through the use of a label, or name. The labels applied to sociological concepts are frequently everyday words, such as "role," "group," "family," "class," "culture," and "deviant." But just as "work" has a technical meaning to the physicist, and "reaction" a technical meaning to the chemist, so the definitions of sociological concepts are technical and frequently differ considerably from the same term as it is used in everyday life. The development and use of proper sociological concepts is important for research, for we must be as precise as possible about what we are attempting to measure or observe.

Before a sociological concept can be used in research, we need to have an **operational definition** of it. That is, we must define it in a way that can be measured, and we must state clearly what measure we will be using. For research purposes, we may define a "broken home" as one in which there is only one parent because of divorce or the death of the other parent. This operational definition does not include homes in which the husband and wife have separated or those in which an unmarried mother or father is rearing children alone. In the research reported in Box 2.1, willingness to report rule-breaking behavior, which sociologists call "deviancy" (see Chapter 17), is operationally defined in terms of how freely customers in a store reported an incident of shoplifting they observed. In another study, the same variable may be operationally defined in terms of how people respond to a questionnaire that asks them how willing they would be to report an act of deviancy.

And so it is with other concepts, such as "role" or "social class." The researcher must identify how the concepts used in a study have been operationally defined; otherwise, a hypothesis will be vague and subject to different interpretations.

As we mentioned earlier, a hypothesis states a relationship between various facts that one expects to find. A hypothesis is more than a guess or a hunch, for it is derived from theory—or at least, it is based on previously observed phenomena or previously discovered generalizations.

Typically, researchers will first use general concepts to phrase a hypothesis. For example, they might state as a hypothesis, "The higher the social class, the better will be the quality of marriages." This hypothesis, you will notice, predicts a certain relationship between two concepts: social class and the quality of marriage. This prediction is possible because we know some things about marriage, and because we know some things about the behavior of people in various social classes. We know, for example, that upper-class people tend to marry at a later age than middle-class or working-class people. We know, too, that people who marry later in life are less likely to get divorced than those who marry young. These two facts alone might lead us to expect that there will be fewer divorces in the upper class. But we also have some other facts about upper-class people that increase the likelihood that our hypothesis will be correct. We know, for instance, that upper-class people tend to stress kinship ties and to be more concerned than other classes with the larger family group of which the married couple is a part. Upper-class people, by definition, have money, and so financial problems are unlikely to interfere with their marriages. Therefore, later marriages, concern with the extended family, and financial security are all characteristics of upper-class people. Knowing these characteristics allows us to predict that there will be fewer divorces among the upper class than among other classes of people. Finding out whether or not our hypothesis is correct will require the collecting of additional data.

COLLECTING DATA

To test a hypothesis, facts are needed. The hypothesis and the theory being tested will determine which facts, or data, are appropriate and also how this information should be collected. A researcher may use the **survey research method,** which involves mailing questionnaires or asking questions in personal interviews. For some studies it might be better to use an **observation method,** which we will discuss soon. But in large-scale survey research, no matter what groups are being studied, it is usually neither feasible nor necessary to gather data from the entire group, so the technique of **sampling** becomes essential.

Sampling:
Some Represent All

If you wanted to discover how many marbles of each color are in a large barrel filled with marbles, you could, of course, dump out the barrel and painstakingly sort and count the marbles of each color. But often, such precision is not necessary, and simply drawing out a representative sample of marbles will give you a very close approximation of what you would obtain by mak-

---

**BOX 2.1
PUTTING
A THEORY
TO THE TEST:
SHOPLIFTING**

To see how the steps outlined in Figure 2.1 actually occur in a piece of research, let us take the example of an observational study of reactions to shoplifting done by Darrell J. Steffensmeier and Renée H. Steffensmeier in 1973.

The shoplifting study was designed to test a theory of human behavior and to determine whether or not a certain general theory could be used to explain the specific kind of behavior called "shoplifting." The theory tested in this particular study is called labeling theory (see Chapter 17). Technically, shoplifting is considered deviant behavior because it violates the rules of society. Labeling theory is an approach to deviant behavior that deals with how people in the larger society react to behavior that is against the rules of the group. The act, or behavior, is defined by those who know about it—they may consider it a delinquent act or just a harmless prank—and the individual committing the act is given a label, such as "juvenile delinquent."

Labeling theory thus emphasizes other people's reactions to certain behavior rather than the behavior itself. A logical deduction from this theory would be that people will judge similar acts differently, depending on who is committing them and on the circumstances under which they are committed. A five-year-old who takes the neighbor child's tricycle is not labeled a thief, but a fifteen-year-old who takes the neighbor's car may be labeled as such. According to the deduction from labeling theory, certain attributes of a person committing an illegal act would affect, for better or for worse, his or her chances of being labeled deviant. One such attribute would be appearance. If a person looks like the kind of person who gets into trouble, the chances of his or her being labeled deviant would be higher than if he or she looked more "respectable."

In the study by the Steffensmeiers, the shoplifters were actually research assistants who, with the store owner's knowledge, were to steal items in plain view of ordinary customers. Half of the shoplifters looked like hippies, with long, unruly hair, no socks, and soiled, patched jeans; the others had trimly cut hair, were clean shaven, and wore neatly pressed clothes. One hypothesis of the study was that store customers will be more likely to report a shoplifting incident when the shoplifter has a hippielike rather than a "straight" appearance.

ing a total count. Obviously, it is easier, quicker, and less costly to use a sample than to do a complete count (Simon, 1969).

Before drawing a sample, the researcher must define the group about which he or she wishes to generalize. This group is called the *universe,* or *population*—for example, people over sixty-five years old living in Austin, Texas; all college students in the United States; or the patients in City Hospital. To be good, a sample must give an unbiased picture of the total universe being studied.

Data used to test the hypothesis were gathered by having both types deliberately steal merchandise in a way that an ordinary customer could readily observe their actions. After the shoplifter moved away, another research assistant, dressed as a store employee, moved into the immediate vicinity of the customer and began rearranging stock on the shelves. This gave the customer an easy opportunity to report the shoplifting incident. If the customer did not report it, the "employee" moved on and another research assistant, also dressed as a store employee, came to question the customer. At first, he simply asked if the customer had seen anything suspicious. If the customer still did not report the shoplifting incident, the employee probed further, saying, in effect, that he was sure he saw "that guy there" (pointing to the shoplifter) stuff something under his coat.

The findings of this study are reported in Table 2.1. Some of the 178 customers in the study voluntarily reported the shoplifting incident; these people were said to exhibit a high degree of willingness to report deviancy. Others reported it only after being questioned, and still others only after the "store employee" questioned them more vigorously. These people were said to show medium-high and medium-low willingness to report shoplifting, respectively. The remaining customers would not report the incident, even after vigorous questioning.

The "hippie" shoplifters were much more likely to be reported than were the "straight" ones. Statistical tests of the data indicated that the relationship between appearance and being reported was not accidental. Therefore, the researchers were able to conclude that their findings supported the hypothesis that was being tested. Relating the findings back to the original theory from which the hypothesis was derived shows the utility of labeling theory. Although it may not explain all deviancy, it does show that it is not just an illegal act but also people's reaction to the act that results in an offender being considered deviant. Had this been a real-life situation instead of a research study, it would be reasonable to conclude that those shoplifters who were identified, and thus labeled deviant, would be more likely to think of themselves as deviant than those who were not labeled as such.

TABLE 2.1 Willingness of Customers to Report Shoplifting by Appearance of Shoplifter

Appearance of Shoplifter	High (voluntarily reported)	Medium High (first prompting)	Medium Low (second prompting)	Low (would not report)
Hippie	48.5	39.7	7.4	4.4
Straight	20.9	40.3	19.4	19.4

Source: Adapted from Darrell J. Steffensmeier and Renée H. Steffensmeier "Who Reports Shoplifters? Research Continuities and Further Developments," *Internation Journal of Criminology and Penology* 5 (1977), 79–95.

One method of obtaining a good sample is called *random sampling*. Every unit in the universe is given the same chance to be selected as every other unit. The major advantage of random sampling is that a simple statistical formula indicates what size the sample should be to give confidence that, within a given margin of error, it resembles the universe. Suppose that we wanted to know whether the adults of the United States favor the legalization of marijuana. A properly drawn random sample of 2,500 people would be enough to give us an answer that will be accurate to within 5 percent. That is, if it were found that 60 percent of the sample was in favor of legalizing marijuana, we could be confident that the true percentage for the nation ranges from 55 to 65 percent. It should be noted that this random sample, to give a true picture of the feelings of all adults in the United States, would

To discover the kinds of organisms in the water you don't have to bring the whole lake to the laboratory—an adequate sample will do.

TABLE 2.2   Comparison of a Probability Sample and Actual Population of the United States*

Region	Percentage Distribution Actual Adult Population	Percentage Distribution Completed Interviews in Sample
East	27.6%	25.6%
Midwest	29.9	29.8
South	28.9	31.3
West	13.6	13.3
	100.0%	100.0%

*Sample size, 4,933.

Source: From Samuel A. Stouffer, *Communism, Conformity, and Civil Liberties* (New York: John Wiley & Sons, 1955), p. 237.

have to include respondents from all social classes, from a variety of ethnic groups, from all age levels, and of both sexes. In other words, the sample would have to be a miniversion of the population as a whole.

The data in Table 2.2 are taken from an actual study. They compare the proportion of interviews completed in different sections of the country with the proportion of the population determined by the census to be living in those sections. The biggest difference is that 2.4 percent more people from the South were interviewed than the proportion of people living in the area would indicate. All in all, the sample in the national study resembled the regional distribution of the people in the United States to a remarkable degree. Similar analyses of the sample used in a particular study could be done to see whether it accurately represents a cross-section of income levels, educational levels, religious affiliations, and so on.

Research by Observation

The survey research method is not the only way in which sociologists study human interaction. Another basic method is *observation*. In **nonparticipant observation** the researcher carefully witnesses interaction from outside the group. In **participant observation** the researcher is or becomes a member of the group and takes part in the interaction to be observed. Nonparticipant and participant observation are not clear-cut categories. For example, you might approach a commune and explain that you would like to live with the group and conduct a sociological study of it. If you are housed with the group, eat your meals with group members, and accept work assignments as others do, you are obviously not observing the group from outside. Still, you are not a full member of the group, but rather a sort of sociologist in residence.

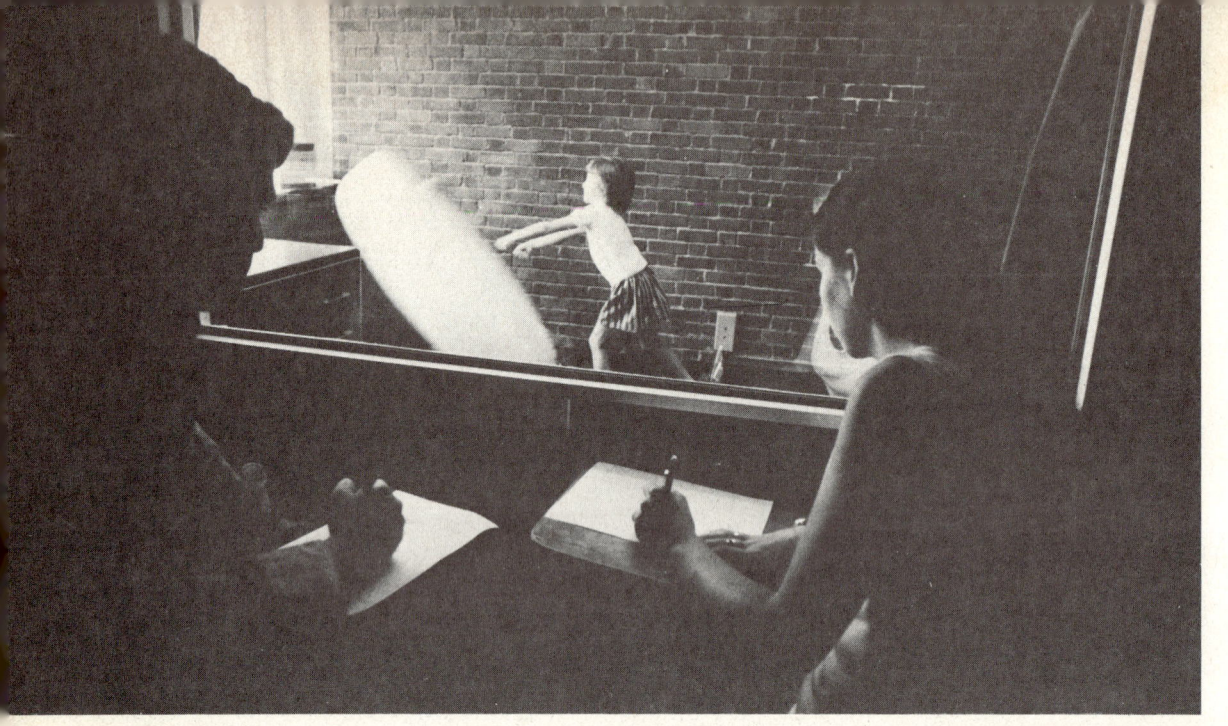

Nonparticipant observation, with careful note-taking, is an excellent way for these students to learn about the development of children.

As a true participant observer, you actually would have to be a member of the group you are studying (see Box 2.2). You would join a dance band, as did one sociologist, move into a community and join groups there, or take a job in a factory as a normal employee, and not as a sociologist conducting a

---

**BOX 2.2
THE ETHICS OF PARTICIPANT OBSERVATION**

Presumably, every science has limits to its permissible areas of investigation and methods of research. What are the limits sociologists must respect? Their scope of study is all social behavior, and different kinds of studies are suited to some methods of research and not to others. Can a sociologist choose a research topic that interests him or her and then adapt any method of investigation to suit the topic, with the only limitation being, perhaps, that no outright physical or social harm come to the human subjects of the research?

In the late 1960s, the sociologist Laud Humphreys (1970) undertook a study of "impersonal sex in public places"—homosexual activities in "tearooms" (homosexual slang for public restrooms used for homosexual encounters). To conduct his study, Humphreys used a modification of the participant observer method. Concealing the fact that he was a sociologist, he allowed himself to be used as a "watchqueen," a third person who acts as a lookout to protect the homosexual participants from discovery by the police or by a nonparticipant.

By recording the license numbers of cars, he was able to get the identities of many participants (which he scrupulously kept concealed). He took notes on their homes and neighborhoods and acquired data on

study. The basic techniques are similar, however, for both participant and nonparticipant observation (Wiseman and Aron, 1970).

Sociological Observation: For a Purpose Anyone can observe a group in action and give some kind of report on what was observed. The differences between an average person's observations and those of a trained sociologist lie in three areas: why the observation is made, how the observation is conducted, and what is done with the findings.

Sociologists observe for a purpose: they would like more knowledge about some aspect of social interaction. In designing a given study, sociologists specify what they want to observe, and often, they write out in advance what they expect to find. For example, sociologists living in or joining a commune may want to learn whether the phenomenon of territoriality exists in this particular group. *Territoriality* is the tendency of individuals and cliques to stake off physical space that becomes, in a sense, their own. For example, a corner of the cafeteria may be the meeting place of a certain group of students; a woman may have her favorite living-room chair in which to read her paper; a given park bench may be reserved informally for the daily use of several elderly men; or designated city blocks may be the turf of a boys' gang, which will defend it vigorously from invasion by rival gangs. Such possessive attitudes toward space would seem to conflict with the idea of communal living, but since territoriality is a basic trait of human

---

them from city and county directories. A year later, his appearance deliberately changed, he interviewed many of those same participants (often in the presence of their wives) on subjects unrelated to their homosexual activities.

Using these methods, Humphreys drew up a sociological profile of people whose lives were mysteries to society—people whose activities, motives, and characteristics had, up to that point, been described only by the police.

Despite Humphreys's care that his subjects' identities never become known, and despite the possible social value of his study as a guide for future public policy, Humphreys has received criticism for this study, chiefly for his method of research.

Should sociologists allow themselves to invade the individual's privacy without his or her knowledge? Many nonsociologists say "no." Humphreys himself says, "You do walk a . . . tightrope in regard to ethical matters in studies like this, but unless someone will walk it, the only source of information will be the police department, and that is dangerous for society."

groups and is found among many animal species as well, sociologists are intrigued by the question of how communes would deal with this tendency.

We should not assume that observers restrict themselves to only one research problem at a time. Sociologists studying communes, for example, may also want to investigate how the group gets the necessary work done without passing out rewards, whether problems of personal jealousy arise, or whether leaders tend to emerge. All of these problems are sociologically important, and the results of the observations would thus contribute to sociological knowledge.

Sociological Observation: Systematic Just as participant and nonparticipant observers are systematic in their statement of a research problem, they are also systematic in their observations. While they do not know exactly what they will find, they know what kinds of interaction they are interested in, and so they focus their attention on the people and the situations that will provide them with relevant information. They must be alert to subtleties of interaction as well as to the more obvious spoken word and physical action.

For example, some years ago I conducted an observational study on family decision making (Kenkel, 1957). In their own homes, couples discussed how to spend a hypothetical gift of money. To make it easier for them to allocate the money to different purchases, they were given $300 in stage money. The money was given to the couple and physically placed between the husband and wife. The focus of the study was on whether the husband or wife would have more influence on the use of the gift. Careful records were made of how much each partner spoke and how frequently each submitted ideas. It was of more than passing interest that in all cases the man took physical charge of the stage money, counted it, and sorted it into piles. This occurrence illustrated and helped to explain the man's influence in family decision making. It would be interesting to repeat this study today and see whether such male dominance still prevails.

Participant observers are not usually able to take notes while observing. As soon as possible, however, a written record must be made of the sociologically relevant facts observed. It is desirable to go over these notes from time to time while in the group being observed, to make sure that one is getting the kind of information needed or to detect an area where more observation is required.

Participant and nonparticipant observation are particularly fruitful methods to use in research areas that have not been well explored and to get a thorough description of the interaction patterns of the group. The sociologist Jacqueline Wiseman (1970), for example, composed a description of a typical day spent by men on Skid Row, by repeatedly and thoroughly observing their activities. Sometimes, observational and other research methods are combined. Another sociologist, Lloyd Birch (1971), had an organist in a funeral home record specific points in ministers' sermons, such as whether they mentioned the deceased by name. A few months later Birch interviewed the ministers and asked them what they would do at hypothetical funerals closely resembling ones they had actually conducted. Birch found that the earlier observed behavior of ministers differed from their reports of how they said they would conduct a funeral.

The raw findings of observational research usually consist of copious written notes and perhaps long strings of numbers representing who talked to whom, whether or not a behavior was observed, and so on. These findings need to be analyzed. What this analysis often amounts to is a systematic presentation of the findings as answers to the questions that guided the research.

ANALYZING DATA: FINDING THE MEANING IN FACTS

When sociologists talk about analyzing data, they frequently mean that they will be using **statistics**—mathematical methods for summarizing data that have been obtained by measurement or enumeration. Some statistics provide a summary description of a sample or a population, such as the average grade of students on a test, rather than a listing of every student's score. Other statistics are helpful in deciding whether to accept a hypothesis. In a study that hypothesizes that grade-school girls will score higher than boys on a standardized English test, an appropriate statistic will indicate how much of a difference in scores is necessary before the difference can be considered significant, rather than just a matter of chance.

Some statistical methods are quite simple, others more complex. It must be kept in mind that the only reason any kind of statistic is used is to help us interpret data we have collected to test hypotheses, and ultimately, to understand human interaction.

Measures of Central Tendency

One simple descriptive kind of statistic is a **measure of central tendency.** Instead of simply listing the scores on a test, for example, we can present them in a condensed or more meaningful manner by determining the mean, median, and mode for the raw scores. As most people know, the arithmetic **mean**, or average, is computed by adding up all the scores and then dividing that figure by the number of scores; the **median** is the middle score—when the scores are arranged from high to low, half will be above the median, and half will be below it; and the **mode** is the score that occurs most frequently.

Measures of central tendency can be quite useful. Rather than listing and trying to make sense of, say, the incomes of millions of men and women, it is more concise to compare the average income of men with that of women. Of course, averages can also be misleading. The average height of the

Increasingly, sociologists use a computer to analyze data statistically in order to make sense of the facts and determine whether or not they support the research hypothesis.

members of my family is five feet six inches. Yet a pair of pants designed for someone of that height would fit no one in the family. It is hard to say who would look more ridiculous in such pants—the youngest child, whose height is five feet, or her older brother, who stands at five feet ten inches. There is a creek near our home with an average depth of four feet three inches. Despite the fact that it is less than the average height of our family members, we would all drown if we attempted to wade across it, for it drops off to about twelve feet in the middle. Thus, with heights, depths, scores, and many other values, it is also frequently desirable to know the *range* from high to low, as well as the mean or the median. It is also helpful to know how many scores center around the middle value. There is another statistic, called the *standard deviation*, that shows how closely the data cluster around the mean or spread out from it.

Correlations

Sociological research cannot stop at merely describing the distribution characteristics of a given set of scores or values, for such an exercise would not explain much. There are other statistical techniques that allow us to discover whether, and how closely, one characteristic we are studying is associated with another one. If we have two sets of scores for the same group of people, we can determine statistically whether they are related, or

correlated. One such measure is the Pearson Product Moment Correlation Coefficient, often called Pearsonian *r*. Consider Table 2.3. From its title, it is clear that it deals with the relationship between income and the belief that there is life like ours on other planets. In the left-hand column, incomes are arranged in decreasing order. Reading down the right column, you can see that the percentage values also decrease. In other words, there is an association between income and belief in life on other planets. The higher the income level, the more likely people are to think that there are people like us on other planets. We speak of this as a *positive* correlation. If it were found that the lower the income, the more likely people are to believe in extraterrestrial life, the two variables would be related, but we would refer to the association as a *negative*, or inverse, correlation.

The actual value of the Pearsonian *r* for the data in Table 2.3 is .96. If there were no correlation at all, the *r* would be close to .00. A perfect positive correlation would be designated as +1.00, a perfect negative correlation as −1.00. Thus, our correlation coefficient of +.96 is actually a very high positive correlation, indicating a strong relationship between income and the belief in extraterrestrial life.

There are other statistics that sociologists use when they wish to know more about the scores obtained by two categories of people, such as males and females. In Table 2.3 we see that 48 percent of the males polled believe in extraterrestrial life, while 45 percent of the females hold this belief. A statistical test of significance indicates that such a difference could occur by chance in more than 20 cases out of 100, which is not an acceptable level for the difference to be considered significant.

The finding of a sex difference, therefore, does not really help us under-

---

TABLE 2.3   Income Level and Belief in Extraterrestrial Life

Income	Belief in Extraterrestrial Life	
	Number	Percent
$20,000 or more	216	57
15,000–19,999	202	51
10,000–14,999	412	48
7,000–9,999	228	43
5,000–6,999	175	42
3,000–4,999	150	38
Under $3,000	133	34
All males	786	48
All females	764	45

Source: The Gallup Opinion Index (Princeton, New Jersey: Gallup International, Inc., 1973).

stand why some people believe in extraterrestrial life and others do not, nor does it add much to our knowledge about the real or presumed differences between the sexes. Statistical tests are valuable tools, in that they let us know how much confidence we can place in a given set of findings. But they cannot substitute for the judgment of the sociologist, who must decide whether the findings of a study provide support for a hypothesis or add to our store of knowledge on human interaction.

Interpreting Findings

Once data have been analyzed, either statistically or otherwise, the result is a collection of facts. On the basis of the study, a certain relationship can be said to exist or not to exist. But a science does not develop by a mere accumulation of facts. The ultimate goal of any science is the discovery of principles or rules that explain certain classes of facts rather than isolated facts or relationships. Not every research finding will yield a general law or principle. What we call *interpretation* of the findings should, at the very least, include an effort to relate the findings to previous research. Do the new findings support the old? If not, is it because the present study was made at a time so far removed from earlier studies that circumstances have significantly changed, or because the study used different methods, or perhaps, because a different kind of sample was studied? Whatever the explanation, the finding must be fitted into the existing body of knowledge. Only in this way will laws be formulated that specify the conditions under which certain categories of relationships will prevail.

The intellectual process of interpreting and analyzing data, like all the steps that go before in research, poses for the sociologist many hazards of error. For example, in our everyday life we commonly talk of *causes:* "Cigarette smoking causes lung cancer"; "The oil companies caused the energy crisis"; "Violence on television causes violence in children"; and so on. But, in sociology, it is not common practice to speak of the causes of human behavior, partly because the concept of causality is loaded with philosophical complexities and ambiguities. For example, a newspaper account of a fire says the fire was caused by a person smoking in bed. Perhaps, if the man had not been drinking, he would not have fallen asleep with a lit cigarette; and if his boss had not been unusually rough on him, he would not have gotten drunk; if the mattress had not been made of flammable material, it could not have caught fire; and of course, if our atmosphere did not contain so much oxygen, neither the cigarette nor the mattress would have burned. What, then, was the cause of the fire?

Why worry about it? Often, it is sufficient to talk about an *association*—that is, our knowing that a certain relationship (or correlation) exists allows us to predict human interaction, and if it is so desired, to control it. Let us say that we know, for example, that people of different social classes live in different parts of the city and that the lower the social class, the more children in the family. From this information we can predict which areas of the city will need schools, even if we do not believe that having a low income is what causes a woman to become pregnant.

If a study discovers that minority-group children learn more in racially integrated schools than in segregated ones, we could control the outcome of the educational process by integrating the schools, even without knowing the whys and wherefores of the relationship. If we know that the younger the couple is when they marry, the more likely they are to get a divorce, we could reduce the divorce rate by discouraging marriage at a young age. Of course, the better we understand why a relationship exists, the sounder will be our basis for predicting or controlling the behavior in question. But the important thing to remember is that establishing an association between two factors is not the same as showing that one factor caused the other. The association *could* indicate a cause, as in the case of a high correlation between the administration of a poison and subsequent death. On the other hand, as we have seen, there is no clear-cut causal link shown in the association between social class and family size.

Spurious Relationships When two things are statistically associated, there is always the possibility that it may be a **spurious relationship**—that is, a false or accidental one. *A* may appear to be related to *B* when, actually, it is not; it may be that *C* is linked to both of the others. Let us suppose that a study found a relationship between the sale of Bibles and the sale of alcoholic beverages. As Bible sales increase, so does the sale of alcohol, and as less of one is sold, less of the other is sold. Does reading the Bible turn one to drink, or does drinking turn one to the Bible? Neither of these things is true. The sale of most goods is related to economic conditions; the more money people have, the more they spend on lots of things, including Bibles and alcohol.

Studies have found a positive relationship between college grades and the smoking of marijuana: the average grades of pot smokers are higher than those of nonusers (Gergen, Gergen, and Morse, 1972). Which causes which, and why? Does smoking marijuana expand the mind or otherwise make it easier to learn, or does studying harder for high grades lead one to seek relaxation and the release of tension in smoking grass? Perhaps neither of these is true. It may be that pot smoking and high scholastic achievement are two causally unrelated results of growing up in a modern suburban family marked by permissive child rearing. In such an environment we may expect a tolerance for smoking marijuana as well as an availability of good elementary and high schools that provide sound preparation for college. Or perhaps the academically more successful students have more self-confidence and are thus less inclined to follow social rules without first testing alternatives for themselves. To date we do not understand how marijuana use and college grades are related. We suspect that the explanation is complex and that the association does not indicate a simple causal relationship.

Dangerous Extrapolations To **extrapolate** means to estimate a value or extend a series beyond its observed range. For example, one could extrapolate from the sales figures for the past several years to estimate how many cars will be sold next year. At times this can be quite useful. But it should be obvious that we cannot take a sociological trend and mathematically extend it indefinitely. The fact that the birth rate is going down in the United States does not mean that no one will be having babies in the foreseeable future. The fact that the divorce rate is going up does not mean that everyone getting married will someday get divorced. Anyone with elementary skills in arithmetic could take current trends in birth or divorce rates, extrapolate them, and reach startling but farfetched conclusions. Mark Twain (1883) gave us all the warning necessary to avoid this misuse of data:

> There is something fascinating about science . . . the wholesale returns of conjecture out of such a trifling investment of fact. . . . In the space of one hundred and seventy-six years the lower Mississippi has shortened itself two hundred and forty-two miles. That is an average of a trifle over one mile and a third per year. Therefore, any calm person, who is not blind or idiotic, can see that in the old Oolithic Silurian period, just a million years ago next November, the Lower Mississippi was upwards of one million three hundred thousands miles long, and stuck out over the Gulf of Mexico like a fishing rod. And by the same token any person can see that seven hundred and forty-two years from now the Lower Mississippi will be only a mile and three-quarters long, and Cairo and New Orleans will have joined their streets together (p. 129).

REPORT OF THE RESEARCH

The final step in the scientific method is to make a written record and report of the research. The results of sociological research may be reported in a paper read at the meetings of the American Sociological Association, or they may appear as an article in the *American Sociological Review* or in one of the more specialized journals, such as the *Journal of Marriage and the Family* or *Social Problems*. It is important to report research findings for many reasons. A science grows by the steady accumulation of knowledge. Once in a while, to be sure, a major discovery or breakthrough is destined to have a major impact on the discipline. It is not too often, however, that an Archimedes of sociology runs naked down the street yelling "Eureka" upon gaining some sudden insight into the workings of reality.

Generalizations and laws usually grow gradually as the findings of one research effort add to the existing body of knowledge or as an existing generalization is modified by more recent research. If research findings are to contribute to the general body of knowledge, they must, therefore, be carefully and fully reported. Not only must findings be reported, but the methods of research and the interpretation of the findings must be described. Only then can others conduct similar studies to verify the findings or to discover

Sociological research has found that the higher the low-income population density, the higher the rate of crime and other social problems. These high-rise apartments for low-income people proved a failure and had to be torn down.

whether a relationship found to exist in one group can be generalized to apply to other groups.

Many research findings in sociology ultimately have implications for the lives of people. Research results with such immediate implications reach the public in various ways. Formal courses in areas of sociology, such as Juvenile Delinquency, the Family, or Race Relations, are continually updated to take into account the most recent findings and generalizations. The results of some studies reach still wider audiences through newspapers, magazines, and books. The findings that youthful age at marriage is associated with divorce and that the greater the density of a housing unit, the smaller the space with which people identify, and the greater the crime rate have received fairly good coverage in the popular press. The latter has been vulgarized as "the taller the building, the higher the crime rate," but at least the finding is out in the open where citizens and city officials can, if they wish, take it into account when planning multiple-family housing units.

Thus, the research process that begins with the formulation of a problem ends with a report of the findings. It is exciting and intellectually stimulating, even though it involves much tedious work. There are frustrations, such as being unable to get the sample size one would like or not having enough money in the budget to run the data through a computer. There are worries, such as wondering whether one has made the right judgments. Did the researcher phrase the questions so that people understood what he or she meant? What should be done about the fact that five percent of the sample failed to respond to a question? All these questions, and more, are counterbalanced by the realization that one is making a contribution to the field and adding to the ever-expanding store of knowledge.

MAKING PREDICTIONS

Despite the sociologist's use of the scientific method, some people question the scientific nature of the discipline, particularly its ability to predict human behavior. Others, including professional sociologists, argue over what should be done with research findings. These points are related, for if accurate prediction is not possible, it would be foolish—even dangerous—to use the findings of sociological research in an attempt to control future events.

Some people claim that patterns of human interaction and behavior in groups are too elusive and complex ever to be predicted and that the scientific nature of sociology is questionable. Yet sociologists can and do predict the rates of birth, marriage, divorce, death, and other social phenomena. Although lacking precision, a method to predict the success or failure of marriages has been worked out and tested (see Bowerman, 1964). We can predict where in a city the number of arrests for juvenile offenses will be the highest. In these and many other instances we can state what will probably occur, because we think we understand the phenomena or have a grasp—sometimes admittedly slight—of an underlying principle.

Sometimes predictions about human behavior can affect later behavior. The sociologist Robert Merton (1949) adapted to sociology the concept of the **self-fulfilling prophecy,** meaning that a prediction can come true simply because it is made. For example, a teacher might wrongly predict that a certain group of boys will become delinquent and then watch their behavior carefully, crack down on their infringements of minor rules, and perhaps segregate them from the "good boys." If the teacher's actions are sufficiently intense, the close scrutiny could impair the boys' self-images or provoke their hostilities toward a suspicious authority figure, sparking them to rebellious activities. Thus, the boys would become delinquents simply because the teacher predicted it. In addition to the obvious harm to the boys, the false-prediction-come-true could confuse our understanding of the roots of delinquency.

There seems to be a similar concept of **self-defeating prophecy**—that is, some predictions may not come true precisely because they are made. For example, if it is predicted that the spring rains will bring flooding in the suburbs, the citizens can construct better storm sewers; and therefore, the prediction, because it was made, will not come true. Although the self-defeating prophecy may pose a methodological difficulty for the sociologist, it can also be used strategically by those wishing to bring about social change. For example, Zero Population Growth (ZPG) has actively publicized predictions of a future world plagued by overpopulation, massive famine, and shortages of materials and energy. It may be that as people become aware of the dangers of unrestrained population growth they will decide to limit the size of their families. Thus the prediction becomes self-defeating, and the goal of ZPG — the reduction of population growth — will be achieved.

VALUE JUDGMENTS, SCIENTIFIC NEUTRALITY, AND SOCIAL RESPONSIBILITY

For many years sociologists have been debating the place of value judgments in sociology. The issue gets muddled, for sometimes the focus is on what kind of research sociologists ought to do, while at other times, it is on how it ought to be done, and at still other times, on whether the sociologist ought to accept responsibility for seeing that his or her findings are correctly applied. Note that the word "ought" was used three times in the preceding sentence. "Ought" implies an obligation or moral responsibility, and it is this notion, indeed, that is at the heart of the concern over value judgments in sociology. Let us delve into this a little deeper.

Values are the meanings or definitions of worth that we attach to any object, condition, principle, idea, or goal. Self-employed persons may value their relative freedom more than financial security. One group may value the ease of traffic flow over the preservation of an historic building that stands on the site of a street that could be widened. When we make a value judgment, we are expressing a preference for one activity over another. We are saying, in effect, that pursuing one course of action is better, or worth more, than pursuing another. Do scientists, in the course of their research, make value judgments? Should they? The simplistic answer that there is no way to avoid making value judgments hides a very complex issue.

In conducting research, the scientist does not judge whether it is good or bad for chemicals to combine in a certain way or for the birth rate to go up or down. He or she is seeking the truth, whatever it might be. Clearly, it is unethical to fake the results of an experiment or other research so that one can report the kinds of results he or she would like to find. But sometimes the researcher's desires unconsciously affect the results of the study. A team of sociologists may be so convinced that older people have problems, and so distressed over this situation, that the members flavor the kinds of questions they ask of older people, spend more time talking to certain people in the sample, and interpret the old people's responses in light of what they expect to hear. Because the researchers have assumed ahead of time that old people have problems, all they find are problems. The lack of scientific detachment has thus led them to use improper procedures; no sociologist would approve of this kind of research.

There are still other ways in which values affect research. Judgments enter into the choice of research, whether the kind of research an individual wants to conduct or the kind a given society is willing to support (see Box

2.3). If a medical researcher chooses to study techniques for cosmetic plastic surgery, he or she cannot be conducting cancer research at the same time. He or she has made the judgment that it is more interesting, challenging, or profitable to study one and not the other. In a similar manner, sociologists who choose to study urban problems usually cannot be studying decision making in small groups as well. Allowing the researchers in any field to choose the problems they will study and those they will ignore has some obvious advantages. Interest, creativity, and enthusiasm for one's work should run high if one is doing something one has judged to be worthwhile, and consequently one's productivity should be enhanced.

Freedom to conduct research of one's choosing can, of course, result in an overemphasis of some types of problems and an underemphasis of other types. Because of our concern with overpopulation, there is more interest in, and public support for, research into how to control fertility than there is in research that would help couples with a fertility problem to have children. So we learn more about the one problem than the other. To take another example, more sociologists can be found working on problems that affect the poor, the disadvantaged, and the unfortunate than conducting research that would be helpful to the affluent and to big business. You may or may not agree with the value judgments sociologists have made in their selection of research problems, but the main point is to recognize that choices are made in regard to which issues research will be directed toward.

**BOX 2.3
SHOULD ANY SOCIAL ISSUES BE OFF-LIMITS TO THE SOCIOLOGIST?**

Whole societies or particular groups have held certain beliefs as virtually sacred, and scientists have often disagreed with these beliefs—at their own peril. Centuries ago, the Ptolemaic theory of the universe fitted in with the teachings of the Catholic Church, and the Church was not interested in making any changes in that theory. But in 1632, Galileo Galilei published research support for the Copernican theory. The Inquisition promptly invited Galileo to denounce his findings. He pondered the alternatives (which included a very good chance of burning at the stake) and accepted the invitation.

Many sociologists have come up against a modern-day version of Galileo's choice. They have noted broadening political interference in their research and in the treatment of their reports. Many universities have set up review boards to limit the boundaries of research. And in 1973, the United States Department of Health, Education, and Welfare issued a lengthy report on a broad system of control that now applies to all federally funded research.

The area of research where sociologists feel most threatened is that of race relations. Apparently, a combination of factors is at work in this area. Minority problems and proposed solutions have, of course, long been sources of controversy. Minorities have developed their own identi-

A second aspect of scientific neutrality is even more knotty than that of dealing with value judgments and the choice of research topics. It has to do with the application of research findings. We have seen that the goals of every science are understanding and prediction. Along with prediction comes the possibility of control. The practitioners of pure science exclude control from their activities and concerns. But the fact cannot be ignored: the better our knowledge and ability to predict, the better able we are to control matters. If we know when a swollen river will crest, we can build dikes, or at least evacuate the area. The better we understand the causes of a disease, the more likely we are to be able to cure or prevent it.

But we do not have to use the knowledge. Or do we? This is one of the controversies in sociology today, and it has been with us for some time. What responsibility, if any, do we sociologists have to study issues related to the welfare of society or to see that the findings of our studies are applied to the improvement of social ills?

According to one position, sociologists should take a neutral stance. We may want to investigate, for example, the factors associated with divorce. But we should not judge the morality of divorce, nor should we feel compelled to see that our findings benefit couples with marital difficulties. Physicists, chemists, astronomers, and other scientists pursue knowledge in their fields without applying it or being concerned—at least in principle—with its applications. Sociologists, it is held, are scientists, too, even if their

---

ties and have sought to reestablish their own cultures, but they have also become conscious of themselves as victimized groups. In effect, they have become politically significant.

In the politically charged atmosphere of recent years, violent controversies have been triggered by certain sociological reports. To name only a few, the Moynihan report of 1965 concluded that a major black problem was the matriarchal family inherited from the slave past; in 1966 James Coleman reported on the inequality of achievement among black and white school children; and, perhaps most notorious, the so-called Jensen report (see Chapter 16) of 1969 concluded that blacks seemed innately inferior to whites in intelligence.

Many sociologists have been condemned not only for their conclusions but for even having conducted and published their studies. They have gotten the message that "the scientist represents a threat to politically motivated interpreters of reality, and certain things are better left unsaid." The goals of sociologists and politicians appear to be in conflict, and in 1972, sociologist Wilson Record reported that most sociologists who had been specializing in race relations were no longer doing so. Is this a gain for social harmony or a loss for social knowledge? Can you really have the first without the second?

field of study is society and their theories are not as rigorous as those in other sciences. As scientists, they should report what is; it is not their concern to say what should be or to show how their findings can be used to change conditions in society (Lundberg, 1947). They do not work for "the establishment" or against it; science is their only master.

Others claim that sociologists have a moral responsibility to choose research problems that have a bearing on the welfare of society and to see that the findings of their research are applied to the common good. The sociologist should take a stand for or against such social phenomena as a high birth rate, a low infant mortality rate, or an increase in the rate of extramarital sex relations. The sociologist should be involved in changing society, not just in studying it. In 1939 the sociologist Robert S. Lynd, in his book *Knowledge for What?*, argued that sociologists should apply their knowledge to the solution of human ills. More recently, other sociologists have supported this position (Becker, 1967; Friedrichs, 1968; Gouldner, 1962; Mills, 1956).

It is not just sociologists who are concerned with the application of scientific findings. The development of the process called *amniocentesis* is a case in point. This process consists of inserting a hollow needle into the uterus of a pregnant woman, drawing out a little of the amniotic fluid, and analyzing it. Through this procedure, it is possible to determine whether the fetus has certain genetic defects, and somewhat incidentally, whether it is male or female. If the fetus is found to be defective, it could be aborted.

There now exists, therefore, a method whereby couples can effectively choose the sex of their children. It has been suggested that amniocentesis could be used solely to determine the sex of the fetus, so that the parents could choose to abort a healthy fetus that is not of the sex they prefer. Should use of this procedure be allowed, discouraged, or absolutely forbidden? And who should decide these questions? If many people choose the sex of their children, the social implications could be staggering. In the short run, there would probably be an excess of males, for studies repeatedly show that more couples want boys, particularly for the first child. The excess of males would eventually affect the marriage rate, and for a time, men would have to marry women considerably younger than themselves, if they wished to marry at all.

Presumably, the excess of males would make females scarce and desirable, and in the next generation, more couples would choose to have girls. There is no assurance that things would ever even out. Should couples therefore be denied the right to choose the sex of their children? How does one weigh the unhappiness of couples produced by having children of the "wrong" sex against the common good of having approximately half of the births male and half female?

There are those who would say that biologists cannot remain indifferent to the implications of their research and that sociologists have a moral responsibility to speak out concerning the consequences for society, as best as we can determine them, of such research. It is contended, also, that sociologists should be even more willing to interpret their own research for the general public and to speak out on the probable consequences of trends they discover. Meanwhile, as we have seen, others do not feel that it is correct to put sociologists in the position of advocating one course of action over another or of promoting, so to speak, certain social policies and not others.

The controversy between adherents of value-neutrality and social responsibility is not the sort that will be easily resolved. The main thing is to recognize that the controversy exists. Both types of sociologists continue to "do their thing"—and actually, they do much of it in the same way. They differ mainly in the stance they take toward the responsibility of the sociologist in determining how sociological knowledge is applied, but they agree on the procedures necessary to acquire sociological knowledge in the first place.

In the following chapters we will not be referring to controversies over the application of the studies we describe, nor will we discuss, in detail, the research methods used in the studies. We should recognize, however, that these studies followed, in a general way, the procedures set forth in this chapter. By now you should be getting a feel for what sociology is and for how sociologists go about their work. In Part Two, we will come to grips with the basic sociological concepts on which the science is based.

SUMMARY

1. As a scientific enterprise, sociology accepts the basic assumption of science that the universe is orderly. Because there is assumed to be order to social behavior, sociologists believe we can understand social behavior and predict many sorts of social interaction.

2. The process of sociological research begins with **theory**—a set of systematically related propositions. Theories are used to make sense out of collections of facts and to predict new events.

3. In order to do research, the sociologist must develop a **hypothesis**—a statement of a relationship expected to exist between two facts, based on the theory being tested. A hypothesis is stated in terms of **concepts**—labels representing generalized ideas about human interactions.

4. The next step in research is to test the hypothesis by gathering data. One method of gathering data is **sampling**—studying representative members of a larger, overall group. In order to be unbiased, a sample should be random.

5. Most sociological research is in the form of **observation.** In **nonparticipant observation** the researcher witnesses interaction from outside the group; in **participant observation** the researcher is a member of the group being studied. Sociological observation is directed at a specific purpose and is done systematically.

6. Once data have been collected, they must be analyzed. One method of data analysis is to determine the **measures of central tendency**—the **mean, median,** and **mode**—for the set of scores. Averages can be misleading, so it is a good idea to determine the *range* of scores as well.

7. Two sets of scores can be statistically related, or correlated. If the **correlation** between two scores is +1.00, the two are perfectly related; if the correlation is .00, they are not related at all; and if it is −1.00, then they are perfectly inversely related. Correlations do not indicate cause and effect—they merely show a statistical relationship between two sets of data.

8. Once data have been analyzed, they are related back to the original hypothesis, and the findings are related to other research in the same area. Finding that two things are related may allow one, for example, to make predictions and to give advice. However, sociologists must be careful to avoid **spurious relationships**—those that occur accidentally or that reflect the fact that both sets of data are related to a third factor but not to each other. Sociologists must also be careful not to take their **extrapolations** too far.

9. The final step in doing research is to report the findings, either in a journal or at a meeting of sociologists.

10. The findings of sociological research are often used to make predictions. In some cases predictions can result in a **self-fulfilling prophecy**—an event comes about because it was predicted to happen. At other times, predictions result in a **self-defeating prophecy**—the prediction does not come true precisely because it was made.

11. Some sociologists say that sociological research should be treated as any other type of scientific research and that sociologists should remain neutral about how research findings are used. Other sociologists feel that they are obligated to use their work for the good of society and that they should choose research projects with this aim in mind.

KEY TERMS

concept
correlation
deduction
exchange theory
extrapolation
hypothesis
mean
measures of central tendency
median
mode
nonparticipant observation
observation
operational definition
participant observation
sampling
self-defeating prophecy
self-fulfilling prophecy
spurious relationships
statistics
survey research
theory

SUGGESTED READINGS

Braybrooke, David, ed. *Philosophical Problems of the Social Sciences.* New York: Macmillan, 1965.
A collection of essays dealing with the meaning of social reality and the extent to which the social scientist might intrude into that reality.

Forcese, Dennis, and Stephen Richer, eds. *Stages of Social Research: Contemporary Perspectives.* Englewood Cliffs, N.J.: Prentice-Hall, 1970.
A collection of essays on the basic issues in methodology. Such issues include the scientific approach, conceptualization of research problems, measurement, research strategy, sampling, data collection, analysis, and interpretation.

Liebow, Elliot. *Tally's Corner.* Boston: Little, Brown, 1967.
A fascinating account of participant observation research in an urban ghetto.

Matson, Floyd W. *The Broken Image.* Garden City, N.Y.: Doubleday, 1966.
A critique of the relationship of the scientific enterprise to people and society. The author's forcefully presented thesis is that science has reduced and destroyed the human image.

McCall, George J., and J. L. Simmons, eds. *Issues in Participant Observation.* Reading, Mass.: Addison-Wesley, 1969.
A group of essays dealing with such issues as the relationship of field workers to their subjects, the quality of the data gathered, and the difficulties of generating and evaluating hypotheses in participant observation studies.

Philips, Bernard S. *Social Research: Strategy and Tactics.* New York: Macmillan, 1971.
A comprehensive work on the research process, data collection, and data analysis. The book contains a particularly good section on measurement and scaling.

Rosenberg, Morris. *The Logic of Survey Analysis.* New York: Basic Books, 1968.
The author aims at constructing a logical method for the interpretation of survey research data. The book is especially helpful to those interested in learning how to analyze statistical tables.

Schoek, Helmut, and James Wiggins, eds. *Scientism and Values.* Princeton, N.J.: D. Van Nostrand, 1960.
A collection of essays that deal with the question of whether a science of human beings is possible.

Simon, Julian L. *Basic Research Methods in Social Science: The Art of Empirical Investigation.* New York: Random House, 1969.
One of the better works on sociological research. The author views social research in terms of the problems and obstacles that particular approaches have to overcome.

Zetterburg, Hans. *On Theory and Verification in Sociology.* Totowa, N.J.: Bedminster Press, 1965.
The author develops a scheme for the conceptualization of theory and for the deduction of working hypotheses from theory. A good source on what is known in the area of axiomatic theory.

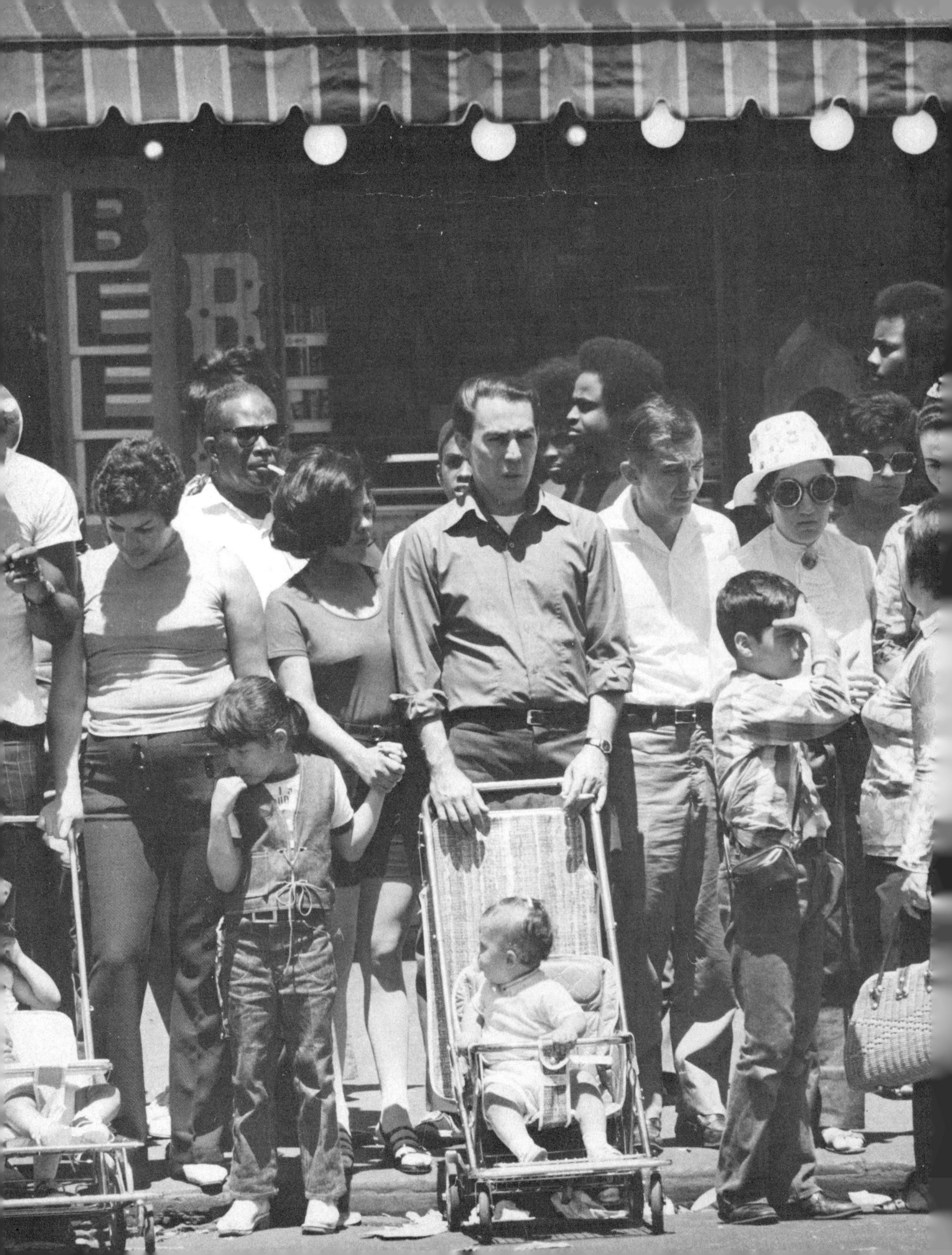

Part Two

Understanding Social Organization

To understand how society is organized, sociologists have developed broad concepts to describe human interaction and the results of such interaction. One such concept is that of culture. It is necessary to realize that this is an example of a familiar word being given a special meaning. In everyday use, the word "culture" may suggest the arts—music, literature, painting, theater; or it may suggest boredom and pretension or excitement and discovery. But does it suggest your ten-speed bike, or your car, or the hot plate in your room, or the belief that men and women should marry before having sexual relations? Do you think of your individual rights and freedoms, your love of chicken, or your calculator as being "culture"?

The word "culture" suggests none of these things to you, but sociologists include all of these objects, ideas, beliefs, and preferences in their concept of culture. Just about everything you believe, everything you own or would like to own, every idea you cherish is part of your culture. The sociologist defines culture very broadly as "a historically derived system of explicit and implicit designs for living, which tend to be shared by all or designated members of a group." As little as this definition may convey to you right now, you should be able to see that culture does pervade our society.

You will soon see, also, that your "humanity" is a product of your culture. We think of ourselves as human beings. However, if by some process of abstraction we were able to remove from ourselves the beliefs, ideas, values, and feelings that we derive from our culture, the only human characteristics remaining to us would be our bodies and our basic physical and psychological needs.

How did we come to be so dependent upon culture that it determines who we are and whether or not we survive? Sociologists would reply that we have reached this point through socialization, the complex process of bringing us from the helpless condition of the newborn to the state of being full-fledged, functioning members of our society. As you can see, the process begins at birth. Child rearing in any society is both the collection of techniques for ensuring the infant's survival and the process of teaching the child the first rudiments of social behavior. During childhood we learn to feed ourselves, to control our bowels and bladders, and to dress ourselves.

Even in early childhood, however, we are not only learning techniques for self-sufficiency, but we are also learning attitudes, beliefs, values, rules, and all of the elements that make up a personality. Some of these are taught us deliberately; others we learn through no one's apparent effort. By observing those around us, particularly our families, we pick up ways of behaving; attitudes toward others; and values about life, society, property, and work. In addition, we augment our observations by imitating others.

Despite the immense human capacity for learning, we would not become true members of a human society were it not for one other crucial element in the human makeup, the capacity to develop a self. Without this capacity, societies probably couldn't survive. Individuals could then simply play at being responsible, functioning members whenever it suited their purposes, and they could violate the needs of others whenever doing so proved profitable. True, almost every society has a certain portion of members who do disregard the people around them, and the rest of us are not always angels and good little scouts. But enough of us are sufficiently dependable that we do not jeopardize society.

Thus, socialization has not only given us ideas, values, and norms, but it has also so formed us that we are committed to the things it has given us, and we identify with them. But to say that we are now members of a society tells us as little as to say that we are human beings. You're a young man or woman, a son or daughter to parents, brother or sister, college student, a friend to many. Perhaps you're already a parent yourself, or you have been in the armed forces as a soldier, sailor, or pilot. The sociologist calls all of these capacities social positions. You are no doubt aware that you are expected to act in certain ways. You are expected to be obedient and respectful to your parents, to give them affection (and you expect to receive it in return), to be studious at college, and to make an earnest effort. The behavior demanded of you in any of your positions is called your role.

The concept of role, as well as that of socialization, can be applied to an important issue in American society: the roles and role relationships of men and women. I'm sure you've heard of women's liberation and may have given some thought to how the situation arose in which women came to occupy subordinate roles. Perhaps you are not aware of the true extent of the inequality between the sexes that exists in education, employment, earnings, and the home. When the concept of socialization is applied to sex-role learning, we gain insight into how society has traditionally produced adult males and females with different kinds of personalities and abilities, and we can see, too, what needs to be done if we wish to release the human potential of both sexes.

The learning of sex roles takes place in groups, first in the family and then in the school and other groups. The concept of group is basic to sociology. Groups have three basic traits: they allow physical and symbolic interaction, or communication, between members, who are aware of one another; they are made up of people who think of themselves, and are thought of by others, as group members; and their members accept roles and obligations as well as privileges and rewards. Undoubtedly, you have belonged to many groups—a family, a play group of children in your neighborhood, hobby groups, friendship cliques, work groups, and so on. You will recognize that some of these groups were quite informal, even intimate, while others were formal, and you didn't get to know the "whole person" of the people in the group. Sociologists study this difference between groups, as well as leadership patterns and other group characteristics.

Nearly all societies are divided not only into different groups, with their positions and roles, but also into classes that vary according to the social rewards their members receive. These rewards can take the form of wealth, prestige, power, or all or any combination of these. Although most societies need most of the positions and roles they encompass, they seem to consider some worthy of more rewards than others, as you can easily observe in our own society. Doctors, lawyers, and other professionals are handsomely rewarded in money and prestige.

Our social class affects more about us than simply how much money we make or how much social prestige and political power we have. Class plays a crucial role in our lives, for it affects our life chances, for example, the likelihood that we will marry early or late, will get divorced or not, will continue long in school or not, or will have larger or smaller families. We are therefore more fortunate than members of many other societies, in that our society allows a relative degree of vertical social mobility—the possibility of moving up (as well as down) the strata of social classes—and thus the possibility of improving our own or our children's life chances.

Only humans have developed tools, beliefs, and values to help ensure their survival; thus, only humans have developed culture. Like many inventions, culture can call necessity its mother, for our lack of instincts to guide our behavior is counterbalanced by our great capacity to learn and communicate. Since humans rarely survive outside of groups, cultures include ways of living harmoniously together and meeting human psychological needs. Because cultures are the invention of many minds, they vary from one to another. An important difference among cultures lies in the ideas and tools that people have developed to solve the practical problems of life in a particular environment. At the hunting and gathering stage of human evolution, there were few tools and few ideas for coping with the environment. Then came the horticultural and agricultural stages, and finally, the industrial stage, which is marked by a vast wealth of ideas and tools for dealing with the environment. Cultures are continually changing, because elements are constantly being added or dropped and because there is imperfect transmission of elements from one generation to the next. Such changes, however, are not always smooth, for often, we change our tools and methods more readily than we change our ideas and values.

3
Culture

Imagine that, while probing into space, we happen to anger aliens living on a distant planet. Imagine, further, that these aliens return the visit and spray the earth with a substance that erases all human memory of everything that has been learned from previous generations and of everything stored prior to the moment of spraying. Men and women would remain intelligent and in other ways human, but they would have no memories of the customs, habits, or abilities passed on by their predecessors—including the ability to use language.

Within a month, most people in our cities would be dead, and the remaining few would probably last less than a year. Shortly after the attack, hunger and thirst would be humankind's main concern, but people would not be able to communicate their needs to their fellows, nor would they be able to tell others about chance findings of food or water. Grunting, upright apes would wander aimlessly in search of food. The stronger would snatch what little is found from the weaker in a desperate effort to survive. Perhaps, after many had already died, some would explore the supermarkets that smelled of rotting meat and vegetables, but they would have no way of knowing that those boxes and cans on the shelves contain food.

Sanitation would be a gigantic problem, because it would never occur to anyone to bury the rapidly increasing numbers of dead. Disease would be rampant. A broken arm would lead inevitably to death. On the farms, people would probably be afraid of the larger animals, but they would survive for a time by eating the smaller ones and any obvious foodstuffs that are stored up or ready to be harvested. In the northern and the temperate zones, the few people who survived for six months or so would perish during the winter. Perhaps some primitive groups in the tropics, where there are fewer threats to physical survival, could stay alive long enough to develop some simple way of life. These primitive people might be all that would stand between the human race and utter extinction.

WHY CULTURE?

What these people would have been robbed of is **culture:** the total way of life of a group. Culture consists of all of the ideas and things that humans have created, that they share with other members of their group, and that they pass on to the next generations. It is culture that affects how life is and should be lived. To study culture is to concentrate on humanity rather than animality, for it is culture that gives humans their unique place in nature. Life without culture is not pleasant to think about, for without culture we would not be human. We desperately need the culture we have created.

Only by responding in one of two ways can any living thing survive in its environment: by *instinct* or by *learned behavior*. Among the lower animals, instinct is supreme. Although animals do learn—often by trial and error,

We understand the message sent by raised eyebrows, pursed lips, and head scratching because the meanings of such acts, like other aspects of culture, are shared by members of our society.

and sometimes by imitation—they are governed mainly by instinct. Learned responses have a tremendous advantage over instincts, for what has been learned can be either modified or replaced by a new and better response. If the learning capacity is high, as in humans, reliance on learned responses provides a truly remarkable advantage in the struggle for survival.

Our tremendous capacity to learn sets us apart from every other animal. Our learning ability is so much greater than that of any other species that this difference is not merely one of degree but one of kind. Equally important in setting humans apart from other animals is our ability to use **language** (see Box 3.1). One person's ideas can be shared with others, and all the ideas that a group creates and collects can be passed on from generation to generation. In the dim past, for example, one person's chance discovery of fire was shared quickly with others and was eventually taught to the children, who in turn, taught it to their children. Thus, culture provides the fundamental means by which human beings store and pass on what has been learned.

Sociologists fascinated with the idea of culture have pursued answers to four broad questions:

1. Why do humans create culture?
2. How do humans create culture?

3. How does culture affect human interaction?
4. How have cultures evolved through the years?

Our chapter-opening fantasy about humans without culture provides a clue to the answer to the first question. Stated simply, humans need culture to solve their problems. In a later section, we will classify these problems and discuss human attempts to deal with them.

The question of how humans create culture can be approached in two ways. The first is by studying the forces, such as geographical environment, that affect the building of culture. The second is by studying cultural change. Because no human group lacks culture, we cannot observe how one would start from scratch and develop its culture. We can, however, study how a group changes the behavior and ideas that form its culture.

BOX 3.1 LANGUAGE AND CULTURE

When Alice objected to Humpty Dumpty's use of the word "glory" to mean "a nice knock-down argument," Humpty said, "When I use a word it means just what I choose it to mean—neither more nor less." Alice then questioned whether one can make words mean different things. "The question is," said Humpty Dumpty, "which is to be master—that's all." In one sense, we are clearly the master of words for, after all, words and language were invented by humans. But as so often is the case, there is another side to the question.

Language is both a part of culture and the means by which the elements of a culture can be shared by a group and transmitted to the next generation. By language, we mean a system of symbols that allows us to transmit and store information—in our minds and elsewhere. A symbol is something that stands for or represents another thing. The word "tree" is not a woody plant of certain dimensions, but rather, a symbol that represents such an object. To be part of a language, the symbol must have a distinctive meaning that is agreed upon by those using it. Otherwise, instead of using language to transmit information, we would merely be making unintelligible sounds at each other. In this sense, words are the master of us all. To communicate effectively, we must adopt the conventional meanings of words.

The importance of conventional symbols for sharing elements of a culture can be illustrated by the difficulty people report in trying to communicate the mental and bodily state reached through Transcendental Meditation (TM). Words like "sleep," "trance," and "unconscious" are clearly inaccurate, while the expression "achieving pure awareness" fails to transmit information to most people. By contrast, the Sanskrit language has some twenty different words to communicate varying states of Nirvana—the states, presumably, achieved in TM.

Answers to the third question, how culture affects human interaction, can be found throughout this chapter, and indeed, throughout the entire book. In this chapter, culture's effects on interaction can be seen with particular clarity in the section on cultural variability. Its effects can also be seen in the discussion of human ingenuity in devising ways to meet group needs. Later chapters, such as those dealing with the family, religion, and the class system, indicate how profoundly culture affects our lives.

Many sociologists have explored the fourth question—how cultures evolve—by studying cultures of both the past and present, in order to develop theories of how cultures change over time. Some of these theories will be explored later in this chapter. First, however, it is necessary to investigate a little more fully what the important concept of culture means to the sociologist.

The importance of shared meanings of symbols is also illustrated in the poor communication that results when people speaking different languages try to communicate. In a discussion with President Kennedy, Soviet Chairman Nikita Khrushchev used a Russian expression in his assertion that the Soviet political and economic system would be around long after our own disappeared—after ours had died and was buried. The Russian expression was translated, "We will bury you," which is clearly a threat and not the statement of conviction that was intended.

But there is more to language than just the verbal aspects. Humans also communicate with gestures and facial expressions. We point our fingers, raise our eyebrows, nod our heads, wink an eye—and in doing so, usually transmit information in a way that other people understand. But gestures have different meanings in different cultures. When the crew of the captured ship Pueblo was made to pose for a group picture in North Korea, several of the men had a finger raised in what is considered by Americans to be an obscene gesture. The ideas of contempt for their captors and lack of cooperation with them were effectively communicated to Americans seeing the picture. When the North Koreans learned the meaning of the gesture, the men were severely punished.

Language comes in still another form: writing. This mode has obvious advantages for providing a lasting record of communications and for transmitting information to people separated by great distances. Laws, decrees, and statements of religious principles, as well as poetry and literary works, can be transmitted from generation to generation more readily in writing than by the spoken word. Language in its various modes, therefore, is the key to how culture is transmitted and has much to do with how it is created as well.

THE MEANING OF CULTURE

Culture has been defined by anthropologist Clyde Kluckhohn (1957) as "a historically derived system of explicit and implicit designs for living, which tend to be shared by all or specifically designated members of a group" (p. 23). Kluckhohn's phrase "historically derived" means that, at any given time, a society's designs for living have come down to the group from earlier generations. In other words, culture is learned, and it is transmitted from generation to generation by the process of socialization (a concept treated more fully in Chapter 4).

Most of the behavior and characteristics we consider human come from culture rather than from biological makeup. Thus, much of what we consider normal or natural is not really so in any ultimate sense. For example, although Americans think it is natural to be competitive in economic affairs, we are competitive only because we have learned to be. It is no more natural for individuals to be economically competitive than it is for them to be cooperative. From our culture we can learn to worship many gods or one, to love several wives or husbands or only one, and so on.

In Kluckhohn's definition, culture is "shared by all or specifically designated members of a group." The idea that culture is shared is very complex and fraught with semantic and other difficulties. How many people must hold a belief or follow a practice before it can be considered a shared cultural element of the group? For example, Americans supposedly share a common language. But do we? A narcotics agent would show little interest in a middle-aged person's remark that he intends to cut the grass. The same statement overheard coming from a college student would elicit quite a different reaction from the same agent. Furthermore, there are regional differences in pronunciation and vocabulary within the United States, and some ethnic minorities make very little use of the English language. Nevertheless, if we think of the similarities rather than the differences, it is apparent that a common core to our language permits adequate communication. It is therefore appropriate to say that Americans really do share a language. In a similar way, other cultural elements can be considered shared if they provide a dominant thread in the goals and destinies of a group, even if not all members of the group make equal use of them.

Although some aspects of a culture are fully shared by only "specifically designated" members of a society, the elements nevertheless belong to that culture. For example, although attitudes and behavior are now changing, much of the behavior of women around the home and in connection with child rearing is still not shared by men. A society's religious leaders have specific knowledge, beliefs, and practices that are unique to them and that are not shared by society as a whole. Political leaders, steam fitters, farmers, and many others in specific occupations share knowledge and behavior among themselves but not with the entire society.

All or most members of society have a general knowledge of the culture shared by those in a specific category; therefore, in a way, all share these aspects of culture. Many Americans of both sexes, for example, have an idea of what is involved in baking bread, even if most men and women do not share with bakers the knowledge and skill required to perform the job. City people have a general knowledge of what is involved in farming, even though they probably do not know enough to be very good at it.

Ethnocentrism

Note that we have used the term society a number of times, and probably from the context you have been able to understand what was meant. By **society** sociologists mean a relatively self-sufficient, independent group that shares a common culture, perpetuates itself, and has an organization that regulates behavior among its members. Often, a society is a political unit—we can speak of the United States or Japan as a society. The political boundaries of primitive societies may not be so clear-cut, but if the people have organized themselves into a group in which most of their needs are met and most of their interaction occurs, and if they share a common culture, they constitute a society. Thus, society refers to the *people* and their organization, while culture refers to the people's way of life.

There is a decided tendency for people in a society to view their own customs and way of life as better, more natural, or superior to corresponding practices in other societies. This tendency is called **ethnocentrism.** The term implies that the world revolves around one's own group, in the same way that "egocentrism" refers to the idea that the world revolves around oneself. Sociologists have discovered that ethnocentrism exists in all known societies, a fact that is not difficult to understand. Most people live out their lives in the society of their birth, learning about and participating in one particular culture. Sometimes they are deliberately taught that their economic system, family system, or some other aspect of their culture is the best or the most natural arrangement. But even without direct instruction, those who know only one way of life find it easy to conclude that this way of life is the best. It is ethnocentrism—the belief that the Christian religion is superior to others—that persuades many Americans to send missionaries to primitive societies throughout the world. And it is ethnocentrism—the belief that their own gods and religious practices are best—that makes such societies resist missionary attempts at conversion to Christianity.

The universal tendency to ethnocentrism can be both functional and dysfunctional. One positive function of ethnocentrism is its tendency toward promoting social solidarity, a sense of unity of opinion and purpose in the group. Belief in the goodness of one's way of life prevents radical social changes in important areas of culture—changes that may be disruptive to the society. But a group that is fully convinced of the superiority of its own values may fail to recognize the worth of other people's values. For example, many Americans so fully accept our nation's emphasis on technological progress, economic growth, and an abundance of consumer goods that they cannot appreciate the fact that "the good life" can be defined in interpersonal or spiritual terms and not economic ones. Furthermore, ethnocentrism can make it difficult for the many societies of the world to understand one another and to engage in cooperative ventures. How many Americans can really accept the fact that millions of people in the world believe that Communism is the best of all possible social systems? And, how many people in Communist societies understand that Americans have faith in their economic system and believe it to be superior to all others?

Sharing Cultural Alternatives

A society that shares a common culture also shares common alternatives. In other words, a given culture may provide more than one belief or practice for use in a given situation or for the achievement of a certain end. These beliefs and practices can be used by almost any member of the society. The culture of the United States, for example, contains a wide range of religions, with no cultural requirement to select a certain one.

Yet, even the widest range of alternatives excludes some of the possible choices. Thus, our variety of religious beliefs and practices does not include human sacrifice to the gods or polygynous marriage (marriage of one man to two or more women at the same time). We can choose to travel by airplane, train, or automobile, but our culture does not offer us the choice of ox cart or camel. These examples should make clear that some things are prohibited in a culture (human sacrifice, for example), while others are simply absent from it (an ox cart or a camel is of no real use in our culture, but their use is not prohibited).

Culture: Material and Nonmaterial

The designs for living shared by a society can be either tangible or intangible. Thus far, most of our examples have been of intangibles, such as language, culturally prescribed marriage forms, and religious beliefs. These and other intangible products of the human mind are nonmaterial aspects of culture. The material aspects of culture are known as *artifacts:* the things that humans have produced. **Material culture** and **nonmaterial culture** are closely related. The automobile, for instance, is quite a tangible object; yet this aspect of our material culture has affected our living patterns, allowing people to live at some distance from their place of work and giving rise to the development of suburbs. An automobile can be a status symbol, a recreational vehicle, a necessary part of a profession, and much more. Only if both the material and the nonmaterial aspects of the automobile are taken into account can we understand how this part of our culture fits into the total way of life of American society.

We humans are idea-making animals. We think up ideas on how to wrest a living from our environment, how to regulate our lives in society, how to amuse ourselves, and how to explain the order of things in nature. Often, these ideas produce material objects. For example, early humans not only came up with the idea that it would be good to have fire, but they also invented tools to produce it. We "modern" humans not only have elaborate systems of ideas that we refer to collectively as our religions, but we have also produced temples, priestly vestments, and sacred objects.

Material objects are inventions, but so are the ideas behind these objects. It would seem logical, therefore, to suppose that no two groups would develop exactly the same culture, either material or nonmaterial. Such is, indeed, the case. Because culture has come from human minds, with countless people helping to shape and modify it, it is unimaginable that even two young cultures could be alike in every detail.

On the other hand, although no two cultures are exactly alike, all cultures should have some features in common. Cultures are invented by men and women, and as biological creatures, all men and women have certain common needs. We may expect, then, that everywhere, basically similar methods will be invented to meet basically similar needs.

FUNCTIONS OF CULTURE

The function of any culture is to assure the survival and well-being of the society. All societies face basic problems that interfere with the group's survival and well-being if they are not solved by the culture. The common problems of people in society everywhere are how to ensure physical survival, how to maintain orderly and satisfactory group living, and how to provide for the psychological needs of the society's members. The results of efforts to solve these problems constitute the three *universal functions of culture,* or **cultural universals** (Linton, 1955). Let us examine each of these functions in detail.

Ensuring Physical Survival

Every culture contains ideas about securing food, providing shelter from the elements, and assuring protection from enemies. The culture directs the way in which people should behave in order to achieve these fundamental goals. Culture further dictates what objects people should make for physical survival and how these objects should be made. The primitive digging stick and the combine of modern wheat farmers are both material culture objects developed to assist people in securing food. In a similar sense, the knowledge of how to construct a thatched-roof hut or a split-level home and the skill of making stone weapons are expressions of the function of culture to help people survive.

A society could not survive for long unless it replaced the members who died. People are easily taught how to make babies. But, they must also be taught how to take care of these babies, so that at least some of the offspring will live to adulthood. Thus, in every culture there are ideas about who should assist the mother during a birth and of how the newborn should be treated. The culture also specifies who will provide food and other necessities for the mother, what and how often the young child should eat, and so forth.

Furthermore, these new members of society must be trained, or socialized, so that they will know how to function in their society. Not only what a child learns, but also how it learns, is determined by culture. For example, if a child is to survive, it must receive nourishment. But what to eat, when to eat, and how to eat—whether with chopsticks, fingers, or knives and forks—are all culturally determined. How this learning takes place is also a matter of cultural determination. In some societies, parents reward their children for culturally approved behavior. In other societies, children are punished for behaving in inappropriate ways. Many societies, including our own, use both reward and punishment. Still other societies depend mainly

---

BOX 3.2 CAUTION: CULTURE IS AN ABSTRACTION

There is no such thing as culture. That is, culture is an abstraction—an idea, not a thing. We form an abstraction by using the same mental process that we use to form concepts. We form an idea about the properties or qualities of an object or about the relationship between objects, and then we mentally separate the idea about the objects from the objects themselves (much as we did with the concept of "table" in Chapter 2).

The important step in forming an abstraction, whether it represents things or people, is that we mentally separate the idea from the actual things or people. The abstraction can be thought of or spoken about without reference to particular people or objects. We can think of tallness without having a person, a tree, or a building in mind. Likewise, honesty is an abstraction. We can observe honest behavior, but we cannot observe honesty. Yet we can talk about honesty, and we believe we know what we mean when we do so.

The abstraction "culture" was invented by early sociologists and anthropologists to stand for the system of shared beliefs and practices of an enduring group and for the material objects that are the products of group behavior or that are in some way related to it. As an abstraction, culture is not the behavior or the objects. It is an idea about them. The idea of culture was derived from observing behavior and objects and from thinking about those observations. In this sense, the idea of culture is much like the ideas of honesty and tallness.

on imitation: the child learns by watching the behavior of adults and older children.

Maintaining Group Living

If a group merely worked out ways to secure its food and shelter and still allowed extreme friction, rivalries, fighting, and killing among its members, the society would be doomed to extinction. Every culture must contain ideas for allowing people to live together without undue friction. Ways of behaving must be established that result in orderly relations between individuals, between groups within a society, and often between one society and others.

Later in this chapter we will look at the evolution of human cultures, noting that one of the results of the improvement in technology is that there are more different kinds of work to be done. At the hunting and gathering stage, for example, the division of labor was simple: most of the men were hunters and most of the women were responsible for gathering nuts and fruits. At later stages of culture there were farmers, tool makers, and various

---

Although everyone knows the difference between an idea and a material object, we sometimes tend to think of the ideas that we create as real objects. This tendency is called reification. When we reify an abstraction, we treat the idea as if it had material substance. Reification may be convenient, but the danger is that we may not always be fully aware of what we have done. For example, we talk of a changing culture. Yet, since culture is an abstraction, it cannot change, for an idea has no ability of its own to change. Again, no culture can compel people to act in any manner. And yet we talk of behavior that is prescribed or dictated by culture. We say, for example, that the practice of female infanticide is prescribed by the culture of some nonliterate group. However, the culture does not drown the babies, some person does—probably the baby's own parent. The various expressions that tend to ascribe life or substance to culture are figurative statements; they are not to be taken literally.

Although the people of a society behave in ways that implement their culture, and although people transmit their culture from one generation to the next, culture can be studied without reference to specific people. Culture tends to persist over long periods of time, while individuals do not. Not everyone in society behaves in a way that implements all aspects of culture. We can therefore study culture in the abstract, charting the changes of a given culture and comparing the culture of one group to that of another. But we must always keep in mind that what we are studying is simply a useful abstraction—there is no such thing as culture.

craftsmen. With the greater division of labor, it became necessary to assure that the work of the various people was somehow coordinated for the common good. One of the cultural techniques invented to coordinate work was the idea of **positions:** medicine man, pottery maker, food gatherer, husband, daughter—all of these are positions that people can fill. To each position, there is attached a **role:** a designation of the behavior that is expected or demanded of the person in that position. (The concepts of position and role are more fully discussed in Chapter 5.) If all members of society learn their roles and how these roles relate to other roles, each person's behavior will contribute to the needs of the group. Each person's conduct will mesh—and not conflict—with the behavior of others. Of course, such a state of affairs is hypothetical and idealistic. For not even the smallest society has been able to develop a network of positions and to define roles in such a way that there are no areas of ambiguity or conflict. Also, no society has been able to get everyone to accept all positions as they are defined or to learn all of the behavior expected of them.

Positions and roles are not by themselves enough to ensure orderly behavior within the group. We have referred already to the need for socialization to teach behavior and attitudes appropriate to various roles. Every society must impose a system of morality—rules of right and wrong—and a system of reward and punishment designed to enforce good behavior. Rules of conduct (or **norms**), like positions and roles, have something important in common with fire-making tools, thatched-roof huts, and animal-skin clothing: they are all human inventions produced to meet human needs, and they all have developed and changed over time. But not one of them was developed as a conscious donation to culture, by a cultural committee as it were. In other words, we should remember that culture is an abstraction invented by social scientists. It is not a thing that people consciously serve, contribute to, or organize (see Box 3.2).

Meeting Psychological Needs

All human beings have basic psychological needs. A society that fails to meet deep-seated human needs will produce discontent among its members and will endanger its own survival. The sociologist William I. Thomas has developed one system for classifying human needs (Thomas and Znaniecki, 1927). In Thomas's view, the needs of humankind produce four basic wishes: (1) the desire for new experience, (2) the desire for security, (3) the desire for response from other individuals, and (4) the desire for recognition. A culture thus must contain diversions, play, creative activities, and other ways for the members of a society to escape boredom and find new experiences. A culture's various aesthetic activities—painting, dancing, writing—provide new experience and an opportunity to gain recognition and response from other members of the group. Security of a long-term sort is provided by the culturally prescribed behavior, beliefs, and rituals that deal with unknown forces and the meaning of life. Sometimes, we derive a sense of security, too, from our government and economic systems, which provide a regularity to life, physical protection, and a means of satisfying our many wants and needs.

We need look no further than our own society to see the discontent that can arise when human needs are not adequately met. Some of the complaints of women, as articulated by those in the women's liberation movement, are that women have been systematically deprived of equal opportunities for new experiences, for response from individuals other than their children, and for recognition in occupations and professions (Morgan, 1970).

The three functions of providing for physical survival, orderly group living, and fulfillment of individual needs are performed by the total culture, not by just a single element. In addition, a given element, whether a material object like a sports car or a complex institution like marriage, may have a variety of functions. A sports car may serve as a student's mode of transportation, but it also may be a source of recognition among his or her peers. Its owner may, very likely, find it a thing of beauty, and keeping it clean and in good condition may help to satisfy his or her aesthetic urges.

To take another example, the cultural rules and practices of marriage and the family serve many functions. By living together in a small, intimate group, individuals can meet their needs for response and recognition from

Cultures everywhere provide ways to allow people to escape boredom and to derive new experiences.

other people. Permitting or encouraging sexual intercourse between marriage partners not only meets the needs of the husband and wife, but it also provides the society with new members. The family provides a sense of security, particularly for the young, but also for the adult members. Regardless of which specific tasks are considered the man's work, which the woman's, and which are shared, the culture of a group contains some ideas on the division of labor within a family, and these ideas, in turn, help to assure that society's members meet their needs for physical survival.

It is also true that the same general function, such as physical survival, is usually served by more than one aspect of culture. The cultivation of food, the construction of dwellings, and the manufacture of clothing are different aspects of culture; but each of these activities contributes to the function of assuring physical survival.

WHY A SPECTRUM OF CULTURES?

Even though all cultures serve the same three functions for society, their methods vary considerably. Digging sticks and tractors are two very different tools with the same function: helping people to secure food. Earlier, we suggested one explanation for cultural diversity. Since every culture and element within it is an invention of human minds in response to basic needs, it is highly unlikely that the collective ideas of any two groups will be exactly alike. Other influences contribute to cultural diversity, however. Among these are geographical environment and race. But how great are these contributions? Let us examine them in some detail, and then return for a further consideration of human versatility.

Geographic Environment

Most geography texts show Eskimos living in igloos and South Pacific islanders living in thatched-roof huts; they present a picture of Chinese junks on the Yangtze River; of scantily clad, spear-throwing Bushmen on the African plains; and of the great cities of Western civilization. The notion of cultural variability—that humans secure their food and protect themselves from the elements in many different ways—is learned early. But this textbook presentation can lead to a false conclusion. Having learned that geographic environments vary considerably and that cultures also vary considerably, one might conclude that geography somehow produces the cultural variability. Such a conclusion is wrong, or at best, a gross exaggeration.

Geographic environment imposes some limits on a culture. A particular environment poses certain problems and usually limits the variety of possible solutions. To survive, people must somehow reckon with the temperature, terrain, animal and plant life, and other features of their environment. Eskimos could not have invented bamboo dwellings, because bamboo is not

Geography places some limits on human cultures but the ideas of growing rice and using a boat came from the minds of humans and were not dictated by the geographic environment.

available to them. And bamboo would not provide an effective arctic shelter, even if it could be obtained. Tribes deep in the interior of Africa, no matter how hungry they become, could not develop new and better ways of harpooning whales.

The presence of wild, fruit-bearing trees might well have tempted people to taste the fruit, and much later, perhaps, to cultivate the fruit trees. Fur-clad animals may have given our shivering ancestors the idea of slaying the animals and wrapping the fur around themselves. Even for early humans, though, the mere presence of certain resources in the environment by no means guaranteed that these resources would be used. The American Indians did not see in the Great Lakes the possibility of a great inland water route, nor did they feel obliged to improve on nature by digging the Erie Canal. The forests of our continent did not suggest a lumber industry or the processing of wood pulp for newspapers to them. They never used the coal that lay beneath their campgrounds to warm a dwelling or cook a meal. Groups in the Siberian Arctic, such as the Chukchi and Yukaghir, live in an environment quite similar to that of the Eskimo, yet they have never built an igloo. Instead of using the snow around them, they make shelters of skin attached to a framework of wood; and they do so even though wood is scarce in their environment (Herskovits, 1955).

Even when geographic features suggest certain functions, the environment does not tell people how to carry out these functions. River and lake dwellers may eventually try water transportation, but rivers and lakes do not tell them what kind of boat to build or how to build it. Different groups along the same river can and do develop different kinds of boats. Only the available animals can be hunted, but they can be killed in many different ways. Only the available fruits and vegetables can be eaten, but they can be carried home in a basket, wrapped in an animal skin, or eaten on the spot. The environment of early humans, therefore, placed some limits on early culture and suggested some strategies for survival, but it did not determine cultural development for these people.

The nonmaterial aspects of culture seem even less traceable to geographic environment. It is indeed farfetched to think of the presence of rivers and mountains as accounting for the existence of religions, even though both have been personified and worshipped. Neither trees nor rainfall nor temperature can explain the variability of marriage systems throughout the world. Only in a loose sense can the physical environment affect human artistic endeavors or play activities. There is, then, only a very limited connection between the physical environment and the strategies developed by different cultures for assuring their survival.

Race and Culture

By the same reasoning that derives cultural variety from geographic variety, we can observe that there are different physical types, or **races,** of humans and that humans have different cultures. You will recall from Chapter 2 that to propose a relationship between two observations is to state a hypothesis. In this case, we observe that people differ in their physical make-up, and that cultures differ from one another. When it is maintained that the physical differences cause the cultural ones, we have a hypothesis. A hypothesis is not a fact, but it can be tested; that is, we can gather evidence and discover whether or not the hypothesis is supported. In this case, the evidence strongly suggests that differences in race do not cause differences in culture.

By "race" we mean major groupings of people who share inherited physical characteristics. The people of the world are often classified into three

---

BOX 3.3 DO ANIMALS HAVE CULTURE?

In 1953, social scientists in Japan observed a monkey pick up a sweet potato covered with sand, soak it in water, and wash off the sand with her hands. While raccoons customarily wash their food, presumably by instinct, such behavior is not considered instinctive in the monkey. In human terms, washing the sweet potato was an idea a particular monkey invented. A month later, one of her playmates began to wash sweet potatoes, and a few months after that, the mother of the monkey who invented the custom was observed doing the same thing. The behavior spread, and in ten years about 75 percent of the troop members were washing their sweet potatoes before eating them.

The potato-washing behavior was learned, rather than instinctive. Eventually, it was shared within the group, became a part of their way of life, and was transmitted to succeeding generations. Apparently, potato-washing proved to be functional or useful, perhaps making the food more palatable or easier to eat. The monkeys observed one another engaging in all sorts of behavior but only began to share and transmit that

major races: Mongoloid, Negroid, and Caucasoid. Chinese, Japanese, Koreans, Okinawans, American Indians, and many smaller groups make up the Mongoloid race. From this short list, alone, it is immediately obvious that different cultures have been developed by people of the same race. The corollary to this is also true: different races can participate in and help develop the same culture. We need look no further than our own society for evidence of this fact. Caucasians, Negroes, and Mongolians share a common culture. Could this be possible if a given race customarily produced a single type of culture?

The hypothesis that race determines culture could be true only if one of two conditions prevailed. Because culture exists to satisfy human needs, either the different races have different needs, or the different races have different abilities to satisfy their needs. Some 20 years ago, social scientists proved both assumptions false (Comas, 1956; Montagu, 1963). It is no accident, therefore, that the same race can produce different cultures or that different races can contribute to the same culture. Most differences among races are superficial and are not of the sort that would lead to the development of different cultures. In other words, such trivial characteristics as skin color, hair texture, and shape of eyes could scarcely be related to the ideas and products of ideas that constitute human culture.

Human Inventiveness in Meeting Needs

Remember that culture is invented, maintained, and transmitted by human behavior. So, to explain the variability of culture, perhaps we should first look at the human species. (Is culture limited to human beings? See Box 3.3.)

---

which was of some use in their daily lives. Nor is this potato-washing an isolated instance of learned, shared behavior. Bathing habits, the care of infants, and cries indicating danger have been found to be learned by the young from the mature members of an animal group, to be shared by that group, and to be more or less distinctive from the patterns found in other groups of the same species.

Do animals have culture? If we define culture as something possessed only by humans, then clearly they do not. But this is playing games with words. The essence of culture seems to exist among animals even though most of their behavior is not learned, shared, or transmitted. It is still correct to say that humans have a distinctive place in nature by virtue of the complexity of their cultures and the great number of ways in which culture, and not instinct, governs human behavior. It is tempting to conclude that the differences between human and animal cultures are so great that they are different kinds of phenomena rather than differing degrees of the same thing. Or is this just an example of ethnocentric thinking?

84
UNDERSTANDING SOCIAL ORGANIZATION

Two human characteristics make it highly unlikely that any two groups would develop precisely the same way of life: our intelligence, and our physiological flexibility. First, human intelligence allows the invention of more than one solution to almost any problem. Second, human physiological characteristics are such that many different solutions to a given problem will work. Let's take the examples of food and sexual behavior.

Food: A Biological Need and a Cultural Artifact Like the lower animals, humans need food to survive; but unlike them, humans have surrounded their procuring, processing, and consuming of food with a variety of mean-

All cultures contain some ideas on what is food and how it should be prepared but the specifics vary considerably from culture to culture.

ings. No dog or chimpanzee seems to have developed the idea that it is wrong to eat certain foods. Yet, in modern as well as primitive societies, food taboos abound. Jews eat no pork; Hindus eat no beef; until recently, American Catholics ate no meat on Fridays; and many sects and individuals eat no meat at all.

What is considered food also varies from culture to culture. We may choose not to eat, say, chicken, beef, or pork. Whatever our taste, though, we recognize these items as food. But what about snakes, eels, grasshoppers, and rats? Many Americans would maintain that these are not food. Yet for people in other cultures—and even for some Americans—these foods are rare delicacies.

Just as humans have come up with different meanings for the food sources they see around them, so they have invented a host of ways to process their food. They fry their fish, smoke it over a fire, or eat it raw. Some people have regular meals; some just eat whenever they are hungry. Some cultures may designate that only certain foods are appropriate for feasts or parties. These values, attitudes, meanings, and emotions associated with food and the eating of it are human inventions. Once acquired and shared by a group, these meanings tend to be transmitted to later generations, so that great cultural variability develops with respect to food.

Sexual Variability   No known society is completely indifferent to the sexual behavior of its members: all cultures contain values, regulations, and emotions concerning this behavior. And again, from culture to culture, there is a great variety in the ways in which this behavior is handled.

Societies must both permit sexual behavior and limit it. Without sexual reproduction, the society would die out from lack of replacements. In addition, total prohibition of the expression of the adult sex drive would provoke serious discontent and thus jeopardize the society. But at the same time, a society completely indifferent to its members' sexual behavior would be in jeopardy. (As we said, no such group is known. This is probably because the human sexual drive and its expression have the potential for so much conflict, jealousy, and guilt that without regulations the harmony of group life would be seriously threatened.)

All societies, therefore, must reckon with the same biological facts of human sexuality. True to form, humankind has been extremely ingenious in the variety of ways it has invented to cope with the dual social needs for permission and prohibition of sexual expression. To be sure, as a legitimate relationship for sexual expression, marriage has been a universal invention. But the forms this invention has taken are various.

Among the many variants of marriage are: monogamy (one man married to one woman, a common but not universal form), polygyny (one man married to more than one wife at a time, common in the Old Testament and often found today, particularly in nonliterate societies), polyandry (one woman with more than one husband at a time, found less frequently than polygyny), and group marriage (several men and women living together as a family group).

Marriage is only one method of dealing with human sexuality that societies have invented (see Murdock, 1949). The other customs and regulations invented to deal with this show the same variety as that found in the custom of marriage. For example, every culture prohibits sexual intercourse between close relatives, but the definition of "close relative" differs widely—first cousins may be either tabooed as marriage partners or considered the best possible mates. Premarital sexual relations may be tolerated under some circumstances in one society, severely punished in another, and encouraged in a third; adultery may be either mildly criticized or punished by death; prostitution may be part of religious rites, it may be condoned or defended, it may be considered a great social ill, or it may not even exist. Human ingenuity, therefore, has resulted in a wide range of sexual practices, customs, and values.

The diversity that societies show in food practices and control of the sex drive extends into every area of social life—political systems, economic systems, and so on. Our ability to invent various ways to satisfy our needs explains most of the differences between cultures. But only principles governing cultural change can supply a satisfactory explanation for the variety of cultures in the world today. For even if two or more cultures happened to be similar at the time of their origins, the principles of cultural change assure that they would not be similar today.

There is much variation in marriage from culture to culture. Not so long ago, Hindu parents were expected to select marriage partners for their children and a couple like this might meet for the first time on their wedding day.

THE EVOLUTION OF HUMAN CULTURES

By its very nature, culture must change. Because culture is a human invention, there is little reason to assume that the development of a certain culture will bring an end to inventiveness. On the contrary, it is much more reasonable to assume that the same general processes of invention that formed the culture will continue to change it. In addition, culture is transmitted from one generation to the next. But culture does not transmit itself; people transmit it. Furthermore, each person has his or her own interpretation of what is to be transmitted. So, even if faithful transmission were attempted, some changes would be introduced. Culture is developed to satisfy human needs and desires. But needs and desires change. As people learn more about their environment and what can be done with it and to it, they come to have different expectations. The desires of humans go far beyond the wish to develop ever better means to assure physical survival. In any ultimate sense, people's desire for a better way of life, however it is defined, is insatiable. Finally, when people encounter other societies, they discover new needs and wants. To provide for these new expectations, a culture must be able to change.

Technology and Change

You will recall (from Chapter 1) that late nineteenth-century social theorists—Comte, Spencer, Marx—developed theories on the stages through which human societies progress. These theorists were more concerned with broad, general descriptions of the dominant mode of thought at different stages and less concerned with the content or nature of the culture at different stages of human development. Comte, for example, posited an early stage in which people gave theological explanations for everything, but he wasn't too concerned with what cultures were like in that early stage or with how they moved from that stage to the next.

At about the same time as Comte, a Danish anthropologist, Christian Thomsen, was busy developing a system for classifying the artifacts that had been dug up at many prehistoric dwelling sites. It became apparent to him that the *kinds* of material from which tools and other artifacts were made—stone, bronze, iron—had each been the dominant material during a certain stage of cultural development. From his observations came the designations Stone Age, Bronze Age, and Iron Age for the chronological stages of cultures.

As time went on, anthropologists and sociologists shifted their emphasis from the time stages of human existence to the nature of the technology at different stages and how this technology, in turn, affected the social organization of human groups. By **technology** we mean the information, techniques, and tools with which humans utilize the material resources of their environment to satisfy their needs and desires (Lenski, 1970). Technology thus includes all of the ideas and things that are developed to manipulate or use the material environment to solve the practical problems of life. Technology plays a vital role in the evolution of human societies and their cultures. The anthropologist Walter Goldschmidt (1959) has identified five broad, fundamental changes that generally result from significant changes in technology:

1. With better technology, whatever resources the environment has to offer can be utilized more easily and efficiently; this usually results in *population growth.*
2. With better technology with which to work the natural resources, there is less need for migration, and *settlements can become more permanent.*
3. Better technology leads to an *increase in the production of goods and services.* (This helps to support the greater population, but the production increase should occur whether or not the population increases.)
4. As technology advances, it becomes increasingly difficult for everyone in society to master all aspects of it; accordingly, *division of labor and specialization of work roles are likely to increase.*
5. Advanced technology implies that *some people are released from the production of the basic necessities of life,* such as food and shelter. Some individuals are thus free to devote their time to such things as art, politics, and religion.

**BOX 3.4
THE TASADAY: THE STONE AGE AS THE GARDEN OF EDEN**

Since the vague beginnings of the social sciences, workers in the field have gathered evidence that all societies and cultures share certain fundamental traits. It had long been thought by anthropologists and other social scientists that primitive people who subsisted by food gathering, and therefore spent all their time scrounging for the bare essentials, would not be settled enough to invent a technology.

But in 1971, in the dense mountain jungle of the Mindanao rain forest on one of the Philippine Islands, anthropologists made contact with the Tasaday, a tiny, peaceable tribe of 24 persons who did no hunting or farming and who knew neither war nor hatred. Their food could be gathered in a few hours each day, and the rest of their time was leisure. Yet, they had not developed a technology any more advanced than the classic Stone Age tools of the stone axe, for opening roots and sharpening bamboo tools, and a fire-making tool.

Except for a bamboo version of the jew's-harp for music, they exhibited no arts, and they lived in natural, unadorned caves. They had some fears and taboos, such as a fear of thunder and a taboo against venturing far

This list could be greatly expanded. We could show, for example, how increased productivity coupled with division of labor leads to greater inequalities in a society. Some people, by virtue of their specialized roles, thus come to demand greater rewards and power than others. But our purpose here is to look at the kinds of societies that have resulted from the significant changes in the technology throughout the long course of human history. Let us examine more closely one scheme for classifying stages of society.

A Classification of Human Societies

The classification of human societies that follows is based on the kind of technology used to secure the basic necessities of life (Lenski, 1970). Such a classification system does not imply that there are forces that inevitably propel societies from one stage to another and that always bring about certain social organization effects (see Box 3.4). Rather, the stages should be thought of as representing the typical progression of human groups, and the effects of technology at each stage should be recognized as those that are usually associated with each technological stage.

Simple Hunting and Gathering Societies These societies existed more than 35,000 years ago. The people in them subsisted by gathering wild plants and hunting game. Basically, human energy was the only element used in these and other subsistence pursuits; the best of the technology at this first stage was the wooden spear.

---

from their caves at night, but they had no articulated religious beliefs or myths to explain to themselves where they came from and why they were here. Asked if they had souls, their young spokesman said, "We don't know."

When a hunter and trapper of a neighboring tribe had accidentally come across some Tasaday in 1966, he gave them various hunting tools and weapons and taught them how to trap. But they remained nonhunters and became only casual trappers, using their new steel-blade knives in their old food-gathering pursuits, adding only two edible plants to their diet. About animal flesh they said, "We found that their meat is good, but we do not need it."

Although this newly discovered tribe has been little studied, we can tentatively state that, while adversity retards technological development, the absence of adversity makes such development unnecessary. And this rule might also apply to the nonmaterial elements of culture, such as religious beliefs and creation myths.

FIGURE 3.1 Basic Types of Human Societies

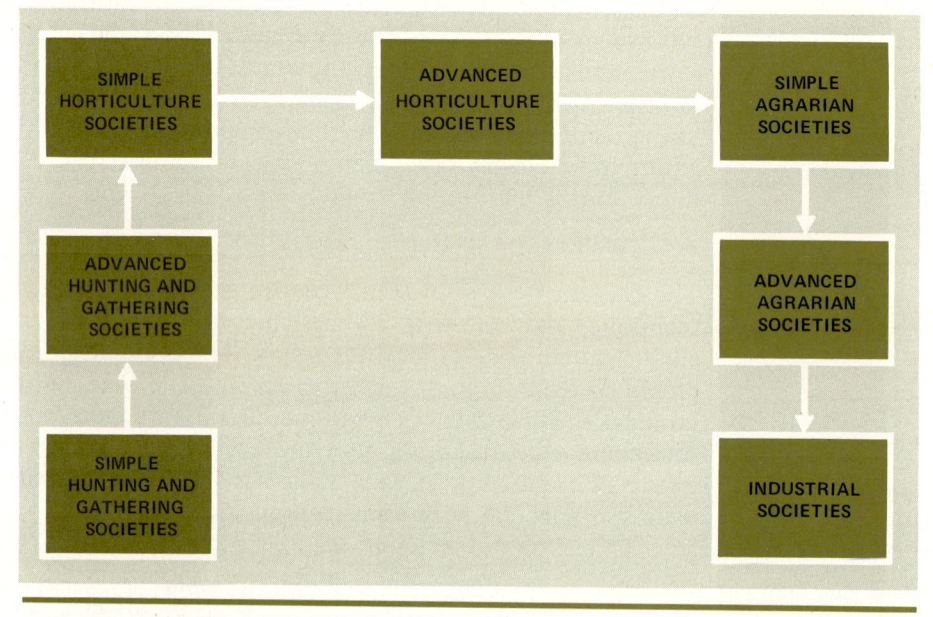

Source: Gerhard Lenski and Jean Lenski, *Human Societies,* 3rd ed. (New York: McGraw-Hill, 1978), p. 90. Used by permission.

Advanced Hunting and Gathering Societies The important technological developments distinguishing this stage from the first one were the bow and arrow and the spear thrower. Food became somewhat easier to obtain, leading to population growth and some increase in leisure time.

Simple Horticultural Societies About 10,000 years ago, humans came up with the idea of deliberately planting roots or seeds. Cultivated plants then became the major source of food. At first, the only tools for cultivation were the wooden hoe and the digging stick. Nevertheless, settlements could be more permanent, and somewhat larger numbers of people could live within a given geographical area. The male, by virtue of his size and strength, was responsible for clearing the land. Control over the strategic resource of land made it possible for inequalities in wealth and power to develop.

Advanced Horticultural Societies A major change in the culture of horticultural societies was the invention of metal (chiefly bronze) tools and weapons. This made food production a lot easier and accentuated the various results of the horticultural stage, such as population growth and permanent settlements.

Simple Agrarian Societies   It is not farfetched to say that the invention of the plow was the forerunner of a cultural revolution. With the plow, soil could be turned over to a greater depth than with the hoe, thus bringing back to the surface the nutrients that were leeched below root level. Weeds that competed with crops for moisture and nutrients could more easily be controlled. The same fields could be used over and over again, and human dwelling sites became permanent. The plow dates back to about 3000 B.C., and early versions were but modifications of the hoe (which shows how culture builds on existing traits).

Advanced Agrarian Societies   The distinguishing feature of this level of society is the use and manufacture of iron tools and weapons. The use of iron made a significant improvement in such tools as the plow, particularly after people thought of using animals to pull it. The potential for a large agricultural surplus increased dramatically. More and more people were released from the necessity of working the land to provide sustenance for themselves and their families. It was in this period that cities arose, writing was invented, empires were developed, and considerably more time was devoted to the arts and to religion. Occupational specialization increased dramatically, resulting in great differences in wealth among craftsmen, landowners, peasants, and rulers. Birth rates were high but were offset by the high death rates that accompanied urban living.

Industrial Societies   In the middle of the eighteenth century there occurred what is commonly called the Industrial Revolution. Entire books have been written on the subject, cataloging the many inventions that came one after the other. A key feature of this stage was the large-scale use of mineral energy sources. This led to a tremendous increase in the efficiency with which goods could be produced, great surpluses of goods beyond what was needed for mere sustenance, and eventually, a fantastic increase in the *kinds* of goods that were available. Control over the natural environment, the ability to wrest new materials from it, and the ease of traveling over it were radically changed from what they had been before.

The effects of industrialization have been truly tremendous. Some of them will be dealt with in various later chapters, particularly those on education, the family, social change, government, population, and the city. Suffice it to say, at this point, that the label "revolution" is an apt one.

PROCESSES OF CULTURAL CHANGE

The long evolution from hunting and gathering societies to the modern industrial state did not just happen. People made it happen by changing the technological and other aspects of their cultures. We have seen *what* changed in human cultures. Now let us look at *how* cultural change occurs.

There are only three essential ways in which a culture can change: (1) new elements can be added, (2) elements can be dropped, and (3) elements can be redefined or reinterpreted, so that they have a new meaning to the group. At times the three methods are intertwined, but it is best to examine them separately.

Adding Cultural Elements

Whether it is a complex, intangible pattern like Christianity or a simple cultural object like the longbow or the airplane, any new item is added to a culture by the same three-step process: (1) the society learns of the potential addition to the culture; (2) the element is accepted by the group; and (3) the new element is integrated, to some degree, into the existing culture.

A society can learn about a potential addition to its culture in several ways: the new item can be discovered, invented, or borrowed from another group.

Invention and Discovery The term **invention** refers to a new combination of existing material and nonmaterial elements of a culture to produce something distinctive. For example, everything that "went into" the first airplane existed in many cultures prior to the time that a number of inventors, working independently, put the various elements together to make the airplane.

The most important factor affecting the rate of invention is the magnitude of the elements in the existing culture. The more elements there are—whether material or nonmaterial—the more different ways they can be combined to form something new. Regardless of the size of the culture base, however, people still have to *want* to invent new ideas and objects.

Most of us have heard the expression, "Necessity is the mother of invention," which suggests a rational explanation for inventions. If there is a problem, human ingenuity will be turned to solving it. History gives us many examples of this sequence. Machines are invented to release people from toil, medicines and surgical techniques are developed to fight disease and restore health, and systems of traffic control are devised to ease movement in large cities.

It makes equal sense, however, to reverse the idea and claim that, "Invention is the mother of necessity." In other words, the invention may create the need. Television provides an excellent example of this. Before its invention, there was no need for it. Today, millions are highly dependent on it and find it difficult to imagine life without it. The giant field of advertising, of course, rests on the assumption that once something is invented, people can be convinced that they need it.

The term **discovery** is reserved for situations in which something entirely new is added to a culture. It is proper to talk of the discovery of a principle of genetics, of the properties of the atom, or of a previously unknown form of plant life. A discovery may be the result of a deliberate search, or it may be a more or less accidental result of human curiosity about the unknown. The motivation behind a discovery can affect the use to which it is put. The New World, for example, was discovered because a shorter trade route was being sought to the Indies. But consider that, in fact, Columbus *re*discovered a continent that the Scandinavians had discovered centuries earlier. (Obviously, the Native Americans had discovered the continent earlier still.) Apparently, the Scandinavians had little need to incorporate their discovery into their culture. But the fifteenth and sixteenth century Spanish, Portuguese, French, and English were at a stage of economic and social development that made Columbus's discovery immensely useful to them.

Not all inventions and discoveries are made to fill needs, or even to create needs. The private notebooks of Leonardo da Vinci, who died in 1519, are filled with detailed scale drawings of such military items as the machine gun, the helicopter, and the tank. Apparently, da Vinci invented these ideas for his own entertainment, and they were not even made public within his lifetime. In our own society, many longstanding needs remain unfulfilled. Despite immense efforts, we still do not have a cure for cancer. Nor have we managed to alleviate poverty and great economic inequality.

Cultural Diffusion: Borrowing Among Cultures New cultural elements can be introduced into a society when ideas or practices spread from one society to another. This process is called **cultural diffusion.** Probably every society that has come into contact with another has borrowed some cultural traits. Thus, almost all human societies owe parts of their culture to other groups.

Contemporary industrialized societies that have been in contact with many other groups sometimes seem to have a hodgepodge of cultural traits liberally borrowed from a host of groups over many years. For example, the dominant religion in Western Europe and the United States came from the Middle East, our alphabet from the Phoenicians, the dishes we eat on from China, and so on. It is important to remember, however, that every cultural trait that is diffused was invented by somebody somewhere.

Particularly when we deal with complex ideas, it can be difficult to trace the diffusion of the cultural elements. For example, the concept of democracy shows its roots in the Athenian Constitution of 508 B.C., while the Magna Carta of A.D. 1215 revived the notion of individual rights and liberties. The ideas of many thinkers in other countries as well as the United States in the last several centuries have added to and modified the principles of democracy. By now it is almost impossible to say how much of the current American meaning of democracy was borrowed and how much of it was invented. So it is with other ideas and practices.

The process of cultural diffusion is essentially the same, whether the ideas are actively sought by one society or are brought into it by an outside group. Almost a thousand years after Christianity had spread through

Europe, it was still practically unknown in Russia. Prince Vladimir sent emissaries to both Rome and Constantinople to learn more about this religion. Following the emissaries' glowing reports, he embraced the Greek Orthodox religion and persuaded other princes to join him. They, in turn, brought their subjects into the church. A new culture pattern, one that was destined to have a profound effect on the lives of the masses, was thus deliberately sought out and brought into the culture from another society.

At other times, the initiative for cultural diffusion rests with a group that attempts, peacefully or otherwise, to teach its way of life to other peoples. A little more than 100 years ago, Commodore Perry sailed into Yokohama Bay and opened the ports of Japan to world trade. A nation that had long shut itself off from the rest of the world became a world power in about fifty years. Today most Americans are acquainted with the various kinds of economic, technological, and agricultural assistance that their country is providing to the developing nations. On a smaller scale, our own and other countries have for years been sending religious missionaries, doctors, and teachers to less developed nations for the purpose of teaching them aspects of our way of life.

Sometimes a conquering group will attempt to eradicate parts of the culture of a defeated group and teach the people a new way of life. During the Japanese occupation of Korea, for example, the Koreans were forced to change many aspects of their life, including the long, braided hairstyles of the men. Many decades earlier, it seemed that the manifest policy of the European American was to force the Native American Indians to change their way of life to conform with that of the invaders. Diffusion, therefore, is not always a slow and peaceful process but can occur relatively quickly and by force.

Acceptance of a Cultural Element Whether a society learns of a cultural trait by invention or diffusion, that trait must be accepted at least to some degree by the group before it becomes a part of the culture. It is sometimes difficult to explain why a group will accept some new traits but not others. Late in the eighteenth century, a commission of French scientists developed a new system of weights and measures, called the *metric system*. Objectively, this system seems superior to the English system of inches and feet and is now used in most industrialized countries. Certainly, the idea of the metric system was diffused to the United States a long time ago, but it has not yet been accepted as a part of our general culture. Very likely we will adopt the metric system, and possibly soon, but we have not yet done so.

The source of a new idea can sometimes influence whether it will be accepted or rejected. This may explain our prolonged resistance to the metric system—countries under English control or influence were not prone to accept foreign ideas, especially from a political enemy like eighteenth-century France. As another example, imagine the fate of a congressional bill to broaden our social security program if its backers were to say that they got the idea from the Russians. Before World War II, Japan had a reputation as an exporter of cheap, inferior merchandise that accounts for our resistance, in recent years, to accepting Japan as a producer of high-quality optical and electronic goods.

The sheer utility of an element does not guarantee its acceptance, for the element must be seen as useful by the potentially borrowing group (see Chapter 13). Also, new elements that seem to fit in with the existing culture — that are not contrary to the group's values — are more likely to be accepted than are other types. The Eskimo is not likely to borrow the bikini, nor the Hindu to borrow some new technique for preparing beef. Yet much is unknown. Just a few decades ago it would have seemed ludicrous to predict that Japan would adopt democracy so quickly and with so much enthusiasm. The introduction of Christianity in some primitive societies has also met with outstanding success, despite its apparent contradiction with existing religious beliefs.

Integration of the New Element The third step in the addition of a cultural element is its integration into the existing culture. If the new element is a borrowed one, new meanings are often assigned to it, so that it can merge with the existing culture. Thus, for example, in some areas where Catholicism has been introduced and accepted, the gods and spirits of the native religion have become fused with the saints of the Catholic church. In Haiti, converts to Catholicism merged the personalities of the Dahomean rainbow serpent with Saint Patrick, who is often portrayed amidst snakes. The Haitian god Lagba, who dressed in rags, was fused with Saint Anthony, the patron of the poor.

Invented cultural elements also must be integrated into the culture. The element must be assigned meanings, and its relationship with existing elements must be defined. Consider the invention of television. As TV became integrated into our culture, radio and its functions and meanings had to be redefined. Daytime soap operas and evening drama and variety shows shifted to the new medium, leaving radio with music, news, and call-in shows. In addition, new rules of etiquette for visiting patterns have been developed. For many, the meaning of the family mealtime has been altered by the fact that some meals are taken in front of the TV set. Schools, churches, airlines, and bars have all developed ways to integrate this invention into their particular segment of the culture. Many more aspects of our culture have been changed as we have worked television into our total way of life.

Loss and Redefinition of Cultural Elements

For some reason, how and why some cultural elements are lost have been studied less than the ways in which these elements are acquired. Perhaps a trait is dropped by a culture because a new one is introduced that performs a similar function better or more efficiently. But not all elements are dropped when a new and better one is introduced, and some traits are lost without being replaced by an invented or borrowed one.

When a society learns of a new and better idea, it may drop the older element reluctantly or altogether refuse to give it up. The old order of Amish use the horse and buggy as a form of transportation. For almost everyone else in the United States, the horse and buggy has, for all practical purposes, been dropped from the culture. Newer methods of transportation have supplanted it, so that all that remains is its history. But this does not always happen.

The fireplace is still a very real part of our society's culture. It is found in public buildings, lodges, camps, offices, and most of all, in quite a number of American homes. When more effective ways of heating homes were developed, the fireplace was not dropped. The existing cultural element was reintegrated into the culture when other methods were developed. New meanings have been assigned to the fireplace, and new functions have been devised for it. Today, the fireplace is used because it is considered attractive, because it serves as a focus of interest in room decoration, and perhaps, because fire symbolizes psychological warmth and comfort.

Someday, unless the energy crisis becomes more severe or is taken more seriously, the electric table fan will be widely replaced by air conditioning. But the fan is not likely to be kept for some aesthetic reason or otherwise reintegrated into the culture. What is the difference between the fan and the fireplace? Quite possibly, the fireplace had other meanings, even when it was valued chiefly for its utilitarian functions. The aesthetic and psychological meanings came to be emphasized as the utilitarian meanings became less important. The more numerous the different functions a given cultural trait serves, the more likely it is that the trait will be retained when one of its functions is replaced by a newer trait.

Although our examples have focused on simple material culture traits, it can be seen that it is difficult to establish basic principles that explain the loss of cultural elements. With more complex matters—particularly ideas—the task of explaining cultural losses is more difficult still.

By now, it should be clearer what is meant by the simple statement that culture is the way of life of a group. The knowledge and practices of early humans were meager, but they were nevertheless shared with others in the society and were passed on to succeeding generations, who modified them and built upon them. What culture is and how it operates illustrate the primary themes of sociology: human interaction and the behavior of men and women in groups. Only by social interaction is culture developed, only by interacting with others can we learn our culture, and only by interacting within groups can culture be passed on. We are members of a group that shares a culture, although at birth, we are simply individuals who have been born to members of a group. How we become members—the process of socialization—is the subject of Chapter 4.

SUMMARY

1. **Culture** is the total way of life of a group. It is learned by each generation and passed on to the next. A major way in which culture is transmitted is through the various modes of language.

2. **Society** is a relatively self-sufficient, independent group that shares a common culture, perpetuates itself, and has an organization that regulates behavior among its members. When people in a society consider their culture to be superior to that of other cultures, such thinking is called **ethnocentrism.**

3. People who live in a society share a common culture; sharing certain aspects of culture may simply involve a general knowledge of those aspects rather than a direct participation in them. The culture of a society also offers a range of alternatives in a number of areas, although this range is limited either by direct prohibitions or by circumstance.

4. Culture has both material (human-produced artifacts) and nonmaterial (beliefs, roles, ideas) aspects.

5. Culture serves three *universal functions:* (1) to ensure physical survival, (2) to maintain group living, and (3) to meet individuals' psychological needs. These psychological needs include (1) new experience, (2) security, (3) responses from other individuals, and (4) recognition.

6. Many different cultures have appeared to fulfill these universal functions. How did these cultures arise? One explanation is geographic environment, although the effects of this actually appear to be minimal in a number of aspects of culture. Another explanation is racial differences, but there seems to be little proof that racial differences produce cultural diversity. It is most likely that cultural diversity is a product of human inventiveness and ingenuity and the fact that our basic problems have a number of workable solutions.

7. Human cultures have gone through several evolutionary stages over time; these stages have been identified on the basis of the technology in each. According to Lenski, the basic stages are: **the hunting and gathering stage, the horticultural stage, the agrarian stage,** and **the industrial stage.**

8. There are three ways in which a culture can change: (1) by adding new elements (by invention, discovery, or borrowing from another group); (2) by dropping elements; and (3) by redefining or reinterpreting existing elements. The process of borrowing from another group is called **cultural diffusion.** For a new element to be added to a culture it must be learned of, accepted by the group, and integrated into the existing culture.

KEY TERMS

agrarian stage	material culture
cultural diffusion	nonmaterial culture
cultural universals	norms
discovery	position
ethnocentrism	race
horticultural stage	reification
hunting and gathering stage	role
industrial stage	society
invention	symbol
language	technology

SUGGESTED READINGS

Barnett, H. G. *Innovation: The Basis of Cultural Change.* New York: McGraw-Hill, 1953.
An analysis of the conditions that allow new additions to culture.

Barnouw, Victor. *Culture and Personality.* Homewood, Ill.: Dorsey, 1973.
A complete text on culture. It defines culture and its basic concepts, surveys the various classic studies on culture, and covers methodological approaches to culture and personality research.

Benedict, Ruth. *Patterns of Culture.* Boston: Houghton Mifflin, 1934.
A classic anthropological study that uses examples from primitive societies to show how culture influences human behavior.

Duncan, Otis Dudley, ed. *William Ogburn on Culture and Social Change.* Chicago: University of Chicago Press, 1964.
A collection of essays that deal with various forms of sociocultural change and explanations for change, such as the cultural lag theory.

Edgerton, Robert B. *The Individual in Cultural Adaptation.* Berkeley, Calif.: University of California Press, 1971.
A comparative study of the people in four tribes in East Africa. A good treatment of the emergence of similar and unique cultural patterns in a common physical environment.

Linton, Ralph. *The Study of Man.* New York: Appleton-Century-Crofts, 1936.
Drawing from a wide variety of cross-cultural materials and examples, the author deals with the functions, components, and universals of culture. A basic anthropological treatment of culture.

Marcuse, Herbert. *One Dimensional Man.* Boston: Beacon Press, 1964.
A critical approach to the organization of thought and ideology in modern America. Marcuse argues that mass-produced culture has restricted the alternatives necessary for desirable qualitative changes in American society.

Miner, Horace. "Body Ritual Among the Nacerima." *American Anthropologist,* 58 (June 1956), 503–507.
A satirical essay on American culture and behavior, poking fun at many of our customs and practices.

Roszak, Theodore. *The Making of a Counter Culture.* Garden City, N.Y.: Doubleday, 1969.
A historical reconstruction of the counterculture of the 1950s and the 1960s. Roszak speaks about what issues and to what extent the youth culture conflicted with the dominant culture.

Slater, Philip. *The Pursuit of Loneliness.* Boston: Beacon Press, 1970.
A critique of the emphasis placed on individualism in American culture. Slater argues that Americans who seek community involvement and dependence are frustrated by opposing American values and norms.

At birth, we know nothing and have everything to learn. Who sets about the awesome task of teaching us? Usually, it is our parents who first socialize us —that is, who first teach us what we need to know to take our place in society. But we learn a great deal from other sources—other agents of socialization—as well. Television, for example, has become an important agent of socialization for children of all ages. And when the child reaches age five or six, the school manifests itself as a socializing agent. From our family and other agents of socialization, then, we learn beliefs, values, prejudices, and a great variety of skills and abilities, the descriptions of which are contained in our culture. What the various agents of socialization do is to interpret these descriptions for the child. The culture also contains ideas on many aspects of child rearing. By following these child-rearing rules, and by interpreting the culture, agents of socialization prepare children for adult roles in society.

As we grow up and are being socialized, we are also developing a self. Your self is what you think of you. We develop feelings about our self, such as ideas about our looks, intelligence, and emotional stability, through interaction with others in our society. Our self is thus a result of what we think others see when they look at us.

Socialization and the development of the self are most intense in the childhood years, but neither of these processes ends when we enter adulthood. As we go to college or take a job, we still need to learn from others before we can do what is expected of us adequately. You can probably recall taking a summer job or joining a new group in which you had to learn not only new skills but the whole way of life of the group before you could feel comfortable. Later, you showed the ropes to newcomers—you helped to socialize them into the group.

4
Socialization

UNDERSTANDING SOCIAL ORGANIZATION

This year three million babies will be born in the United States. Think about this for a minute—three million creatures who are human biologically but who are, in every other way, like little animals. They are all born naked but unashamed, male or female but ignorant of the difference or of the profound effect it will have on their lives. They are born black or white or brown or yellow, but they neither care nor judge. They have no status aspirations, no religious faith, and no political convictions. They are soon hungry but are totally unable to get food, prepare it, or even get it into their mouths. For all of these reasons, they are not really very human; and, most of all, they are utterly helpless. (Alas, only their lungs and bladders seem to work persistently and well!) Without the care of other people, they would survive only a few days, or perhaps, hours.

Most of these little animals will someday be human adults able to feel shame, pride, guilt, love, anxiety, hate, and ecstasy. They will have a great many mental and physical skills, attitudes and values, beliefs and judgments. Each will be different, but each will share with other members of the society into which he or she is born a remarkable number of traits and characteristics.

How do we account for this fantastic metamorphosis from helpless infant to human, social adult? Part of the answer is, of course, simple biological maturation. But to develop into a truly human adult, one requires **socialization:** the process through which a person learns the rules of behavior of a society and how to conform to them, learns appropriate values and atti-

---

BOX 4.1 THE WOLF-GIRLS OF INDIA

What would human beings be like without socialization? The answer to this question may be found in the few isolated cases of children who have grown up in the wilds without the benefit of human interaction. One such case was reported by the missionary J. A. L. Singh, who in the 1930s in India discovered two "wolf-girls" (Singh and Zingg, 1939). After hearing reports of a strange "man-ghost" in a jungle area of India, Singh set up watch near a wolf's lair. He observed three wolves and two cubs leave the hole, followed by "a hideous-looking being—hand, foot, and body like a human being; but the head was a big ball of something covering the shoulders and the upper portion of the bust, leaving only a sharp contour of the face visible, and it was human." This animal was followed by a smaller, similar being.

The next day, Singh captured the two girls, who he named Amala and Kamala. Amala was about one and a half years old and died about a year after her capture. Kamala, who appeared to be about eight, lived for almost nine years and was probably not related to Amala.

The missionary took the girls to his orphanage, where he observed their

tudes, becomes imbued with a sense of oneness with the group, and does all of this to a degree sufficient to command at least the tolerance of others. Furthermore, a socialized person has acquired a myriad of physical, mental, and social skills that take their form and content from the culture in which the person lives. Socialization is, thus, education in its broadest sense; it includes all of the results of learning from other people (see Dager, 1964).

Socialization is actually a lifelong process of learning. As we go through life, we join new groups, engage in new activities, and take on different responsibilities. But even though socialization continues to be important throughout life (we will be exploring *adult socialization* later in this chapter), sociologists tend to emphasize *childhood socialization,* for it is of the greatest importance for the individual and society. In simple terms, it allows the individual to become human, and it allows the society to continue its existence. (For an example of what can happen to humans without socialization, see Box 4.1.)

We will look at the process of socialization in more detail shortly, but first, it is necessary to investigate what can be thought of as the raw materials for socialization—that is, the individual characteristics with which a person is born. No matter how or by whom a person is socialized, the person's unique, inherited characteristics are bound to have some effects on what he or she is like and will become. The question is, how much influence do inherited characteristics exert?

---

unusual behavior. They moved by running on all fours or crawling on their knees—they could not stand erect at all. During the night, they howled like wolves. To eat, they lowered their mouths to plates on the floor, like dogs—they did not eat with their hands. They preferred carrion to the food in the orphanage, and Kamala was observed chasing vultures away from a carcass in a field, in order to have it for herself.

After Kamala had been in the orphanage for about three years, she was able to stand upright. Mrs. Singh gave her special attention and helped her to lose some of her wolflike characteristics. Still, six years after her capture, she preferred to run naked and only wore clothes when going out-of-doors. She learned a few words and had a vocabulary of about 40 words at the time of her death.

Even with nine years of living among other humans, Kamala never became fully human. Similar discoveries have been made with other "wild" children. It thus seems that socialization is particularly critical early in life in order for human beings to become human beings.

THE RAW MATERIALS FOR SOCIALIZATION: HEREDITY VERSUS ENVIRONMENT

Each person is human in his or her own unique way. Thus, although we all share many traits and characteristics with humans everywhere, each of us is different from everyone else. How much of the sameness and how much of the difference is the result of our inherited characteristics, or **heredity**?

All normal humans have basically the same body—the same number of organs located in the same places and performing the same functions. We share the same basic reflex actions, such as the eye blink and the knee jerk. And we all have the same basic needs for food, sleep, and sexual satisfaction.

Our essential sameness is, of course, why we can be called "human." But we each inherit a physical appearance that is a unique combination of such physical traits as body size, hair type, and eye color. Even the capacity to learn is an inherited characteristic—some people learn more easily than others. It also seems that traits of temperament, such as excitability or lethargy, are inherited.

Our inherited characteristics do not determine what we will become, but they can affect what we can (or cannot) become. For example, a mentally slow person will have difficulty becoming a nuclear physicist, a very short man is unlikely to become a basketball player, and a tone-deaf person will have problems in trying to become a professional musician. Most of us do, nevertheless, have the inherited capacity to fill many roles and perform many tasks in our society.

In a given culture, certain inherited characteristics may be selected for special attention. For instance, in France or Germany, an extremely tall boy may not receive any special attention, except, perhaps, teasing. But, in the United States, an extremely tall boy, if he is physically adept, will be encouraged to play basketball. If he is good, he may eventually be offered one or more college athletic scholarships. If he excels at college basketball, he may be offered a place on a professional team, at a tempting salary. In college, this young man may develop a passionate interest in medicine, law, chemistry, or any one of a number of fields. In our society, he will be faced, at the time of college graduation, with choosing between the immediate prestige and monetary rewards of the professional athlete and the rigorous study and riskiness of building a career based on his other interests. The choice is his to make, but his culture has presented the choice to him.

Just as culture can favor certain inherited characteristics, it can regard others with disfavor. For example, only in recent years, and only after much personal and social struggle, have women begun to enter the professions in any numbers. Although their numbers are growing, women lawyers, doctors, architects, and stockbrokers still represent only a small percentage of their respective professions. Similarly, being black, Indian, or a member of another minority has a major influence on the opportunities offered by society.

The interplay of social roles and cultural values with individual traits makes it extremely difficult for the social scientist to isolate what is biologically inherited from what is culturally learned. In the late nineteenth century, for example, the importance of heredity was greatly stressed. "Blood will tell" was a popular phrase. Gradually, however, evidence began to accumulate that different life experiences and learning processes are a major influence on human development. By the 1920s, emphasis on the importance of environmental factors had become so extreme that the psychologist John B. Watson (1928) said, "Give me a dozen healthy infants, and my own world to bring them up in, and I'll guarantee to train any one of them to become any kind of specialist I might select—doctor, lawyer, artist, merchant, chief, and even beggar man or thief" (p. 35).

Neither Watson nor anyone else carried out such an experiment, and social scientists no longer believe that Watson's guarantee could have held. Although much is still unknown, social scientists today are trying to achieve, in their theories, some kind of balance between inheritance and environment as factors in human behavior. Still, it is difficult to separate the two factors when focusing on any one characteristic. Say, for example, that a social scientist wanted to discover how much intelligence is inherited. The scientist might administer intelligence tests to a group of young subjects and then test the parents, grandparents, and others in the subjects' families. Test results could then be compared to see how closely the children scored in comparison to their relatives.

But how does one construct a test that will isolate intelligence from differences in age, education, motivation, attitudes toward tests and toward social scientists, and other such factors? Lively controversies are raging in the popular media and social sciences today over just such ambiguities in social science research. Some say that IQ tests show that blacks, as a group, are inherently less intelligent than whites (see Chapter 16). Others say that this is nonsense—that the data are being naively and wrongly interpreted. They argue that such basic factors as poor diet, cultural disadvantages, apathy, and low self-esteem adversely affect test performance among blacks.

What it all boils down to is that social scientists have not yet refined their research methods to a level that can provide accurate data on the influence of heredity versus environment in such areas as intelligence, personality, and emotions. What they can do, however, is acknowledge that inborn biological characteristics do play a role in human behavior and that they provide the raw materials for shaping the individual into a member of his or her society. Let us now return to socialization and see how this shaping process occurs.

THE SOCIALIZATION PROCESS

Figure 4.1 schematically shows the major forces that contribute to socialization. The process begins with the culture of the society. But a culture cannot simply descend upon an infant and produce a social adult. An *agent* is

FIGURE 4.1   The Socialization Process

```
            CULTURAL FACTORS
            Fund of common experiences
            Rules for child-rearing
                    │
                    ▼
            AGENTS OF SOCIALIZATION
            Family
            School
            Peers
            Mass media
                    │
                    ▼
            METHODS OF SOCIALIZATION
            Instruction
            Rewards and punishment
            Imitation
                    │
                    ▼
UNIQUE EXPERIENCES → ADULT PERSONALITY ← INHERITED CHARACTERISTICS
                                       ← BIOLOGICAL MATURATION
```

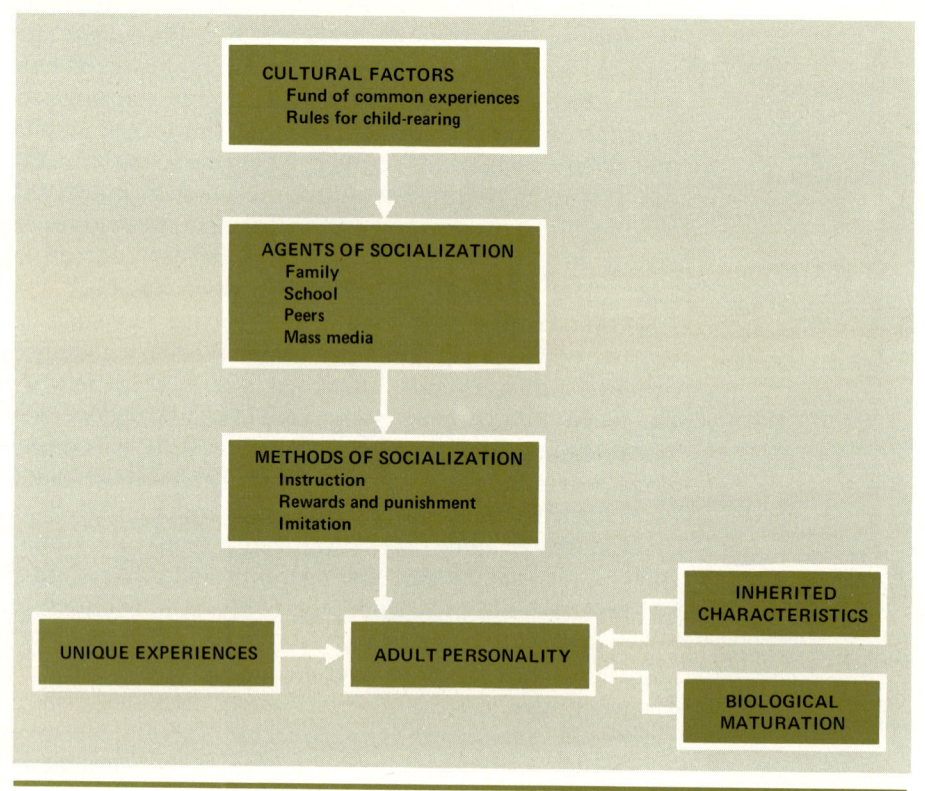

needed to put the cultural prescriptions into practice and to interpret and transmit the culture to the child. The first agents of socialization are usually, of course, the child's parents; but very soon, other agents, such as babysitters, older brothers and sisters, and teachers, begin, each in their own way, to socialize the child. Because each agent interprets the cultural prescriptions in his or her own unique way, no two children, not even members of the same family, are ever reared in exactly the same way.

As the child grows up, he or she is taught the rules of society in a number of ways: by direct instruction, by reward and punishment, by being offered models to imitate. The end-product of the process of the input from culture, socialization agents, and learning is an *adult personality*—a set of unique characteristics and traits—capable of living in a particular society. (Other influences on personality, such as inherited characteristics, biological maturation, and the person's experiences that are more or less unique to him or her, are downplayed here, as our present concern is to elaborate on the process of socialization.)

Cultural Factors in Socialization

In Chapter 3 we noted that culture is the way of life of a society. We also found that there is an extreme variability among the cultures of the world. Herein lies the clue to one way that culture influences personality: each society has its unique culture that it presents, as it were, to the newborn. The second way that culture influences the individual is more direct: it consists of the specific requirements, rules, and techniques for child rearing that are part of the culture.

Content of Culture The culture of any society contains the definitions and descriptions of the many roles and positions in that society. Culture contains the beliefs of the people concerning the world around them; it contains their values, their definitions of the natural and the supernatural, and the

Most children are exposed to the culture of only one society. Simply by living in China this girl has learned to think and act much like other Chinese.

norms that govern their behavior. These and other aspects of culture are shared by the members of a society. The shared patterns constitute, at the same time, a fund of common experience for the infants and children of the society.

As the adults enact their roles of parents or providers, as they express their beliefs through their magical or religious practices, as they conduct their courtships and engage in play, and as, in many other ways, their behavior expresses or reflects their culture, they are, in a sense, acting out their culture for the newcomer. They are providing the child with his or her first — and perhaps only — experience with a society in action. As the culturally prescribed behavior is repeated over and over again, the developing child gradually comes to accept the fact that what he or she sees around him or her is the way of all life, or at least, the way life should be led.

Since no two cultures are precisely the same, nowhere is the fund of experience to which a given newborn will be exposed exactly the same as it is in his or her own society. Each child usually sees but one drama of life acted out before him or her. Merely by being born in Samoa, for example, the total experiences of the Samoan child will, in some measure, be different from those of a child born anywhere else in the world. As the child witnesses, and later participates in, the Samoan culture in action, he or she gradually learns to talk, think, and act like a Samoan.

The members of a society are not identical. Nevertheless, they do have certain basic traits in common and exhibit a general personality pattern more frequently than do members of another society. Thus, if we say that the Arapesh are cooperative, it does not mean that an uncooperative Arapesh cannot be found; but it does mean that life in the Arapesh society calls for considerable cooperation. Consequently, throughout life, the Arapesh child witnesses cooperative behavior in a variety of situations.

Child-Rearing Practices No society leaves how children are to be raised to chance or to the whims of parents (see Whiting, 1963; Bronfenbrenner, 1970). All people seem to understand, no matter how vaguely, that child-rearing practices shape the personality of the future adult. As the saying goes, "As the twig is bent, so the tree inclines." Every culture approves only certain kinds of behaviors, attitudes, and child-rearing techniques for the parents or guardians of the newborn child.

A catalog of all the many different child-rearing practices throughout the world would be nearly endless. In fact, the rules for child care begin even before birth. In our society, a woman is expected to begin regular visits to an obstetrician as soon as her pregnancy is certain. And she is to follow faithfully the doctor's instructions in matters of diet, rest, physical exertion, and so on. If she neglects to visit a doctor or ignores the doctor's instructions, many people will consider her irresponsible. If she is too poor to see a doctor regularly, she and the baby are likely to be considered victims of social inequality. But, in many industrial societies (and even in parts of the United

States), the woman rarely if ever sees a doctor. Instead, she may visit a midwife occasionally, and the midwife may be the one who actually delivers the baby. In some societies, a woman may deliver her baby alone; in others, she may be helped by female relatives; and in still others, she may receive the aid of *shamans* (magic-using priests) and their rituals.

The culturally approved child-rearing practices begin to influence the child at birth. In the Soviet Union and some other places, babies are tightly swaddled; some American Indians strap their infants to cradleboards; American parents allow their babies to kick freely. In our society, babies are usually taken from their mothers and placed in cribs in the hospital nursery; in other societies, the infant spends most of the first days in its mother's arms.

Thus, a society's culture permeates the newborn's life and gradually reveals itself in every new experience. It influences the child simply by being there, and it also exerts its influence in the rules it prescribes for the rearing of children. As the child grows older and its mental abilities increase, the socialization process becomes more intense, and the child learns about his or her culture in a number of ways.

Agents of Socialization

It takes a long time to become an adult in a modern, industrial society. On the road to adulthood, we are typically exposed to the socializing influences of many people. Groups or individuals who have special responsibility for socializing the young—or who, while not given such responsibility, nevertheless play an important role in socialization—are called **agents of socialization.** In American society, the important agents of socialization are the family, the school, the peer group, and the mass media, particularly television. (The agents may be different in other societies. For a society in which the government is a socializing agent, see Box 4.2.) As they interpret the culture for the child and teach the child countless skills and attitudes, these agents have a strong influence on what the child will be like and will become.

The Family In almost every society the family is extremely important in socializing the young, and it is usually the first socializing agent. This primacy of contact is significant, for never again will individuals be as pliable as they are in infancy and early childhood. The learning and experience of later years will reinforce or contradict what was learned in the home, but later learning must always reckon with the family's early influences on personality development.

The family has another advantage as a socializing agent: the long duration of its contact with the child. Some very young children rarely leave the home and thus are exposed almost solely to family influences. Those children who go to day-care centers return home daily. As children get older,

**BOX 4.2
CHILDHOOD
SOCIALIZATION
IN COMMUNIST
CUBA**

In 1958, Batista's government was overthrown, and it was replaced by a Communist regime. Fidel Castro and the other leaders of the new order sought a new society, one organized on principles different from, and often diametrically opposed to, those of the previous regime. As the Communists saw it, the old society bred individualistic and selfish persons whose lives were directed by thoughts of personal benefit and personal ambition, not by thoughts of what was for the good of the state or for the good of all. Castro sought a quite different society: "To live in a Communist society is to live without selfishness, to live among the people and with the people, as if every one of our fellow citizens were really our dearest brother" (Leiner, 1978, p. 16). In the new, Communist Cuba people would find fulfillment in their work and would consider work to be respectable. They would want to share the fruits of their labor with their countrymen; thus, there would be no great differences in wealth and possessions within the society. The ideal person for the new order would be a collectivist, selfless worker, loyal to the society and to the Communist party.

To help insure that the dreams of the revolution would become a reality, the leaders felt that it would be desirable, if not necessary, for the government to be heavily involved in the socialization of young children. Hundreds of day-care centers were established, and today, their numbers continue to grow. There is no charge for working mothers, and the day-care centers take children as young as 45 days and keep them until they are old enough for school. The centers operate from 6:00 A.M. to 6:00 P.M. Thus, the bulk of the child's waking hours is spent in the center, not in the home; much of the rearing of preschool children is done by center workers and not by parents. Some centers are actually boarding nurseries, where the children stay twenty-four hours a day, five days a week, going home only on weekends.

How are children reared in government day-care centers so that in time they will become the new Cuban citizens? Training for life in a collectivist society begins in infancy. At least six infants are put together in a large playpen to get children used to being members of a group. As the children get older, the day-care workers do not allow them to play alone but make special efforts to see that all children participate in whatever activity is designed for the group. Children are discouraged from bringing their favorite toy or "security blanket" from home. The toys used in the center belong to the group and are not personal possessions. In many ways, sharing, cooperation, and the group are emphasized, while individualism is deemphasized. For example, a birthday party in the center is for all children who have a birthday during a given month, so that no one child is singled out for recognition and attention.

The activities and schedules of day-care centers are carefully planned by child psychologists and other experts. As would be expected, political awareness and loyalty to the new social order find their part in socialization in the day-care centers. The curriculum guide suggests, for example, that in the sixth week of the fall session children be involved in a program called "Our Friends the Guerrilla Fighters." Suggested activities for four-year-olds include: "Show pictures of guerrilla fighters. Explain in a simple way how these companions fought in the mountains to liberate their nation. . . . Tell of the events in the life of a guerrilla fighter. Have the children learn the Hymn to Che. Carefully observe the pictures of the guerrillas. Comment on what the guerrilla fighters are doing" (Leiner, p. 24).

The proper attitude toward work is taught in a number of ways. Some work in the center, such as the serving of meals, is assigned to older children as a reward—children who have been particularly cooperative are permitted to be servers. Children also learn about adult work through what is called the padrino (godfather) system. Most day-care centers have been adopted by a shop or factory. At the practical level, this means that the factory workers come to the center to build play equipment, paint, and make repairs. It also shows the children that workers are unselfish people who labor for the good of the group. The padrino system makes children aware of various occupations and is supposed to help them develop a respect for work.

There are no private day-care centers in Cuba. Children of the leaders, government officials, professionals, factory workers, and field hands associate together and have the same experiences in the centers. Upon arrival at the center each morning, children are dressed in uniforms supplied by the state. This not only gives children decent clothes to wear but gives them a daily lesson in equality of treatment. Meals are carefully planned from a nutritional standpoint, and of course, all children get the same food, regardless of what their parents do for a living. Medical care, including vaccinations, is provided through the centers and the schools, and again, all children are treated alike.

In Cuba, the state is more heavily involved in childhood socialization than in most other societies, but parents continue to be important agents of socialization. The parent-education arm of the day-care center movement publishes pamphlets and magazines and puts on radio and television programs to teach parents principles of child development. Close family-school relations are encouraged. These measures provide the child with a certain continuity in his or her experiences. Ideally, children do not learn one thing in the center and another at home. It also helps assure that the principles that guide day-care center socialization—preparation for collective living, deemphasis of personal property, respect for work, equality—are expressed in family socialization.

When the day-care centers were first established in Cuba, some felt that parents would not like them, out of fear that they would "sovietize" their children. But parents have responded quite favorably to state day-care. According to Marvin Leiner (1978), an American educator who lived in Cuba and sent his children to Cuban schools, through the day-care centers the new generation is growing up healthier, better fed, and better educated than did children in the old society. The main goal of collectivist child-rearing, of course, is producing a generation capable of taking on responsible adult roles in Communist society. The best indications are that this goal is being achieved.

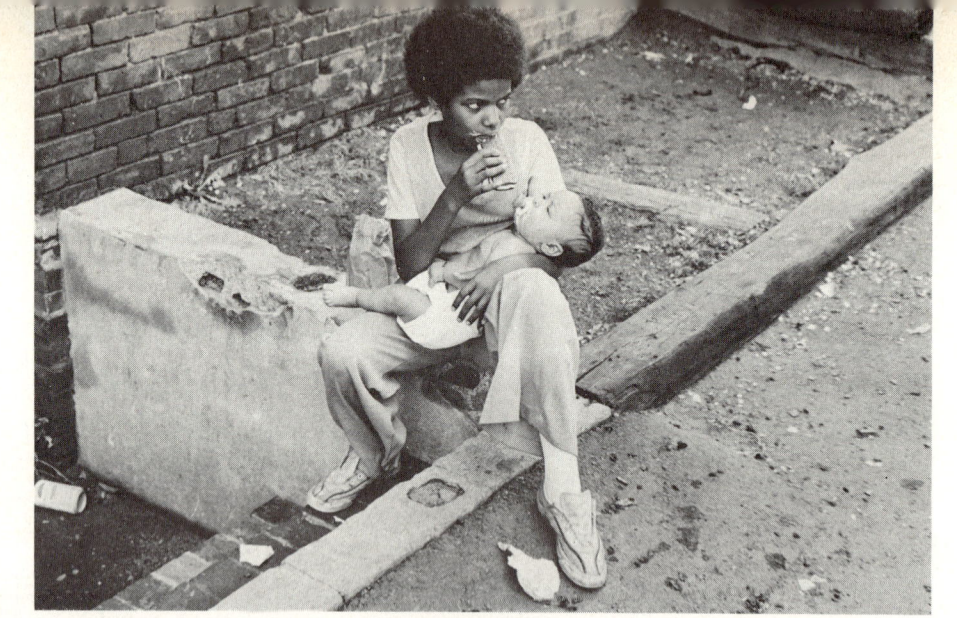

A child's personality is strongly influenced by interaction with its parents. Try to imagine the many differences that could result from the family experiences of these children.

they spend more time away from home, but almost every day for perhaps 18 years, they spend part of their time with family members. The repetitiveness of family contacts is particularly important for the formation of such basic personality characteristics as self-worth and feelings of security and belongingness.

In Chapter 6, we will discuss the family as a primary group. One characteristic of primary groups is that total personalities are involved in member relationships. In the family, therefore, children are exposed to a wide variety of learnings. They are exposed to basic emotions, such as love, grief, and anger, and they learn how these emotions should be expressed—or repressed. Children interact with their parents and perhaps their brothers and sisters in a variety of situations and thus have the opportunity to learn several different skills and what we sometimes call "everyday knowledge." Some things are "caught" in the home, rather than deliberately taught. Children catch on to the parents' attitudes toward race, the importance they attach to money, their feelings about the roles of the sexes, and so on, even if the parents say little about such things.

So the family has the children first, has contact with them for a long time, and provides an atmosphere in which a wide variety of skills, facts, and values are taught and caught. It is, thus, no wonder that sociologists consider the family to be the most important agent of socialization. But it is not the only agent.

When ours was a rural economy, parents taught their children many of the skills needed to be successful adults. This is no longer the case. To become an adult capable of functioning adequately in today's society requires specialized knowledge and skills that most families cannot provide for their children. Even such skills as dancing and swimming often can be taught more easily and effectively by specialists outside the family. And when it comes to knowledge and skills needed to make a living in the modern world, specialists outside the family become essential. Parents can rarely teach their children to become sociology professors, computer programmers, or nurses. Although the family has lost its prominence in the socialization function, it is to society's advantage that other agencies share the task of socializing the young. An extremely important socializing agent is the school.

The School We expect schools to teach academic subjects—an aspect of socialization necessary to the producing of adults who can take their place in society. But a little thought will reveal that there is much more taught in schools than the typical academic subjects. For example, schools often offer such basic "social" courses as driver training, homemaking, and family life education. In addition, they provide guidance counselors to help students with their plans for adult life. In school, children learn basic values, such as the importance of getting ahead, and paradoxically, the importance of not being too different from other children. In Chapter 11 we will discuss the "hidden curriculum" of the school, which includes all the rules that children must learn to get along in the school system.

For many children, entrance into kindergarten or first grade marks the first time adults other than their parents are in a position to teach, reward, or punish them. As adults, we are members of all sorts of formal groups in which there are rules for behavior and people in positions of authority who supervise our behavior and give or withhold rewards. School is thus a training ground for a very important aspect of adult life. The school also provides a setting in which children can interact with others of their age and thus socialize each other. This is referred to as *peer group socialization*.

The Peer Group A child's **peer group** is the group of children of approximately the same age and background with whom he or she interacts. The peer group is an interesting agent of socialization, for, unlike the family and the school, it is not charged with the responsibility for socializing the young. Yet, during the school years, children prefer to spend their time with their peer group rather than with their parents, and they actually spend about twice as much time with their peers (Bronfenbrenner, 1970).

One important feature of the peer group is that it is a voluntary association of near-equals. There may be informal leaders, but they are not in the same authoritarian position as a parent or a teacher. The children in a peer group socialize one another by exchanging experiences, telling each other about new events, and teaching each other new skills. Groups are formed on the basis of mutual likes and dislikes and remain intact on the same basis. Interest in learning is, therefore, usually high. The desire to continue to be accepted by the group leads to a willingness to incorporate the views of the dominant group into one's own.

Most people will admit that disapproved forms of behavior — skipping school, smoking, cheating on tests, petty crimes — are learned from peers and not from parents. But this is just the tip of the iceberg. Almost anything can be discussed in the peer group, and in the process, children learn about things that are not taught at home or in school, and they learn different interpretations of things that their parents and teachers do talk about. The peer group is important in the formation of attitudes toward sex, money, the importance of education, and other such issues.

Peer group socialization begins early in life, frequently before a child goes to school. During the grade-school years, the peer group becomes increasingly important in the child's life, and peer group loyalty becomes stronger. Peer group influence reaches its peak in the adolescent years, when the opinions and behaviors of one's age-mates become all-important.

Mass Media Television, radio, newspapers, and magazines are the prominent mass media. They are so designated because they reach large audiences, or the *masses*. Of the mass media, television is probably the most important socializing agent. Children spend many hours a week — sometimes several hours a day — watching television. It is impossible to determine exactly what children learn from it, but sociologists and most parents know that they learn a great deal. A parent who makes a remark to a child about a circus, a city on the other side of the world, the life of beavers, or any of a million other topics, has come to expect the response, "Oh yeah, I saw it on

Television is helping to rear our children. It teaches children things their parents don't know, shows them places their parents know nothing of, and maybe instills values that are different from the parents'.

TV." In Chapter 7, we will discuss a major way in which television exerts its power, when we examine its influences on maintaining the idea that the woman's place is in the home. In countless other ways, television affects our ideas and values. We learn of tragedies and how people respond to them; we see vivid contrasts between the lifestyles of the rich and the poor. Sometimes these accounts are fictionalized, but they nevertheless affect our ideas and values. Through television advertising, children learn our society's definitions of the good things in life—the things we are supposed to have to be happy. Children learn important lessons about the standards of physical attractiveness, about success, and about how adults behave toward each other by watching countless adults demonstrate these things for them on the television screen. Other mass media perform a similar socialization function but are probably not as far-reaching in their influence as TV.

Other Agents of Socialization Commercial groups, church groups, and community groups also help socialize the young. Many children participate in such groups as the Girl Scouts, the YMCA, and church youth groups, and many also take lessons in music, dancing, skating, riding, swimming, and so on. Of course, not all children can afford these socialization experiences, but those whose families can are learning all sorts of skills outside the home. They may also be learning new values through interaction with adults who are not members of their family, and they may be participating in segments of the culture unexperienced by their parents. They may be learning skills that will affect their recreation pattern during much of their lifetime, and they may even explore activities that will affect their choice of jobs. Then, too, by participating in these groups and activities, children expand their friendship groups and have still more opportunities to learn from peers.

It is a long road from infancy to adulthood, this acquiring of all the values, attitudes, and behaviors necessary to function in society. Many agents of socialization play a part in this process, and how these agents actually exert their influences is our next topic of discussion.

Methods of Socialization

Learning to be a member of a particular society is sometimes a conscious process: behaviors and ideas are directly taught. At other times, values, attitudes, and beliefs seem to be "caught" from parents and other socializing agents more than consciously taught by them. The major methods by which these aspects of life are learned include direct instruction, rewards and punishment, and imitation.

Direct Instruction Many skills, attitudes, and kinds of behavior were taught to you by direct instruction. For example, when you first started school at five or six years of age, your parents probably told you that you must be attentive and obedient to the teacher and nice to the other children. As a child, you also had to learn the behaviors appropriate to particular roles, such as how to behave as a student, a son, a sister, or a friend. And you had to learn more specific kinds of behavior as well—how to hold a fork, how to dress yourself, and how to speak your language. You were also taught many facts and beliefs about the world, such as "rattlesnakes can hurt you" and "the stove is hot." Your parents made a special effort to teach you right from wrong and told you what was "good" and what was "bad."

Rewards and Punishments To be instructed is not necessarily to learn. Sometimes you must be instructed over and over again before you learn a certain skill or piece of knowledge. Rewards, punishment, or both can encourage learning. Rewards and punishment may be large or small, tangible or intangible. Your mother's smile or approving nod may have been reward enough for you to repeat a desired response. Her frown may have stopped you from behaving in a disapproved manner. To be effective, rewards and punishment need not to be immediate, especially with older children. An American teenage boy may wash the car in the morning in order to earn a dollar from his parents in the evening or to increase his chances of using the car on the weekend.

Imitation Parents and other adults can unwittingly teach the child important lessons about himself or herself, about the parents, or about society simply through their own actions. By acting out their roles and by expressing their attitudes and beliefs to one another, the adults of society inevitably influence their children's behavior.

Such unconscious teaching and learning partly explains the transmission of attitudes and values from one generation to the next. For instance, the child in Alor observes how careful his or her parents are not to waste food.

The child hears them talking about recurrent food shortages in the past. Before anyone deliberately teaches the child the proper attitude toward food, he or she has learned that food is something precious and scarce.

Some American parents, to take another example, appear mystified when their children display racial prejudice, and they stoutly deny that such beliefs were taught in the home. What the parents mean is that they never sat their children down and told them that blacks are untrustworthy, inferior, or whatever. Such direct instruction is not necessary, though. Children observe that blacks have never been guests in their home. Perhaps the only blacks they see around the house are those employed by the parents to do menial and undesirable work. And the child notices how the parents talk

Like mother, like daughter. Through direct instruction and imitation this girl is learning a skill, but she is learning also that homemaking tasks are women's work.

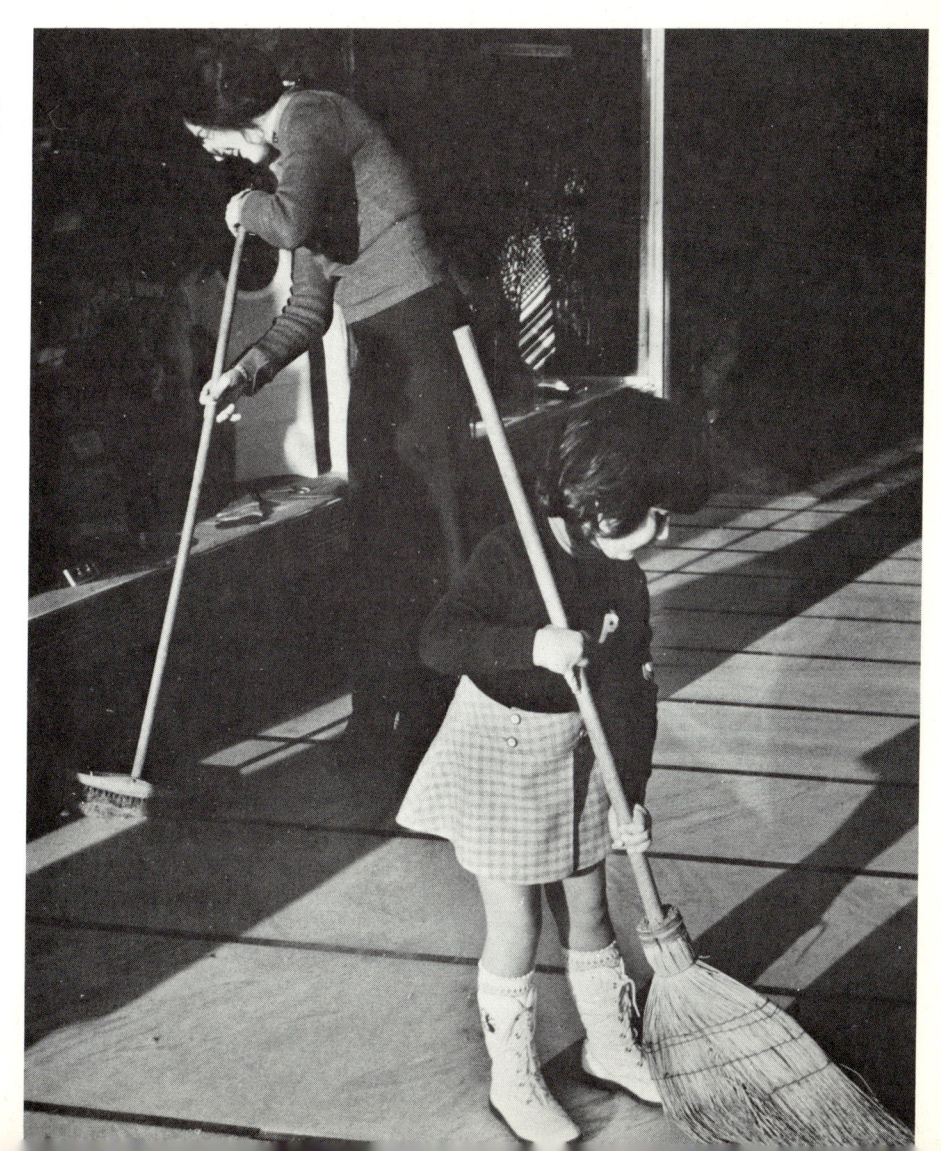

about and interact with blacks. In these ways—and without any direct instruction—a child may absorb the attitudes and prejudices of the parents quite easily.

Children are influenced by more than what the parents say and do. They also learn values and attitudes from their parents' gestures, tones of voice, and emotional reactions. A child is quick to learn when its mother is angry. By the emotions the mother shows as she describes how the supermarket clerk almost cheated her out of 59 cents, she teaches her child much about the meaning of money and financial injustices. Adults' reactions to a child's handling of a snake or worm are noticed by the child, even if the adults try to conceal their true feelings. The parents' amused reaction to a little boy's announcement that he would like to be a garbage man when he grows up may teach him that this is a goal that they—and therefore, he—should not take seriously.

THE SELF: A SOCIAL CREATION

While you are learning the elements of your culture and how to fit into society, you are developing a **personality**: a set of traits and characteristics that make you a unique individual. As we noted earlier, personality is developed through contributions from hereditary make-up and environmental influences. Personality traits range from shyness and timidity to generosity and meanness. Your personality is what you display to other people.

At the same time that you are developing a personality, you are acquiring a **self**. Odd as it may seem at first, no one is born with a self. The self is developed only through social interaction, during which you gradually form attitudes and beliefs about yourself—for example, that you are smart or not so smart, good-looking or plain, bold or shy, and so on. These beliefs and attitudes develop as you compare yourself with others, as you imagine what others think of you, and as you draw conclusions about others' reactions to you.

Your self is you, as you perceive yourself. When you consider your self, you are both subject and object. That is, you attempt to look at yourself from the standpoint of another person. For instance, if you are ashamed of yourself, you have gone outside yourself mentally and are looking at your behavior as others might view it, and you feel a sense of shame before these mental others.

The Looking-Glass Self

The self we each develop is an inevitable product of socialization. It follows from the human trait of not merely learning values, beliefs, and rules but also *internalizing* them. That is, we come to describe and judge ourselves by how well we meet these cultural standards of belief and behavior. Thus, our development of a self is inseparable from our experience of socialization and from our interaction with others.

Soon after the turn of the century, Charles Horton Cooley (1902) developed the theory of what he called the *reflected,* or **looking-glass self,** to describe the feelings about ourselves that result from our imagining of how others view us. Cooley saw the looking-glass self as having three parts: (1) *What I think you see* when you observe me. As if in a mirror, we see ourselves in the mind of another. (2) *What I think you think* upon observing me. We imagine not only what another sees when looking at us, but also how the other judges us. (3) *How I feel about myself* because of how I think you see me and judge me. Having imagined how I am seen by another and how I am judged, I feel pride, joy, shame, or some other emotion. Self-feelings result not from how we appear or behave but from how we think another judges our appearance or behavior.

We begin to develop a looking-glass self when we are two or three years old. From then on, throughout our lives, we gradually build up, reinforce, or modify a great many attitudes about our self. Through repeated perceptions of how we are judged by others, we conclude that we are good-looking or plain, smart or dull, good or bad, poised or clumsy, well-versed or ill-informed, emotional or stable. Whether these perceptions are completely right or partially or totally wrong, they will influence our self-appraisal. Thus, someone who has an "inferiority complex" may actually be judged more highly by others than by himself or herself.

Our attitudes and beliefs about ourselves influence how we act. A woman who does not feel terribly smart or informed may not add her opinions to a discussion. A man who thinks that women find him unattractive will not ask them for dates. Often, we may act in ways that conceal how we really feel about ourselves. For example, you may feel insecure enough to refrain from expressing your opinions, but the expression on your face may suggest knowledgeable agreement with a particular person or, perhaps, superiority and boredom at the silliness of it all. Or an insecure person who is uneasy at a party may be too talkative and, perhaps, too loud. We may not know what the person's true self-feelings are, but we can see that they are influencing his or her behavior.

The Social Steps to the Self

Two decades after Charles Horton Cooley had contributed his looking-glass self theory to sociological thought, the great sociologist George Herbert Mead made important theoretical contributions to the knowledge of the stages of development the individual goes through on the way to the self (Mead, 1967). Cooley showed that the self is a social creation, in that the looking glass reflects our own imaginings about how others see and judge us. Mead theorized about how various stages of social interaction contribute to the development of the self, and he stressed language, play, and games as essential to this development.

Language and Ideas All animals interact and communicate with one another, but only humankind has a true language. (An interesting discussion of how language affects our thinking process can be found in Ross, 1957, pp. 11–26.) A bee that returns to the hive and dances to communicate the direction and distance of food to other bees is guided by a built-in, instinctive code of movements (von Frisch, 1962). The code is fixed, and it can communicate only the kind of information that other bees are able by instinct to receive. But the human mind and its product—language—are capable of creating and communicating *ideas*.

The ability to create and communicate ideas is essential to the development of the self. For example, as children, we learned the meaning of the word "happy." Once we had the idea of happy, we could apply that word (idea) to our own experience of the feeling it describes or stands for. When we saw the outward signs of happiness in another person, we could apply the word to him or her. We could now think about our own happiness or that of another person. Although, as children, we had only simple understandings of simple ideas at first, we had acquired a basis for developing the self, and we were then able to go outside ourselves to see how our behavior would appear to someone else.

Play: Being Others Once we were able to imagine how others would react to our behavior, we could behave in ways that would elicit the reaction we wanted. With this, we were beginning the actual development of a self. In Mead's description, we had passed into a **play stage,** in which we acted out specific roles that we had observed. More or less indiscriminately, we acted out the roles of mother, father, cowboy, or even cat or dog. We pretended to be the people or animals, and we behaved as though we were in their positions. We imagined what is expected of someone who occupies a certain position and we acted out the role as we interpreted it. In other words, we acquired the ability to take the role of the other, a capacity that is of great use in further social development.

Games and the Generalized Other At the play stage, we became able to take the role of others—but only one role at a time. According to Mead, we passed next into the **game stage.** To take part in even a simple, organized game like hide-and-seek, we had to learn to imagine the roles of several people simultaneously. We needed to imagine where each of the other children would hide and where the child who was "it" was likely to look, and we had to take all these facts into account when choosing our own hiding place.

An organized game, such as baseball, requires even more of the ability to simultaneously anticipate what other players are going to do and how they will react to what you do. You need to know the rules of the game. And so it is with the game of life. We must understand the rules governing interaction in the social world, and we must have the ability to apply them in such a way that we can anticipate what others will do and how they will react to us.

This process started in the game stage, when we began to view our behavior as we imagined it was viewed by the group, and we began to regulate it accordingly. In responding to a group instead of to an individual, we responded to what Mead called the **generalized other.** While at the play stage we chose our behavior to fit how we imagined it would appear to a single other person, at the game stage we behaved according to how we thought we would appear to a collective, or generalized, other, such as our play group. As we matured, we gradually expanded the idea of the generalized other

In their play children try to imagine what it is like to enact specific adult roles and to have adult feelings and responsibilities.

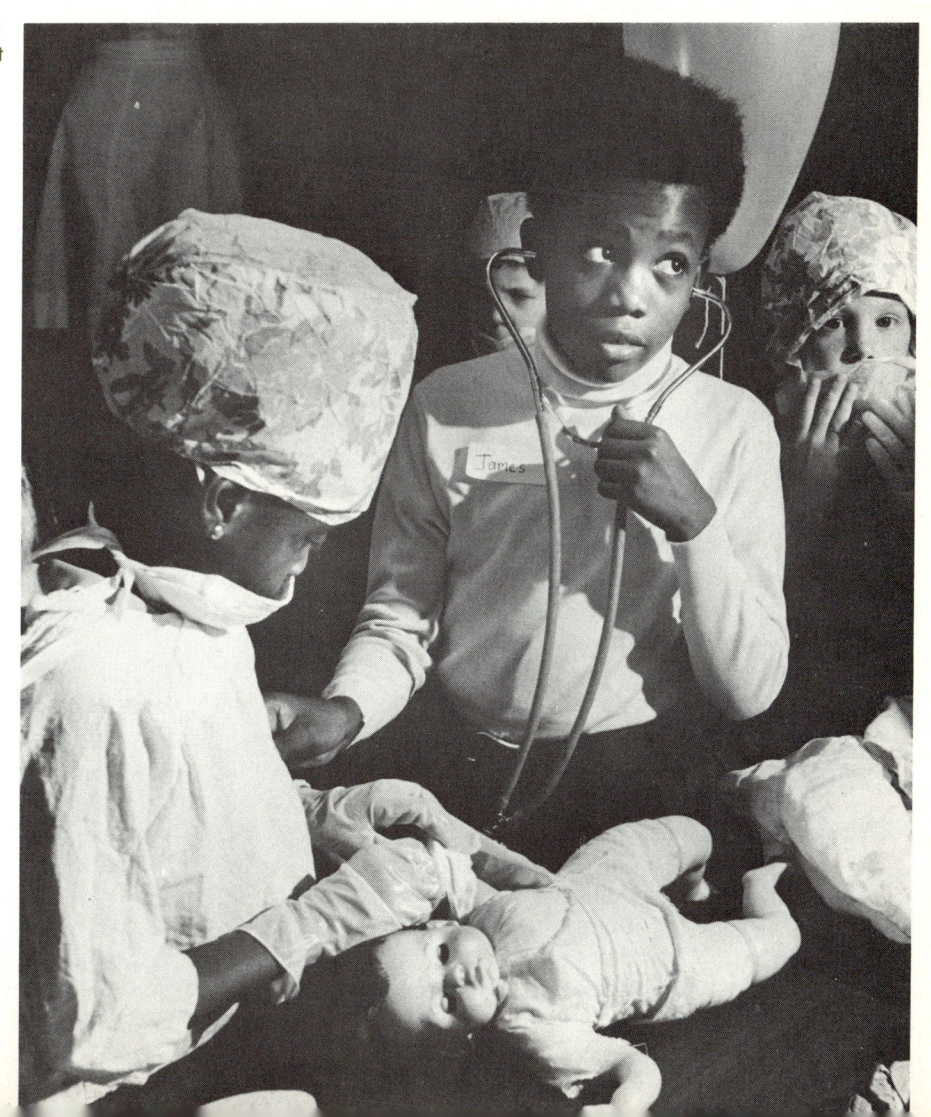

until it included the society. In this way, society has entered each of us and has become part of our self.

There is always a part of us that is not completely socialized. As Mead conceptualized it, there are two parts of the self, the "I" and the "me." The "I" consists of the spontaneous, impulsive, self-interested self, whereas the "me" is the social self, in which the rules of society have been incorporated. In adult life, the "me" is dominant, but the "I" continues to exist.

SOCIALIZATION IN ADULT LIFE

If our socialization has been reasonably complete and successful, we will have the requisite skills, abilities, and feelings to take on adult roles. Some of these adult roles are sex-typed—that is, considered appropriate for the male or the female but not both. The process of being socialized to become an adult who is capable of enacting a masculine or feminine role, the nature and effect of these sex roles, and the changes taking place in sex roles in our society are major topics of interest to the sociologist. We have, therefore, devoted an entire chapter to the subject of sex roles (Chapter 7). Because of the changing nature of sex roles, many adults are undergoing resocialization, so that they can enact the new and emerging roles.

Adult socialization is an ongoing process that occurs in many areas. We become members of new groups and will probably continue to join new groups throughout much of our lives. We move to new communities, take a new job, or go to a different college. To be successful members of these new groups, we must continue to learn new skills and acquire new attitudes.

Adult socialization is not much different from childhood socialization (see Brim, 1966). Those who are doing the socializing—the members of the ongoing groups that we join—are both instructors and models for us to imitate. As newcomers, we listen to instructions, observe what is going on around us, and adjust our behavior and attitudes according to our imagined reactions of the generalized other.

A vivid example of *attempted* adult socialization is contained in the novel *One Flew Over the Cuckoo's Nest* (Kesey, 1962). The story deals with how an adult is socialized to become an acceptable member of a particular group. In this case, the group is a mental hospital, and the role the principal character must learn is that of patient. Despite what the head nurse, the patients, and the doctor do to him and how they react to him, the hero, Randall McMurphy, steadfastly refuses to adopt the proper behavior of a mental patient. Until his eventual prefrontal lobotomy, he remains a poorly socialized member of the ward.

When we enter college, we must be socialized to a new way of life, albeit not as vigorously as in the case of McMurphy. As freshmen, we learn to adjust our actions and feelings to the expectations of the group. Perhaps not until we go home for the holidays will we notice the changes we have undergone. We think of ourselves as college students, and consciously or unconsciously we have discarded attitudes and modified values that we feel are inappropriate to the new role. Soon, we will no longer be obvious newcomers and can, ourselves, serve as models for the next group of freshmen.

As we move through life, there are other times when socialization is required. For example, men who enter the military go through such a process (see Box 4.3). Even if one has the requisite job skills, such as being able to weld, teach, or type, taking a job in a particular organization entails being socialized in the way things are done for that group. Similarly, young married couples learn how married people are supposed to act from parents, friends, books, movies, and just by living in a world with married people. And, so vast is the new learning involved in becoming a parent—of having complete 24-hour responsibility for a new life—that some sociologists refer to parenthood as a *crisis*.

Socialization for old age is a particular problem in our society. To be comfortable with themselves and others, older people need to develop new attitudes toward work, leisure, and physical vigor. Getting ahead in the world of work is no longer necessary, or for that matter, is often no longer possible. It becomes necessary, therefore, to find new meanings in life and to seek activities that are satisfying and give one a sense of worth. The older person can

Socialization does not stop at childhood. The adults in this group had to learn how to meditate, had to learn the meaning of the act, and how to interpret their feeling states.

learn about these activities and can learn the new values and attitudes appropriate to old age through interaction with other older people.

Although adult socialization produces fewer and less drastic personality changes than occur in childhood socialization, the adult self does not escape

---

**BOX 4.3
JOIN
THE SERVICE
AND BECOME
A MAN**

Becoming a member of the military is an excellent example of adult socialization. The individual must learn many new skills, attitudes, and values in the process that transforms a civilian into a member of the armed forces. The total person is so reshaped that it is difficult for anyone who has not experienced the transformation to appreciate it. The primary socialization into the military occurs over a relatively short period—two months or less. The profound change that must be produced and the short time for doing so probably account for some of the extreme measures used in military socialization.

The sociologists William Arkin and Lynne Dobrofsky (1978) have taken a new look at military socialization and have found that strongly embedded in socialization for the military is socialization for the masculine role. The military is not just turning civilians into soldiers; it is turning boys into men. Socialization for masculinity by the military occurs at the point of transition from adolescence to adulthood, as new recruits are typically between seventeen and twenty years of age. At the very time in life when young males are attempting to define the masculine role and to become comfortable with it, millions come under the influence of military-masculine socialization.

Socialization to military life begins when the recruit is transported to a basic-training camp set apart from towns or cities. Ties with the home community are completely broken, and the only ties with one's family are through the mails. Military-masculinity socialization then begins in earnest. The recruits' heads are shaved. This sets them apart from others on the base and symbolizes that they are targets for special discipline and taunts. And, as Arkin and Dobrofsky point out, the head-shaving eliminates the possibility that recruits will spend time fixing their hair or becoming vain about their appearance—traits presumably associated with women. Years ago, recruits were addressed by a variety of vulgar terms. Today, drill instructors call them "ladies"—presumably, they have not yet earned the right to be called "men."

The meshing of military and masculine sex-role socialization is seen in many of the activities of basic training. Combat training and long hours of marching teach skills and discipline, but they are also tests of endurance. The weak falter; the men learn to take it. Inspections and drills teach respect for authority and conformity to rules, but they also form the personality of a strong, silent, obedient man.

A combat team must function as a unit, so cooperation and pride in one's outfit are fostered. But competition is also stressed, and each recruit

some change. But the self is not a sort of chameleon, assuming new colorations with each new interaction; once self-feelings have been built up during childhood, they become relatively fixed. In later life, reactions to the generalized other strike against already established, solid self-images.

tries to beat his teammates at target practice, obstacle course runs, and endurance tests. Because one's buddy is also one's competitor, one must conceal any signs of weakness. Recruits thus learn that masculinity implies a lack of closeness with other males and a reluctance to talk about personal problems, fears, or doubts.

In the Marine Corps, a recruit is taught to love his rifle. A common punishment for dropping one's rifle is to be forced to sleep with it. This teaches respect for the rifle on which one's life may depend, but it also subtly suggests that all one has to do to make things right with a love object is to sleep with it. If a recruit makes the unpardonable mistake of calling his rifle a gun, he will probably be required to go through a humiliating exercise with it, first raising it over his head and then lowering it to approximately crotch position, while chanting:

> This is my rifle
> This is my gun
>
> This is for war
> This is for fun.

In countless other ways the recruit is taught that the masculine sex role implies viewing women as sex objects.

The recruit's separation from his family teaches self-reliance, a desirable trait for a future combat soldier. But it also prevents him from obtaining emotional support or receiving advice from his parents or wife—actions that would be considered characteristic of a sissy or cry baby, someone tied to his mother's or wife's apron strings. Military socialization and masculine sex-role socialization are thus never completely separated from each other.

There are approximately 27 million veterans of military service in the United States as well as two million men current in the services. It has been estimated that about 20 percent of all males will be socialized by the military. The particular version of the masculine sex role taught in the service has affected and will continue to affect a sizable portion of our nation's men. The influx of women into the Armed Forces is now posing a challenge to the military socialization in masculinity. You can turn civilian women into soldiers, but you cannot turn them into men. At present, the role of military women has been one of "little brother" or, sometimes, even neuter. It remains to be seen whether a clearer role will be developed for military women, or whether the role of military man will be modified to include both sexes.

By joining this accordion band restricted to older women, a woman admits she is old, but she also learns a skill, enjoys the company of others, and finds new meanings in life.

If as children we are consistently accepted and liked for what we are, we probably develop a basic self-respect that will not be altered by an occasional contrary looking-glass encounter later in life. Also, as we get older, we generally become more selective in receiving looking-glass reflections. Adults can become quite effective at screening out reflections of themselves that are incongruous with previously established self-feelings. For example, even though a doctor may know that a few people in his community think that medicine is a fraud and that doctors are unscrupulous charlatans, he does not alter his image of himself as a member of an important profession. Most parents firmly maintain their beliefs, values, and self-images, despite conflict or criticism from their teenage children. Furthermore, adults tend to associate with others who think and feel more or less as they do. Such people are unlikely to present each other with reflections that are seriously at odds with their own prior self-conceptions. Thus, the looking-glass process operates differently with adults, whose personalities are relatively fixed, than it does with children in formative years of personality- and self-development.

During the process of socialization, we learn much of what makes up the culture of our society—our beliefs, values, and rules of behavior. We develop a personality, and we acquire a sense of self. Just as "socialization" is a single term covering this series of interrelated changes, the word "society" itself covers a complex whole made up of interrelated parts. Even before we are aware of the fact, we have assumed some roles or positions in society that make us one of its interrelated parts—we are sons or daughters, brothers or sisters, and so on. In Chapter 5, we will examine more closely the network of roles and positions that make up any society.

SUMMARY

1. **Socialization** is the process through which a person learns the rules of behavior of a society and how to conform to them. Although socialization is a lifetime process of learning, it is particularly important in childhood.

2. Individuals are born with inherited characteristics that influence, to some extent, the kind of people they will become. Environmental factors interact with **heredity** to produce the adult personality. How much each factor—heredity, environment—contributes is a matter of great controversy.

3. The socialization process that eventually produces an adult personality involves three major inputs: cultural factors, agents of socialization, and methods of socialization.

4. Culture influences personality in two major ways: (1) it presents the individual with a way of life and a set of roles; and (2) it prescribes how children should be reared.

5. The family is the major **agent of socialization,** because it is usually the first socializing agent; it has influence over the child for a long period of time; and it provides an atmosphere in which many skills, attitudes, and values are both taught and "caught."

6. Other major agents of socialization include the school, the child's **peer group,** mass media (especially television), and the formal groups to which children belong.

7. The major methods by which children learn behaviors, attitudes, and values include direct instruction, rewards and punishment, and the imitation of adults.

8. **Personality** is a set of traits and characteristics that make one a unique individual. The **self** is one as one perceives oneself. Each person develops a self as a result of socialization. Cooley used the term **looking-glass self** to describe the feelings about oneself that result from imagining how others view one.

9. Mead suggested that the development of the self goes through three major stages: (1) the learning of language stage, which enables one to think about abstract ideas and about one's own behavior from another person's viewpoint; (2) the play stage, in which one imagines oneself in other people's positions and acts out their roles; (3) and the final, or

game, stage, in which one is able to imagine the roles of several people simultaneously and thus begin to respond to the opinions of the **generalized other**—the group.

10. Socialization continues to occur in adulthood as people take on new jobs, join organizations, or enter new institutions. For older adults, socialization consists of adapting to a new phase of life with different activities and different needs.

KEY TERMS

adult socialization
agents of socialization
game stage
generalized other
heredity
looking-glass self

peer group
personality
play stage
self
socialization

SUGGESTED READINGS

Cooley, Charles H. *Human Nature and the Social Order.* New York: Schocken, 1964.
Originally published in 1902, this classic work presents Cooley's concept of the looking-glass self.

Danziger, K., ed. *Readings in Child Socialization.* New York: Pergamon Press, 1970.
A collection of essays covering such areas as the family's role in socialization and the effect of different value orientations on the child.

Devos, George. *Socialization for Achievement.* Berkeley: University of California Press, 1973.
Essays on Japanese cultural psychology, basic value orientations, and achievement motivation. An excellent cross-cultural examination of socialization.

Hoppe, Ronald A., G. Alexander Milton, and Edward C. Simmel, eds. *Early Experiences and the Processes of Socialization.* New York: Academic Press, 1970.
A collection of readings dealing with genetic, psychological, and sociological factors that influence personality development.

Langton, Kenneth P. *Political Socialization.* New York: Oxford University Press, 1969.
The author focuses on the agencies in the political socialization process—the family, the school, and the peer group.

Leiner, Marvin. *Children Are the Revolution.* New York: Penguin Books, 1978.
A penetrating account of government day-care centers in Castro's Cuba and their role in socializing children.

McNeil, Elton B. *Human Socialization.* Belmont, Calif.: Brooks/Cole, 1969.
An excellent treatment of socialization, providing a wide view of the concepts, factors, agents, and consequences necessary for understanding socialization.

Mead, George Herbert. *Mind, Self, and Society.* Chicago: University of Chicago Press, 1934.
   A collection of several of Mead's lectures and essays on social psychology, the development of the self, and the interaction that forms the basis of human society.

Rosow, Irving. *Socialization to Old Age.* Berkeley: University of California Press, 1973.
   The author reviews socialization theory and recommends better and more humane ways to socialize people for old age.

Skinner, B. F. *Beyond Freedom and Dignity.* New York: Random House, 1972.
   Skinner presents his extreme but thought-provoking behaviorist position on socialization. Many consider his approach an assault against freedom and dignity.

Wrong, Dennis H. "The Oversocialized Conception of Man in Modern Sociology." *American Sociological Review,* 26 (1961), 183–193.
   A critique of modern sociology's overemphasis on environmental factors in explanation of personality. Wrong points out the need to be aware of biological and instinctual factors as well.

Ever since birth, we've been playing a number of parts in a complicated system: we've been sons, daughters, playmates, students, workers, and so on. Sociologists call these parts positions, and each position includes a role, which is the behaviors expected of those who occupy a particular position. Role is an important sociological concept. The fact that there are roles in groups, which specify the behavior of people in different positions in the group, explains how groups can continue, even though members leave and are replaced. New members enact the roles in much the same way the old members did. But roles do change, and no two people play the same role in exactly the same way. After all, roles are learned, and the learning process is never perfect.

Although roles usually help to make our lives run more smoothly, there are times when things go wrong—when we experience role failure. For one thing, all of us play many roles, not just one, and the various roles can conflict when the behavior expected of us in one role clashes with that expected of us in another role. The role of part-time worker, for example, may conflict with the role of student. Sometimes the role failure is due to a discrepancy between how a person in the opposite position—someone enacting a counter role—expects us to behave, and how we think he or she should behave. For example, a student and a teacher are in counter roles, and their expectations of each other are often widely different. Another kind of role failure is role strain, or the negative feelings we sometimes have about our own role performance. Other people may consider a man to be a good parent, but the man himself may feel somehow inadequate in the role.

The various role concepts discussed in this chapter should provide you with a better understanding of the groups to which you belong—how they work or fail to work and how they might be made to work better.

5
Positions and Roles in Society

The !Kung Bushmen live in a semiarid region of the Kalahari Desert area of Africa, where food and water are not very plentiful. With bows and poisoned arrows, the men hunt large and small animals, sometimes traveling great distances from the camp in search of game. The man who kills an animal first shares it with the other men in the hunting party. Each man who gets meat distributes it to his wife's parents, his wife and children, and his own parents, in that order.

Each morning, the women of the group travel 5 to 10 miles from camp in search of roots, berries, and mongono nuts. They take their children with them and return in the afternoon with the food, which they then prepare for their families. The meat furnished by the men is highly desired, but the food gathered by the women constitutes over half the group's regular diet (Friedl, 1975).

The !Kung Bushmen are living in the hunting and gathering stage, a stage that was typical of all human societies thousands of years ago (see Chapter 3). Life could be hard, but it was simple. With their crude weapons, the men and older boys roamed an area to trap or hunt animals. Women worked equally hard at digging edible roots and gathering fruits and nuts. Yet, even at this simple stage, it was evident that there was some kind of social organization. The food obtained by the adults was often distributed in a certain order within some designated group, and of course, it had to be shared with those who were too young, too old, or too infirm to get their own food. The group had to decide who was to do what, in order to ensure that all the necessary jobs got done. It was not a matter of each individual functioning independently or more or less randomly deciding what to do. Rather, the people functioned as a group.

As technology improved, a number of things happened to increase the complexity of human groups. With an increase in the kinds of work that needed to be done, it proved efficient to have people specialize in different kinds of work. The specialization of activities that began with a simple division of labor—men doing one kind of work and women another—became more and more intricate. The advanced agrarian stage, marked by the invention of the iron plow and other tools, led to a sizable agricultural surplus. Now that fewer people were needed to produce food, more could live in small cities, where they worked at crafts, engaged in business and trade with other societies, and delved into the arts. Then came the Industrial Revolution, with the proliferation of production jobs in factories and an accompanying increase in supervisory, managerial, selling, and advertising jobs. Today it is estimated that there are over 100,000 different job titles in the United States alone.

So far, this discussion has emphasized only the work roles of people at different stages of civilization. Even at the hunting and gathering stage, however, people were acting out the parts of mother, father, husband, wife, medicine man or woman, elder, and the like. In more complex societies, such as our own, each of us belongs to many groups—familial, political, religious, recreational, community service, and so on. Yet, it is clear that there is a certain predictability to the parts, or roles, that each of us enacts in our many groups. And the parts themselves, which we can think of as positions in a group, mesh with other positions in the group, so that some kind of an organized network emerges. This network, or organization of positions, is called a *social system.*

The purpose of this chapter is to increase our understanding of human behavior in groups. To accomplish this task, we must explore three basic sociological concepts to which we have briefly referred: *social systems, positions,* and *roles.* In this chapter we will see how these concepts relate to one another and how sociologists use them to analyze human interaction. We will be concentrating on the concept of "role," showing how roles promote group stability, how roles change, how we learn roles, and how, for different reasons, we sometimes fail at role performance.

THE SOCIAL SYSTEM AND ITS PARTS

A *system* is a unity, or whole, made up of interdependent parts (Miller, 1965; Parsons, 1951). Thus, we can speak of the solar *system,* or a supply *system,* or the digestive *system* of the human body. What all these systems have in common is a number of parts that interact with one another in a patterned and predictable way. But a system, we must remember, is an abstraction. What we actually observe are the component parts and their effects on one another. But from these observations we can establish the system's rules of interaction. Once we know these rules, we can predict behavior within the system—even behavior that has yet to be observed. For example, we know that the planetary orbits are maintained by a balance between gravity and centrifugal force. An orbit, therefore, results from a certain relationship between a planet and the sun. If either the sun or the planet changes, the orbit will change. If the change is great enough, the planet will either crash into the sun or fly off into outer space. We can say this with some certainty, even though we have never seen it happen. But we know that under certain circumstances it will happen, because we know about the solar system's rules of interaction.

Sociologists use the concept **social system** to describe the pattern that exists or could exist whenever two or more people interact. The elements, or parts, of a social system are not particular people but rather the **positions** they each occupy in the system. Of course, real people fill the positions and act out their parts with other people who are filling other positions. But the social system itself—the abstraction—is simply the network of interrelated positions. It should be noted that some sociologists use the term **status** for what we are calling "position" (Bates, 1956). But, because many people find it difficult to separate status from the idea of a high or low ranking, "position" seems the less confusing term.

The Network of Positions

A position can be described and studied without studying the individuals or their particular behavior, just as the positions on a basketball team—guard, forward, center and so on—and the relationships among them can be described without ever referring to the particular players. Although a position exists apart from the person who fills it, a position cannot exist without at least one other position. You cannot occupy the position of son or daughter unless someone else occupies the position of father or mother; you cannot be an employer unless there are employees; and you cannot be a teacher unless there are students.

The network of positions in a social system can be simple or complex—from two campers in the wilderness to a giant industrial bureaucracy, with its many different positions. In a complex system, not only are there many different kinds of positions, but also many people who simultaneously fill, or could fill, a single position. For example, there may be twenty men filling the position of foreman in one industrial plant, but we can think of this system as having a single position called "foreman," rather than 20 such positions. This is possible because all persons in the position of foreman stand in

Study this picture. There may be a dozen family positions—mother, husband, daughter, cousin, older sister, and the like—these people could be filling. How many do you count?

the same relationship to persons in the positions of plant manager, inspector, or assembly-line worker. Many other social systems also have more than one person in a single position. In a college class, there are usually two positions, instructor and student. Although usually only one person occupies the position of instructor, the position of student can include as few as 4 or 5 in a small seminar or as many as hundreds in a large lecture class.

Roles and Role Analysis

Just as positions can be studied apart from the people who fill them, the *behavior* expected of people who fill the positions can be separated for analysis from the positions themselves and from the people who fill them. Some positions have titles that describe what a person filling them would be expected to do: drill instructor, shop manager, street cleaner, housekeeper. But whether or not the title is descriptive, each position in any social system carries with it a set of expectations. The **incumbent,** the person who is filling the position, is expected to do certain things. We expect, for example, that a person who fills the position of drill instructor will, in fact, teach the troops close-order drill. We expect that the housekeeper will keep house and that the street sweeper will sweep streets.

We also have expectations about what the incumbent will be like, apart from what he or she will do. In our society a mother is expected to feel love and affection for her child and to be concerned about the child's well-being, health, and safety. And she is expected to know how to act on these concerns. In addition, the incumbent of any position will have expectations about how other people in other positions will behave toward that incumbent—what they will do to or for him or her. To be effective, the mother must expect obedience and cooperation from her child, as well as love and respect. The holder of any position thus has rights and privileges as well as duties and obligations. Others expect certain things of the incumbent, and he or she in turn has legitimate expectations of them.

The sum of what we expect from someone who occupies a position, and what he or she can expect of others, is called a **role** (or sometimes, a *social role*). *A role is the sum of culturally prescribed duties, characteristics, and rights expected of and granted to the incumbent of a particular position* (Biddle and Thomas, 1966). For every position there is a role, and for every role, a position. Although role and position can be studied separately, in real life the two concepts are inseparable.

Role is a powerful concept for understanding human behavior in groups—so much so that some sociologists have made role analysis, or role theory, their specialty. In the sections that follow, we will explore some of the major ways in which the concept of role is employed to help us understand human groups and the behavior of individuals as they enact their different roles.

HOW ROLES PROMOTE GROUP STABILITY

A single role can be played by different people. In our history, almost 40 different men have acted the role of President of the United States. The role of junior partner in a business firm may be enacted first by one person, then by someone else. You can probably think of many examples of roles that have been filled by a number of people. Take the example of a small rock group that needs to replace a member. After the position is refilled, the group continues to function more or less as it had previously; the role in the group remains the same, even though a new person had to be found to enact it.

Roles not only give a certain stability to human groups, they render human behavior fairly predictable. In the research experiment on guards and prisoners reported in Box 5.1, it is apparent that the roles were interpreted similarly by those who assumed them. In the example of the rock group, the new musician can be expected to behave in predictable ways and to have certain skills, attitudes, and values. It can be expected that the rock group's new guitarist will come to practice, follow directions, and play the guitar. Such expectations, and others, will influence how the older members of the band interact with the new one. They will know what to do and what to say to him or her because they know what behavior is associated with the role of guitarist. Because of the relative stability of the roles in the group, the

**BOX 5.1
THE GAME
OF GUARD
AND PRISONER**

Whether or not we think the prison system is in need of reform, we should all be familiar with certain criticisms frequently leveled against prisons: that they punish rather than rehabilitate; that the guards are often insensitive at best, brutal and sadistic at worst; that the prisoners are dehumanized by life behind the walls, are treated like animals, and are made less fit to reenter society.

Many proposals have been made to improve the system, from locking up only those convicted of violent crimes to giving applicants for guard positions psychological tests. But a possible kink in the entire notion of prison reform has been found as the result of an experiment conducted by psychologist Philip Zimbardo (1972) at Stanford University.

Zimbardo and his colleagues set up an experiment to study deviant behavior. They built a mock prison in a laboratory basement. They then selected 22 young volunteers from those who answered an ad offering fifteen dollars a day for participating in a prison experiment. They administered personality tests to be sure all 22 were emotionally stable. By random selection, eleven volunteers became prisoners, and the other eleven became guards. The guards were instructed only to maintain order.

band will continue to perform its functions in more or less the same way as before.

It is often useful to distinguish between *role,* on the one hand, and **role behavior,** or *role enactment,* on the other. *Role behavior* refers to what a person actually does, while the concept "role" is reserved for what he or she is supposed to do. Normally, of course, the expected and the actual behaviors coincide to a great extent, but they are rarely identical. This is because each incumbent brings to the role a unique background of experience and a unique interpretation of what is expected. A replacement guitarist will not interpret the role in exactly the same manner as did the original incumbent. Sometimes, too, an incumbent will deliberately attempt to modify a role. President Carter does many of the same things as president that others before him have done, but he has brought his own interpretation to the role, beginning with his walk down Constitution Avenue in the inauguration parade.

Earlier, we noted that the existence of roles in a group allows the group to continue to function, even when it is necessary to change incumbents. When we take into account the additional fact that incumbents help shape and define the roles they enact, it is apparent that groups *do* change as the positions are filled first by one person and then another. Often, this is not a problem, but should the role incumbents change rapidly, the group itself may change substantially or find difficulty in performing its functions. For

---

The experiment was to last 14 days, but it lasted only 6. Prisoners and guards quickly began to show the behavior attributed to their counterparts in actual prisons. Prisoners became passive and anxiety-ridden; guards became abusive and cruel. Several prisoners had to be released after only a few days. Almost all the remaining prisoners were desperate enough for release that they were willing to sign away the right to the money they had earned to that point. The guards, on the other hand, were eager to continue the experiment. Several guards worked for longer than their regular shifts, without extra pay. As one guard later said, "Power can be a great pleasure."

Why did the middle-class college students so quickly and thoroughly fall into roles that were alien to their experience? Since the roles of guard and prisoner were assigned randomly, it is unlikely that the behavior of the guards was due to their unique personality characteristics. A more likely explanation is that the role of guard, which carried with it control over another human being and little accountability, encouraged the role incumbents to go beyond the role somewhat and to act cruelly and abusively. Similarly, the role of prisoner was one of powerlessness and inability to control one's fate. Almost anyone assigned to this role would be apt to become passive and anxiety-ridden.

this reason, formal groups often stagger the election of officers or members of a board, for instance, by electing two each year rather than replacing, say, all six at one time. Groups also avoid radical changes by defining the roles as fully as possible, so that each successive incumbent will have a good understanding of his or her role. Some groups, such as the military, have a formal, written job description that describes the expectations and requirements of a given role and how the role relates to others in a given group.

HOW ROLES CHANGE

Most people have positions in many different social systems and thus enact many different roles. Even a preschool child plays several different parts. Certain characteristics and behaviors are expected of a little girl or boy as a child of parents, as a little sister or brother of an older child, as a playmate among neighborhood children, and so on. Children learn that when a grandfather comes to visit they have a position in still another social system, for interaction with a grandfather is somehow different from interaction with a father.

Throughout our lives in society we give up positions in groups and take on other positions. Since there is a role attached to every position, our roles change. The roles we enact can change in four major ways: (1) new roles can be added to the cluster of roles; (2) roles can be given up, willingly or otherwise; (3) one role can be substituted for another; and (4) the nature or content of one or more roles can change over time.

As children grow older, they enact more and more roles: student, church group member, club member, and so on. In adulthood, they continue to acquire roles—taxi driver, computer programmer, husband or wife, member of a professional society, parent. Any person can add new roles to existing ones or substitute one role for another—by changing jobs, by divorce, and in many other ways. One can lose roles, as a person does who retires and gives up not only a job but also union and other job-related memberships. Being required to give up a role can, in fact, be quite distressing. Erving Goffman (1952) refers to it as a person losing one of his or her social lives.

Not only does a person's number of roles change, but the content and nature of each role can change over time. What is expected or demanded of a three-year-old son or daughter is not what is expected of a teenage or adult son or daughter. The roles of newlyweds differ so clearly from those of spouses who have been married for a while that even a casual observer can usually distinguish between the two groups, even if all the couples are about the same age. Thus, roles change even while a person is enacting them.

Changes that occur in roles over time in the same society can be studied. And a role in one social system can be compared with a similar role in another system. For instance, a study of changes in the role of women in the United States over the last 100 years might note that, in the earlier period, women were expected to possess certain domestic skills, to observe the strictest decorum in speech and dress, and to be subordinate to men. The study might also note that, over time, these expectations were modified, and new abilities and attributes came to be expected of women.

Such a study of the changes in the role of women could have important practical implications. It might explain why two generations of women, even a mother and her daughter, frequently have a difficult time understanding each other. In times when roles are changing rapidly, a woman who attempts to teach her daughter the role she learned in her youth is, indeed, "old-fashioned."

No less valuable than a historical study of roles would be one that compared roles in different societies. For example, the role of the adult male in the United States requires that men not cry when sad, that they not hug male friends in greeting, and the like. In other societies, such as in France, males are freer to express their emotions and their feelings of friendship. By such a comparison, we learn that different cultures have different role expectations for the same position.

HOW ROLES ARE LEARNED

In Chapter 4, we found that roles are learned as part of the socialization process. Since so much of a child's life consists of learning, it is usually impossible to separate the various learning processes. However, we can identify a few major ways in which roles are learned and developed: by instruction and observation, by playing a reciprocal role, and by generalizing and imagining. A closer look at these mechanisms will help us to understand and deal with the various role problems we will be discussing later in the chapter.

Learning by Instruction and Observation

You will recall from Chapter 4 that some aspects of roles are learned by direct instruction. A little girl is taught part of the traditional role of wife and mother by instruction from her own mother, and probably, also, from school courses, such as home economics. She is taught by her mother how to make beds, how to cook, and how to clean house. In short, she is *taught* how to act out certain portions of a role. At one and the same time, she learns certain skills and certain expectations that others will have for her if she assumes the position of housewife.

Instruction is required for many roles throughout life: soldier, clergyman, office worker, and so on. Even prostitutes, as a study by James Bryan (1965) has shown, must be instructed in the many elements of their role. The novice call girl is taught her trade by an established prostitute or a pimp. She must learn how to solicit customers, how to converse with them, and how to collect the fee. She must also learn what not to do. As one woman put it, "Don't take so much time, the idea is to get rid of them as quickly as possible." Bryan concludes that what makes the prostitute's training period necessary is not the level of the skills that are required but rather the secrecy of the occupation.

Although a woman aspiring to the position of prostitute does not have the opportunity to watch others enacting all aspects of that role, most individuals who may play a certain role one day usually have early opportunities for observing how others play the role. By continued observation throughout the years of her childhood, a girl enlarges her knowledge of the traditional role of wife and mother. Through observing her father's reaction to the way in which the mother plays her role, the daughter may modify her ideas on how the role of wife should be played. She also learns by observing how

Direct, formal instruction is one way in which all of us learned about the duties and responsibilities accompanying some roles. By being a student, we also learned something about the role of teacher.

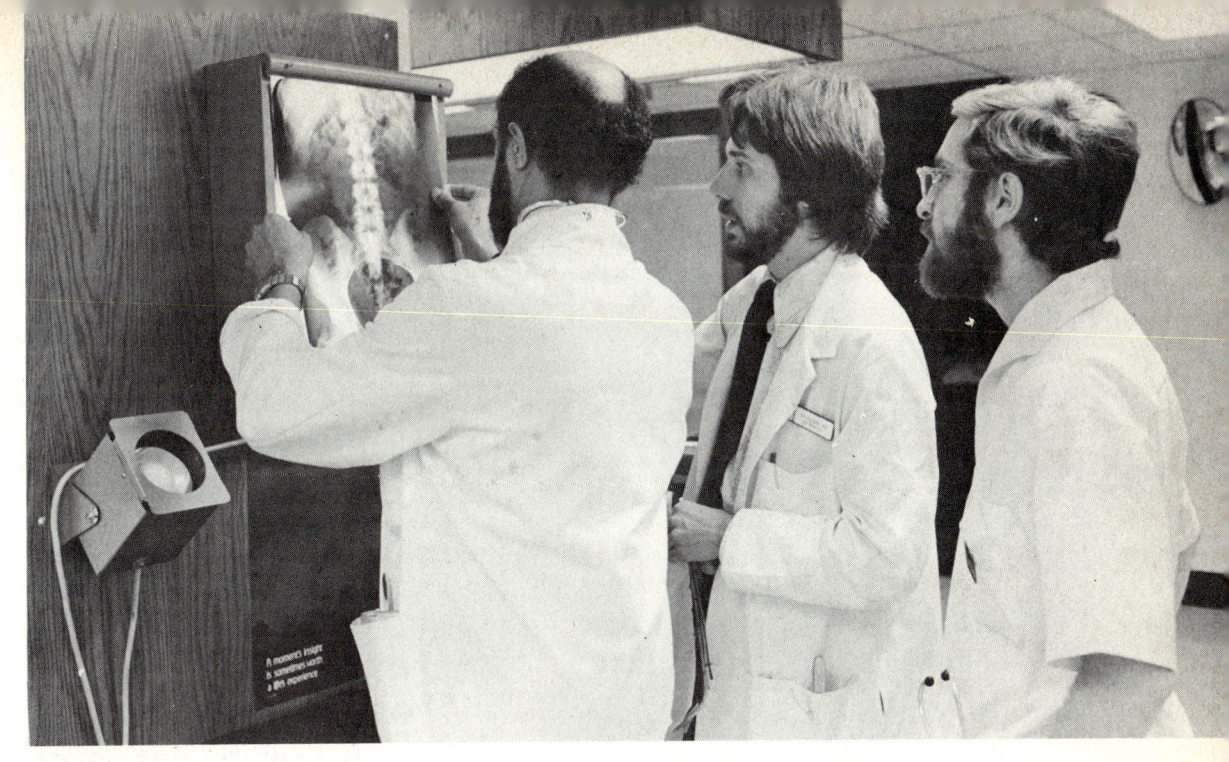

Observation as a method of learning roles is not restricted to childhood. Throughout our lives we learn some aspects of roles by watching others perform them.

other women interact with their husbands, either in real life, as at a friend's house, or in novels or on television. Over the course of many years, all of these observations influence how she later acts out this role, if she chooses the position of wife and mother.

Learning by Playing a Reciprocal Role

Some roles can be partly learned by playing the **reciprocal role,** or **counter role,** in a specific social system. Even though it may sound odd at first, a boy learns to play the role of father partly by playing the role of son. Playing a reciprocal role differs from observation in that the boy is not merely watching someone act out the role of father, but rather, he is interacting with the person in the other role. He learns not only what a father does in interacting with his son but also how he himself reacts to what his father says or does. In other words, he evaluates the role performance of his father in terms of his own reaction to that performance. The boy will remember both how the role of father was played and how well he thought it was played.

If, when the boy becomes an adult, he chooses the position of father, his own performance of the role will depend partly on how he evaluates his father's role performance and partly on what he has learned elsewhere about the role of father. Even when a man is determined to act as much unlike his father as possible, he is highly influenced by his father's behavior. By having played the reciprocal role of son, he has learned enough about his father's role performance to choose to act in ways that are unlike those of his father.

A person learns roles by playing counter, or reciprocal, roles in many areas of life. As people act out their roles as members of a church congrega-

The role of parent is partly learned through playing the role of child. This child is learning how a mother interacts with children and how she feels about the interaction.

tion, they are learning about the role of minister; the role of teacher is learned partly by being a student; the role of boss is learned by being bossed.

Learning Through Generalization and Imagination

Sometimes we learn how to play a role largely by having had experience in similar roles. We recognize tasks and functions common to different groups and then apply what we've learned in an earlier group experience to a later one. Suppose, for example, that at a children's summer camp, a child is discovered to be lost one evening just before dark. A search party is formed at once, but the camp director is unavailable. The immediate task is to send out the searchers in a way that best ensures the finding of the child. Unfortunately, no one at the camp has ever had experience as a leader in such a situation. However, one of the counselors has had experience in organizing other groups. Without necessarily realizing that she is doing so, she draws on this previous experience and takes charge, selecting the members of the search party, instructing them in what has to be done, setting up channels of communication, and soliciting advice of group members. Although she has never enacted this particular role before, her experience in a similar role has prepared her to perform it. This process of applying learning from one role to another is called *generalization.*

In addition to generalization, we learn to enact roles partly by using our imagination and mentally picturing ourselves in certain roles. A person may plan mentally what to do when he or she arrives home an hour and a half later than expected. He or she will most likely imagine how those at home will respond to the late arrival. The person will go on to mentally develop his or her own response to how others enact their roles: "Then Mom will say . . . , then I'll say . . ." People can mentally rehearse various kinds of roles they anticipate enacting. Although some experience, observation, or instruction may be drawn on in the imaginative role playing, part of the learning process will consist of mentally trying out the role and rejecting some ideas on how it should be played and keeping others.

Even though we learn the behavior, attitudes, and knowledge expected of us in a certain role, we are not always able to put this learning into practice. Difficulties in the performance of a role are referred to as **role failure,** but the word "failure" does not imply that the problem is irreversible. Let us now examine several different types of role failure, so that we can understand the sources of failure and see how failure can be reduced.

ROLE FAILURE: KINDS AND CAUSES

In any type or size of social system things sometimes go wrong. Every day people are dismissed from jobs for failure to perform their roles adequately. In families, parents are accused of not bringing up their children correctly, husbands and wives divorce each other for not fulfilling certain role expectations, and children are punished for failure in role performance. Even though the individual is surely affected by these situations, the sociologist is concerned not so much with the individual as with the role. The sociologist looks at such problems as being social rather than personal.

Sociologists commonly distinguish the main types of role failure as *role discrepancy, role conflict,* and *role strain.* The main causes of such role failure are inadequate role preparation and discontinuity in socialization. We shall look at each of these types and causes of role failure in some detail.

Role Discrepancy

As we have noted, the simplest social system consists of two positions that in some way relate to each other. When difficulties occur in such a small social system, the problem is often one of **role discrepancy** — the failure of one person to behave in ways expected by a person in the reciprocal position. Take the example of a young college couple who are married or living together. What the woman does will not necessarily conform to what the man expects her to do, and vice versa. For instance, she may want to have friends over to study with her, while the man may consider this an infringement on his need for a quiet place to study.

Often, there is not much point in trying to discover who is right and who is wrong, for the point is that each time that a person attempts to act out a role, his or her behavior may be inconsistent with what the person in the counter position expects. Because roles are learned, there is no guarantee that two people who one day enter reciprocal roles will have learned them in exactly corresponding ways. Even if a man and woman have had similar experiences as students, have talked with other college couples, and have known each other for some time before marrying or deciding to share an apartment, they can still enter an arrangement with diffcrent conceptions of the proper roles of man and woman. Each brings his or her unique expectations of how the roles should be played. These expectations serve as a guide to the person's own behavior and as a standard for evaluating the other person's behavior.

The first step in resolving role discrepancies is to appraise them accurately. There are three possible ways of resolving discrepancies, and which one should be used depends on the nature of the role discrepancy, the specific social system in which it occurs, and the willingness and ability of the role incumbents to modify their behavior or expectations. The role behavior of a given actor can change, the expectations of the person in the counter position can change, or both behavior and expectations can be modified until they are compatible with one another. In our example, the woman could change her behavior by not having friends over to study with her. Or, the man could accept her point of view and go to the library to study. Or, perhaps, role behavior and role expectations could be modified by the couple's agreeing not to have friends over, except on weekends or at times that will not inconvenience the other person.

Role Conflict

A **role conflict** occurs when one of a person's roles conflicts with one or more of the other roles the person plays at the same time (for examples, see Campbell and Pettigrew, 1959; Preiss and Ehrlich, 1966). Since each person plays many roles, it is understandable that serious role conflicts will arise now and then. The conflict is internal and personal, for it is the individual who must act out the parts, or refrain from doing so. But the conflict is also social, because the conflicting demands come from a social system or systems in which the person has positions. (A discussion of role conflicts in business organizations can be found in Box 5.2.) For instance, several years ago, cadets at the Air Force Academy discovered that some of their friends had been cheating on examinations. Under the honor system, the cadets were required, in their role as students, to inform their superiors of the

It is unlikely that a drill instructor could take on the role of friend to a new recruit for it would conflict with the duties and expectations of his formal role.

cheating; but, as members of friendship groups, the cadets were also expected to remain silent. The roles were clearly in conflict; one could not successfully play both roles.

Most of us have experienced role conflict at one time or another. Often, teenagers cannot simultaneously be both the child their parents expect them to be and the group member their friends expect. The demands of the role of wife may conflict with those of mother, and both may conflict with the demands of a woman's job. As a worker, the woman is expected to be efficient and productive; as a mother, she is expected to give her child the time, attention, and guidance required for proper child rearing; as a wife, she may be expected to cook and look after the house. It is a rare woman who can fill all these roles without experiencing at least some conflict.

Role conflicts are seldom easy to resolve. One method is to avoid, or give up, one of the conflicting roles; another is to make compromises between the two roles, in order to minimize conflict; a third is to rationalize the conflict and reduce its importance in one's own perceptions; and still another is to try to live with both conflicting roles, by pursuing, at proper times, each role as if the other were nonexistent.

The choice of method depends on the circumstances. For instance, a man whose religion requires pacifism can *avoid* the role of combat soldier by not enlisting in the military. Even when the draft was still in effect, he could apply for conscientious objector status. And, if all else failed, and he firmly wished to avoid a combat role, he could elect imprisonment or self-imposed exile as alternatives.

Another man may have a conflict between the role of father and that of provider. The more time and energy he spends on the job, the less time he has for his children, and vice versa. *Compromise* is one of the most common resolutions of such a conflict. But compromise may be unsatisfactory if it leads to the feeling that both of the conflicting roles are being neglected.

Finally, an individual may *rationalize* the problem away, by rearranging his or her ideas, so that the conflict appears either unreal or unimportant (Wispé, 1955). A person may be concerned about pollution of the environment and yet work for a company that is a source of pollution. Such an individual might think up all sorts of reasons why, "for now," pollution is inevitable. That person may also come to feel that it would be futile to express

---

**BOX 5.2
ROLE CONFLICT ON THE JOB**

Each of us plays many roles. We play the role of student, friend, daughter, parent, Boy Scout, voter, customer, driver, and so on. And, as this chapter points out, some of these roles may come into conflict with one another from time to time. To further complicate things, roles can conflict in a number of different ways. Let us take the example of one person—a foreman in a factory—and look at the kinds of role conflict he might encounter.

First, the foreman may be caught in the middle, between the supervisors and the workers. The supervisors may expect him to hold the workers strictly to company rules and to high production schedules, whereas the workers may let him know that they want loose supervision or they will produce at low levels. This type of role conflict is termed inter-sender conflict. That is, the foreman is getting contradictory messages from two sources, and he must somehow please them both. Similar to this problem is that of intrasender conflict, in which one person sends contradictory messages. For example, a supervisor may tell the foreman to do something that is against company regulations while also telling him not to violate the regulations.

Another type of role conflict the foreman might be faced with is inter-role conflict. This type of conflict occurs when two or more of a person's roles clash. For example, the foreman's need to work overtime may interfere with his performance of his roles as husband and father.

Finally, role conflict can arise from a conflict in values. The foreman may feel pressured by his work role to participate in a strike or in union activities, despite personal antiunion feelings. Or, he may act on his true feelings and be ostracized by others who feel that he is not performing his role correctly.

Researchers at the Institute for Social Research at the University of Mich-

any objections, since it would not change the situation and might result in loss of the job.

Let's return now to the woman who is a worker, a mother, and a wife at the same time. Her job may demand as much of her time, attention, and energy as her husband's job demands of him. Thus, the demands of her job and her husband's expectations of her role in the home may come into conflict. Suppose that avoiding either role is impossible (the second income is essential to the family, and divorce is unthinkable). Compromise has failed, for her husband is thoroughly socialized in the traditional male-female roles. Rationalization won't work, because there is nothing for it to work on. The woman will not give up either role, and the conflict is produced outside of her, by her husband's refusal or inability to change his expectations of her role as a wife. Her only choice, then, is to live as best she

igan (Kahn, 1972) found that certain positions are more susceptible to role conflict than others. Salesmen and others who often must work outside their company have added problems because they are faced with demands and criticisms from people both inside and outside the company. Stress is also greater for creative people, who have to fight to get their ideas heard and who rebel against the time-consuming paperwork that keeps them from pursuing their creative activities. Middle management is also an area in which there is high conflict. Those in middle-management positions feel pressure from above, below, and both sides. Finally, shift workers run into role difficulties, because their work role often interferes with their roles as fathers, husbands, friends, community members, and sex partners.

What are the costs of role conflict? Those who experience the greatest conflict often suffer such physical problems as digestive upsets, infectious diseases, headaches, insomnia, ulcers, and arthritis. Emotionally, they may become withdrawn and apathetic. They may feel dissatisfied with their job and have low confidence in the company they work for. As a consequence, role conflict has great costs for organizations: it reduces productivity.

What can be done to reduce role conflict for people on the job? According to Kahn (1972), there is strong evidence that the negative effects of role conflict can be eased by close and positive relations between workers. Furthermore, the higher one's self-esteem, the more easily one can cope with conflicts. Organizations that are anxious to keep conflict in control and want to improve worker performance might, therefore, consider measures that would promote good relations between workers and contribute to the individual worker's self-esteem.

can for as long as she must—or for as long as she *can*—with both conflicting roles. She must try, in effect, to handle each role as if the other were nonexistent or not conflicting. This is the fourth way of handling conflict, and one that is probably in widespread use in our society.

Role Strain

Role strain refers to the negative feelings one may have concerning his or her role performance. F. Ivan Nye studied this concept in his research of Washington families, which was reported in his *Role Structure and Analysis of the Family* (1976). He measured role strain by asking husbands and wives whether they ever worried or felt guilty about how they performed such activities as teaching their children, caring for small children, meeting their spouse's sexual needs, and trying to help the spouse with his or her problems. These measures allowed him to locate the area of role strain in a family. He found, for example, more strain reported concerning the child socialization role than the child care role.

Role strain could well result from role conflict. A person may feel guilty about his or her role performance as a parent or spouse if it is felt that one role cannot be performed well without slighting the other. The strain could also stem from role discrepancy, as in the case of a husband who feels that he is not living up to his wife's expectations as a person who will listen to her problems and help her solve them. Again, role strain refers to how one feels about one's role performance, rather than to the actual performance itself. For the smooth functioning of a family or any other group, it clearly would be best if people felt good about their role performance rather than feeling role strain.

Since role strain exists solely in the mind of the role incumbent, it is basically up to the individual to reduce worry or guilt about role performance. Sometimes it takes professional help, such as from a marriage counselor, for a person to understand why he or she feels guilty. Understanding the common causes of role failure—which include inadequate role preparation and discontinuity in socialization—may also help a person to understand what needs to be done to feel better about how a particular role is being enacted.

Inadequate Role Preparation

A common cause of the role failures we've been discussing is that the incumbent is not prepared to fill the new position and its role. If the behavior and attitudes of the new role can be learned quickly, role strain is usually only temporary and mild. But, sometimes, so much preparation is required for a role that learning to enact it before failure occurs is extremely difficult, or even impossible.

We see examples of role failures caused by inadequate preparation all around us. At most colleges and universities each fall, a small but predictable number of freshmen drop out of school after only a week or two of their first semester. Many of those students are not yet able to direct their own lives: they miss classes and appointments, fail to complete their assignments, and in various other ways prove unable to take care of themselves without supervision and direction; others have never left home emotionally; and still others have never learned how to get along in small groups of their peers. Many young couples marry with as little preparation for marriage as such students have had for college.

Inadequate role preparation frequently appears to be the fault of the ill-prepared individual. Some individuals do fail to perceive what is required of them or are otherwise unable or unwilling to prepare for a new role. But, often, poor role preparation can be traced to the specific social system in which the person is supposed to take the new role or to the social system that should have prepared the person for that role. Perhaps the college is forbidding to certain students—it is too large or too demanding or too impersonal. Or perhaps the student's family or high-school counselor urged him or her on to college without taking into account the person's expressions of self-doubt or lack of self-confidence. Or perhaps parents and teachers did not make clear the immense differences between high school and college.

Discontinuity in Socialization

Ideally, our preparation for life's sequence of roles has a certain continuity. The characteristics we acquire while enacting a certain role can be carried over into our next role, allowing us to go from one to the next with little strain. At times, though, there are *discontinuities* in the sequence of roles we play. That is, before we can enact a new role, we may have to unlearn previously learned behaviors or attitudes. When the tendency toward discontinuity is society-wide, it is a **discontinuity in socialization,** or a discontinuity in cultural conditioning (Benedict, 1939).

In the United States, we find discontinuity in socialization in the many contrasts between the role of the child and that of the adult. Most children today are not supposed to be responsible for their own maintenance and welfare; someone almost always takes care of them. Children are not expected or allowed to be truly independent, to make their own decisions, or to direct their own lives. Yet, as adults, they are supposed to be responsible for their own welfare, and usually, that of others. They are expected to be autonomous free agents, capable of directing their own adult lives.

The transition from the role of child to that of adult can be smooth or harsh, and the time for the role change can be clearly demarcated or left ambiguous. In our society, discontinuity in socialization prevails, because the contrast in successive roles is great. There is much unlearning involved before the adult role can be fully assumed, and often, there is no clear-cut signal to the incumbent that the time has come to change roles.

Many primitive societies have a special **rite of passage** that signals the passing of a person from the status of child to that of adult. The rite usually corresponds with the attainment of physical maturity, but its true significance lies in the fact that it reduces ambiguity and counteracts any discontinuity in the socialization, for it signifies clearly that one has entered the adult world and is ready to take on the roles of an adult.

Only a few decades ago, many more children than is the case now were introduced to the adult world in early or middle adolescence, when they got their first real jobs. They entered a transitional stage in which they had to please employers, hold down a job, and bring home wages, while still being dependent offspring. In fact, it was once fairly common for offspring to live at home until they married, no matter what their age. Since World War II, however, our higher standard of living has freed many teenagers from the need to work, and our requirement of a college education for so many jobs and careers has prolonged the dependency of adolescence, often well into the person's twenties.

A common discontinuity in socialization is the lack of preparation for the change from the role of mature adult to old adult. This transition is just as ambiguous as the one from child to adult, and often, a considerable amount of unlearning is required. Among the Comanche, for example, the adult male was a warrior and was expected to be self-reliant, competitive, and to some extent, self-seeking. An old man was expected to be gentle, to work for

These modern Apache Indians still use their ancient puberty rite which clearly signifies to the participant and her tribe that a girl has become a woman.

the welfare of the tribe instead of his own, and to settle feuds between the warriors. As the anthropologist Ralph Linton (1936) put it, "Young men strove for war and honor, old men strove for peace and tranquillity" (p. 121). It was often only with great difficulty that the older Comanche admitted to himself and to others that he had reached the point of old age.

In our society, people find the transition to older adult every bit as uncomfortable as did the Comanche warrior. The role of older adult is unclear. It is difficult to know what it includes—other than keeping out of the way of younger people—and the unlearning required can be formidable. Men and women have to somehow forget their lifelong strivings in the world of work, to play down competitiveness generally, and to change their attitudes toward the meaning and use of leisure time. For those in the work force, old age is ushered in dramatically with forced retirement at age 65. Suddenly, there is lots of leisure time. Many older people complain that they have too much time on their hands and have difficulty finding socially useful activities that give them a sense of self-worth. Eventually, most somehow adjust to the situation, but the strain in doing so points up the discontinuity of the socialization process. Like the Comanche warrior who must become an arbiter for peace, the old people in our society find it difficult to suddenly adopt new values and new lifestyles.

In this chapter we have seen how the roles designated by a society help to shape the behavior of individuals, and when all goes well, how they help insure the smooth functioning of groups. But, we have not yet dealt at length with the group itself, its properties, and the varied functions of different types of groups. These topics are the subject of our next chapter.

SUMMARY

1. A **social system** is the pattern of relationships that exists whenever two or more people interact—it is a network of interrelated **positions.** Positions exist apart from the people who fill them, but each position cannot exist without at least one other position existing in relation to it.

2. The sum of what we expect from someone who occupies a position is called a **role.** The **incumbent** of a position is expected to fulfill the role for that position.

3. Because a single role may be played by different people, roles function to promote group stability. Roles also allow us to predict human behavior. **Role behavior** refers to what one actually does in a role, while "role" refers to what the incumbent is supposed to do.

4. Roles can change in four major ways: (1) new roles can be added; (2) roles can be given up; (3) one role can be substituted for another; and (4) the nature of a role can change over time.

5. There are several mechanisms by which roles are learned: (1) by direct instruction or observation; (2) by playing a **reciprocal role** to the role one is learning; (3) by *generalization* from one role to another; and (4) by imagining oneself in the role.

6. **Role failure** takes three major forms. (1) **Role discrepancy** occurs when the individual fails to behave in ways expected by a person in a reciprocal role. (2) **Role conflict** occurs when one of a person's roles conflicts with the person's other roles. Methods used to resolve role conflict include avoidance, compromise, and rationalization. (3) **Role strain** occurs when the individual has negative feelings about his or her role performance.

7. Role failure can result from *inadequate role preparation* or from **discontinuity in socialization,** in which previously learned behaviors or attitudes interfere with smooth acquisition of the role.

KEY TERMS

discontinuity in socialization
incumbent
position
reciprocal role (counter role)
rite of passage
role
role behavior

role conflict
role discrepancy
role failure
role strain
social system
status

SUGGESTED READINGS

Biddle, Bruce J., and Edwin J. Thomas, eds. *Role Theory.* New York: John Wiley & Sons, 1966.
  A collection of essays dealing with many aspects of the concept of role and role-related research.

Dobriner, William M. *Social Structures and Systems.* Santa Monica, Calif.: Goodyear, 1969.
  The author emphasizes social systems and their components and analyzes them from a functional perspective.

Goffman, Erving. *The Presentation of Self in Everyday Life.* Garden City, N.Y.: Doubleday, 1959.
  Using theatrical performance as a model for studying social behavior, Goffman provides an insightful view of man the actor performing for various social audiences.

Lopata, Helen Znaniecki. *Occupation: Housewife.* New York: Oxford University Press, 1971.
  A study of the many roles played by the housewife, socialization into these roles, and the areas in which role conflict occurs.

Merton, Robert K. *Social Theory and Social Structure.* New York: The Free Press, 1968.
A thorough discussion of role conflict and the mechanisms that operate to reduce various types of conflict.

Nye, F. Ivan. *Role Structure and Analysis of the Family.* Beverly Hills, Calif.: Sage Publications, 1976.
A research report that applies many role concepts to the study of the family. The book deals with the measurement of various roles in the family and relates role behavior to marital satisfaction.

Simmel, Georg. *The Sociology of Georg Simmel,* Kurt Wolff, ed. New York: The Free Press, 1950.
A collection of Simmel's most important essays. The book includes essays on the dyad, the triad, collective behavior, rituals, the secret society, the stranger, and the city. One of the most insightful works in classical sociology.

Smelser, Neil J., and William T. Smelser, eds. *Personality and Social Systems.* New York: John Wiley & Sons, 1970.
Readings on the relationship of social systems to individuals. The book deals with both macroscopic systems, such as society, and microscopic systems, such as small groups.

Whyte, William Foote. *Street Corner Society.* Chicago: University of Chicago Press, 1955.
A classic participant observation study of a neighborhood group of young men. Whyte focuses on the way that group membership affects individual behavior.

From your study of positions and roles in Chapter 5, you have become aware that groups are not just collections of people. Groups represent the interaction of many people in many roles, and the kinds and quality of these interactions vary. This chapter focuses directly on the major types of groups that humans form and shows what constitutes a group and the ways in which groups can affect our functioning as human beings.

Sociologists make an important distinction between primary groups—in which there are intimate, face-to-face relationships—and secondary groups—in which there are more formal, less personal relationships. Sociologists are also interested in the influence of size on group functioning and in the differences between formal and informal groups. Most groups have leaders of some sort, and sociologists have discovered that, in many groups, there are actually two leadership positions: one of these is meant to assure that the group works toward achieving its goals, while the other serves to keep the group running smoothly and harmoniously. Learning about groups and how they can be efficiently organized can help us to function more effectively in the voluntary associations to which we belong.

One special kind of group that deserves our attention is bureaucracy. In America, large, impersonal bureaucracies are often criticized and lampooned. Nevertheless, bureaucracies do offer one solution for the efficient organizing of large numbers of people. The sociological study of bureaucracies can help us to understand such organizations better, by focusing on their key features, including division of responsibility, chains of command, and the importance of formal rules. However, as we well know, the same features that help ensure that jobs get done can also lead to problems.

We will consider many kinds of groups in this chapter, from such small, personal groups as newlyweds, to such large, impersonal groups as the United States government. Because you are a member of many kinds of groups—family, school, friendship, work, volunteer—you should benefit personally from a better understanding of the problems and needs of groups in general. You should begin to get the picture, too, of the links between person and person, group and group, that hold society together.

6
Human Groups

> What a commentary on human life, that human beings must associate to endure it.
> —BALZAC

> The most natural privilege of man, next to the right of acting for himself, is that of combining his exertions with those of his fellow-creatures, and of acting in common with them.
> —ALEXIS DE TOCQUEVILLE

What Balzac describes as "an unfortunate necessity," de Tocqueville calls "a natural privilege." But both agree that humans are not solitary creatures —that we must live in association with our fellows. Thousands of years before the beginning of sociology, philosophers were aware that humans were accustomed to joining together in groups, and they knew that such groups possessed some organization and sense of unity. It remained for sociologists to focus on the human group as something that could be studied and analyzed in and of itself. In the course of such study, much has been learned about the different kinds of groups that people form, the interaction patterns within these different groups, the various purposes of groups, and how groups function and mesh together to form an integrated society.

To the sociologist, the everyday term "group" has a technical meaning. Two or more people are considered a **group** if four important criteria are satisfied:

1. *The people are mutually aware of one another and interact physically or through the use of symbols, such as communication by words or gestures.* Reciprocity is implied in the ideas of mutual awareness and interaction. In a group relationship, action follows a two-way path between and among members.
2. *The people must think of themselves as a unit (group) and must be thought of by others as members of a unit.* It is almost as if those observing the interaction among the people cannot help thinking of them as a whole, a unity—a *group*. Similarly, the people interacting think of themselves collectively and have a sense of common identity, in addition to seeing each other as separate human beings.
3. *The people accept roles, privileges, and obligations as members of the unit or group.* This acceptance results in at least a minimal amount of organization and regularity, for the members share expectations regarding one another's behavior.
4. *The people share and accept some rules that govern their interaction.* These rules for behavior (**norms**) can range from quite informal, agreed-upon standards regarding acceptable behavior to formal, even written, rules.

The concept "group" implies nothing about the quality of the interaction among members, the number of people involved, or the purposes for which they have joined together. Interaction can be warm and intimate, or it can be formal; size can range from two people to millions; and groups can be formed for any number of purposes, from that of meeting people's recreational needs to that of providing a collective effort to remedy a social ill. These are some of the differences among groups that we will study in this chapter. We will begin with a discussion of *primary groups,* which are small and intimate, and will work through to larger groups, such as bureaucracies and communities.

PRIMARY GROUPS

Early in the history of American sociology, Charles Horton Cooley (1956) developed the concept **primary group,** using the family as the best illustration of such a group. The term "primary" seems an apt designation for several reasons. First, the family is the first group of which the human infant is a member. Second, it is primary in the sense that it has a primary influence on the child's personality development, for, particularly during the early years, the family is the chief agent of socialization. Finally, the family is primary in that it is the group toward which most people feel intense, deep, and, often, first loyalty. Most of us recognize the fact that the interaction between and among family members is quite different than that in most other groups to which we belong. Cooley attempted to describe these differences, and later, other sociologists elaborated on the nature of primary relationships. Sociologists have identified a number of other groups that fit the description of a primary group. Even criminal gangs can be primary groups—see Box 6.1.

Primary Group Relationships

People in a primary relationship see, value, and interact with one another as whole persons. Thus, primary relationships involve the *total personality* (to the extent that it is possible for any relationship to do so). By contrast, we may know, say, the service station attendant or the store clerk by name, but usually, we know only one aspect of his or her personality, that of attendant or clerk. One of the reasons, therefore, why primary relationships involve total personalities is that in such relationships we interact in a variety of roles, not just one. We get to know each other's feelings about work, politics, religion, leisure, and family. Some members of a campus organization may interact with one another only in the role of club member; while others may study together, work on their cars together, trade records, go to parties together, and through other such interaction get to know each other as whole persons.

Another characteristic of primary relationships is that interaction is spontaneous and relatively free. In a primary group, we can be ourselves, sharing our fears and doubts without worrying that the others will think less of us. We can share our joys and talk of day-to-day happenings, because we feel free to do so, and because we sense that those in our primary group will want us to do so and will understand us. Communication is free, generally easy and unrehearsed, and little is deliberately held back. Communication is deeper in primary relationships, for we expose our feelings, not just our thoughts and ideas. To those with whom he or she has a *secondary relationship,* a high school student may explain the logical reasons for his or her family's move to another community; but to those in the primary group, the student would describe how he or she feels about moving away from friends and the old home, about missing the old school and being unable to graduate

---

BOX 6.1
SOCIAL OSTRACISM OF JAPANESE GANGSTERS

Japan is a very group-oriented country. All aspects of life there are built around the group—the family group, the work group, and so on. If a child misbehaves, the worst punishment he or she can receive is to be sent outdoors, away from the family group. It is no surprise, then, that in such a group-conscious society, many crimes are committed by groups—Japan's criminal gangs. The city of Osaka, for example, has been likened to Chicago, because of the long series of gangland feuds occurring there; it has been estimated that, in Osaka alone, there are 316 criminal groups, containing about 10,000 gangsters.

These gangsters are involved in the same sorts of activities as American gangsters. According to the New York Times (March 17, 1977), "The smaller gangs operate like baseball farm teams, training the men in their prime activities—gambling, prostitution rings, some narcotics sales, cabaret and bar operations, the protection racket, and loan-sharking. Members, some of whom chop off parts of a little finger to demonstrate their sincerity, work their way up to the major groups."

Until recently, these gangsters were accepted as part of life in such cities as Osaka. The gangsters were proud of their groups and even had the gang's name and symbol on their office doors and windows. They were easily recognizable on the street, as they all wore dark, wide-striped suits and drove flashy foreign cars. Like American gangsters, they had perfected ways of avoiding legal prosecution for their criminal activities.

But today, in Osaka at least, the gangsters have lost their social acceptability. Public warfare between rival gangs has frightened the citizens enough to make them want to do something about the gangsters in their midst. Working with police, they have launched an antigangster program that is totally unique. Its strategy is based on the Japanese fear of social ostracism, a powerful weapon in this group-oriented society. The basic approach is to avoid dealing with the gangsters and their families and to shame them into quitting their gangs. For example, parents tell their

with the class, about nagging doubts about being able to get along in the new town, and so on.

Primary group relationships are personal and intimate. The idea of *intimacy* refers to how members feel about one another: they feel close to one another, are held together by emotional bonds, and develop a "we feeling" with respect to the primary group. This does not mean that all interaction is warm or affectionate. It may be quite the opposite, but unless the stressful interaction becomes extreme, group members will continue to view themselves as closely bound to one another.

Primary group relationships, finally, are relatively enduring. We can drop a class or stop doing business at a record store with relative ease, but our

---

children not to play with gangsters' children, housewives refuse to exchange traditional greetings with gangsters' wives, and the whole family is treated coolly by shopkeepers.

The gangsters undoubtedly derive a great deal of personal satisfaction from the primary relationships in their gangs. Yet, the men and their families also have extragroup linkages—ties with other groups. What the citizens have done, then, is to interfere with the extragroup linkages of the gang members, leaving them with only their primary group. Meanwhile, the police are focusing their attention on the primary groups—that is, the gangs themselves. The police have been picking up elderly gang leaders one by one and subjecting them to denouncements of their activities and to urgings that they break up their gangs. For these proud old men, such an experience is humiliating.

Citizens have also banded together in crime prevention associations and have engaged in nonviolent activities designed to force gangsters out of their neighborhoods or to get them to change their professions. As Osaka's police chief described this strategy, "We are trying to change the waters the gangsters swim in, to deny them support, to render them weak, to make them feel estranged and socially isolated" (New York Times, March 17, 1977).

Has this strategy worked? It is still too soon to say, but so far, a few leaders of the smaller gangs have disbanded their groups, and other gangsters have moved away. The citizens realize that it will take many years to get real results. But, in the meantime, don't they fear retaliation? As one community leader has said, "We tell these gangsters that they are welcome in our group if they change their ways. How could there be retaliation? It would hurt them further because our movement is based on good will" (New York Times, March 17, 1977). Thus, the citizens are both trying to break up the criminal gangs and are offering gang members a place in more socially acceptable groups.

Primary groups are characterized by close, intimate interaction. Who among us does not value primary relationships?

primary relationships tend to last. People want their primary groups to endure and find it difficult to break such relationships and establish new ones. Primary groups, such as the family and close friends of either sex, tend to last, and when they do not, it is not easy to establish new relationships to replace them. The physical closeness of primary group members and the face-to-face nature of their interaction helps to keep these relationships intact and to produce other characteristics, such as ease of communication and the involvement of total personalities. Despite their wishes and efforts, people who become separated physically find, more often than not, that, in time, their primary relationship tends to fade.

The Importance of Primary Groups

Sociologists have recognized the importance of primary groups, both for children and for adults, for a long time. The family is the group into which almost all children are born. The close, intimate association of parent and child, and the depth of their emotional involvement with each other, is important for the child's learning of a very basic human skill: the developing and maintaining of social relationships with other human beings. Through socialization in a primary group, the child learns to trust others, to communicate with them, and to get along with them. Later, the skills first learned in the family are practiced and developed further in such primary groups as play groups and school friendship groups.

Primary groups, then, play a major part in the formation of our basic personality. The emotional bonds in primary groups are a key element in socialization, because the values and norms we are taught are not merely abstract social rules, but rather, they are expectations for us that we tend to incorporate into our personality because we want to gain the approval and the sustained emotional support of primary group members. The young child in the family, for example, not wanting to risk losing the deep and personal relationship with parents, tries to learn what they are teaching, and indeed, tries to be like them in many ways. In short, the transfer of knowledge, skills, and basic values—all a part of childhood socialization—is easier when it is attempted in a primary group.

Because of this importance of primary groups to socialization, in recent years sociologists have been concerned with the fact that the primary group relationships in our society have been weakening. With increased urbanization, our relationships have become more impersonal. At one time whole communities, neighborhoods, and extended families (families including grandparents and often aunts and uncles in the same or a nearby home) served as primary groups in the socialization of young people. Most mothers in a neighborhood once felt it was their social responsibility to deal with any child caught deviating from community norms. Today, however, we rarely become involved in raising anyone's children but our own. Many social scientists, including Urie Bronfenbrenner (1967), believe that today's children are socialized more by their peers and by television than by their parents. Whether or not this is true, the shift from the extended to the nuclear family structure (see Chapter 9) has meant that children have fewer primary group members with whom they can identify and from whom they can learn. Consequently, they have fewer sources of motivation and social control.

The need for primary group relationships is not restricted to children. Apparently, it is part of our human nature to desire and to seek out response from other humans in personal relationships. Witness how quickly all of us move toward establishing primary relationships when we find ourselves cut off from our more familiar primary groups. Before the semester is long underway, students in a large dormitory have sorted themselves into small friendship groups in which interaction is more personal and communication deeper than that among dormitory members as a whole. A similar phenomenon takes place among people who go on a group tour, work in the same office or factory, are in the military service, and so on. The friendship cliques formed in such situations do not necessarily develop into true primary groups, but the interaction at least approaches that characteristic of primary relationships. The size of our settlements and the mobility of our population hinder the development of primary relationships among adults, but we keep striving to attain them, nevertheless, because they satisfy a basic human need. (One way in which many people seek primary group ties is through religious cults—see Box 6.2.)

SECONDARY GROUPS

Sociologists who studied Cooley's theories perceived a set of traits basic to groups other than primary groups, so they called these other groups **secondary groups.** Secondary group relationships are impersonal rather than intimate and superficial and businesslike rather than deep, meaningful, and spontaneous. Unlike primary relationships, they affect only one aspect of an individual's life, and interaction takes place between *roles* rather than between persons. For example, a taxi driver acts out a role and takes you to your desired destination; you, in turn, perform a role by paying for the driver's services.

A society like ours must have positions, such as taxi driver and passenger, store clerk and customer, business executive and client, in order to function smoothly. Because we cannot possibly know everyone with whom we come into contact, as we might in a small group, we must rely on expected role be-

---

BOX 6.2 THE NEW CULTS AND THE SEARCH FOR PRIMARY RELATIONSHIPS

The Unification Church of Sun Myung Moon, the International Society for Krishna Consciousness, the Church of Scientology, and the Church of God are all examples of religious cults. A cult is a highly cohesive group of religious believers who have joined together voluntarily. Cults usually ignore the existing social order and expect active participation, conformity, and personal commitment on the part of their members. Although these groups are based on religious tenets, they often have strong rules of their own controlling such aspects of members' lives as eating habits, sexual activity, and use of drugs and alcohol. (One religious cult, The People's Temple, is examined in detail in Box 10.2.)

During the past decade, thousands of young people have joined the new cults. Why? Marvin Doress and Jack N. Porter (1978) suggest a number of reasons: the spiritual search for awareness, adolescent rebellion, a search for adventure, the need for attention. But, certainly, one of the most important explanations they offer for the current popularity of cults is that young people are looking for a familylike primary relationship that is missing in their own families. In their homes, young people may hear their parents praising honesty, helpfulness, and other virtues while practicing the opposite of what they preach; or the young person's home may be a battleground, with constant bickering and physical violence.

Where does one turn if the family does not furnish a sense of security,

havior in dealing with others in a more impersonal, secondary group situation. Social roles and positions tend to bind our secondary groups together, while face-to-face relationships in primary groups give more personal meaning and direction to the lives of individuals.

One advantage of secondary group relationships is that, in them, we are likely to treat one another equally and without favoritism. A teacher who has not moved toward a primary relationship with any of his or her students is not likely to show preferential treatment to any of them. Another advantage of secondary relationships lies in the ease of interaction they provide. Bluntly, most people do not want to take the trouble to establish primary relationships with all of the many people with whom they interact, and it is doubtful whether a large society could operate if they did want to do so. Secondary groups are necessary for day-to-day life in society, but something quite human is lost when they overshadow primary relationships or when society is so organized that the formation of primary ties is difficult.

Group Size

An obvious difference among groups is that some are larger than others. The importance of the size of a group on the characteristics of the group and the interaction within it was noted by the early sociologist Georg Simmel

---

closeness, and love? Some young people in such a situation turn to religious cults as a sort of replacement family. The Unification Church, for example, constantly stresses the breakdown of the American family and contrasts it to the work of the church toward the "perfect family." Another religious cult calls itself simply "The Family."

In the ideal family, one should receive a measure of recognition as a worthwhile person. If the family does not provide such recognition, the individual may look to a cult that warmly welcomes converts. In addition, the dress of the cult may ensure that one gets attention—even if it is of a negative sort. Being stared at while wearing the saffron robe of the Hare Krishna is better than being ignored by one's parents. Overpermissiveness —letting children do just about anything they want to—can be interpreted by children to mean that their parents don't care what they do or, perhaps, don't care for them. But the cult cares, and often, direction in the cult is provided by a strong father figure, such as the Reverend Moon.

Humans have a strong need for security, recognition, closeness, warmth, and a sense of belongingness. When these things cannot be found in the family or in a primary friendship group, there is a void in people's lives. Religious cults, whatever their other merits or drawbacks, offer a way to fill this void.

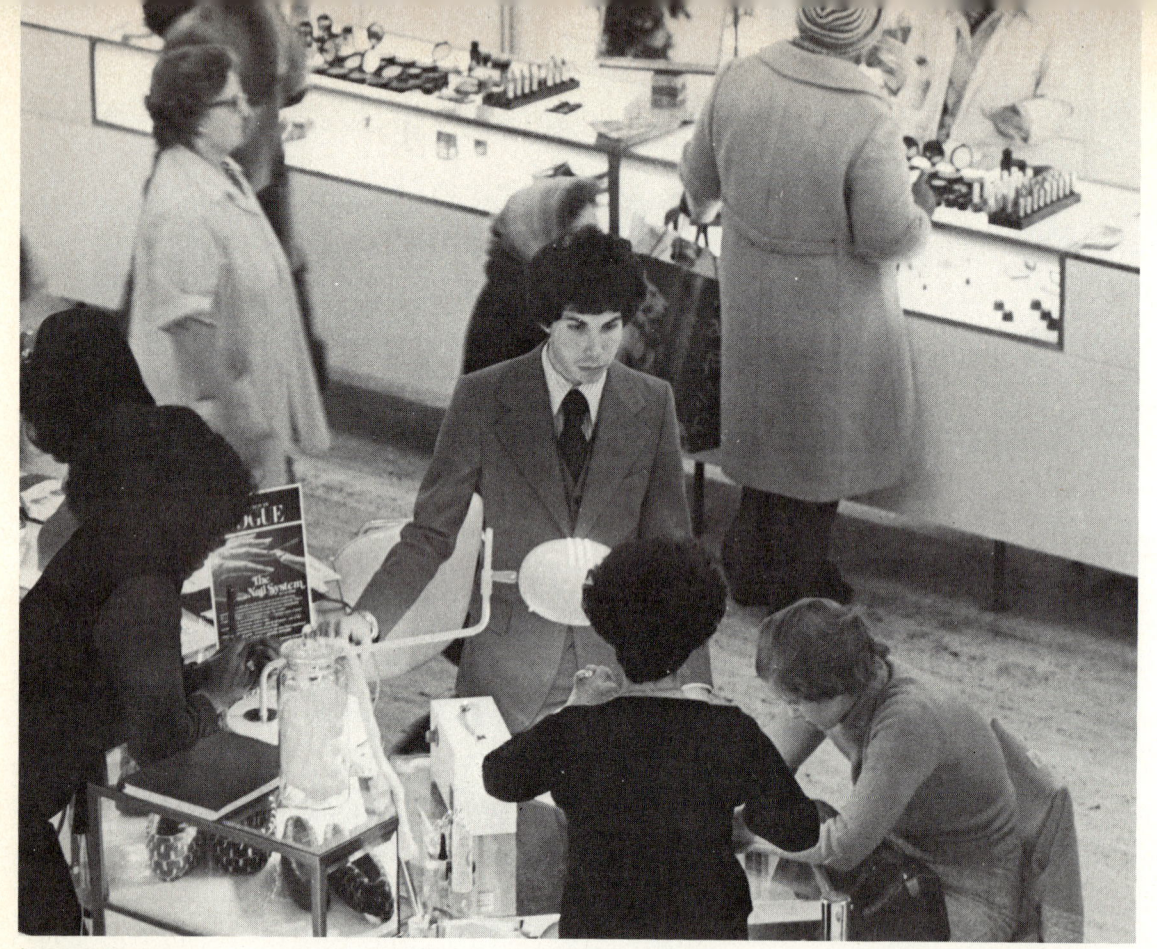

In secondary groups we exhibit only a small portion of our personality and interact with others in terms of our roles.

(1950). If we begin with the smallest possible group—two persons—and look at what happens when the number of members increases, the importance of group size will become apparent.

A two-person group is called technically a **dyad**. In the dyad, there is but one relationship. When a dyad is increased by the addition of one person, creating a *triad,* the number of relationships jumps from one to three. A dyad of a husband and wife, for example, is one set of relationships. But with the addition of a child, there are three sets of relationships: (1) mother and father, (2) mother and child, and (3) father and child. If two children were added to the original dyad, there would be *four* persons but *six* sets of relationships: (1) mother and father, (2) mother and child A, (3) mother and child B, (4) father and child A, (5) father and child B, and (6) child A and child B. And, if we extrapolate to a group with 20 members, often the sociologist's upper limit for small groups, we find 190 relationships (Bossard and Boll, 1966).

There is a simple formula that can be used to determine the number of pair relationships in groups of different sizes: $N = (Y^2 - Y)/2$. N represents the number of possible pair relationships, and Y the number of people in the group. In a five-person group, the number of possible relationships is 10 (25 minus 5, divided by 2); in a seven-person group, there are 21 possible relationships (49 minus 7 divided by 2). Note that while the group size increases by two members, the number of possible relationships increases from 10 to 21.

If you apply this formula to your own family, you will see what it does *not* tell about interaction in groups. It is likely that the interaction between two family members, say a ten year old and his infant brother, occurs less frequently and is less intense and personal than that between two other family members, such as the father and the infant or the ten year old and his eleven-year-old brother or sister. The formula, nevertheless, shows vividly how the number of *possible* relationships in a group increases with group size.

In a dyad, there can be a special closeness between the group members and an openness of communication that is not so readily attainable in larger groups. While persons in a dyadic relationship do not have to develop strong emotional ties to each other, the degree of intimacy possible among group members *is* affected by group size. The folk saying, "Two's company, three's a crowd," expresses how the level of intimacy can change merely by adding one member to the group.

Still another influence of group size is the different *kinds* of relationships that are possible. Beginning with the triad, it is possible for a coalition to develop within the group—the familiar two against one. In larger groups, there can be a number of cliques, factions, or coalitions. Sometimes, the existence

A dyad is the smallest possible group. Would you call this dyad a primary or a secondary group? A formal or an informal group?

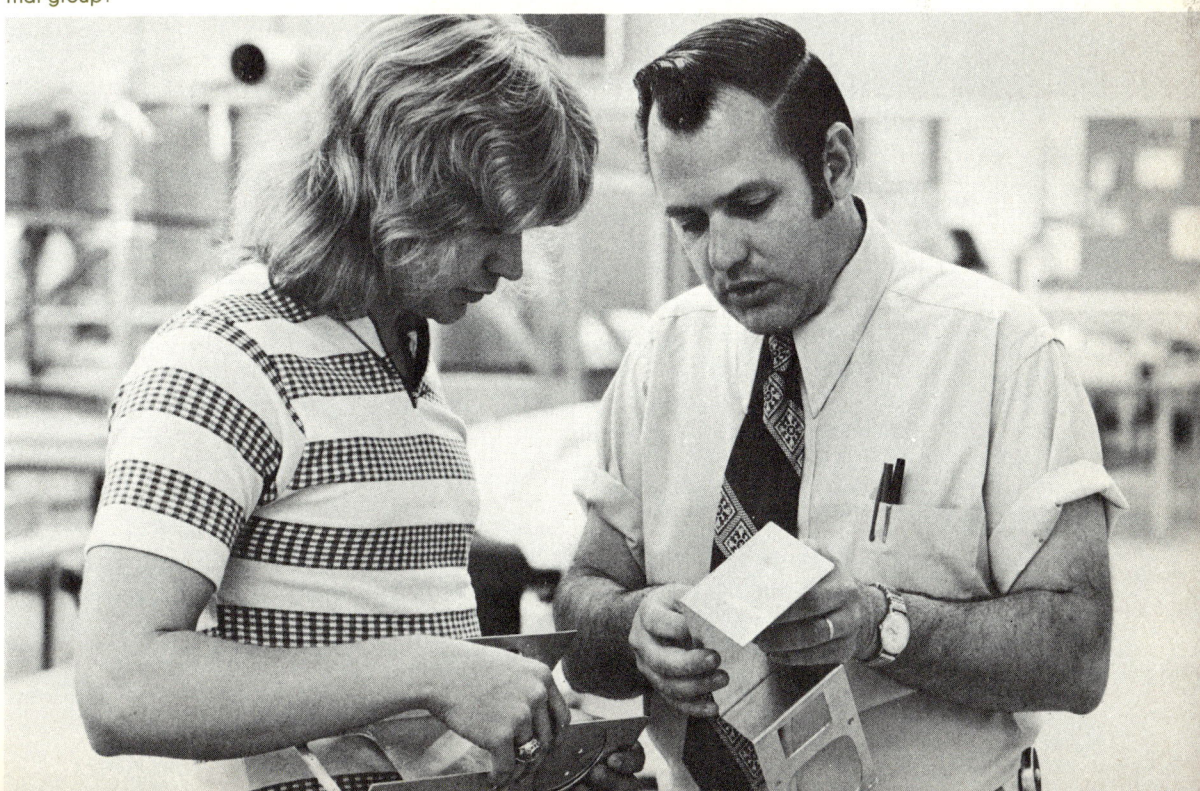

of such subgroups can interfere with the smooth functioning of the larger group. You may have noticed this happening in a club or a fraternity or sorority to which you belong. A certain clique or faction can almost be relied upon to oppose new ideas or to be against some proposed group activity.

Formal versus Informal Groups

Another difference among groups is in how formally they are organized. All groups are organized in the sense that patterns of interaction develop between and among members and that, therefore, there is a certain predictability to interaction patterns. In an informally organized group, the roles of group members are understood; in a formal group, they are specifically defined, often in written form. Through the give and take of their interaction, a husband and wife reach an understanding in regard to who takes care of the lawn, who writes out checks and keeps records, who turns down the heat and locks up the house at night, and so on. However these things are done in your family, two safe guesses can be made: (1) the roles are regular and therefore predictable, and (2) the duties and responsibilities are not written down but are merely understood. There is probably also some flexibility in the roles and other aspects of informal groups. By agreement, a family may usually eat dinner at 6:30, but the time can vary and be changed relatively easily. In a formally organized group, however, the time at which activities start, the length of the activities, and other rules governing behavior are precisely organized.

The degree of formal organization of groups is related to other properties of groups that we discussed previously. Although formal organization tends to increase with group size, this relationship is not inevitable. Most of us can think of a moderately large group that deliberately tries to keep its organization informal, or of another group of about the same size in which rules are more explicit and duties are more clearly defined. In general, however, primary groups are informally organized, while secondary groups tend to be more formally organized. The primary-secondary distinction involves more than organization, however, for secondary groups do not allow for involvement of the total personality or for a high degree of intimacy. The formality-informality dimension is restricted to how loosely or tightly groups are organized. Later in this chapter, we will see the ultimate in formal organization—bureaucracy.

Leadership in Groups

Sociologists have long been interested in the emergence and maintenance of leadership roles in groups. The work of Robert F. Bales (1951) is particularly insightful in this regard. Bales developed a method for classifying the behavior of people in small-group interaction. The method is most applicable to groups that are faced with some problem to be solved, decision to be made,

Often the task leader of a group can be distinguished by his or her physical position in the group or by body language like standing while others are seated. The social-emotional leader is less easy to spot.

or issue to be resolved. Bales's technique allows the observer to record who talks to whom, how often the various people interact, and the nature of their interaction (such as asking questions or contributing ideas).

Bales's studies of small, task-oriented groups revealed that two types of leaders emerged. The actions of one, called the **instrumental,** or **task, leader,** were directed toward the actual solving of the problem confronted by the group. This person would submit ideas, ask for suggestions, and keep the group oriented toward the task at hand. The other type of leader that emerged, the **social-emotional leader,** would direct his or her behavior toward keeping the group running smoothly, by relieving tensions and easing any conflicts that arose.

Bales's theories and methods have been applied to many different kinds of groups. In my own research (Kenkel and Hoffman, 1956), reasoning from his theories, I hypothesized that even in the husband-wife dyad there would be a tendency for one spouse to lead in the task-related area and the other to lead in the social-emotional area. The findings of the study showed that over two-thirds of the husbands excelled in giving ideas and suggestions on how a hypothetical gift of money should be spent, while about 80 percent of the wives did more talking that was directed toward keeping the decision-making session running smoothly. Men were clearly the task leaders, women the social-emotional leaders. (With today's movement toward equality of the sexes, the division of leadership functions may no longer be as sex-linked as it was 20 years ago, when these studies were conducted.)

An important finding, nevertheless, is that, in many groups, there are two distinct types of leadership and that people tend to specialize in one or the other. It may be that an officially designated leader, such as a club president, is the task leader but that, off to the side as it were, there is another leader, an individual who jokes around to relieve tension, who shows satisfaction with the "idea person," and who otherwise keeps the group's meetings running smoothly. You can probably spot these two types of leadership roles in groups to which you have belonged.

Extragroup Linkage

Still another property of most social groups is **extragroup linkage.** Each member of a group establishes relationships with other individuals and other groups, thereby forming an intricate network of relationships contributing to the integration of our society. Take, for example, a college student. This student is a member of several dyadic relationships: teacher-student, mother-daughter, father-daughter, sister-brother, girl friend-girl friend, boyfriend-girl friend, and so on. In addition to these one-to-one relationships, the student has established relationships in larger groups at school and in the community; and her teacher, parents, siblings, and friends all have other groups to which they, too, belong. Some of these extragroup linkages are primary, while others are secondary. Individuals in each of these groups have their own constellations of dyadic and extragroup linkages. Individuals participate in society through this interlocking system of groups. Therefore, when we look at our society as a whole, it becomes apparent how intricately this complex network of interrelationships is established among individuals, between individuals and groups, and among groups.

We shall now look at some of the kinds of groups to which people belong, dealing first with voluntary associations and then with the giant bureaucracies in which millions of people work.

VOLUNTARY ASSOCIATIONS

In the 1830s, the Frenchman Alexis de Tocqueville visited the United States to gain an understanding of our way of life, especially our government. In his book *Democracy in America* (1847), de Tocqueville described a very American characteristic, our eagerness to form voluntary associations:

> Americans of all ages, all conditions, and all dispositions constantly form associations. They not only have commercial and manufacturing companies in which all take part, but associations of a thousand other kinds, religious, serious, moral, futile, general or restricted, enormous or diminutive. The Americans make associations to give entertainments, to found seminars, to build inns, to construct churches, to diffuse books, to send missionaries to the antipodes . . . If it is proposed to inculcate some truth or foster some feeling by the encouragement of a great example, they form a society (pp. 128–129).

Americans have been called a nation of joiners. Only a few of the many types of voluntary associations in Deerfield are represented in this display.

The associations described by de Tocqueville cover a wide range of activities. Given a little thought, most of us could come up with a list of hundreds of specific groups—garden clubs, CB radio groups, square dance clubs, car clubs, bowling leagues, consciousness-raising groups, the Rotary Club, and so on. Such variation in kinds of groups makes it difficult to define a voluntary organization precisely. The essence of a **voluntary association** is that it is a group deliberately formed to achieve certain goals. Whatever the purpose, a voluntary association is an effort to bring together people with similar interests, so that their combined activities can be directed toward a common goal. As the designation implies, people *voluntarily* band together for a common purpose.

Functions of Voluntary Associations

Although the tens of thousands of voluntary associations in America almost defy classification, it is useful to consider some of the types of such groups and the functions they serve.

Achieving Social Goals One function of voluntary associations is to achieve social or political goals that cannot be handled or are not being dealt with by branches of the formal government. For example, the Sierra Club was formed in 1892 by a group of naturalists to preserve a wilderness area in California's Sierra Nevada mountains. The association grew, and its activities led to the creation of the National Park Service and the preservation of forest and other land. When the Sierra Club was formed, there was no arm of the government concerned with environmental protection, so individuals who were concerned banded together to do something about it.

The League of Women Voters (whose membership, incidentally, is open to men), has among its goals the creation of an informed public that can vote intelligently. While not supporting political candidates, the league studies current local, state, and national issues and proposed legislation. It disseminates the information widely, so that people will be aware of the issues and

---

**BOX 6.3
SELF-HELP
GROUPS**

Judging by the burgeoning number of groups based on shared problems—groups for alcoholics, cancer victims, the recently divorced, battered wives, gambling addicts—the old saying, "Misery loves company," certainly seems to be true. For just about any human problem you can name, there is a self-help group. A self-help group is any voluntary association with the manifest function of providing help and support for its members through the members themselves rather than through outside professionals.

People with a shared problem—overeating, drug addiction, recent breast surgery—meet together, share experiences, and help one another to deal with the problem. One reason that people turn to self-help groups is that they feel the helping professions—medicine, psychiatry, social work—have failed them. Members of self-help groups often mention that the care furnished by professionals is cold and impersonal. People want to learn how to cope with their problems, but many feel that they can learn to deal with their difficulties better in a primary group relationship than in the secondary relationship between professional and client. Certainly, one of the latent functions of self-help groups is the providing of a sense of belonging and community—a feeling that one is not alone.

The psychologist Leon H. Levy (1976) is one of a number of social scientists who have studied self-help groups, because they feel such groups have the potential for meeting important needs of troubled individuals. One of Levy's research interests was to discover whether there are processes and methods common to most self-help groups, regardless of their particular problem area. He studied a number of groups, such as Alcoholics Anonymous, Take Off Pounds Sensibly (TOPS), Overeaters Anonymous, Make Today Count, Recovery, Inc., and a woman's consciousness-raising group. He observed actual sessions of these groups and recorded what went on. He also interviewed participants after the meetings to determine members' attitudes toward the group. He asked the members how they thought the group operated, what techniques were used by the group, and which methods were most helpful in group meetings.

Levy found that there are common processes (techniques) used in self-help groups. Some of these processes have a behavioral focus—members help one another to reduce certain behaviors and increase others. Other processes have a cognitive focus—they deal with how members think about their problems and with beliefs members have about themselves and others. In both the behavioral and the cognitive processes, a given member is both an agent of and a target for help.

be able to make wiser decisions. No branch of government has such a mission, and certainly, political parties cannot be expected to present clear findings on all sides of all social issues. There are many other voluntary associations with goals that bear similarly on broad social policies.

Unlike the professional-client relationship, group members both help others and receive help.

One of the common behavioral processes used in self-help groups is reinforcement techniques for the development of desired behavior and the elimination of problem behavior. A meeting of TOPS, for example, begins with the weighing-in of all the members, and the announcing of weight gains and losses to the group. Those who have gained have to pay a small monetary penalty, while those who have lost are applauded. In many self-help groups, members also compliment and praise one another as they recount how they are dealing with their problems.

Another behavioral process used in self-help groups is training and indoctrination in self-control. Overeaters Anonymous teaches its members that they should never think or talk about the pleasure they once got from certain foods; and other groups use similar direct instruction methods. Self-help group members also serve as models for one another. Typically, members give testimonials, telling how they have achieved some degree of success in dealing with their problems.

In addition to such behavioral processes, Levy observed several types of cognitive processes in these groups. He noted that all types of groups provide some rationale for the problems faced by their members or an explanation of the problem and of how the group can deal effectively with it. All groups also provide an atmosphere in which members can receive specific advice and information relative to their problem. At a TOPS meeting, for example, a member may learn methods for avoiding the temptation of between-meal snacks. A common process at self-help meetings is the mutual sharing of problem-solving methods, which increases the knowledge and range of solutions of all members.

By sharing their problems in the group setting, members discover that they are not unique in their difficulties. Members have expressed relief at discovering that they are not alone in their fears. When they see that others have managed to deal with similar problems, they begin to feel hope for their own situation.

As a result of his studies of self-help groups, Levy sees the possibility of developing guidelines or manuals that would describe how such groups should operate to best serve their members. Such guidelines should be welcomed by those wanting to establish new groups or to improve the effectiveness of an ongoing group. Levy's study thus illustrates one way in which knowledge of human groups can benefit society's members.

Providing Services Other voluntary associations have social goals that are expressed more through the direct provision of some service for their members or for some particular group of clients. For example, private associations have been formed to operate day-care centers for poor people, to find jobs for ex-convicts, to provide meals for old people who live alone, or to help alcoholics help themselves. In a number of communities, people have formed rape counseling services, where victims can get immediate, personal, and supportive help. And drop-in centers for young people who want help with personal problems have been established and maintained by concerned citizens. Again, the list of such organizations is almost endless, and the clients they serve are extremely varied. Some see these organizations as performing work that should be provided by the state or local government. Yet, there are many people in need, and there are many, too, who want to provide help for their fellow citizens. (Some even group together to give help to themselves and others like themselves—see Box 6.3.)

Sharing Interests Still other voluntary associations are formed because people with similar interests want to come together to share ideas or to engage in activities. The need for such groups may not seem to be as compelling as that of the helping organizations, but interest groups do play an important part in the lives of many people. There are clubs for those interested in folk dancing, antique autos, comic books, CB radios, dramatics, and a host of other activities and hobbies. Sometimes the goals of such groups are mixed. Amateur radio clubs provide a community service by establishing communications links in times of disaster, and they often have training classes in electronics and Morse code to help others get their ham radio licenses. What brings people together in such groups is a desire for activities that can be expressed better by joining with likeminded people. And sometimes the major interest may lie in just being together and sharing one another's company.

Latent Functions If asked why they joined a voluntary association, many people would give the group's formalized objectives as their reasons. But, as the sociologist Robert Merton (1957) first noted, it is necessary to distinguish between two distinct functions of a group: its manifest functions and its latent functions. Those functions whose consequences are "intended and recognized by participants in the system" (that is, those that refer to the group's objectives) are its **manifest functions;** and those "which are neither intended nor recognized" are its **latent functions.** To take a specific example, an association may be formed with the manifest objective of preserving and restoring the historical sites in a community. A number of unintended, or latent, functions may also be built into the group; for example, through the group, some members may learn more about the pollution and slum housing that exist in certain neighborhoods and join or form groups to remedy these problems; other people may use the group to fill leadership roles that are denied them in their jobs; and for others, the association may serve as a training ground for the learning of group procedures and democratic processes. Another latent function may be that of providing an opportunity for people to make new friends and form primary attachments. However, none of these functions was intended by the founders of the organization. To take another example, a nudist camp may have the manifest function of allowing people to develop healthy bodies in a natural setting. But it may also have a latent function for those members seeking an acceptable setting in which to view naked bodies or to exhibit their own bodies. Recognition of the latent functions of groups gives us a deeper appreciation of the importance of voluntary associations in the lives of people and in society as a whole.

Organizational Needs of Voluntary Associations

We have seen that there is a wide variety of voluntary organizations. Yet, since all such groups are attempting to direct the activities of their members toward a specified goal, all have certain organizational needs. These needs can be seen if we take a moment to determine what you would have to do if you wanted to form a voluntary association.

First, you would have to specify and publicize the goals of the group. After all, it is the manifest functions of the group that will attract members. You cannot expect people to be turned on by the objectives unless they know what they are. Next, you would need to provide an incentive for joining and participating in the group. The incentive may be implied in the objectives, but it would be best to spell out why people should join more directly. You could stress personal rewards, altruistic reasons, such as community betterment, or both. A third area to which you would have to give attention is the need for effective communication within the group. Translated into direct activities, this refers to such things as providing for meetings, establishing subcommittees, keeping records of activities, and publishing a newsletter.

Another organizational need would be that of establishing a system to ensure that the activities of group members are directed to achieving the goals of the group. Like other organizational needs of the group, the specific way this is done can vary, according to the group's size and purpose. A constitution specifying the responsibilities of the leadership roles with regard to guiding the group toward its goals could be drawn up, bylaws providing for periodic review of activities could be enacted, and so on.

Finally, a voluntary association must be prepared to deal with external conditions that could interfere with the group's activities, or even threaten its existence. The group does not exist in isolation. For example, the group you are forming may draw its members from a college population and meet on a college campus. Thus, the activities of your group will have to take into account other college activities. In arranging trips out of town, scheduling meetings, rehearsing musical numbers, or whatever else the group may do, it must take into account the other activities of its members, other activities going on at the same time, and the reactions of nongroup members who may be affected by the group's activities.

Extent of Participation

How many Americans belong to voluntary associations? The answer is not easy to supply. Should we count as voluntary associations such groups as labor unions or professional organizations, such as the American Medical Association? It is almost compulsory to join such groups for some kinds of employment. What does "belong" really mean, in reference to voluntary groups? Does one belong to a group if he or she pays dues but never attends meetings and seldom even reads the organization's newsletter or magazine?

Regardless of the difficulties in defining participation, it is clear that millions of Americans—probably the majority of us—belong to some voluntary association. This conclusion is easy to reach, if we think of the largeness of some organizations. There are many that have more than five million members, including the YMCA, the American Association for Retired Persons, 4-H Clubs, and the Boy Scouts. Among the many associations with more than a million members are the Girl Scouts, the Loyal Order of Moose, the National Rifle Association, the National Jewish Welfare Board, the Knights of Columbus, and the YWCA. Of course, some people belong to more than one of these as well as to other large associations. Still, when we think of all the large groups, as well as the smaller local ones, in American society, it is not hard to accept the fact that most of us belong to *some* voluntary association.

Membership in voluntary associations is unevenly spread through society. As we will see in Chapter 8, belonging to, participating in, and accepting leadership roles in groups varies systematically by social class, with the working class being less group-oriented than the middle and upper classes. Whatever recreational, social, or political benefits can be derived from banding together in an association, the poor reap fewer of them than do the rich.

BUREAUCRACIES

Many people think of bureaucracies in terms of hopeless snarls, red tape, and a tangle of rules and regulations that plague their lives. Others view bureaucracies as a tribute to human genius, an illustration of human ingenuity in organizing the efforts of large numbers of people toward a common goal. In studying bureaucracies, we must be careful to remain objective and to examine them without preconceived ideas about the desirability of this type of organization. To the sociologist, a **bureaucracy** is a particular type of formal organization with certain identifiable characteristics.

Characteristics of Bureaucracy

Bureaucratic organization has its problems and its merits, but our chief concern is with its fundamental nature—what distinguishes it from other human groups. A typical bureaucracy has four characteristics: division of responsibility, a chain of command, governance by formal rules, and a mechanism for coordination.

Division of Responsibility
A key feature of a bureaucracy is that the organization, whether an army, a government, or a college, is divided into a number of units. Sometimes these units are even called *bureaus,* but designations like "department" and "division" also convey the idea that there are separate units within the larger organization. Each unit has responsibility for certain clearly designated tasks. Often, there is a written statement of the objectives, goals, or responsibilities of the unit. The sociology department in your college probably has a written statement of objectives. With or without a formal document, it is undoubtedly known that the sociology department is *not* responsible for teaching German, caring for the grounds, or

To be sure that rules and procedures are followed, bureaucracies need to keep detailed records of their activities. And then more rules and procedures are needed on how to keep the records.

176 UNDERSTANDING SOCIAL ORGANIZATION

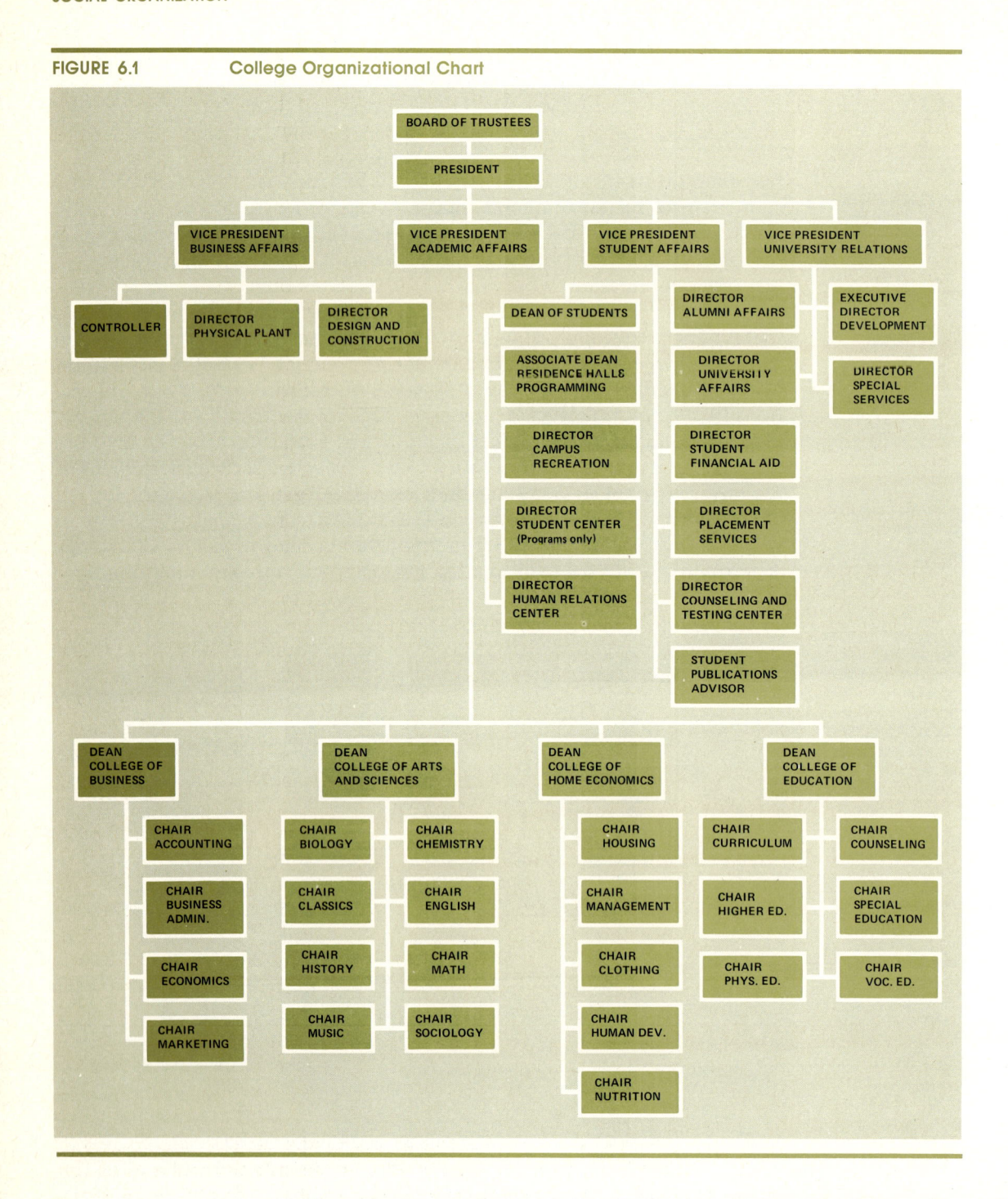

FIGURE 6.1   College Organizational Chart

- BOARD OF TRUSTEES
  - PRESIDENT
    - VICE PRESIDENT BUSINESS AFFAIRS
      - CONTROLLER
      - DIRECTOR PHYSICAL PLANT
      - DIRECTOR DESIGN AND CONSTRUCTION
    - VICE PRESIDENT ACADEMIC AFFAIRS
      - DEAN COLLEGE OF BUSINESS
        - CHAIR ACCOUNTING
        - CHAIR BUSINESS ADMIN.
        - CHAIR ECONOMICS
        - CHAIR MARKETING
      - DEAN COLLEGE OF ARTS AND SCIENCES
        - CHAIR BIOLOGY
        - CHAIR CLASSICS
        - CHAIR HISTORY
        - CHAIR MUSIC
        - CHAIR CHEMISTRY
        - CHAIR ENGLISH
        - CHAIR MATH
        - CHAIR SOCIOLOGY
      - DEAN COLLEGE OF HOME ECONOMICS
        - CHAIR HOUSING
        - CHAIR MANAGEMENT
        - CHAIR CLOTHING
        - CHAIR HUMAN DEV.
        - CHAIR NUTRITION
      - DEAN COLLEGE OF EDUCATION
        - CHAIR CURRICULUM
        - CHAIR HIGHER ED.
        - CHAIR PHYS. ED.
        - CHAIR COUNSELING
        - CHAIR SPECIAL EDUCATION
        - CHAIR VOC. ED.
    - VICE PRESIDENT STUDENT AFFAIRS
      - DEAN OF STUDENTS
      - ASSOCIATE DEAN RESIDENCE HALLS PROGRAMMING
      - DIRECTOR CAMPUS RECREATION
      - DIRECTOR STUDENT CENTER (Programs only)
      - DIRECTOR HUMAN RELATIONS CENTER
      - DIRECTOR ALUMNI AFFAIRS
      - DIRECTOR UNIVERSITY AFFAIRS
      - DIRECTOR STUDENT FINANCIAL AID
      - DIRECTOR PLACEMENT SERVICES
      - DIRECTOR COUNSELING AND TESTING CENTER
      - STUDENT PUBLICATIONS ADVISOR
    - VICE PRESIDENT UNIVERSITY RELATIONS
      - EXECUTIVE DIRECTOR DEVELOPMENT
      - DIRECTOR SPECIAL SERVICES

arranging athletic events. If each unit within the organization fulfills its responsibilities, then the overall objectives of the organization are met.

The division of responsibility affects workers in that, typically, each is assigned to a particular unit. The workers' tasks may be highly specialized, but the tasks of all should contribute to the mission of the unit. While a bureaucracy allows division of labor among workers, its essential characteristic is that it purposely divides the responsibility for the work of the organization among various units.

Chain of Command In a bureaucracy, the lines of authority, or chain of command, are clear-cut. A formal organizational chart allows people to keep the chain of command straight and makes it clear who sends directives to whom, who reports to whom, and so on. For example, if you follow the vertical lines in the college organizational chart in Figure 6.1, you can trace a line from the Board of Trustees to the President, the Vice President for Academic Affairs, the dean, and then, the chair of an academic department. This shows which position has authority over another, and it also indicates how authority within this organization has been delegated. While the Board of Trustees has ultimate authority for the operating of the university, the authority to run the College of Arts and Sciences is delegated to the position of dean of that unit. The position of dean, of course, does not carry absolute control over the division, for the Vice President for Academic Affairs has certain authority over the various divisions.

The chain of command facilitates communication within the organization. Information needed to perform work is sent down through the channels, theoretically assuring that all who need it will receive it. Similarly, requests for information, clarification of rules, and the like go up through the channels. The chairman of a department does not go directly to the Board of Trustees for permission to introduce a new course (although it might prove easier to get new courses if it could be done this way).

Finally, it should be noted that authority is vested in positions, not individuals, and that the communication link is technically from position to position rather than from person to person. For the proper functioning of the bureaucracy, it is the position, not the individual filling it, that is important. The individual is dispensable and can be replaced by another individual with the same training and expertise. But the position, or job, is indispensable to the functioning of the organization, and its accompanying role must be fulfilled. In a corporation, for example, the vice president in charge of purchasing issues instructions that are followed, not because of his or her personal reputation as a decision maker, but because of the specific authority that accompanies the position.

Governance by Rules Max Weber was one of the earliest sociologists to write on the nature of bureaucracies. Besides describing the bureaucratic features we have already discussed, Weber emphasized that bureaucracy represents a rational or logical way to organize the activities of many for a common goal (Weber, 1946). The element of rationality shows up in the many rules and regulations that exist and that are expected to be followed in a bureaucracy.

Some of the rules govern work procedures. Work must be done in a certain way to achieve the organization's goals with a minimum waste of time, effort, and money. True to the concept of rationality, efficiency experts are employed to examine an organization. Once the most efficient way of doing something is discovered, rules are drawn up to describe the proper procedure. Other rules govern employees—the qualifications they should have for a given job, their duties and benefits, and the requirements for advancement within the organization. Still other rules cover the proper exercise of authority and control the communication procedures.

With a rule or regulation for every possible situation, decisions should be made as objectively as possible. Within a university, for example, a person is not promoted from, say, assistant to associate professor just because the department chairman decides that it would be a good idea. In most universities, there are specific rules governing promotion, including objective assessment of job performance, letters of reference, evaluations of teaching submitted by students, consultation with the tenured faculty, evidence of research activities, and so on. As students, you are well aware of the myriad rules that govern your academic life. And the activities of the bureaucrats who administer the academic and other programs are also controlled by a host of rules and regulations.

Coordination If a family is packing up for a picnic or a short trip, the members may check back and forth with one another to be sure that each has done his or her tasks. Often, no one person assumes the role of coordinator, as the whole procedure is handled informally. In a large organization, however, the coordination function is quite important. Positions need to exist for people whose responsibility it is to assure that the goals and objectives of the various bureaus or units mesh with and contribute to the overall objectives of the organization.

Problems with Bureaucracies

If one looks at organization charts, mission statements, job descriptions, standard operating procedures, and the like, bureaucracies appear to be neat, rational, and orderly ways of organizing human activities toward the achievement of certain goals. Yet, the structure can be too rigid for the organization's own good. The creativity of bureaucrats may be stifled, for they often find that it is easier, and less likely to get them in trouble, if they "go by the book" rather than try new and possibly more efficient procedures.

An unbending attitude toward the organization's rules may result in the organization not meeting its own objectives. Following a recent flood in eastern Kentucky, for example, the county was declared a disaster area—that is, it was determined that the area met the specific criteria to be so designated. According to the rules, many of the homeless were eligible for emergency food stamps, and they were taken by bus from their temporary shelters to a place where they could get them. Some authorities felt, however, that the state would not be reimbursed by the federal government for the stamps unless there were signs at the distribution center warning of the penalties for fraudulent acceptance of food stamps. Moreover, some felt that the signs had to be the official ones produced by the federal government and obtainable from a regional office in Atlanta, Georgia. The result was that the homeless, hungry people were bused back to their temporary shelters without food stamps, and later, when the proper signs were obtained, they were bused back to the center, where they finally received them. The objective of providing emergency help to the needy was thus frustrated by the bureaucracy's inability to work with its own rules.

Bureaucracies run the risk of becoming too impersonal. As we noted, communication routes and authority channels are from position to position. In the process, the people who occupy the positions can become overlooked as real human beings, and this puts their morale and efficiency in jeopardy. What often happens to offset this is the formation of informal networks of interaction that are outside the formal organization chart.

Several years ago, partly at the request of big businesses to discover ways of improving productivity, sociologists began applying their methods of study to large bureaucracies. Using such techniques as participant observation, checking office records for levels of productivity, and questionnaires and interviews, sociologists gathered intimate data about the actual day-to-day operation of a bureaucracy. Some of these studies produced *sociograms*—maps of how members of a department, or of several coordinated departments, actually interacted, according to personal preferences.

The results of many studies conducted over the past decades have indicated that inside the highly formal, secondary structure of the organization, there are informal primary groups and relations. Informal regulation of production levels was discovered to be common. That is, it was found that employees frequently worked out maximum and minimum quotas of production and applied sanctions (punishments) to those who worked outside the quotas. Because the impersonal goals of the formal structure provided no fulfillment of personal needs, the workers found such satisfaction among themselves, providing each other with acceptance, recognition, and so on. It was found, in some cases, that the primary links among executives facilitated communication and understanding and thus actually helped the organization achieve its goals.

Many large corporations have responded to such discoveries by incorporating into their formal structure elements that encourage productive primary interactions at all levels. Executives have been urged to join sensitivity-training groups. Tennis courts and golf courses have been made available to all of a corporation's employees. And the coordination of positions within departments has been made more flexible to accommodate—and to benefit from—the primary relations that arise.

COMMUNITY AND SOCIETY

So far, we have looked at voluntary groups, both large and small, and at the giant bureaucracies in which millions of us work. But sociologists are interested in some even larger groupings: the people who live together in a territorial area.

The German sociologist Ferdinand Tönnies (1957), writing in the 1880s, was one of the earliest sociologists to draw attention to the social and organizational differences that exist between humans who live together in a fixed territory. He designated one type **Gemeinschaft,** meaning "community"; and he called the other **Gesellschaft,** which translates as "society." Groups

In a Gemeinschaft-type community there is a sense of shared values. The group is held together by their strong sense of belongingness.

Interaction in a Gesellschaft-type group is purposeful and impersonal. The group is held together by commitment to group objectives.

are not of one or the other type, but rather, they approach one or the other type.

A *Gemeinschaft,* or community, is characterized by a sense of unity and solidarity. The whole social order seems permeated by a sense of shared values and sentiments. Interaction among the people is often much like that in primary groups. The usual small scale of the community both enables and requires its members to constantly interact either directly or through intergroup linkages. (One symbol of such a community is the cracker barrel or the pot-bellied stove of the old country store, where everyone gathers to swap yarns and gossip.) As with primary groups, there is a deep sense of belongingness in a community, a "we feeling," and a tendency for people to be involved with one another as total personalities. Small towns and religious communities are examples of *Gemeinschaft*-type groupings.

A *Gesellschaft*-type group is characterized by its rationality: it exists for a well-defined purpose. Accordingly, interpersonal relationships are secondary, for people tend to view one another as role incumbents who have banded together to achieve an objective. In the *Gesellschaft,* the commitment made is more to the objective of the group than to the group members as total personalities. Most voluntary associations are *Gesellschaft*-type groups, as are governmental, educational, business, and other bureaucracies.

Sociologists use the concepts of *Gemeinschaft* and *Gesellschaft* to both describe the social patterns in a specific group, such as a monastery or an industrial plant, and to characterize an entire society. A peasant society, of course, would fall close to the *Gemeinschaft* end of the scale; whereas industrialized societies would be characterized as *Gesellschaft,* for, while communal groups and communities are found within them, the dominant mode of the larger society is *Gesellschaft.* Robert Redfield (1941) gets at this dominant mode in his classification of societies as "folk" or "urban." Both Redfield's and Tönnies's classifications show that societies are held together and that the activities of members are integrated by different *kinds* of mechanisms. An important concept for further understanding of the integration of societies is the idea of "institution."

INSTITUTIONS

Suppose that in a high school, the custom of "senior skip day" somehow arises. That is, on a certain day in the spring of their last year, seniors can stay out of school without fear of punishment. Rules develop around the custom, such as those defining precisely who is eligible, which day is to be selected as the skip day, and so on. In time, roles are clarified. There are expectations regarding how teachers should react to senior students who skip school, how parents should behave, and how students should deal with juniors or other noneligibles who skip school on the designated day. Perhaps an informal norm develops to the effect that while all seniors should be encouraged to participate, those who choose to attend classes should not be harassed. An outsider looking at the practice of senior skip day after it has developed for a number of years would be impressed with the regularities and organization. He or she might say that the senior skip day is "practically an institution" at the high school. If such words were chosen, the person would come close to using the word "institution" as it is defined by sociologists. The observer would be mentally separating the fairly complex idea of skip day from the actual students who are skipping school and the teachers who are reacting to them.

In Chapter 3, we noted that there are universals in cultures because people everywhere are faced with common problems involved in ensuring the survival and well-being of their society. Customs, practices, norms, and roles gradually develop around these "survival problems," on a larger scale but in much the same way as in our example of senior skip day.

The sociologist Kingsley Davis (1949) defined **institution** as "a set of interwoven folkways, mores, and laws built around one or more functions." Sociologists commonly number the basic social institutions at five, corresponding to the five broad areas of human needs that are considered universal. Each institution has the social function of fulfilling those needs. For example, the *family* fills the infant's needs by providing food, shelter, protection, and emotional interaction; and it fills society's needs by controlling sexual behavior, ensuring constant replenishment of its membership, and producing fully socialized members.

The four other social institutions are *education,* which also functions as a socializing agent; the *economy,* which fulfills our material needs for goods and services; *government,* which meets society's need for constant forms of social control; and *religion*, which fulfills our need for a sense of meaning in life. (These five institutions are discussed in detail in Part 3.)

Sociologists have ample evidence that every human society has some version of these five basic social functions and their attendant cluster of cultural elements. This is true even though the corresponding institutions of two different societies may not appear to be similar in their collections of norms and folkways. For example, our economic institution is dominated by gigantic corporations and conglomerates and by advertising agencies that persuade us to participate heavily in the economy as consumers. The economic activities of the African bush people, in contrast, revolve around hunting by men and the gathering of edible roots by women. Yet, in both instances, the economic activities are regularized and organized and are governed by all sorts of norms and customs.

It is important to realize that the term "institution" is an abstraction. As such, it is used apart from the people or groups whose activities lend expression to the institution. We can see a tall building and we can feel a hot day, but we cannot perceive tallness or heat in the abstract. Similarly, we can observe a family group and we can watch people produce or distribute goods, but we cannot observe the family institution or the economic institution. Groups tend to express institutional values, but groups and institutions are not the same thing.

This chapter has dealt primarily with the kinds and characteristics of human groups. We have seen that the ways in which people interact are often influenced by the groups to which they belong and by the roles they hold in these groups. One type of role in our society has had such a major effect on our interactions that we have devoted a whole chapter to it: the sex role. In Chapter 7 we will examine the nature of sex roles, how sex roles are learned, and how changes in American society both affect and reflect the changing nature of our sex roles.

SUMMARY

1. Two or more people make up a **group** if: (1) the people are aware of and interact with one another, (2) the people think of themselves as a group and are considered a group by others, (3) the people, as members of the group, accept its roles, privileges, and obligations, and (4) the people share and accept some of the rules (**norms**) that govern their interaction.

2. A **primary group** consists of two or more people who share their total personalities with one another; marriages, families, and friendships are good examples of primary groups. Primary group relationships are personal, intimate, relatively enduring, and held together by strong emotional bonds. Primary groups play a key role in socialization.

3. **Secondary group** relationships are impersonal, superficial, and businesslike. They usually affect only one aspect of an individual's life; interaction is between roles rather than between persons.

4. The larger the group, the more interaction patterns are possible, but the less intimacy is possible. **Dyadic** (two-person) groups offer closeness and free communication; in larger groups, coalitions, cliques, and factions may appear to interfere with the smooth functioning of the group.

5. Formal organization tends to increase as the size of the group increases; secondary groups also tend to be more formally organized.

6. In small groups, two types of leaders may appear: **task leaders,** who keep the group oriented toward solving the problem at hand; and **social-emotional leaders,** who resolve conflicts and keep the group running smoothly.

7. A **voluntary association** is a group deliberately formed to achieve certain goals. Voluntary associations exist for a number of purposes: (1) to achieve social ends, (2) to provide services, (3) to share ideas or common interests, and (4) to fulfill latent functions for members (such as providing leadership opportunities or a training ground for learning certain skills).

8. In order to survive as a group, a voluntary association must: (1) specify and publicize the goals of the group, (2) provide incentives for joining the group, (3) provide for effective communication within the group, (4) establish a system for guiding the group toward its goals, and (5) deal with external conditions that can interfere with the group's activities.

9. A **bureaucracy** has four major characteristics: (1) division of responsibility, (2) a formal chain of command, (3) a set of rules by which it is governed, and (4) overall coordination of the whole organization.

10. Tönnies distinguished between two types of groups: **Gemeinschaft** (community) and **Gesellschaft** (society). Groups usually contain elements of both types. A *Gemeinschaft* is characterized by a sense of unity and solidarity, while a *Gesellschaft* is more like a secondary group, committed to some purpose or objective.

11. Sociologists have identified five major **institutions** that serve universal human needs: the family, education, the economy, government, and religion.

KEY TERMS

bureaucracy
dyad
extragroup linkage
Gemeinschaft
Gesellschaft
group
institution
latent function

manifest function
norms
primary group
secondary group
social-emotional leader
task leader
voluntary association

SUGGESTED READINGS

Blau, Peter, and Marshall W. Meyer. *Bureaucracy in Modern Society.* New York: Random House, 1971.
A study of the meaning of bureaucracy, the organization of bureaucratic authority, and the operation of particular bureaucracies.

Cartwright, Dorwin, and Alvin Zander, eds. *Group Dynamics.* New York: Harper & Row, 1968.
A reader on small-group research. The book covers group leadership, power, structural properties, pressures to conform, and membership.

Cooley, Charles Horton. *Social Organization.* New York: Charles Scribner's Sons, 1909.
A classic treatment of social organization on both the macroscopic and microscopic levels. The chapter on primary groups is especially valuable.

Hinton, Bernard L., ed. *Groups and Organizations.* Belmont, Calif.: Wadsworth, 1971.
A collection of articles on small-group formation and processes. This reader is especially oriented toward understanding small groups that exist within the context of formal organizations.

Liebow, Elliot. *Tally's Corner.* Boston: Little, Brown, 1967.
A participant observation study of black streetcorner men, their relationships to their wives, children, and each other, and the effects of their economic situation on their lives.

Stein, Maurice. *The Eclipse of Community.* Princeton, N.J.: Princeton University Press, 1960.
Stein synthesizes the findings of a number of community sociologists into a macroscopic view of American society. He theorizes that the processes of urbanization, industrialization, and bureaucratization have resulted in the breakdown of communities and the rise of mass society.

Warren, Roland. *The Community in America.* 2nd ed. Chicago: Rand McNally, 1972.
The author presents the various perspectives for studying community and then deals with sociological processes that are now affecting American communities.

In previous chapters we showed how a number of sociological concepts—role, culture, socialization—are important for understanding human groups and the interaction of their members. This chapter takes a different approach. Here, we apply a variety of sociological concepts (roles, culture, socialization, status) to the single, but far-reaching, issue of sex roles in modern society.

Instead of tracing the influence of technology on the development of culture, for example, the focus is on how technological influences on culture affect the positions and roles of men and women. The general topic of how social roles influence the behavior and attitudes of the incumbents is applied to the influence of the culturally approved roles of male and female on the men and women who enact the roles.

In Chapter 4, we saw how the socialization process results in people with the kinds of personalities that allow them to take on adult roles and have the skills, abilities, and attitudes that enable them to function in the society in which they were reared. The subject of sex-role socialization focuses on how humans develop the particular kinds of personalities labeled masculine and feminine. Sex roles and their effects on society and on the human potential of its members are important issues. The application of sociological concepts should further your understanding of the issues, as well as your understanding of the concepts themselves.

7
The Sociology of Sex Roles

The Women's Liberation movement, the Equal Rights Amendment, sex discrimination in jobs and income, day care, abortion on demand—all have been hot issues in the United States in the last decade. And American women have not been unique in their desire for equal rights. Other countries around the world have felt the winds of change as women have begun to express their dissatisfactions with their roles in life. From Portugal to Egypt, women are making advances in such areas as politics, work, marriage, and education. Laws banning sex discrimination have been passed in Great Britain, Portugal, and other Common Market countries, where recognition is finally coming to the sex that makes up 51 percent of the world's population.

In Europe, the women's movement has brought some notable changes: women in Holland's armed forces are trained to go into combat; in West Germany, a man may choose to adopt his wife's surname; in Italy and Portugal, divorce has been legalized; Sweden has six women cabinet members (30 percent of the total); in Switzerland, women have finally achieved the right to vote; and in Great Britain, antidiscrimination laws have resulted in such job renamings as "chamberperson" for "chambermaid" (Bradley, 1978).

Despite these advances, however, and despite much lip service paid to equal rights for women, long-standing discriminatory practices remain firmly entrenched. Women in many countries still work primarily in "women's" jobs, receive lower pay than men, have little political clout, and are still hampered by restrictive laws governing divorce, abortion, illegitimacy, and property rights.

The fact of the matter is that in societies all over the world, women are treated as second-class citizens. How did this situation come about? To understand the reasons for the present condition of men and women in our society, we must understand the concept of **sex role:** the part a person is expected to play by virtue of being born male or female in a particular culture. In this chapter, we will be exploring the biological, cultural, and historical roots of sex roles, and we will be examining sex roles in other societies as well as our own. We will also be looking at *sex-role socialization* and at the consequences of *sex-role stereotyping*—for both men and women. Finally, we'll be speculating a bit on the future of sex roles in America.

BIOLOGY AND SEX ROLES

When discussing socialization in Chapter 4, we acknowledged that inborn biological characteristics play a part in human behavior and that they provide the raw materials for shaping the individual into a member of his or her society. The question now is, how important are biological differences between men and women when it comes to determining social differences between the sexes? Is it true that "biology is destiny"—that men are designed to be dominant and women to be submissive? Let's look at three major biological ways in which males and females differ—anatomically, genetically, and hormonally—to get at the answer to this question.

Anatomical Differences

Perhaps the most obvious biological difference between men and women is in their anatomy—their body structures. Men and women have distinctively different genitalia and secondary sex characteristics (such as breast development in women and facial hair in men). There is also a different distribution of fat and muscle by sex. Dr. Barbara Edelstein, in her diet book for women (1977), suggests that the extra layer of fat under a woman's skin exists because females are designed to be "baby receptacles." The fat is there to ensure that the fetus will be physically protected and to provide extra food or heat if needed.

In addition to differences in genitalia, fat, and muscle, on the average, men are heavier and taller than women. How important are these anatomical differences? One socially significant effect is that they allow us to classify people as male or female and to recognize each other's sex. If this sounds like a trivial consequence, try to imagine what life would be like if we could not differentiate males from females.

There are other ramifications of anatomical differences, some of which are trivial unless society chooses to make them important. For example, the distribution of body fat in women makes it harder for them to lose weight than it is for men, according to Edelstein. This anatomical fact can be a deficit in a society that places a high value on thinness in women. Edelstein claims that male doctors fail to appreciate this problem and stress willpower in treating their overweight female patients, making them feel like "weak-minded failures." Thus, we see one way in which anatomical differences can be made socially significant.

Hormonal Differences

Hormones are chemical substances produced by the endocrine glands and secreted into the bloodstream to affect other organs of the body. Males and females produce the same hormones, except when it comes to the hormones secreted by the sex glands. An important male sex hormone is **testosterone,** which is also produced in very small amounts in females. There is some indication that testosterone is related to aggressiveness. Levels of testosterone vary among males, and one study of prisoners found that those with higher levels of this hormone had a history of violent or aggressive criminal behavior throughout childhood and adolescence (Kreuz and Rose, 1971). Judith Bardwick (1971) reports that adult females who were administered testosterone experienced increases in physical activity and aggressiveness to levels normally found in males.

Estrogen and **progesterone,** hormones that are present in very small amounts in males, are the important female sex hormones. Estrogen is responsible for preparing the uterus for ovulation and possible conception. Progesterone allows the uterus to maintain a state of pregnancy or produces the end of the menstrual cycle if pregnancy does not occur. Because female hormones affect the menstrual cycle of women, it is possible that they are also responsible for the mood swings, or changes in emotions, that many women report in relation to their menstrual cycle. However, in Western societies women have been taught to expect mood shifts, premenstrual tension, muscle cramps, and the like. It is therefore likely that the self-fulfilling prophecy is more responsible than hormones for premenstrual depression and similar "female problems."

Hereditary Differences

The hereditary characteristics transmitted from parent to child are carried in the **genes,** which in turn, are carried on the chromosomes found in the nucleus of all our body cells. All human beings have 23 pairs of chromosomes. One pair, called the **sex chromosomes,** determines whether the individual is male or female. There are two types of sex chromosome: X and Y. If an individual receives two X chromosomes, a female results; if an X and a Y pair up, a male is born.

Some very important differences are created by this one chromosome pair: not only do the sex chromosomes influence hormone production and sexual characteristics, but they can also regulate the expression of certain hereditary traits. Color blindness, for example, is a trait found primarily in males; females are more likely to carry the trait and pass it on to their sons without expressing it themselves. As a result of having only one X chromosome, males do not receive immunity or resistance to a number of other disorders that are genetically transmitted. Ashley Montagu (1975) has listed 60 such disorders, including such serious illnesses as hemophilia (the bleeder disease) and such mild problems as webbing of the toes.

A few males are born with an XYY chromosome pattern, receiving a double dose, so to speak, of the male sex chromosome. Studies done with prison and nonprison samples found that the XYY pattern is more prevalent among prisoners and that there is some evidence that this abnormal pattern is related to violent and aggressive behavior (Money and Ehrhardt, 1972). But, even if the presence of an extra Y chromosome does increase aggressiveness, it does not necessarily follow that the normal XY pattern is associated with aggressive behavior.

What, then, can be concluded about the role of biological differences in accounting for behavioral differences between the sexes? It is possible, although not definitely proved, that the higher level of testosterone and the Y chromosome in males produce a predisposition to greater aggressiveness. This characteristic, in turn, can be rewarded, ignored, encouraged, or discouraged in the socialization process. In societies where aggressive tendencies are encouraged and praised in males and discouraged and punished in females, we are likely to find a systematic psychological difference between the sexes. Similarly, if physical differences in musculature, fat distribution, and size are emphasized in childhood, we are likely to see males taking on the more physically demanding roles.

Thus, we can see that although there are biological differences between the sexes, there is very little evidence of a biological basis for psychological differences. And when biology does play a role, it does so, most often, in conjunction with socialization influences.

CULTURE AND SEX ROLES

Because socialization forces play such a major part in the development of men and women, what is considered "masculine" and "feminine" varies from culture to culture. An interesting illustration of sociocultural influences on personality can be found in Margaret Mead's (1935) work in three primitive New Guinea tribes: the Mundugamor, the Arapesh, and the Tchambuli.

In the Mundugamor, formerly a head-hunting and cannibalistic group, both males and females are expected to be competitive, aggressive, and even violent. The women are not at all maternal and do not like to nurse babies or to take care of them physically. The striking features of Mundugamor personalities are the similarities in the temperaments of males and females and the fact that both sexes seem to exhibit what we would consider masculine characteristics. Among the Arapesh, in contrast, both men and women exhibit traits considered feminine in Western societies. Both sexes are cooperative, passive, and gentle, and both seem to enjoy taking care of children. Aggressiveness and violence are vigorously discouraged in childhood, and these traits are largely absent in adults of either sex. In the third tribe, the Tchambuli, women have many traits that we would consider masculine, whereas men have what we would think of as feminine personalities. Women are competent and efficient in economic affairs. They are the aggressors in sexual activity, and they do not adorn themselves with ornaments. Men are artistic and are considered to be more sensitive, emotional, and nervous than women.

Mead concluded that most of the traits we generally link with one sex or another are the result of social conditioning, not biology. This does not contradict the idea that the hormonal influence of testosterone generally results in males being more aggressive than females. Rather, findings such as Mead's suggest that biological predispositions or tendencies are weak and can be overridden by cultural conditioning that emphasizes traits opposite to such tendencies. In most societies, however, the culture works with the predispositions, so to speak, and encourages males to be aggressive—or at least does not discourage them. Females are encouraged to work with biology and to nurse and care for their babies.

There is no reason to challenge Mead's conclusion, reached over four decades ago, that personality differences in the sexes are largely the result of social conditioning. Yet, there is another difference frequently attributable

---

**BOX 7.1
NONVERBAL
BEHAVIOR
AND SEX-ROLE
STEREOTYPES**

Language may be the most important method of communication between humans, but it is not the only one. We also communicate by the nonverbal signals we send out, such as our facial expressions, gestures, and body positions. Often, we are not fully aware that we are communicating nonverbally, nor do we intend to send some of the messages we do. When and how we smile, how we look at someone to whom we're talking, and how we sit and walk all have meanings that are shared by people with a common culture. The social psychologist Irene Frieze has investigated the differences in nonverbal behavior of men and women, and she has found that nonverbal behavior tends to maintain the higher power and status associated with males and to preserve sex-role stereotypes in general (Frieze et al., 1978).

Frieze was particularly concerned with two types of nonverbal messages: those indicating dominance or status, and those communicating emotional warmth and expressiveness. Her findings revealed that there are significant differences in male and female nonverbal messages. For example, the sexes differ with regard to how they sit, or are supposed to sit. Girls are trained to sit "properly" or in a "ladylike" position, whereas boys have fewer restrictions. Women sit so that their closed legs cover their genital area, or else they cover that area with their hands. Men, on the other hand, typically expose the crotch area. If a woman sits in a relaxed position with legs spread widely apart and the crotch area of her pants exposed, she may be viewed as being sexually receptive, or even aggressive. The tighter, straighter arm and leg positions of women, which take a minimal amount of space, are associated with lower status. Leaning back, with legs and arms somewhat sprawled, occupies greater space and is associated with higher status.

Frieze also noted that the amount of physical space that a person uses or controls seems to vary by sex. Personal space is that distance immediately surrounding one's body. If another person purposely comes into our personal space, we react by withdrawing or by aggressing, if the person is of equal or lower status. Higher-status, or more powerful, people can and do violate the personal space of a lower-status person, since they need not fear reprisal. Thus, a man can come quite close to his secretary when he gives her an order, but she keeps her distance when she needs

to sex, and that is the difference in roles that men and women play and enact in society. As we noted in Chapter 5, roles affect behavior, encouraging incumbents to behave in some ways and not in others. The purpose of such roles is to give a certain stability to the group. Societies customarily differentiate between masculine and feminine roles. Men and women are assigned to different work positions, home positions, and other niches on the

---

to ask him a question. In general, women are more tolerant and accepting of personal space invasions, especially when the invader is a male.

There are other ways in which men control more space than women. In the home, the kitchen is often considered the woman's space, but it is also a public space that can be entered by anyone. The man is more likely to have a personal area, such as a workshop or a study, which is less frequently invaded by others. In work situations, lower-status individuals work in public areas, such as on assembly lines, while higher-status individuals have a private office. Thus, control of space comes to be associated with high status or dominance.

There is some evidence that men are more likely to stare at women than women are to stare at men. Women are more likely to look downward, which is a submissive nonverbal response. Once again, the nonverbal behavior of the sexes follows the traditional patterns of dominance-submission in the sexes.

As the stereotyped sex roles have it, women are supposed to be more emotional and more caring than men. One nonverbal method of communicating caring is through smiling. Women smile more than men. We could thus conclude that women, as warmer and more emotional persons, are quicker to express their pleasure and satisfaction. But we could also interpret the more frequent smiling of women as meaning they are more accustomed to deferring to others, by showing approval through smiling. Women are less likely to indicate disapproval of others, particularly males, by failing to smile or by having a stern appearance.

All in all, there is considerable evidence that women communicate low status and subordination through the nonverbal messages they send. And in this way, sex-role stereotypes are perpetuated. Yet nonverbal behavior is hard to change, since it is deeply ingrained in our personalities and comes out unconsciously. When women try to change their nonverbal behavior, it sometimes comes out wrong, almost like a caricature of men, for they have not had the years of practice that make such behavior seem natural in a man. More than this, both men and women are likely to object to women who don't "act like a lady." Women are thus in a bind. The nonverbal behavior expected of them communicates submission and low status, yet efforts to act in nonsubmissive ways bring derision and criticism.

basis of their sex. They are expected to take different positions in the group and to behave differently, regardless of whether or not they are taught to have different temperaments.

How did it happen that societies developed sex roles, so that the sexes customarily have performed different kinds of activities? How did we reach a position in which men are considered dominant and women submissive, so that even the subtlest of everyday behaviors reflect these roles (see Box 7.1)? Let us look to the evolution of human societies for some clues for the answers to these questions.

SEX ROLES IN HISTORY

No one can know for sure how sex-role differentiation began, but one theory is that it was related to biological changes in the human species. The development of the species was accompanied by a loss of various physical advantages but a gain in other areas—the development of language, the use of tools, and so on. There came to be a real advantage in larger brains. But these larger brains required larger skulls, which made childbirth more difficult. There arose a selective factor in favor of women who had the ability to expel a fetus before the head was too large to cause such difficulties. Those women who had this ability lived through childbirth and so did their daughters, who inherited this characteristic.

One result of this biological change was that the "premature" infants needed immediate care over a long period of time in order to survive. They clearly needed a mother who was able to provide milk and physical care. The anthropologists Hockett and Anscher (1964) have theorized that the role of father was invented at about this time in our ancestral history. That is, the nursing mother needed someone to help her get food for herself and to protect her and her helpless infant. Thus, it is theorized, there was a rudimentary division of labor by sex, with women having primary responsibility for the feeding and care of infants and men performing protective duties as necessary. Of course, women were not always nursing babies, and men were not always protecting them. During much of the time, the adults of both sexes were engaging in similar survival activities.

The first real division of labor came when humans developed better weapons, which allowed them to kill larger animals. It made sense to encourage some adults to specialize in the role of hunter and others to specialize in the role of food gatherer. Hunting required absence from the home. Days or weeks would go by as the animals were stalked through fields and forests. Women, many of whom were pregnant or nursing a baby, seemed better suited to the role of food gatherer. Even if they had to travel some distance from the home, they could still carry their babies with them. And they could also take young children along on the gathering excursions and super-

Early in human history, as in some parts of Mexico today, women were assigned work outside the home that would allow them also to care for young children.

vise their activities. Men, unencumbered by pregnancy, the nursing of babies, and the care of young children, assumed the role of hunter. The food products obtained by both gathering and hunting were considered valuable, for both were sorely needed for survival. There is no reason to believe that the role of either hunter or gatherer was considered superior. The roles of the sexes, while different, were very likely still equal.

The rudiments of agriculture were probably developed by women who domesticated the plants and bushes they found on their foraging trips. But a major leap in technology was required for the development of true agriculture. Tools for clearing the land and for working it, better knowledge of planting, and increased understanding of plant care were all needed before people could produce a surplus of food that could be stored or bartered. At this stage, the male entered the agricultural economy. Men, because of their strength and lack of encumbrances, took on the task of clearing the land for planting.

In an agricultural economy, homes can become fixed, for it is no longer necessary to wander about gathering and hunting food. Typically, this type of economy also produces a surplus of food. These conditions gave us the concept of *personal property.* The fields, the foods produced in them, and the fixed homes came to be thought of as belonging personally to someone. Generally, this someone was the male, because it was he who validated his claim to a piece of land by clearing it for agricultural use. Then, too, when the hunting role became obsolete, the male turned his efforts to working the land and caring for the domesticated animals.

With wealth, in the form of *property,* came power and prestige. The landowner could decide what should be planted, when the harvest should be reaped, and what should be done about any surpluses. He could assign work to his wife and children. There is much power associated with being the primary source of food; and thus, the roles of the sexes were not just different anymore—they were ranked. That of the male had more prestige, carried more power, and was altogether "better." That of the female implied subordination to the male and a relative lack of power, privilege, and prestige.

There have been a few instances of societies in which the development of technology did not result in a division of labor that strongly favored men. In these cases, women became the owners of land and achieved the power and privilege that go with ownership of property. But these have been exceptions. In general, the male's advantage in freedom from childbearing and nursing, his somewhat greater physical strength, and the evolution of the agricultural economy all made for the kind of sex-role division of labor that gave him land ownership and power. The historical exceptions are extremely important, of course, for they indicate that certain kinds of division of labor by sex are not inevitable outcomes of biological differences between the sexes.

SEX ROLES IN OTHER SOCIETIES

We can now see how modern-day sex-role differentiation has come into being, with males in positions of power and prestige and females primarily in subservient roles. This situation exists in most modern societies, and it is one that many people are trying to change. As we saw at the beginning of this chapter, countries all over the world are making efforts to equalize the roles of men and women. It would be useful here to go into detail about such efforts in a few specific societies. We have chosen two: the Soviet Union and the Israeli kibbutz.

The Soviet Union

In October 1917, the Bolsheviks seized control of the government of what is now the Soviet Union. Imbued with the ideology of Marxism, the new leaders sought relief for the oppressed masses, the removal of injustices, and retribution for the exploitation of the weak. Most of all, they stressed the idea of equality for all citizens. This included, of course, equality of the sexes. Steps were taken to bring about this equality.

THE SOCIOLOGY OF SEX ROLES

Soon after the revolution, it became clear that a new role was being developed for women, one that stressed work for pay in the productive economy. Not only would this give women positions equal to those of men, but it would reduce or eliminate a woman's economic dependence on a man. Women were, and are, encouraged to have children, but they are also expected to hold a job. To allow women to fill these dual roles, the government provides maternity benefits, day nurseries for young children, and "schools of the extended day," where children are supervised after the regular school day. The law forbids firing a woman because she is pregnant, and it provides for the granting of maternity leaves. Theoretically, there are no jobs from which women are barred, and equal pay for equal work is the law.

Despite the government's efforts, Soviet women have not really achieved equality in employment. For example, one study found that less than 25 percent of the directors of industrial enterprises or heads of administrative units were women (Brown, 1968). Although about half of all jobs are filled by women, they perform more than half of the manual agricultural work. About three-fourths of all physicians are women, but this position does not afford high prestige or monetary rewards. Soviet physicians earn about two-thirds as much as skilled blue-collar workers. Of course, Soviet women have been able to achieve jobs in important and prestigious occupations. They constitute 34 percent of all Soviet lawyers, compared to four percent for women in the United States. Women are employed in all the sciences. Almost one-third of all Soviet engineers are women, while only one percent of American engineers are female. And the first, and so far only, woman in space has been a Russian. It is fair to conclude that Soviet women are considerably closer to equality in employment than are American women, but

What is your reaction to this picture of working women in the Soviet Union? How would you feel if they were women in the United States?

even 60 years after the revolution, true economic equality has not yet been achieved.

In the political arena, Soviet women hold many important posts, such as ministers in the government and deputies to the local soviets. Yet, in the Communist party, which constitutes the real power structure, women are grossly underrepresented. While more than half of all adults are women, they constitute only 23 percent of the party membership. In the Politburo, which effectively governs the country, there are no women at all. Of the 241 seats on the party's Central Committee, only five are held by women.

There is general agreement among Soviet citizens and writers that equality of the sexes has not been achieved in the home. Housework and child care are still female responsibilities. One study found that women workers average two hours of leisure time a day on a work day, while men averaged four hours (Lapidus, 1975). On their day off, men enjoyed nine hours of leisure time, whereas women had only five hours. Apparently, the typical Soviet male is no more inclined than his American counterpart to share equally with his wife in child care and housework. The extra burden on women is one reason, of course, that many of them cannot take a more active role in the Communist party and in politics in general.

The Soviet picture is, in some ways, discouraging. This society, dedicated to the removal of injustices and to the promotion of equality, has not achieved equality of the sexes in employment, in the political arena, or in the home. Great strides have been made, but more than 60 years have gone by without results that are completely satisfactory.

The Israeli Kibbutz

In Hebrew, the word *kibbutz* means "a group." Since 1921, this term has been used to denote the communal settlements in what is now the state of Israel. The early settlers in Israel wanted to be reunited with their ancient homeland and to bring about the formation of the legally recognized national state. They chose a communal social organization to lead them to this goal. In a kibbutz, there is very little private property: food, clothing, and shelter are provided without cost to individuals, simply because they are members of the group. All adults have a role in the productive economy, but no member is paid for working. Any surplus or profit produced belongs to the kibbutz as a whole.

The desire for equality, including equality of the sexes, was an important reason for choosing a communal way of life. Much of what was done reflected a lack of sex-role stereotyping and should have promoted equality of the sexes. Most work was assigned without regard to sex. Both men and women worked in the fields, built roads and houses, and worked in the laundry and dining hall. Both were recognized as full-fledged members of the kibbutz and received equal economic support through the group, by means of their collective effort.

No woman in an Israeli kibbutz lists her occupation as "housewife" and none is economically dependent on a man. As these visitors are learning, all women in a kibbutz work for the kibbutz.

Much was done to promote equality in marriage. The woman did not take the man's name, for this could be construed as a mark of her inferiority. The Hebrew marriage ceremony was not used, as it was thought to imply a subjugation of women by men. No woman had to marry to obtain economic support, and none could better herself economically through marriage. All women worked for the kibbutz and received support from it, so they were not economically dependent on fathers, husbands, or any other men.

Children, beginning at birth, were reared in Children's Houses (see Chapter 9, Box 9.1). Thus, in the kibbutz, the tasks that in other countries keep women out of the work force or that overload their working day (child care, cooking, sewing, cleaning) were the responsibility of the group. A woman was as free as a man to work at any kind of job assigned to her by the work committee and to participate in the governance of the kibbutz.

It has been over half a century since the first kibbutz was founded. The movement has succeeded, in that there are now over 200 kibbutzim. But what has happened to sex roles—particularly the role of women?

In most kibbutzim, over the years, there gradually has developed a strong division of labor by sex. Agriculture, the building trades, and management have come to be classified as men's work, whereas child care, teaching, cooking, and sewing have come to be women's work. A thorough study of 34,400 adults found that only 18 percent of the women worked at "male" occupations (as classified above), and only about 12 percent of men worked in "female" occupations (Tiger and Shepher, 1975). In the Israeli army, almost 90 percent of the women hold such "female" jobs as typist, provision officer, and welfare worker. Women pack the parachutes, but men make the jump.

Women in the kibbutz fare no better in the political arena. Lionel Tiger and Joseph Shepher (1975) studied the 15-year records of one kibbutz and found that, except for one year, men had been elected to all important positions. In another kibbutz, not once in 12 years had a woman been elected general manager or treasurer. Furthermore, men in the kibbutz were more likely to attend general assembly meetings and to address the group.

Apparently, only a few women in the kibbutzim are dissatisfied with their sex-typed roles. Most seek out "female" jobs such as working in the dining hall or the nursery, for it is easier to slip away and spend some time with their children than it would be if they were working in the field or in a factory. Women have been instrumental in the abandonment of collective child rearing in some kibbutzim, and it is the men who generally disapprove of this break with the traditional way of rearing children in Children's Houses.

In most societies, women have been required to spend a lot of time in the rearing of children and in home-care tasks. In the kibbutz, these roles are deliberately sought out, even though it means disapproval from the men and constitutes a break with the ideals of the kibbutz. What has happened? Tiger and Shepher conclude that kibbutz women are seeking a more direct and personal association with their own children, and they feel this desire "reflects a species-wide attraction between mothers and their young." So, is biology destiny, after all? The answer is still, "not necessarily."

From almost the beginning of most kibbutzim there was some division of labor by sex. In the early days, most women worked alongside men in all sorts of jobs, but men were still not involved in taking care of little children. This was considered women's work, and this idea was justified, perhaps, by the explanation that masculine muscles were needed in the fields. As time went by, there were more and more children to be cared for and to be taught in the schools. The kibbutzim prospered and could afford to have more people employed in such roles as cook and seamstress. It is likely that women drifted into such jobs because the jobs were unattractive to men. Once sex-role specialization began, it is not difficult to see why it continued. Children observed their mothers working at one kind of job, and their fathers working at other types. Mothers talked about their job in the army as a typist or welfare worker; fathers spoke of their job as soldier.

Thus, women in the kibbutz fell victim to **sex-role stereotyping:** the belief that all women have certain characteristics by virtue of being women and that all men have certain characteristics by virtue of being men. A stereotype is a set of biased generalizations that emphasizes the negative characteristics of persons in a particular category. Sex-role stereotypes include the ideas that all women are soft, pretty, and weak and that all men are strong, brave, and protective. In the kibbutz, such attitudes could have encouraged women to seek less physically demanding roles, and men to let them do so. A recent study in one kibbutz concluded that women rejected harsh physical labor because it "aged and gnarled the young women settlers and prematurely took away their youthful bloom" (Rabkin, 1976, p. 73). This suggests that the women continued to see themselves as sexual objects, with faces and bodies that had to be soft and youthful to appeal to men.

The pioneers of the kibbutz were fairly thorough in their efforts to promote equality of the sexes and to do away with sex-role stereotyping. Yet, in the kibbutz of today, women are often enacting traditional female occupational roles and exhibiting traditional female attitudes. This does not mean that the goals were impossible, but rather that the means for reaching the goals did not take important social conditioning into account. Other societies, such as our own, can learn from the example of the kibbutz just how far-reaching efforts to promote true equality of the sexes have to be.

SEX ROLES IN THE UNITED STATES

One outgrowth of sex-role stereotyping is the development of **sexism**: the belief that women and their roles are inferior to men and their roles and that, therefore, discrimination against women is justified. *Sex-role stereotyping* asserts that men and women have distinctly different personalities and behaviors; *sexism* asserts that men's characteristics are superior to those of women. The attitudes and beliefs associated with sexism are subtle and sometimes difficult to measure. But we can look at the roles of women in the United States in a number of different arenas, and we can see that sex-role stereotyping and sexism have produced discriminatory practices that result in inequality of women in a so-called democratic society. Let's look at some major areas in which women are notably unequal: education, work, income, politics, and the home.

Inequality in Education

Not only is education important in its own right, but formal education is a requirement for almost all jobs in American society. To be denied education is a serious deprivation, and systematic discrimination in educational opportunities is an important indicator of inequality.

In 1976, females were about as likely to finish high school as were males. But in regard to college, the picture changed. The college completion rate of white females in 1976 was less than two-thirds that of males; the completion rate for black females was only 32 percent that of white males; and the

FIGURE 7.1   Median Earnings in 1975 by Years of School Completed for Majority and Black Males and Females with Some Earnings

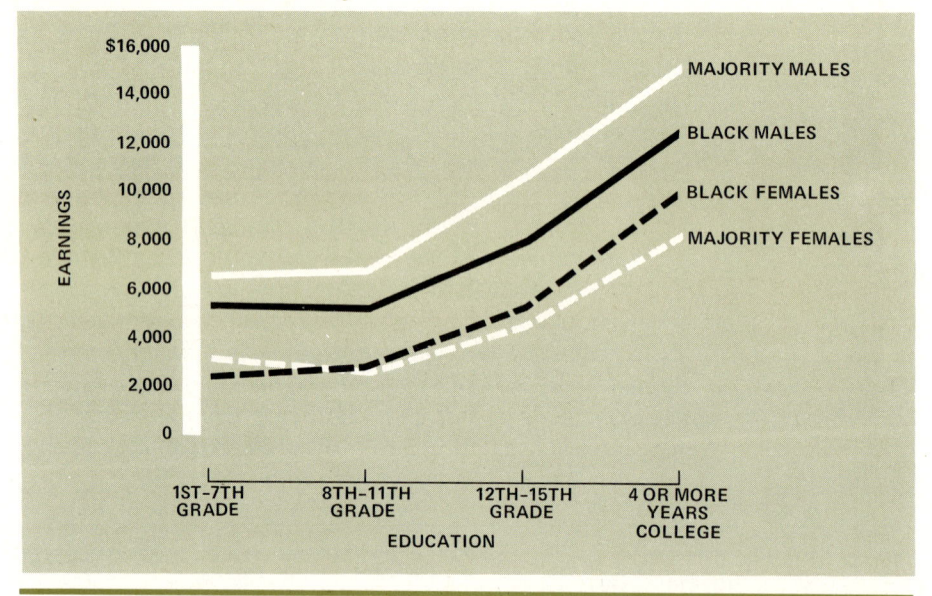

Source: Social Indicators of Equality for Minorities and Women (Washington, D.C.: U.S. Commission on Civil Rights, 1978), p. 23.

rate for other minority groups was lower still (U.S. Commission on Civil Rights, 1978). In other words, women experience more obstacles to the completion of a college education.

Those women who manage to overcome the obstacles find that they are not rewarded to the same extent as are white males. For example, in 1975, women with four or more years of college earned only 53 percent of the average earned by white males with the same education. As a matter of fact, the average earnings of white women with a college education were less than those of white males with only a high school education (see Figure 7.1). Women are, thus, not only more likely to be excluded from higher education, but even those who do make it through receive fewer of the financial rewards that usually go with a college degree.

Inequality in Occupations

The kind of job a person holds has a profound influence on his or her life. It affects how one spends many hours of the day, how much leisure one has, one's feelings of self-worth, and of course, how much money one has to

Gradually people in the United States are getting used to the idea of men and women holding the same job and earning the same pay.

provide for the necessities and niceties of life. Any inequalities in the occupational sphere thus have far-reaching effects.

One of the significant changes in American society in recent years has been the increased employment of women. Today, women constitute over 40 percent of all American workers. This means, of course, that women are still underrepresented in the work force and that a sizable minority do not have earnings they can call their own. One reason that many women do not work outside the home is that they cannot find jobs. The unemployment rate of white women is almost one-and-a-half times that of white males (U.S. Commission on Civil Rights, 1978). Teenage unemployment rates are high for all groups and both sexes, but the percent of teenage females who are unemployed and actively seeking work is higher than that of males.

Another indication of inequality in occupations is the kinds of jobs at which the sexes work. To a large extent, occupations are still sex-segregated, with women working at some kinds of jobs, men at others. For example, women constitute 87 percent of cashiers, 96 percent of nurses, and 70 percent of teachers but only 20 percent of accountants, one percent of engineers, and eight percent of scientists (*U.S. News and World Report,* 1974). Furthermore, women who want to work in male-dominated occupations, such as coal mining, are having a rough time getting work (see Box 7.2).

It has been shown that for women to have an occupational distribution identical to that of white males, about two-thirds of them would have to change their occupations.

Part of the American dream is to get ahead, occupationally and otherwise. People change jobs and get promotions to make the dream more of a reality.

But it is easier to get ahead occupationally if one is a male. In 1970, white females whose jobs were different from those they had had five years earlier had, on the average, increased their occupational prestige by only 71 percent of the white male average increase.

BOX 7.2 WOMEN MINERS CAN DIG IT, TOO

Despite laws forbidding job discrimination on the basis of sex, women have had a hard time getting jobs in certain fields. One of these fields is coal mining. According to the records of the National Institute for Occupational Safety and Health, no women began mining careers between 1969 and 1973, and only one woman was hired in 1973. Since then, however, the number of women coal miners has begun to grow. In 1974, 18 women started digging coal in Kentucky; in 1975, 65 more women joined the coal-mining ranks; 85 were added in 1976; 184 in 1977; and 112 by 1978. In West Virginia, one woman started a mining career in 1973; now there are 724 women coal miners in that state. This growth suggests that many women would like to make careers in the field of coal mining. As of 1978, however, coal mining was still virtually an all-male occupation, since only two-tenths of one percent of all miners were women.

In 1978, the litigation division of the League of Women Voters Education Fund sponsored a conference on women in the mining industry. The purpose was to bring together people involved in female employment in coal mining—union officials, government representatives, women coal miners—to see what can be done to introduce women more fully into coal mining. My wife, Scottie Kenkel, president of the League of Women Voters of Kentucky, participated in the conference and has reported on it.

It was noted at the conference that an estimated 45,000 coal-mining jobs a year will open up between 1978 and 1985. Women are eager to fill these jobs, just as men are, because of the high wages—a starting salary of $60 a day. Will women get an equal chance to compete for these well-paying jobs? Apparently not, unless something is done to change employment practices. Recently, for example, 74 men were hired as miners in Maryland, but no women were hired; in New Mexico, 24 men, no women, were hired. In July 1977, U.S. Steel had openings for 40 miners; and although 96 women applied for the jobs, all 40 positions went to men.

The Kentucky Commission on Human Rights has received a number of complaints of sex discrimination in the hiring of coal miners. After an investigation of the hiring practices of the Island Creek Coal Company, the company agreed to notify 276 female applicants, who previously had been turned down for jobs, of all new openings in their mines. The Kentucky Commission also worked out an agreement with the Gibraltar Coal Company in which one out of four persons hired will be a woman until women make up 20 percent of the work force. While not admitting that

Thus, inequality in the occupational sphere shows up in the higher unemployment rate of women; in occupational segregation, which denies women full access to all available jobs; and in the lower rate of occupational advancement of women as compared to men.

---

they practice discrimination, these and other companies have agreed not to discriminate in the future.

Women who have tried to get mining jobs report that they were told miners are superstitious and feel it is bad luck to let a woman into a mine, even on a tour. Some of those who did manage to get hired reported all sorts of harassment. One woman said she was stripped and rubbed with axle grease as part of her initiation into the mine; another reported finding a "primitive art" object, fashioned from a piece of hose, in her lunchbox; still another talked about the crude and abusive language of the men miners. Women miners were also distressed by the fact that some of the men did not use the portable toilet and chose, instead, to urinate in a corner.

Women miners have also run into the problem of being unable to find good mining clothes. The required steel-toed shoes are not available in women's sizes, nor are good work gloves. Women must wear several pairs of thick socks to be able to wear the shoes, and they must stuff paper towels into hard hats in order to make them fit. Coal mining is hard work under the best of conditions; but it is worse if one's clothes are ill-fitting and uncomfortable.

It became clear at the conference that women were attracted to coal mining because it is a good means of supporting themselves and their families. One divorced woman who used to make $23 a day as a sander in a mobile home factory now makes $66 a day on her mining job. In the counties where many of the mines are located, the only other alternative job for women is store clerking, which pays the minimum wage. It is estimated that about half of the women miners are the sole support for their children, either because of divorce or the death of their spouse.

Coal-mining women were urged at the conference to spend money to support litigation against coal companies and unions. Some had already done so and had received financial settlements to compensate for discrimination in hiring practices. Undoubtedly, newspaper accounts of successful suits are an effective way of persuading other companies not to violate the law. But, meanwhile, there is an extra financial burden on women who have to go to court to get a job for which they are qualified. Recently, the Association of Kentucky-Virginia Women Coal Miners was organized to help women who want to enter the coal industry. Women are serious about wanting to work in the mines and will do what is necessary to get an equal chance for mining jobs. Perhaps, before too long, people will accept the message of the bumper sticker seen around Tennessee coal fields: "Women Miners Can Dig It, Too."

Inequality in Earnings

In 1975, the average income earned by white women was 45 percent of that earned by white males (U.S. Commission on Civil Rights, 1978). In our society, some people earn more than others because of differences in occupation, education, and age. Taking such factors into consideration, it is found that if white females had the same work-related characteristics as men, they would still earn only 57 percent of the amount earned by white males. If men and women have the same work-life history, the discrepancy between their salaries narrows, but it does not disappear. Regardless of how or why it happened, the bald truth is that women workers earn considerably less than men workers.

Earlier, we saw that occupational advancement is harder for women than for men. Generally, as workers get older they gain experience on the job, get promoted to better jobs, and get raises, resulting in increased earnings. For

FIGURE 7.2 Estimated Percentage of Homemakers and Employed Wives Who Do All or Most of Major Homemaking Tasks

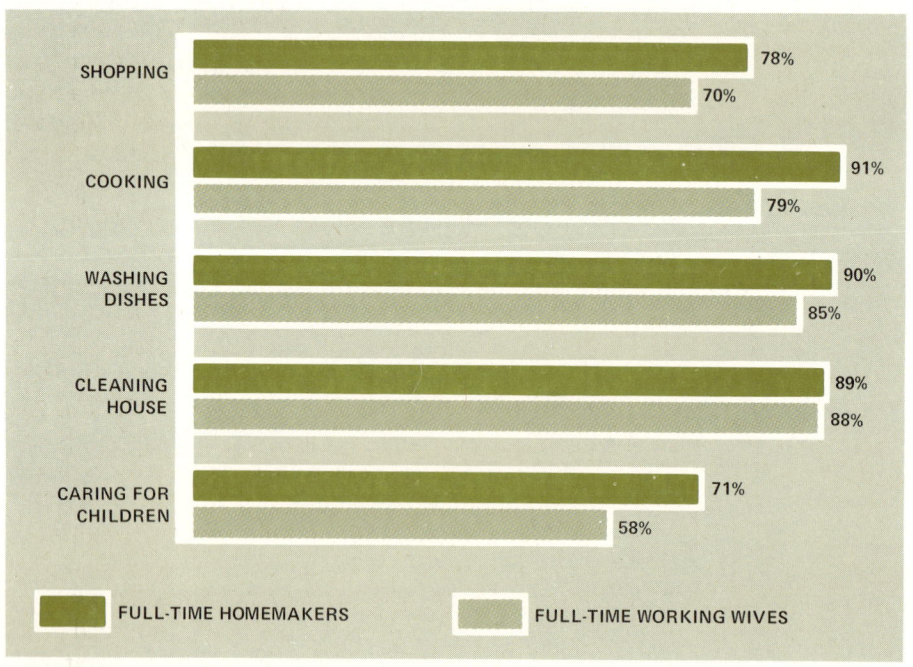

Task	Full-Time Homemakers	Full-Time Working Wives
SHOPPING	78%	70%
COOKING	91%	79%
WASHING DISHES	90%	85%
CLEANING HOUSE	89%	88%
CARING FOR CHILDREN	71%	58%

Wives who are employed outside the home on a full-time basis are only somewhat less likely to do all or most of these homemaking tasks.

Source: Adapted from Morton Hunt, "Women and Their Work," *Redbook Magazine* (April 1978), p. 73. Copyright © 1978 by The Redbook Publishing Company.

males, we can visualize an earnings ladder that many climb steadily; but for females, there is, in reality, no ladder. In 1975, for example, the average earnings increase for white females was only 15 percent of the increase for white males. This indicates that women are more likely to be found in dead-end jobs where the steps up the earnings ladder are very small.

Inequality in Political Power

In our discussion of the Soviet Union, we noted that women have low representation in power positions in that society. In the United States, the situation is distressingly similar. Although over 40 percent of all workers are women, and 51 percent of all Americans are women, in 1978 only two state governors were women, and there were only two women in the United States Senate. As a matter of fact, in our 200-year history, only 11 women have ever been senators, and only five have been governors. Of the 435 members of the House of Representatives, 18 were women in 1978. There has never been a woman on the Supreme Court, and only five women have ever held Cabinet posts. Today, women hold about eight percent of all public offices.

It is rare to find women as university presidents, leaders of major corporations, or mayors of large cities. In roles that require making decisions that affect the lives and fates of others, the incumbent is most likely to be a male, while over half of those affected will be female. Put bluntly, women lack power in American society because they are not filling the power positions. One explanation for this situation, in addition to sexism, is that women are not prepared for leadership roles as part of the socialization process. Another reason is that women are given time-consuming responsibilities in the home.

Inequality in the Home

A study of 1,400 families calculated the dollar value of time spent at housework by husband, wife, and children (Walker and Ganger, 1973). In a family with three children, the daily value of the woman's housework ranged from $14 to $22 if she did not work outside the home, and from $8 to $16 if she was also employed. Husbands of nonemployed wives contributed $2 to $4 worth of work, while husbands of working wives did $3 to $6 worth of work. Teenage children, not usually noted for their generosity in helping around the house, nevertheless contributed about as much work as their fathers. Another study found that 27 percent of men claimed that they shared housework, 22 percent shared child care, and 40 percent shared shopping with their working wives (Hunt, 1978). This is hardly an admirable record for American males.

Still another study discovered that women employed full-time outside the home worked an additional 30 hours or more a week at household tasks, while their husbands did about five hours of housework (Barrett, 1976). The extra work load of working wives means that they have less time than their husbands for self-improvement or for preparation for job advancement, not to mention leisure pursuits.

Why Inequalities?

The facts on inequality should make those who contend that we do not need the Equal Rights Amendment at least question their stand. Why do inequalities persist? There are three major reasons: (1) the legacy of sex-role differentiation, (2) the cultural idea that men and masculine roles are more important than women and feminine roles, and (3) the belief system that holds that, in many respects, the sexes have different personalities.

We saw how sex-role differentiation developed when we looked at the

Outside the home, women frequently are in jobs where they help a man or take directions from a man—not much different than the traditional role of wife.

history of sex roles. At the agricultural stage of society, men had primary responsibility for clearing the land, planting and harvesting the crops, and caring for the larger animals. Women often helped at these tasks, but their primary jobs were those that could be performed around the home: child care, housekeeping, cooking, laundering, sewing. As the society became industrialized, men's jobs took them outside the home, to the shops, factories, and offices. In time, more and more women began working outside the home, but their work roles were similar to their domestic ones. As school teachers, they continued to rear children; as secretaries, receptionists, and nurses, they continued to help men; and as factory workers, they were supervised by men. What's more, society still held to the idea that the most important roles for women were the domestic ones.

The cultural tradition of our society also contained the idea that men's occupations were more important than women's occupations. Thus, not only were sex roles differentiated, but they were ranked. Even as increasing numbers of women worked outside the home, they still were restricted to certain kinds of jobs—ones that were less prestigious and that paid less than men's jobs. Even today, with the same education as men women earn about half as much as them. The idea that women's roles are less important than men's roles led to the idea that women *themselves* are inferior to men. Does this sound extreme?

Well, parents in this country seem to think that boys are superior to girls. If parents could preselect the sex of their babies, they would choose boys, especially for the first child. Studies have consistently found that boy babies are preferred to girl babies, not only for first births but for subsequent births as well. Even recent studies find that almost two-thirds of married *women* would like their first child to be a boy (Westoff and Rindfuss, 1974). This is a not-too-subtle indication that boys are considered more valuable or more worthwhile than girls.

Not too surprisingly, girls catch on to their parents' evaluation of them as less important than boys, and in time, some accept the idea of their basic inferiority. Studies have repeatedly found that although very few men ever wish that they were female, at least one-fifth of all women at some time in their life seriously wish that they were male. The lower self-image of women has also been illustrated in a study of college women who were asked to evaluate six research articles (Goldberg, 1968). Half of them were told that the articles were written by John T. McKay, while the rest were told they were written by Joan T. McKay. The women who thought the author was male rated the articles higher than those who thought the author was female—even though the articles were identical.

We have seen, then, that according to our cultural heritage, the roles of the sexes are expected to be different, and that the roles of men are seen as superior to those of women. Our cultural heritage also contains the idea that men and women have different abilities, are naturally inclined toward different skills, and have different personalities generally. Independence,

FIGURE 7.3 What Men and Women Most Want in Life for a Daughter and a Son

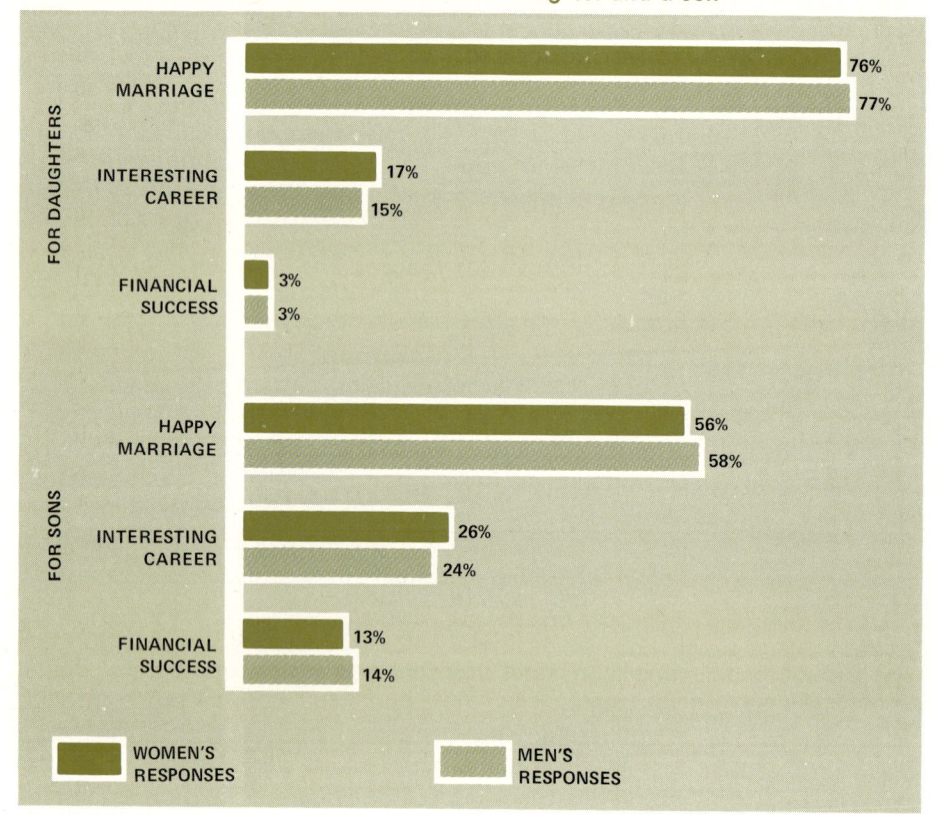

FOR DAUGHTERS
- HAPPY MARRIAGE: 76% / 77%
- INTERESTING CAREER: 17% / 15%
- FINANCIAL SUCCESS: 3% / 3%

FOR SONS
- HAPPY MARRIAGE: 56% / 58%
- INTERESTING CAREER: 26% / 24%
- FINANCIAL SUCCESS: 13% / 14%

WOMEN'S RESPONSES   MEN'S RESPONSES

In a national cross-section sample, 3,000 women and 1,000 men were asked what they most wanted in life for their children. Both more men and more women ranked a happy marriage first for a daughter than for a son. In addition, men and women agreed that an interesting career and financial success are more important for sons than for daughters.

Source: The Virginia Slims American Women's Opinion Poll, vol. 3, "A Survey of the Attitudes of Women on Marriage, Divorce, the Family and America's Changing Sexual Morality," conducted by the Roper Organization (Spring 1974), pp. 52, 84.

rationality, competitiveness, courage, roughness, and risk-taking are considered to be masculine traits, while their opposites—dependence, emotionality, cooperativeness, timidity, daintiness, and security-seeking—are said to be feminine traits. How do children learn about these traits and come to acquire them? We saw earlier in the chapter that biology is a weak influence and that culture is a major one. How does culture exert its effects in order to produce "masculinity" and "femininity"? The answer to this lies in the phenomenon of sex-role socialization.

SEX-ROLE SOCIALIZATION

Sex-role socialization begins early and is done quite thoroughly. Jerome Kagan's (1964) research found that children as young as three "know that girls are cute and dependent while boys are strong and that mommies are nurturant while daddies are aggressive." Beginning as early as infancy, little boys and little girls are reared differently. The female infant is handled and cuddled more than the male. Parents spend comparatively more time teaching their daughters how to smile (Lake, 1975), and in numerous other subtle ways, they respond to the maleness or femaleness of their baby.

As children grow, aggression and roughness are permitted or encouraged for boys but not for girls. It is "understandable" that little girls will at times cry or pout, but their brothers are told that "big boys don't cry." Gradually, children develop what our society believes to be sex-appropriate behavior and attitudes. Most children become comfortable with sex-appropriate roles, attitudes, body movements, and interests. They begin to seem "natural" to them and are accepted as natural by those around them.

The Role of the Schools

As in the socialization process in general, the school is an important agent in the socialization of sex roles; for example, the sexes are frequently segregated in games and activities. Sometimes the segregation is self-imposed, as boys and girls (as a result of their self-definitions) seek out others of their sex for games, play activities, and friends. At other times, the segregation is imposed on them, as when certain areas and types of equipment are designated for boys only or girls only. The idea that there are masculine and feminine roles and that the sexes have different likes and abilities is thus subtly reinforced.

When the books used in school are analyzed for sex-role stereotyping, it is found invariably that texts typically portray men and women in traditional sex roles and frequently devote a lot more attention to men and boys than to women and girls. A study by Marjorie U'Ren (1971), for example, found that only 15 percent of the illustrations in school textbooks included women. As recently as 1977, a study of textbooks used in Pella, Iowa, schools found that about two-thirds of the books mentioned twice as many job possibilities for men as for women. Women were almost always depicted as secretaries, teachers, or other traditional female workers. A mathematics textbook contained problems dealing with men purchasing insurance or shares of stock, while the only woman mentioned in this book was buying a rug for her home. Throughout all the books used in this school system, it was invariably a man, and not a woman, who showed initiative, skill at making decisions, and courage (*Carnegie Quarterly,* 1978).

Until recently, high schools had some courses that were reserved for females, and others for males. Today, most schools let females enroll in shop

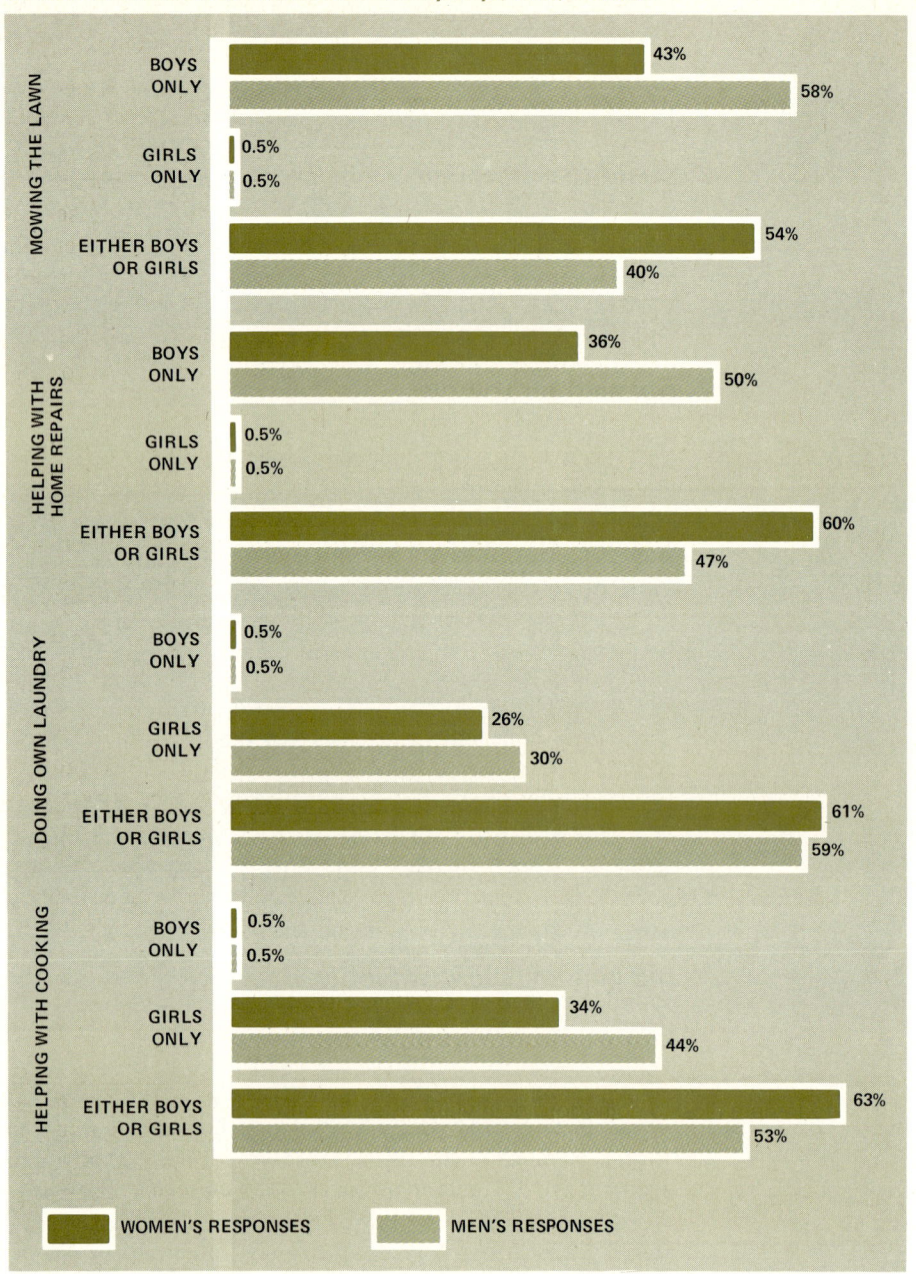

FIGURE 7.4 Household Chores that Should Be Done by Boys, Girls, or Either

MOWING THE LAWN
- BOYS ONLY: 43% (women), 58% (men)
- GIRLS ONLY: 0.5% (women), 0.5% (men)
- EITHER BOYS OR GIRLS: 54% (women), 40% (men)

HELPING WITH HOME REPAIRS
- BOYS ONLY: 36% (women), 50% (men)
- GIRLS ONLY: 0.5% (women), 0.5% (men)
- EITHER BOYS OR GIRLS: 60% (women), 47% (men)

DOING OWN LAUNDRY
- BOYS ONLY: 0.5% (women), 0.5% (men)
- GIRLS ONLY: 26% (women), 30% (men)
- EITHER BOYS OR GIRLS: 61% (women), 59% (men)

HELPING WITH COOKING
- BOYS ONLY: 0.5% (women), 0.5% (men)
- GIRLS ONLY: 34% (women), 44% (men)
- EITHER BOYS OR GIRLS: 63% (women), 53% (men)

WOMEN'S RESPONSES   MEN'S RESPONSES

Greater numbers of women than men believe that these household chores should be performed by either boys or girls. Yet, a fairly high proportion of both men and women consider some chores appropriate for boys only, and others for girls only. For example, no woman or man felt that the traditionally masculine roles of lawn mowing or making home repairs should be done by girls only, and none felt that doing laundry and cooking should be done by boys only.

Source: *The Virginia Slims American Women's Opinion Poll,* vol. 3, "A Survey of the Attitudes of Women on Marriage, Divorce, the Family and America's Changing Sexual Morality," conducted by the Roper Organization (Spring 1974), p. 25.

and auto mechanics courses, and males in home economics courses. Still, there are none-too-subtle pressures to choose "sex-appropriate" courses of study. Imagine a counselor's reaction to a boy who wants to take a sewing class or to a girl who wants to take auto shop. Imagine, too, the boy talking to his parents and friends about his plans to take sewing. It isn't so bad for the girl to take auto mechanics, for after all, she is emulating the "superior" sex. It is interesting that in some high schools where boys showed an interest in home economics, a special course called "Bachelor Living" was designed. Thus, the idea is perpetuated that the sexes have different interests and abilities and should prepare themselves for different roles in life.

The Role of the Mass Media

The entertainment media are notorious for sex-role stereotyping. Even today, in most movies and television programs men and women are shown in traditional roles. Efforts are presumably being made to change this situation, and the number of women in roles such as doctor, judge, and police officer has increased. Yet, even when women are shown in assertive roles, as in "Charlie's Angels," they are often depicted as enjoying serving men and dressing and acting as sex objects for the pleasure of men.

In TV commercials, we can also note sexual stereotyping. Women are shown going into raptures over products that promise brighter clothes, shinier floors, and cleaner-smelling toilets. Men are depicted marveling at chain saws, drinking beer at parties, and purchasing tires. It is a man who manages the store where women come in to squeeze the toilet paper. The roles of the sexes are not merely different in TV commercials and programs—it is obvious that women's roles are less important and less exciting than those of men.

Growing Up Female

The end-products of socialization are individuals who have values, skills, knowledge, and interests that equip them for pursuing adult roles in their society. The end-products of sex-role socialization are people who are equipped to handle roles assigned to one or the other sex. Through socialization in the home, the school, and other places, women incorporate into their personalities those traits that will make them good mothers, housekeepers, and helpmates to men. Meanwhile, women are not socialized to develop traits that are necessary or desirable in the world outside the home. As Janet Chafetz (1978) puts it, "Females are trained to be sensitive, emotional, intuitive, passive, unaggressive, and so forth, but the modern work environment increasingly requires rational, logical, aggressive, ambitious, competitive, and mechanical traits" (p. 128).

A number of women are further ill-prepared for careers and responsible positions because of the low self-image, or inferiority complex, they have acquired by growing up female in our society. A woman will find it difficult to be a success if she has incorporated into her personality a basic attitude that she is not as good as a man. Finally, women reaching adulthood today have not had sufficient *role models*—that is, women who are successfully acting out a variety of occupational and leadership roles to which the younger woman can aspire. In view of the socialization experiences that teach stereotyped roles, that encourage personality traits ill-suited to the world of work, and that produce a poor self-image, it is little wonder that women are less likely than men to go to college, and particularly, to pursue advanced degrees.

Those women whose socialization experience has been less rigid or who have forced their way out of the sexual stereotype still have difficulties in achieving equality. For one thing, they have to live and compete educationally and occupationally in a society where many people still believe that sex-role differentiation is somehow part of the natural order of things. Such women may be prepared to buck the system in order to achieve equality, but it is still rough going. Despite the Civil Rights Act of 1964, which made it illegal to discriminate on the basis of sex with regard to employment, promotion, and pay, some employers continue to avoid hiring women and to withhold promotions and pay raises from those they do hire.

CONSEQUENCES OF SEX-ROLE STEREOTYPING

There are many far-reaching consequences of the sex-role stereotyping that is still found in the United States. We will examine these effects in terms of their consequences for society, for women, and for men.

Consequences for Society

At the societal level, the resultant economic dysfunctions are enormous. Roughly one-half of the adult population does not have full access to all of the roles in the productive economy. Functionally, it would be better if all the occupational roles—doctor, judge, engineer, teacher, child-care worker, coal miner—were open to all who wish to pursue them. In this way, we would come closer to getting the best-qualified persons filling the various occupational roles, rather than getting the best-qualified persons of a given sex. Our society is not fully utilizing the talent of half its adults.

The relative lack of women in leadership and decision-making roles is another important dysfunction of sex-role stereotyping. Our society has many problems, nationally and internationally; and it is the loser when only the creative and imaginative skills of men, and not women, are turned to the solution of these problems.

The talents of women are underutilized in another sense as well. You will recall that the unemployment rate for women is higher than that for men. But this unemployment rate underestimates the underutilization of women, as it is based on a count of only those actively seeking work. When the rate is high, people get discouraged, and if they stop looking for work, they are not counted as unemployed. Consider the middle-aged woman who is thinking about taking a job. She may have little job experience, and the salable skills she had when she graduated from high school or college 20 years earlier have become obsolete. Understandably, she is not eager to enter a low-paying job; and if, because of this, she does not look for work, she is not counted as unemployed, and society is losing the benefit of her potential economic productivity. More women than men are found in part-time and temporary jobs, another indication of the underutilization of their talents.

The economic costs of sex-role stereotyping are substantial, but there are still other social costs that must be considered. Certainly, a price is exacted, in terms of the mental health of us all, when as a society we encourage or merely tolerate practices that fill people's minds with myths, false stereotypes, and other justifications for systematic discrimination against any of our citizens. It is a frightening thought that many Americans are not living in a real world populated with real people, but in one populated with people who must conform to certain stereotypes lest they be considered odd, radical, or worse.

Another noneconomic cost of sex-role stereotyping is its effect on the moral fiber of our society. Something happens to such fundamental ideas as justice, fairness, and equality of opportunity when they are not applied to the same degree to all categories of citizens. To be sure, America is not on the brink of disaster, but this does not negate the fact that there are serious economic and noneconomic dysfunctions associated with sex-role stereotyping.

Consequences for Women

As a result of living in a sexist society, women bear both economic and psychosocial costs. As we have seen, women earn less than men. This means that whether the woman is supporting only herself, supporting herself and her children, or co-providing for an intact family, she has less money at her disposal than she would if her wages were on par with those of males. Of all the American families living in poverty, 40 percent are headed by women. And those women who are unemployed or who are too discouraged to look for work are also suffering economically.

Another cost to women in our sexist society is their comparative lack of control over their own destinies. If married, a woman usually defers to her husband in many important areas. He and his job usually have a strong effect on where the family lives, when they move, their lifestyle, when and where they go on vacation, and so on. The single woman has more control over her fate, but not if she cannot get into a desirable occupation or is discouraged from continuing her education. Both single and married women, even when employed, have difficulty getting bank loans, opening charge accounts in their own name, and buying items on credit. Many women still find it difficult to be treated as independent adults capable of making their own decisions and directing their own lives.

Still another cost to women is the psychological damage that results from being treated as second-class citizens. As we have seen, many have a poor self-concept, or inferiority complex; they are thus psychologically burdened with traits that make them unfit for roles other than ones in which they are dependent on men. Lacking assertiveness and self-assurance, many women are unable to improve their lot in life or to take on occupational and other roles that allow them to use their talents, follow their interests, express their individuality, and otherwise achieve the full measure of their potential.

Consequences for Men

Have you ever thought about the expression "the *opposite* sex"? According to popular stereotypes, whatever women are like and whatever they do, men are supposed to be completely opposite. Thus, men are trapped in a stereotype, just as women are. Some men would like to go into "feminine" occupations, such as nursing and child-care work, and some, of course, do so. But only the most secure among them can stand the criticisms, suspicions, and often the accusations of homosexuality accorded those who cross role boundaries by taking a role opposite to the one they are supposed to assume.

In a similar manner, men are trapped by the stereotype, which dictates that their personalities and behaviors must be "masculine." Where women are expected to be weak, men must be strong; where women are expected to be dependent, men must be independent and able to take care of others; where it is "natural" for women to cry and to express gentle emotions, men should do neither; where women are cooperative, men must be competitive. But gentleness, cooperativeness, feelings of doubt and weakness, and wanting to be cared for are all *human* traits and feelings. Men can be taught to suppress these emotions, but they do so at their own cost.

When a baby boy is born, a label should be affixed to his body: "Warning: The Male Role May Be Dangerous to Your Health" (Harrison, 1978). The lifelong pressures on the male to be strong, to suppress his feelings, to be and to remain successful, and to be aggressive and competitive are intense, and many men break down, in one way or another, under the strain. Men are more likely than women to suffer from peptic ulcers, heart attacks, asthma, and hypertension, all of which are associated with tension and stress. Men are about fifteen times as likely as women to become alcoholics, although the rate among women is rising. Men commit suicide five times as frequently as women, even though women *attempt* suicide more often. This latter fact suggests that women, less ashamed to be dependent, use a suicide attempt as a cry for help; while the stoic male, expected to solve his own problems, uses suicide as the only way out.

"Women's liberation" is a household term, but "men's liberation" is a term still whispered softly by a handful of men who have discovered how the male stereotype inhibits them, limits their role options, and just generally hurts them. One men's liberation group, the Berkeley Men's Center, produced a manifesto that reads in part:

> We, as men, want to take back our full humanity. We no longer want to strain and compete to live up to an impossibly oppressive masculine image—strong, silent, cool, handsome, unemotional, successful, master of women, leader of men, wealthy, brilliant, athletic, and "heavy" (Pleck and Sawyer, 1974, p. 174).

It takes courage to join a men's liberation group and to admit to the absurdity of the stereotype of masculinity. The men who join such groups are witnesses to the hurtful and repressive nature of the stereotyped male sex role. And they are also aware of the fact that women's liberation *is* men's liberation, for men can benefit greatly from the advances made by the women's movement (see Box 7.3).

THE FUTURE OF SEX ROLES

As most people realize, our society is in the throes of profound changes with regard to sex roles. The tempo of the movement toward a nonsexist society, one devoid of sex-role stereotypes, is strong. The movement is affected by and intermingled with other social changes. Already, there have been changes in the socialization of the young, and adults of both sexes have been resocialized for life in a nonsexist society.

Sex-role liberation interacts with a number of other trends in our society. The trend toward smaller families, somewhat older age at marriage, greater acceptance of the single person, the availability of day-care centers, and the increasing willingness of men to share in child care and housework all mean that more women will have more years during which they can be employed outside the home. Laws such as the Civil Rights Act of 1964, state equal rights laws, and the Equal Rights Amendment should make it easier for people to choose and fill roles without regard to sex. Affirmative action programs, which encourage the entry of women into nontraditional roles, should also help in the erosion of sex-role stereotypes.

Changes now going on in the socialization of the next generation should also lead to a reduction in sex stereotyping. Some parents agree to take nontraditional roles in the home (father doing the laundry, mother mowing the lawn), in order to provide models for their children. They are careful to see that their children are given the opportunity to play with all sorts of toys, and not just "sex-appropriate" ones. And, of course, by both parents working outside the home, as well as in it, they serve as models of the emerging order.

Schools are moving in the same direction, carefully watching the textbooks that are used, the athletic programs, and the course offerings. Even college textbooks, such as this one, are carefully checked for sexism in the use of examples and in the use of the pronoun "he" to refer to all human beings. Sex-role stereotyping still exists, but more and more educators are

BOX 7.3
WOMEN'S LIBERATION AS MEN'S LIBERATION

Undoubtedly, some men have been threatened by the Women's Liberation movement. They may fear competition with women in the job market, fear that they will lose power, or maybe even fear that they will lose their masculinity. Warren Farrell, author of The Liberated Man (1974), challenges the assumption that men must necessarily be threatened by the liberation of women. As he sees it, there are a number of areas in which men will actually benefit from women's liberation. Here are a few of the points Farrell makes:

1. If a woman has her own life and destiny to control, she will not need to control her husband. Men sometimes complain that their wives manipulate them or control the whole household. This complaint should be voiced less frequently when women are pursuing their own interests and not living their lives through their husbands.
2. Sharing the breadwinner role frees the man from a great deal of pressure. A man who is not the sole support of his family can afford to take some risks, such as trying a more interesting job or going into business for himself.
3. A man can devote more time to his children, in a more positive atmosphere. Not having to work overtime, and relieved of some of the pressures to "make it," the man can share in the rearing of children in a more relaxed manner.
4. In poverty homes, if both parents work, the additional money gives the man and his family the basic freedom to keep food on the table and the option of holding the family together. Middle-class families with two bread winners will find it easier to afford travel, longer vacations, and better education for the children.
5. The responsibilities of the man within the home will, in some situations, be lessened. Traditionally, chores such as mowing the lawn, painting, and repairing furniture have been defined as part of the male role. The liberated husband of a liberated wife will find that he is not necessarily stuck with chores he doesn't like. The couple may choose to paint a room together, the wife may do the "handyman" chores while

aware of the problem and are at least attempting to eliminate it. Two of the key agents in socialization, the family and the school, are thus moving in the direction of nonsexist socialization.

It should be recognized that even while children are being socialized for life in a nonsexist society, some of the current generation of adults are being *resocialized,* so that they are no longer sexist in their behavior and attitudes. More men and women are rejecting the notion of the basic inferiority of women and the pressures that force people into rigidly designed roles. They feel that both sexes should have ample opportunities for achieving their full potential and that both should be able to pursue their personal ambitions

---

the husband prepares meals, or having two salaries, they may hire someone to do the chores that neither likes.

6. The liberated woman can allow a man more independence in his personal life. Since a working wife is not alone at home all day without companionship, she is less likely to mind if her husband stops off for a drink on the way home, goes off on hunting trips, or has a night out on his own from time to time.

7. Men who learn to listen to women acquire a new set of values. In an egalitarian relationship with a liberated woman, the man takes her seriously. By really listening, he can learn new viewpoints and acquire new information, just as he can by listening to other men.

8. Men become free of many of the practices that discriminate against them. There are still barriers to men's obtaining of paternity leaves from their jobs, so that they can share in child rearing in the baby's early months, and still be assured of their jobs. For many years, the Social Security system discriminated against widowers by not allowing them to claim benefits upon the death of a wife unless they could demonstrate they were dependent on her; women did not have to do this. In the area of divorce, the law discriminates against men with regard to alimony, and traditionally, women have been awarded custody of the children. Equal treatment of the sexes under the law can help men, too.

9. Upon retirement, men's lives will not be empty. The man whose life has centered around his job and around being a good provider will feel a great loss when he retires. The man and woman who have shared responsibilities and have interests of their own should be better able to continue this pattern after retirement.

Farrell has outlined a number of other ways in which men can reap rewards from the liberation of women. Perhaps if more men thought about the benefits, instead of worrying about presumed losses, they would be less fearful of women's liberation.

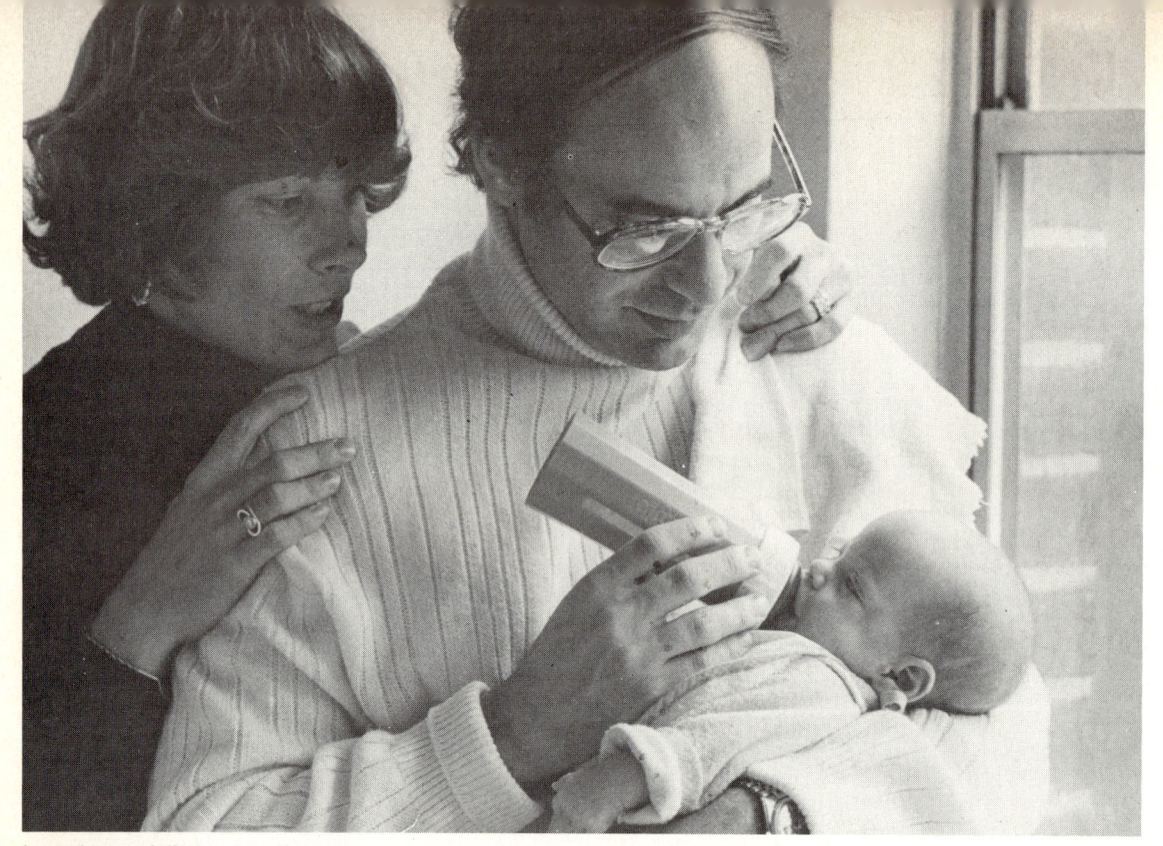

In modern societies men can feed and otherwise care for an infant. The question becomes how many men, and women, feel comfortable with such an arrangement.

without the restriction of traditional sex-typed roles, attitudes, and behavior. People who espouse such beliefs are not yet in the majority, so they do meet with opposition.

Opposition to major social change of any sort is not difficult to explain. After all, there is a certain comfort in the familiar, even if one secretly admits that it is not the best. In Chapter 3, we discussed the concept of ethnocentrism, the belief in the goodness and rightness of the way of life in one's society. Accepting major changes means that the universal human tendency toward ethnocentrism must be combatted. In Chapter 4, we discussed the idea of discontinuities in socialization—the pattern in which people are socialized for the enactment of some roles only to find that the rules have been changed abruptly and that they must take on new roles. Adults of both sexes today are finding that, to some extent, the rules have been switched, and the strain they experience is no less than that which occurs when a child must enter the role of adult or an adult must enter the role of older person. Despite these and other barriers to change, it still seems that the movement toward a freer, nonsexist society will continue. But it will not come as rapidly as its proponents hope or as its opponents fear.

In this chapter, we have traced the ways in which inequalities have developed between the sexes—inequalities in income, power, and prestige. In the next chapter, we will tackle the general topic of social stratification—the division of a society into classes based upon inequalities in money, power, and prestige. We will see how such inequalities developed and discuss whether they can be reduced or erased in the same way that sex-role inequalities are being eliminated.

SUMMARY

1. Biologically, males and females differ anatomically, genetically, and hormonally. Aside from differences in sexual characteristics, men are larger and more muscular than women. Men have higher levels of the male sex hormone, **testosterone,** while women have higher levels of **estrogen** and **progesterone.** Men have an XY sex chromosome configuration, while women have an XX configuration.

2. The higher levels of testosterone in males and the existence of the Y chromosome may predispose men to greater aggressiveness than women. But cross-cultural studies, such as that done by Margaret Mead, demonstrate that cultural factors have a much greater influence on sex-role differences than do biological factors.

3. **Sex roles** are roles assigned to men and women by their society. The predominant sex-role differentiation we see today probably had its origins in the agricultural economy, where men came to own the land because they cleared it and planted it while women were encumbered with pregnancy and child care.

4. Since the Russian Revolution, the Soviets have stressed the idea of equality for women. The government has instituted many programs to help bring this about. Nevertheless, Soviet women still experience inequalities in employment, politics, and the home.

5. The Israeli kibbutzim were founded on the idea of equality, and much was done in the early years to promote equality of the sexes. Yet, traditional sex-typed roles have developed, and the women seem to be happy in these roles because of the pervasiveness of **sex-role stereotyping:** the idea that all women have certain characteristics and that all men have certain other characteristics.

6. In the United States, women have been the victims of both sex-role stereotyping and **sexism** — the belief that the sex role of men is superior to that of women. Women in the United States experience discrimination in education, occupations, job promotions, pay, and politics. They are also saddled with the bulk of the housework and child care, even when they work full-time.

7. These inequalities between men and women have developed because of three major factors: (1) the legacy of sex-role differentiation, (2) the cultural idea that men's roles are superior to women's roles, and (3) the belief that men and women have distinctly different personality characteristics.

8. Beginning in infancy, children learn the appropriate behaviors for their sex role. **Sex-role socialization** begins in the home and is reinforced by such socializing agents as the school and the mass media. The socializing of girls focuses on preparing them for a life as a wife and mother and neglects to teach them skills necessary for success in a career.

9. Sex-role stereotyping has negative consequences for society, for women, and for men. On the societal level, it deprives us of the creativity and productivity of a large segment of our population, and it erodes our mental health and moral fiber to permit injustices to continue. The costs to women are both economic and psychological. And sex-role stereotyping traps men into "masculine" roles that inhibit them and that are even harmful to their health.

10. The trend toward sex-role liberation can be seen in nonsexist child-rearing practices, resocialization of adults, and economic and political changes that are creating equal opportunities for the sexes. Opposition to such changes is rooted in ethnocentrism and the strains of discontinuities in socialization.

KEY TERMS

estrogen
genes
hormones
progesterone
sexism
sex chromosomes
sex role
sex-role socialization
sex-role stereotyping
testosterone

SUGGESTED READINGS

Chafetz, Janet S. *Masculine, Feminine, or Human?* Itasca, Ill.: Peacock, 1978.
   A book for those who share the author's interest in bringing about changes that will encourage males and females to explore and develop their human potentials. Areas covered include socialization for sex roles and the costs of role stereotypes.

Duberman, Lucile. *Gender and Sex in Society.* New York: Praeger, 1975.
   An exploration of the differences between men and women in their roles at home and at work and of the factors responsible for these differences. Sexuality is also examined.

Farrell, Warren. *The Liberated Man.* New York: Bantam Books, 1975.
   Using the findings of social research and the experiences of consciousness-raising groups, the author shows how men can go beyond masculinity to truly human liberation.

Friedl, Ernestine. *Women and Men.* New York: Holt, Rinehart, and Winston, 1975.
   An anthropological study of how the level of technology affects the roles of the sexes. The author concentrates on societies at the hunting and gathering stage and the horticultural stage.

Frieze, Irene H., et al. *Women and Sex Roles.* New York: Norton, 1978.
    A wide range of topics is covered from a social psychological point of view. Included are theories of feminine personality, biology and sex differences, women's adult development, sex roles of women, psychological disorders, and women in politics.

Komarovsky, Mirra. *Dilemmas of Masculinity.* New York: Norton, 1976.
    A study of college males—their sexual activity, their images of femininity and masculinity, and their relationships with women. An important study of the masculine role, with its strains and contradictions.

Yorburg, Betty. *Sexual Identity.* New York: John Wiley & Sons, 1974.
    The author considers both male and female sex roles from a social change perspective.

One rather obvious aspect of our society is the fact that some people are richer than others, some have more power than others, and some receive more respect than others. You have probably used phrases like "working class," "middle class," and "upper class" to refer to a person's social standing. And you are probably aware of some of the differences among the social classes. Knowing a person's social class, or place in the social stratification system, is important to sociologists, because the more they know about social stratification, the more they know about many other aspects of human behavior. Divorce rates, family size, incidence of mental illness, and participation in formal groups are just a few of the social factors that are related to social class.

Where do social classes come from? Inequality in money, power, and prestige had its beginnings in the division of labor. Those who had the talent and the ability to take on the more complex jobs had to be offered greater rewards as an incentive to acquire the necessary skills. In this chapter, we focus on the situation in America today: how much inequality exists, how that inequality affects our life chances and our lifestyles, and how we can change our social status by moving up and down the social ladder.

Is some system of social stratification, with its unequal distribution of rewards, really necessary? <u>Functional theorists</u> say "yes," if a society wants its most able people to accept important positions. <u>Conflict theorists</u> disagree, saying that the struggle over scarce rewards is the basis for a class system. Conflict theorists, notably Karl Marx, envision an ideal society in which there are no classes.

8
Stratification and Mobility

Throughout recorded time, and probably since the end of the Neolithic Age, there have been three kinds of people in the world, the High, the Middle, and the Low.

The aims of these groups are entirely irreconcilable. The aim of the High is to remain where they are. The aim of the Middle is to change places with the High. The aim of the Low, when they have an aim — for it is an abiding characteristic of the Low that they are too much crushed with drudgery to be more than intermittently conscious of anything outside their daily lives — is to abolish all distinctions and create a society in which all men shall be equal.
—GEORGE ORWELL, *1984*

High, Middle, Low; Upper Class, Middle Class, Working Class; the "haves" and the "have nots" — all these expressions describe the inequalities in human societies, and *inequality* is what **social stratification** is all about. The dream of living in a classless society is ancient and persistent, but the real world in which people live is marked by inequalities in rewards, privileges, prestige, and power.

In Chapter 5, we explored the organization of human societies, noting that in any social system there are a number of interrelated positions. As long as these positions are merely different, we can think of them as *horizontal* divisions of the social system. But there is also a *vertical* dimension to societies that has to do with the *ranking* of positions, and consequently, of the people who fill them. In societies with a stratification system, whole categories of positions are ranked, giving rise to expressions like the "High," the "Middle," and the "Low," as used by George Orwell. Orwell also noted that people are concerned with what sociologists call **social mobility:** movement up or down the social status ladder. Those at the top, Orwell claimed, want to prevent their own downward mobility, while the others want to achieve upward mobility. Orwell described those at the bottom as being "crushed with drudgery," an accurate description of the lives of people who are, as we put it in the United States, "below the poverty level."

There are many questions about social stratification that sociologists have tried to answer, among them:

1. How long has there been a vertical dimension in human societies? How did class, or stratification, systems come into being?
2. What kinds of inequality exist in modern societies, such as the United States? How much inequality is there? What difference does it make?
3. To what extent are places in strata inherited? What is known about the process and extent of social mobility?
4. Are stratification systems functionally necessary for the survival or well-being of modern societies?

Many sociology departments devote entire courses to the study of stratification alone. In this chapter, we cannot possibly deal comprehensively with the extensive research and theory on the subject. But we can at least address ourselves to these four sets of questions and present some of the answers to them that sociologists have developed.

THE ORIGINS OF INEQUALITIES

At the hunting and gathering stage of civilization, small communities of humans divided the work on the basis of age and sex. As among the !Kung Bushmen described in Chapter 5, the men and older boys were expected to hunt, while the women and children were expected to gather fruit, nuts, and berries. No one owned the land that yielded up the food, so there was no substantial property to pass from generation to generation. Rewards, in the form of food, were more or less equally distributed, and there was no way for wealth to accumulate in certain families or in certain groups of families. To be sure, there were a few special roles, such as *shaman*, or medicine man, that were rewarded more than the usual work roles, and the incumbents were treated better than the rest of the men and women; but, basically, there was little inequality at this stage of human culture.

As the hunting and gathering stage moved into the horticultural stage, and particularly, as agriculture developed, the vertical organization in human societies became more pronounced. With agricultural surpluses, more people could withdraw from the age-old task of producing food. The division of labor became more complex: there were carpenters, potters, metal workers, and other craftsmen, as well as such positions as scribe, priest, city official, merchant, and tradesman.

Try to imagine the evolution of human society from a stage with a simple division of labor to one with an increasingly complex division of labor. Just as at earlier stages, it was necessary that the various jobs be performed, but the jobs could no longer be assigned on the basis of age and sex. Recruitment for occupations became a new challenge. The response to this was the creation of a system of differential rewards that would persuade people to compete for the jobs. The more important jobs, and those requiring greater skill, carried higher rewards, so that they would be filled by people who had or were willing to acquire the necessary skills. The menial tasks, also very necessary, went to those who were less skillful or who could not avoid being compelled to perform them. It was unnecessary to reward these tasks greatly, for there always seemed to be more ordinary people than truly talented ones. The system of assigning differential rewards to occupations, while assuring that all jobs would be filled, led to more rigid vertical dimensions in society: the rich and the poor, the "haves" and the "have nots." Land, small shops, and trades were passed from father to son, giving a certain rigidity to the new system of classes.

Going from a stage of assigning work on the basis of sex and age to one in which occupations were grouped and rewarded unequally represented a major change in human societies. And with the agricultural and industrial revolutions, the division of labor became vastly more intricate. More and more people were allowed, and indeed, were required, to seek work off the farm. In addition, it was during this period that there was a spurt in the growth rate of human populations. So, we find both more people and more positions in society. The basic societal task of assuring that the many intermeshing positions were filled assumed greater proportions. Coordinating the work of thousands of new workers, so that all the jobs would somehow fit together, became a managerial problem; and persuading people to fill the positions became the function of the stratification system.

There may be other ways of getting positions filled in societies with an intricate division of labor, but the system of rewarding incumbents differently and treating them differently was one solution to the problem.

BASIC STRATIFICATION CONCEPTS

We will return to the question of the necessity for social stratification at the end of the chapter. The bulk of the chapter will be spent investigating the stratification system in one society, the United States, in hopes of providing a better picture of the total impact of a stratification system, with its desirable and undesirable features. But, first, let us take a brief look at some basic stratification concepts.

Class, Stratum, and Rank

Early sociologists borrowed the term *strata* from geologists, who used it to describe layers of rock. A vertical cut into a mountainside reveals these layers, each one more or less distinct and laid atop another. The early sociologists saw the term as descriptive of societies in which people could be placed in different categories and in which the categories themselves could be ranked one above the other. The criterion that separated each layer, or *class*, from the others was its level of social rewards—wealth, power, prestige, and other related social traits.

The analogy is more descriptive of some societies than of others. Under feudalism, for example, there were noblemen, freemen, and serfs. Although some differences in privileges and rewards could be found within each group, feudal society clearly had three distinct classes of people. Everyone knew to which class he or she belonged, and all agreed on which class was highest and which was lowest.

A large, complex society does not exactly fit the analogy to geological strata. In a society like ours, the vertical hierarchy of social rank does not seem to break down into a given number of distinct categories, or strata, as it did in feudal times. In the United States, differences in prestige, wealth, and other variables seem to shade into one another as we go up or down the status hierarchy (see Cuber and Kenkel, 1954).

Without distinct, separate strata, it is not literally correct to talk of social classes in the United States, but the concept of **social class** is still useful for describing our society. We can talk of the upper, middle, and lower class in much the same way that we speak of old age, middle age, and youth. That is, there may not be distinct lines between such categories, but broad differences are discernible. For some purposes, finer gradations, such as upper-upper or lower-lower class, may be useful. As long as some approximate portion of the status hierarchy is being distinguished from other segments, there should be no confusion in calling these portions *social classes.*

Although we have talked about social stratification as if it were a single system, the sociologist Max Weber distinguished among three stratification systems in society: (1) the economic order, (2) the honorific, or prestige order, and (3) the power structure (see Gerth and Mills, 1946; Henderson and Parsons, 1947). According to Weber, each of us has not one rank in society but *three,* and our three ranks do not necessarily match one another. The same person could rank very high in the power hierarchy, not quite so high in prestige or esteem, and lower still in economic position. Our behavior is affected by each of our three positions. To understand the totality of our behavior, the sociologist would have to determine all three of our ranks.

Much of the stratification research in the United States today concentrates on two of the dimensions identified by Weber: the economic and the prestige dimensions. Further, there has been considerable research into **status consistency**—that is, how similarly a person ranks on different dimensions of social class (see, for example, Kelly and Chambliss, 1966; Malewski, 1966). It has been proposed, for example, that people whose income places them lower in the status hierarchy than does their education would probably feel a certain dissatisfaction. This dissatisfaction, in turn,

Sanitation workers have low prestige but relatively good income—a good example of status inconsistency.

would affect their ideas and their behavior, such as how they vote or the likelihood of their joining a protest movement.

Social Mobility versus Social Rigidity

As we will see later in the chapter, ours is a society that offers *social mobility*—the possibility of moving up (as well as down) in the ranks of privilege, prestige, and power. But some societies today, like many societies in past history, have rigid systems. A society with a rigid stratification system—marked by classes clearly set apart from one another and with practically no movement among them—is said to have a **caste system.** A person born into a certain caste is totally restricted to its lifestyle, its privileges (if any), and its occupation or range of occupations. A person's friends and possible marriage partners come from the same caste, and one's children will be born, grow old, and die in the same caste.

For most of the Middle Ages, the feudal system was close to being a pure caste system. The caste system of India, which was ended by law only a little over a decade ago, was one of the oldest in the world (Gist, 1954; Hutton, 1946). There were originally four castes in India. From highest to lowest, they were the priestly, warrior, merchant, and worker castes. Over time, thousands of castes developed, each based primarily on a particular occupation. An intricate system of approach and avoidance governed social interaction between members of different castes. For example, if a lower caste person were to come closer than a certain distance to a higher caste person, the higher caste person would be polluted. A high caste person would also be polluted if the shadow of a low caste person fell on him or her, and he or she would have to be purified ritually.

Until the recent past, there were castelike qualities in the stratification system of the United States, with blacks constituting one caste and whites another. The rules governing social interaction and marriage between members of the two castes were about as rigid, as well understood, and as faithfully followed as those in the castes of India. Blacks, as members of the lower caste, could hold only certain jobs—those that carried the fewest rewards. Superimposed on the racial caste system was a sexual caste system. Women, as members of the lower caste, were restricted in their ability to own property, to vote and otherwise participate in the governance of society, and to hold prestigious and financially rewarding jobs. The castelike qualities, with regard to both race and sex, have crumbled in the United States, but they certainly have not disappeared completely.

In the ideal **open class system,** although differences in prestige and privilege would exist, the higher ranks could be readily attained by anyone with ambition and the necessary abilities. The occupation of physician, for example, might carry high prestige and financial rewards; but if one could get into medical school, one's abilities to learn and to perform would be the only requirements for becoming a doctor. In such a system, we would expect

For a caste system to work effectively there must be ways to distinguish caste membership. The shawl on this man's shoulder, the way he wears his turban, and particularly the mark on his forehead show that he is from a high caste in Northern India.

to find many people moving up and down the status hierarchy from the classes into which they were born, for there would be no arbitrary or artificial barriers to such movement.

There is no known society that has such an ideal open class system, however. Continuing with our example of the physician, in the United States, a person is not barred from this position by virtue of his or her birth. However, those from wealthier families can better afford the cost of an education and the necessity to prolong the time before they will be working for a living than can those from poorer families. Industrialized societies, such as our own, are certainly much closer to the open class system than to the caste system. And, it is possible to designate where in the range from caste to open class any given society falls. Later in this chapter, we will deal with mobility and the barriers to it in the United States. But now, let's turn to the existing social stratification in this country.

DIFFERENTIAL REWARDS IN THE UNITED STATES

In any stratified society, people at different ranks receive different rewards. Almost anything that is valued by a group, that is scarce, and that is distributed unequally can be considered a reward. In industrial societies, the three common rewards are money, prestige, and power. **Money** enables a person to compete in the acquisition of scarce, valuable goods and to obtain privileges, such as hiring someone to perform undesirable tasks. **Prestige** is attributed to someone who does something, has something, or is something that is valued by the group. An individual receives prestige, admiration, or esteem by occupying a position of importance or by having possessions that are valued. **Power,** the ability of a person to control the behavior of others, even over their opposition, is also distributed unequally in society. The sociologist Gerhard Lenski (1966) sees power as the basic element in a stratification system, for with power one can acquire privileges and be granted prestige. Lenski sees prestige as a function of both power and privilege: the more power and privilege people have, the more esteem they have.

The relationships among the basic inequalities—wealth, prestige, power—are quite complex. Money, for example, can be translated into power. A wealthy person may win election to a political office because of a well-financed campaign. The power that comes from the office can, in turn, be used to increase the politician's wealth. Furthermore, someone with high prestige will have an easier time getting a loan than someone with low prestige. The loan can be used to finance a business enterprise, thereby increasing the person's wealth. Or it can be used to finance a political campaign, which, if successful, will increase the person's power. It is such relationships among prestige, wealth, and power that give credence to the saying, "The rich get richer while the poor get poorer."

Income Inequalities

Income inequalities are a fact of life in American society. Adding some of the percentages in Table 8.1 shows that 47 percent of white families have an income of $15,000 or more, whereas about 18 percent make less than $7,000 (about $134 per week). Fifteen percent of the white families are very well off, with $25,000 or more in annual income; while seven percent of the white families are very poor, making less than $4,000 a year.

Table 8.1 also shows that race is part of our stratification system. About

TABLE 8.1   Income Distribution in the United States, 1975

Total Annual Income	Percentage of White Families	Percentage of Black Families
Under $2,000	1.8	5.2
$2,000–2,999	1.9	7.0
$3,000–3,999	2.9	7.9
$4,000–4,999	3.6	8.3
$5,000–5,999	3.9	6.3
$6,000–6,999	4.0	5.9
$7,000–7,999	4.2	5.4
$8,000–8,999	4.4	5.1
$9,000–9,999	4.0	5.0
$10,000–11,999	8.9	9.8
$12,000–14,999	13.8	10.8
$15,000–24,999	31.7	18.2
$25,000–49,999	13.6	4.9
$50,000 and over	1.5	0.1

Source: U.S. Bureau of the Census, *Current Population Reports* (Washington, D.C.: U.S. Government Printing Office, 1977), series P-60, no. 105, p. 37.

TABLE 8.2   Median Annual Income of Full-time Workers 18 Years Old and Over, by Race, Sex, and Education

	Median Annual Income			
	White		Black	
Years of School Completed	Male	Female	Male	Female
Elementary				
0–7	$ 8,879	$ 5,193	$ 7,623	$ 4,549
8	10,592	5,856	9,552	4,733
High School				
1–3	11,358	6,317	8,545	5,914
4	12,921	7,283	10,171	7,454
College				
1–3	14,379	8,533	12,115	8,767
4 or more	18,321	11,067	13,418	10,158

Source: U. S. Bureau of the Census, *Current Population Reports* (Washington, D.C.: U.S. Government Printing Office, 1977), series P-60, no. 105, pp. 198, 203.

41 percent of black families, as compared with less than 18 percent of white families, have an income of $7,000 per year or less. A much higher percentage of blacks than whites fall below $4,000 annual income. At the other extreme, only 23 percent of black families as compared to 47 percent of white families have a yearly income of $15,000 or more.

Table 8.2 presents the median annual income of workers. (You will recall from Chapter 2 that in a ranking from highest to lowest, the *median* is the midpoint; half earn more and half earn less than the median.) The data show that not only race but also sex is part of our stratification system.

In an industrial society with a heavy demand for skilled and managerial workers, it is reasonable to expect that those with little education would not earn as much as the better educated. But look at the data. At each educational level, black males earn less than white males; in other words, a high school or a college education is worth less for black than for white males. Data in the table also show that with the same education, women, whether black or white, earn less than men. Since the data are for year-round, full-time workers, the differences in earnings of men and women cannot be accounted for by the fact that more women than men work part-time.

In part, this inequality stems from the fact that women often drop out of the labor force to bear and rear children, and upon their reentry into the job market, they find that the value of their work skills has diminished. This inequality, however, is also built into the stratification system. In general, it is the skills of women, and not those of men, that lose value. Moreover, women are more likely than men to be *underemployed*—that is, to be working at less than their full capacity; for example, a female college graduate working as a typist would be underemployed. The underemployment of women is also part of our stratification system. In a similar manner blacks, Chicanos, and other minorities are often underemployed, because they have difficulty finding jobs in keeping with their education and training.

Over the last 30 years, the average family income in the United States has increased more than threefold. Part of the increase is due to inflation—it takes more dollars to buy goods or services. It is also true that real purchasing power has increased, which means that as a nation we are wealthier than we were 30 years ago. From the standpoint of our stratification system, the important question is whether the various income groups have participated equally in the increasing wealth of the nation. If the incomes of the poor, the middle groups, and the rich have all increased at the same rate, their relative positions have not changed at all.

Some claim that income inequalities in the United States are narrowing and that this aspect of our stratification system is becoming less extreme. The truth of this claim can be tested by comparing the shares of the total national income received by various income groups at different times. We can determine, for example, whether the 20 percent of the families with the lowest income now receive a larger or smaller share of the total national income than they did 10, 20, or 60 years ago. If we look at Table 8.3, we can see that the top 20 percent of income recipients have received a larger share of the national income than the bottom 60 percent for the last 65 years. What is more, since 1910, the lowest 20 percent has experienced a definite loss in its share of income, even though it has regained a little since 1960. Thus,

TABLE 8.3 How the Total Income is Distributed: Percentage Share Received by Each Fifth of Families, 1910–1977*

	Lowest Fifth	2nd Fifth	3rd Fifth	4th Fifth	Highest Fifth
1977	5.2	11.6	17.5	24.2	41.5
1970	5.4	12.2	17.6	23.8	40.9
1960	4.8	12.2	17.8	24.0	41.3
1950	4.5	11.9	17.4	23.6	42.7
1910	8.3	11.5	15.0	20.0	46.2

*While the distribution has generally remained about the same, the lowest 20 percent of all families now receive a smaller share of the national income than they did in 1910.

Source: Data for 1910 from Gabriel Kolko, *Wealth and Power in America* (New York: Frederick A. Praeger, 1962), p. 14. Other data from U.S. Bureau of the Census, *Current Population Reports* (Washington, D.C.: U.S. Government Printing Office, 1978), series P-60, no. 116, p. 11.

in general, for the last 65 years the extent of inequalities in income has remained about the same.

Prestige Inequalities

Many sociologists who study the effects of the stratification system on social interaction and human behavior use *occupational prestige* as an indicator of a person's rank in the system. The scales measuring occupational prestige were developed by determining, through questionnaires distributed to large samples of people, how Americans rate certain occupations.

The prestige scores of occupations in the United States, as given in Table 8.4, changed very little between 1947 and 1963, and they have remained about the same up to the present. The prestige of the policeman and the nuclear physicist have increased a little, while that of the radio announcer has dropped some, but basically, the prestige system has been remarkably stable. As a matter of fact, the sociologists who conducted the 1963 study report that the prestige of occupations in the United States has not changed very much since 1925 (Hodge, Siegel, and Rossi, 1964).

Cross-cultural studies suggest that an occupation carries essentially the same prestige in different societies. Alex Inkeles and Peter Rossi (1965) studied the prestige of occupations in six industrialized societies: the United States, Great Britain, the Soviet Union, Japan, New Zealand, and Germany. Robert Hodge and others at the National Opinion Research Center compared occupational prestige in the United States and 23 other countries, both industrialized and developing (Hodge, Treiman, and Rossi, 1966). These studies found a striking similarity in the prestige of occupations from country to country. (Hodge and his associates caution, however, that only occupations found in all of the societies studied can be used in comparative analyses.)

The Hodge study concludes with the intriguing hypothesis that in order for a country to develop economically it must first adopt a modern stratification system for occupations. Developing countries must persuade people to train for the skilled, clerical, managerial, and professional positions necessary in an industrial economy. One way of doing so is to afford these positions the same sort of prestige they carry in already industrialized countries.

As you look down the list of occupations in Table 8.4, note that almost all of them are jobs traditionally held by males. The underlying assumption of early stratification research was that the husband's occupation alone defined the social class of the family. It was the husband's link to the economic system that determined how the family lived and how it was ranked by others. In the past, when few women, married or single, worked outside the home, these assumptions may not have been in error, but today they have become increasingly questionable. More and more married women are pursuing careers, a fact often not reflected in the statistics.

TABLE 8.4   Occupational Prestige Ratings, 1963 and 1947

Occupation	1963 Score	1947 Score
U.S. Supreme Court Justice	94	96
Physician	93	93
Nuclear physicist	92	86
Scientist	92	89
Government scientist	91	88
State governor	91	93
Cabinet member in the federal government	90	92
College professor	90	89
U.S. Representative in Congress	90	89
Chemist	89	86
Lawyer	89	86
Diplomat in U.S. Foreign Service	89	92
Dentist	88	86
Architect	88	86
County judge	88	87
Psychologist	87	85
Minister	87	87
Member of the board of directors of a large corporation	87	86
Mayor of a large city	87	90
Priest	86	86
Head of a department in state government	86	87
Civil engineer	86	84
Airline pilot	86	83
Banker	85	88
Biologist	85	81
Sociologist	83	82
Instructor in public schools	82	79
Captain in the regular army	82	80
Accountant for a large business	81	81
Public school teacher	81	78
Owner of a factory that employs about 100 people	80	82
Building contractor	80	79
Artist who paints pictures that are exhibited in galleries	78	83
Musician in a symphony orchestra	78	81
Author of novels	78	80
Economist	78	79
Official of an international labor union	77	75
Railroad engineer	76	76
Electrician	76	73
County agricultural agent	76	77
Owner-operator of a printing shop	75	74
Trained machinist	75	73
Farm owner and operator	74	76
Undertaker	74	72
Welfare worker for a city government	74	73
Newspaper columnist	73	74
Policeman	72	67

Occupation	1963 Score	1947 Score
Reporter on a daily newspaper	71	71
Radio announcer	70	75
Bookkeeper	70	68
Tenant farmer — one who owns livestock and machinery and manages the farm	69	68
Insurance agent	69	68
Carpenter	68	65
Manager of a small store in a city	67	69
A local official of a labor union	67	62
Mail carrier	66	66
Railroad conductor	66	67
Traveling salesman for a wholesale concern	66	68
Plumber	65	63
Automobile repairman	64	63
Playground director	63	67
Barber	63	59
Machine operator in a factory	63	60
Owner-operator of a lunch stand	63	62
Corporal in the regular army	62	60
Garage mechanic	62	62
Truck driver	59	54
Fisherman who owns his own boat	58	58
Clerk in a store	56	58
Milk route man	56	54
Streetcar motorman	56	58
Lumberjack	55	53
Restaurant cook	55	54
Singer in a nightclub	54	52
Filling station attendant	51	52
Dockworker	50	47
Railroad section hand	50	48
Night watchman	50	47
Coal miner	50	49
Restaurant waiter	49	48
Taxi driver	49	49
Farm hand	48	50
Janitor	48	44
Bartender	48	44
Clothes presser in a laundry	45	46
Soda fountain clerk	44	45
Share-cropper — one who owns no livestock or equipment and does not manage farm	42	40
Garbage collector	39	35
Street sweeper	36	34
Shoe shiner	34	33
Average	71	70

Source: Robert W. Hodge, Paul M. Siegal, and Peter H. Rossi, "Occuptional Prestige in the United States: 1925–1963," *American Journal of Sociology* 70 (November 1964), 286–302.

The lower the social class, the larger the family size. What are some of the disadvantages these children are likely to experience because of their class position?

One recent study of 566 married women found that they derived class position from their own occupation, not from their husband's (Kanter, 1976). Such research calls into question the whole matter of whether families or individuals should be considered the unit of social class. If whole families have a single class position, how does one take into account the different occupational rankings of a husband and wife? When both husband and wife are employed, does the family's class depend on the higher of the occupational prestige rankings, on the lower, or on some kind of average of the two? There are similar problems with using income as an index of social class in two-career families. Surely, there is a difference, in terms of prestige and social recognition, between a family where two members earn a total income of $20,000 and one in which one member earns the same amount. But how do you measure the difference? As our society and its stratification system change, sociologists need to develop new research methods to determine how people rank each other. To date, only a limited amount of work has been done in this area.

THE IMPORTANCE OF SOCIAL CLASS

The study of social stratification is one of the most significant areas of sociological research. Part of its importance stems from the fact that knowledge of a person's social status is extremely crucial in understanding and predicting his or her behavior. From birth to death, in almost countless ways, our social status affects what happens to us, what we do, and even how we think and what we believe. (To which social class do you belong? See Box 8.1.) Because social traits are generally so closely linked to social class, it was once commonly believed that the link was biological—that is, that social traits were genetically determined. Ample sociological evidence has proven otherwise. And we now know that a person's social traits tend to change as he or she moves from one social class to another. Nevertheless, the social class into which we are born affects both our *life chances* and our *lifestyles*.

FIGURE 8.1 Infant Deaths per 1,000 Live Births, by Family Income and Race

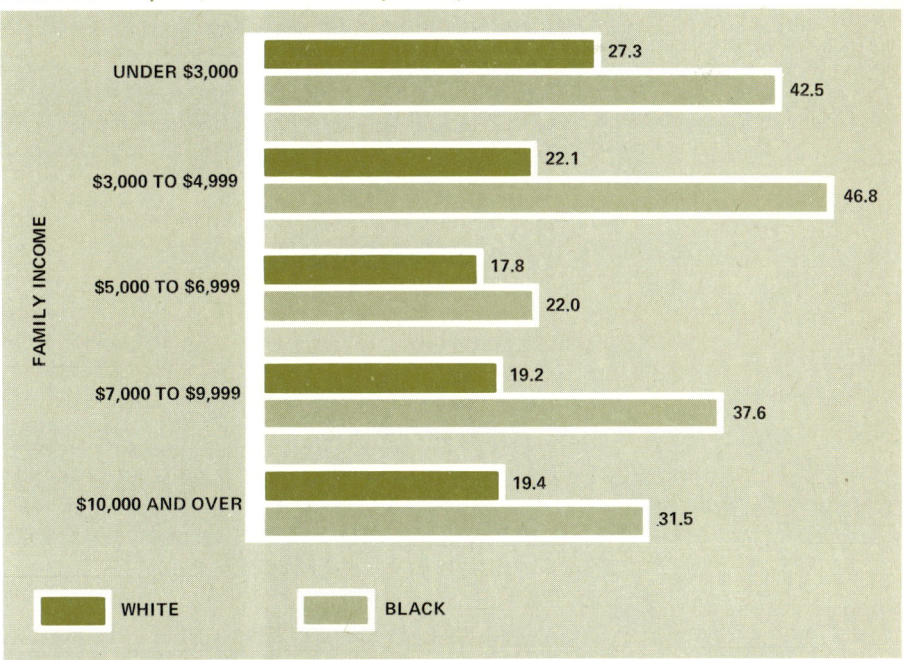

Family Income	White	Black
Under $3,000	27.3	42.5
$3,000 to $4,999	22.1	46.8
$5,000 to $6,999	17.8	22.0
$7,000 to $9,999	19.2	37.6
$10,000 and over	19.4	31.5

The lower the family income, the less the chances are that an infant will live through the first year of life. The odds are even lower for the infant if its parents are black.

Source: U.S. Department of Health, Education and Welfare, *Infant Mortality Rates: Socioeconomic Factors: 1972* (Washington, D.C.: U.S. Government Printing Office, 1973), p. 13.

Social Class and Life Chances

When we say that **life chances** vary with social status, we mean that the odds of receiving an advantage or suffering a disadvantage in some impor-

---

**BOX 8.1
TO WHICH SOCIAL CLASS DO YOU BELONG?**

Would you like to know to which social class your family belongs? Sociologists use a variety of methods to discover how people rank one another. One of these is the Index of Social Position developed by the sociologist August B. Hollingshead (Hollingshead and Redlich, 1958, pp. 389–398). The index is based on the assumption that a family's class can be estimated if one knows a few important characteristics of the family. First, one must know the occupation of the family head, for occupations differ in the amount of prestige assigned to them, and it is the occupation, usually, that provides the family income. One must know where the family lives, for residential area tells us much about the family's lifestyle, and to some extent, about how the family spends its money. Finally, one must know the educational level of the family head, for people at a given educational level have similar tastes and attitudes, and education reflects the general social and cultural values of a family.

It is not too complicated to compute your family's social class if you know these three status characteristics. The first step is to assign numerical values to the residential, occupational, and educational rank of the family. Next, the three scores are each multiplied by weights determined by Hollingshead. The weights reflect the fact that some status characteristics are more important than others when it comes to why and how people rank one another.

The residence scale is the most subjective and perhaps the most difficult to use. It amounts to assigning a score value of 1 to 6 to all homes in a community. The finest homes in the best section of the city receive a value of 1; the poorest tenements or most run-down houses get a score of 6. Try to score your family's home. It may help, first, to determine whether it is about average (score 3 or 4), below average (score 5 or 6), or above average (score 1 or 2). Now, you should be able to narrow it down a little more. For example, if you rank the house about average, give it a score of 4 if you think most people in your community would consider it on the low side of average, but otherwise, give it a 3.

The occupational and educational scales each have seven points, as follows:

Score	Occupation	Education
1	Executives of large corporations; major professionals, such as physicians	Received a professional or graduate degree (beyond B.A.)
2	Managers of medium-sized businesses, lesser professionals	Completed four years of college and received a degree

tant aspect of our social lives is dependent on social status. For example, we know that juvenile delinquency, at least as it is officially measured, occurs less frequently in the upper class than it does in the lower class. We know, too, that more lower- than upper-class people are hospitalized as schizo-

3	Administrators in large concerns, owners of small businesses, semiprofessionals	Some college but did not complete four years
4	Owners of little businesses, clerical and sales workers, technicians	Graduated from high school
5	Skilled workers	Some high school
6	Semiskilled workers	Completed ninth grade
7	Unskilled workers	Less than seven years of school

From these scales, select the score that best fits your father's occupation and education. Now, multiply the occupational score by 9, the educational score by 5, and the previously selected residential score by 6. Finally, add the three weighted scores for the total social class value.

For example, if the head of the family is a skilled worker in a factory, the weighted occupational score would be 5 × 9, or 45. If he completed high school, he would get an educational score of 4 × 5, or 20. And if the family home is on the low side of average, the residence score would be 4 × 6, or 24. The total is 89.

The final step is to determine the social class that corresponds to the total score, using the following values:

Range of Scores	Class
20-31	I
32-55	II
56-86	III
87-115	IV
116-134	V

You may have had some trouble determining your family's social class. A specific occupation may be hard to relate to the categories listed. Or perhaps both your parents work, and the combined income allows the family to live better than if only one parent were employed. Or maybe your mother's job or education ranks higher than your father's. Sociologists are working on problems like these in order to develop better measures of social class.

For most families, the Hollingshead method gives a good approximation of social class position. Remember, what it reflects is not how Professor Hollingshead ranks your family but what your social standing is as judged by other people in this society.

phrenics (Hollingshead and Redlich, 1958). This does not mean, however, that schizophrenia and juvenile delinquency occur *only* in the lower class. It is a matter of probability. Although both occur in all classes, it is also true that both occur more frequently in the lower class.

Many other advantages and disadvantages vary with social class. But sociologists generally restrict the concept of "life chances" to important events and to characteristics that have fairly high social approval or disapproval, even if these terms must be rather loosely defined. Take, for ex-

FIGURE 8.2 Occupations and Poverty Status of Fathers of Servicemen Killed in Vietnam Compared to Fathers of High School Seniors

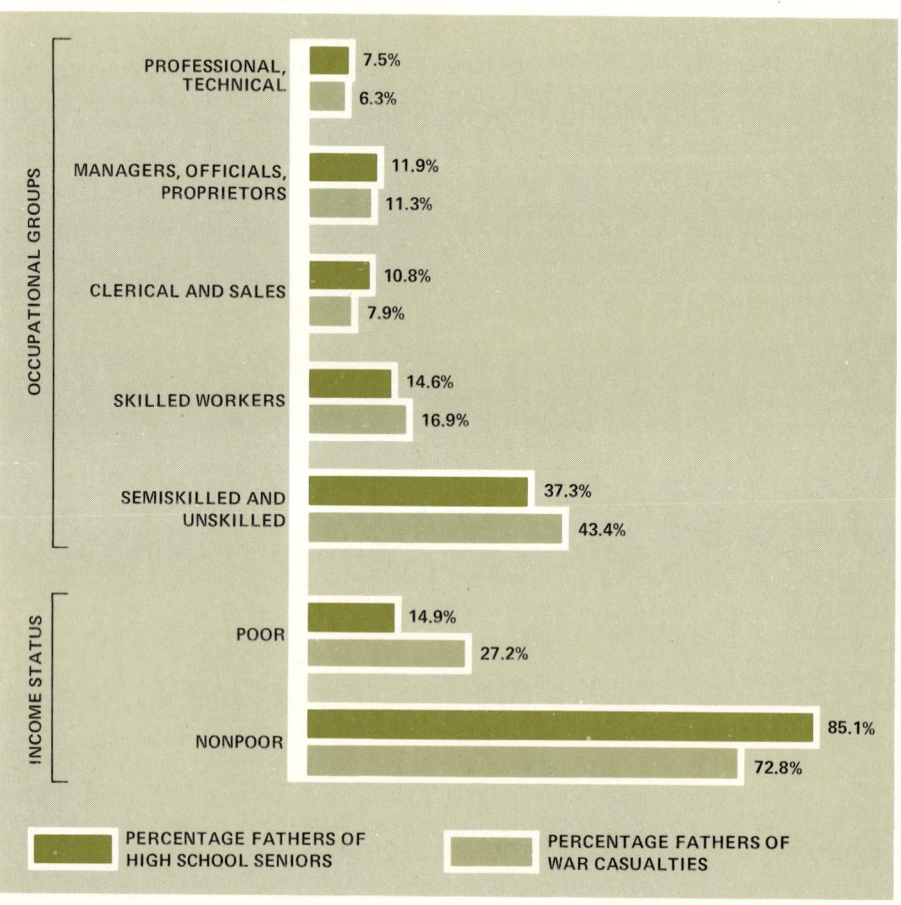

OCCUPATIONAL GROUPS

Group	Fathers of High School Seniors	Fathers of War Casualties
PROFESSIONAL, TECHNICAL	7.5%	6.3%
MANAGERS, OFFICIALS, PROPRIETORS	11.9%	11.3%
CLERICAL AND SALES	10.8%	7.9%
SKILLED WORKERS	14.6%	16.9%
SEMISKILLED AND UNSKILLED	37.3%	43.4%

INCOME STATUS

Status	Fathers of High School Seniors	Fathers of War Casualties
POOR	14.9%	27.2%
NONPOOR	85.1%	72.8%

■ PERCENTAGE FATHERS OF HIGH SCHOOL SENIORS
▪ PERCENTAGE FATHERS OF WAR CASUALTIES

These graphs compare the occupations and incomes of fathers of servicemen from Wisconsin killed in Vietnam with the occupations and incomes of fathers of Wisconsin high school students in general. Zeitlin et al. conclude: "The sons of the poor and of the workers have borne by far the greatest burden of the war in Vietnam, in the measured but immeasurable precision of death" (p. 328).

Source: Maurice Zeitlin, Kenneth G. Lutterman, and James W. Russell, "Death in Vietnam: Class, Poverty and the Risks of War," *Politics and Society* 3 (Spring 1973), pp. 313–328.

ample, infant mortality. It may be inhumane to inform a group of new mothers that the probability that their child will survive its first year depends on their social class, but it is true statistically. For a long time, the infant mortality rate has varied inversely with social class. Why? For one thing, low-income mothers are less able to afford proper nutrition while they are pregnant. They are also less able to afford good medical services during pregnancy and for the child after it's born.

Another aspect of American society that has varied by social class for the last 100 years is family size: the higher the social class, the fewer the children in the family—although the size of the difference is now narrowing (see Kenkel, 1977, pp. 221–227). A child's life chances are affected by this inverse relationship because the scarce financial resources of the lower-class family have to be spread among many people, while the greater resources of the middle- and upper-class families are distributed among fewer people.

Throughout our lives, our destinies are affected by social status. Lower-class children are less likely than upper- or middle-class children to do well in school. From their parents, they have probably picked up the notion that school is dull and that education is not really important. From parents, too, children learn how to speak and dress and relate to adults. Lower-class children often do not speak correct (that is, educated) English. Nor are they as clean and as well dressed as their middle-class teachers think they should be.

Thus, while middle-class children meet with a certain consistency in their lives—parents and teachers reinforce each other and seem to agree on

FIGURE 8.3   Percentage of Unwanted Births Between 1956 and 1970, by Education of Mother

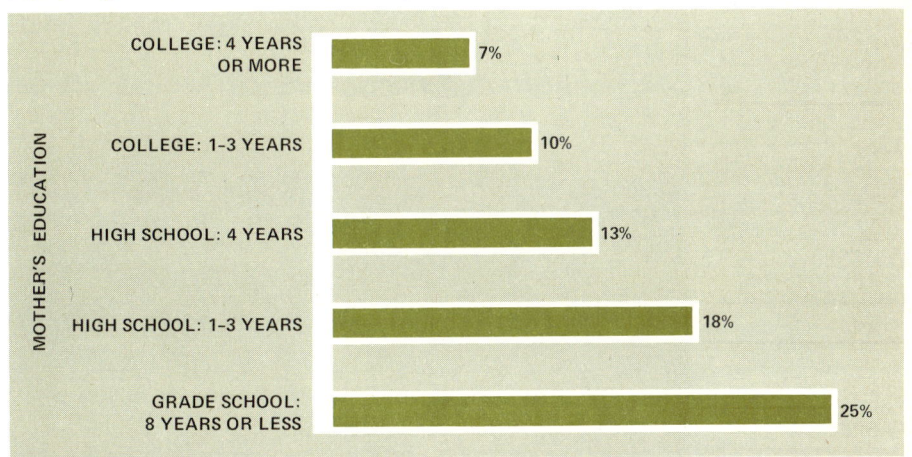

MOTHER'S EDUCATION

- COLLEGE: 4 YEARS OR MORE — 7%
- COLLEGE: 1–3 YEARS — 10%
- HIGH SCHOOL: 4 YEARS — 13%
- HIGH SCHOOL: 1–3 YEARS — 18%
- GRADE SCHOOL: 8 YEARS OR LESS — 25%

Whether or not the birth was planned, a child deserves to be wanted. The lower the social class, as measured by the mother's education, the more likely that one starts out in life as an unwanted child. The percentage presented in these graphs show the births to white women that were unplanned and unwanted.

Source: U. S. Bureau of the Census, Statistical Abstract of the United States: 1975 (Washington, D.C.: U.S. Government Printing Office, 1975), p. 57.

what is important in life and what is necessary to get ahead in the world—lower-class children meet, instead, with contradictions. Their teachers are not like the other adults they know: the teachers speak differently, dress differently, and most of all, expect different behavior of children. It is not surprising, then, that lower-class children do not like school and are more likely than middle- or upper-class children to decide that school is not for them. The school dropout rate has a strong inverse relationship with social class.

The lower the social class, the younger the age at which individuals marry, the more children they have, the greater the chance that they will divorce, and the younger they will be when they die. (Despite the presumed tensions, businessmen and professionals live longer, on the average, than unskilled and semiskilled workers.) As we look over the cycle from birth to death, it is quite apparent that the lower classes receive more of the disadvantages of life and fewer of the privileges than the higher classes. We must remember, though, that the relationship between social class and life chances is a matter of probability and therefore may not hold true for any particular individual. Nevertheless, we may whimsically conclude that the best advice to give a child is "Choose your parents carefully."

Social Class and Lifestyle

Although there are many differences in the **lifestyles** of people at different status levels, it must be remembered that not all lower-class people think or act one way, all middle-class people another way, and all upper-class people still a third way. Rather, there is a gradual shading in lifestyles as we ascend or descend the status ladder, and at every status level there are exceptional individuals.

Nevertheless, knowing a person's social status allows us to predict many

Low income means wearing older clothes, doing without a car, living in a poor and crowded neighborhood, in short, being denied many of the things that make for the good life.

STRATIFICATION AND MOBILITY

FIGURE 8.4 The Relationship Between Income and Happiness

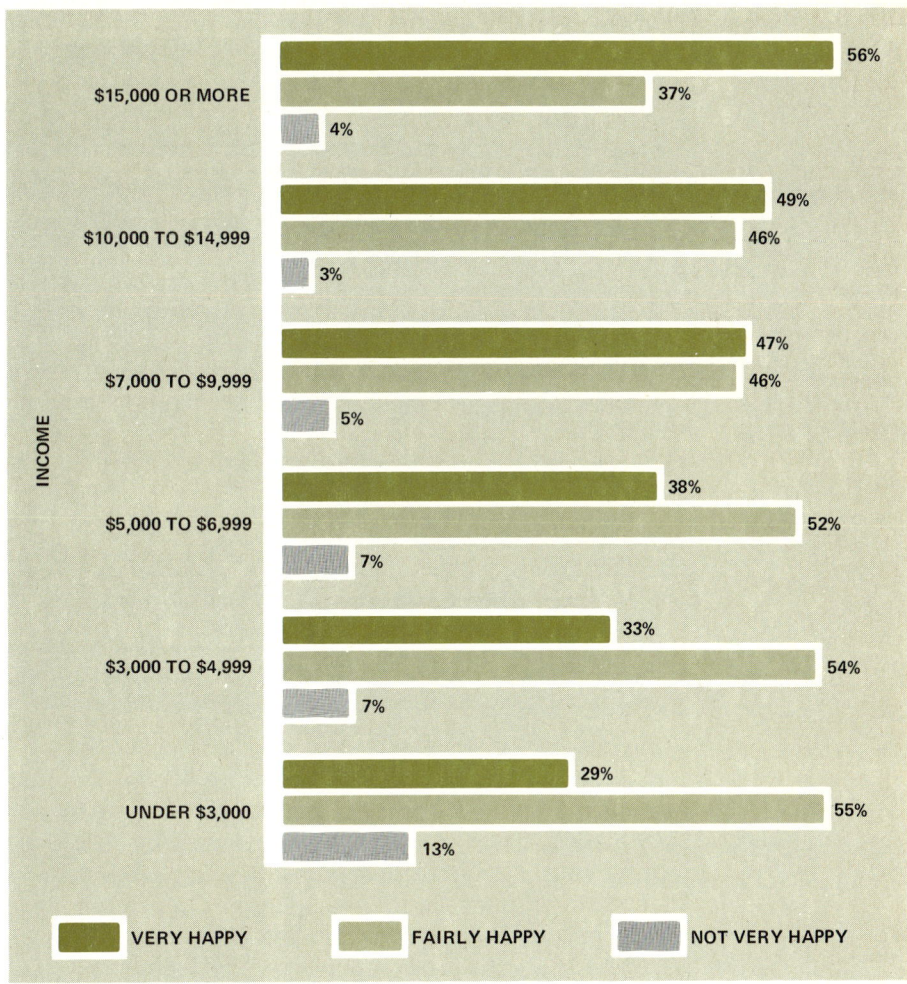

Income	Very Happy	Fairly Happy	Not Very Happy
$15,000 OR MORE	56%	37%	4%
$10,000 TO $14,999	49%	46%	3%
$7,000 TO $9,999	47%	46%	5%
$5,000 TO $6,999	38%	52%	7%
$3,000 TO $4,999	33%	54%	7%
UNDER $3,000	29%	55%	13%

Studies repeatedly find that the higher the income, the more likely persons are to report that they are "very happy," and the less likely they are to say that they are "very unhappy." Some, of course, are "poor but happy," but often, being poor, and therefore being denied much of "the good life," takes its toll on human happiness.

Source: *Gallup Opinion Index* (Princeton, N.J.: Gallup International, December 1970).

aspects of his or her style of life. In various significant ways, people of different social statuses think and feel differently, behave differently, and have a different way of life.

Material Possessions One of the more obvious differences among people of different classes is their possessions—the things that money can buy. Homes, automobiles, and clothing are among the more conspicuous posses-

FIGURE 8.5　Family Income and Household Burglary Rates

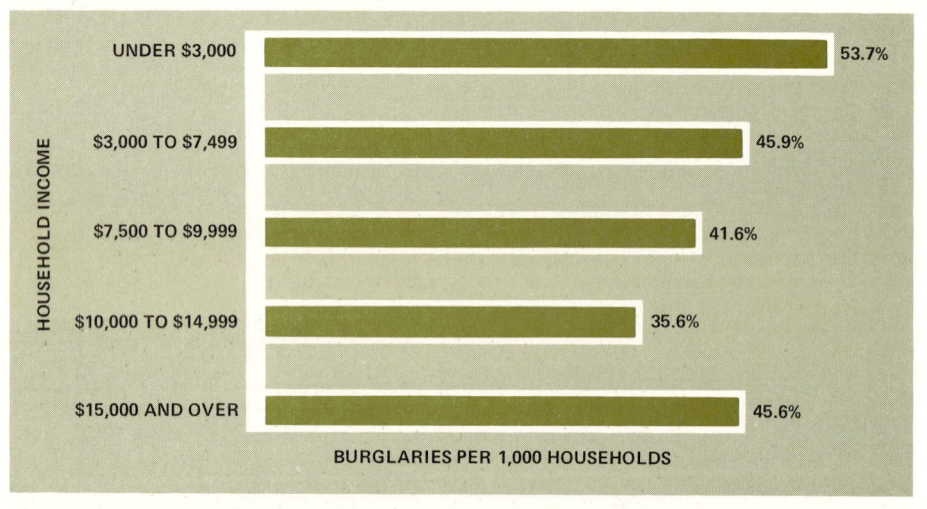

Household Income	Burglaries per 1,000 households
UNDER $3,000	53.7%
$3,000 TO $7,499	45.9%
$7,500 TO $9,999	41.6%
$10,000 TO $14,999	35.6%
$15,000 AND OVER	45.6%

Common sense might suggest that the homes of richer people would get burglarized more often than those of poorer people. Except for the highest income category, however, this is not the case. For those with an annual income of less than $15,000, the less money they have, the more likely it is that their home will be burglarized, showing another disadvantage of being poor.

Source: U.S. Bureau of the Census, *Statistical Abstract of the United States: 1975* (Washington, D.C.: U.S. Government Printing Office, 1975), p. 154.

sions that differentiate the social classes. These and many other goods are not distributed uniformly, either in amount or in quality. Some goods become *status symbols:* outward signs that the possessor has attained a certain economic or social rank. Those who are moving up are usually quick to acquire the symbols of their new rank. They buy a bigger home in a more prestigious area, trade their modest car for a larger one, and perhaps purchase fur coats for the women of the family.

The effects that material possessions have on a person's way of life also constitute major differences among the classes. Living in an overcrowded tenement is different from living in a modest tract house or a spacious mansion. One may have no fine clothes, only one set of Sunday clothes, or a closetful of fine clothing. The poor person may have to buy a worn-out used car, while the wealthy person can afford to buy a new Mercedes or Cadillac and trade it in for a new model every year. Such differences in material possessions affect how we feel about ourselves, how others see us, and how we behave.

Political-Economic Attitudes　Questionnaires, opinion polls, and area analyses of voting patterns all yield ample sociological evidence that people of different social classes think differently about political and economic issues; they perceive the world and its problems in different ways. (Many

The rich, of course, have more money than most people. They also have a wide range of social experiences and enjoy a full social life.

stratification theorists have stressed the different political and economic attitudes expressed by people of diverse ranks; this phenomenon has been called the *interest group theory of social classes.* For an early study in this area see Centers, 1949.)

Studies have shown, for example, that the lower the social class, the more likely one is to favor labor unions. Working-class people view various government regulations of business and industry as desirable, while the upper classes regard them as unnecessary interference. On the other hand, political scientists and sociologists have discovered that the exercise of constitutionally guaranteed civil liberties is positively related to social status. One study found that about two-thirds of professional and semiprofessional men had tolerant attitudes toward civil liberties, whereas about one-half of the clerical and sales workers and only 30 percent of the manual workers expressed tolerant attitudes (Lipset, 1959). Another study revealed that 66 percent of college graduates said that they voted in the most recent presidential election; yet only 58 percent of the high school graduates, and 43 percent of those who did not go beyond grade school voted in that election (U.S. Bureau of the Census, 1975, p. 450). What is more, there is a strong tendency for working-class people to vote Democratic and for upper-class people to vote Republican.

The list of specific differences in political and economic attitudes among social classes could be extended considerably. Actually, it is not hard to understand why the "haves" and the "have nots" perceive society and its problems differently, and why they hold different beliefs about how society's problems should be corrected.

Social Participation In many ways, our relations with others are affected by social class. The higher our social status, the more likely we are to belong to and participate in formal organizations and to hold leadership roles in them. Yet, lower-class people do not seem to compensate for their low participation in formal groups through informal contacts with close friends. One study found that while 30 percent of unskilled workers reported that they had no close friends, only 13 percent of skilled workers and 10 percent of the professional and businessmen reported no close friendships (Kahl, 1957).

The range of social contacts also varies by social class. Typically, upper-class people travel extensively, both in this country and abroad; their social sphere is often international, and they may maintain homes in different parts of the United States. Upper-middle class people may have vacationed in Europe once in their lives, but their sphere of activities is usually in their own section of the country. Many lower-class people live out their entire lives in one geographically restricted area.

In part, the patterns of social participation differ among the classes according to differences in the availability of money for traveling, the joining of formal groups, and the giving and attending of parties. Also, the knowledge and skill required to seek out compatible groups in one's own town or city are not distributed evenly by social class. And the social activities of the classes differ according to the values placed on belonging to groups and on interacting with others.

SOCIAL MOBILITY

Social mobility refers to the movement of a person from one position to another—**horizontal mobility** being a change in position without a change in prestige, and **vertical mobility** being movement up or down the status hierarchy. When sociologists use the term "social mobility," they usually mean *vertical mobility*. Most Americans believe that there is, or should be, a great deal of social mobility in the United States. "There's room at the top." "Any boy can grow up to be President." Although probably few believe the second claim anymore, if indeed they ever did, many people seem to believe that most individuals can improve their lot in life and rise above their parents' social position.

Before examining the social mobility pattern in the United States, let us first look at some basic concepts and at how social mobility is measured.

Types of Social Mobility

There are two kinds of vertical social mobility. First, and most commonly, we can move above or below the social status of our parents; this is called *intergenerational mobility.* One way that our status could be compared with that of our parents is by means of an occupational prestige scale, such as that in Table 8.4. We could see whether our occupational status is higher or lower than that of our parents, and if so, by how much. Although occupation is only one of many status characteristics, it can be used to determine how many mobile people there are. Further, if the data are available, we could compare the rates of vertical mobility in different societies or in one society at different periods of time.

The second type, *intragenerational mobility,* is movement upward or downward within a person's own working lifetime. Sociologists look at different periods of an individual's work life to see whether, in the course of his or her career, the person's status rose or fell. Not all career lines provide the same opportunities for advancement or promotion, so a rise in income or prestige that is normal in one type of job may be unusual upward mobility in another type. For this reason, intragenerational studies of upward mobility do not tell as much about the open or closed nature of the stratification system as do intergenerational studies.

Measurement of social mobility is more difficult than it might seem, particularly in specific cases. Take, for example, the son of an uneducated, unskilled worker. The son graduated from high school and operated a small business for a while. When the business failed, the son accepted unskilled employment, much like his father's. The son was upwardly mobile and then downwardly mobile, but the net lifetime result was no mobility at all. Studies of the same person at different times would reach quite different conclusions. And, what about the rise or fall of an entire occupation in the prestige hierarchy? We noted in Table 8.4 that the prestige of policemen rose and that of radio announcers declined from 1947 to 1963. Should a person who remained in either profession during that period of rise or decline be considered vertically mobile? These and other measurement difficulties make our conclusions about social mobility less precise than we would like them to be.

Technological Change and Social Mobility

When a society becomes industrialized, the increased need for workers is usually filled by taking people away from the farms. Industrialization, then, is bound to change the occupational structure of a society by creating new kinds of jobs. As it continues, industrialization moves people about in the stratification system. At the present stage of industrialization in the United States, more top-level, high-prestige positions are being created, and low-status, unskilled jobs are becoming increasingly scarce. People to fill the new top-level executive positions can come only from someplace lower in the status hierarchy. The growing complexity of our industrialized society demands more skilled workers and foremen, who come chiefly from the ranks of the unskilled. Thus, technological changes in the United States today have assured social mobility, much of it upward.

Fertility Differentials and Vertical Mobility

Traditionally, social status has been inversely related to family size. At times, the higher economic, educational, and occupational classes were not even replacing their numbers, and for a long time, they have not contributed their proportional share to the total population growth. This circumstance alone has made some room at the top. For example, assume that a society needs a certain proportion of professional workers in the general population. As the population grows, more professional workers are required in order to fill that need. Even if the children of every professional worker were to become professionals themselves, there would still be unfilled professional positions. These positions could be filled only from below, thus assuring some upward mobility. In recent years, the social class differences in family size have narrowed, but they have not disappeared. Thus, class differences in reproduction still help assure that there will be some social mobility in the United States, although these differences are not as strong a factor as they once were.

Extent of Occupational Mobility

Entrance of blacks and women into many areas of the labor market is so recent, and it is still on so minor a scale (although it is growing), that the main information on social mobility available deals with white males. The best estimate is that one-half to three-fourths of those in professional, business, clerical, and skilled labor positions have a higher position in the occupational prestige hierarchy than did their fathers. At least one-half of the men at any one of these levels see men like themselves around them—that is, men who have been upwardly mobile from the status of their fathers. It is no wonder that the stratification system appears to them to be open and fluid.

At the higher levels, both the total number of workers and their percentage of the total work force are relatively small. Even recruitment of half the professional workers from below produces upward mobility for only about three percent of the male labor force. It is true, too, that the sons of upper-level fathers tend to stay at that level. Their chances of remaining at the top are from five to eight times greater than for those who fill top positions from below. Thus, technological change, and not the downward mobility of the sons of high-status fathers, has produced upward mobility.

Between any two generations, advances in the status hierarchy are more likely to be short moves than dramatic "rags to riches" changes. This fact results in more mobile people; for, when one new top-level position is created, the odds are that it will be filled by someone from the middle ranks, thus creating a new vacancy in the middle. Perhaps three or four individuals can be mobile because of one new top-level position. If the new high-level position were filled by someone from the very bottom, as occasionally happens, only one person would be mobile. Although such major intergenerational changes do sometimes occur, the more modest rises of the masses are what produce our relatively high rate of vertical mobility.

Although international comparisons are difficult, the rate of social mobility, as determined by occupational changes, appears to be only slightly greater in the United States than in most European countries. This suggests that wherever massive technological change is to be found, it results in a certain amount of social fluidity.

Education is an excellent route for upward mobility, but it works better if you are white.

The surest pathway to upward social mobility is through education—at least for white males. Even though education has not yet worked so well for blacks and females, the data presented in Table 8.2 indicate that, even in these categories, the better educated earn more than the less educated. It is true that education, alone, will not allow a person, even a white male, to reach the very top, for it is almost impossible to enter the upper class, except by birth. For the masses, however, the more education one has, the better one's chances of moving upward and of competing successfully for the economic rewards of society. Current programs, such as Headstart and massive efforts to reduce the school dropout rate, should make the educational avenue of mobility available to more people. To the extent that such programs work, in the future there should be more competition for middle- and high-level positions.

IS SOCIAL STRATIFICATION NECESSARY?

In the opening section of this chapter, we saw that social stratification is an extremely old phenomenon. It goes back to the agricultural stage of human civilization, when specialization in work roles became too complex to allow the assignment of jobs solely on the basis of age and sex. The tremendous impact of the stratification system on the lives of all of us is bound to lead to one question: How necessary is it to have a stratification system? Even though it is an old social invention, is it inevitable that we retain a system of unequal distribution of rewards and privileges?

The *functional theory of stratification* holds that no society beyond a simple stage of civilization could exist or survive without a system of differential rewards and privileges. The reasoning of this theory begins with the fact that division of labor requires the creation of a number of different jobs, so that all the work will get done. But some jobs are more pleasant than others, some are more difficult than others, and some are more necessary than others. Because, in all societies, talent and intelligence are distributed unevenly, every society must have some system of differential rewards to motivate the most talented people to prepare themselves to fill the most important positions. (For a vision of a society in which even talents are equalized, see Box 8.2.) Lesser rewards are attached to less important positions, and the fewest rewards are attached to those positions requiring the least talent or training. Although this reasoning may seem persuasive, the question of whether a system of differential rewards and privileges is the only way to motivate talented people to undergo necessary training and to accept the important jobs still remains.

It is useful to consider groups that have tried to establish a classless society. One such group is the Israeli communal settlement, or kibbutz. In the kibbutz, it is held that all necessary work is good and that everyone should work for the good of the group, without regard for personal gain (Spiro, 1956). Each does what he or she is able to do, in accordance with the needs of the group, and all are rewarded equally. These small communal societies

BOX 8.2 EVERYONE HERE IS EQUAL

Many people have dreamed of living in, or of creating, a society in which everyone is equal. But how can this utopian vision be reconciled with the obvious fact that people are not equal? Some are more intelligent than others, some are healthier or stronger or prettier than others, some are more artistic than others, and various other talents and abilities are distributed unequally. You can't force people to be equal. Or can you? In his short story "Harrison Bergeron," Kurt Vonnegut, Jr. describes a society that achieved absolute equality and the price the society's members paid for it:

The year was 2081, and everyone was finally equal. They weren't only equal before God and the law. They were equal every which way. Nobody was better looking than anybody else. Nobody was stronger or quicker than anybody else. All this equality was due to the 211th, 212th, and 213th Amendments to the Constitution, and to the unceasing vigilance of agents of the United States Handicapper General.

In Vonnegut's fictional future, the government has been thorough in its efforts to produce equality. Those with above-average intelligence are required by law to wear a mental handicap radio in their ears. It is tuned to a government transmitter that sends out a sharp noise every 20 seconds to distract them from taking unfair advantage of their unequal intelligence. One man with above-average endurance has a canvas bag filled with 47 pounds of birdshot padlocked around his neck. Ballerinas performing on television wear masks, so that the plain and the beautiful are indistinguishable. The better dancers wear weight belts, so that they perform no better than the average dancers. People with particularly

have been able to avoid a stratification system up to a point. But the Israeli kibbutz is not a complete, self-sufficient industrialized society, for its members depend on the larger society for some key services, such as medical and dental care. They operate no banks, railroads, hospitals, or heavy industries. But the division of labor is more complex than that of a peasant society, for in the kibbutz there is light manufacturing, farming, and building of roads and houses. These societies, with egalitarianism as a core feature of their value system, have existed since the 1920s. While we cannot generalize from the kibbutz to modern, complex industrial societies, it is nevertheless apparent that, for some types of societies, a system of differential rewards is not necessary to assure that the various positions will be filled.

The functional theory of stratification has been sharply debated by some sociologists. Melvin Tumin (1953), for example, has dealt in detail with the dysfunctions of a stratification system. Such a system, Tumin maintains, limits the discovery and use of talent, because the talented among the poor are unlikely to develop or to be found. As a result, the productivity of society is impaired. In addition, according to Tumin, social inequalities encourage hostility, suspicion, and distrust among the social classes.

Other critics, such as Richard Simpson (1974), have pointed out that the

---

good eyesight are required to wear glasses that make their vision only normal.

The penalties for not wearing the various handicaps are severe, for such behavior indicates that one is basically antisocial or wants to return to the "dark ages," when people were not content to be average but liked to compete against their fellow citizens.

Few people would really like to live in the society portrayed by Vonnegut, with its absurd emphasis on equality. Yet we cannot dismiss the idea that there is a better way of life than one in which person is pitted against person to determine who is better or who gets more of something. How do we mesh the reward system of society with the fact of individual differences in talent and ability? This is at the heart of stratification problems. One solution would be to let people keep their differences but not to pass out rewards on the basis of such differences. In terms of Vonnegut's story, the person with above-average intelligence would work at a more responsible job but would not live better than someone of average intelligence. The talented ballerina, rid of her body weights, would perform better than a less-talented dancer, but both would receive the same pay and other rewards. The differences among us, whether innate or acquired, would not necessarily be played down, but neither would they carry differences in rewards.

What do you think about this plan? Would it work? Would it be good for society? For individuals?

importance of a position, in terms of the social welfare, is difficult to determine. Often, it seems that highly rewarded jobs, such as those of entertainers, are not intrinsically necessary for the survival of society but are important because the public thinks they are. In other cases, it appears questionable whether the magnitude of the reward is warranted, even if the position is necessary for our type of economic system and the talent required for the position is relatively scarce. For example, is it necessary to pay the chairman of the board of a large corporation 20 times the amount paid a school teacher in order to insure that a competent person will aspire to the executive position? Perhaps a fivefold difference in rewards would work as well. Criticisms, such as these, have not persuaded the functionalists that systems of differential rewards are not necessary or inevitable, and so the debate continues.

The *conflict theory of stratification* sees the roots of stratification in the continuing struggle between groups in society over scarce or limited rewards. Conflict theorists thus not only point to weaknesses in the functional theory but offer a substitute theory to explain why social classes exist.

Karl Marx was an important conflict theorist who dealt extensively with the importance of social classes. According to Marx, the key to where one belongs in the class system is whether or not one owns or controls some means of production. A factory, a shop, and land are all means of production, because goods are produced through this kind of property. A car or a house is property but is not usually a means of production. If, however, the car is used as a taxicab, or the house as a boarding house, these types of property would be considered means of production.

As Marx saw it, there are two basic classes. One, the **bourgeoisie,** consists of those who own or control the means of production. The other, the **proletariat,** consists of those who do not own any means of production and must sell their skills to those who do. The proletariat is the poorer but larger class; the bourgeoisie is much smaller but richer and more powerful.

No society has an infinite supply of goods or resources. The basic struggle, according to Marx and other conflict theorists, comes down to who gets how much of the scarce, or relatively scarce, goods and resources. Marx contended that the bourgeoisie realize that what gives them their many advantages in the struggle for scarce rewards is the fact that they control the means of production. They keep the workers poor, ignorant, and powerless and thus prevent them from achieving means of production of their own. The proletariat generally are not aware that their position will never improve unless they get control of the means of production. Marx felt that, eventually, the proletariat would recognize that they are being exploited and would revolt against the bourgeoisie. The numerically stronger proletariat would be the victors in such a conflict and would set up a "people's state" or "workers' society"—one in which the means of production would be held in common by everyone. There would thus be no more classes, no more struggles. Modern conflict theorists do not accept all of Marx's propositions, but they do hold that he made an important contribution, by showing us that conflict over scarce rewards is an important element of social stratification.

Modern structural-functionalists do not hold that the functional necessity for some stratification system dictates the *kind* of stratification system. Early functional theorists seemed to assume that the stratification system that has evolved in a given society is somehow the best possible system. This assumption ignores the fact that societies can tolerate a lot of inefficient and dysfunctional features. But societies can and do change. With regard to stratification, a society could come to stress honorific rewards instead of tangible rewards, such as income. There seems to be no inherent reason why there must be *great* differences in the rewards, whatever they are. A society can change from a rigid stratification system to one that is relatively open, allowing people to move up or down readily—and it can also change in the opposite direction. In sum, it is difficult to see how a modern society can avoid stratification entirely, but there is no reason to assume that our, or any other, system is the best possible human invention.

In the last several chapters, we have studied how societies are organized and held together. We have looked at the process of socialization and at the ways in which we become contributing members of our society. We have looked, too, at the positions we fill and the roles we play in groups, institutions, and social classes. It is now time to examine, in more detail, the five major institutions that are designed to meet our enduring physical and social needs. The next part of this book takes up each institution in turn, starting with the fundamental institution of the family.

SUMMARY

1. **Social stratification** is the division of society into layers based on the ranking of positions. **Social mobility** refers to movement from layer to layer, up or down. Social stratification evolved because division of labor leads to jobs with differential rewards—the greater the rewards, the higher the social status.

2. The layers, or strata, of society are referred to as **social classes.** Classes are differentiated by variations in wealth, power, and prestige. In some societies, these strata are clear-cut; in others, such as our own, classes seem to shade into each other.

3. According to Weber, there are three stratification systems in society: the economic order, the prestige order, and the power structure. One person could rank differently in each of these areas.

4. A **caste system** is one in which there is no social mobility—people are born, grow old, and die in the same caste. In an **open class system** there are no barriers to movement up or down the status hierarchy.

5. There are three basic inequalities in American society on which social stratification is based: money, prestige, and power. These three elements are highly interrelated.

6. In American society, black families have a significantly lower average income than white families, and women have lower incomes than men with comparable education.

7. Scales that measure occupational prestige have indicated that the prestige system in the United States has remained remarkably stable over the past 30 years. Furthermore, occupations appear to have similar prestige in all countries studied.

8. One's social class affects one's **life chances** and one's **lifestyle.** For example, infant mortality is high among the lower social classes; family size is smallest among the upper social classes. Overall, the lower the social class, the more one will experience the disadvantages of life. Lifestyles at various social levels vary with respect to material possessions, political-economic attitudes, and extent of social participation.

9. **Horizontal mobility** refers to a change in social position that does not involve a change in prestige; **vertical mobility** refers to social movement up and down the status hierarchy.

10. There are two types of vertical social mobility: *intergenerational mobility* (status change between generations) and *intragenerational mobility* (status change within one's own lifetime).

11. Among factors that affect social mobility in the United States are technological change, fertility differentials, and education.

12. According to the *functional theory of stratification,* advanced civilizations cannot exist without a system of differential rewards and punishments. Critics of this approach say that social inequalities impair productivity, because they limit the discovery and use of talented people. Other critics point out that some positions are disproportionately rewarded and that rewards could be less diverse between positions.

13. According to the *conflict theory of stratification,* social classes have developed out of the struggle over scarce resources. Marx proposed that those who own the means of production—the **bourgeoisie**—keep the workers—the **proletariat**—from acquiring their own means of production. Marx predicted that the struggle between these two major classes would end only when the means of production became commonly owned and classes ceased to exist.

KEY TERMS

bourgeoisie
caste system
horizontal mobility
life chances
lifestyle
open class system
power
prestige
proletariat
social class
social mobility
social stratification
status consistency
vertical mobility

SUGGESTED READINGS

Bendix, Reinhard, and Seymour Lipset, eds. *Class, Status, and Power.* 2nd ed. New York: The Free Press, 1966.
A collection of essays on theoretical approaches to class, differential class behavior, social mobility, and stratification issues in postindustrial society.

Bottomore, T. B. *Classes in Modern Society.* New York: Pantheon, 1966.
The author offers an interesting discussion of the basis of class, the effects of class on technology, and the development of modern class ideologies.

Davis, Kingsley, and Wilbert E. Moore. "Some Principles of Stratification," *American Sociological Review,* 10 (April 1945), 242–249.
An article that summarizes the functional approach to stratification.

Dollard, John. *Caste and Class in a Southern Town.* Garden City, N.Y.: Doubleday, 1957.
A study of a Southern town, emphasizing the aspect of stratification along racial lines. Dollard points out the gains of whites from segregation.

Domhoff, G. William. *Who Rules America?* Englewood Cliffs, N.J.: Prentice-Hall, 1967.
A study aimed at discovering whether or not the upper class is also a governing class. Domhoff shows the extent to which the upper class controls the corporate structure, the political institutions, and the institutions that affect public opinion in the United States.

Gans, Herbert J. *More Equality.* New York: Pantheon, 1973.
Gans discusses the functions poor people serve, such as comprising a market for second-hand goods and leftovers. Despite this situation, Gans argues, it is possible to have more equality.

Heller, Celia S., ed. *Structured Social Inequality.* New York: Macmillan, 1968.
A reader in comparative social stratification, covering theories, types, dimensions, and consequences of stratification.

Lopreato, Joseph, and Lawrence Hazelrigg. *Class, Conflict, and Mobility.* San Francisco: Chandler, 1972.
The authors begin with the theories of Marx, Pareto, Dahrendorf, and Weber and show how these theories have been applied to social phenomena.

Lundberg, Ferdinand. *The Rich and the Superrich.* New York: Grosset and Dunlap, 1968.
A brilliant analysis of the upper class in American society, focusing on how the rich got their wealth and how they keep and control it.

Veblen, Thorstein. *The Theory of the Leisure Class.* New York: Random House, 1934.
This classic work, first published in 1899, criticizes the upper class for their failure to perform any meaningful function in society.

Warner, William Lloyd. *Yankee City.* New Haven, Conn.: Yale University Press, 1959.
This classic community study focused on the stratification system of Newburyport, Massachusetts, and on the effect of bureaucratization on that system. An excellent source on the methodology used to study and analyze stratification.

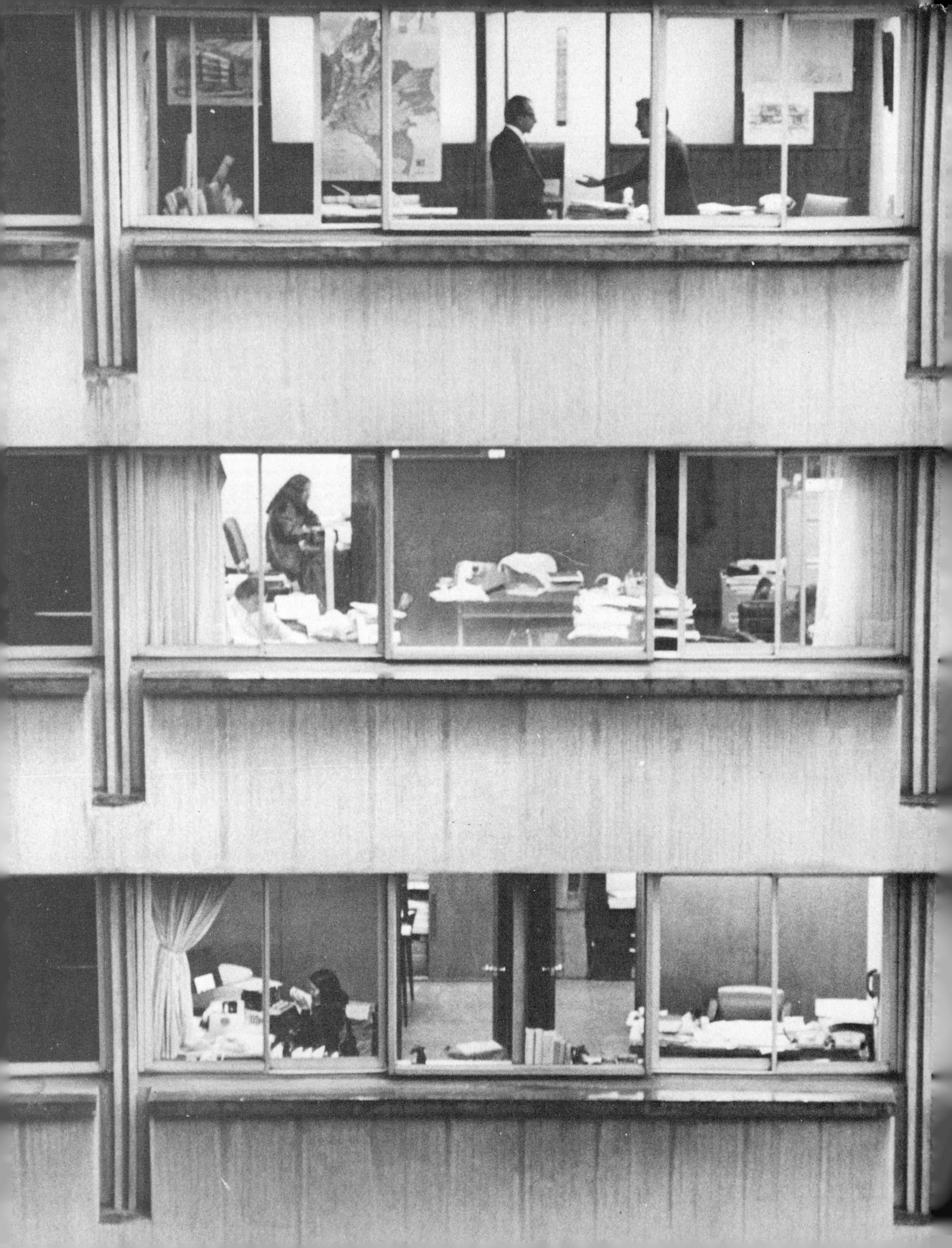

Part Three

Understanding Social Institutions

Sociologists define institutions as enduring social groupings and their interwoven folkways, mores, and laws built around one or more functions. The concept "institution" is an abstraction, but it is expressed through real groups. For example, the educational institution is expressed through the schools. The functions of institutions are as old as human life, for they correspond to permanent human needs. And once again, although we can use the sociological method to isolate the social institutions, in the real world these institutions are interdependent, interlocking, and interacting. Several will combine to perform one function, and any one institution will perform, in whole or in part, more than one function.

What are the basic functions that institutions combine to fulfill? There are three functions, and we've seen them before in this book. The first function is to ensure physical survival; the second, to maintain order and harmony within the group; and the third, to provide for the individual's psychological well-being.

Sociologists find the same five institutions in every society, although in many societies the expression of two or more institutions may rest with the same group of people. For example, in many primitive tribal societies that subsist by hunting game and gathering roots, the institution of the family and the economic institution may be expressed by the same group; and this group might also be the educational institution.

In our own society, large bureaucracies, division of labor, and specialization make the five social institutions visible as distinct, separate entities. The family, education, religion, government, and the economy, while interwoven in a complex network, are each nevertheless separately recognizable. However, over the last couple of centuries, and especially in the past several decades of our century, each institution has changed markedly.

The family, for example, although still the major socializing agent, has given up much of that role to education. It has even given up part of the socializing role to television, thus accelerating the entrance of secondary groups into our lives. Marriage was once the unchallenged regulator of sexual conduct. Premarital and extramarital sex go back at least as far as Biblical times, but they were considered immoral, and in most societies, were illegal. In our society, notions of acceptable sexual conduct are changing; more and more people think sex outside of marriage is not wrong.

The immense changes in our economic institutions over many generations gradually made the education institution stronger as a socializing force in our lives. To be productive members in society, we have to know much more than our ancestors had to know. At the same time, these economic changes have gradually shrunk the economic importance of the family. The family has been transformed from a productive unit to a consumer unit. And although the extended family was common in our agrarian past, it is virtually nonexistent in our present urban, industrial society.

The increased importance of education, and its growth into a major bureaucratic institution, have made the schools an arena of controversy. Traditionalists maintain that schools are meant only to impart information and train the young in mental skills essential to the economically productive good citizen. Progressives maintain that the schools must live up to their recently acquired duties as socializing agents. They must deal not only with minds but with the whole person. Still others attack the schools for failure to provide equality of opportunity. Blacks, most minorities, and the poor of all races get less from our schools than does the white middle class.

As you can conclude from the chapter on stratification, education is not the only institution that is doing a less than perfect job of fulfilling its basic social functions. As we have grown from our agrarian roots into an advanced industrial society, we have also become a mass society. More and more, gigantic industrial, business, and government bureaucracies have come to dominate our lives and determine our fates. As our industrialized economy spawned immense trusts and monopolies, government necessarily began to grow in order to control them.

Government itself reached its bureaucratic maturity in the Great Depression of the 1930s, when the economy broke down and left millions in utter poverty and misery. The government took upon itself the task of running the economy, and to this day, it still tries to manage the economy. Once government stepped into the economy, not only did it never step back out entirely, but also, it began to assume other social responsibilities as well. A survey of current government regulatory and social agencies would be staggering, especially if compared with a survey of 1930, or even of 1950.

Much of what happens in society, from the economic, political, and social welfare of minorities to the relations between consumer and producer, is no longer left to the conscience of the individual or the group. Government has assumed a significant role as the conscience of society. Whether this is good or bad is not for sociologists to say. But they can ask, among other questions, where this puts the institution of religion in relation to the social functions that institutions are supposed to perform.

In the past several centuries, religion has undergone constant changes in its social power and importance. In the early Middle Ages in Europe, religion <u>was</u> society. In those disjointed times after the fall of the Roman Empire, the Church was the only institution with unquestioned authority. The Church possessed the word of truth, and it was the earthly representative of God.

The situation of religion in our own society is clearly quite different. Our constitutional separation of church and state protects each religion or sect from the others. But it also limits the social power of religion itself. Over the centuries, religion has surrendered one area after another to secular authority. Few in Western societies take the Biblical account of creation literally. The Church once burned at the stake people who claimed that the earth is round or that the sun, not the earth, is the center of the solar system. Today, a scientist can say that many planets in the universe are likely to have intelligent life, and not a murmur of objection is heard from churchmen.

What, then, is the social function of religion in our present-day society? Religion offers to its believers the solace of ultimate answers to the questions that we bewildered humans have always raised. Its beliefs and rituals, its sacred objects and prayers enable believers to face life and its tragedies as something other than meaningless and cruel. But can't religion, by its claims to supernatural sources of truth, create problems, if society is changing against the wishes of a powerful religious body? It can and it has, as you will see. But religions have also been the sources of social change, often when society has not been living up to its professed cultural values. Ministers, priests, and nuns were in the forefront of civil rights activities in the 1960s and the antiwar movement of the late '60s and early '70s. But whether religion, or any other institution, group, or person, resists or promotes change, it is not for sociologists to say that the change is desirable or undesirable.

The family is considered by many to be the basic institution in human societies. Why? Some form of marriage and the family is found in all societies. Why? The answers to these questions can be found in the family's contribution to the welfare and survival of the group. The family has been entrusted with the bearing and rearing of the next generation. Furthermore, the adjunct institution of marriage provides a socially approved means by which most adults can find satisfaction of their sexual needs.

How families provide these functions—child rearing, sexual gratification, and so on—varies greatly from culture to culture. In some cultures, "family" means a married couple and their children; in others, the family may extend to many other relatives or may involve multiple spouses. In addition, societies vary in their rules for who shall marry whom and who may have sex with whom.

In recent years, the functions of the family in America have gone through some changes. In the past, the family has been charged with bearing children, socializing the young, ascribing status, controlling sexual behavior, providing love and affection, and fulfilling economic needs. In this chapter, we investigate each of these functions, how it has changed, and how the changes have affected society and its members. An objective study of the American family shows that it is not without problems, that it will continue to change, but that it will survive, for it is unlikely that we will devise a better way of meeting so many needs of children and adults alike.

9
The Family

> When the social functions of the family are all lost, affection within the family, and in fact the family itself, will also be lost.
> —KINGSLEY DAVIS (1949)

In this simple statement, the sociologist Kingsley Davis calls attention to the fact that the institution we call the family contributes to the survival and well-being of society. Were it not for this function, Davis feels, no one could seek love and affection in the family, for the family would not exist. There is concern today that the family is in trouble, precisely because it is losing functions or is failing to perform them well. Yet, over the long course of human history, wherever humans have been found, there has been some form of a family. Why?

To explain the universality of the family, and to investigate contemporary concerns with its fate, this chapter focuses on the functions of the family: what they are, how they were performed at various stages of civilization, and how they are performed today. But, first, we need to take a look at the biological characteristics of the human species that underlie formation of families, and we need to define the nature of the family and of marriage.

BIOLOGICAL ROOTS OF THE FAMILY

The human family is universal because certain human biological characteristics are universal. Humans have a long period of dependency after birth. It takes at least 14 years for a human to achieve physical maturity, while most other mammals achieve maturity in no more than a few months. The human animal, with very few instincts to guide behavior, is highly dependent on learning. Humans, therefore, desperately need the help of others to survive and to learn how to continue to survive. There is thus a biological basis for a relatively stable and enduring group to meet the survival needs of the species.

What form the family originally took will never be known. Some sociologists and anthropologists speculate that the earliest family unit was the mother and her offspring (Briffault, 1931). The mother provided the only food the infant could receive and digest. She cared for the child and taught it until it was able to fend for itself. According to this theory, only later in human history did the adult male become a member of the group: the family existed before marriage.

Other sociologists speculate that because the newborn needs constant and intense care, its survival would be in jeopardy if the mother had to leave it alone while she foraged for her own food. Because the mother needed food, and because both the mother and child needed protection, another person, the male, was probably part of the original family group. According to this theory, male and female joined together out of sexual attraction and remained together to rear their offspring: marriage came before the family (Westermarck, 1921).

The second biological basis for the family is human sexual reproduction, which obviously requires the participation of both sexes. Humans have no rutting season (a recurring period of sexual excitement in many animals), and the female does not have to be in heat to mate. There is no human instinct to assure that males and females pair off during a mating season and remain together afterward. On the contrary, with their unflagging sex drive, males and females would be more likely to continuously search for sexual partners. It is speculated that uncontrolled sexual activity would create conflict, jealousy, and disruption. The sexual nature of males and females thus requires some controls, such as those provided by marriage and the family.

WHAT IS A FAMILY?

Without a modifier, the term "family" is not very precise. "Family" could mean any of several groups. If a college woman says that she will be spending the holidays with her family, what does she mean? If she is married, she could mean that she, her husband, and their baby will spend the holidays together. But whether married or single, she could also mean that she is going to her parents' home. She may also mean that she, her brothers and sisters, and their spouses and children, aunts, uncles, cousins, and grandparents are all going to gather for a family reunion.

Although what is meant by "family" is often apparent from the context, the social sciences have more precise designations for the various types. Most basic is the **nuclear family:** a married pair and their immature offspring (Murdock, 1949). Every society recognizes this family form. Because the nuclear family is so important in the United States, you may not be impressed with the fact that it is universally found. But, true cultural universals are so rare that it is quite remarkable to find no known exception to this rule: every society recognizes the nuclear family as a unit distinct from the rest of society. Sometimes it is the only type of family recognized; more often, the married pair and their offspring form the *nucleus* of other complex family forms.

In societies such as ours, people customarily belong to two nuclear families. We are born into a **family of orientation:** the family group that rears us and gives us our basic orientation to life. The family that a married pair begins with the birth of their first child is called their **family of procreation** (which, of course, is also their child's family of orientation).

In 92 out of 192 societies he studied, the anthropologist George P. Murdock (1949) also found instances of the **extended family**—that is, two or more nuclear families joined by an extension of the parent-child relationship. The extended family of the ancient Hebrews, for example, contained three generations: an older man and his wife or wives, his unmarried sons and daughters, and his married sons and their wives and children. Typically, all the members of an extended family live together in a common residence, in nearby dwellings, or in some clearly designated compound. People in extended families have closer bonds to fellow members than to their other relatives outside the group.

Societies with extended families distribute some functions of the family beyond the nucleus throughout the larger family. Child rearing, although considered the primary responsibility of the parents, must be shared by other adults, such as grandparents or uncles and aunts. Anthropologists have found that in some extended families roles are strictly assigned. Young sons are disciplined by their fathers and given affection and played with by their uncles; daughters are disciplined by mothers and loved and played with by aunts. Because most parents are also aunts and uncles, they usually play both roles at the same time—but with different children, of course.

This Frenchman and his great-grandson illustrate the point that in the extended family members other than the parents help with the rearing of children.

The extended family may be an economic unit in which all its members cooperate in a joint enterprise, such as hunting or farming. Various forms of security are provided by the extended family: older people are assured support and comfort; substitute parents are readily available for children whose parents die; and all members receive some form of aid and affection. Thus, the affectional function of the nuclear family is diluted. Even loyalty to one's spouse is limited by the demands of loyalty to the larger family group.

MARRIAGE: UNIVERSAL BUT VARIED

Marriage is a relationship between two sexually interacting adults that is sufficiently enduring to provide for the procreation and rearing of children. In our definition, marriage is not just any relationship between the sexes but one that is approved of by society. Furthermore, children are not necessary to the concept of marriage, although the ability to have them and rear them is. To be considered marriage, a relationship must permit sexual intercourse, and it must be an enduring state rather than a temporary liaison.

Marriage is found in all societies, and every society regulates who may marry whom, how marriages are to be formed, and what rights and duties are to be given to the spouses. Despite considerable variation in the specific regulations, every society regulates marriage and prescribes approved behavior for the spouses.

For example, every society regulates how many spouses a person may have. Since there are only two sexes, the possible combinations are rather limited. The approved form of marriage may be **monogamy**—one man married to one woman; or it may be **polygamy**—one spouse of either sex having two or more spouses of the opposite sex at the same time. **Polygyny** is one man being married to more than one woman; **polyandry** is one woman married to more than one man; and **group marriage** refers to two or more men married to two or more women. Each basic form of marriage shows considerable variation from society to society. In polygyny the co-wives may be unrelated or they may be sisters, and in either case, they may or may not have equal status. In polyandry the co-husbands are usually but not always brothers.

Marriage forms also vary as to the roles of the marriage partners, the authority pattern of the family, and the ease with which the marriage bond can be severed. In almost every primitive society, the role of husband includes those tasks that require more physical strength and absence from the home. The woman, periodically incapacitated by pregnancy and bound to the home to nurse and rear children, is customarily assigned tasks that can be carried out around the home.

Such a division of labor frequently makes the woman dependent upon and subordinate to her husband. This dependency may explain the prevalence of the **patriarchal family**—in which the male has the power and authority—as opposed to the **matriarchal family.** The sociologist Betty Yorburg contends, "Male superiority within the family, in prestige, authority, and privilege, is a fact of life in almost all known societies. No valid instances of true matriarchal societies have been known to exist" (1973, p. 16). In modern, industrialized societies, the biological bases for woman's dependency are greatly reduced, and the patriarchal family is more difficult to justify. This has given rise to **egalitarian marriage,** in which authority is shared.

Whatever the marriage form, all societies also regulate who may marry whom. Such rules are generally divided into two types: endogamous and exogamous. **Endogamous rules** stipulate that a person must select a mate from *within* a certain group—say, from the same tribe or even from some smaller group within the tribe. Racial and religious endogamy are often found. Until recent decades, certain religious denominations in our society strictly enforced religious endogamy, and racial endogamy is still predominant. Racial and religious endogamy are irrelevant in primitive societies, for members share the same race and religion. Class endogamy is fairly common, even if it means only that the rulers and the ruled should not intermarry.

Exogamous rules stipulate that a person must select a marriage partner *outside* some designated group. Generally, exogamous rules have a kinship basis: marriage is forbidden between persons related by blood or marriage. All societies have exogamous rules that define persons as being too closely related to be acceptable marriage partners. Those outside the nuclear family who are prohibited by the exogamous regulations are not necessarily one's closest blood relatives. For example, one may be permitted to marry a first cousin but prohibited from marrying a more distant relative. Exogamous rules are often considered an extension of the primary incest taboo, which forbids sexual relations between parents and children and brothers and sisters. (The incest taboo is treated more fully later in this chapter.)

Societies do not merely specify acceptable mates. They also regulate *how* a mate is to be obtained. In many places the marriage is arranged by the woman's or man's parents, a go-between, or a special functionary, and some marriage partners do not meet until their wedding day. Arranged marriage is no mere oddity of a few primitive societies but has been practiced in such ancient, highly civilized societies as Japan, China, and India. Throughout history, millions and millions of marriages have been arranged. The practice is said by some advocates to result in wiser choices of marriage partners because those who know the young people try to make reasonable choices without the complications of passion or romantic love. Whether for this reason or some other, the divorce rate is lower in societies where arranged marriage prevails.

David and Vera Mace (1960) report that in some societies, young people, particularly girls, defend the practice of arranged marriage on the grounds that adolescence is more relaxed if it is uncomplicated by the necessity of

This Lapland wedding is probably different from any you've seen but it serves the same function as marriage rites everywhere. It announces to the group that the parties are changing their status from single to married.

attracting a mate. They see the "free enterprise" mate selection system as one in which there would always be uncertainty and the secret fear that one might be unsuccessful in finding a mate. With arranged marriage, they know that their parents will strive diligently to find them the best possible marriage partner. As we will see later, however, the higher incidence of failure among marriages that have not been arranged could result from many factors besides the emphasis on romantic love.

Whether marriages are arranged or the partners choose each other, all societies have a marriage rite or ceremony. It may be a simple ritual, such as publicly exchanging gifts, or a very elaborate affair accompanied by feasting and celebration. In any case, the function of the marriage rite is to announce to the group that the parties are changing their status from single to married and that they are assuming all the responsibilities, rights, and privileges of their new positions.

FUNCTIONS OF THE FAMILY

In Chapter 3 we noted that all societies face basic problems that must be solved if the group is to survive. Every human society has three common needs: (1) to ensure physical survival; (2) to maintain orderly group living; and (3) to provide for the psychological needs of its members. The family helps fulfill these needs through its major functions, which include reproduction, socialization, status ascription, sexual regulation, intimate interaction, and economic survival.

Producing Children

In order to perpetuate itself, a society must have offspring. It must, therefore, endorse the value that reproduction of the species is good, and it must encourage the birth of young. The biology of reproduction does not require marriage, yet all societies have adopted a general norm concerning child bearing: it should occur *in* the family, not outside the family. Many societies differ as to how they define this norm and adjust it to their own situation. Some societies encourage few children, others many (and the infant mortality rate may determine how many births are encouraged). Societies are not equally successful in restricting child bearing to the family nor equally tolerant when children are born outside the family.

Family Size Throughout most of human history, population grew slowly. For this reason, societies encouraged couples not only to have children but to have many children. The Soviet Union is an example of a modern society that still encourages a high birth rate. In 1944, that country began making payments to families who had additional children. Payments ranged from

FIGURE 9.1 Average Number of Births to Date, Additional Births Expected, and Total Births Expected by Married Women

Year	Age of Women	Births to Date	Additional Births Expected	Total Births to Date and Expected
1967	18–24	1.2	1.7	2.9
1967	25–29	2.3	.7	3.0
1977	18–24	.8	1.3	2.1
1977	25–29	1.5	.7	2.2

This graph illustrates the change in the child-bearing function of the family. The birth rate started to fall in 1958, and it continued to fall in the decade 1967–1977. Note that as recently as 1967, young married women expected to complete their families with about three children, while ten years later, the average size of the completed family was expected to be about two children.

Source: U.S. Bureau of the Census, *Current Population Reports*, series P-20, no. 301 (November 1976) and no. 325 (September 1978).

400 rubles for the third child to 5000 rubles for the tenth and subsequent children (Kenkel, 1977). Honors were also bestowed: a Motherhood Glory award to those who had seven, eight, or nine children; Heroine Mother to those who had ten or more. Between 1950 and 1969 almost 100,000 women received the Heroine Mother award. During the same period, 11 million women were given Motherhood medals or Order of Motherhood Glory awards. In part, the drive for a high birth rate can be explained by the severe loss of male population in World War II. Yet, as far back as 1936, the Soviets forbade abortion (except for serious medical considerations) in order to encourage large families.

Today in the Soviet Union abortion is free and easy to obtain. However, the Soviet Union views itself as an underpopulated country with a chronic labor shortage and still officially encourages a high birth rate. The example of the Soviet Union reminds us that emphasis on overpopulation and the value of small families is a relatively recent one and that acceptance of it is still found chiefly in industrialized societies.

What has been happening to the birth rate in the United States? The **crude birth rate**—the number of births per thousand people in the total population—is one measure of the reproductive situation. In 1915 the crude birth rate in the United States was 25. The rate began to drop in the 1920s and reached a low of 16.7 in the depression year of 1936. Thereafter it began to climb slowly, reaching 25 again after World War II. From 1947 to 1958 the crude birth rate remained at or close to 25. What at first appeared to be a slight decline is now more pronounced. The crude birth rate in 1965 was 19.5, and it now stands at about 15.

In 1973, married women between the ages of 45 and 49 (beyond their child-bearing years) had an average of 3.99 children during their fertile years. By contrast, the total number of children young married women of today have had, and the number of additional children they anticipate, averages out to just over two children per mother. Some people may be skeptical about accepting women's statements about the number of children they expect to have in the future. Yet there are other indications that Americans have come to value small families. In a recent Roper poll, almost half the people polled stated that two children make the ideal family. In the 1940s and 1950s only one-quarter of the people chose two as the ideal number of children; the rest regarded larger families as ideal.

It is safe to conclude that in the United States the small family is back in style. What's more, the number of childless couples is beginning to increase. It is apparent that the value of low reproduction is basically accepted. Today, couples are rarely criticized for being childless or for having only one or two children. In response to changing conditions, the expression of the reproduction function of the American family has changed. From the standpoint of the survival of society, the function is being performed adequately, for there are sufficient births to offset deaths.

Illegitimacy The social rules of reproduction restrict child bearing to the family. Not all countries keep records on illegitimacy, so it is difficult to determine how our ratio of legitimate to illegitimate child bearing compares to the ratio in other societies. For instance, in 1918, Russia removed all distinctions between legitimate and illegitimate children; it thus legally abolished illegitimacy and stated that "actual descent is regarded as the basis of the family" (Kenkel, 1977). The name of the father of the illegitimate child could not be used on the birth certificate or on school records, and the father was not required to support the child. Although difficult to determine precisely, the number of children born out of wedlock in the Soviet Union is substantial. There is also some evidence that there will be a return to an earlier policy of requiring fathers to support their children born out of wedlock.

Until the mid-1950s, fewer than four percent of all births in the United States were illegitimate. Now the figure is about 13 percent born out of wedlock—more than 400,000 babies a year (U.S. Department of Health, Education, and Welfare statistics). In recent years some of the stigma has been removed from illegitimacy, and some women are choosing to have babies outside of marriage because they want to be mothers but not wives. Thus, the reproductive function of the family has increasing competition, but not nearly enough to threaten its continued existence.

Socializing Children

A sufficient crop of infants each year does not in itself assure the survival of a society. Enough of the infants must live to adulthood and must have children of their own who live to adulthood. More than simple physical survival of individuals is needed, however. As we discussed in Chapter 4, all infants must undergo extensive training to acquire the correct personality traits, to internalize the group's values and norms, and to acquire the skills and knowledge necessary for participating in and perpetuating society. No society that wishes to avoid extinction can escape socializing its young. It can, however, determine what is to be included in the socialization process and who is to do the socializing.

As we saw in Chapter 4, in almost all societies the family is the chief socializing agent. The family usually maintains its socializing influence throughout most of preadult life; the repetition and continuity in training and experience assist in establishing basic values and personality traits. Many of the basic values of society—its fears, superstitions, taboos—first reach the young through the family.

But the family is not the only socializing agent. Most societies devise other ways to help socialize the young. Modern societies have schools, churches, youth groups, and the like. But, even in nonliterate societies, adults outside the family have some part in teaching children the beliefs, values, and practices of the culture. In the Israeli **kibbutz,** from birth on,

The socialization function of the family is often carried out quietly and insignificantly as a parent teaches children about everyday things in their environment.

children live separately from their parents in children's houses, where they are reared by trained nurses (see Box 9.1). Children visit their parents for an hour or two daily, but parents are not the chief agents of socialization. Some of the kibbutzim have given up this practice, and children now live with their parents. In those settlements that still have communal child rearing there seems to be a growing dissatisfaction with it, particularly on the part of the mothers. An important lesson of the kibbutz experiment, however, is that a couple of generations of children were raised with apparent success in a system in which parents had only a minor role in the socialization of the young.

Long ago, the Soviet Union developed day nurseries for children from about two months to about three years of age. These are multifunctional institutions, feeding and clothing the children, checking their health, instructing them on many matters, and carefully supervising play activities during the day while the parents work. Although there are not enough places in the day nurseries for most Russian children, millions have been reared this way. From all indications, this sharing of socialization between family and nursery has worked well (see Bronfenbrenner, 1970).

The American family has always had a central role in the socialization of children. Today, however, nine million children under the age of eighteen are being reared by one parent only, most often the mother. It is common to call such units "single-parent families," but however we designate them, they represent a dramatic change in the socialization function of the family. In the past, when a mother or father died prematurely there were usually grandparents, aunts and uncles, or others from the extended family to help rear the children. Today's single parent is more often divorced or separated and may find help only in day-care centers—if they are available and if she or he can afford them. The rate of single-parent families has grown three

In almost all societies members of a nuclear family share a common household where they can be socialized by their parents. In the kibbutz, children live with their agemates apart from their parents and are socialized by special counselors.

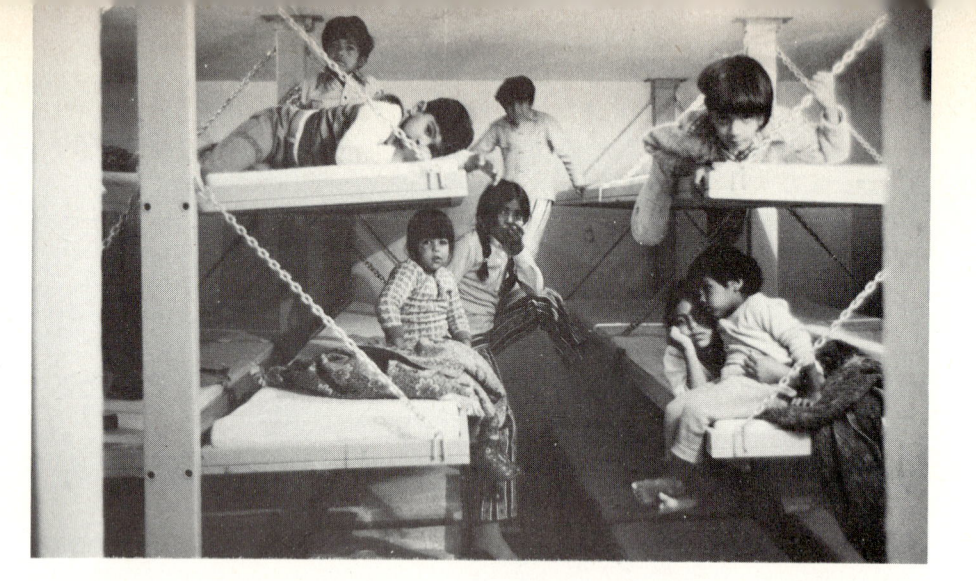

BOX 9.1
THE "FAMILY" IN THE ISRAELI KIBBUTZ

Are marriage and the family found in all societies? At one time, it was thought that one exception could be found in the Israeli kibbutz. A look at the family in the kibbutz is fascinating, for it shows how resourceful people can be in their efforts to satisfy human needs.

In Hebrew, kibbutz means "a gathering" or "a group." Since 1921, the term has come to be associated with a particular kind of group: a communal farm in what is now the national state of Israel. The young people who founded the first kibbutz had a dream: to unite themselves with the ancient homeland and to establish communities marked by democracy, equality, and communal ownership of all property. Kibbutz members did not (and still do not) receive wages for their work. No one owns land, homes, or other goods. Work is assigned by an elected work committee, and all profits belong to the group. People are given clothes, goods, and a dormitory room simply because they are members of the group.

In the early days of the kibbutz, if a young couple fell in love and wanted to live together and establish an exclusive relationship, they simply asked the room committee for a double room and moved their beds into it. The term "marriage" was not used, but once a man and woman had moved into a common room they were referred to as a couple, or a pair. Was this marriage? We conclude that it was. There was a relatively enduring sexual relationship between two persons of opposite sexes, and there was a ceremony that marked the beginning of the relationship. It does not matter whether a society requires the principals to a marriage to join their hands, exchange gifts, or dance around an oak tree in the nude. If there are two positions in a society—married and single—then there needs to be a way to indicate when a person has given up the one position and accepted the other. The bed-moving ceremony serves this purpose well in the kibbutz society.

Unlike almost all other societies, marriage serves no economic function in the kibbutz. Everything one needs is furnished by the group, not by one's husband or wife. Meals are eaten in the communal dining hall, and

times as fast as that of two-parent families. When we speak of the socialization function of the family, therefore, it must be recognized that it often occurs in an incomplete family unit.

Ascribing Status

To maintain orderly group living, a society must assign statuses or positions to its members. The family plays an important role in this status ascription function, a process that begins when the family gives a name to its newborn child. With its name, the child acquires a position in the family and an answer to the question, "Who am I?"

---

clothes are cleaned in the communal laundry. In the early days, and in many kibbutzim today, children did not live with their parents but in separate children's houses, where trained nurses took care of them. As they grew older, they lived in groups of eight with a counselor, who remained with the group until they completed high school. Parents visited their children each day, and as the children got older, they went to their parents' room for an hour or so daily. Nevertheless, the socialization function was largely performed by the nurses and counselors, not the parents. Furthermore, the family served no economic function for the children. But parents and children remained greatly attached to each other. During the hours when children and parents were together, work in the kibbutz came to a virtual standstill. When children spoke of "my room," they meant their parents' room, which was a sort of psychological home, even though the children did not live in it.

The family is thus a source of affection for both the couple and their children in the kibbutz. While couples may separate as easily as they came together, they do so no more frequently than couples in many societies that have marriage and divorce. For the children, the family also serves a status-giving function, for every child knows who his or her parents are. No one is confused about whether they belong to a family, to which family they belong, or why they belong to one.

Many studies have been conducted in which it has been found that kibbutz children are as psychologically adjusted and socially mature as children elsewhere. Men and women fare well, too, for they have a personal commitment to each other uncluttered by financial worries, economic interdependence, and the need to provide for children. The kibbutz marriage and family system is admittedly unique in human cultures, and presumably, not everyone could be happy with such an arrangement. A few, of course, do leave the kibbutz, and others would like to change the system, so that it would allow parents to rear their own children. But the kibbutz spirit lives on, and more importantly, its unique marriage and family system is working.

As children grow older, they learn their various positions. Some people are cousins, aunts and uncles, and grandparents, and the child is a grandchild, a cousin, and a nephew or niece. In primitive societies children learn that they are members of a large kin grouping, or *clan*. Children in modern society learn of their family's social class, religion, and race. Although children may eventually change some of their statuses, such as class or religion, their initial placement is made by the family. Through the status ascription function of the family, members of a society learn who they are and how they fit into the larger group.

Controlling Sexual Behavior

The family function of regulating sexual behavior helps to solve all three of the basic problems facing any society (physical survival, orderly group living, and the individual's psychological needs). We have seen that sexual behavior must be permitted and encouraged if the group is to perpetuate itself. Sexual behavior must also be regulated to maintain harmonious group living, for the sex drive is a powerful force, and its uncontrolled expression would disrupt the group. Yet, because sex is a strong basic human drive, any society that attempts to prohibit all sexual behavior would risk serious discontent among its members.

All societies, therefore, must regulate and control the sex drive while also providing for its expression. In every society, the principal source of sexual satisfaction is supposed to be found in marriage. Even while allowing for

---

BOX 9.2 ARE PARENTS SEXUAL BEINGS?

High school and college students often feel that their parents do not understand and accept the sexuality of youth. There seems to be a sexual gap between parents and youth—so much so that some sex educators feel that sex education in the home is not really possible. The incest taboo creates a barrier between parent and child that prevents the parent from seeing the child as a sexual being with his or her own needs, problems, and frustrations. But what about children? Are they any better able to accept the fact that their parents are sexual beings?

The sociologist Ollie Pocs and the psychologist Annette G. Godow (1977) decided to pursue this question. They hypothesized that college students would estimate their parents' sexual behavior to be far less frequent than one would expect of married males and females, as based upon the research findings of Kinsey. A questionnaire was completed by 239 male and 407 female college students. Among the items, students were asked how frequently their parents engaged in marital coitus each month. Their answers were then compared with Kinsey's statistics for males and females of different ages. Most of the mothers of the college students were between ages 41 and 45, and the fathers between 46 and 50. Students of

sexual expression, marriage limits and restricts sexuality. Many primitive societies, for example, have taboos on sexual relations between husband and wife during menstruation or for some stipulated period before and after the birth of a child or even before a big hunt or a religious festival. Most important, marriage limits sexual expression by stipulating that one cannot have sexual relations with anyone but one's spouse(s).

The Universal Incest Taboo   One control over sexual behavior found in all societies is the primary **incest taboo,** which forbids sexual relations between parent and child and between brother and sister. The primary taboo is always extended to include other relatives. Which other relatives are taboo — whether cousins, uncles and aunts, or grandparents — depends on the society's method of reckoning descent and on the residence rules that affect family groups that live together (Murdock, 1949).

No natural horror of incest has been proven by investigators. Children are not born with a reluctance to enter into sexual relations with close relatives. Even so, societies everywhere teach their children that such relations are not appropriate. It has been speculated that the universality of the incest taboo arises from the recognition that allowing sexual relations between close relatives would be extremely disruptive of the family group. Sexual jealousy and conflict would be rampant within the family, and orderly family living would be in peril. The family's status ascription function would be in jeopardy, because many confusing relationships would result from such sexual behavior. The female offspring of a father and his daughter would be

---

these parents estimated that their parents engaged in sex 2.8 times per month — Kinsey found that the frequency for couples this age was about 7 times per month. For other age categories, the results were the same — students greatly underestimated how frequently their parents engaged in sex.

There is no reason to suspect gross error in Kinsey's findings, for other studies have found similar, if not higher, frequencies of marital sex. A probable explanation is that the incest taboo not only prevents parents and children from desiring one another sexually but even from thinking too much about one another's sexuality. Some students in the Pocs and Godow study wrote in comments that indicated that they were defensive or possibly upset by having to think about their parents' sexuality. One wrote, "Who even thinks about their parents' sexual behavior — except perverts?" Another wrote, "Why didn't you send (the questionnaire) to them, I don't sleep in the same bed with them." By suppressing thoughts about their parents' sexual behavior and underestimating their sexuality, the students protect themselves from incestuous feelings. In the process, youth-parent communication suffers, but perhaps that is unavoidable.

both the granddaughter and daughter of the father and both half-sister and daughter to her mother. The socialization function of the family would also be threatened if the typical parental responsibilities of training, controlling behavior, and punishing were mingled with sexual desire and seduction. The roles of disciplinarian and lover would seem to be difficult to combine. The incest taboo thus fills an important social function. (An interesting extension of the incest taboo is examined in Box 9.2.)

Sexual Activity Outside Marriage Other restrictions on sexual behavior have a logic similar to that of the incest taboo. They are designed to provide sufficient restraints on who relates sexually with whom, so that orderly living within the larger society is not jeopardized. Societies vary considerably as to what controls are believed to be necessary and proper. *Extramarital relations*—sexual intercourse between a married person and someone other than his or her spouse—are customarily forbidden. In 120 societies for which information was available, George P. Murdock (1949) found only five that freely allowed adultery. Societies are not equally vigilant in preventing such behavior, though; nor are they equally severe in punishing offenders. The death penalty for adultery is found in some societies, but far less severe punishments are also found, and much more frequently.

It is with regard to the unmarried, however, that societies show the greatest differences in their sexual values and practices. Some societies, both primitive and modern, attempt to prohibit all sexual intercourse among the unmarried. In some societies, premarital chastity may be considered extremely essential and may be preserved, particularly among females, through the use of considerable precautions. In other places, young people are allowed to have premarital intercourse. Murdock found information on premarital sex taboos, or their absence, in 158 societies. Premarital sex was forbidden in 44 societies, mildly disapproved in 6, conditionally approved in 43, and fully permitted in 65. Societies that approve of premarital sex often see it as a prelude to marriage, and in such societies, young people have no reason to feel guilt or shame about their sexual behavior.

Sexual Regulation in the United States Because sexual intercourse is a private, personal act, it is somewhat surprising how much is known about the sexual activity of Americans. Even so, the interpretation of the facts—what they mean with regard to the sex regulation function of the family—remains difficult. It is clear that most of the sexual intercourse that takes place in the United States is marital. On a given day, or night, most of the sexual intercourse that takes place is between spouses who are married to each other. What is more, by far, most of the sexual intercourse a typical individual experiences throughout his or her lifetime is with his or her spouse.

It thus appears, or can be made to appear, that American society is fulfilling its task of regulating and controlling sexual behavior. Despite appearances, however, various recent studies indicate that much sexual intercourse takes place outside of marriage and that the rates are higher than they were in the 1940s and 1950s. The 1972 Research Guild study, reported by Morton Hunt under the title *Sexual Behavior in the 1970s* (1974), found that 95 percent of men aged 24 had sexual intercourse before marriage. In the older generation of men (those who were 55 and older at the time of the study), the comparable rate was 84 percent. The more religious men were less likely to have sex before marriage, and if they did, they experienced it less frequently.

In the early 1970s, it was estimated that 28 percent of young American women aged 15–19 had had premarital intercourse. This was one of the findings of the Kantner-Zelnick (1972) study, in which interviews were conducted with a national sample of 2,839 white and 1,401 black women. Those who attended church frequently, who were from wealthier families, who lived with both parents, and who generally confided in their parents were considerably less likely to have premarital sex. Since the oldest respondents were only 19, this study does not give us a complete picture of all women who engage in sex sometime before marriage. Other studies suggest that the proportion of unmarried women having sexual intercourse is almost as high as the proportion of unmarried men.

The statistics on extramarital intercourse reveal a considerable departure from the stated norm that sexual relations should be restricted to marriage. On the basis of his studies in the late 1940s, Alfred Kinsey (Kinsey, Pomeroy, and Martin, 1948; Kinsey, Pomeroy, Martin, and Gebhard, 1953) estimated that at least half of all married men had extramarital intercourse sometime during their married life and that about one-fourth of married women had extramarital relations by the time they were 40 years old. Hunt's (1974) more recent study found only somewhat higher rates of extramarital sex among males than those reported by Kinsey. For young

The fact that many people find this motel sign humorous suggests a tolerant attitude toward extramarital affairs. Can this be the same society that years ago made adulterers wear a scarlet "A" about their necks?

FIGURE 9.2 Is Sexual Intercourse Outside of Marriage Morally Wrong?

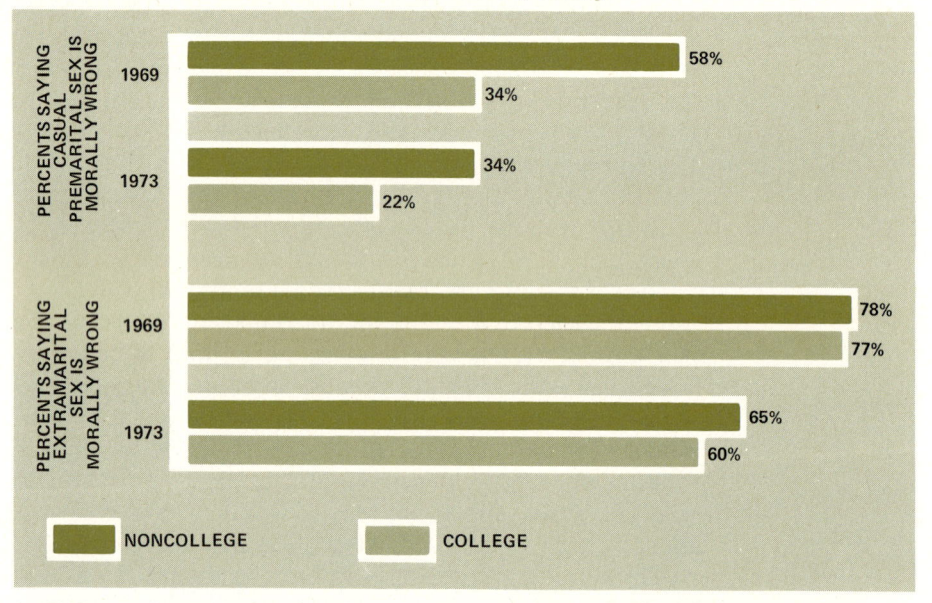

PERCENTS SAYING CASUAL PREMARITAL SEX IS MORALLY WRONG

1969: Noncollege 58%, College 34%
1973: Noncollege 34%, College 22%

PERCENTS SAYING EXTRAMARITAL SEX IS MORALLY WRONG

1969: Noncollege 78%, College 77%
1973: Noncollege 65%, College 60%

■ NONCOLLEGE   ■ COLLEGE

In 1969, over three-fourths of college and noncollege youth felt that it was morally wrong for married persons to have sex with someone other than their spouses, and over half of the noncollege youth felt that premarital sex was also morally wrong. More recently, a cross-sectional study of over 3,000 American youths between the ages of 16 and 25 found a decided drop in the number of both college and noncollege youth who consider casual sex before marriage morally wrong. In addition, less than two-thirds of the nation's youth now feel that extramarital sex is morally wrong. Many young people are saying, thus, that marriage is not the only approved outlet for sexual behavior.

Source: Daniel Yankelovich, *The New Morality: A Profile of American Youth in the 70s* (New York: McGraw-Hill, 1974), p. 93.

married women, the picture is quite different. Hunt found three times more married women in the under 25 age group reporting having sex with someone other than their husbands than Kinsey had found.

Various studies thus point to the fact that the rates of premarital and extramarital sex have increased, particularly for women. This means that the double standard, which allowed men more sexual freedom than women, has changed considerably. Men and women are becoming more similar in their attitudes and behavior with regard to sex outside of marriage (see Smigel and Seiden, 1968).

No known society has been able to enforce all of its sexual regulations all of the time, just as none has enforced rules on property rights or other matters with complete success. The existence of too great a discrepancy between what a society says *ought* to be done and what people actually do opens two courses to the group: it can either make new rules or attempt better enforcement of the old ones. Many Americans, as judged by their actual behavior and their stated beliefs, do not seem to accept the value that sex belongs only in marriage. Others accept a liberal sexual code for the unmarried but hold to a code of sexual fidelity for the married. While the rates of extramarital sex are increasing, the majority of married men and women are faithful to their spouses.

In the United States, the family function of regulating sexual behavior leaves much to be desired. For one thing, the existence of different codes for sexual behavior creates doubts and indecisions for individuals and does not provide an adequate guide for behavior. For another, the weakening of the norm for sexual exclusivity after marriage does not seem to be in the best interests of maintaining stable marriages, despite the fact that some individuals are able to hide their extramarital affairs, and some marriages seemingly are not harmed by the infidelity of husband or wife. For most people, however, a sexually exclusive relationship in marriage is a strong bond between husband and wife and is related to another family function, the giving and receiving of affection.

Meeting the Need for Love

Researchers in all of the social sciences have recognized the human need for some kind of intimate interaction with other persons. Any society that failed to provide for the satisfaction of this need for love, response, and deep companionship would neglect a critical psychological drive of its members. In all societies the family has some affectional function, and in most societies the family is the major group that meets these affectional needs.

The human need for a warm and loving relationship is evident in infancy. Psychologically, and even physiologically, infants fare better when reared by someone who gives them love. Even very young infants seem to need and respond to hugging, cuddling, and soothing talk. Infants reared in orphanages or in similar institutions where they are deprived of physical affection do poorly physically (Ribble, 1943; Spitz, 1945). They become listless and may even suffer permanent damage to their capacity to respond emotionally. In extreme cases, they are said to suffer from *marasmus,* a slow wasting away to death. Fortunately, the instances of total deprivation are rare, but children who grow up in less than a warm and loving relationship are far from rare. The consequences of such deprivation may be serious—delinquency, unhappy marriages, or other symptoms of a poor ability to relate to people.

The need for affection and intimate response does not end with childhood. Every society recognizes that adults, as well as children, need affection. And most societies expect that adults will satisfy this need within the family. In some societies marriage and the nuclear family are looked upon as the prime sources of emotional satisfaction. In others, the affectional func-

The need to give and receive love is deeply rooted in our humanity. Most people seek fulfillment of these needs in the intimacy of marriage and the family, but all do not find what they seek.

tion may be shared by other groups. The extended family or men's and women's groups (which are sometimes secret and may serve a religious function as well) often serve as a source of emotional gratification for adults. Yet the family always performs some affectional function, for it provides an intimate, close relationship in which one receives intense emotional response from others.

Today, the American family is as much a source of affection and companionship for its members as it has always been. One reason for this is that the increased geographic mobility of nuclear families has deemphasized the extended family; thus, children must look to the nuclear family for love and security, because grandparents, uncles and aunts, and cousins frequently live far away. Other adults may help to train the child and give or withhold praise, but it is in the family that the child is loved unconditionally. For at least a couple of generations, experts have stressed the idea that children need love. It is extremely difficult to determine whether the modern family is performing the affectional function better than the family of the past. By and large, modern parents seem to take this function seriously and to try hard to provide their children with love and affection.

To Americans, the need for love and companionship in adulthood is almost synonymous with marriage, and it is definitely the basic reason why people marry. The need for a helpmate is really no longer important economically. Today, society accepts the fact that adults of either sex can find a comfortable way of life without marriage, yet few of them choose the single life. Most adults seem to need an enduring affectionate relationship with a partner of the opposite sex, and many adults seek this relationship in marriage. The high divorce rate and the increase in extramarital sexual liaisons attest to the fact that those who seek love and affection in marriage do not always find it.

In Chapter 7 we saw that the socialization process still stresses the dif-

FIGURE 9.3 Things Considered "Very Important" to a Good Marriage

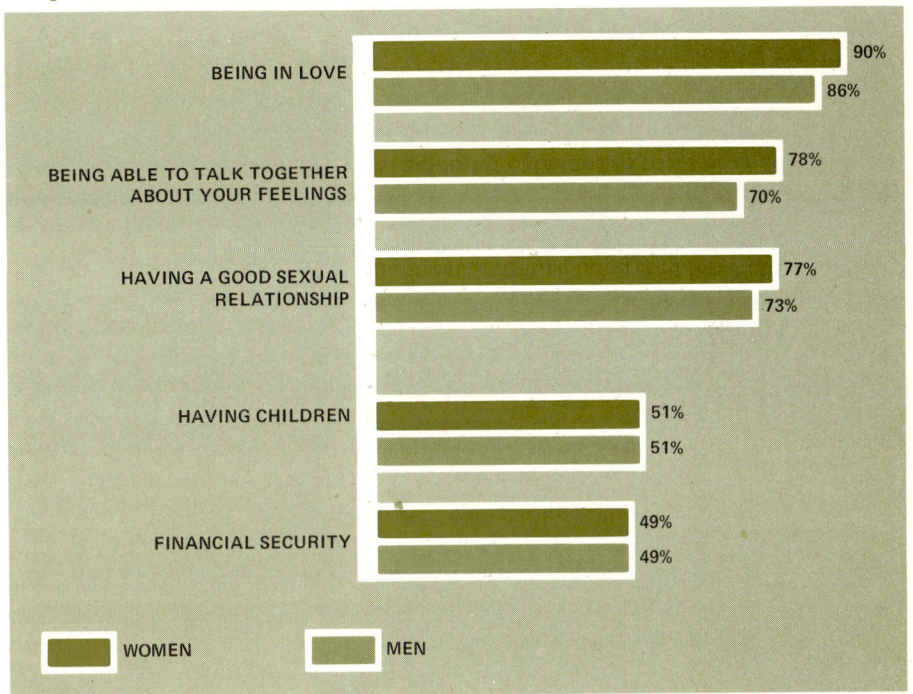

	Women	Men
BEING IN LOVE	90%	86%
BEING ABLE TO TALK TOGETHER ABOUT YOUR FEELINGS	78%	70%
HAVING A GOOD SEXUAL RELATIONSHIP	77%	73%
HAVING CHILDREN	51%	51%
FINANCIAL SECURITY	49%	49%

Men and women basically agree that various aspects of the affectional function of marriage are things that are very important in it. (Note the lesser stress on the childbearing and economic functions.) When love and companionship are not sufficiently strong in their marriages, many couples find that there is not much else to hold them together.

Source: The Virginia Slims American Women's Opinion Poll, vol. 3, "A Survey of the Attitudes of Women on Marriage, Divorce, the Family and America's Changing Sexual Morality," conducted by the Roper Organization (Spring 1974), page 45.

ference between the sexes and conditions males and females to think, feel, and act differently, as well as to act out different roles in society. One result of this training is a certain amount of distance being created between the sexes. Men and women, even those married to each other, are not fully comfortable with the opposite sex and often find it difficult to understand each other. In other words, our sex-role stereotyping has created a barrier to intimacy between husbands and wives and strains the affectional function of the family.

It is true that sex-role stereotyping was more pronounced in the past than it is today. This suggests that the barriers to intimacy were also stronger and that the affectional function of the family was under more strain than it is now. In the past, it was probably difficult for husband and wife to achieve a highly intimate relationship. But the spouses had closer ties with members of the extended family, and in that way, they received and gave affection within the group. Then, too, husbands and wives were more bound to each other economically, and there were more children in the family to care for and rear. Thus, although affection between the spouses was important, there were other strong ties between them that were equally important.

The women's movement is often praised for its liberating effect on women, for making them better able to achieve their potentialities and find fulfillment as individuals. Others note that the movement benefits men, also, for it produces wives who are more stimulating and exciting. It should also be noted that modern trends are reducing the barriers between the worlds of men and women. Each sex should become better able to appreciate the problems, joys, and frustrations of the other. These shared experiences and feelings should allow husbands and wives to understand each other better and to achieve an intimacy that is deep and full.

There are indications that the American family may soon be performing its affectional function better than ever before. However, the strong emphasis on the affectional function of marriage can be a source of strain as well as a source of strength. Believing that love is all they need, some people marry too young, before they are emotionally mature or aware of the obligations of marriage. Others choose mates unwisely or expect too much of the affectional potential of marriage. To be sure, many find emotional refuge from a cold and uncaring world in the closed circle of the marriage. But it may simply be too much to ask that all the strains and frustrations of the world of work be smoothed away daily in a loving husband-wife relationship.

Meeting the Need for Clothes, Food, and Shelter

The part the family plays in producing and distributing goods and services needed for its members' survival constitutes the family's economic function. For a group to survive, its members must be fed, clothed, and sheltered from the elements. These basic needs must be met in such a way that people can live in harmony with one another, without disruptive conflict over scarce resources.

Almost everywhere, marriage involves some kind of division of labor between husbands and wives, so that they and their children can obtain the goods and services they need. This division of labor sometimes involves members of the extended family as well, and in some cases, even the children play a part in producing goods and services. The technological aspects of culture affect not just what is produced and the means used to produce goods but also the economic function of the family.

Evolution of the Economic Function At the hunting and gathering stage of societal development, it was advantageous for the units of production to be small, so that people could move freely in search of game and fruit. The primary division of labor was within the nuclear family, with the men and

Generally, women have been assigned the role of caring for children but in Laos it is common for fathers to feed little children and otherwise participate in their daily care.

older boys going on the hunt, and the women and younger children searching for nuts and berries. Often, the meat from larger animals was shared within the group that banded together, as among the !Kung Bushmen described in Chapter 5, but even so, it was distributed only to specific nuclear families. Since neither men nor women owned the property that was used to produce a living for the family, it is likely that, at this stage, there was an egalitarian relationship between husband and wife.

With the coming of the horticultural stage, and particularly with the agricultural stage that followed it, homes became fixed. Larger family units cooperatively worked a plot of land. As we saw in Chapter 7, almost all societies assigned the task of clearing the land for cultivation to the male, and this led to male control of—and eventually ownership of—the land. Since the many tasks involved in working the land were divided among a number of people, it was desirable to have a leader or someone to assure that the various tasks were completed and that the proper agricultural practices were followed. Thus, the male who controlled or owned the land began to exercise more control over the people who worked it, and the egalitarian relationship of husbands and wives was replaced by the family with a strong male head. Usually, the extended, rather than the nuclear, family prevailed, but in any case, the family was still the basic unit of economic production.

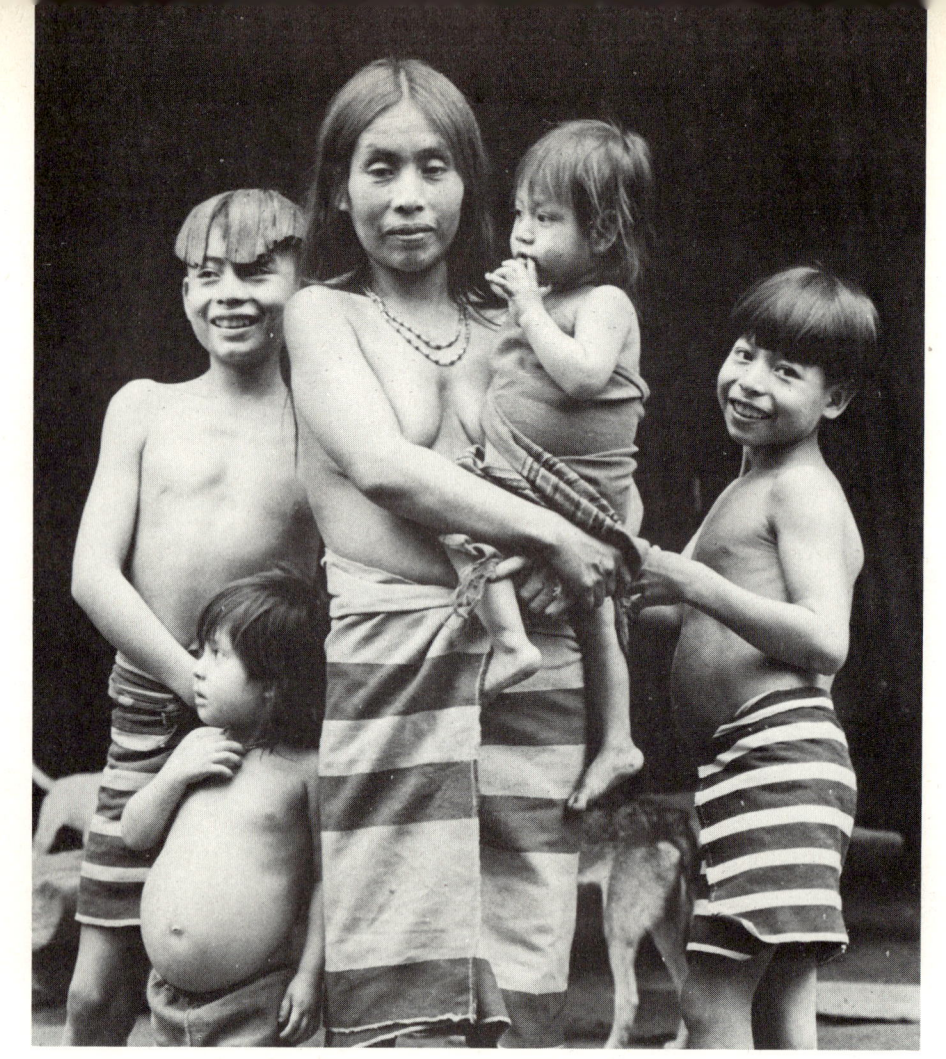

The distended abdomen of one of these children is a sign of malnutrition. The economic function of the family may be deficient but it seems to be performing its affectional function very well.

Even at the pioneer stage of our own society, the family had a major economic function, in that it was the group by which most goods were produced and within which most were consumed. Family members built the family home, raised their own food, and made their own clothing. Because there were few surpluses, the family consumed most of what it produced.

Finally, we come to the industrial stage of civilization, which like the stages before it, has had its effects on the family. In the first place, industrialization led to urbanization, and the small nuclear family was better suited for life in the crowded cities than was the extended family. In modern industrial societies, workers must be willing to move to where work is available, and the small nuclear family is an easier unit to move from place to place than is the larger extended family. The twin forces of industrialization and urbanization are responsible for lowering the birth rate and reducing the size of the family that customarily lives in a common household. The average number of people per family household was 5.7 in 1790 and about the same in 1850. Fifty years later, it had already dropped to 4.8 persons and has been declining ever since. Today, the average household has 3.4 persons. In 1790, just over half of all families had six or more persons; today, only ten percent of all households are that large, and over one-half consist of but two or three members. Industrialization and small family units go hand in hand.

Still another way in which industrialization has affected the family is by reducing the importance of the family group itself as a functioning economic unit—in particular, the family's role as producer of goods and services. Industrialization requires an intricate division of labor and specialization. It brings together people from many families according to their individual skills at producing a great variety of goods. The individual, not the family, becomes the unit of production. Even the family's economic function as consumer is modified as family members eat their meals and obtain many services away from home. As with other family functions, the economic function varies considerably from society to society, and it is strongly influenced, in particular, by the technological stage of the society.

The Changing Economic Function of the American Family In today's American family, the unit of economic production is the individual. The husband, and increasingly, the wife also, contracts to perform some work for a business or firm. In return, he or she receives a wage that is used to provide for his or her own needs and for those of the nonproductive family members. Although highly efficient, this system is quite different from a common economic venture among family members in which the family produces and consumes what it needs.

The family's economic function has changed the most in regard to the number of married women employed outside the home. In 1900, only 5.6 percent of married women held jobs. Today, about 50 percent of all married women who are living with their husbands work outside the home. It has been estimated that 90 percent of American women will be employed at some time during their married life. Although employment rates vary with the presence and age of children in the family, more than 37 percent of married women with children under six years of age work outside the home, as shown in Table 9.1. The employment rate for this category of women is increasing, despite the meagerness of day-care facilities for young children.

TABLE 9.1 Employment of Married Women, Husband Present, 1975

Stage in Family Cycle	Percentage of Working Wives
Wife under 35, no children under 18	77.2
Wife under 35, child under 6	37.2
Wife under 45, child 6–17	55.6
Wife 45 or older, no children under 18	33.4

Source: Data provided by Allyson Grossman, Division of Labor Force Studies, U.S. Department of Labor.

Despite stresses and strains, the family as an institution will survive as long as people of all ages find in it emotional gratification and a sense of belongingness.

From the discussion of roles and positions in Chapter 5, we would be able to predict that a major change in the role of wife would affect the counter-role of husband. But curiously, food purchasing, cooking, cleaning, and other housework still tend to be considered woman's work, whether or not the woman is employed outside the home. But there is a whole new generation of women today who anticipate working, just as men do, whether or not they marry or have children. Younger women, and the men they marry, seem more concerned with sharing both the breadwinning role and the homemaking role, rather than assuming that the one belongs primarily to the husband and the other to the wife. This represents a major change in the economic function, but the basic function of providing family members with the goods and services they need is still being performed within the family.

THE FUTURE OF THE FAMILY

Will marriage and the nuclear family survive in the United States? Should they? These questions are frequently voiced today, for in America, the family is often blamed for the troubles that beset society. Some predict that, having failed to perform its functions, the family is doomed to extinction. Others simply conclude that the family must be in serious trouble, for if not, there would not be so much emphasis in the popular media on how to deal with marriage and family problems.

TABLE 9.2   Divorces and Divorce Rates, United States, 1870–1978

Year	Number of Divorces	Divorces per 1000 Married Females	Divorces per 100 Marriages Performed in Year
1870	10,962	—	3.1
1900	55,751	3.0	7.9
1920	170,505	8.0	13.4
1940	264,000	8.8	16.5
1960	393,000	9.2	25.8
1970	715,000	14.6	32.8
1972	845,000	17.0	37.0
1974	970,000	19.3	43.6
1976	1,077,000	19.9	45.0
1978	1,107,000	21.0	50.2

Source: Data adapted from U.S. Department of Health, Education, and Welfare, *Vital Statistics of the United States and Monthly Vital Statistics Report,* various issues, and *100 Years of Marriage and Divorce Statistics, United States, 1867–1967.* Data for 1978 are provisional.

Divorce

There is much evidence of difficulties in the institutions of marriage and the family in the United States. One indication is our divorce rate—the highest in the industrial world—which is still increasing. As shown in Table 9.2, after the close of the Civil War, about 10,000 divorces were granted each year; 50 years later, around 1920, there were over 170,000 a year; and after another 50 years, in 1970, there were 715,000 divorces annually. Today, the figure is over a million.

In part, the increase in the number of divorces reflects the growth in population. To get a better idea of what these numbers really mean, let us look at some divorce rates. Table 9.2 contains two different rates of divorce. The first one, calculated as the number of divorces per 1,000 married women, shows the proportion of all marriages now existing that will end in divorce in a given year. Thus, for recent years, we can say that about two percent of all marriages end in divorce each year. This rate is analogous to a statement of the probability of your being in an automobile accident this year.

The other figure relates the number of divorces granted in a given year to the number of marriages performed during that same year. There are technical problems with this statistic, but it attempts to measure what proportion of all marriages will *someday* end in divorce. It is analogous to a statement of your chances of ever being in an automobile accident, rather than your chances for such an occurrence this year alone. From this second divorce rate, we would estimate that about 50 percent of all marriages being formed will eventually end in divorce. However we measure divorce, it is apparent that the rate is very high, indicating that millions are not finding in marriage what they are seeking.

Cohabitation

There is other evidence of strain in our contemporary marriage and family system. The number of couples who live together outside of marriage increased eightfold between 1960 and 1970 and doubled again by 1976, with 1.3 million people cohabiting outside of marriage. A survey of 100,000 women by *Redbook Magazine* found that three percent had, at one time, lived with a man outside of marriage (Levin and Levin, 1975). Some college campuses report a considerably higher rate of couples living together. Again, there are people who live in what they consider group marriages, and there are cases in which one woman lives with two or more men or one man lives with two or more women. These plural unions cannot be considered legal marriage in our society. The actual number of people involved are few, but the various arrangements for cohabiting outside marriage do attest to the discontent and disillusionment with traditional marriage. It is significant, too, that these extralegal arrangements are more or less tolerated by the rest of society.

Restructuring Marriage

There are many specific complaints about contemporary marriage, but the overriding criticism of those who opt for other arrangements is that marriage is an affront to equality and interferes with personal growth. Meanwhile, there is a countertrend toward redefining and strengthening marriage, as exemplified by the marriage encounter and marriage enrichment movements. Couples involved in these groups believe that human growth is facilitated in an atmosphere where there is love, mutual help and support, and a long-term commitment to the relationship. These values, it is contended, are best articulated in egalitarian, monogamous marriages. Couples dedicated to marriage enrichment are discontented with the traditional, authoritarian marriage and family and are striving to make marriage more compatible with human needs, as they are seen today.

Economic Stress

It is not just the marital relationship that is in trouble today. There is evidence that there are considerable strains on the economic function of the family, too. The nuclear family, as a system, seems incapable of providing health, education, and sometimes even support for its members, particularly the very old and the very young. The economic function of the family can, and probably will, be modified by state provisions for more medical care, better support for the aged and the poor, more day-care centers, increased aid to dependent children, and the like.

We can still safely predict, however, that marriage and the nuclear family will survive well beyond this century. The affectional function of the family seems absolutely necessary. As yet, nowhere have people been able to delegate to nonfamily groups the function of providing completely for the emotional needs of infants and children. Similarly, adults have a need for an enduring relationship in which they can obtain emotional gratification. The nuclear family can fulfill this need for most people, and even today, it does so for many.

The important emotional gratification function of the family will, no doubt, continue to dominate its other functions. Although there are strains in this function, many of them can, and probably will, be eliminated when, as a society, we work through some of the confusions and contradictions of male-female roles and provide better socialization for marriage. As the sociologist Betty Yorburg puts it, "Marriage and the nuclear family will continue as basic institutions in human societies, functioning imperfectly and inefficiently, and sometimes malevolently, but persevering because it is not possible to come up with anything more workable to provide for the basic emotional needs of human beings—young or old" (1973, p. 197).

We have seen that the family combines many of the major social functions in a single institution. As a socializing agent, it is the first and most important teacher of the values, roles, and norms of a society. Although, in advanced industrial societies, the economic function has lessened considerably, other functions essential to smooth human interaction are still performed by the family—reproduction, sexual regulation, status ascription, and affection. But, even in these functions, the family has undergone change. There are now many socializing agents besides the family. And, for decades, traditional sexual rules have been followed by decreasing numbers of people: couples are living together without marrying, and some women are choosing to be mothers without being wives. Moreover, there is evidence that the heavy stress put on the affectional function of marriage, along with the role conflicts arising from changes in values, norms, and roles, is largely responsible for our rising rate of failed marriages.

Although we can predict that the family will survive in the future, today it is surely in the midst of heavy weather, as, indeed, are all of our institutions. Major changes have also occurred, for example, in the institution of religion, which was the major source of values in Western societies for many centuries. It is to this institution that we will turn our attention in Chapter 10.

SUMMARY

1. There are two biological bases for the family: (1) human infants are helpless and need someone to care for them, and (2) the sexual nature of human beings requires controls such as those offered by marriage and the family.

2. The term "family" has many different applications. The **nuclear family** is a married pair and their immature offspring. We each belong to two nuclear families: the **family of orientation** (the one we are born into) and the **family of procreation** (a married pair plus their offspring). The **extended family** is two or more nuclear families joined by an extension of the parent-child relationship.

3. **Marriage** is a relationship between two sexually interacting adults that is sufficiently enduring to provide for the procreation and rearing of children. Marriage is found in all societies, although it takes a variety of forms, from **monogamy** and **polygamy** to **group marriage.**

4. All societies regulate marriage in some way. **Endogamous rules** stipulate that a person must select a mate from within a certain group; **exogamous rules** stipulate that a person must select a marriage partner outside some designated group. Societies also have rules for how mates are selected and how the marriage ceremony is performed.

5. The major functions of the family are reproduction, socialization of children, status ascription, sexual regulation, emotional gratification, and economic survival.

6. Societies differ in their attitudes toward family size and toward illegitimacy. In America, the family plays a central role in socialization, but other agents are beginning to have a great influence. Still, through the family, children learn who they are and how they fit into the larger society.

7. In every society, the principal source of sexual satisfaction is supposed to be marriage. All societies have the primary **incest taboo,** but they vary in their attitudes toward premarital and extramarital sex.

8. In all societies, the family has an affectional function. Children who are deprived of affection in infancy suffer from both physical and psychological disorders. Adults also look to the family as a source of emotional satisfaction.

9. In earlier stages of civilization, the family was the primary economic unit—it was the group in which most goods were produced and consumed. With the industrial revolution came a drop in family size and an emphasis on the nuclear family. Today, the unit of production has become the individual, as opposed to the family, and women are fulfilling more of the economic function than they used to.

10. The American divorce rate is the highest in the industrial world and continues to increase. Another indication of strain in the American marriage system is the fact that many people are turning to cohabitation as an alternative. There appear to be strains in all of the family's functions, as various other agencies take over aspects that had previously

belonged to the family. But, it appears that as long as the family is the major source of emotional gratification, it will continue to survive.

KEY TERMS

crude birth rate
egalitarian marriage
endogamous rules
exogamous rules
extended family
family of orientation
family of procreation
group marriage
incest taboo

kibbutz
marriage
matriarchal family
monogamy
nuclear family
patriarchal family
polyandry
polygamy
polygyny

SUGGESTED READINGS

Billingsley, Andrew. *Black Families in White America.* Englewood Cliffs, N.J.: Prentice-Hall, 1968.
 A structural-functional approach to the problems of America's black families.

Farber, Bernard. *Kinship and Class.* New York: Basic Books, 1971.
 A sociological study of kinship relations in two midwestern cities.

Fullerton, Gail Putney. *Survival in Marriage.* New York: Holt, Rinehart and Winston, 1972.
 A view of the family in modern mass society. The emphasis is on factors that lead to family conflict and breakdown.

Kenkel, William F. *The Family in Perspective.* 4th ed. Santa Monica, Calif.: Goodyear, 1977.
 A basic text in family sociology. The book deals with the family in our own and in other cultures and provides a number of different approaches to the study of the family.

Kenniston, Kenneth. *All Our Children: The American Family Under Pressure.* New York: Harcourt Brace Jovanovich, 1977.
 Kenniston documents how families, and the circumstances of their lives, are the most critical factor in determining children's fates.

O'Neill, Nena. *The Marriage Premise.* New York: Evans, 1977.
 The author examines the reasons for the continuing appeal of marriage as an arrangement for meeting basic human needs.

Rossi, Alice S., Jerome Kagan, and Tamara K. Hareven. *The Family.* New York: Norton, 1978.
 A cross-cultural approach, with chapters on family life and sex roles in western Europe, Japan, Kenya, and the United States.

In the dim past, humans did not separate the seen from the unseen world, nor did they believe that there were gods to be worshipped. It is fascinating to trace the ways in which human societies changed, so that religion ultimately became an important institution. One major anthropologist, Sir James G. Frazer, has traced these changes through three major phases, based on three major means people have used to understand the world and deal with its problems: magic, religion, and science.

To the sociologist, there are three aspects of religion: the belief system—ideas about gods, supernatural life, and sacred objects; ritual—the behavior and practices dictated by the religion, such as kneeling in worship or singing sacred songs; and the addressing of questions on the ultimate meaning of life—the nature of humanity, the eventual fate of humans, and the meaning of human existence. Beliefs and rituals help people to deal with the latter aspect of religion.

With its emphasis on ultimate meanings, it would seem that religion could be a powerful force in human societies. We will see that religion does serve a number of functions, including the endorsement or validation of society's values. Religion can both keep a society stable and help to bring about social change: these are social functions. Religion also has personal functions and dysfunctions—beneficial or harmful effects on the individual. It can help people achieve peace of mind and contentment, or it can lead to torment and unhappiness.

In the United States, religion is characterized by both pluralism—a diversity of religions—and ecumenism—a move to unite all Christian religions. Americans have made an effort to separate church and state, which has not always been an easy task. The religious behavior of Americans has been studied by examining religious preferences, church attendance, church membership, and measures of religiosity.

Despite the fact that some feel religion is not a relevant social force, and despite problems such as the secondary role of women in most churches, it is likely that organized religion will continue as long as people have ultimate concerns that cannot be answered by science.

10
Religion and Society

Walking down the street in any large American city today can be quite an adventure and a chance to be exposed to some fascinating aspects of our culture. For example, recently, on a sunny day in New York City, there was a group of Hare Krishna members dancing, chanting, and beating tambourines on one corner, while across the street, a Salvation Army band was beating on its tambourines. Further down the street, there was a soapbox preacher lecturing on the topic of abortion and handing out pamphlets on the rights of the unborn. Among those wandering by as he spoke were a group of Japanese parochial school students in their uniforms and an Orthodox Jew in his skull cap and beard. A few blocks from all that, there was a group of "Moonies" handing out tickets to a giant rally at which Sun Myung Moon was to appear; and not too far away from there, some Black Muslims were peddling their publication, *Muhammad Speaks.* Wandering past the giant skyscrapers, one could observe nuns entering one of the impressive Catholic churches; and while windowshopping, one could see a Christian Science Reading Room, a number of delicatessens featuring kosher foods, and novelty store windows filled with plastic Jesus statues.

One's power of observation need not be great to realize that religion is not only a pervasive part of American society but also a greatly diversified aspect of our culture.

In Chapter 3, we noted that the culture of every society contains three broad elements: (1) ideas for physical survival, (2) ideas for living together in an orderly way, and (3) ideas for meeting the psychological needs of the society's members. In this chapter, we explore how, as a basic social institution, religion is related to these universals of culture, and particularly, how religion gives meaning to the various ways humans have invented to meet their needs.

We could begin this chapter by trying to present a terse definition of religion. It would, of course, have to be sufficiently broad to encompass such modern movements as Jim Jones's Peoples Temple, Sun Myung Moon's Unification Church, and the followers of Maharaj Ji in the 1970s in the United States; such ancient religions as Buddhism, Islam, and Christianity; and all else that we tend to think of as religious in primitive and modern societies. Rather than attempting a formal definition of religion at this point, we will approach the subject by first discussing some of the problems scholars have encountered in their attempts to chart the evolution of religion and to distinguish it from related phenomena.

We will look briefly, first, at how religion has evolved and at the interrelationship of magic, religion, and science: the three systems humanity has developed to give meaning to its world. We will then be better able to explain what we mean by religion, and to discuss how sociologists study religion to expand their understanding of human social interaction.

THE EVOLUTION OF RELIGION

Sociologists and others have long been interested in religion among early humans and how it evolved to the present-day systems. We noted in Chapter 1 that Comte, the "father of sociology," maintained that the earliest humans offered theological and supernatural explanations for all phenomena. Other sociologists have gone into the origin and evolution of religion more deeply. For example, Robert Bellah (1964), a sociologist of religion, traced religion through five stages: primitive, archaic, historic, early modern, and modern. At the *primitive stage,* humans did not recognize a duality of the seen and unseen world. Their single world was inhabited by ancestral spirits and animal figures from the past, but these were not gods, and they were not worshipped. Primitive humans ritualistically acted out their identification with mythical beings and with elements in the seen world, such as rocks, trees, and mountains.

At the *archaic stage* of religion, according to Bellah, there was still only one world, but it contained nonhumans, or gods, who sometimes interfered with daily life. Religious rituals were seen as a way to maintain communication between humans and gods in the unified natural-divine cosmos. At the *historic stage* (during which stage Judaism, Christianity, and Buddhism arose), religion underwent a profound change. It became transcendental; that is, it posited a world beyond the limits of human experience, a world that is not a part of the material universe.

Bellah sees the Protestant Reformation as the turning point from the historic to the next, or *early modern,* religious stage. The key feature of the early modern stage was the rejection of the idea that it is necessary to withdraw from worldly activities to achieve salvation. The world was seen as an arena in which to work out the divine command and to serve God in every walk of life. In the emerging *modern stage,* according to Bellah, the essential dualism between the world of our senses and the world apart from them is collapsing. The search for meaning is bound up intricately with the search for personal maturity and social relevance. Each individual must work out his or her own ultimate solutions, drawing not only on the church but on secular doctrines as well.

There is still much to be learned about the evolution of religion and how it affects, and is affected by, the organization of societies. The journal *Ethnology* regularly publishes systematically coded information on hundreds of existing primitive societies in all parts of the world. Gerhard Lenski (1970) analyzed these records for the dominant conception of God, if any, found in the many cultures. He found that in those societies at the least complex stage of civilization (the hunting and gathering stage) most often there is no conception of a supreme creator. Where such a belief does exist, the supreme being is considered to be unconcerned with human affairs. This is consistent with Bellah's idea of the primitive stage of religion. In advanced horticultural societies—those in which plant cultivation is the primary means of subsistence and in which metal tools are used—belief in a supreme creator becomes more prevalent. It is not until the agrarian stage that the predominant belief is in a supreme being who created the universe and who remains actively concerned with what was created and with the moral behavior of humans. (This stage corresponds to Bellah's historic stage.)

This orderly sequence in the evolution of religion in human societies suggests that as society becomes more complex, people seem to have a greater need for explanations of their world. But there is more than one way of explaining reality; other explanations come from magic and from science.

MAGIC, RELIGION, AND SCIENCE

Lenski's analysis of the evolution of religion by societal types—hunting and gathering, horticultural, agrarian—rests on a rather complex relationship between the technology that humans develop and the social organization it permits them. A somewhat different view of the evolution of religion was taken by Sir James George Frazer. In 1890 Frazer published *The Golden Bough,* a classic study of magic and religion that linked our ancient taboos, rituals, superstitions, and beliefs with our perennial problems and wants. Frazer concluded that the needs and wants of people everywhere are basically the same, but that throughout the centuries different modes of seeking solutions have been used.

As Frazer saw it, humanity has progressed from magic to religion to science in its unending search for control of the forces of nature. Magic assumes a certain order to nature, which humans, by their own means, can control to suit their needs. When early humans discovered that their powers to control nature were imaginary, they threw themselves on the mercy of invisible beings, or gods, to whom they ascribed the power they once thought themselves to have. Thus, in Frazer's view, magic was gradually superseded by religion. The gods of primitive religion were thought to be vastly more powerful than humans and to have the ability to control the forces of nature. But this concept assumes an irregular and variable universe, one that is controlled by the whims or capriciousness of the gods.

Frazer theorized that, in time, humans became impressed with the order of natural events. They came to realize that, if understood properly, such events could be predicted with some degree of accuracy and acted upon accordingly. As Frazer put it, "In short, religion as an explanation of nature, is displaced by science." Interestingly, Frazer did not consider science the final stage in the sequence of humanity's attempt to understand and deal with nature, but only the current stage. According to Frazer, "as science has supplanted its predecessors, so it may hereafter be itself superseded by some more perfect hypothesis, perhaps by some totally different way of looking at the phenomena—of registering the shadows on the screen—of which we in this generation can form no idea" (pp. 649–650).

Frazer's theories on the progressive sequence of magic, religion, and science provide a useful point of departure for discussing these phenomena. Clearly, there is *some* connection among these three systems. What is magic, and how does it differ from religion? Is there actually a conflict between science and religion? And what is the relationship among these three modes of thought?

Magic and Religion: How Do They Differ?

It is not easy to make a rigid distinction between magic and religion. Both systems of belief assume that there is a supernatural or unknown world, and both assume that there is a power in this supernatural world that can affect life in the natural world. The supernatural is what is beyond the world of the senses; it is scientifically unknowable and incapable of proof or disproof.

It should be noted here that when we talk about **magic** we are not refer-

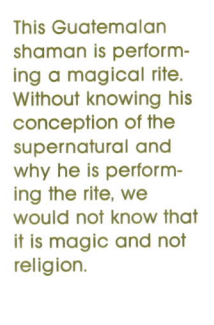

This Guatemalan shaman is performing a magical rite. Without knowing his conception of the supernatural and why he is performing the rite, we would not know that it is magic and not religion.

ring to stage magicians' tricks or sleight of hand. We are referring, rather, to the belief that there are supernatural forces that human beings can learn to control in order to achieve some goal. Religion, too, involves a belief in supernatural forces, and it is often difficult to distinguish the two concepts. Nevertheless, we can begin to understand how the two concepts differ by comparing and contrasting them. Their differences are in: (1) the assumptions each makes about the supernatural, (2) the ends or goals pursued, (3) the means used to seek those ends, and (4) the effects of the systems on society and on the individual.

Assumptions About the Supernatural Characteristically, religions include a belief that the power that influences the unknown world is a being or beings of some sort. These beings may have the physical form or other characteristics of humans. While it may be stretching the matter to say that the wind, the sun, or a mountain has animate power, these, too, should be included, for power is sometimes ascribed to this type of "being." In what is called *animate power,* the source of power is given a definite location, equivalent to a person or personality.

Magic, in contrast, is more frequently characterized by a belief in *inanimate* rather than animate power. The unknown world of the supernatural contains forces that can be manipulated by those who understand them. This type of power can be compared to modern humanity's conception of electricity. It is just there. He who has the knowledge can use it, for good or evil. So, if two different groups were seeking the same results—say, rain to end a drought, or someone's return to health—and one group believed in magic and the other religion, they might both use some kind of ritual. However, the religious ritual would be directed to an invisible *person* with power over rain or health, whereas the magic ritual would be used to directly tap invisible, impersonal *forces* that control rain or health.

Goals In magic, the goal relates to the observable world, is usually desired immediately, and is usually personal. A man might consult a magician or witchdoctor to assure the fertility of his field—or for that matter, of his wife. A witchdoctor might be sought out to heal a sore or cure a disease. These are personal goals, and the results are anticipated almost immediately. The magician is consulted because it is felt that he has learned the secrets that enable him to tap the power in the unknown world.

Goals pursued by religious means can also be practical and personal. One may pray for health or success, for the life of a loved one, or for rain for one's crops. But often, the ends, though personal, are expressed differently by the religious person than by the magic-oriented person. A Christian may pray for guidance to cope with life's problems or for the strength to endure what cannot be cured. There is no formula for such ends in any system of magic. Religion offers a philosophy of life and addresses itself to ultimate values; magic generally does not.

Rituals Magic and religion also differ in the means used by each to reach the desired goal. Sometimes their rituals, whether bodily movements, incantations, or the offering of a sacrifice, appear similar. But if one investigates the symbolic *meanings* of the behavior and the *spirit* and *attitudes* accompanying it, striking differences can be noted. Magic is a businesslike affair, with the magician performing his rites in an impersonal manner. A contractual relationship is established between the practitioner of magic and his or her "customer." When a witchdoctor is consulted to break a spell, his superior skill is recognized, but he is not considered a superior being. The magician, or witchdoctor, is not beseeched or entreated. He or she is simply hired to do a job at hand. Behind the religious ritual, on the other hand, is the tacit recognition that an appeal is being made to a vastly superior being (the god), who is approached with deference, awe, and piety. There is thus a difference — admittedly sometimes subtle — in the behavior and accompanying attitudes of the participants in a religious as opposed to a magical ritual.

Social and Personal Consequences By almost any definition, magic can be considered beneficial. Millions of people have been "cured" by witchdoctors, and millions more have experienced great emotional relief to learn that an evil spell has been broken. Magic has also been used to cast evil spells, to bring about the death of an enemy, or to gain another's property illegally. Such "black magic" is not only harmful to the believing victim but may be harmful to society as well. It may force individuals to use life's precious moments engaging in countermagic or guarding their hair or nail clippings from a wicked enemy. To be sure, religion can do and has done both good and harm to individuals and societies, and we will deal with this later. Generally, however, religion has not been used to achieve ends contrary to group goals, whereas magic has been.

Again, it is not easy to make a rigid distinction between magic and religion, even though there are observable differences. As a further complication, the two systems can co-exist within a single society, and either or both can co-exist with science.

Science and Religion: Competition and Co-existence

As we have seen, religion deals with the supernatural. Its system of beliefs, accepted on faith, seeks to determine the values and to describe the forces that, in some ultimate sense, affect human destiny. By definition, then, *religion* deals with the extraordinary, with phenomena that are not knowable in any ordinary way. There is a profound difference between the questions, "Is there a heaven?" and "How many people believe there is a heaven?" Science cannot tell us that there is or is not a heaven. A scientific survey showing that belief in an afterlife is declining might make people question their beliefs, but the findings could not be construed as challenging the belief itself or providing evidence contrary to it. Why, then, is there any problem? If science and religion use different methods and deal with different phenomena, how can there be a conflict?

Well, for one thing, the distinction between the knowable and the unknowable is not clear-cut. Sometimes it cannot definitely be said that a certain phenomenon is incapable of being studied by scientific means. It may be true today but not tomorrow. Not too many years ago, science could tell us nothing about the origin of human life on earth; when, where, and how life began were unknowable by scientific means. Christianity, as well as other religions, had strong beliefs about these matters. Questions about the origin of human life were considered to be religious matters, and just about every religion had long ago offered answers with its own account of creation.

Over the years, people came to believe that to seek knowledge about the origin of their species was legitimately within the scope of science. Beginning in the Renaissance, questions on the origin of human life were transferred from the domain of religion to that of science. But as late as 1929, the contest was still alive. It was so alive, in fact, that John Scopes was convicted at the famous "monkey trial" in Tennessee for teaching Darwin's theory of evolution in a public school, in violation of state law. For a considerable time, then, religion and science were in conflict on this issue. One cannot accept both a literal interpretation of Biblical creation and the biological theory of evolution.

Other examples of the impermanence of the boundary between science and religion, between the knowable and the unknowable, are not difficult to find. The Copernican theory that the earth and other planets revolved around the sun was once considered heresy, for it conflicted with the official belief of the Church that the universe was earth-centered. Galileo first gave and then withdrew his public support for Copernican theory. He was treading on the shifting boundary between religion and science. Even though he had confirmed Copernican theory with his telescope, under the threat of excommunication and death at the stake, he cast his lot with religion. Ultimately, the battle was won for science, for the Christian denominations now consider it legitimate for scientists to study the moon, the stars, and the planets objectively and to report their findings factually, whatever they may be. The proper source of knowledge of the physical world has shifted from religion to science.

A current example of the shifting boundary between the knowable and the unknowable can be found in the reports of persons who have been clinically dead and have given accounts of their experiences "after death" (Moody, 1976). The reports are remarkably similar. Almost all of them describe the sensation of floating a few feet above their bodies and watching the doctors and nurses work on them or give up on them. The afterlife described by those who have "died" and come back is beautiful beyond comprehension, and often, they report meeting relatives who died years before. Do reports such as these indicate that life after death can be studied scientifically? Is the source of knowledge concerning the hereafter shifting from religion to science, and if so, to what will religion address itself?

It may appear that religion has been forced again and again to surrender to science. Often, however, it has not been a total surrender. By reinterpreting its views or by shifting the issue to a more philosophical and less literal plane, religion has erased the contradictions between religious beliefs and scientific facts. Thus, Christians can believe that the earth and its inhabitants have a special place in the eyes of their God, so much so that He sent His son to dwell here and sacrifice Himself for human salvation. But they can also accept the scientific fact that the universe is not earth-centered. Discovery of intelligent life on another planet could also be reconciled with religious beliefs. Could not this be what Jesus meant when he said, "Other sheep I have who are not of this fold"? As science has advanced, people have looked to it for answers to more and more questions. Yet, questions remain about ultimate causes, the meaning of human existence, and human destiny, and these questions cannot—yet—be answered by science.

THE NATURE OF RELIGION

Perhaps, in a chapter on religion, it is not too much to ask the reader to have a little faith—not unquestioning belief in a specific dogma, but rather, faith that we will soon show why understanding religion is important to the sociologist. But, first, a formal definition of religion will enable us to agree on just what is important and consequential.

According to the sociologist J. Milton Yinger (1957), we can define **religion** as "a system of beliefs and practices by means of which a group of people struggle with [the] ultimate problems of human life" (p. 9). Charles Glock and Rodney Stark (1965), other authorities on the sociology of religion, define religion as "one variety of value orientations, those institutionalized systems of beliefs, symbols, values, and practices that provide groups of men with solutions to their questions of ultimate meaning" (p. 17). Let us examine these definitions to see what they include and exclude.

Ultimate Meanings

Probably the most abstract but most significant aspect of both definitions is the idea that religion deals with **ultimate meanings.** We noted in our discussion of magic and religion that humans have always been concerned with a reality beyond experience. A system of ultimate meanings describes this reality, gives the reasons for human existence, and defines the nature of humanity: its origins, its purpose, its relationship to the natural world, and its eventual fate. A system of ultimate meanings allows one to answer, even if

FIGURE 10.1 Cross-Cultural Comparison of Religious Beliefs

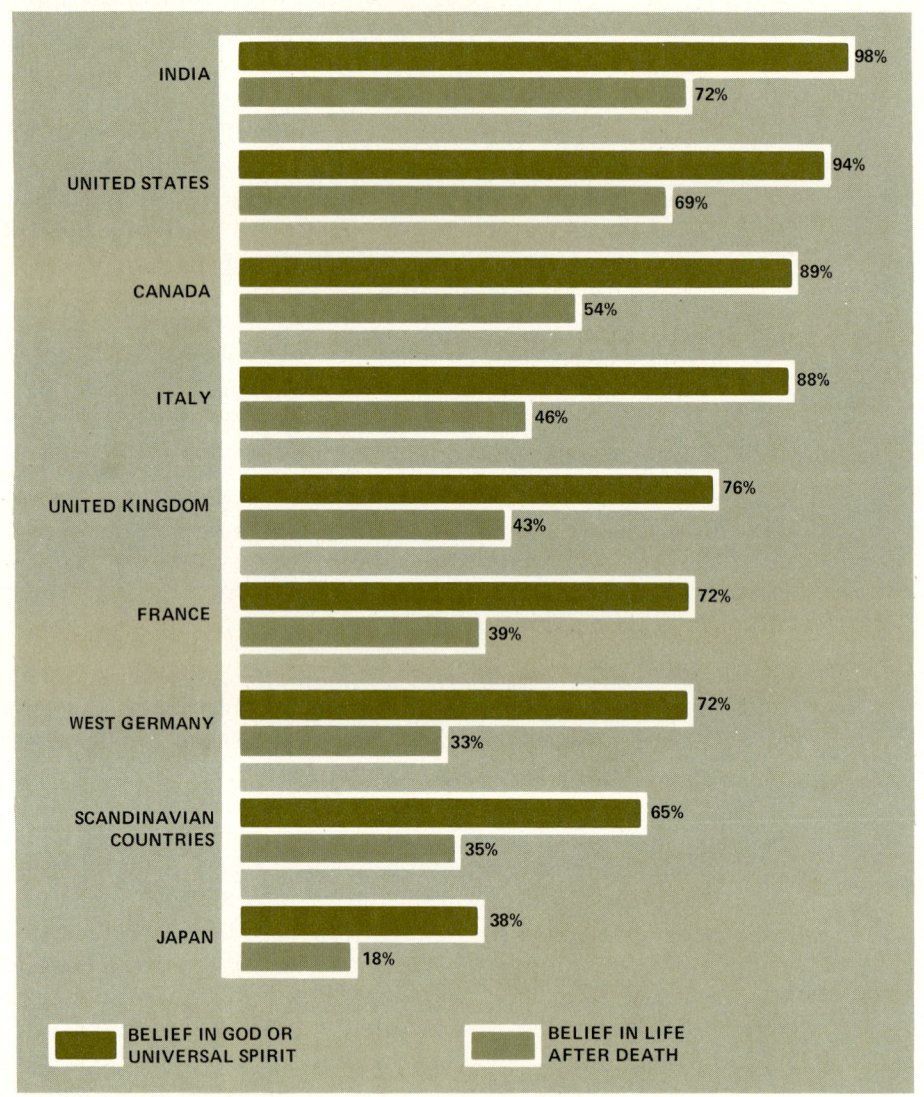

Country	Belief in God or Universal Spirit	Belief in Life After Death
INDIA	98%	72%
UNITED STATES	94%	69%
CANADA	89%	54%
ITALY	88%	46%
UNITED KINGDOM	76%	43%
FRANCE	72%	39%
WEST GERMANY	72%	33%
SCANDINAVIAN COUNTRIES	65%	35%
JAPAN	38%	18%

In Italy, often considered a Catholic country, less than half of the people believe in life after death, and fewer Italians than Americans believe in God or a Universal Spirit.

Source: *Gallup Opinion Index* (Princeton, N.J.: Gallup International, 1976), p. 6.

tentatively, the universal and pervasive question, "What am I doing on this earth?"

It would be next to impossible to find agreement on some listing of the ultimate human concerns. The following, however, are among the questions to which human societies and individuals have sought answers through their religions:

What is the purpose of life?
What is death, and what is beyond it?
Is there a central meaning to life that can help us to understand life's disappointments, sufferings, and tragedies?
Can interpersonal and intergroup hatred and hostility be controlled, or even neutralized?

Religion cannot supply scientifically testable answers to these and other fundamental questions, but it can furnish a system of beliefs about these ultimate concerns.

Beliefs

Every religion contains a set of **beliefs.** The essence of any belief is the conviction that an idea is correct. What is believed is accepted as being true: empirical or logical proof is not required. To the sociologist, it does not really matter whether a religious belief is "true." The essential thing is to ascertain and to understand what it is that a group believes.

Emile Durkheim's definition of religion, in his classic work *Elementary Forms of Religious Life* (1926), provides a starting point for a fuller appreciation of religious beliefs:

> All known religious beliefs, whether simple or complex, present one common characteristic: they presuppose a classification of all things, real and ideal, of which men think, into two classes or opposed groups, generally designated by two distinct terms, which are translated well enough by the words *profane* and *sacred* (p. 36).

What is regarded as **sacred,** or holy, is set apart from the ordinary, the secular, or, in Durkheim's term, the **profane.** Sacredness is in the minds of the believers. People define what is sacred, and people develop and display attitudes of awe, respect, and reverence toward what they consider sacred, whether it is in the supernatural or the natural world.

In the great religions of the world, much of what is defined as sacred deals with the supernatural—that which is beyond what we can see, hear, or touch. Belief in an existence beyond the grave, in a power that manifests itself in the universe, in gods, angels, eternal reward, or eternal damnation—all these are extraordinary, or supernatural, matters that groups have defined as sacred. Within the supernatural, specific personages—such as the Holy Spirit of Christian religions, Allah and Mohammed, his prophet, Zeus, or Jupiter—may also be considered as sacred.

Sacredness is also attributed to objects in the natural, material world. To Moslems, the Black Stone of the Kaaba is sacred. To Jews, the Ark of the Covenant is sacred. To Hindus, the cow is sacred (see Box 10.1). And to Christians, the cross is sacred. Books, prayer wheels, candles, cows, rosary beads, ikons, fire, and water have all been considered sacred by one religion or another. These and many other objects are not sacred because of built-in natural qualities, but because they have symbolic connection with a group's beliefs about the supernatural.

Religious beliefs, whether about the natural or the supernatural realm, may be highly articulated and specific, as in the Nicene Creed, which recites the fundamental articles of Christian faith; or they may be implicit, as in a systematic and intricately organized theology. In any case, religious beliefs define for the believers what is sacred and what is not. More than this, the beliefs relate the sacred to the nonsacred. They specify, in other words, how the unseen and the unknowable are related to the observable world. Although beliefs themselves rest in the mind, they have a bearing on behavior—at the very least, on the behavior known as religious practices, or rituals.

**BOX 10.1
INDIA'S
SACRED COW**

In the Hindu religion, cattle are considered sacred, and Hindus are forbidden to eat beef. Many people consider this religious taboo to be totally irrational, for as cows wander city streets nibbling produce off market stands, thousands of people starve rather than eat them. However, anthropologist Marvin Harris (1978) has challenged this viewpoint and has suggested that the sacred cow is, in fact, the foundation of India's economy. Without the taboo against beef-eating, India would be in far worse shape than it is.

The species of cattle revered in India is the zebu, a large, humpbacked type. Although the zebu cow produces milk, this is not her main economic function (in India, female water buffalo are the main source of dairy products). The primary function of sacred cows is to produce male calves, from which come the oxen that are the main work animals of India. Oxen are used to plow the fields, to break grain from stalks, and to transport goods and people. As Harris puts it, "The ox is the Indian peasant's tractor, thresher, and family car combined; the cow is the factory that produces the ox" (p. 31).

In order to survive, each family must have a cow and a team of oxen. If an ox dies, replacements are so expensive that the farmer eventually loses his land trying to make the payments. Having a fertile cow allows the family to raise replacements for the ox team. All cattle are sacred, but because the cow produces both bulls and oxen, it is considered the most sacred. "The peasant whose cow dies is not only crying over a spiritual loss but over the loss of his farm as well," Harris writes (p. 31).

India is a country plagued by droughts, and its agriculture is highly dependent on the capricious monsoon. Zebus weather drought periods well, as, like camels, they store food and water in their humps and can

Ritual

Religious groups prescribe behavior and practices that relate to their beliefs. That type of practice is called religious **ritual.** This ritualistic element is what distinguishes religion from a philosophy of life, which is the closest thing to religion, in that it contains beliefs about the nature of the universe or about the ultimate meanings of human existence. A philosophy of life would undoubtedly influence its holder's day-to-day behavior, yet it would have no prescribed rites or rituals.

Some religions have elaborate rituals; others have simple ones. Some expect frequent performance of rituals: five times a day, Moslems face Mecca and pray; each week, they are expected to join in the noon prayers at the mosque; during Ramadan, the ninth month of the Moslem year, they are ex-

---

last for long periods without either. It is during the dry months that farmers allow their cows to wander along roads and into market places to scavenge food for themselves.

In Western countries, a large percentage of arable land is devoted to growing food for livestock. In India, the cattle eat the inedible remains of crops left in the fields, and they munch on weeds and grass along roads. Thus, they cost virtually nothing to maintain. Furthermore, zebus convert their food into an important product—dung—which is used as fertilizer and as fuel for cooking. If India were to purchase coal for fuel to replace the dung that is used, it would cost the country 1.5 billion dollars. And replacing the manure that is used as fertilizer would cost even more.

Even after a cow dies, it continues to be useful. Members of the Untouchable caste haul the dead cows away. They skin them and use the hides or sell them to leatherworks, and they cook and eat the meat. In this way, the lower sector of the population manages to get animal protein in its diet.

Harris concludes that the practice of cow worship came about to prevent people from consuming the animal on which the country's economy depends. He suggests that abstention from eating beef originated as a practice among farmers, who felt it more important to keep their cows as producers of oxen. An unwritten taboo gradually developed and was incorporated into the Hindu religion. In this way, the starving populace was prevented from yielding to the temptation of slaughtering the all-important cattle.

Thus, according to Harris, the sacredness of the Indian cow is not just an ignorant religious belief that stands in the way of progress. It is a practice that actually plays a crucial role in the maintenance of Indian society.

pected to fast; and at least once during his or her lifetime, each Moslem is expected to make the pilgrimage to Mecca. Other religions have less demanding rituals, but all religions have some.

Almost every type of behavior has, at one time, been used as a religious ritual: fasting and feasting; kneeling and standing; singing and shouting; lighting fires; immersing oneself in certain waters; offering human sacrifices; taking drugs; and making specific movements of the head, hands, or body. Sacred objects are manipulated, and sacred words are spoken. Special articles of clothing are worn, such as tie-dye vestments, ermine cloaks, or skull caps. The list is almost limitless, and the variety of behavior is staggering.

A Moslem observing a Roman Catholic walking to a church altar and accepting a wafer of unleavened bread would not see the act as self-evidently religious, nor would the Catholic recognize the religious significance of the Moslem's walking seven times around the Kaaba and kissing the Black Stone in its wall. Both have been taught that their behavior is religious. They have learned that seemingly ordinary actions can be extraordinary and have special meaning or symbolism. Rituals, then, provide people with a way of relating to the unseen, supernatural world. Rituals can also serve as a reminder of an event in the group's history. This function can be observed in the Christian's reverence for the cross or in the breaking of a wine glass during a Jewish marriage ceremony in memory of the destruction of Jerusalem and its temple. You can probably think of many other examples of rituals in religions.

No ritual is self-evidently religious and no object is self-evidently sacred. With Biblical justification, these worshipers have assigned meaning to snake handling.

FUNCTIONS OF RELIGION

As noted in Chapter 1, the functionalist theory holds that all systems, or institutions, have some effect on the larger society. Religion, like other institutions, has consequences for the well-being and survival of society. At times, it serves to maintain and strengthen the ongoing society; at other times, it serves as a vehicle for change and can disrupt the smooth functioning of the group. Practicing a particular religion or holding specific religious beliefs also has consequences for the individual. We should, however, keep the societal and personal functions of religion separate. One deals with the impact of religion on society as a whole; the other deals with the individual consequences of belonging to religious groups, holding religious beliefs, or engaging in religious rituals. Let us first examine the social functions of religion.

Social Functions

As we discuss the social functions of religion, two points must be remembered. First, sociologists do not endorse functions of religion, nor do they hold that religion should have particular consequences. Second, it is often difficult to evaluate the consequences of religion, even by the group's own value system. For instance, religion may give its believers a strong sense of stability, which the group values. Yet, this very stability may make the group tradition-bound and unable to keep pace with the developing world. On the other hand, the group may value some functions of their religion but not others, or it may value certain consequences in the present, but at a later time consider them dysfunctions. For example, Catholics in Latin America value many features of their religion today but may later consider the Church's stand on contraception as dysfunctional.

Most sociologists of religion consider its most valuable social function to be its *integrative* role. Kingsley Davis (1949) goes so far as to say that religion makes an "indispensable contribution to the social integration" (p. 529). Any ongoing group is somewhat integrated if its members perform specialized but interrelated activities and are, therefore, dependent on one another. Religion often produces a special kind of group unity and a strong social cohesion. It can supply the bond or force that holds members of a group together, and it can give them strong, positive feelings toward the group.

Endorsement of Society's Values Religion can contribute to group integration in many ways. Perhaps the most significant is that religion can forcefully help to legitimize society's most cherished values. When religion justifies and affirms a system of values, a compelling dimension is added to the value system. We need look no further than our own Declaration of Independence for an example. It does not state that a handful of intelligent men, borrowing liberally from the thinking of past philosophers, put together an attractive list of norms for judging the rightness and wrongness of things. But it states, instead, that people were endowed by their Creator with certain inalienable rights. What higher appeal can be made? The value statements are not only legitimized, they are sanctified.

On a less abstract level, religions endorse and reinforce our society's norms of honesty and personal rights. Note how often newspaper reporters seek out the opinions of religious leaders as a way of testing what values society should endorse. Recent examples of this are the printing of religious leaders' positions on the test tube babies born in England and on the removing of life-support systems from comatose patients.

Guides to action and standards for judging one's own and others' behavior in the natural world are infused with beliefs about the supernatural. So, by offering the highest-order explanation for group values, religion can persuade members to agree with and accept the group norms and goals. By providing sacred objects and religious rituals, religion also contributes to social integration, by providing a means for expressing and reinforcing the beliefs of the group.

Resistance to Change   Some theorists emphasize the dysfunctional effects of religion, showing how it slows down progress, resists necessary change, and interferes with human development. Marx, for example, posited that with the development of social classes, people became alienated from their work and their societies. The meaninglessness of life in the typical class societies led people to yearn for liberation and freedom. Unable to change social conditions, humans projected their need for liberation into the heavenly sphere and looked for a better way of life, not in the here and now but after death. This made the workers more accepting of their lot and less inclined to attempt radical changes. In class societies, furthermore, superior-inferior and command-obey relationships were solid facts of life, and these types of relationships were reflected in the religions of the times. Marx thus saw religion as "the opiate of the people," a drug administered by those in power to preserve their command positions and to keep the masses obedient and tolerant, if not content, with their position in society.

Marx paid little attention to Eastern religions or to primitive religions, so his theories on the repressive nature of religion cannot be universally applied. It is, nevertheless, true that religion has taken the stance of convincing people to be content with their lot in life and to resist social change. Nor is this difficult to understand. Those who stress the supernatural can easily be indifferent, or even opposed, to worldly progress and accomplishments. Then, too, the major world religions lean heavily on the past, by holding as sacred the beliefs of their founders or the form of their ancient rituals. As Gerhard Lenski (1963) has pointed out, "Creeds formulated fifteen hundred or more years ago are still accepted as definitive statements of faith by major groups. Scriptures originating two and three thousand years ago continue to be regarded as sacred documents" (p. 355).

Instances abound of religious support for the status quo and inhibition of social change. The gross inequalities of the caste system of India received justification from the Hindu religion. The higher castes felt morally justified in their greater privileges, for these privileges were signs that they had led moral and pious lives in previous existences. Lower caste members accepted their fates, believing that by performing their humble tasks ungrudgingly they would be better off in a future existence. The Russian Orthodox Church, to take another example, supported what we now consider the harsh subjugation of women, likening the father of the family to God, and giving him the moral right to beat his wife and children. In Christian European countries, for centuries Jews were treated as outcasts and forbidden to pursue certain occupations or to own land. With some notable exceptions, clergymen in the United States found religious justification for slavery. These beliefs and actions were considered right by the religious standards of the times. These historical examples show that religion's resistance to change and its support of "unworthy" conditions are not new.

Working for Change Religion has also been a force behind social change. The Ghost Dance, which spread among the American Indians from 1870 to 1890, expressed, in religious symbols, the return of the land to the Indians, the expulsion of whites, and the rebirth of their culture. While the results were unsuccessful, the force of religious ritual was nevertheless used in an attempt to direct social change. Long before the Peace Corps and the United Nations' technical assistance programs, Christian missionaries were serving as agents of change in Africa, Asia, Latin America, and elsewhere. They built and operated hospitals and schools, taught the latest agricultural techniques, and took other deliberate steps to foster social change. Recently, the Catholic clergy in Chile, Brazil, and other Latin American countries have engaged in socioeconomic reform through such means as distributing church land to peasants and operating technical training institutes (Vallier, 1962, 1965). Today in the United States, many religious denominations are seeking to produce change in inner-city ghettos and to improve the lot of the rural poor, the worker, and the minority-group member.

The Black Muslims in contemporary America are using the vehicle of the new religion to challenge society and to alert both the members of the religion and society in general to the grave injustices and suffering that have been the lot of black people for so long. The Black Muslim religion is not an opiate but a stimulant for its believers. Similarly, the Reverend Martin Luther King, Jr., in his "Letter from Birmingham Jail," said that "Jesus Christ was an extremist for love, truth and goodness," and this gave him religious justification for civil disobedience and extremism. The dream of Dr. King was for a better tomorrow right here on earth.

Of course, religious support for change can be judged differently by dif-

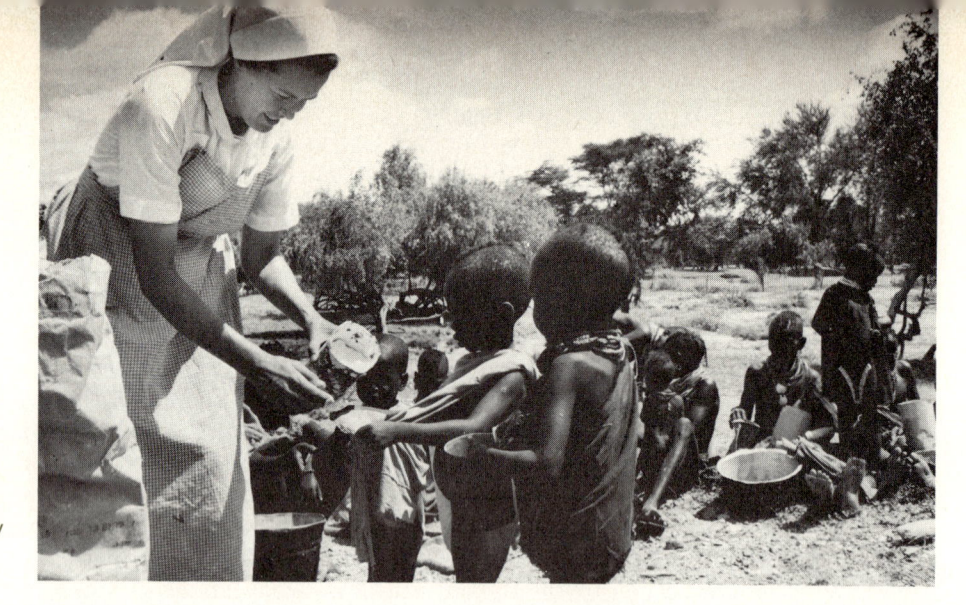

By furnishing food and teaching nutrition, missionaries try to promote social change.

ferent value systems. Is it right or wrong to attempt to win converts to Christianity, even if the effort is accompanied by measures to improve people's health and welfare? Was it right or wrong for many Protestant denominations to seek to change the way of life in America by vigorously supporting national prohibition of alcoholic beverages? Were Protestant and Catholic clergy who resisted the status quo by teaching civil disobedience in such matters as civil rights and the military draft behaving rightly or wrongly? Regardless of one's evaluation, such activities illustrate that religion has been for change as well as against it.

Personal Functions

People everywhere experience frustrations, crises, tragedies, and disappointments. The young person may dream of the future only to awaken, in middle age, to the stark realization that those dreams will never come true. Anyone reasonably sensitive to the plight of humanity realizes that many people are living in poverty and deprivation. Injustices abound in almost any society. There are sometimes rational, scientific reasons for these injustices and inequalities, but often, they are not fully satisfying explanations. A historian or psychologist can explain Stalin's murder of thousands or Hitler's execution of millions by describing the totalitarian mentality. But no one can scientifically explain why the world is the kind of place in which such types of mentality and cruelty can exist and gain power.

Human beings are thinking, but also feeling, creatures. Intellectually, parents might understand the medical explanation of why one of their children was born blind and another mentally retarded. Still, the nagging, unanswerable question is, "Why did it have to happen to us?" Religion offers many people an interpretation for the crises and tragedies that beset us all, and in so doing, provides solace and peace of mind. People are able to live with their sorrows, because they believe in a guiding force, a final cause, a God who in His wisdom—which we may not understand—permits such things to happen.

Benefits and Costs Research findings generally support the idea that religion can have positive effects on the happiness and serenity of believers. In a national study, *Americans View Their Mental Health* (Gurin, Veroff, and Feld, 1960), it was found that both Catholics and Protestants who attended church regularly reported a better self-concept, less general distress, and more happiness on the job than those who did not. The most striking finding, however, was the relationship between church attendance and marital happiness. Those who reported extreme unhappiness in their marriages were the Protestants who never attended church and the Catholics who attended church only a few times each year.

A recent Gallup poll found that those who considered themselves "very religious" were much more likely to rate themselves as "very happy" than were those who thought of themselves as "not at all religious" (Gallup and Davies, 1974). Finally, a poll of 100,000 women conducted by *Redbook Magazine* discovered that women who rated themselves as "very religious" were more likely to describe their marital sex life as "very good" than were the less religious women (Levin and Levin, 1975). Sex and sin have been equated for so long that many were amazed to find that the religious, devout women were so highly satisfied with the sexual side of their marriages. The very religious women were also more likely than the others to describe themselves as happy most of the time; they were quite content with their marriages and thus seemed to have a basic satisfaction with life. The various studies seem to indicate that many people find in religion an inner contentment that keeps them at peace with their fellow humans and brings them satisfaction in their marriages and in life in general.

But modern-day religions have also proved damaging to the well-being of some individuals. People throughout the world will long remember the over 900 members of the Peoples Temple who followed their leader to suicide in 1978 (see Box 10.2). Each year children die because their Christian Scientist parents cannot, in good conscience, allow them to receive a blood transfusion or undergo surgery. In parts of Kentucky and West Virginia, some religious sects ascribe to a literal interpretation of the New Testament passage, "They shall take up serpents; and if they drink any deadly thing, it shall not hurt them" (Mark 16:17–18). Part of the religious rituals of these sects requires the handling of poisonous snakes, and though most believers remain unscathed, now and then a person is bitten and dies. As another example, during the war between West Pakistan and East Pakistan, out of which came the new state of Bangladesh in 1972, approximately 200,000 Moslem women were reported to have been raped by West Pakistan occupation forces. According to Moslem custom, the victimized women were considered unclean and were, therefore, deserted by their husbands.

BOX 10.2
CULTISM
IN THE
EXTREME:
THE PEOPLES
TEMPLE

In November 1978, Congressman Leo J. Ryan made a fact-finding tour of a California religious cult, the Peoples Temple, that had settled in Jonestown, Guyana. The investigation was being conducted as a result of complaints and stories Ryan had heard about the cult. As Ryan was boarding the plane to leave Guyana, he and four other members of the fact-finding group were killed by Peoples Temple gunmen. Following these murders, cult leader James Jones and over 900 members of the Temple committed mass suicide.

Was the Peoples Temple a unique group, somehow different from other cults? Why would so many people have been willing to die for their leader and their group? What sort of social climate would allow such a cult to develop? Perhaps we can learn something about religious cults in general by exploring the history and structure of this tragic group.

At another point in history, it is probable that Jim Jones would have remained a somewhat radical, erratic preacher in a storefront church in downtown Indianapolis. In order to thrive, cults need a particular social climate, and the climate was just right for Jones's Peoples Temple to develop into a full-blown cult that attracted thousands. Cults flourish in times of turbulent social change—times when people tend to experience uncertainty, lack of direction, and rootlessness. For example, many cults came into being after the fall of Rome, after the French Revolution, and during the Industrial Revolution.

In 1966, the sociologist John Lofland published his research on the Doomsday Cult, a religious cult, and a number of the principles he discovered can be applied to the Peoples Temple. One aspect that Lofland focused on was the recruitment of new members. He found that conversion to the group had to be built on ties between a member and the prospective member. Some converts in the cult studied by Lofland had been the spouse or lifelong friend of a member. Others had formed an emotional tie to a member and then converted. Similarly, in the Peoples Temple, there were a number of married couples and families represented.

Those who have studied cults have noted that conversion to a cult proceeds better if the potential convert lacks ties to other groups, such as family or close friends, or if such ties can be neutralized. It is reported that in his active recruiting stage, Jim Jones sought out college dropouts and former drug users—people who had lost their ties to meaningful others (Tracy, 1978). Jones would offer these social misfits love and concern in exchange for their loyalty.

Once people converted to the cult, their ties with the outside world were systematically cut off. Temple members were not allowed to go anywhere, except to work, without a guardian. Members were not even supposed to talk to strangers. Moving the community from California to a cleared jungle in Guyana was the ultimate effort in neutralizing the effects of any ties people may have had with the world outside the temple.

Isolation of the group also facilitated the achievement of another requirement for cult growth and survival: intense day-to-day interaction between members. Long periods of interacting only with fellow members reinforces each other's beliefs and rewards each other's behavior. Apparently, Jim Jones interpreted Congressman Ryan's visit as a threat to the cult's isolation. He feared that Ryan's investigation would focus attention on Jonestown, bring other investigators, and draw the people of Jonestown back into the mainstream of society. This fear, coupled with Jones's growing insanity, led to his decision to start the bloodshed that eventuated in the deaths of over 900 men, women, and children.

Cults demand unusual conformity and commitment on the part of their members. The loyalty that the cultists exhibited as they drank the cups of grape drink laced with cyanide had been carefully developed, tested, and checked upon while the group was still in California. At first, demands were made for lesser things, such as work, money, or having parents send their children out on the street to beg. Then the tempo picked up. Jones would conduct all-night sessions in which individuals would stand in the middle of a circle while their friends and families heaped personal criticism on them. Jones announced that marriage and enduring sexual partners were evidence of corruption. Husbands and wives were forced to sleep with different partners in preparation for life in the egalitarian society that Jones began to speak of as "the Marxist Republic of Guyana."

As the demands on the loyalty of the members escalated, Jones became more and more concerned with any evidence of lack of full commitment. Spying within the group was systematized, with members being required to report on each other's conversations, attitudes, and personal behavior. Church members had to report to counselors, who were made responsible for the behavior of from ten to twenty members. The counselors would report any unusual behavior or suspicious attitude, and Jones himself would decide what punishment was needed. Members would be beaten, humiliated before their friends, and made to say "thank-you" for being reformed (Tracy, 1978).

At first the measures used by Jones to build and test loyalty were not that different from those used in other cults. But, during the five years prior to leaving California, the loyalty demands, tests, and punishments surpassed the bounds of methods used by other cult leaders. Hundreds dropped out of the Peoples Temple, but those who remained constituted an intensely committed group, conditioned to follow their leader's every wish. Their final act of conformity, the drinking of cyanide, was not as bizarre an act as it may seem. The suicide rite had been practiced, and it had been given meaning. Jones had described to his followers the better life that awaited them after death and had explained how enemies from the outside might seek to destroy their community.

It will take some time to document the life histories of those who joined the Peoples Temple. Studies such as Lofland's have found that, generally, cults attract lower-status people who have less to lose by not conforming to society's norms. Often, converts have experienced severe interpersonal strain or tension, such as job trouble or marital discord. Because of a religious background, those who join cults seek answers in this manner rather than looking to psychologists, counselors, or other such alternatives. Potential converts also define themselves as persons who are open to new religious ways of dealing with their problems.

Perhaps we will never fully understand the cult phenomenon and the people who make cults a way of life. But the tragedy of the Peoples Temple may at least spur social and psychological research that will give us enough insights into religious cults so that such a situation can be prevented in the future.

These examples show the damage that can come from the prescribed beliefs and rituals of organized religions. In addition, some individuals make their own interpretations of religious belief and either suffer terror or guilt or become what are generally called "religious fanatics." Far from strengthening social ties and helping individuals, such religious beliefs can bring about psychological and physical suffering.

Sense of Identity As we have seen, religion is a group experience. An individual's sense of belonging to a group of fellow believers and participants in rituals should have a positive function. Indeed, membership in a community of believers may be what gives members their inner security and sense of well-being.

Not all religious groups seem to offer an equal sense of community. In Chapter 1, we referred to Emile Durkheim's study, *Suicide* (1951). As part of that study, Durkheim attempted to explain why the suicide rate was lower for Roman Catholics than for Protestants. The relevant belief systems of the two groups are similar: both consider suicide sinful, and both hold that, in the next life, one would be punished for one's sins. Durkheim noted, however, that Catholics had a stronger attachment to their religious groups and participated more in their group-centered activities than did Protestants. The greater individualism of Protestants, and their lower reliance on group participation, according to Durkheim, accounted for their higher suicide rate.

There is much sociological evidence that human beings derive great satisfaction from associations with others and that most people require warm

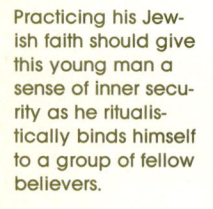

Practicing his Jewish faith should give this young man a sense of inner security as he ritualistically binds himself to a group of fellow believers.

primary group associations. Yet, religion has often failed to provide meaningful groups to which the members of a society can anchor themselves. What is more, it has been suggested that modern religious groups in the United States are failing in this respect at the very time when more and more of us are living in the impersonal anonymity of urban areas (O'Dea, 1970). Individuals are now satisfying their need for group identification in a variety of functionally equivalent groups, some clearly secular, others with religious overtones.

A fascinating development in the United States is the interest in the occult, which expresses itself most vividly in Satanism and witchcraft. Few people practice witchcraft singly; almost all witchcraft practices are group activities. Some of the rituals, such as a double-spiral dance performed in the nude or the ritualistic sexual intercourse practiced in some covens, suggest a need among practitioners to gather with fellow worshipers who share beliefs about the mystery of the unknown world. One interpretation of the growing interest in the occult is that people have a deep-seated need for *myth* — stories that express values and beliefs in emotionally expressive ways — and a strong desire to relate to the unseen world, neither of which is being met by organized religious groups. As indicated in Box 10.2, one reason why some people are attracted to cults, such as the Peoples Temple, is that they fill an emptiness in their lives that is not being filled by the major organized religions. They nevertheless feel a need for some kind of religious experience and some kind of religious interpretation for their lives.

We have reviewed some of the functions that religion serves for the individual. However, for many people in our own and other societies, religion has no place. They do not seem to need or to miss the religious experience. To the sociologist, the behavior of such people is neither laudable nor blameworthy; it simply must be taken into account as we attempt to develop a full picture of the consequences religion has for the individual.

RELIGION IN THE UNITED STATES

We hope our study of religion and its social and individual functions has persuaded you that this institution is both important and complicated. As we turn now to a sociological treatment of religion in the United States, you should recognize that what we present is only an overview of this complex and changing institution.

Separation of Church and State

One feature of organized religion in the United States, separation of church and state, is so generally accepted by Americans that we may forget how unique it is, and how radical an idea it was at the time of its inception. It is only partly a joke to say that the early settlers came to these shores to prac-

As these worshipers stop for public noon prayers in Cairo, Egypt, it probably wouldn't occur to them that religious practices and secular life could be separate.

tice their religion—and make everybody else do likewise. In some of the colonies, religious differences were not tolerated. Rhode Island was founded by religious fugitives from Massachusetts; and in Virginia, the Church of England was, in essence, the established church of the colony. At the same time, the seeds of religious freedom were being firmly planted. While Maryland is often thought to have been a Catholic settlement, the original charter clearly provided for religious freedom. And other colonies that attempted to have an established church also changed rapidly.

For centuries in most European countries, one Christian denomination or another was the established church or was definitely intertwined with the political order. Presumably, the rulers felt that a cohesive system could be maintained best by loyalty to a single religion. Even today, the governments of many European countries endorse, in varying degrees, a single religion. The Islamic religion has generally sought a close connection between church and state, as evidenced by the official name of Pakistan, which is the Islamic Republic of Pakistan.

The radical idea that developed during the colonial period was that a social order could exist without compulsory allegiance to a common religion. By the time the colonies gained their independence, this new idea was widely, although not completely, accepted. Consequently, the First Amendment to the Constitution specified that "Congress shall make no law respecting an establishment of religion, or prohibiting the free exercise thereof." What its drafters and ratifiers meant by this was that there should be no one official denomination and that the government should not support any religious denomination, financially or otherwise. All people should be free to worship in the religion of their choice, or not to worship, without penalty or harassment.

For 200 years we have lived with the idea of separation of church and state, and if anything, the principle is more strongly endorsed today than ever before. Even so, almost from the beginning, the principle has been violated periodically. The wave of immigrants from Catholic countries aroused anti-Catholic feelings. The Know-Nothing party maintained that no one who owed allegiance to "any foreign prince or potentate" (the Pope) should be a candidate for public office. The Mormons, whose religion endorsed polygyny, were persecuted until they fled to the territories where United States law did not yet hold.

Today, many norms and values of the larger, secular American society continue to come into conflict with religious norms and values, producing lengthy court battles between the government and a religious sect. Only after considerable litigation did members of the Native American Church win the right to use peyote, an otherwise illegal hallucinogen, in their religious ceremonies. The Amish have only recently won the right not to violate their religious convictions by sending their children to school beyond the eighth grade. Mennonites do not have to wear legally required safety helmets on construction jobs, for such a requirement violates their clothing taboos. Jehovah's Witnesses and others are mistrusted, at best, and persecuted, at worst, because they believe it idolatrous to salute the flag.

Not only do secular and religious norms sometimes conflict, but many controversies have raged over the exact extent and intent of the First Amendment in matters of religion. Probably the greatest controversy followed the Supreme Court decision that mandatory prayers in schools and other public assemblies are unconstitutional. Some people feel that there is nothing wrong with the government providing transportation or books for children attending a parochial school, but others feel it is a gross violation of the First Amendment. Some feel we are compromising our principles by not levying taxes on church property, while others feel that to do so would constitute government harassment, by making it difficult for people to practice their religion freely.

Despite these and other conflicts and controversies, the separation of church and state appears to be relatively functional for our society. In a society of many religious denominations, with no single one having political sanction, controversies seem inevitable.

Pluralism and Ecumenism

Although most of us are accustomed to thinking of the religious variety in our society as threefold—Protestant, Catholic, and Jewish—our religious spectrum is far more diverse. There are almost 250 Protestant denominations; there are small Catholic groups, such as the Polish National Church of America and the Old Catholic Church; and there are Orthodox, Conservative, and Reformed Jewish congregations. But there are also about 100,000 Americans in the Buddhist Churches of America, and over two million other people belong to religious groups that cannot be classified as Protestant, Catholic, or Jewish.

Nevertheless, about 60 percent of the population is affiliated with one of three broad Christian denominations: Catholic, Baptist, or Methodist. If we

UNDERSTANDING SOCIAL INSTITUTIONS

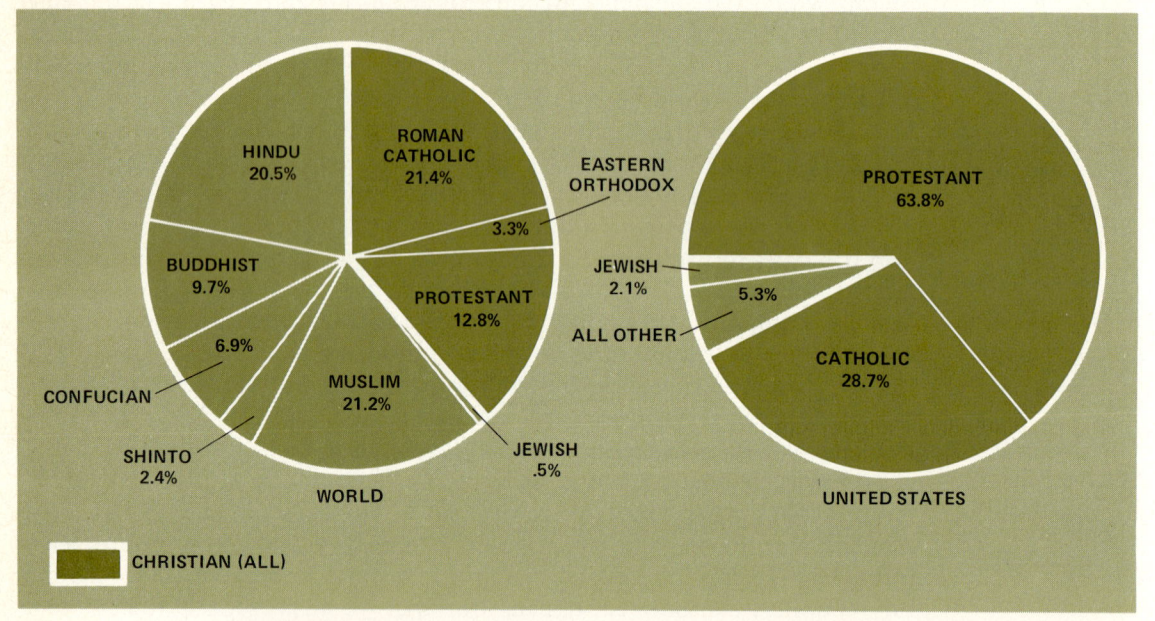

FIGURE 10.2 Populations of the Major Religions in the World and in the United States

World:
- HINDU 20.5%
- ROMAN CATHOLIC 21.4%
- EASTERN ORTHODOX 3.3%
- BUDDHIST 9.7%
- PROTESTANT 12.8%
- 6.9%
- CONFUCIAN
- SHINTO 2.4%
- MUSLIM 21.2%
- JEWISH .5%
- ALL OTHER

United States:
- PROTESTANT 63.8%
- JEWISH 2.1%
- 5.3%
- CATHOLIC 28.7%

CHRISTIAN (ALL)

It is interesting to compare the populations of the major religions in the United States to those in the world. A few important differences can be noted from these graphs: (1) Most Americans are Christians; most of the people in the world are not. (2) In America, Protestants greatly outnumber Catholics; in the world, there are considerably more Catholics than Protestants. (3) Three religions, Muslim, Hindu, and Buddhist, claim half the people in the world; in the United States, these and a number of other religions account for only about 5 percent of the population.

Source: Data compiled from *Information Please Almanac, 1978,* 32nd ed. (New York: Information Please Publishing, 1978), p. 351; percents of those claiming church membership computed from *Gallup Opinion Index, Religion in America, 1977–1978,* Report no. 145 (Princeton, N.J.: 1978), p. 12.

add four more religious bodies—Lutheran, Presbyterian, Episcopalian, and Jewish—we account for 80 percent of the population. Each of the Protestant denominations, however, has several subgroups that can be considered separate denominations. Members of the Lutheran Church, Missouri Synod, usually make it clear that they are not merely Lutheran, as Southern Baptists make it clear that they are not merely Baptist. The diversity within broad denominations, the numerous small religious bodies, and the seemingly endless formation of splinter groups and new sects are all part of the denominational **pluralism** that is a prominent feature of religion in the United States.

Another characteristic of religion in the United States, but one that is neither new nor unique to our society, is **ecumenism.** The goal of ecumen-

Numerous sects and cults compete with organized religions in the United States, a society characterized by denominational pluralism.

ism is the universal integration and unity of all Christian bodies. Landmarks in the movement include the international conference in Edinburgh in 1910 and the formation of the World Council of Churches in 1948. In the United States, however, Christian unity is receiving more attention and effort than previously.

The impact of the ecumenical movement in the United States is difficult to assess. As a goal, it seems to have considerable support, and some denominations, but not an impressive number, have merged. Bridges have been built between Protestant bodies and the Catholic Church. Under some circumstances, clergymen of both faiths can officiate at a mixed marriage involving a Catholic and a Protestant. And recently, the Catholic Church stipulated that Protestants can participate in the Catholic communion service, again, under certain circumstances.

How Religious Are Americans?

No sociologist who begins a research project by asking, "How religious are Americans?" is going to find a single, final, definitive answer. However, religious preference can be measured, as can official church membership and actual church attendance. Some sociologists even use a scale of five dimensions (which we will examine shortly) for determining *religiosity.*

Religious preference is the denomination, if any, with which an individual identifies or to which he or she claims some allegiance. It is the answer a person gives when asked his or her religion. "Protestant" has become a catchall category for an unmeasurable number of Americans who know they are neither Catholic nor Jewish but feel they should indicate some religion. It is partly for this reason that the number of religious people arrived at by using stated religious preference is quite large. Very few Americans—less than ten percent of all adults—claim to be atheists, agnostics, or otherwise have no religion. (An *atheist* is someone who holds that there is no God or Supreme Being; an *agnostic* holds that it is impossible to know whether or not there is a God.)

Offical membership in a church gives us a different picture of the religious nature of Americans. Even though these figures are at best misleading—the records of most churches are incomplete and out of date—we come up with far fewer religious people by using church membership rolls than by using stated preference. Records for the very early years of our country are sketchy and of questionable validity, but some contend that, in 1800, only about ten percent of the population belonged to a church and that it was the large mass of unchurched people that led to the great revivals (Yinger, 1957). Whether or not it was caused by the waves of revivalism, by 1900, about 43 percent of the population belonged to some church. Church membership increased steadily, so that by 1977, almost two-thirds of all Americans were church members.

You can claim to be a Protestant, and you can hold membership in a specific Methodist church, but if you never attend church, are you a Protestant or a Methodist? *Church attendance* is another method of describing how religious Americans are. In 1975, about 40 percent of all Americans reported attending church in a typical week. Church attendance varies among the major denominations: 55 percent of Catholics, 37 percent of Protestants, and 16 percent of Jews attend weekly. Church attenders are more likely to be women than men, and more churchgoers are found among the college educated, among the wealthy, and in the rural segments of society.

TABLE 10.1 Proportion of Adults Attending Church During a Typical Week

Year	Percent
1940	37
1950	39
1955	49
1960	47
1965	44
1970	42
1975	40
1977	42

Source: Gallup polls for the respective years.

During the last 30 years, as shown in Table 10.1, church attendance in the United States increased and then declined. The high point was the middle to late 1950s. Although the rate today is declining, it is still higher than it was in the 1940s. The changing religious behavior of Catholics can account for much of the drop in church attendance. As recently as 1964, over 70 percent of Catholics attended church during a typical week, while since the early 1970s, the rate has declined to 55 percent. The current attendance rate of adults under 30 years of age is particularly noteworthy: about half of the Catholics between the ages of 21 and 29 attend weekly, while 70 percent of those over 30 go to church once a week; the comparable rates for Protestants are 32 percent and 45 percent, respectively.

Because a person can be "religious" in different ways, considerable research effort has been spent developing concepts of **religiosity** and scales to measure how religious people are and in what ways. Sociologists now commonly refer to different *dimensions of religiosity,* such as those developed by Charles Glock and Rodney Stark (1965), who distinguish five dimensions:

1. The *experiential dimension:* the religious emotions and feelings expressed by an individual.
2. The *ideological dimension:* the religious beliefs of an individual; how many of the basic principles of the particular religion are accepted, and how strongly.
3. The *ritualistic dimension:* the extent to which a person engages in the rituals and practices of his or her religion.
4. The *intellectual dimension:* how much a person knows about the basic tenets of his or her faith — its origin, history, and literature.
5. The *consequential dimension:* secular effects of the first four dimensions; the degree to which religious principles are acted out in daily life.

We might expect some overlapping among the five dimensions of religiosity, but not that much is found. People can score considerably higher in one dimension than in another. In other words, people can be more religious in some aspects than in others. More refinements are needed in such scales of religiosity, for if religious commitment has significant behavioral consequences, we must be able to measure it with some precision. We do know, for example, that religion varies somewhat with social class. Gerhard Lenski has found statistical relations between religious affiliation and occupation, political views, social mobility, and other such variables (see Box 10.3).

The Future of Religion in the United States

The facts gathered in recent years by sociologists indicate that religion is still a living institution in the United States. After all, less than ten percent of the population claims no religious affiliation, and even though church attendance is low, about 40 percent of Americans do attend church during a typical week. This percentage equals Canadian attendance and is about twice that of Great Britain, Australia, and several other countries. A cross-cultural opinion poll found that 94 percent of the people in the United States profess to believing in God or in a universal spirit (Gallup poll, September 1976). Only in India was the proportion of believers higher; while in West Germany, belief in God was expressed by 72 percent of the people; in the Scandinavian countries by 65 percent; and in Japan by 38 percent. The same poll found that 69 percent of Americans believe in life after death—about twice the proportion who hold that belief in West Germany and Scandinavia.

A little over one-half of all Americans (56 percent) believe that religion is losing its influence on American life (Gallup and Davies, 1974). Twenty years ago, only 14 percent of the population felt that way; but in 1970, 75 percent thought that religion was losing influence. About 60 percent of the population feel that religion can answer all or most of today's problems; but

---

BOX 10.3 RELIGION AND SOCIAL CLASS

Sociologists have long known that when Americans are categorized by their religious affiliations, major differences become apparent. For example, it has become apparent that religion is intertwined with the class system in America. Studies repeatedly find that different denominations draw the bulk of their memberships from different levels of society. People of higher social status tend to be concentrated in the Episcopal, Presbyterian, and Congregational churches. The churches of the middle class tend to be the Methodist, the Lutheran, and the Disciples of Christ, while lower-class people are overrepresented in the Baptist, Holiness, and Pentecostal congregations. The Catholic Church draws its membership disproportionately from the lower and middle classes, in that order.

Unfortunately, most of the research relating social class and religion has been more descriptive than explanatory, giving statistics but venturing no firm conclusions. But, Gerhard Lenski's study, The Religious Factor (1963), stands as a landmark of research that went beyond a description. By studying a Detroit-area sample of Jews, Catholics, and white and black Protestants, Lenski sought to discover how religious belief and practice affected family life, economic behavior, political involvement, and so on. Lenski's treatment of the interrelationship of these variables is notable. To take but one example, he found that Catholics generally are more closely attached to their family and kinship groups than are Protestants. This difference is shown by visiting patterns, the influence of the family on voting behavior, and the migration pattern of the groups. The attachment to family and relatives—particularly as shown by an unwillingness to

in 1957, 80 percent of the people felt that way. Two-thirds of the people have a lot of confidence in organized religion; this should be compared with the 58 percent who have confidence in public schools, 44 percent in the Supreme Court, 30 percent in labor unions, and 26 percent in big business. Americans do not go to church as much as they did 20 years ago, nor do they have the same confidence in religion as they once did. Nevertheless, it is difficult to conclude from the various studies that organized religion is in the throes of death and is merely awaiting a decent (Christian?) burial.

The Young: A Major Unknown The older adults who make pronouncements on our churches and schools will not be around much longer. Wherever they are going, they will be followed with discomforting swiftness by those in their middle years. It makes sense, then, to look at the behavior and attitudes of young people for some insights into the future of religion in our society.

We have already noted that far fewer people under 30 years of age attend

---

move geographically—is seen as a partial explanation of why Catholics are less likely than Protestants to achieve upward social mobility (Mack et al., 1956; Lenski, 1963). By its effects on the institution of the family, religion affects the class system in America as well.

Lenski summarizes a few of his findings as follows:

Depending on the socio-religious group to which a person belongs, the probabilities are increased or decreased that he will enjoy his occupation, indulge in installment buying, save to achieve objectives far in the future, believe in the American Dream, vote Republican, favor the welfare state, take a liberal view on the issue of freedom of speech, oppose racial integration in the schools, migrate to another community, maintain close ties with his family, develop a commitment to the principle of intellectual autonomy, have a large family, complete a given unit of education, or rise in the class system (p. 349).

Extrapolating from his study, Lenski traces the growth of our industrial state to the predominance of Protestants in American society and speculates on the consequences that religion has for economic development elsewhere: "In view of the social heritage of contemporary Catholicism, it seems unlikely that in the forseeable future any devoutly Catholic state will become a leading industrial nation.... Catholicism seems to contain too many elements which are incompatible with such a role" (p. 320). We have not, to be sure, done justice to Lenski's wealth of research findings, his detailed analyses, and the theoretical arguments that are based on his research. But we have tried to show that religion and social class are intimately connected and that the nature of the connection is complex and far-reaching in its implications.

Young people in America differ greatly. Some seek out religious experiences and practice their religion with devotion. Others feel that religion is old-fashioned and seldom attend church.

church than do those over 30. In addition, more younger than older people profess no religious affiliation. One Gallup poll found that more young than older people hold that religion is largely old-fashioned, out-of-date, and cannot answer most of today's problems (Gallup and Davies, 1974). Of those who subscribe to a religion, fewer young than older people consider themselves "very religious." Of course, we cannot tell from such studies whether we are witnessing a lasting change or simply a difference between generations. That is, as the younger adults grow older, will they become more like their parents in religious participation and attitudes? To add to the complexity of the prediction problem, it is primarily young people who were in the Jesus Movement of the early 1970s and who currently are followers of Sun Myung Moon or Maharaj Ji. Many youth, in other words, show a deep concern for religious experiences.

Women and the Church In many countries where Christianity prevails, women greatly outnumber men in church attendance and in other outward signs of religiosity. Today in the United States more women than men typically attend church, and more women than men consider themselves "very religious." Yet, there are signs of strain between women and the organized churches, and to some extent, the future of religion in the United States depends on the resolution of these problems.

There can be little doubt that Christianity and Judaism, the dominant religions in the United States, have a definite male bias. Historically, the religious leaders were patriarchs, and traditionally, men have held the positions of power and authority in the churches and in the seminaries where the new church leaders are trained. To be sure, a few more women are entering the clergy, but often only with great difficulty. The ordination of women as Episcopal priests in 1977 threatened to cause a major schism in that denomination. More and more women are, nevertheless, questioning why it takes a deep voice to deliver the word of God or why the hands that administer the sacrament must be male. Some even see elements of sinfulness in women's acceptance of submission to men and their consequent failure to utilize their God-given humanity for work and service. Many churches are

Women priests are rare in the Episcopal church. Is this due to theology or sexism? For how long will women accept their second-class status in most organized religions?

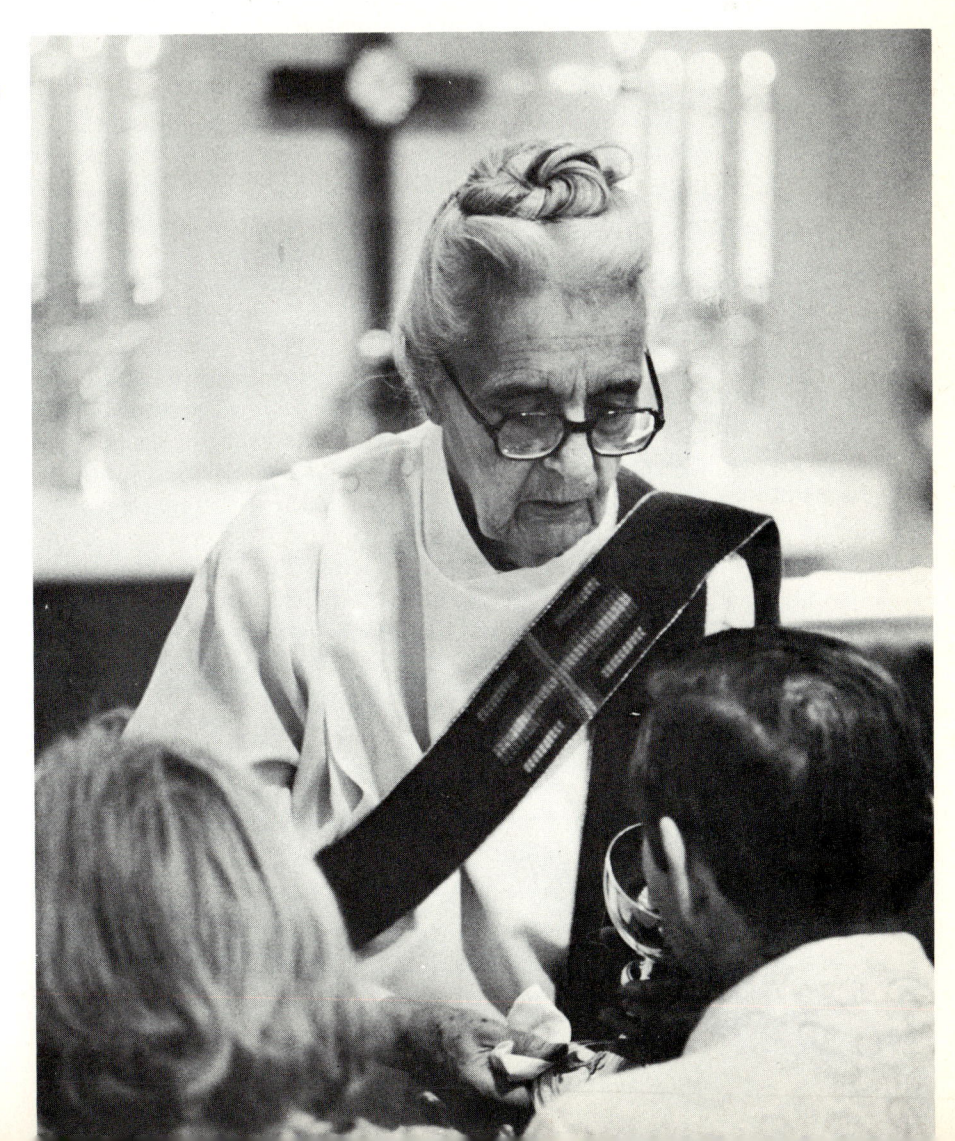

responding to the call for equal status for women, but unless the response is thorough and genuine, women are likely to become disenchanted with organized religion.

By now, it should be clear that we cannot predict, with any certainty, the future of organized religion in the United States. Religion will continue to change, of course. In the immediate future, we will probably see the churches attempting to address themselves to relevant social issues without compromising theological principles. For the thoroughly disillusioned, these efforts will seem to be in vain. Some already see organized religion not as an agency for dealing with modern problems but as a part of the problem. We must not forget, however, that religion includes a lot more than church attendance, liturgy, and changing emphases on social issues. As long as people have ultimate concerns that cannot be answered by the best of their science, and as long as people seek rescue from their cosmic loneliness, they will need religion. It is safe to predict that these conditions will continue for a long, long time.

The religious institution generally comes closer than any other social institution to dealing exclusively with beliefs, values, norms, and other aspects of nonmaterial culture. The place of religion in our society is complicated by the fact that although our society is secular, and is kept so by our constitution, most of our social values come from a long history in which church and state intimately shared the guiding role and were, for centuries, virtually inseparable.

The power of the religious institution depends on how many members of a society choose to share its stated beliefs and values. Because religion is expressed in voluntary associations—that is, groups having only members who choose to join or to remain—it has, perhaps, not suffered strains quite as severe as those suffered by other institutions in recent years. The institution we examine next, education, also deals with the nonmaterial elements of culture. But education is currently suffering from unprecedented stresses and conflicts. This is partly because participation in the school system is compulsory and partly because changes in other institutions have had a variety of confusing consequences for the schools.

SUMMARY

1. According to Bellah, religion has evolved through five stages: primitive, archaic, historic, early modern, and modern. These stages correspond well with the evolutionary stages of society identified by Lenski.

2. Frazer saw humanity as progressing from magic to religion to science in its search for control over the forces of nature. And, according to him, science is not necessarily the final stage in the progression.

3. **Magic** is a belief in supernatural forces that can be controlled by human beings in order to achieve some goal. Magic differs from religion in four areas: (1) its assumptions about the supernatural, (2) the ends or goals pursued, (3) the means used to seek those ends, and (4) its effects on society and on the individual.

4. Religion deals with the unknowable, while science deals with the knowable. Sometimes the distinctions are not clear-cut, however. In most cases, religion has had to surrender to science, but by redefining issues and putting them on a more philosophical plane, religion has been able to erase many contradictions between beliefs and scientific facts.

5. A major aspect of religion is the fact that it deals with **ultimate meanings,** such as the purpose of life and the meaning of death. Religion also involves a set of **beliefs** — it defines the **sacred** as opposed to the **profane.** Practices and behavior related to religious beliefs are termed **rituals.** What is sacred and what rituals are to be practiced are specified in each religion.

6. Religion serves many social functions. Perhaps its most important contribution is to *social integration* — it produces group unity and social cohesion. Religion also contributes to social integration by endorsing society's values, by resisting social change, and by also working *for* social change.

7. Among the *personal functions* of religion are: providing people with peace of mind in times of sorrow, increasing marital and job happiness, and providing a sense of identity. However, religion can also be detrimental to people who take their beliefs too seriously or to those who make their own interpretations of religious belief, which may result in personal suffering.

8. Religion in the United States is characterized fundamentally by a separation of church and state. However, secular and religious norms have come into conflict from time to time. The United States is a **pluralistic** society in which a great variety of religions can be found. Another trend in the United States is toward **ecumenism** — universal integration of all Christian bodies.

9. Sociologists study the religious habits of Americans by examining three types of statistics: religious preference, official church membership, and church attendance. Some sociologists have also developed scales of **religiosity** to measure how religious people are.

10. Compared to other countries, the United States appears to be quite a religious nation. Organized religion has come under a great deal of fire in recent years, but the future of the institution cannot be predicted, and

it seems likely that the youth and the women of today will play a major role in the direction it takes.

KEY TERMS

beliefs
ecumenism
magic
pluralism
profane

religion
religiosity
ritual
sacred
ultimate meanings

SUGGESTED READINGS

Berger, Peter L. *The Sacred Canopy: Elements of a Sociological Theory of Religion.* Garden City, N.Y.: Doubleday, 1967.
  The author applies a theoretical perspective derived from the sociology of knowledge to the phenomenon of religion. He shows how religion functions in the construction of a world view, and how the process of secularization affects this world view.

Carrier, Herve. *The Sociology of Religious Belongings.* New York: Herder and Herder, 1965.
  This book deals with the need for people to belong to meaningful groups. The author holds that the religious group experience is a source of identification for people, that it provides a self-image, and it integrates the individual into a secure social community.

Durkheim, Emile. *The Elementary Forms of the Religious Life.* New York: The Free Press, 1965, originally published in 1915.
  A classic in the area of the sociology of religion. Durkheim contends that the function of religion is to integrate persons into society and that this integration is accomplished through rituals, sacrifice, and beliefs.

Freud, Sigmund. *The Future of an Illusion.* Garden City, N.Y.: Doubleday, 1964, originally published in Vienna in 1927.
  Freud argues that religious ideas are born out of the need to make tolerable one's feelings of helplessness, which stem from one's memories of the helplessness of childhood.

Glock, Charles Y., ed. *Religion in Sociological Perspective.* Belmont, Calif.: Wadsworth, 1973.
  This collection of articles provides an overview of the kinds of research on religion being done by sociologists.

Greeley, Andrew M. *Unsecular Man: The Persistence of Religion.* New York: Schocken Books, 1972.
  Greeley presents the thesis that there are basic human religious needs, that these needs have not changed throughout history, and that the modern unsecular mood is only temporary.

Herberg, Will. *Protestant-Catholic-Jew.* New York: Doubleday, 1960.
    A historical treatise on the rise of three religious communities in the United States.

Seligmann, Kurt. *Magic, Supernaturalism, and Religion.* New York: Grosset and Dunlap, 1968.
    A history of magic and its influence on Western civilization.

Weber, Max. *The Sociology of Religion.* Boston: Beacon Press, 1964, originally published in Germany in 1922.
    A classic work on the sociology of religion. Weber deals with the difference between religion and magic; offers classical definitions of the prophet, the priest, and the magician; and discusses asceticism, mysticism, and salvation religion.

What can be more important than socializing the young, so that they can fill adult roles in society? In modern societies, socialization outside the home is formalized through the educational institution. You have been to different schools, and no doubt, you are aware that there are problems with the American school system. Sociologists look at these problems from two perspectives: the structural-functional approach and the conflict approach.

Looking at the functions of education, we see that the most obvious one is the imparting of knowledge. But we also expect schools to help implement equality of opportunity, preparing students so they can make of their lives what they really want them to be. We expect the schools to keep students enrolled up to a certain age, which, incidentally, keeps them out of the job market and out of trouble. We expect schools to find out how well students are doing, to let the students know how well they're doing, and to guide them toward goals appropriate to their performance and ability. According to the structural-functional model, problems with education today are a result of problems in fulfilling these many functions.

A closer look at the American educational institution reveals a number of controversies over what should be taught in the schools, what results schools should produce, and who should control the schools. These controversies can be seen in terms of conflicts between groups of people with different views, interests, and investments in the educational system. Thus, problems in the educational institution can also be examined in terms of the conflict model.

Sociologists can only examine, and to some degree, try to explain the nature of the American educational institution. Unfortunately, their research has not revealed any easy solutions to the problems we are experiencing in the schools today.

11
Education and Society

The biggest disappointment of the Scarecrow in the land of Oz was that he could not think, because he had no brain. The Wizard of Oz led him to see that he was really just as smart as everyone else and that he simply lacked a certification of his intelligence. The Wizard then awarded him the degree Doctor of Thinkology. The Scarecrow's problems were solved, and the Wizard showed that he was, indeed, a wizard.

Outside of Oz, there is a lot more to learning and being educated than a certificate — or, at least, there should be. In its broadest meaning, education is the same as socialization. All societies educate their preadults to enable them to participate in their society and to assume the occupations and other roles required by the group.

Education, as an institution, has necessarily become more complex and more formalized as societies have developed over the centuries. Consider the function of education at the hunting and gathering stage of societal development. Education was largely informal. It could be so, because the store of knowledge was not great, and it was transmitted verbally. When a young girl gathered nuts and berries with the women, no one labeled it "schooling"; in fact, the concept "school" as a place where learning takes place had not yet been invented. She watched her "teachers" — that is, her mother and other women in the group — and as we would put it today, she "learned by doing." As civilization advanced, it became increasingly difficult for parents and other adults to educate children informally. The great diversity of adult roles had led all but the simplest societies to formalize education — to assign that function to organizations whose primary function is to educate. Of course, the tremendous store of knowledge that has built up, and the consequent dependence on the written word have also forced the formalization of education.

In this chapter we will investigate what today's formalized educational institution does to and for society. We will look at the major functions of this institution and their applications in our own society, and we will examine what goes into the organizations that embody the institution and what we receive in return for the resources devoted to them.

You know much about our schools from your own experiences in them. A sociological study of the educational system should add a different dimension to your knowledge, one that shows how the schools fit into the broader social system. A sociological study should also be interesting, maddening, challenging, upsetting, and possibly action-provoking. This is a big order. Read on.

THE FUNCTIONS OF EDUCATION

The educational institution in any society serves a number of functions. Most obviously, it functions to transmit knowledge. But it also (in our society, at least) is supposed to provide equality of opportunity by giving all

In this Bhutan village high in the Himalayas, formal education is needed to transmit knowledge and to prepare children for adult roles. Throughout the world, informal education by parents has given way to formal education by specialists.

members of the society an equal chance to acquire the skills and knowledge to become what they want to become. Education also serves as a source of new knowledge: students are encouraged to apply what they learn by doing research and potentially coming up with new inventions and new ideas. Finally, the educational institution provides a method for **placement**—the sorting of people into their proper place in society. Let us now look at each of these functions in greater detail.

Transmission of Knowledge

If people were asked why we have schools (and if they didn't think the question too absurd to merit an answer), most would probably say that we have schools so that children can learn. That, of course, is true: one of the major functions of our formal education system is to transmit knowledge. But, fulfilling this function is not as simple as it may appear at first.

For all practical purposes, we can consider that knowledge is infinite. There is no end to what we can learn about ourselves, our world in all its dimensions, and the universe. Thus—and this is sometimes overlooked—some *selection* must be made. Of all the knowledge that has been accumulated by and about past and present cultures; of all the languages, both living and dead; of all the information that we have about biology, optics, chemistry, and so on; of all the mental and physical skills that can be taught to humans; we must select what knowledge and skills should be taught.

In the early generations of our society there appeared to be agreement on what sorts of knowledge were important enough to transmit to the next generation through formal schooling. Children were expected to spend several years in school learning how to read and write and do arithmetic. These skills were felt necessary to prepare children for life in the kind of world in which their elders thought they would live. Once educated, they could read the Bible, engage in commerce, and participate in the budding democracy.

These were highly utilitarian educational goals, for they were related to living and working in the real world.

To be sure, there were institutions of higher learning—here and abroad—for those few who wanted to study the classics or to prepare themselves for the professions, particularly the ministry. In time, more years of public education were provided, and eventually, compulsory attendance laws were enacted. Private and public colleges sprang up all over the nation. As a society, we seemed to be saying that more of the infinite storehouse of knowledge should be transmitted to more people.

We now have the same educational institution as we had in colonial days, but the way in which it must perform its function has changed drastically. Herein lies one of our problems. We nod our heads vigorously, and sometimes woefully, whenever we hear mention of the "knowledge explosion," but sometimes we act as if we do not understand its profound implications. What knowledge should be transmitted, and to whom? Why? Think about it. Later in the chapter we will look into the problems of what is sometimes glibly called "the transmission of knowledge."

Equality of Opportunity

An important stated function of our school system is to provide equality of opportunity: education for all who want it and who are mentally able to profit by it. Presumably, most people in our society feel that money and the good things in life should *not* be distributed equally—that every one of us should have a chance to do what we want to do and reap the rewards according to our ability, motivation, and personal desires. Some would end up richer than others, some would be in more prestigious occupations than others, and some would have more knowledge and skill than others. But the chances for success should be equal, even though the result is inequality of rewards.

The value of equal opportunity means that our chances for success should depend not on how well we chose the family we were born into, but on what we ourselves want to do and are able to do. Success would not be guaranteed to anyone, but everyone would be offered the same opportunities for it. Society should gain from a such a value system. Important positions would be filled by those who best use the opportunities offered them. The reservoir of talent from which we could draw would be broad, for the abilities of people from all backgrounds would be used.

Whether or not the school system can actually provide equal opportunities is a question being widely explored today. There is general agreement that the schools are not providing equal opportunity, but there is little agreement on the reasons for this failure. One side claims that culture and environment are the problem; the other, that inherited differences are the cause. Let us assume, first, that the conclusions of Arthur Jensen (1969) are correct and that intelligence is substantially influenced by genetic factors.

In this case, equality of opportunity could be assured by giving all children the chance to be educated to the limits of their ability to learn. Innately superior children, regardless of race, family background, or finances, could be educated in such a manner that they would have an equal chance to attend college and professional schools if they wished. Some compensatory educational program, such as Head Start, might be necessary to make up for the absence of preschool learning for intelligent children of humble birth, thus equalizing their chances of profiting from formal education.

But, what if intelligence is culturally and environmentally determined, and early childhood socialization and the presence or absence of a stimulating home environment radically affect the preschooler's ability to learn? In this case, more individual attention to children from disadvantaged homes would fail to produce equality of opportunity, for strong countervailing forces would still be operating to stifle the child's intellectual motivation and ability to learn. (The role of IQ in perpetuating inequalities is highly controversial; see Jencks et al., 1972.) And, what if intelligence is partially genetic but strongly influenced by early childhood socialization? Finally, what can, or should, the schools do with children who have the ability to learn but are not motivated to do so, or with those who are motivated but apparently lack the ability?

Our educational system continues to have the manifest function of providing equal opportunities for all to attain academic success, and ultimately, success in life. Later in this chapter, we will investigate how, and how well, this function, so basic to the American value system, is actually being achieved.

Creation of New Knowledge

Another function of education is to discover new knowledge. In most universities, this function is defined explicitly: the university professor has the responsibility to conduct research as well as to teach. Whether the field is marine biology, physics, English literature, animal science, or sociology, the collective efforts of researchers should generate new facts, new explanations for phenomena, or new solutions to problems. As a result of these efforts, we should find out more and more about humanity, society, the physical world, and so on.

New knowledge is not sought or discovered only in universities. Private enterprise spends large sums of money for research and development, and a high value is placed on new knowledge throughout our entire educational system. In elementary school, for example, students learn about classic inventions and discoveries, and science fairs encourage students to apply the principles of the scientific method. In high school, students gain more practical experience in conducting experiments in various fields. Implicitly, at least, children are taught both the value of new knowledge and one method by which it can be developed. Students are supposedly taught to think for themselves; that is, they should be able to generate new knowledge, new ideas, and fresh ways of looking at familiar problems.

If students learn these lessons well, the educational system should be an instrument of change. Many people are able to accept this consequence in some areas of knowledge but not in others. The development of safer automobiles, of antipollution devices, and of cheaper methods of producing energy all require the willingness and the ability to consider new ideas. But, when students who have been taught to think for themselves apply their innovative skills to other areas, their efforts are not always applauded. Investigating new methods of taxation, better ways of caring for the poor, or more effective abortion methods often leads to ideas that challenge the status quo or conflict with cherished traditions. It is clear that our society is beset by many "people problems," and social innovations of various kinds are sorely needed. One of the functions of the educational system is to encourage innovative thought and new knowledge, which in turn, could lead to rational, humanitarian change. Paradoxically, we are often threatened when our schools work this way and are critical when they do not.

Placement

Still another function of our educational system is placement, or sorting. Throughout our school careers we are tested and evaluated as to how well we are doing and what course of study we should be encouraged to pursue. Whether or not labels such as "slow learner" and "college material" are used, children are steered along different paths according to evaluations of their performance. Indeed, if placement tests and course prerequisites are part of the system, the term "steer" is too gentle. (For an account of how this works at the junior college level, see Clark, 1960.)

The placement function would, at first, seem to be socially useful, for every society must be sure that all the necessary work is done. In a complex society with many adult roles, it would seem logical to have some kind of a sifting and sorting process, based on reasonable criteria, that would place people in jobs for which they are best suited. But there are problems with this function and the way it is actually performed.

The validity of placement criteria has been seriously questioned. What do test scores and similar measures *really* tell us about what children can, or should, do with their own lives? The evaluation devices sometimes appear logical. For example, repeated failure in high school math indicates rather well that a person will not be able to pursue a successful career in engineering. This logic sounds reasonable until we venture into the touchy area of what kind of mathematics courses are offered, how they are taught, and how it is determined that some children have real ability, and others little talent in this area. The problem is magnified when we look at the overall placement function rather than at individual performance. Each year, thousands of students drop out of school, others switch into vocational programs or trade schools, while still others remain on the so-called "academic track."

This variation brings us to another aspect of the placement function; that is, the schools not only place children, they also teach them their place. The methods used to convince children where they belong are not subtle. Testing and grading are the most obvious means, and children are usually convinced that such evaluative devices are legitimate. If these evaluations are accepted, repeated failures or low scores or the recognition that he or she is near the bottom of the class can be powerful devices for persuading the child to drop out of the academic program. Children learn their place, even if they suffer loss of esteem in the process.

Many bright students are turned off by the whole educational process, while not-so-bright ones may have career aspirations beyond their abilities, and many others seriously mismatch their chosen careers with their true interests and abilities. Perhaps in simpler societies there are gentler and more humane ways of encouraging people to prepare for and accept the necessary adult roles.

Other Educational Functions

Our system of formal education performs still other functions, both manifest and latent. First, schools perform a **custodial function:** they keep children out of the home a good many hours a day, five days a week. This function should not be viewed lightly. Many women go back into the labor force once their youngest child is in school, and recently, there has been great demand for day-care centers that would allow mothers of preschool children to work outside the home. Apparently, we need or want responsible agencies to keep children out of the home. If this function makes the schools seem like isolation wards, a world apart from the real world where children and youth can be kept until they are cleansed of the awful stain of youthfulness (see Box 11.1), consider that most jobs in our society are for people of adult years, and this fact is not likely to change. In 1976, there were about 16 million young people between the ages of 16 and 19. Over ten and one-half million of them were in school. Imagine how high our national unemployment figures would be if even half of those now in schools suddenly were to drop out and look for work. If we did not have schools, we would have to invent something very much like them to give our young people something to do.

Schools also allow young people to be socializing agents for one another (see Coleman, 1961). This function works more dramatically if the students come from different backgrounds than if there is segregation by class or race. Through their interaction, children can learn both important and trivial information from each other: the lives and hobbies of their peers, the different jobs held by their parents, the differing political or religious convictions of their parents. Perhaps most important of all, they can learn that such differences exist. Of course, children also teach one another how to blow bubble gum, how to whistle through their fingers, how to smoke cigarettes or pot, how to do the latest dance steps, and the like.

Finally, the schools provide children with an ongoing experience in a hierarchical, bureaucratic organization. They notice that test grades and attendance records are kept, that memoranda regularly flow from the principal to the teachers, that they need proper identification before they can borrow a book from the library, and that they need "hall passes" if they are not to get in trouble for being out of the classroom. Just as surely, they learn that there are ways to beat the system, to get by without conforming to the rules, and that for every rule there seems to be a bewildering array of exceptions. They learn, too, that there is a ranking system of authority and prestige within the school and, if they are at all perceptive, that the real power

---

BOX 11.1
HIGH SCHOOLS AS PRISONS

"Our nation's schools have turned into prisons, with guards posing as teachers, and students learning how to be docile prisoners." This is the view of social psychologists Craig Haney and Philip Zimbardo (1975), who have studied both prisons and high schools and have come up with many parallels between the two institutions. Just as the prisons have developed ways of fulfilling their custodial function for prisoners, so high schools have developed similar ways for dealing with their custodial function for students. Here are some of the parallels Haney and Zimbardo have identified:

1. <u>Physical facilities.</u> Like prisons, high schools have an oppressive appearance—they are huge, stark buildings isolated from the rest of the community by walls and fences. The interiors are drab and depressing, with a series of identical cubicles for students to occupy. The schools "have been designed for efficiency, security, and surveillance, rather than beauty or the comfort of their inmates," Haney and Zimbardo point out. They suggest that school vandalism by students represents a "striking out against the most obvious symbol of their oppression."

2. <u>Authoritarianism.</u> Teachers are the guards of the high school "prison." They have almost absolute authority over student "inmates." In all but two states, teachers are allowed to use corporal punishment to keep students in line, but they have a number of other methods of control at their disposal, from embarrassing a student in front of his or her classmates to giving bad grades or suspending the students. Furthermore, if school officials are asked to arbitrate between teachers and students, it is the teacher they will support.

3. <u>Control of inmates' lives.</u> As in prisons, students in high schools must obey the rules and regulations of the institution as long as they are within its walls. Schools control students through schedules (signaled by bells), roll calls, hall passes, dress codes, and regulations about ev-

and prestige are not always in keeping with the formal system. All this, and more, teaches them how things work in the bureaucracies they will encounter beyond the school.

EDUCATION IN THE UNITED STATES

Education in the United States is an enormous enterprise, with all the merits and imperfections of a big business. In 1975 there were about 111,000 schools from elementary to college level, with about 56 million students. On a typical day, more than 3 million children were in kindergarten, and 1.6 million in nursery schools, bringing the total to almost 61 million in schools at all levels. When trade and business schools, training schools

> erything from when they can eat to when they can go to the bathroom.
> 4. <u>Symbols of power.</u> In prisons, authority is maintained through such symbols as bars on windows, gun towers, uniforms, and the like. In high schools, such symbols are less obvious, but they take the form of special status for teachers: the teacher's large, impressive desk, special faculty lunchrooms and lounges, and other faculty areas that are off-limits to students.
> 5. <u>Psychological techniques.</u> In both institutions inmates/students outnumber guards/teachers. Thus, various techniques must be employed to prevent the inmates from uniting against authority. In prisons, guards use the "divide and conquer" strategy, pitting prisoners against each other by giving special favors and promoting the development of antagonistic groups (usually racial). In schools, students are encouraged to compete against each other in academics, sports, and other areas. In this way, student aggression is channeled toward each other and away from authority.
> 6. <u>Functional autonomy.</u> Both prisons and schools tend to lose sight of their original goals and come to see themselves as ends rather than means. Prisons try to maintain themselves, often at the expense of rehabilitating criminals. Similarly, high school rules and regulations are often designed to make the school run smoothly at the expense of turning out educated students.
>
> Haney and Zimbardo conclude that the major result of the prisonlike school setup is to turn out students who have been so regimented and controlled that they have lost the desire for self-expression, and who have "accustomed themselves to passive nonidentity and nonparticipation." Thus, in an effort to carry out one of their functions—the custodial—schools may, in fact, be thwarting their other primary functions.

operated by industries, and correspondence schools are included, the best estimate is that, on a typical day, almost one-third of our population is attending some type of school.

Education in the United States is expanding, as Table 11.1 shows. Though sometimes difficult to grasp, sheer numbers are both a measure of our success and a part of our problem. Between 1950 and 1976, the number of students in kindergarten increased by over two million, those in elementary and high school by 18 million, and in college by more than seven million. The total number of students at all levels went from about 31 million to almost 60 million in about 25 years. A couple of decades can be an excruciatingly short time for any society to create places for almost 30 million additional students in its schools. But we did it, and at the same time that we were building homes and cars, feeding an increasing number of people, getting men on the moon, and engaging in two wars.

The recent decline in elementary school enrollments (see Table 11.1) is due to our lowered birth rate. Soon, the high schools will be experiencing declining student populations. It is more difficult to predict college enrollments, since they depend not only on how many people are of the appropriate age but also on what proportion of them choose to attend college. Kindergarten enrollments have increased, despite the declining birth rate, because more school districts have established kindergartens as part of the school system. The overall growth in school enrollments is quite impressive. In 25 years, school enrollments at all levels increased 89 percent, whereas the total population of the United States grew only 41 percent.

More students require more teachers. In 1976, there were over two

The United States spends vast sums for new school buildings. Recently, half or more of all bonds for new schools were turned down by the voters, who have become disenchanted with the schools.

TABLE 11.1   U.S. School Enrollments, 1930–1976

Year	Kindergarten	Elementary	High School	College	Total
1976	3,490,000	29,774,000	15,742,000	9,950,000	59,956,000
1970	3,183,000	33,950,000	14,715,000	7,413,000	59,261,000
1960	2,293,000	30,119,000	9,600,000	3,216,000	45,228,000
1950	1,175,000	21,032,000	6,453,000	2,659,000	31,319,000
1940	661,000	20,466,000	7,130,000	1,494,000	29,751,000
1930	786,000	22,953,000	4,812,000	1,101,000	29,652,000

Source: U.S. Bureau of the Census, *Statistical Abstract of the United States; 1972* (Washington, D.C.: U.S.Government Printing Office, 1972), p. 102 and U.S. Bureau of the Census, *Current Population Reports,* P-20, no. 247, February 1973; no. 294, June 1976; no. 309, July 1977.

million teachers in the nation's public elementary and high schools, more than double their number in 1950. Actually, the combined teaching staffs at these levels increased by a higher percentage than school enrollments. Millions of other workers are toiling less visibly in the educational vineyard. Architects design school buildings, service workers keep them clean and repaired, and others make the furniture, publish the textbooks, and make and maintain our schools' machines and equipment. The list could go on and on.

Another indication of the vastness of our expanding educational enterprise is the amount of money our society devotes to education. Scarcely 9 billion dollars was spent for education in 1950, whereas in 1975, about 110 billion dollars was spent. About 97 percent of this went to public schools at all levels. Even allowing for inflation, it is obvious that there has been a tremendous growth in school expenditures over the 25-year period. The cost of education rose more than twelvefold in that interval, significantly more than the increase in the number of students. In 1975, eight percent of our gross national product went for public education, as compared with three percent in 1950.

What is our society getting for the money and other resources it devotes to education? The question is crucial, but unfortunately, there are no easy answers. Perhaps the easiest approach to an answer — although not necessarily the best one — is quantitative: the percent of the population in the appropriate age groups who are in school, retention rates, degrees awarded, and other such statistics.

In 1975, practically every child between the ages of seven and thirteen and 90 percent of those between fourteen and seventeen years of age were enrolled in school. The schools thus reach most of the clientele that they should be reaching. The school retention rates and their changes over the years give another view of the payoff we receive for our educational dollars.

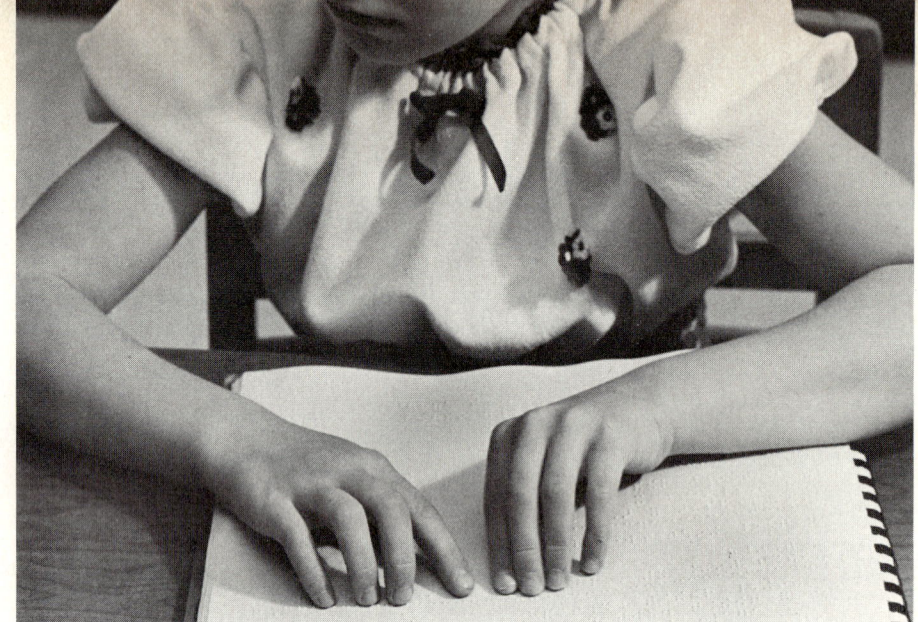

Practically every young child in America goes to school. This means that resources must be available for those with special needs.

Out of every 1000 students who entered the fifth grade in 1926, 400 entered the twelfth grade, and 333, or exactly one-third, graduated from high school. Out of the original 1000, 129 went on to enroll in college (but this does not mean they graduated). But look at a more recent picture, the high school class of 1974. Of each 1000 children who entered the fifth grade in 1966, 75 percent graduated from high school, and almost half of the original group of fifth graders enrolled in college. The increase of from one-third to three-fourths graduating from high school is impressive.

The data on those who completed college round out the picture on the educational achievements of our society's students. In recent years, over a million college degrees have been awarded annually (U.S. Office of Education, *Earned Degrees Conferred*, published annually). The increase in the number of college degrees has been fantastic. In the 15 years from 1960 to 1975, the number of bachelor's degrees awarded more than doubled, master's degrees increased threefold, and doctorates increased three and a half times. Another way of looking at the growth in college degrees awarded is to see how it affected the proportion of our population of young adults who have one or more college degrees. In 1940, six percent of the people between the ages of 25 and 29 had completed four or more years of college. The comparable figures for 1950, 1960, and 1975 are 8 percent, 11 percent, and 21 percent, respectively.

However, these figures on what our society puts into our educational system and what we get out of it do not reveal what most people would consider *issues* in education. Do those who are enrolled in schools attend regularly? Do those who attend learn anything? Do retention rates mean the students have learned whatever it is they are supposed to be learning at one level before being promoted to the next, or are they just being moved along through the system? Among those who are learning—and surely there must be some—what are they learning? Is it what they should be learning? Are our total educational dollars spent in such a way as to provide the same quality of education for all children, or do some receive a bigger slice of the educational pie than others? These are blunt and perhaps unpleasant questions, but they are persistently raised. The straight answers to them can be equally unpleasant.

MAJOR ISSUES IN AMERICAN EDUCATION

The concerns that Americans have about their schools are many and varied, ranging from the serious to the trivial. We have hinted at only a few of them. We can discuss these concerns by looking again at some of the major functions of our educational system, this time concentrating on how well they are being performed.

Problems Concerning the Transmission of Knowledge

Presumably, no one would deny that one function of our schools should be to transmit knowledge. But, as we mentioned earlier, serious questions can be raised about what knowledge should be transmitted to whom, and for what purpose. Rational humans should be able to develop logical guidelines for determining what knowledge is sufficiently important to transmit to the next generation through formal education. In other words, we should have sound *educational goals.*

If any general statement can be made, it is simply that educational goals have become less related to working and living than they were in the past. Today, it is charged that the main purpose of the early years of grade school is to prepare students for the later years; the purpose of the later years is to prepare students for high school; and an important goal of our high schools is to prepare students for college. Then what? The basic problem does not seem to lie in the function of transmission of knowledge but in the educational goals that serve as guidelines for this transmission.

Three major criticisms are commonly leveled at today's educational goals. First, our goals are poorly defined. Second, our goals, however poorly defined, are not being achieved, at least not enough to justify the vast time and money spent. Third, and most devastating of all, our educational goals are bad, or—less bluntly—they are ill-suited to the present and emerging social condition.

Poor Definition of Educational Goals It is possible to find general statements of educational goals, but they are often vague. Such vagueness makes it almost impossible to evaluate a given course of action. Take, for example, the question of how much choice students should have in selecting their high-school courses. Should they have a great deal of choice or very little? Should we have several different "tracks," or should all students basically meet the same requirements? These questions can be answered meaningfully only if we can agree, first, on the purpose of high school education.

For another example, sex education was rapidly introduced into our grade and high schools, presumably because "somebody" thought it desirable. But in some communities, it was just as swiftly withdrawn when various groups strongly objected to the way it was handled (see Baker, 1969; Calderone, 1969).

Why are modern foreign languages taught? If children should learn a foreign language, why are they not taught one in grade school? Studies have shown that young children learn another language more easily than do older children. What should be part of the physical educational program: archery? dancing? golf?

These and many other questions are continually answered in the form of decisions on what should or shouldn't be done in the schools. Many have an uneasy feeling that important decisions may not be guided by well-formulated goals. It has been said that if you don't know where you're going, any path will get you there. For a leisurely hike in the woods, perhaps it makes no difference which path you take or which destination you reach. There would seem to be much to be gained, however, by making our educational goals as explicit as possible. At the very least, it would allow us to see where the many paths are taking our children—and all of us.

Nonachievement of Educational Goals Even though it would be foolish to make a blanket indictment of the entire school system, there is ample evidence that schools are failing to reach their own goals, however poorly defined. Nationally, our literacy rate is high, but anyone who has gone through our grade and high schools knows that a certain proportion of pupils did not learn what they were supposed to learn and were, nevertheless, passed through the grades. The present system of "social promotion" may be more humane than the older system of keeping students back. But, at least the older practice implied that students were supposed to learn something, and those who didn't had to repeat the grade until they did. In the practice of passing nonlearners, there is the cynical suggestion that teaching and learning may not be important functions of our educational system at all.

The evidence that students are not learning as much as they used to cannot be ignored. Since 1963, there has been a downward trend in the average scores attained by students on the Scholastic Aptitude Test (SAT), a requirement for admission to many colleges. In 1963, the mean score on the verbal portion was 478; in 1975 it was 434. The mathematics portion of the test showed a decline in mean scores of from 502 in 1963 to 472 in 1975. Analyses have shown that, if anything, the SAT has been getting easier, not harder, over the years and that the pronounced decline in average scores is not due to the fact that a higher proportion of all high school students are now taking the test. Furthermore, declines similar to those of the SAT have been found in the American College Testing Program (ACT) scores as well.

Other specific studies also point to a decline in learning among students. At the University of Wisconsin, for example, over 60 percent of those taking

EDUCATION AND SOCIETY

FIGURE 11.1   Average Scores on the Scholastic Aptitude Test (SAT)

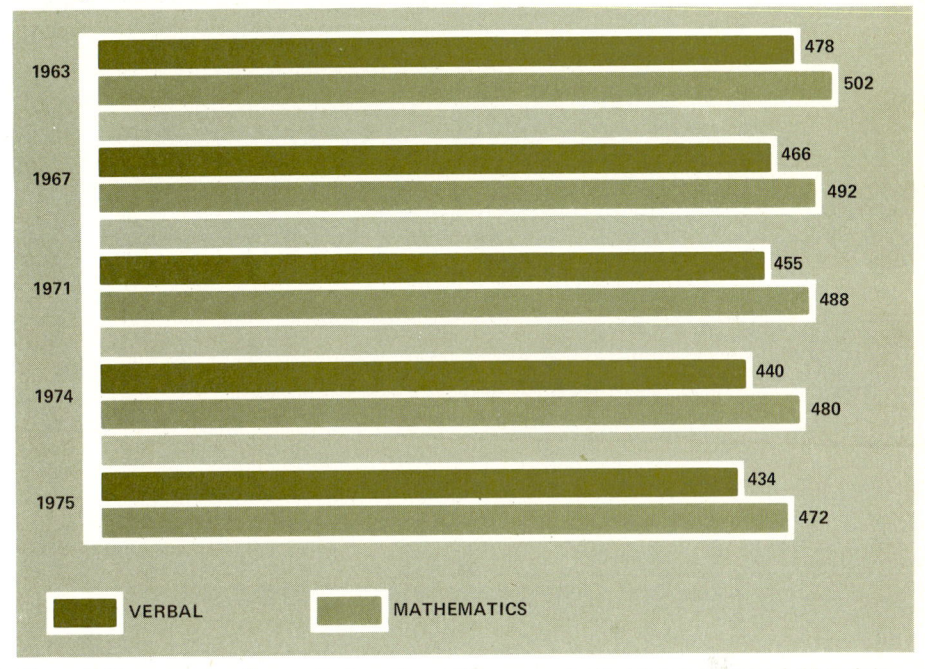

Year	Verbal	Mathematics
1963	478	502
1967	466	492
1971	455	488
1974	440	480
1975	434	472

Since 1963, scores on the verbal portion of the examination have plunged 44 points, and on the mathematical portion, 30 points. Analysis has shown that the biggest decrease was in the number of students scoring in the higher bracket (600–800), which means that the lower average scores are not the result of more students taking the examination.

Source: *U.S. News and World Report* (September 15, 1975), p. 60.

an English usage test to qualify for majors in journalism failed; the failure rate previously had been 25 percent. Another study found that a high percentage of young adults were unable to balance a checkbook, use an income tax table, or apply simple mathematical concepts in buying canned goods at the supermarket (Reys, 1976). Getting more specific, there is the case of the 1976 valedictorian from a Washington, D.C., high school whose SAT scores were only half as high as they should have been to obtain admission to George Washington University. The dean of the university is quoted as saying that the student had been conned: "He has been deluded into thinking he's gotten an education" (*U.S. News and World Report,* October 18, 1976).

College instructors are notorious for their complaints that many of their students have come to college poorly prepared in logical reasoning, have trouble reading and writing their native language, and lack mathematical skills. The blame can be passed to the high schools, and then to the elementary schools, where it can be returned to the college professors who taught the teachers. Wherever the blame lies, our educational system is failing in what presumably is one of its major functions—to educate.

FIGURE 11.2 Average Scores of Final-Year Secondary Students on International Achievement Tests, Selected Countries: 1970

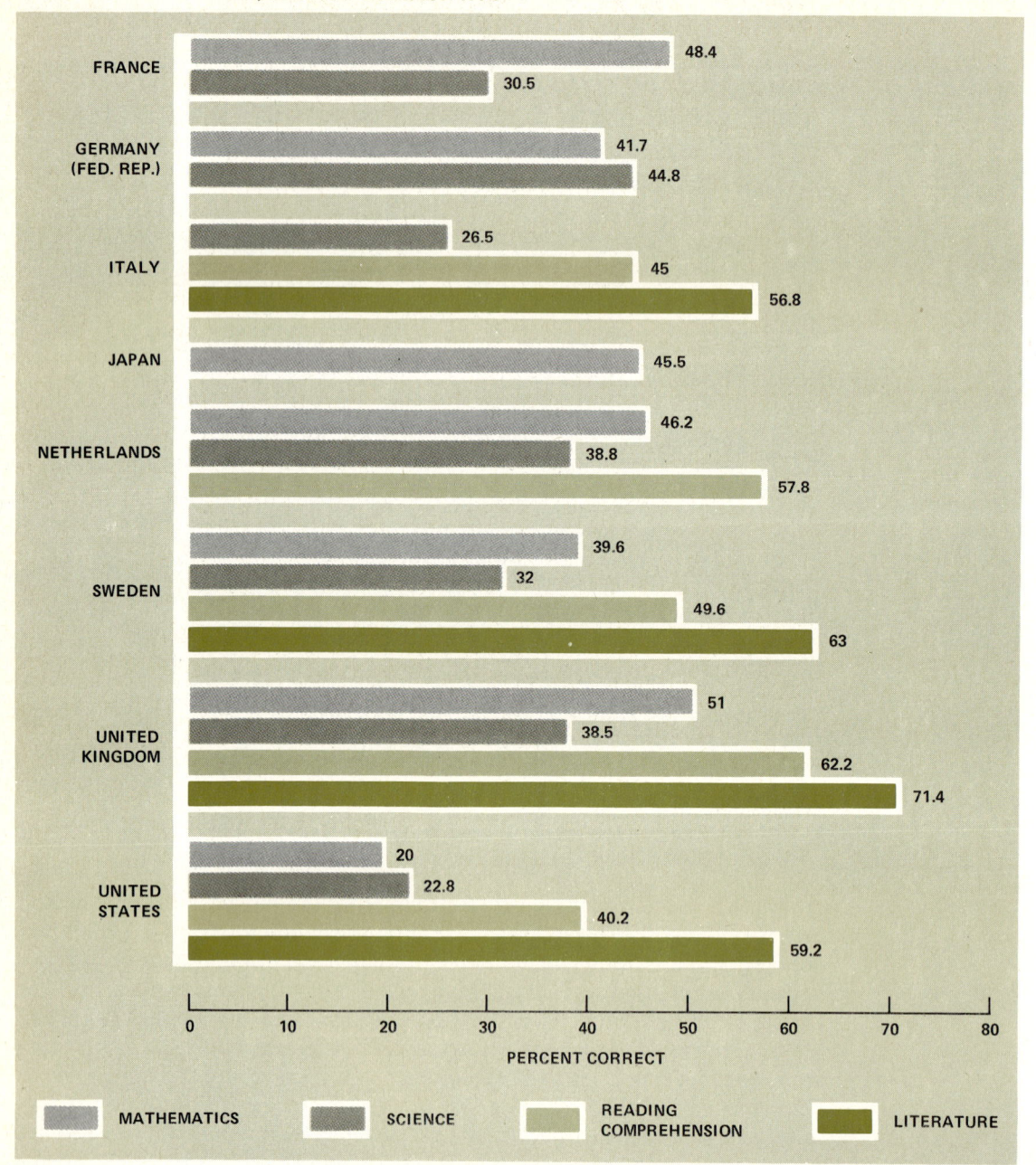

Country	Mathematics	Science	Reading Comprehension	Literature
FRANCE	48.4	30.5		
GERMANY (FED. REP.)	41.7	44.8		
ITALY	26.5		45	56.8
JAPAN	45.5			
NETHERLANDS	46.2	38.8	57.8	
SWEDEN	39.6	32	49.6	63
UNITED KINGDOM	51	38.5	62.2	71.4
UNITED STATES	20	22.8	40.2	59.2

PERCENT CORRECT

Legend: MATHEMATICS — SCIENCE — READING COMPREHENSION — LITERATURE

On the average, high school seniors in the United States score much lower on standard achievement tests than do their counterparts in a number of other countries. Scores of American students in mathematics and science are particularly low. Of course, a higher proportion of American youths are in school than is true in the other countries. This suggests that we have not been able to educate the masses up to the level that can be achieved when it is not expected that almost everyone will graduate from high school. (All scores not available for all countries.)

Source: Executive Office of the President: Office of Management and Budget, *Social Indicators, 1976* (Washington, D.C.: U.S. Government Printing Office, 1976), p. 293.

EDUCATION AND SOCIETY

Educators are beginning to take this decline in learning seriously. The Los Angeles City School Board has ordered that, starting in 1979, students must pass a reading proficiency test before being awarded a high school diploma. Students in the tenth grade can take the reading test up to four times and will be given remedial instruction if they fail. Virginia and New York have also imposed reading proficiency requirements for high school graduation. A recent public opinion poll found that almost two-thirds of the general population now favor the idea that high school students should be required to pass a standard, nationwide examination in order to receive a high school diploma. Apparently, more and more people recognize that the schools are not performing the function of transmission of knowledge as well as they should and would like to see the situation remedied. (Many parents are calling for a return to fundamentals in the schools—see Box 11.2.)

The Question of Relevancy Many students have speculated that the real problem is not the failure to meet educational goals but the irrelevance of

FIGURE 11.3   Changing Objectives and Attitudes of College Freshmen, 1970–1974

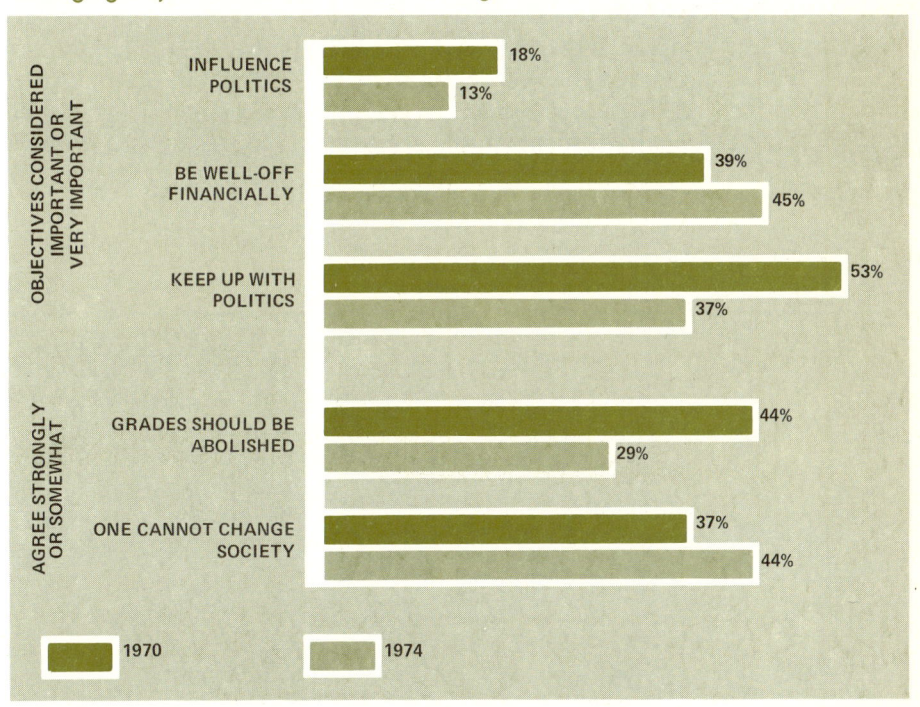

OBJECTIVES CONSIDERED IMPORTANT OR VERY IMPORTANT

- INFLUENCE POLITICS: 18% (1970), 13% (1974)
- BE WELL-OFF FINANCIALLY: 39% (1970), 45% (1974)
- KEEP UP WITH POLITICS: 53% (1970), 37% (1974)

AGREE STRONGLY OR SOMEWHAT

- GRADES SHOULD BE ABOLISHED: 44% (1970), 29% (1974)
- ONE CANNOT CHANGE SOCIETY: 37% (1970), 44% (1974)

1970   1974

If new jobs are scarce, social concerns decline and students concentrate on their own economic security. Grades become more important. In a few short years, the mood on college campuses has changed dramatically.

Source: Richard B. Freeman, *The Over-Educated American* (New York: Academic Press, 1976), p. 44.

the goals themselves. They claim that the schools, or certain courses of study, are simply not relevant to contemporary life. We can dismiss such complaints as idle prattle of the immature, or we can admit that, just possibly, those who are supposed to be profiting from the system have discovered a serious flaw in it.

Formal education, as part of the broad socialization process, should be future-oriented. Ideally, it should prepare children to live in the world they will find when they become adults. But, neither parents nor educators can possibly know, for certain, what tomorrow will be like. The best we can do is to equip the adults of the future, so that they will be able to build and rebuild it for themselves. Nevertheless, critics contend that our schools are attempting to prepare our children to live in a world that no longer exists.

In a 1939 satire on education, *The Sabre-Tooth Curriculum*, J. Abner Peddiwell describes a mythical paleolithic society in which the elders insisted that children be taught how to kill sabre-tooth tigers—long after the tigers were all but extinct. Children were also expected to learn how to club the wooly horse, even though the animals had long since deserted the area. Educators were not addressing themselves to the real problem of the day: the danger of the fierce glacial bears who migrated to the area and who could not be dealt with by the same tactics used on tigers. The teaching of antelope snaring was considered somewhat subversive, even though the antelope had replaced the wooly horse in the ecosystem. Clubbing would not capture antelopes, whose skins and meat were sorely needed by the group. Many of today's students could see parallels to the present system quite readily and would assert that today's school is seriously out of phase with their own and with society's real needs.

What, then, should be taught in the schools? Sociologists are not special-

---

**BOX 11.2
BACK
TO THE
FUNDAMENTALS**

Schools in a few cities across the country are trying a "radical" new approach to education—a return to "fundamentals." In this case, "fundamental" means the traditional approach of teaching the three R's. Apparently, there are more than a few parents who are unhappy with their children's progress in the modern "open classroom," with its emphasis on self-paced instruction, and they are skeptical about the value of other faddish educational "alternatives." They suggest that going back to the basics is what children really need.

One city in which the fundamental approach is being tried is San Diego. According to the San Diego Reader, two of the city's elementary schools have been set up to provide "the type of grade-school education that was taken for granted in the 1950s and 60s." This means grades, homework checked and signed by parents, and a dress code, among other things.

An interesting aspect of the San Diego fundamental schools is their role

ists in curriculum development. They only look at the society and try to relate our institutionalized system of learning to what they know about the society. Ours is a society of onrushing change. Routine assembly-line work is rapidly disappearing, and it will continue to do so. Within the lifetime of individuals now graduating from high school, whole career lines will fold and new ones will open up, forcing many to change careers perhaps several times if they wish to stay employed. Many other changes will occur. In this type of society, as George Leonard (1964) puts it, "the school may best serve society by serving the individual capacity to keep learning, to keep changing, to keep creating" (p. 104).

The rapid pace of change will require individuals who are able to cope with such change. Increasingly greater abilities to judge and to make choices, to be imaginative and creative, and to be adaptable will be required in the postindustrial society (a society in which the production of services is more important than the production of goods). If our physical climate were changing drastically because a new ice age was approaching and we did not change our institutions to enable individuals to deal with the change, the survival chances of our society would be low. In a similar sense, to serve society, our educational system must alter its goals to respond to the profound social, economic, and political changes of today and tomorrow.

Problems with Equality of Opportunity

When evaluating the function of providing equality of opportunity, we must keep in mind that it actually entails two functions: the providing of equality *in* the school system and the providing of equality *through* the school system. First, are children treated equally and otherwise given equal chances of

---

in school desegregation. Before the switch to the fundamental approach, one of the elementary schools was 98 percent black and Chicano. Wanting their children to have a good fundamental education, many white parents enrolled their children in that school, reducing the minority percentage to 70. Similarly, the other school, which was predominantly white before the change, increased its minority enrollment from 15 percent to 35 percent.

Many parents who pushed for the fundamental program were worried that the racial integration issue would cloud the point they were really trying to make (the school board originally instituted the program as one means of satisfying a court decree that local schools be integrated). But a peek into the classrooms shows children working together peacefully to learn their three R's. Whether they are learning better than their counterparts in modern schools is yet to be seen. Meanwhile, parents have shown that they really do care about what their children learn.

succeeding in school? Second, how well do the schools provide all children with equal chances for success in life? If the educational experience is in any way related to success in later life, the two aspects of equality of opportunity should be related. Nevertheless, they are not identical.

One way of evaluating how well the schools are providing equality of opportunity is to use the familiar *input-output model.* We look, first, at the various resources that go into different types of schools, and then we look at the extent to which students of different backgrounds are receiving an equally good education and equal chances for success in life. Finally, we should look at the long-term output to see whether there are systematic differences in actual success in life, particularly with respect to lifetime occupation and income.

School Inputs One measure of **school inputs** is the amount of money spent per pupil. Nationally, we spent about $1400 in 1976 for each student in our public elementary and high schools. New York spent $2179 per pupil; and eleven other states, including some of the middle Atlantic states, Wisconsin, Minnesota, and Montana, spent over $1600. By contrast, Arkansas spent $881 per pupil; and Kentucky, Mississippi, and Tennessee each spent less than $1000. A recent study of the per pupil expenditures in 20 large cities found great differences among them: San Antonio, Houston, Indianapolis, and San Diego all spent less than $1000 per pupil, while cities such as San Francisco, Washington, D.C., and Chicago spend over $1800.

There are thus gross inequalities among the various states and cities in the amount of money spent per pupil in our schools. In addition, it is generally found that within a city or metropolitan area there are great differences, with the schools in the wealthy suburbs spending considerably more per pupil than those in the inner city. Wealthy suburbs have a predominantly white population, whereas inner-city populations are mainly black. Some school systems with a high proportion of minority students, such as those in New York City and Washington, D.C., have high per pupil dollar inputs. Two major points are, nevertheless, true throughout the system: (1) in the United States, there has long been a great disparity among schools in the amount of financial resources per pupil; and (2) the differential has not been random but systematic: the poor, blacks, and other minority groups are much more likely to be attending inferior schools than are the whites and the more affluent.

One of the main reasons for these differences in financial input is related to the way in which school funds are obtained. Basically, money to run the schools is obtained partly from the state and partly from local taxes. Although the proportion derived from the state varies with each state, as long as local property taxes are used to finance local schools, those who live in more expensive homes pay more property taxes and can afford better schools in their areas. Theoretically, a state could develop a formula that would yield more state aid to poorer school districts, thus equalizing the

The great inequalities in per pupil expenditures mean that the schools do not provide all children with equal chances for success in life. What educational experiences are the Montana ranch children who attend this school missing?

total amount of money available for each school. States have indeed attempted to do so, but, apparently, with little success. In some states, it has become a legal issue. In 1972, Michigan's Supreme Court ruled that the formula for state aid did not, in fact, equalize the money available to school districts and was therefore unconstitutional. Equalizing the amount of money available per pupil within a state would not solve the problem either, however. We would still have state-by-state variations. Is it fair that $881 per pupil is spent in Arkansas, while $1618 is spent in Wisconsin?

The problem of equality and racially segregated schools is still unresolved. In 1954, the United States Supreme Court ruled that separate educational facilities for the races is inherently unequal. Even if teachers' salaries, library facilities, lunch programs, and all else were identical in white and black schools, the mere act of separating the races, it was reasoned, generates a feeling of inferiority on the part of blacks. And this deprives them of an educational experience equal to that of the majority of students. Following the Court's decision, efforts were made—sometimes peacefully, sometimes under protest—to integrate the races in the schools.

As late as 1972, however, official school records indicated that, nationally, 46 percent of black children were attending schools where minority students constituted 95 to 100 percent of the school enrollment. The South had the least segregated schools, with about 20 percent of blacks in predominantly black schools; while in the border states, the percentage was over half; and in the northern and western states, over 40 percent of all blacks were in schools where minorities made up at least 95 percent of the student body.

It is by no means easy to remove the inequality in American education resulting from segregation. Busing has been tried with varying degrees of success, but it is a controversial measure and is disfavored by most politicians. School districts have been redrawn, but at times with such ingenuity that racial integration has been prevented rather than achieved. Accepting the harsh reality that true integration will not be achieved very soon, some

College is one route to becoming a productive member of society. Studies generally find that more blacks than whites want to go to college but even today blacks are less likely to do so.

blacks now prefer segregated, but otherwise equal, schools for their children. Other people, both black and white, view this as a sorry surrender. As scientists, sociologists are supposed to report their findings without making judgments; yet, it can be reported that if one function of our educational institution is to provide equality of opportunity in the system, the schools have failed rather dismally in performing this function. This is true of both the various economic inputs and of the subtler inequalities resulting from racial segregation.

Educational Outputs One could argue that whether or not school facilities are equal, the critical question is how good an education—the output of our school system—children from different backgrounds are receiving. **Educational outputs** can be measured in many ways, and they deal, most often, with quantity of education rather than quality. But each tells us something a little different about what happens to our children in the schools.

If the number of years of school completed are compared, white and nonwhite groups under 30 years of age differ considerably, as shown in Table 11.2. In 1977, over 14 percent more whites than blacks had completed high school, and 56 percent more whites had completed four or more years

TABLE 11.2   Percentage of Persons, by Race, Ages 25-29, Completing Specified Years of School

White

Year	Less Than Five Years of Elementary School	4 Years of High School	4 or More Years of College	Median School Years Completed
1977	0.8	87	25	13
1970	1	78	17	13
1960	2	64	12	12
1950	3	55	8	12
1940	3	41	6	11

Nonwhite

Year	Less Than 5 Years of Elementary School	4 Years of High School	4 or More Years of College	Median School Years Completed
1977	1	76	16	13
1970	2	58	10	12
1960	7	39	5	11
1950	15	23	3	9
1940	27	12	2	7

Source: U.S. Department of Health, Education, and Welfare, *Digest of Educational Statistics, 1977-1978* (Washington, D.C.: U.S. Government Printing Office, 1978), p. 14.

of college. But this disparity is less than it was years ago: in 1940, over three times more whites than blacks completed high school, and three times more whites than blacks completed college. Blacks are better educated today than in the past, but even in the "enlightened" 1970s, the amount of formal education received is still related to race.

School dropouts are those persons of roughly school age who are not enrolled in school and who are not high school graduates. Here, again, we note a systematic difference by race. As Table 11.3 shows, in 1976, 7 percent of all white females and 11 percent of all black females were school dropouts. Among males, there was not as much difference in the dropout rates of blacks and whites, except among nineteen-year-olds where we see that 21 percent of blacks as compared to 15 percent of whites were high school dropouts. While the odds are still greater that a black rather than a white will be a school dropout, the gap has been narrowing considerably.

One of the goals of formal education is to prepare people to be *productive, participating,* and *successful* members of society. There are many ways of defining these terms; but, whatever else may be included, a person's *job* is one measure of productivity and success. *Income* is another measure of success, even if it is sometimes overrated and overemphasized.

TABLE 11.3　Percentage of High School Dropouts by Race and Sex, 1976

	Black		White	
Age	Male	Female	Male	Female
Total: 14–19	9	11	9	7
14	*	1	1	*
15	1	2	2	2
16	4	8	6	3
17	12	14	9	8
18	18	23	19	10
19	21	18	15	15

*Less than one percent.
Source: U.S. Bureau of the Census, Current Population Reports (Washington, D.C.: U.S. Government Printing Office), series P-20, no. 319, February 1978.

Many interesting facts and relationships can be discovered from the data in Table 11.4. First, the more years of formal education you have had, the better are your chances of being employed in a white-collar occupation. Although that relationship is the focus of our present discussion, two other points are noteworthy: (1) among males with comparable education, blacks are less likely than whites to hold a white-collar job and more likely to be service workers; (2) women at the same educational levels as men are more likely to be engaged in service jobs (and those in white-collar jobs are more likely to be employed as secretaries, clerks, and typists). One could also compare black women with white women, black men with black women, and so on. Nevertheless, education indeed affects the kind of work that you do. When you think of the hours per day and the years per lifetime spent on the job, the effects of formal education on your life are almost incalculable.

Because occupation and income are related, the more years of school you complete, the higher will be your yearly and lifetime income. The differences in lifetime income are particularly revealing. The average person with four or more years of college earns $758,000 over the course of his or her life. This is $279,000 more than what is earned by a high school graduate, and $414,000 more than a grade school graduate (U.S. Bureau of the Census statistics).

Cynics claim that it is not how much you know that counts but whether or not you have the proper credentials—the right piece of paper, the diploma. There is some truth in this. The lifetime earnings of those who have had some high school are considerably less than the earnings of those who graduated, and persons with only some college earn much less than college graduates. Apparently, completion of a given level of education affects the kind of job you can find, and thus, your potential earnings.

TABLE 11.4 Percentage of Persons in Occupational Groups by Race and Years of School Completed, 1976

	Employed Males			
	White		Black and Other	
Percent, by Occupation	Less than 4 Years of High School	4 Years of High School or More	Less than 4 Years of High School	4 Years of High School or More
White collar	15.9	53.8	9.0	37.4
Blue collar	63.3	36.8	62.9	46.0
Service, including private household workers	12.3	6.6	21.0	15.3
Farm	8.5	2.8	2.1	1.3

	Employed Females			
	White		Black and Other	
Percent, by Occupation	Less than 4 Years of High School	4 Years of High School or More	Less than 4 Years of High School	4 Years of High School or More
White collar	30.6	76.7	12.5	62.7
Blue collar	31.3	8.3	27.6	13.8
Service, including private household workers	36.1	13.8	59.4	23.4
Farm	2.0	.7	.5	.1

Source: U.S. Bureau of the Census, *Statistical Abstracts of the United States: 1975* (Washington, D.C.: U.S. Government Printing Office, 1977), p. 140.

Schools and Cultural Bias We have seen that there are systematic differences in how far a person will progress through the school system and how this, in turn, will have profound effects on his or her life. It would take an unscrupulous wizard, fast with rhetoric but loose with facts and logic, to maintain that the schools are performing their function of providing equal opportunity. But, what has gone wrong? To explain why some people continue in school longer than others and achieve more than others, we must look at the schools, the students, and the interaction between the two.

Studies have shown that the inequality of resources that go into our schools accounts for some, but not much, of the difference in achievement test scores (Coleman et al., 1966). As we discussed in Chapter 8, the public school system is basically a middle-class institution, reflecting and instilling middle-class virtues and values. An obvious bias favors those who are obedient, who learn by rote when it is demanded, who learn how to take tests, and who, in short, catch on to the rules of the educational game and are willing to play by them. The child who has or acquires these traits will get along in our present-day schools without too much difficulty. The child who does not master these things will be at odds with teachers, and often, unhappy and frustrated as well. (Students who do not accept the middle-class values are often defined as "troublemakers." See Stinchcombe, 1969.)

It has generally been found that attitudes and beliefs are highly related to achievement in school. People who believe that they can control their lives and environments will do far better in school than those who feel that fate, luck, or the facts of life control them. Life has taught some children, cruelly but with certainty, that what middle-class people would term an unduly fatalistic attitude is, basically, a correct one. Groups that are discriminated against do not have much control over what happens to them. In addition, while some children learn good grammar at home merely by hearing it spoken, have reading and reference materials in the home, or have parents who praise schooling and defend its competitiveness and reward system, other children are what is euphemistically called "culturally deprived." Of course, such children have culture in the sociological sense; but what they do not have are some aspects of the culture of the middle class. This lack can hardly be said to be the fault of the schools. Perhaps the schools cannot be expected to perform the function of providing equal opportunities until, or unless, some basic social changes are made.

Problems with the Custodial Function

Simply stated, the custodial function refers to the role schools serve in keeping children and young people out of the home and out of the work force for many hours a day. In view of students' complaints that what goes on at school is not relevant to the real concerns of the world in which they will have to live, it should come as no surprise to find that schools are having troubles with their custodial function.

For about ten percent of youth between the ages of 14 and 19, the school is serving no custodial function at all, because they have dropped out of school. The Children's Defense Fund reports that, annually, at least two million children are suspended from school for a total of eight million schools days missed. Nearly two-thirds of the suspensions are for nonviolent, nondangerous offenses, such as truancy, smoking, cutting classes, and arguing with a teacher. Curiously, when students are suspended for truancy, the crime and the punishment are identical. Suspensions, and the various reasons for them, indicate, nevertheless, that the schools are not performing the custodial function too well.

FIGURE 11.4   Illegal Acts Committed in American Schools During a Typical Month

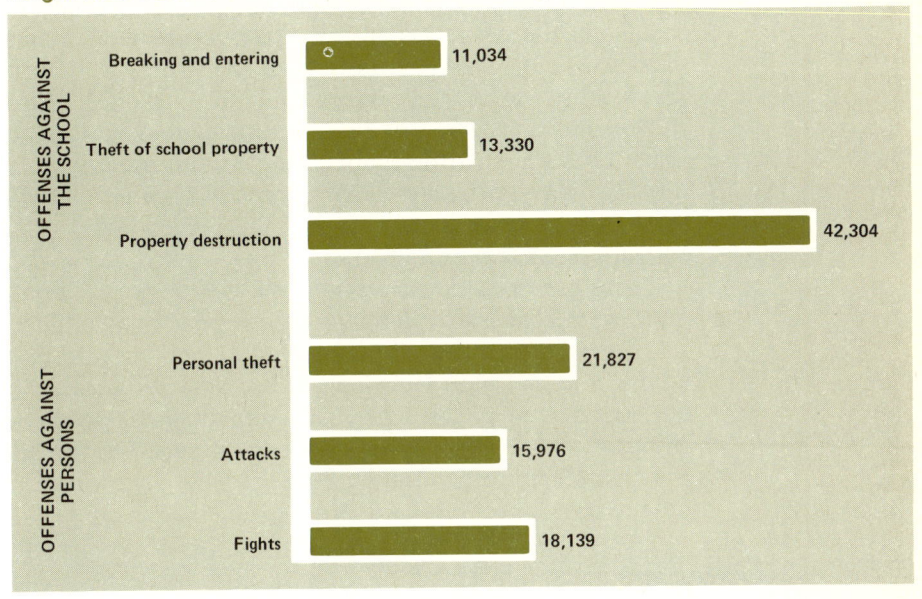

OFFENSES AGAINST THE SCHOOL
- Breaking and entering: 11,034
- Theft of school property: 13,330
- Property destruction: 42,304

OFFENSES AGAINST PERSONS
- Personal theft: 21,827
- Attacks: 15,976
- Fights: 18,139

From principals' report sheets, it is estimated that there were 157,000 illegal acts committed in American schools during a typical month in 1976-1977. (Only the most frequently occurring offenses are shown in the graph.) Crime and violence in our schools appears to have leveled off since the early 1970s, but it is still an important concern.

Source: U.S. Department of Health, Education, and Welfare, *Violent Schools—Safe Schools* (Washington, D.C.: U.S. Government Printing Office, 1978), p. 44.

Other evidence of the schools' failure with the custodial function abounds. Most Americans have read about the terrible conditions in large city schools, where teachers claim to be chiefly disciplinarians (although, from all reports, they are not succeeding too well even in that role). Knifings, muggings, extortion, and physical attacks on teachers are now so common that only the most blatant cases draw the attention of the press. A Senate subcommittee estimated that about 70,000 teachers are victims of serious assaults each year. Its survey of 757 school districts also found that the yearly cost of school vandalism is at least $500 million, equal to the total amount spent on textbooks in every school in the country in 1972. Even the schools in smaller cities and in the suburbs have their share of discipline problems. It is not uncommon, but still a little frightening, to see security guards, with walkie-talkies on their hips, patrolling the halls and playgrounds of elementary and high schools.

Part of the trouble that schools have with their custodial function is that some students do not learn—or perhaps do not want to learn—what Philip

Jackson (1968) calls the **hidden curriculum.** This curriculum consists of everything that students have to learn in order to survive psychologically and socially in the schools. Typically, schools are concerned with order and regulations. Those who get along learn that things start and stop at scheduled times, which do not necessarily coincide with one's interests. Other parts of the hidden curriculum include learning to do what is necessary to secure the praise of teachers without alienating oneself from peers; and learning to put up with delays, rules concerning quiet, and sometimes even rules on how to dress. Those who do not master the hidden curriculum do not like the school system very much and try to get out of it as soon as possible.

There are no easy answers to the custodial problems of schools in the United States. Most Americans believe that every child should be educated, and this value is reflected in our compulsory school attendance laws. Unlike adults, who can quit their job if it becomes unbearable, children and youth are required to go to school. In some places, people are having second thoughts about compulsory school attendance. Under California's new plan, for example, students can quit school before age sixteen, provided they are able to pass a proficiency examination.

What should be done about the fact that some young people hate school and everything connected with it? Money spent as a result of vandalism could well be used for books, teachers, and other purposes.

Problems with Control of the Schools

In the United States, the public schools are supposed to be controlled by the people who live in each school district. The state may set minimums in curriculum standards or in length of school sessions, but the local boards of

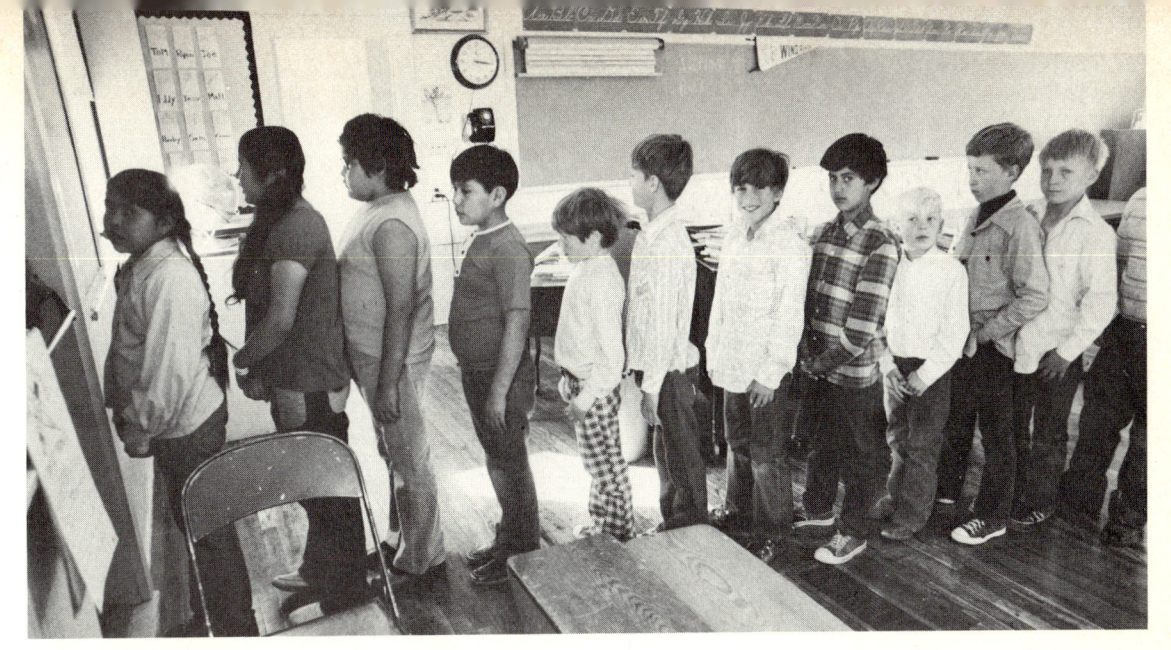

Learning the hidden curriculum of the school means accepting the rules for order, quiet, and regimentation. Some can't learn this curriculum, and some won't.

education implement these standards. The local boards have more direct control over the schools than do the states, since the boards hire superintendents and teachers and approve educational programs. A recent poll found that over two-thirds of the people in the United States would like to see even more local control of schools. But there are dissatisfactions with local control, even if it is preferred to control and influence by the state and federal governments.

School boards have been severely criticized for not actually representing "the people." It is typically charged that most of the members of most school boards are power figures in the community, such as bankers, clergymen, and business leaders. Although extremely unpopular individuals can be removed at the next election, this takes time and organization, and people are often afraid that the new members will be no better than those they replace. Minority-group members and the poor are rarely found on school boards.

One problem is that there is no such thing as "the people"; the phrase is rhetoric meant to suggest that some vague, undefinable group has greater legitimacy than others. Not only is such a claim for greater legitimacy not true in law, but each of us is of "the people." So, to say without qualification that the boards should represent the people is almost meaningless. As we shall see, every group that claims to be, or to represent, the people excludes other groups that have equally legitimate claims.

Control by the people sometimes means that the parents of those children now in school should have the most influence on how the schools are run. Suggestions have been made for giving such parents more direct control, and one method proposed has come to be called the **voucher system.** Under this arrangement, parents of a school-age child would be given a certificate worth so many dollars to spend on education. They could then shop around and enroll their child in the public or private school most to their liking. The theory is that this would bring competition into the educational system and would thereby improve it. Schools would have to shape up to the demands of parents or close their doors.

The utter administrative confusion that the voucher system would presumably create is not the most serious complaint against it. If schools shape the minds of students who, in turn, will shape and reshape society, should not the unmarried, the childless, and those whose children are out of school also have some control over the schools? Not only do these people pay taxes that fund the schools, but they, too, can be genuinely concerned about the schools and the impact that educational policies will have on the present and future of our society.

Control by the people sometimes means neighborhood control. In some large cities, blacks, Mexican Americans, Puerto Rican Americans, and other minority groups have sought control over schools, so that they could initiate programs and courses of study suitable to their needs (Divoky, 1971; Gross and Gross, 1970). Such arrangements would make the school system less of a white middle-class institution and more responsive to particular needs of certain minority groups.

Professional educators—the teachers and administrators who interact daily with the students—have a different point of view. They claim that their training, as well as the demands of their roles, should enable them to make major decisions about what is taught and how the schools should be run. However, students, too, are people. How much control should students have over what is taught, who teaches it, or how educational dollars are spent? Students are not likely to let us forget them entirely. Having heard participatory democracy praised for many years, they might well want to practice it in the schools that taught it to them.

Much that has been said about the public schools applies also to colleges and universities. To be sure, institutions of higher learning allow much academic freedom. Controversial ideas can be explored without penalty, and research findings can be released without fear of reprisal from groups with vested interests. Although colleges and universities are relatively free in these respects, they are only as free as those who control them allow them to be. Boards of trustees are not noted for their civil libertarian views. Funds to run colleges and universities must come from state legislatures, private endowments, or sometimes, cities. In any case, we have the familiar problem of how much control those who hold the purse strings should be allowed to have.

College faculties can be counted on to take a strong stand for academic freedom, and to seek some control of their institutions. Student control in colleges is a more intensely sought goal than it is at the high school level, possibly because college students are more sophisticated, and because they or their parents are paying tuition in addition to taxes. Between the high school and the college, the question of whether students should control the system or the system should control the students differs only in degree.

The power struggle for control of schools at all levels is likely to continue. Although it indicates a dissatisfaction with how things are presently being done, it at least shows that people care enough about education to be willing to fight about it.

Disenchantment with the Schools

America's faith in education has been deeply shaken. More people are questioning the underlying principle that used to guide our thinking on education (and for that matter, our expenditures): the greatest possible number should be able to receive as much education as they wish and as they can profit from. Education, social progress, and upward mobility were seen as being intricately linked. Through education, each generation could do better than the previous one, and in the process, both society and the individual would gain. Some writers are urging that massive efforts be made to restore the nation's faith in education: "At stake is nothing less than the survival of American democracy" (Hechinger, 1976).

The disenchantment with education and schools shows up in very tangible ways. In 1960, only 11 percent of all school bond issues in the country were voted down, whereas in 1975, 54 percent were defeated—despite the fact that the recession reduced the number and size of bond issues. Legislatures are more concerned than ever with how much money should be spent on education. Many have even suggested that not a single additional dollar be spent on education until there is proof that the public is getting its money's worth. The disenchantment with education shows up in other ways. Some parents have even resorted to suing the schools (see Box 11.3). And many middle-class youths are seriously questioning whether or not they should go to college. They can afford to go, but they wonder whether what they will learn will have any real impact on their lives, or at least, on the kind of lives they wish to live. The Golden Age of education, during which we believed that more education for more people would solve all our problems, is, depending on your point of view, either threatened or over.

Our system of education, from kindergarten to professional schools, has been compared to a mutated octopus that has grown more and more tentacles, while retaining its minuscule brain. This analogy may not be inappropriate, although certainly the idea could be expressed more delicately. The growth of the system itself seems to be matched only by the growth of the conflicting views about what the schools should be doing. The educational functions are obviously in conflict. How can any system simultaneously educate the masses; prepare everyone for jobs; give quality academic education to the few destined for graduate and professional schools; prepare all groups for life, in general; transmit the cultural heritage faithfully, while preparing students for life in a changing society; provide drug counseling; serve meals; smooth out racial and ethnic inequalities; and come down hard on sex stereotyping? Perhaps we are doomed to disappointment if we expect the schools, as presently structured, to be all things for all people.

The current disenchantment with the nation's schools should not be taken lightly. In some cities, parents have pulled out of the system and are operating "free schools," or storefront schools, which reject most of the goals and traditions of the established educational system. None of these schools has been open long enough for us to know whether or not they will do a good job of preparing children for life. Such efforts, nevertheless, demonstrate an extreme degree of dissatisfaction, a magnified version of the disenchantment felt by many. Still, the schools are not about to close their doors, nor has our faith in education been so badly shattered that there will be great pressure for them to do so. In the years ahead, we will see creative and even radical changes in our educational system. For the good of our children and our society, we can only hope that these years will be as productive as they promise to be exciting.

EDUCATION AND THE TWO CHIEF SOCIOLOGICAL MODELS

Our examination of the American institution of education has probably made it clear that, while decades ago, structural-functionalism seemed to be the best model for analyzing the system, today, the conflict model seems

**BOX 11.3
CAN'T READ, JOHNNY?
SO SUE THE TEACHER**

The functions of a given institution may come and go, and changes in these functions can produce social confusion and discomfort. But what happens to a society when an institution is simply failing in its functions? The number of schools and students that are failing is large enough to have made the schools targets of intense criticism for some time now. Year after year, school boards and school districts are embarrassed by the declining level of achievement in their schools. Is the failure in the students or in the schools? Many seem to have decided that the schools have failed the students and have talked of taking the schools to court to force them to shape up.

In late 1972, the San Francisco Unified School District was made the plaintiff in an action brought against it by Peter Doe. Peter Doe is the fictitious name of an actual 18-year-old white male high school graduate. After thirteen years in San Francisco public schools, Peter Doe, who has a normal IQ, had average grades, kept good attendance, and was not a disciplinary problem, was found to have fifth-grade reading abilities. Private tutoring—after high school graduation—improved his reading skills significantly. Throughout his school years, his parents had told teachers they were concerned about Peter's apparent difficulty in reading, but

more apt. In the early days of our history, the family was a far more dominant socializing and economic force than it is today. And, although official church membership was lower in the eighteenth century than it has been in our own century, the religious values of Protestantism also played a major socializing role then. Despite separation of church and state, religious values were more explicitly at work in those days. For these combined reasons, education played a much narrower role in the socializing process. Schools were expected to teach little more than the basic utilitarian skills of reading, writing, and arithmetic. If they did so, there was little complaint. A structural-functionalist could thus show how the educational system meshed with other systems to keep the society in operation.

Today, when we examine the functions of our educational system, it is also necessary to deal with the poor performance of many of the functions, much as we have done in this chapter. More than this, society seems riddled with conflict over everything from the basic worth of education to how to achieve class and racial balance in the schools. At the root of the conflicts are profound changes in society, in general, and in the educational system, specifically, that have occurred in the last hundred years. It became compulsory by law for every child to attend school, and school curricula expanded over the decades. Meanwhile, our society was becoming more complex in numerous ways. The economic institution was growing in complexity and creating more and more jobs requiring hitherto unneeded

---

they were assured that he was an average reader. The schools that Peter Doe attended are now being charged with negligence, false representation, and violation of various statutes.

The courts have been used against the schools before. The historic <u>Brown v. Board of Education of Topeka</u> case (1954) prohibited racial segregation in the schools. Other decisions have required equal public educational facilities for all, regardless of community financial resources. The latest efforts are based on changing the legal status of education from a privilege to a right. Even so, can the courts be made to settle the complex matters of learning? One advocate of educational reform, Gary Saretsky, attended a conference on legal strategies for accomplishing such reform. He was impressed with the legal sophistication of the strategists, but he was appalled at the strategists' ignorance and simplemindedness regarding the theories and practice of education. Could taking the schools to court produce, as Saretsky fears, a cure worse than the present illness of bad performance? Can the complicated, elusive functions of an entire social institution be defined and made enforceable by lawyers and judges?

kinds of training and skills. City dwellers were becoming an even larger percentage of the total population. At the same time, the cities were becoming areas of ethnic diversity, as our growing economy, combined with famines and political unrest throughout Europe, drew waves of immigrants to this country.

In the early decades of this century, education was feeling not only these pressures from outside but also internal pressures. New theories of education and educational psychology strove for dominance within the institution. The traditionalists allowed education only one role: to teach reading, writing, arithmetic, and a few other basic subjects, such as geography, history, and geometry. The progressives, however, sought chiefly to develop the whole person, to socialize children in such a way that they could participate more effectively as adults in a democratic society. Education today is still wavering uncertainly between these two poles.

As if everything we've mentioned weren't enough to tear the institution apart, the racial and ethnic minorities struggling to achieve equality and end discrimination began to realize the importance that contemporary society places on education. They began, at the same time, to see that the schools had their own built-in modes of discrimination. They viewed the schools as extensions of the white, Protestant, middle-class culture into the area of learning; hence, they began making demands, first for integration, and then for community control.

The schools have thus become arenas for social conflict. There is conflict over what functions education itself should perform; conflict over what kind of society we should have; and conflict over how large a role education should play in achieving it. There is conflict over why the schools are generally failing in even the traditional role of teaching basic skills. In recent years, there has even been conflict among many social scientists and parents about what value other social institutions should be allowed to place on educational achievement. Many now claim that the young should have a meaningful choice between vocational training, with early entry into the job market on the one hand, and academic preparation for college on the other. They believe that college and even high school diplomas should be required for fewer occupational positions. We see that, in the present at least, the functions of education are inseparable from the economic and political institutions, from which material well-being and power are ultimately derived. These two institutions are the subjects of the next chapter.

SUMMARY

1. Among the functions of education are: (1) the transmission of knowledge, (2) the provision of equal opportunity, (3) the discovery of new knowledge, (4) **placement** (sorting people into their proper place in society), and

(5) such latent functions as child care (the **custodial function**) and providing an opportunity for peer socialization.

2. The educational institution in the United States is enormous, both in enrollments and financial expenditures. Between 1950 and 1975, school enrollments at all levels increased by 89 percent, while the total population of the United States increased by only 41 percent. Meanwhile, the cost of education for this same period increased twelvefold, much greater than the increase in enrollments. From these inputs of people and money have come the outputs of great increases in the number of high school and college graduates.

3. Schools do not succeed in their function of transmitting knowledge when educational goals are poorly defined, are not achieved, or are not relevant to the students' lives. There has been a significant decline in learning among American students, as indicated by lower SAT and ACT scores and reading levels. These data suggest that American schools are not succeeding in their attempt to transmit knowledge.

4. The function of equality of opportunity can be assessed by examining **school inputs** and **educational outputs.** There are gross inequalities in the amount of money spent per pupil in American schools, varying from state to state and city to city. Less money appears to be spent on the poor, on blacks, and on other minority groups. Attempts to equalize expenditures and to integrate schools have met with great controversy. In comparing outputs, sociologists find that more whites than blacks complete high school and college, and that blacks earn less than whites with the same educational backgrounds.

5. One reason why American schools are failing in their equal opportunity function is that they are culturally biased toward white middle-class children. Cultural background influences one's attitudes toward education, and thus, it influences success in school.

6. Problems with the custodial function of the schools are evident from the extent of truancy and suspensions and the extent of violence and vandalism on school grounds. Those who cause problems in schools may not have learned the **hidden curriculum** — the behaviors necessary to fit into the school system.

7. A major problem of American education today is the struggle for control over the schools; among those seeking control are the federal and state governments, local governments, parents, teachers, and the students themselves.

8. Americans have become disenchanted with the educational institution. They are voting down bond issues, deciding not to go to college, and

expressing their criticisms publicly. They are coming up with such alternatives as "free schools," and are pushing for great changes in the future.

9. When examined according to the structural-functional model, schools can be seen as having specific functions that mesh with the functions of other societal institutions, and they can also be seen as failing in many of their functions. When examined according to the conflict model, the schools can be seen as a battleground—a site of conflict over educational goals, control of the schools, treatment of minorities, and so on.

KEY TERMS

custodial function
educational outputs
hidden curriculum

placement
school inputs
voucher system

SUGGESTED READINGS

Berg, Ivar. *Education and Jobs.* New York: Praeger, 1970.
Subtitled "The Great Training Robbery," this book demonstrates that there is not necessarily a clear-cut relationship between education and job performance or salary. It is possible to be overeducated for one's job.

Jencks, Christopher, et al. *Inequality: A Reassessment of the Effect of Family and Schooling in America.* New York: Basic Books, 1972.
The authors challenge the belief that the schools can bring about social equality. They look at many controversial issues, such as IQ tests and the effects of the family, heredity, and race on IQ scores.

Kozol, Jonathan. *Death at an Early Age.* Boston: Houghton Mifflin, 1967.
An analysis and critique of the educational policies and methods in the Boston public school system, particularly how these policies negatively affect poor children.

―――. *Free Schools.* Boston: Houghton Mifflin, 1972.
The author examines the dissatisfaction of parents with the public school system and the "free school" movement that grew out of this dissatisfaction.

O'Neill, William F., ed. *Selected Educational Heresies.* Glenview, Ill.: Scott, Foresman, 1969.
Essays on education by well-known authors, such as Orwell, Huxley, Carl Rogers, Skinner, Maslow, and Mead. Good discussions of autonomy, alienation, relevancy, and educational values and goals.

Rosenthal, Robert, and Lenore Jacobson. *Pygmalion in the Classroom.* New York: Holt, Rinehart and Winston, 1968.
An interesting discussion of the educational system in relation to the lower-class child. It centers around the influence of teachers' expectations on children's performance.

Silberman, Charles E., ed. *The Open Classroom Reader.* New York: Random House, 1973.
   Essays on the open classroom, the role of the teacher, the curriculum, and the aims of education. An attempt to present alternatives for making education relevant.

Wolff, Robert P. *The Ideal of the University.* Boston: Beacon Press, 1969.
   The author constructs four models of higher education in terms of purpose and then analyzes the type and quality of education that results. The book contains interesting chapters on relevancy, value neutrality, grading, and the governance of the university.

The lives of every one of us are bound up in getting and keeping a job, having money, buying things, dealing with inflation, and other economic matters. We need to remember that this was not always the case. Throughout most of human history, there was no need for a distinct economic institution, as the family was responsible for getting and distributing the food and other goods needed by family members.

As technology improved, more goods were produced than were needed for survival, so there began to be a need for a system to determine who got how much of what. Humans began to live in settlements, so the need arose for some kind of government, a system to organize and control the affairs of the settlement and to protect its members. As the years have gone by, economic and political institutions have grown tremendously in the scope of their activities, and our lives have been touched by them in countless ways. To understand society and the interaction of its members, we need to investigate how these institutions actually work.

In earlier chapters, we saw that other institutions—the family, religion, education—have certain functions and that in our society there are strains on these functions and on the ways in which they are performed. There are strains, too, on the production, distribution, and consumption of goods and services, as well as on the functions of government. One important concern is that of power—who controls people and resources. The more we understand what power is, and who has it, the better we can understand our society and our places within it.

12

Government and Economy: Distributing Goods and Power

The common problems of people in society everywhere are: (1) how to ensure physical survival, (2) how to maintain orderly and satisfactory group living, and (3) how to provide for the psychological needs of society's members.

We the people of the United States, in order to form a more perfect Union, establish justice, insure domestic tranquility, provide for the common defense, promote the general welfare, and secure the blessing of liberty to ourselves and our posterity, do ordain and establish this Constitution for the United States of America.

A comparison of the statement of the three universals of culture (see Chapter 3) and the Preamble to the Constitution of the United States makes it clear why our forefathers needed to establish a government, and why we need one today. The authority of a government is needed to protect society from external threats and to maintain order within it. In performing these functions, government addresses the first two cultural imperatives. Conflict of interest between and among society's members is managed and arbitrated by the government through its establishment and interpretation of laws and regulations. In this way, it helps to provide for the needs of society's members—or, in the words of the Constitution, to "promote the general welfare and secure the blessings of liberty" for all of us.

Government, as an institution, is intimately linked with the economic institution, which is concerned with the production, distribution, and consumption of goods and services. Without the production of goods, our physical survival would surely be in jeopardy; and without an orderly system for the distributing of goods, chaos would exist, for there are bound to be clashes of interest over who gets what, and under what circumstances. The regulation and control of the economy indicate the interrelatedness of the political and economic institutions. Indeed, in a large industrial society, such as ours, it is difficult to think of one without the other. Labor laws control the production of goods. The state itself produces some goods and services, and of course, is a vast consumer of both.

The purpose of this chapter is to analyze the political and economic institutions: what they contribute to the overall functioning of society, and how society's members affect and are affected by the workings of these institutions. In other words, we will deal with the actual workings of these institutions, not with just their formal structure. This will lead us to a consideration of **power**—the ability to control people and resources—as well as of different economic and political systems, and the participation of people as producers and consumers of goods, as voters, and as controlled and controlling members of society. The main focus will be on our own society. But first, to achieve a better understanding of our systems and how they came to be the way they are, we will look briefly at their historical roots, beginning with a discussion of the needs of humans and how they were met in the dim past of human existence.

EVOLUTION OF THE POLITICAL-ECONOMIC INSTITUTION

The hunting and gathering stage represents the technologically simplest and earliest stage of human societies. The !Kung Bushmen of Africa are still living at this stage. Their tribal identity is weak, and boundaries of the territory they occupy are vague and shifting. The typical band or community consists of 40 to 60 members who have kinship ties to one another. During the dry season, each household goes off into a separate part of the territory, thus reducing the size of the group that has to depend on scarce water and food. Under these circumstances, and generally among hunters and gatherers, there is little need for a centralized political system, either within or among the bands of the tribe. Leadership is diffuse and arises in response to specific problems. The leader offers proposals for action but has little power to force agreement.

As we noted in Chapters 5 and 9, among the !Kung Bushmen the family is the major economic unit. Food gathering and hunting are done by family members, and while food is shared within the band, it is distributed by nuclear families. Both the sharing of the food and the control of it by families are thought to be typical of all hunting and gathering societies. Because there is a persistent scarcity of food in such societies, there is nothing for people to fight over—there is no surplus of food, much less of anything else.

Beginning with the horticultural stage, and particularly at the agrarian stage, surpluses of food were created. This, in turn, released some people from the work of producing food and enabled them to work at producing other goods and services. In a real sense, no one needed the surpluses for sheer survival, but there was competition for them, because they were considered valuable. Goods were no longer distributed solely on the basis of need; instead, they were something over which people competed. Goods and services came to be distributed on the basis of power: those who had power could decide who got how much of what. It was at this point in history that a rudimentary form of government arose to maintain orderly relations and to make and enforce rules concerning the use of power and the distribution of goods and services.

As technology improved, human settlements grew in size, and new occupational roles arose. Better organization and control were needed to coordinate the activities of the diverse populations, to promote an orderly system for the distribution of goods and services, to protect the settlement from enemies, and to provide for orderly social living in general. If we skip over tens of thousands of years of societal development, we come to the rise of the city-state in about 1000 B.C. (see Chapter 15). For over two thousand years, the city-state prevailed as an effective form of political and economic organization.

The Rise of the Nation-State

The modern nation-state came into being in Europe in the fifteenth century as a result of the merger, peacefully or otherwise, of neighboring city-states. In terms of the meaning and centralization of political authority, the idea of nation-state was an important departure from the past. In earlier political entities, the political authority of the feudal lord, king, or other ruler was considered limited by the superior authority of the emperor, the parallel authority of the church, and the authority of natural law. The idea of **sovereignty**—that within a definite geographic area, the political unit has supreme and exclusive authority—is thus not very old. But the idea grew, and with it the notion that the authority of a nation-state, whether a monarchy or a republic, should be centrally controlled. By the fifteenth century, England, France, Spain, and Portugal were established as true nations. It was at about the same time that Ivan III drove the Mongols out of Russia and declared himself the first Czar. It remained for his successor, Ivan the Terrible, to break the control of the other princes who previously ruled over extensive areas and to establish an autocracy to govern the nation.

The development of nations has had profound effects on the modern world. It has fostered a sense of belonging for millions of people, it evokes strong loyalties and patriotism, and it allows for collective efforts, such as military encounters and economic development within the state.

The Rise of Mass Society

The modern world is characterized by something more than sovereign nations—a new type of social organization that sociologists call the **mass society.** A mass society is characterized by impersonal and contractual relations, specialization and division of labor, mass production and mass consumption, large-scale organizations, and preference for change. Individuals experience mass society as one composed of secondary group relations, high mobility, and alienation. Although this description is grossly oversimplified, you can see that our political and economic systems cannot be completely comprehended without a broader understanding of mass society and its origins.

Mass society has many sources, one of which is the rise of the nation-state. As nation-states grew in size, they were driven to impersonal and contractual treatment of the citizenry, and they created some of the first bureaucratic organizations. Economically, the modern nation gave support to mercantilism, colonialism, and later, to industrialism.

The Industrial Revolution began in Europe in the late 1700s, and in America in the 1800s. As the industrial stage developed, it contributed to the rise of bureaucracy and the mass society in a number of ways. With the development of national transportation systems, and later, the assembly line, came mass production and consumption, and big business and unions demanded contractual relations enforced by government.

Technology, by providing inventions, gave thrust to the Industrial Revolution. By the twentieth century, the revolution had become self-sustaining. Through research and development, it was actively seeking new inventions and techniques to improve efficiency and generate new products. In the process, technology furthered specialization, mechanized bureaucracy, and encouraged consolidation. In the form of the computer, it epitomized impersonality. Government fell under technology's influence, too, as a glance at a military bomber, a police car, or a utility bill immediately verifies.

The modern state, industrialism, and technology, then, are the three major roots of our mass society — the arena, so to speak, in which modern political-economic institutions perform their functions. Let us now consider each of these institutions separately.

THE ECONOMIC INSTITUTION

As we have noted, **economics** is concerned with the production and consumption of goods and services. These are basic human activities with an obvious relationship to the physical, social, and psychological welfare of people and societies. Of concern to the sociologist is how the economic institution performs its function for the well-being of society, and how individuals affect and are affected by the ways in which the functions are performed.

Economic Production

In order to produce, people all over the world must work, or more technically, perform occupational roles. Many of the world's four billion-plus people labor not for surplus but for bare survival. Much of the struggle for survival is an uphill agrarian battle fought with a minimum of tools and technology. Yet, in the United States, the decline in the number of farmers has been remarkable. At the turn of the century, almost 40 percent of all workers were engaged in farming; in 1977, only four percent were farmers. In other words, fewer and fewer people have had to work to produce the food that all of us need. On the average, one farmer today produces enough food to feed over 50 people; the rest of us are free to perform other occupational roles.

At the turn of the century, only about 17 percent of the labor force held white-collar jobs; in 1976, over 40 percent of all men and 63 percent of all working women were employed in white-collar occupations. Only about one-third of our workers are employed in jobs dealing directly with the production of goods — those jobs dealing with the acquisition of raw materials (such as farming and mining) and with the processing of raw materials (such as production work in mills and factories and the various construction trades). The rest of the workers are employed at jobs where the primary function is to produce some service for society: teachers, doctors, clerks, sales people, government officials, professional athletes, and many others are service workers in this sense.

The changing nature of occupational roles in the United States and in other industrialized countries shows how the economic institution has affected, and has been affected by, the agricultural and industrial revolutions. Occupational roles are occupied by people. How have they fared in the face of these changes?

While escaping the uncertainties of agrarian life, laborers in more industrialized nations still have many complaints. Blue-collar assembly-line work involves relentless drudgery; layoffs or work reductions threaten income; and the chances of promotion virtually cease after a few years. The white-collar worker, despite more pleasant physical conditions on the job, faces bureaucratic intrigue, status anxiety, and pressure to sell self and soul to the corporation.

There is the risk in mass societies that workers will experience greater or lesser degrees of **alienation**—feelings of meaninglessness, isolation, and

---

**BOX 12.1
A NATION
OF
CONSUMERS**

Our economic system results in the production of vast quantities of consumer goods, and to this extent, it "works," or performs its function for society. But, there are problems with the kinds of goods that are produced, which have implications for the economic health of our society. It is becoming common, for example, to hear complaints about the poor quality of consumer goods and services. The flawed quality of many American goods and services is not always a matter of chance. American business often designs products to look obsolete, or it engineers into them varying rates of self-destruction, thereby helping to maintain consumption levels. Furthermore, inferior products are not evenly distributed by class. The stores in which poor people shop may have cheaper initial prices for a given category of goods, but these goods may have a much shorter life span than the somewhat higher-priced versions that those with more money tend to buy.

Despite our irritation with inferior products, to many Americans, maintaining a tremendous rate of production and consumption is a matter of national pride. For the producers, however, it has been a problem. The productive glut is so great in America that a variety of strategies must be employed to avoid a massive surplus of nonessential products. Among these strategies, advertising—a major industry in itself—is used to convince people that luxuries are really necessities and that one's social success may depend on choosing the proper antiperspirant, mouthwash, or shampoo.

Planned obsolescence is another tactic aimed at convincing Americans

Do cars really wear out? I rescued this 1931 Ford from a junk yard and, after a little work, for over twenty years it has provided reliable transportation for my daily drive to the university.

depersonalization arising from their lack of control in the work process. Whether in a blue-collar or a white-collar job, many workers find it difficult to see the meaning in their work—other than the fact that it produces a paycheck. We must be careful not to generalize too much about alienation, however. Many workers enjoy their struggle with the land, factory work, or the opportunities of bureaucracy. Work provides a certain order and regularity to individuals' lives. It is something that has to be done, even if one does

to buy what they don't really need. Automobiles, kitchen appliances, and other products are frequently changed in minor and superficial ways for no other purpose than to make previous models appear outdated. And finally, products that could be designed to provide many years of dependable service are intentionally made to wear out after a brief period. In all fairness, however, American business is not alone in engaging in these practices, although it was among the first to raise the practice of planned overconsumption to a science.

Flawed products and wasteful consumption have done much to keep industrial economies functional. But today, this wastefulness is becoming dysfunctional not only for manufacturers and consumers but also for society in general. Wasteful consumption eats up large sums of money that could be spent on the creating of a better quality of life for all of us. Again, it is the poor who suffer most in a society of inferior goods and conspicuous consumption. We are all socialized to the same values and goals, especially in today's age of mass media. So, the poor overreach themselves in an effort to keep up, or they end up feeling deprived when they cannot buy what they think they should have. In addition, we all consume at the expense of the natural environment, by taking resources in large quantities and replacing them with large quantities of waste. Finally, excessive consumption is an international problem. America and other industrialized nations take a disproportionate amount of resources from the world that cannot be replaced and that will one day disappear.

Millions of workers have routine, dull jobs with not much chance for advancement. No wonder they are alienated and find little meaning in their work.

wonder, now and then, about the sense of it all. For many people, if not most, work remains an important element of their self-definition. The question, "What do you do?" is met with an answer concerning one's work, or if a student, one's preparation for work. In many respects, our work is what we are.

Many view work as one of the great contests of life, a kind of arena in which each person has a chance to win the game. For minorities, though, the chances of winning the game are more remote. Indeed, minority-group members are often not even allowed on the field. Unemployment among ghetto blacks is usually three to four times the national average, and blacks hold about 60 percent of the menial jobs. Their social class and ethnic background hinder them from succeeding in school, acquiring the traits of the dominant culture, and making appropriate social contacts, all of which are so valuable in white, middle-class professions. Women, too, despite their rise, in 20 years, from 30 to 40 percent of the labor force, are prevented from full participation in the job market by stereotyping. Employers continue to feel that the woman's occupational place is in the secretarial pool (97 percent female), behind the store counter (73 percent female), or at the teacher's desk (70 percent female).

The employment problems of minorities and the alienation of workers are both indications of deficiencies in the production aspect of the economic institution. Then, too, there is the problem of unemployment in general. Try as we will, our system seems incapable of providing full employment. Even though individuals may master such disturbing features of our economic system as chronic unemployment, job discrimination, and alienation, we cannot deny that the system itself is failing to some degree in the function it is supposed to perform in society.

Attempts to redress the problems of people's roles in the productive economy have not yet met with great success. American labor unions (about 88 percent white and 80 percent male) do not appear to offer a solution to the employment problems of minorities, and some job-related problems of

GOVERNMENT AND ECONOMY: DISTRIBUTING GOODS AND POWER

other groups receive little attention. Some unions are hesitant to open up apprenticeships to blacks and Chicanos. Women, in their desire to fill newly opened job categories, often have been willing to forego unionization, and even some legislative protection. For many reasons, white-collar workers have opposed unionization, although this norm is beginning to change. Finally, for the blue-collar worker, unions seldom deal with the most obvious irritation—the assembly line and other sources of tedium—or a more ominous one—automation. By the late 1970s, organized labor claimed only 20 percent of the American working force, down considerably from its peak two decades earlier.

Economic Consumption

Naturally, we produce to consume. The Eskimo hunter, the Mekong Delta rice farmer, the Detroit autoworker, the Washington lawyer, and the rest of us must consume to survive. And insofar as we survive, the economic institution is fulfilling its function. But is it really that simple? Consider that one-fourth of the world goes to bed hungry every night. This fact is symbolic of the great and growing inequity between the poor and rich nations of the world. By contrast, America, which comprises only about six percent of the earth's population, consumes more than 40 percent of the earth's produce—almost as much as the other 94 percent of the world's people. (The fact is, we overconsume. See Box 12.1.)

Even though other countries now surpass us in per capita income,

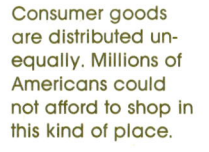

Consumer goods are distributed unequally. Millions of Americans could not afford to shop in this kind of place.

America still ranks high in this area. But, we also rank high among industrialized nations in terms of extremes of wealth and poverty. The total income generated by an economy is a production matter; how it gets distributed — how much each family can spend — is a matter of consumption. As we saw in Chapter 8, the 20 percent of the families in the low-income range receive 5.4 percent of the nation's total income, whereas the highest 20 percent receive 41.1 percent. During the two-thirds of this century in which the income tax has been in effect, it has not redistributed wealth significantly. Whether or not there should be great differences within a society in the people's ability to consume goods and services is clearly a matter of values; that our economic system results in great differences in income and wealth is a matter of fact.

Racial and ethnic minorities, women, and older people are more likely to be found among the lowest income recipients. Our nation espouses the value of equality of opportunity; but when entire categories, such as blacks and women, are found at the bottom repeatedly, it is clear that it is not a matter of individuals losing out in the competition to consume but one of the opportunities of some groups being better than those of others. It is legitimate to criticize the economic institution, in that the system fails in some degree to reflect our societal value of equal opportunity.

THE INSTITUTION OF GOVERNMENT

Like other aspects of culture, the idea of a sovereign state arose in response to human needs, in particular, the need for social controls when large numbers of people live together. As we have seen, it was only a few hundred years ago that the notion of sovereignty became well-articulated. Gradually, the idea of a political body, or state, that has supreme authority for making, interpreting, and applying a system of laws that would apply within a certain territory became accepted. Sovereignty also means that the state has coercive power superior to that held by people and groups within the state, so that it can demand obedience of its citizens and protect its independent existence from groups outside the state.

As the state emerged, political philosophers differed as to the definition of the state and how it should be ruled. Our Declaration of Independence, for example, was strongly influenced by the ideas of the English philosopher John Locke, who suggested that humans have certain natural rights — the right to life, to liberty, and to property — and that it is the function of government to protect these natural rights. Thus, in Locke's view, government has to act as an impartial judge in clashes among citizens concerning their individual rights, and it must have the power to punish those who break the natural law. If a government cannot enforce the natural law, according to Locke, the people no longer owe it allegiance and can set up a new government.

Even a totalitarian government, like Hitler's Germany, needs to assure its sovereignty by fostering a sense of pride in the people and encouraging their sense of belongingness.

The government of the United States clearly performs functions that relate to the protection of life, liberty, property, and the pursuit of happiness. But the enlargement of these functions in the last two centuries, and the growth of other government functions in the United States, has gone far beyond what Locke and other political philosophers could have envisioned. We shall look at the nature of some of these functions and how they are expressed in day-to-day practices.

Maintaining Sovereignty

The governmental function of maintaining sovereignty has three aspects: (1) maintaining the loyalty of a community of citizens, (2) maintaining order within the society, and (3) protecting the society from external threats. Unless citizens are basically loyal to the regime, share a system of beliefs and values, and have a sense of belonging to the state, it will be difficult for the state to remain the supreme authority. Should disloyalty and dissent be severe, it will be hard for any government to maintain order. The threat of force can go only so far in getting people to abide by the rules of the state.

Many methods are used to foster loyalty and a sense of belonging among citizens. Education is important, for through it people learn what their government stands for and how it works. It is hoped that they will develop a sense of pride in the state's history and its accomplishments. Governments also foster a sense of belonging by establishing a community network within the territory, for example, by encouraging railroads to link towns and by developing means for leaders to keep in touch with the people and their needs. Even such rituals as parades, reciting the pledge of allegiance, and singing the national anthem serve to develop in people a sense of pride and a feeling of belonging to their country. It is extremely difficult to estimate what it costs in time and effort to develop such loyalty. Whatever it costs, however, strengthening the attachment of citizens to the state is quite important.

The second aspect of maintaining sovereignty is concerned with keeping order within the society. If the state cannot keep order, then, clearly, it is not supreme. The importance of social control in our own society can be seen in dollars and cents. At the federal level, both the FBI and the National Guard spend millions of dollars to discourage social disorder; and at the local level, a large portion of the incomes of local governments is spent for police forces. Federal and local governments spend billions of dollars a year in their effort to maintain social order.

Most of the judicial system—the making, interpreting, and enforcing of laws—is concerned with maintaining harmony and order within society. Some disputes and conflicts of interest can be settled through the courts. Furthermore, governments are able to define, by legislation, what is orderly behavior. In the words of our Constitution, the government can *establish* justice, not merely help citizens obtain it. But, in defining proper behavior, the government may discriminate for and against various groups. For example, during the 1960s, the possession or sale of small amounts of marijuana was a felony in many states, although it has since been reduced to a misdemeanor. As another indication, laws regarding white-collar crime are vague, making capture and conviction difficult. The legislation involving crimes against private property, most of which is owned by the upper classes, is much more clear.

In promoting domestic order, governments function for the benefit of the people or for the benefit of special interests; further, they protect their own legitimacy and reassert their right to use violence. The advocacy of civil order is both an effort to uphold the laws and a way of opposing any revolution that might threaten government legitimacy.

To accomplish their third function, protection against external threats, governments maintain armies, conduct intelligence activities, and enter into treaties and negotiations with other sovereign states. And ultimately, of course, they have the authority to declare a state of war and engage in warfare. During times of war, the functions of government are often enlarged to include such things as rationing of scarce goods and making restrictions on travel, not to mention compelling citizens to serve in the armed forces.

Much of our national budget goes for salaries, materiel, equipment, physical facilities, and research related to preserving the nation from external threats. Of the major nations, only Russia spends more than America on national defense, be it in absolute dollars, percentage of government budget, or fraction of gross national product (GNP). While, generally, the percentage trend has been a downward one over the past two decades, about 30 percent

Most people recognize that it takes money for the government to protect the country against external threats. But it also takes the willingness of men and women to devote part of their lives to this function.

of the federal budget is still spent on defense. When other military spending categories, such as the space budget and interest on the largely war-incurred national debt, are added, the government may use close to half its income for defense spending. This is the price we pay for protection from external threat, and it is money that cannot be spent, by the government or by private citizens, for other goods and services.

Regulating the Economy

In varying degrees, for a long time governments have been engaged in the regulation of the production, distribution, and consumption of goods and services. This function has been growing in importance and scope in the United States. We have child labor laws and minimum wage laws, and through the Taft-Hartley Act, the government can arbitrate labor-management disputes. Working conditions in the factories and mines are regulated by the government. The government regulates what is produced by establishing standards for pure foods and drugs, by requiring pollution-control devices on automobiles, and less directly, by establishing or refusing to establish tariffs on imported goods. The Federal Communications Commission assigns frequencies to radio and TV stations, specifies the broadcast power they may use, and has numerous regulations that must be followed if one is to get and maintain a license to operate a station. Rates and schedules of airlines are regulated by the federal government. Support prices for agri-

Government regulation of the economy is strongly urged by those who are concerned with what strip-mining is doing to the environment but opposed by those whose major interest is production.

cultural products and regulations on how much can be produced affect the prices consumers pay for food. All this, and much more, illustrates how the government puts the function of regulating the economy into practice.

Control over the economy is one of the major differences among communist, socialist, and capitalistic economic systems. Under **communism,** the state owns the major means of production, such as factories, farms, and communications systems, as well as stores and shops—in short, just about the entire economy. Under **socialism,** only some of the major means of production are owned by the government, and government controls are less rigid. In principle, **capitalism** believes in private ownership of the means of production, but often, as we have seen, the government in capitalistic societies regulates what can be produced, what wages can be paid, and so on. In addition, capitalistic societies, such as the United States, participate more directly in the economic sphere, not only as consumers but also as producers of goods and services.

Participating in the Economy

It is readily recognized that governments like our own are massive consumers of goods—everything from defense materials to the income tax forms we return each April. As a buyer of tons of goods, the government provides profits for firms and stockholders, gives employment to workers, and affects the prices that citizens pay for goods.

Not so well recognized is the fact that the government is also a producer —that is, it is in business to make and sell goods and services. Even a brief listing of government enterprises is impressive. The Tennessee Valley Authority produces and sells electricity. Federal, state, and local governments operate schools and hospitals. The Corps of Engineers builds dams for flood control. The federal government is the largest insurance company in the country, offering life insurance for members of the armed forces and veter-

GOVERNMENT AND ECONOMY: DISTRIBUTING GOODS AND POWER

ans, backing home and farm loans, and insuring bank deposits. Federal money is spent on highway construction and urban renewal. The list is almost endless, and of course, there is the large enterprise of welfare.

America spends huge sums on welfare. In fact, it spends more in absolute dollars than any other nation. Unlike defense spending, welfare spending causes loud complaints in America, even though it amounts to only about 6.5 percent of the GNP, as compared with European expenditures of 10 to 15 percent. Over 16.5 million Americans (8 percent of the population) received direct welfare aid in 1976. With some justice, the opponents of welfare spending point out that these programs are not curing poverty and that, frequently, they may even be perpetuating it. On the other hand, most of the

FIGURE 12.1 Income Security and Health Transfer Payments of the Federal Government, 1965–1975

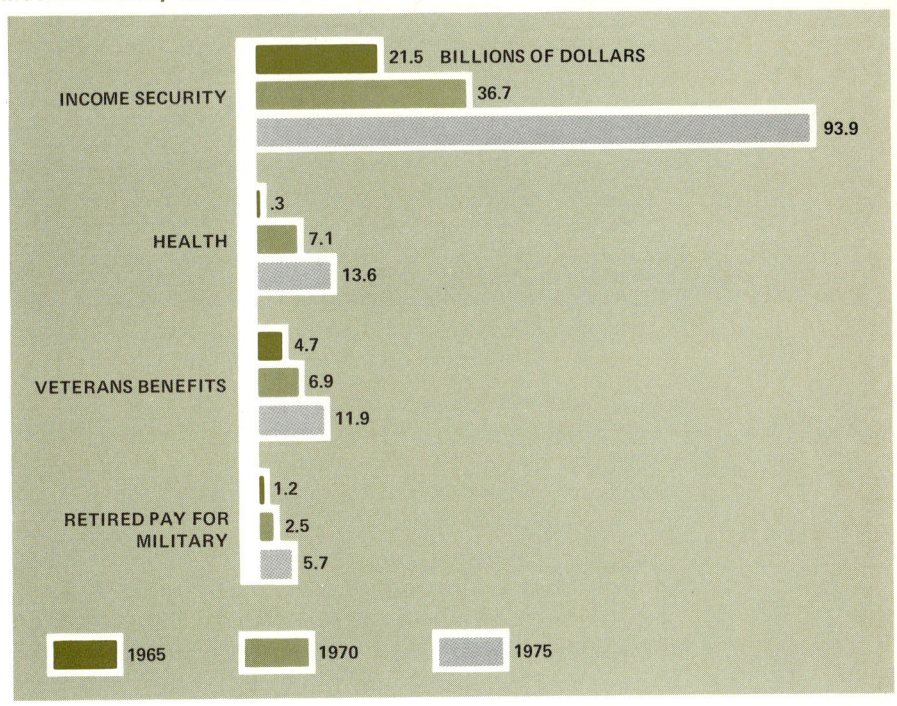

INCOME SECURITY
- 1965: 21.5 BILLIONS OF DOLLARS
- 1970: 36.7
- 1975: 93.9

HEALTH
- 1965: .3
- 1970: 7.1
- 1975: 13.6

VETERANS BENEFITS
- 1965: 4.7
- 1970: 6.9
- 1975: 11.9

RETIRED PAY FOR MILITARY
- 1965: 1.2
- 1970: 2.5
- 1975: 5.7

While not a welfare state like the United Kingdom, the U.S. Government provides income and health security by what is called transfer payments. That is, money is collected by the government from some segments of the population, such as workers, and given to other segments, such as the retired. From 1965 to 1975, income security transfer payments increased over fourfold; they now account for over one-third of the federal budget. Health transfer payments are mostly those given under the Medicare program, which was introduced in 1968.

Source: U.S. Bureau of the Census, *Statistical Abstract of the United States: 1975* (Washington, D.C.: U.S. Government Printing Office, 1975), p. 229.

FIGURE 12.2   Growth in the Percent of the Labor Force Employed by Governments in the United States, 1929–1976

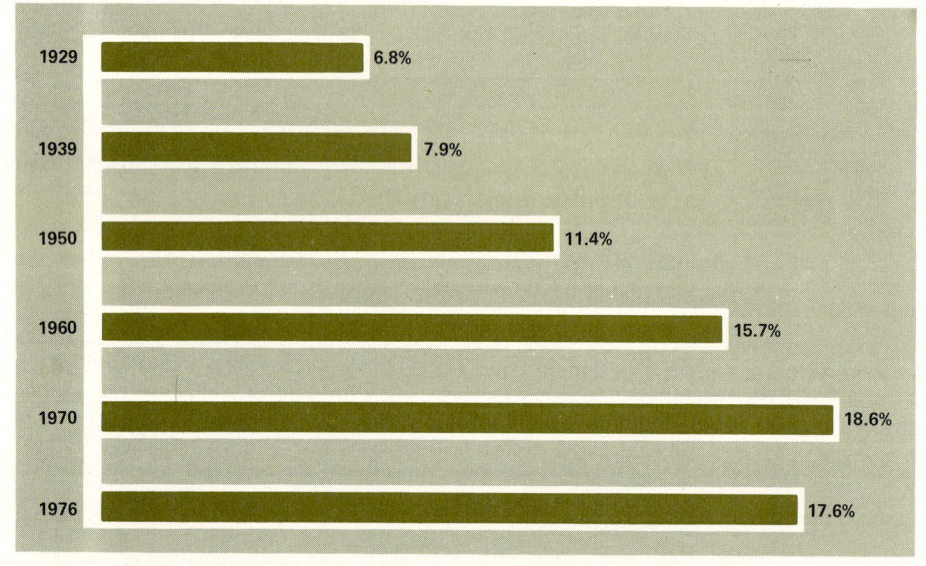

Year	Percent
1929	6.8%
1939	7.9%
1950	11.4%
1960	15.7%
1970	18.6%
1976	17.6%

An easy way to visualize the expansion of government is to compare the proportions of the population that are employed by the government at different periods of time. The proportion of the labor force that works for the government—local, state, or national—has more than doubled since just before World War II.

Source: U.S. Bureau of the Census, *Historical Statistics of the United States, Colonial Times to 1957* (Washington, D.C.: U.S. Government Printing Office, 1960), pp. 70, 73, 710, 711; U.S. Bureau of the Census, *Statistical Abstract of the United States; 1977* (Washington, D.C.: U.S. Government Printing Office, 1977), pp. 306, 367, 387.

people on welfare—children, old people, the disabled, and the like—are unable to help themselves.

In some countries, governments have greatly expanded their welfare responsibilities, giving rise to the concept of the **welfare state.** The welfare state represents a new interpretation of government's function in regulating the economy. In a welfare state, such as Great Britain, it is assumed that the government has the responsibility for ensuring that all citizens have such basic necessities of life as food, housing, health care, and education. In a pure capitalistic system, the government would have the responsibility of protecting people's freedom to secure these necessities and of seeing to it that, in doing so, they do not interfere with the freedom of others. Provision for the sick, the lame, and the old would come from private charity. In the welfare state, the government provides necessities for those unable to help themselves. The welfare state, with its broad interpretation of government responsibility, approaches the doctrine of collective responsibility accepted by socialists and communists. It differs, however, in that, theoretically, people are free to acquire wealth well beyond their subsistence needs. But, the higher income taxes needed to finance extensive welfare programs tend to deter the acquisition of large amounts of personal wealth.

Administering the Government

When many people hear the term "bureaucracy," they automatically think of government. True, there are countless "bureaus" in our own and other governments, whose function it is to plan, organize, execute, and control various programs. Think, for a moment, of the tasks of even a small agency of the government, such as that part of the Federal Housing Administration concerned with homeowner loans. Rules and guidelines have to be drawn up carefully, eligibility and other requirements have to be communicated to lending agencies and consumers, default procedures must be worked out, and the budget for the agency has to be controlled. Thus, a lot of effort and money goes into administering the program. The bureaucracy of the largest part of the government, the executive branch, has 11 cabinet departments, 50 agencies, and some 1800 bureaus, branches, corporations, administrations, commissions, and so on. Altogether, the federal government employs some three million persons and has a payroll of 29 billion dollars. Most of these resources are directly or indirectly related to the administration of federal programs.

MAJOR POLITICAL SYSTEMS

As we have seen, government has many functions. Clearly, there are different organizational forms for performing these functions; these forms are referred to as **political systems.** There are many ways of classifying political systems. Twenty-five hundred years ago, the philosopher Plato classified political systems on the basis of the concentration of power. *Tyranny* was rule by one person; *aristocracy,* rule by an elite few; and *democracy,* rule by the masses. (Plato considered aristocracy to be the best political system.)

The amount of power possessed and exercised by the state—and the amount of freedom allowed to the citizen—is another basis on which the political organization of societies can be distinguished. The two extremes are **anarchism,** in which the state is virtually powerless or even nonexistent, and **totalitarianism,** which involves total state control of the individual. Totalitarianism and constitutional democracy have been the most influential political systems in Western cultures.

Totalitarianism

Germany under Hitler, Italy under Mussolini, and the present states of China and the Soviet Union are examples of totalitarianism. A totalitarian government has a number of important attributes, including concentration of power, a single political party, ideological orthodoxy, and control of the economy.

Concentration of Power   As the name suggests, a totalitarian government is characterized by as near total control of the lives of citizens as is possible to imagine. The center of power may be a single person, a political party, or a small committee. In any of these cases, the power center relies heavily on force, usually in the form of a strong state police. The threat and use of force permeate the entire system and are related to the other aspects of totalitarianism.

Single Political Party   A totalitarian government is further characterized by a single political party. It is from the party that leaders of the army, the police, and the administrators of the various branches of the government are recruited, thus assuring a certain ideological consistency within the government. The party helps to socialize the young. In the Soviet Union, for example, the Communist party sponsors the Octoberists, the Young Pioneers, and the Young Communist League for children and youth. The single political party supplements the government and assists it in many ways.

Ideological Orthodoxy   Ideology is the commonly accepted beliefs and attitudes about social reality. In a totalitarian society, there are no conservative, moderate, or liberal views of social reality—only one official ideology. Deviation from the official ideology is considered as opposition to the government and is not tolerated. A totalitarian state, with its control of the schools, the communications media, and indeed, much of life in general, is able to indoctrinate the citizenry according to the "party line." In Nazi Germany, for example, not only were the radio and press used for indoctrination but artists were commissioned to produce paintings and sculptures that would glorify the Aryan concept—the idea that the Germans were a superrace. Before the invasion of Poland, the Nazi Ministry of Propaganda produced films, cartoons, and "news" items depicting the Poles as inferior, undesirable people. In these and other ways, thought control is very much a part of the totalitarian state.

Control of the Economy   A totalitarian government maintains strong control of the economy. In the Soviet Union, this control takes the form of government ownership and operation of factories, farms, stores, transportation systems, communications media, banks, and so on. The government determines what should be produced and what prices to charge for goods and services. In Nazi Germany, private ownership of some means of production was allowed, but it was closely supervised by the government. In general, totalitarian governments feel that the total power cannot be maintained unless the state owns or rigidly controls the economy.

Constitutional Democracy

The form of government called **constitutional democracy** is currently found in the United States, England, the non-Communist countries of Europe, Canada, Japan, and Australia, among others. While specifics differ from nation to nation, there are some features common to this form of government. Among them are a formal constitution and the idea of consent of the governed.

Formal Constitution An important feature of constitutional democracy is the constitution itself, a formal statement of the essential laws and principles that describe what people can expect of the government and what the government can expect of the people. Generally, a constitution assigns certain specified functions to different branches of the government, such as our executive, legislative, and judicial branches. In this way, it limits the power of officeholders and works to prevent the concentration of power in one or only a few individuals.

A crucial feature of a constitution is its specification of the rights and liberties of citizens. This statement amounts to a declaration of those aspects of life that the state admits are not to be interfered with or controlled. The safeguarding of liberties is one of the most important features of a constitutional democracy. The various freedoms granted by our Constitution, for example, prevent the kind of thought control found in totalitarian countries. Finally, the constitution specifies how it can be amended, thus allowing for peaceable change in the laws by which people live. The Equal Rights Amendment, stating that equality of rights under law shall not be denied because of sex, could only become part of the highest law of our land if ratified by two-thirds of the states.

Consent of the Governed The second major feature of a constitutional democracy is that the people have a real voice in how and by whom they are governed. This is accomplished by granting adults the right to vote. Of course, everyone cannot have his or her own way, but even though the majority rules, the views of the minority are respected and their rights are protected. At least everyone has the ability, through the vote, to try to reshape society and to select its leaders.

Constitutional democracies, unlike totalitarian states, permit more than one political party. This is an important feature, for it provides a way for well-organized and influential groups, such as the Democrats and Republicans, to seek to influence the government along the lines desired by large numbers of like-minded people.

The concept of constitutional democracy is a fascinating example of human inventiveness, of our attempt to bring order to society. Equally fascinating is the behavior of humans within the system—how they interact with one another in a way that allows the political-economic institution to perform its functions and that permits the state to survive. This is not to imply that the interaction is always untroubled. On the contrary, relationships between the governed and the governors are often marked by conflict and clashes of interest. Yet things get done because there are those who can order, direct, and control others. This is what we mean by *power*, a concept that needs to be investigated more thoroughly.

POWER AND POLITICS

Sociologists generally define **power** as the ability to make and carry out—or have carried out—decisions, whether or not there is resistance. If I can get you to do something, whether or not you want to do it, I have power over you. For as long as there have been humans on the earth, some have been able to control the behavior of others. This control has taken many different forms, for power has many aspects.

Dimensions of Power

Power can be exercised in many ways. The use of physical force or physical punishment is called **coercive power.** It can be used to overthrow a government, to maintain one, or to get people to obey the laws of a society. Money or material goods provide another source of power. Were I an employer, I could not very well threaten to hurt you physically if you refused to work in my shop. But I could reward you with money if you did work for me, and I could raise your salary if you worked well. Conversely, I could fire you or fine you for doing poor work or coming in late. Getting others to behave as one wishes through the use of material goods as rewards and punishments is called **remunerative power.** Some groups, such as churches, rely on *symbolic rewards* to affect the behavior of people. The promise of salvation and the threat of damnation are examples of this kind of power. Finally, **persuasive power** can be quite effective in controlling others. Threats or promises may be part of the persuasion, but the major thrust is to use arguments and reasoning to get others to think or act in the way you want them to.

People in a society recognize that it is justifiable and correct for others to have power over them in certain circumstances. This is referred to as **legitimate power,** or **authority.** We see doctors as legitimate authorities who can tell us to take off our clothes and to take certain medicines. We see policemen as legitimate authorities who can penalize us for driving too fast or reprimand us for causing a disturbance. There are many such situations in which authority is vested in a given position or positions. It must be recognized, however, that even though an individual exercises authority, it is attached to the position and not to the person. During World War II, for example, enlisted men were required to salute an officer's uniform draped over a chair to teach them that whoever wore it had a right to expect obedience and respect.

Additional insights into the concept of power, and how it affects life in a society, can be gained by studying such aspects as type, scope, and distribution of power. *Type* of power refers to the broad areas of life that can be controlled. Control of the government is *political power.* Those who can make (and have carried out) decisions concerning which laws are passed, how they are interpreted, and how they are executed, have political power. Similarly, one who can get lawmakers to pass legislation favorable to his or her situation has political power. *Economic power* has to do with control over the production and distribution of goods and services and of financial matters in general. A bank owner has economic power; manufacturers who have control of a market and can set the prices they want, or those who are strong enough to persuade competitors to go along with their pricing also have economic power. Government's economic power can range from practically none, as in laissez-faire capitalism, to complete ownership of the means of production, as in socialism.

The *scope* of power refers to who or what is affected by it—humans, the environment, or whatever. The scope of an office manager's power is limited to control over a few workers, the physical setting in which they work, and the equipment they use. The mayor of a large city has a much larger scope of power, and the president of the country still a larger scope.

Finally, power has varying degrees of *distribution* among its holders. It can be concentrated in the hands of a few people, or it can be possessed and exercised by large numbers of people. Sometimes the distribution of power is referred to as the **power structure.** This simply means that for some social unit, such as a community or a college, it is possible to describe the power figures in the system, what they control, and how they relate to one another. In a democracy, with its emphasis on the power of the people, it is important to investigate how power is *really* distributed. Among sociologists, there are two competing views on the nature of the power structure in the United States.

Power Elite versus Pluralism

Some political scientists and sociologists have reached the conclusion that the nation is controlled by a small, tightly integrated group of people. According to this view, the members of this small, elite group occupy the "command posts" of society—key posts in the military, the government, and industry. These positions allow the **power elite,** as C. Wright Mills (1956) calls it, to make decisions that have the greatest influence on the direction that our society will take.

Despite some differences, the members of the power elite, according to Mills, interact on a personal basis and have a sense of social and psychological oneness; their interaction is not a conspiracy but a matter of common outlook. Many of the command posts of society are located in the large corporations. Major industrialists own and control much of the corporate economy. In 1972, about 200,000 millionaire families owned 35 percent of all corporate stock, 73 percent of all state and local bonds, and 27 percent of all corporate bonds (Chirot, 1977, p. 190). An even smaller group of top managers, lawyers, and financiers runs the major corporations. They serve on the boards of directors of one another's companies, creating what is called *interlocking directorates.* From his study of the power structure, Domhoff (1967) concluded that "interlocking directorates show beyond question that there is a national corporate economy that is run by the same group of several thousand men" (p. 57).

In the political arena, these people may be somewhat invisible, but they are nevertheless influential. By helping to finance both major political parties, for example, they minimize political issues and differences that might otherwise create conflict and unrest and that might produce significant social changes. According to the elitist theory, the key figures in industry, politics, and the military who make up the power elite do not control everything, but they can exert tremendous influence on such crucial areas as foreign policy, defense spending, and the economy in general.

In contrast to the elite theory, other sociologists (Arnold Rose, 1967) have concluded that power in American society is not concentrated but fairly widely dispersed. Political pluralism implies that power is divided among diverse groups—business and industry, the government, labor unions, political parties, special interest groups, and the like. Each of these groups has resources that can be translated into power with respect to *some* issues, but not many—let alone all. The result is that none dominates the power scene, and because of the different interests and loyalties, they do not really get together to form a unified power bloc. In other words, the nation is actually controlled and run by a disunited plurality of groups, each exerting power when it can. The concept of **power pluralism** is closer to the democratic ideal, for it suggests that the competing pressure groups must appeal to the public for support. But, there are more direct ways that the masses can exercise power than merely by supporting competing pressure groups.

People Power

There are a number of ways in which the people in a society can and do affect the running of the society. Not many actually use their power, as we shall see, but the opportunity is nevertheless available. One method is through mass movements, another is through less organized and sometimes short-lived expressions of sentiments, and still another is the more obvious means of voting and participating in political parties.

A **mass movement** is commonly emotional, moralistic, and issue-centered. By the standards of those in power, its ideology may be politically extreme. As in the antiwar and civil rights protests of the 1960s, unconventional techniques, such as mass rallies, marches, and violence, may be used to gain attention and power. Established governments, democratic or not, tend to fear or respect such a movement's potential. Rarely do the governments help or allow the movement to gain its ends. They usually move to

How much power do the people really have? Boycotts, marches, protests, and consumer strikes are direct ways of trying to influence government and the economy but most Americans do not use such means.

weaken or divert it, to give it the appearance of victory without the substance, or to hope it will disappear. The seeming indifference or opposition of governments faced by mass movements arises in part from rational factors, such as ideological disagreement, and in part from less rational ones, such as the inertia of bureaucracy.

Some social movements are so strong that they cannot be ignored by the government, and equally to the point, they produce changes, thus indicating that the people do have some social power (see Chapter 13). The activities of the Anti-Saloon League helped bring about national prohibition through a constitutional amendment. Just as surely, the antiwar movement affected our bringing a close to the war in Vietnam. The women's movement helped raise the consciousness of many Americans to the injustices and inequalities faced by women, and it has brought about the passage and enforcement of various laws pertaining to equal treatment of the sexes. It has also affected the election of officials and is a strong force to be considered in the passage of the Equal Rights Amendment.

Most people in our society do not participate in mass movements. Nor are they likely to engage in protest marches, demonstrations, and the like for or against a specific political issue. A large crowd picketing the White House, a governor's mansion, or a mayor's office represents only an infinitesimal proportion of all adults. The action may be effective, but it is nevertheless true that the great bulk of people do not choose these means of political participation. What, then, *do* they do?

Many Americans claim that they are affiliated with a political party. Yet, few actively participate in the party of their choice, in the sense of attending meetings or giving of time or money to support the party. One study, conducted before it was made possible to donate one dollar of one's taxes to a presidential candidate's campaign through a checkmark on the income tax

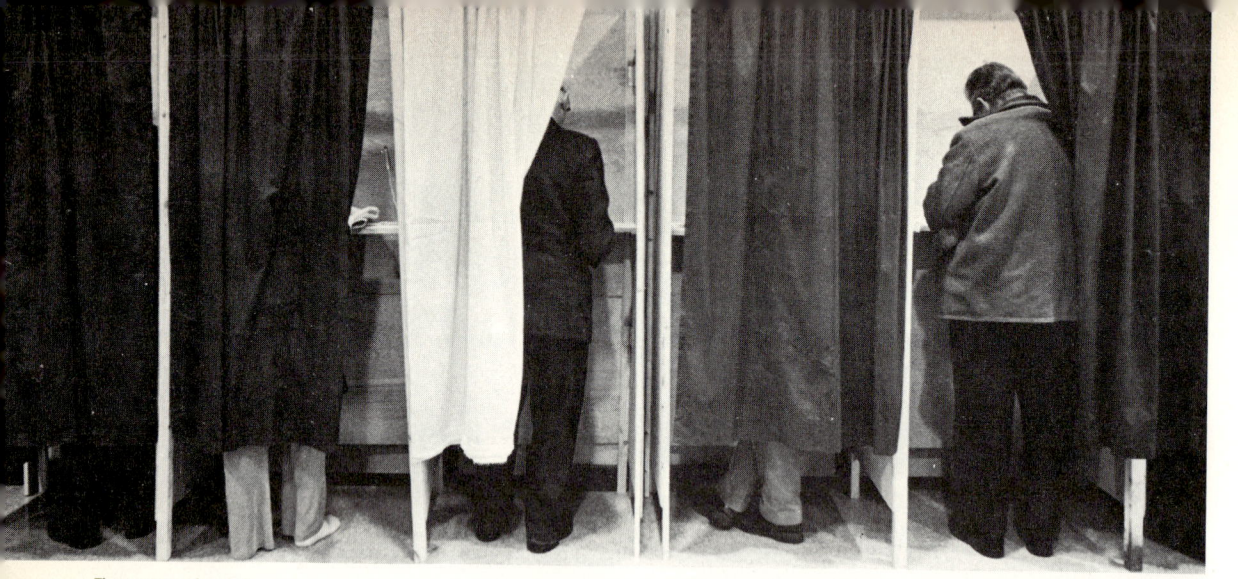

The unemployed, the poor, blacks, and other disadvantaged groups are less likely to vote than are other Americans. Why do you think this is so?

form, found that from 6 to 13 percent of all Americans made a financial contribution to a political party. From 10 to 18 percent wore a political button or had a political bumper sticker on their car. Voluntary political party workers ranged from 2 to 4 percent, depending on the section of the country. This means that the small group of loyal party workers have extraordinary power in the selection of candidates and the drafting of platforms.

In our national elections of recent years, about 60 percent or fewer of the eligible voters actually cast their ballot, a rather low percentage by European standards. Not voting is highest among those who are unemployed, who are

BOX 12.2 POLITICAL SOCIALIZATION

In a nondemocratic society, people may learn the norms and rationale of one-party or two-party politics. This learning may be done by family pressure, under a teacher's manipulation, by peer prodding, or through media suggestion. The young may be drilled in political beliefs, particularly if a totalitarian government pretends to be a "people's democracy." Or they may receive no explicit education in beliefs or methods of political participation. However, even such a conspiracy of silence and inaction teaches a great deal. Just as in some societies people learn to be involved in specific ways, in other societies people learn not to participate at all.

The process is not much different in a democratic system (see Dawson and Prewitt, 1969; Langton, 1969). If anything, it is less carefully regulated and more varied. At a very early age, we learn our basic political affiliation from the family. Thereafter, we may hold as dogmatically to our political party as did primitive people to their totems (their family emblems). The public schools give significant instruction in at least two ways. Outwardly, they teach the democratic myth, which affirms that individuals are of about equal power in politics. In actuality, the schools tend to encourage an uncritical authoritarianism, an acceptance of the decisions and policies of those in power.

poor, who have achieved no more than an eighth-grade education, who are black, and who are young. Men are somewhat more likely to vote than women. These findings indicate that individual behavior, like voting, varies by social characteristics (see Box 12.2). They show, further, that the disadvantaged in our society are less likely to express their views through voting than are the more advantaged.

Attempts have been made to explain the relatively low level of voting and the lack of political participation in general in the United States. It has been found that many Americans feel a sense of futility, because none of the political candidates seems to be of their choosing. Candidates often seem to differ very little in their views and to be unresponsive once they are in office. In addition, some people fear the consequences of political activity, because such involvement can threaten friendships, occupational security, or ego satisfaction. Finally, politics may seem to lack a sense of urgency, because the subject matter is not compelling or because success meets few immediate needs.

A Balanced View of Power

Representative government and free enterprise, in their classical definition, fail to fit the facts of American life. Political and military leaders, business and union directors, technocrats and bureaucrats, and even the people help make our system less than perfectly democratic and capitalistic. Yet, we

---

Other pressures add variety and complexity to the outcome of political socialization. As youth acquire an increasingly distinctive subculture, the peer group may counter earlier family and school socialization. The generation gap, such as it is, may extend to politics. As seen in the protest movements of the 1960s, many young radicals were products of middle-class homes. College, too, can be an ambivalent force. Whereas in the last decade it was a major center of political activism, in this decade the campus is somewhat more quiet, as student interest in careers seems to have gained in relative importance.

The experiences of recent years have taught us that political socialization of minorities is a complex process. What appear to be similar backgrounds may produce an advocate of women's liberation and a quiet housewife. "Uncle Toms" content with the status quo and black militants are produced in the same community, school, and family. In much the same way as in nondemocratic societies, then, Americans learn to participate politically in limited and often ineffective ways. Is it surprising that, as elsewhere, many learn not to participate at all?

FIGURE 12.3   Proportions of Eligible Voters Voting in 1976 Presidential Election

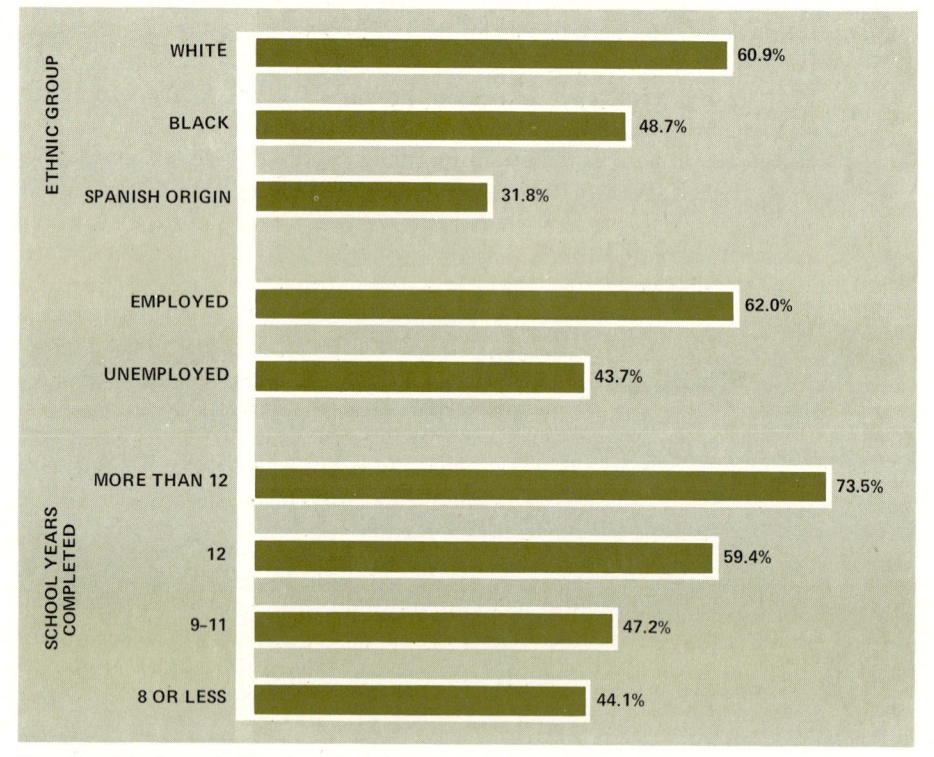

ETHNIC GROUP	
WHITE	60.9%
BLACK	48.7%
SPANISH ORIGIN	31.8%
EMPLOYED	62.0%
UNEMPLOYED	43.7%

SCHOOL YEARS COMPLETED	
MORE THAN 12	73.5%
12	59.4%
9–11	47.2%
8 OR LESS	44.1%

The disadvantaged often feel that there is not much they can do to change society. This feeling of powerlessness is reflected in the lower voter participation of these less privileged groups.

Source: U.S. Bureau of the Census, *Statistical Abstract of the United States: 1977* (Washington, D.C.: U.S. Government Printing Office, 1977), p. 508.

must be careful not to reject these labels, not to substitute other inaccurate descriptions for them, and not to be disillusioned too quickly.

Corporate and state power in America are not absolute. Certain ideologies and norms are boundaries that even the most powerful may hesitate to change or cross, although the Watergate participants produced numerous exceptions to the rule, as did monopolists of the past, such as Commodore Vanderbilt. In some nations, the media may act as a guardian and conscience of public morality. Again, Watergate is a case in point. Also, there is still enough division of power, as C. Wright Mills has admitted, to make a would-be dictator or corporate head think twice before acting capriciously. The people have a fraction of that power. Much of their power lies in the fear that an unpredictable public inspires in its leaders, in no matter what kind of state or economy. Ultimately, such counterpower, or the threat of it, may be the only way to keeping established power in check.

That the people are usually powerless is not necessarily a problem, even in a democratic, capitalistic society. Whatever its structure or label, a system may still serve the interests of the society as a whole or of the people individually. In America, some critics overlook the fact that a less than representative system has, in fact, provided the people with some benefits and reforms. In the part that follows, beginning with Chapter 13 on social change, we will see that, as uncertain as our evaluation of the present may be, the future promises still more uncertainty about our economic, political, and other institutions.

SUMMARY

1. At the hunting and gathering stage of civilization the family was the basic economic unit, and there was little need for a political system. With improved technology came food surpluses and division of labor, eventually resulting in unequal distribution of goods and of power. Systems had to be developed to coordinate the production of goods and services and to provide for orderly social living.

2. The first major political unit was the *city-state,* a form that lasted for over 2000 years. Then came the development of the modern *nation-state,* based on the idea of **sovereignty**—that within a given geographic area the political unit has supreme authority.

3. The modern world is characterized both by sovereign nations and by **mass society,** which developed out of the modern state, industrialism, and technology.

4. **Economics** is concerned with the production and consumption of goods and services. In the United States, the emphasis of production has changed over the last 70 years from farming to services. One problem that has accompanied this change is an increasing **alienation** among workers, who often find difficulty in seeing the meaning in their work. Other problems include high unemployment among minorities and job discrimination against women.

5. Although Americans consume 40 percent of the world's products, there are great inequalities in the American people's ability to consume goods and services.

6. John Locke suggested that the function of government is to protect our natural rights to life, liberty, and property. The United States government encompasses these functions and many others as well.

7. One function of government, maintaining sovereignty, has three aspects: (1) maintaining the loyalty of a community of citizens, (2) maintaining order within the society, and (3) protecting the society from external threats.

8. Another function of government is regulating the economy. Under **com-**

munism, the state owns the major means of production; under **socialism,** the government owns only some of the major means of production and regulates the others; under **capitalism,** the means of production are in private hands.

9. Governments also serve as participants in the economy, providing goods and services, ranging from electricity to insurance. Included in this function is welfare spending. In some countries the government feels responsible for ensuring that all citizens have food, housing, health care, and education; these nations are called **welfare states.**

10. A final government function is administering the bureaucratic structure that comprises the government.

11. Scholars have identified a number of types of political systems. The most prominent systems today are **totalitarianism** and **constitutional democracy.** Totalitarianism is characterized by a concentration of power, a single political party, ideological orthodoxy, and strong control of the economy. A constitutional democracy has a formal constitution and involvement of the people in political processes through consent of the governed.

12. **Power** is the ability to make decisions and have them carried out. One type of power is **coercive power**—the exercise of physical force. The use of material goods as rewards and punishment is **remunerative power.** The use of arguments and reasoning is **persuasive power.**

13. People allow those with **legitimate power,** or **authority,** to have power over certain aspects of their lives. Areas of power include *political power* and *economic power*. Power varies in *scope* and in *distribution*.

14. According to Mills, America is controlled by the **power elite**—a small group of people with key posts in the military, government, and industry. Opposed to this view is the idea that power in America is divided among diverse groups, all exerting pressure in specific areas.

15. The people of a society exercise power through mass movements, short-term political activity (such as demonstrations), affiliation with a political party, and voting. However, few people take advantage of these channels for exercising power.

KEY TERMS

alienation
anarchism
capitalism
coercive power
communism
constitutional democracy
economics

legitimate power (authority)
mass movement
mass society
persuasive power
planned obsolescence
political socialization
political systems

power
power elite
power pluralism
power structure
remunerative power

socialism
sovereignty
totalitarianism
welfare state

SUGGESTED READINGS

Christenson, Reo M., et al. *Ideologies and Modern Politics.* New York: Dodd, Mead, 1971.
A comprehensive account of modern political ideologies.

Dahl, Robert A. *Pluralist Democracy in the United States.* Chicago: Rand McNally, 1967.
A major work arguing for the pluralistic view of power.

Daly, Herman E., ed. *Toward a Steady-State Economy.* San Francisco: W. H. Freeman, 1973.
A collection of essays critical of growth-oriented economies.

Dawson, Richard E., Kenneth Prewitt, and Karen S. Dawson. *Political Socialization,* 2nd ed. Boston: Little, Brown, 1977.
A good survey of the subject of political socialization.

Domhoff, G. William. *The Higher Circles.* New York: Random House, 1970.
An elitist approach that sees economic interests as the dominant force in political life.

Githens, Martha, and Jewel Prestich. *Portrait of Marginality.* New York: McKay, 1977.
The authors examine the political socialization of women and its effects on their influence and power.

Marcson, Simon. *Automation, Alienation, and Anomie.* New York: Harper & Row, 1970.
A discussion of the problems of the worker in industrial and bureaucratic societies.

Mills, C. Wright. *The Power Elite.* New York: Oxford University Press, 1956.
The classic statement of the elitist approach to power.

Mintz, Morton, and Jerry S. Cohen. *America, Inc.: Who Owns and Operates the United States.* New York: Dial, 1971.
A critical exploration of the influence of big business in American life.

Pursell, Carroll, W., Jr., ed. *The Military-Industrial Complex.* New York: Harper & Row, 1972.
The sources, characteristics, and problems of the complex are discussed by outstanding scholars.

Smelser, Neil J. *The Sociology of Economic Life,* 2nd ed. Englewood Cliffs, N.J.: Prentice-Hall, 1976.
Smelser explores the economic system in America and how it is interconnected with other institutions.

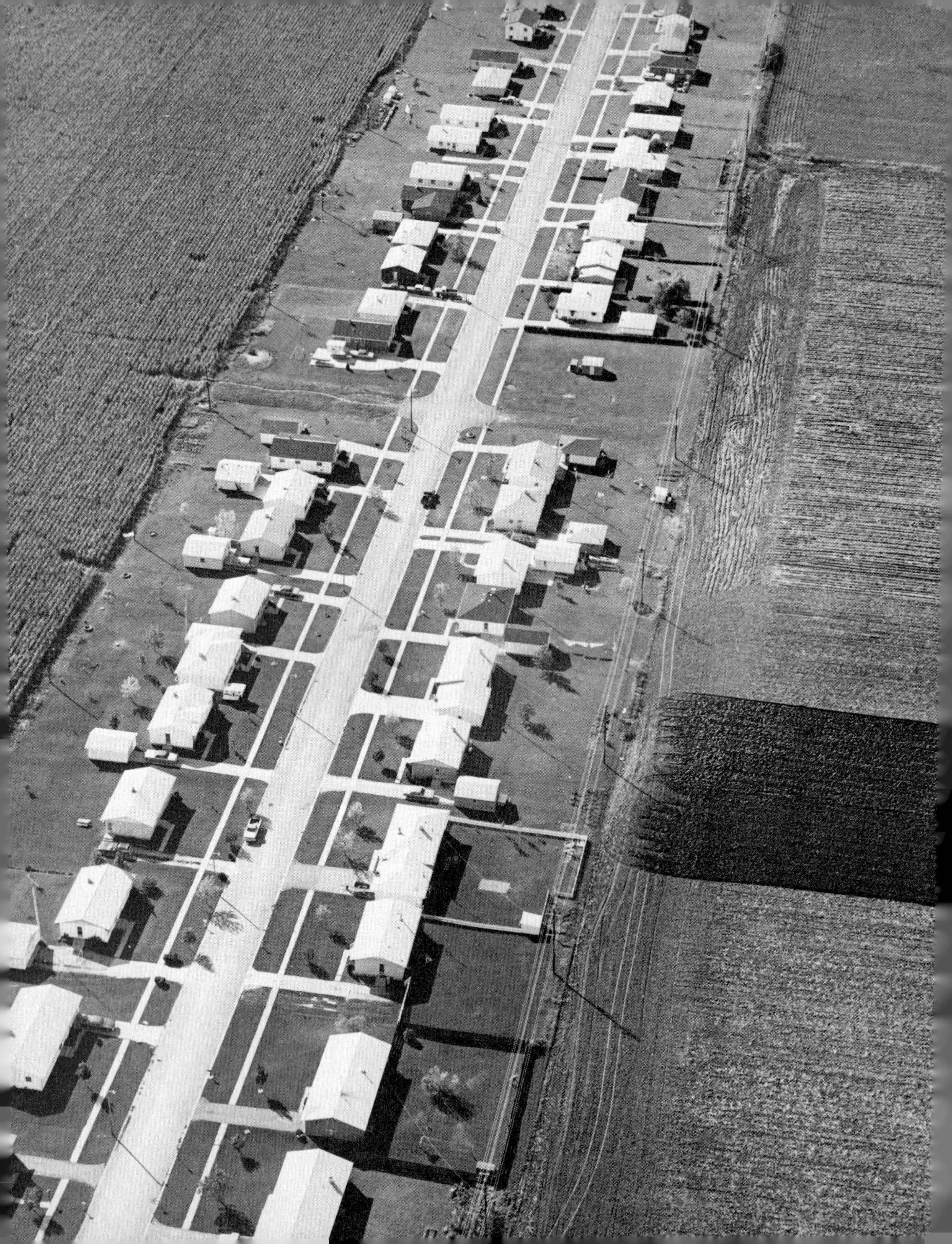

Part Four

Understanding Conflict and Change

All cultures change. Through invention and discovery within a culture or through diffusion among cultures, new objects, beliefs, or needs are introduced. Change is an important factor in our lives today. And, as we saw in the section on institutions, conflict plays a major role in contemporary life as well. In this final part of the text, we will examine the various changes and conflicts that are of special interest to sociologists.

Despite the long service that the structural-functional model has given to sociology, many sociologists today are hard-put to defend it as an accurate description of how societies operate. Yet, the conflict model has proved inadequate as a sole explanation as well. In the absence of another comprehensive theory, sociologists have had to make eclectic use of what they see as the most appropriate elements of both of these major theories. In this part of the book, we use the eclectic view—stressing elements of the conflict model as the more useful—to study several areas of contemporary social conflict and change.

One kind of sociologist, the social demographer, makes change his or her subject of study. Demographers study the growth, decrease, and distribution of populations—on a worldwide scale or in a specific society or community. Birth rates, mortality rates, and migration rates may seem to have little interest, except as curiosities, for people fascinated by large numbers, but they do indeed have immense scientific value. They have value not only as a description of the present condition of a population but also as a sign of what the future will bring.

In addition, demographers can lead other sociologists to pursue answers to questions that otherwise might not have been asked. Demographers have shown that general fertility rates become higher as you descend the social strata of our society. Other sociologists, picking up the clue, asked themselves why this is so. At first, they thought that the lower class probably had different values from those of the classes above it, values that lead lower-class people to want larger families. This is a hypothesis for testing. Sample surveys and questionnaires failed to prove the hypothesis to be correct. Sociologists ultimately discovered that the desired family size is pretty much the same in each socioeconomic class. The difference was that birth control information was not uniformly accessible or sought out, owing partly to financial resources and partly to attitudes toward discussing sexual matters with others.

Demographers also study migration, and they have found that internal migration (movement from one state to another or from one part of a state to another) has become a marked characteristic of our society. In addition, it was migration that was the force that began enlarging our cities long ago. In 100 years, we've been transformed from a predominantly rural to an overwhelmingly urban people. More than three-quarters of our population live in urban areas (in 1800, 6 percent did; in 1900, 40 percent).

Why, then, are the cities in trouble? Because the central, or inner, city is only one part of an urban area. The suburbs must be included as well. The suburbs are not a new feature of our cities, but their phenomenal growth after World War II dwarfs their previous size. This rapid growth has had a devastating effect on the cities, because the suburbs have filled up with the white middle-class families, who could have provided a sound tax base from which cities could draw their operating revenues. Furthermore, cities were needing more and more revenues because, as the middle classes were migrating to the suburbs, the white and nonwhite poor were migrating from rural areas to the cities in search of better jobs and an improved standard of living. The poor, by necessity, rely more heavily than the well-off on public services: health care, transportation, housing, and the like.

Some white middle-class people continue to live in the central city. And whites of the lower middle and working classes are even more numerous in the cities. So nonwhite and ethnic minorities have invariably been forced to live in certain areas of the inner cities. Virtually every American city has slums—decayed, high-crime areas, where the white poor and some of the nonwhite poor live. But most of the nonwhite poor live in ghettos. Although slums and ghettos look very much alike, they are significantly different. Slums are places that people can pass through on their way up the socioeconomic ladder; but ghettos are places that most nonwhite groups are virtually forced to live in. Slums are created by poverty, ghettos by discrimination.

Using the work of biologists and physical anthropologists, sociologists have been able to confirm that racism has social rather than biological roots. The apparent built-in differences among races have been traced to cultural and social class differences. A few people still seek to prove that blacks are inherently less intelligent than whites. But the overwhelming evidence of research is that the only true biological differences among races are the superficial ones of skin color, hair texture, shape of the eyes, average height, characteristic muscle tone, and a few others.

Racism may be built on a myth, but its social consequences are very real. Most nonwhites are "ghettoized" not only in where they live but in just about every other detail of their lives. Compared to whites, their infant mortality rates are higher; their life expectancies are shorter; their family life is less stable; and their economic chances are poorer. Despite the commitment of the federal government and the energetic efforts of many minority groups in past years, progress toward social equality and improved life chances has been tortoise-slow.

Racism and discrimination may one day be behind us, but one element that promises to be with us always is social deviancy. Certain acts, like murder, incest, and theft, are considered deviant by almost all societies. Nevertheless, societies vary widely in what other kinds of behavior are considered intolerable. In our society, various violent and nonviolent acts that have victims are crimes: rape, murder, extortion, burglary. Yet, so are some acts that have no victims (unless you choose to think of the actor as his or her own victim). Use of certain drugs is a crime, and to some thinkers, a symptom of mental or emotional illness. Homosexual acts are a crime almost everywhere in our society. Many consider them expressions of illness. Many others consider homosexuality neither a crime not a sickness, but rather an alternative form of behavior.

Sociologists have not come up with entirely promising theories to explain the group basis of deviant behavior. Of the three major theories in use, each can explain why certain forms of deviancy may occur, but none of the theories truly explains why some people and not others become deviants of various kinds. Perhaps the core of the problem is that much more work must be done to distinguish among the kinds of deviancy. In our society, both habitual criminals and homosexuals are considered deviants. Even so, they have not necessarily become deviants by the same processes or for the same reasons. In addition, society may have different reasons for considering the two kinds of behavior deviant. Before sociologists will be able to produce a better theory of deviancy, they will probably have to explore far back into the past of our Western culture.

Millions of people in the world worry about what—or whether—they will eat today or tomorrow. They worry, too, about the health of their families and about what will happen to their homes or villages if the floods strike again. With such day-to-day problems, it is difficult for them to be concerned about long-term social and cultural changes. In this country, too, we tend to focus on the events of our daily lives. Yet, we are all social beings, and the changes that occur in human societies eventually affect us and thus should be of interest to us all.

Several theorists have taken a long view of human societies and have proposed ideas to explain the changes that occur over time. Some have theorized that civilizations rise, reach a peak, and eventually go through a decline. Others hold an onward and upward view, believing that human civilizations always evolve into something better. And, of course, there are the mainstream structural-functional and conflict views of social change.

Sociologists are primarily interested in the process of change—how change occurs—rather than in what has changed. They look at <u>collective behavior</u>—how people acting together work to produce a change or take some action. One type of collective behavior is the <u>social movement</u>, a long-lasting group effort founded to bring about or prevent some change. Sociologists also look at how people adopt new ideas—the steps they go through in examining and trying out things that will eventuate in social change. The research findings in regard to how ideas are adopted can be used to speed up acceptance of planned social changes in such areas as health practices, family planning, and farming methods.

Finally, sociologists are concerned about how people deal with social change—how it affects our lives. Today, everything points to the fact that the tempo of social change is quickly accelerating. The more we can learn about how social change occurs, the better we may be able to handle the changes as we experience them.

13
Social and Cultural Change

Human beings have been on earth for about 100,000 years. For the vast majority of those years, humans lived at the hunting and gathering stage, using their hands and wits to find the food they needed to keep them alive. For most of human history, this is what human life was all about: finding food, procreating, and keeping alive. When prehistoric humans learned to make and use tools and to use fire, and when they began to develop a language, a vast range of activities opened up to them. With better tools, they could hunt more effectively, and with fire, they could protect themselves from the cold, from wild animals, and from each other. With their language, they could transmit to their young all that they had learned. For thousands of years, they gradually became better and better equipped to cope with their environment. Building on the past, they developed even better ways to shelter themselves from the elements, to gather food, and to protect themselves from enemies. Still, these fundamental necessities occupied most of their time.

It was only about 6000–7000 years ago that humans learned how to grow food, and then, to domesticate animals. Food became more abundant, and the chances for survival increased dramatically. With more food available—and food that could be stored—hunters, fishermen, and food-gatherers were released for other activities. They began to smelt and work metals, they invented the wheel, they developed writing, and small cities arose. Within 1000 years after this change, the rudiments of civilization, as we now think of it, were established.

It took only a few thousand more years for the next major technological change—the Industrial Revolution—to take place. Inventions with vast consequences followed fast upon one another, and the factory system was born. In the past 100 years, human civilization has seen the arrival of the automobile, the airplane, the telephone, radio and television, nuclear power, computers, satellites, and household appliances for every possible purpose.

Even within your own lifetime, human life has changed immensely in almost every way. Many of these changes have been results of the rapid technological progress we have been experiencing over the past century. Others have been the result of the efforts of social movements—the civil rights movement, the women's liberation movement, the human potential movement, and others.

In this chapter, we will be examining the nature of social change—theories of how it happens, the role of social movements, and how people deal with change. Toward the end of the chapter, we will return to a discussion of the rapid pace of changes occurring in our society today and speculate on the future of change and how it will affect society and the people in it.

THEORIES OF SOCIAL CHANGE

Change is a fact of life. It has always occurred, and as you have seen, it is occurring faster now than ever before. The sociologist is not just interested in the fact that change happens; he or she is also interested in *why* and *how* it happens. Many theories have been put forth to account for social change. None of these is entirely satisfactory, but each sheds some light on the process.

Cyclical Theory

The human organism is born, grows, reaches a peak of physical ability, declines, and then dies. There is no known way to alter this pattern. Early in the twentieth century, some social philosophers put forth the idea that societies, too, are destined to go through stages of growth followed by stages of decline. The rise and fall of the Roman Empire provides a good example of the **cyclical theory of change.** Cyclical theorists were not interested in just one or two examples of such change, but rather, they were looking for a pattern of broad social change that could be applied to societies generally. The most notable cyclical theorists were Oswald Spengler, Arnold Toynbee, and Pitirim Sorokin.

Spengler, one cyclical theorist, expressed his views on social change in his book *The Decline of the West,* published in 1918. He studied eight major societies and concluded that each showed the growth-maturity-decline sequence. Western societies, according to Spengler, have reached and passed their "Golden Age." Having gone through the mature, creative stage, they are now in the stage of reflection and material comfort. This is a period of slow decline. Ultimately, our societies will disintegrate, for societies, like living organisms, grow and blossom and decay. There is really no way to reverse the process or to rejuvenate either an organism or a society. A major point of Spengler's theory is that the growth-decay process is built into the nature of human societies. However, few contemporary sociologists go along with Spengler's idea that the decline and disintegration of Western societies is as inevitable as the decline and death of the human organism.

Between 1934 and 1961, the English historian Arnold Toynbee, who was also a cyclical theorist, wrote his twelve-volume work *A Study of History.* In it, Toynbee held that the proper units for studying social change are "civilizations" (a term he did not define precisely) rather than nation-states. He was interested in discovering what history could reveal about *why* civilizations arose, expanded, and decayed. From his intensive studies of 21 civilizations, Toynbee developed the basic idea that the mechanism of social change is challenge and response. Civilizations make a major leap forward when they are able to respond to physical and social challenges thrust upon them by their environment. It is difficult, rather than easy, conditions that propel humans to great achievements. Usually, it is a creative minority that develops the responses, and the masses accept the solutions of the minority and are loyal to them. When the minority cannot develop responses to new challenges, civilizations stagnate or decline. Nations make war against nations, and there are class wars within societies. Toynbee was more optimistic than some cyclical theorists, however, for he held that a troubled civilization could regain its vitality and then continue to meet new challenges.

The social change theories of American sociologist Pitirim Sorokin, an exiled Russian, were not exactly cyclical in the sense of positing a rise and decline of civilizations. Rather, from his detailed studies of many cultures, Sorokin concluded that civilizations alternate between two types of culture: the ideational and the sensate. At the **ideational** stage, the sociocultural system is characterized by dependence on authority, a belief that truth lies beyond the human senses, and faith. Ideational philosophy appeals to the mind and the soul, and religion (whatever its specific form) stresses the reality of the other world. The **sensate** stage, by contrast, depends on and encourages the natural sciences. Its philosophy stresses what can be perceived through the senses and can be studied objectively and empirically.

As Sorokin saw it, cultures contain both ideational and sensate elements, but they tend to develop toward one of the two pure types. As development toward one type reaches an extreme form, it is counteracted by the opposing forces of the other type. The culture then begins to move in the other direction. The alternation between sensate and ideational is common, but Sorokin did not find fixed, regular cycles of change.

Spengler, Toynbee, and Sorokin are sometimes referred to as "grand theorists," for they attempted to discover master patterns of social change by studying the course of human history over thousands of years. In his own way, each found a certain cyclical nature in the development of civilizations. Although modern social theorists do not stress cyclical theories of social change, it is worth keeping one's mind open to the idea that there may be some regular patterns in human history. The ideas of the cyclical theorists are in contrast to those of the evolutionary theorists, to which we now turn.

Evolutionary Theory

In Chapter 1, we discussed the fact that early sociologists assumed, quite confidently, that society is an evolutionary system. Auguste Comte assumed that society evolves in stages and that these stages can be characterized by how people think about the world. First, the world is seen as a playing field for supernatural forces, then, as an arena of human-created abstractions, and finally, as a "positive" creation of scientific principles.

Herbert Spencer and Karl Marx were also evolutionists. Spencer saw society evolving by the same laws that operate in biological evolution. He thought that society, like any living organism, would become perfect through the struggle for survival and through survival of the fittest. To

Modern industrial societies were once at a stage of primitive agricultural technology. How did the fantastic change occur? Will civilizations decline to this stage?

Marx, history had its laws, and they were carried out in human society. Basically, human history has been marked by class struggle—between the masters and the slaves, the exploiters and the workers. In the evolution of the struggle between capitalists and workers, the workers would repress the capitalists and form a "dictatorship of the proletariat," which would evolve into the final stage—the classless society, or communism. As Marx saw it, the evolution toward communism was inevitable. Capitalism, like feudalism before it, would fight to preserve itself, but the laws of history could not be refuted.

The thinking of most of those who propounded the evolutionary theory of change contained the implicit value judgment that change is good, both morally and in terms of the welfare of the people. Marx's classless society, for example, was not just the final steps in social evolution; it was also an ideal stage, a stage of perfection that humans could reach. The sociologist Emile Durkheim was somewhat of an exception among evolutionary theorists, for he suggested that there would be difficulties as societies evolved from the simple to the modern state. In simple societies, there is little division of labor. Durkheim noted that this is accompanied by a sharing of common values, which produces a sense of solidarity among the group's members. As societies become more complex, division of labor increases and there are more and different roles for society's members. This leads to a diversity of values and threatens the solidarity of the group. To hold society together, it is necessary to introduce more formal methods of control, such as laws and civil government. Social evolution, as Durkheim saw it, is more a necessary change than an advancement to a superior state of affairs.

Structural-Functional Theory

Structural-functionalists cannot be classed among the "grand theorists," who seek master patterns to account for social change over the course of human history. Indeed, as we saw in Chapter 1, the **structural-functional model** tends to stress the stability of the social system. Yet, Talcott Parsons (1949, 1950), one of the chief proponents of structural-functional theory, does recognize that changes do occur. As change takes place in one part of the social system, such as the economic sphere, it tends to produce change in other subsystems, such as the family, education, or religion. According to structural-functional theory, however, the overall trend is for the various subsystems to accommodate to the change—for each to adjust itself, as it were, to any changes in other subsystems. Social change is thus seen as leading toward a state of equilibrium.

Structural-functionalists are well aware that, over time, societies become more complex and are marked by increased differentiation of roles and the development of new structures. Yet, the overriding thrust of this theory is that the new will be integrated with the old, so that the functions, albeit changed, will continue to be performed. For example, socialization may be performed by formal agencies, such as schools, rather than by families, but both institutions will accommodate themselves to the situation, and the stability of the social order will not be jeopardized. Major changes in societies, according to Parsons and other structural-functionalists, come about only from forces outside the society.

Conflict Theory

The **conflict model,** you will recall, sees society as being composed of group pitted against group. Clashes of interest abound, and contending forces struggle either to maintain power or to grasp it. From the struggle comes change, which is not only inevitable but meritable. A society in conflict must be dynamic. The struggle for power results in a redistribution of power that, temporarily at least, better reflects the interests of society's members. But the struggle continues, and with each realignment of power, the society changes.

The German sociologist Ralf Dahrendorf (1973) is probably the leading exponent of conflict theory today. In his works, he emphasizes the unequal distribution of power in society. Those who have power and authority want to retain it; those who experience too much control over their lives want to change power relations. Although Karl Marx basically subscribed to evolutionary theory—that societies are moving toward a better state—he also believed that the process by which societies change and evolve is through conflict. The basic conflict, according to Marx, is in the economic sphere. In earlier times, it was between the wealthy landowners and the serfs or peasants. In industrial societies, it is between the owners of industries and the workers. Marx saw conflict between the owners and nonowners as inevitable, and he felt that out of such conflict, a new social order—the classless society—would ultimately evolve.

The various theories of social change we have discussed are intriguing to sociologists and should be so to anyone who is curious about how societies have developed and where they are going from here. No one theory seems to be totally satisfactory in explaining how and why societies change. But we do know that one major way in which societies change is by deliberate action of specific groups of people. So let us now look closely at how social movements can effect changes in society.

SOCIAL MOVEMENTS: PEOPLE AS AGENTS OF CHANGE

When large numbers of people act together to achieve some objective or to take some social action, they are engaging in **collective behavior.** Collective behavior is difficult to pin down, for the concept covers a broad range of social interaction, which includes social movements, crowds, public opinion, rumors, and panics. Some forms of collective behavior, such as **crowds** and panics, are relatively unstructured and short-lived (see Box 13.1). Social movements, on the other hand, tend to be more structured, and the group activity tends to continue over long periods of time, allowing the group to have some effect, large or small, on the society as a whole.

A **social movement** is defined as a relatively long-lasting collective enterprise formed to bring about or prevent social change. There are a number of important characteristics of social movements that allow us to distinguish them from other human groups and associations. In the first place, as noted in the definition, a social movement is intrinsically related to social change. Those associated with a social movement are discontented with the present state of affairs. They believe that, by joining with others and by dedicating themselves to the goals of the movement, they can produce a change or block some ongoing change they disapprove of. Thus, the goal of the temperance movement was to eliminate the production and sale of alcoholic beverages. The Ku Klux Klan movement, on the other hand, was against change and sought, among other things, to block the racial integration of American society.

Social movements tend to involve large numbers of people, to be long-lasting, and to be widespread socially or geographically. While these are relative terms, they serve to distinguish social movements from short-lived, local, small-membership groups that may espouse change. A group of citizens who band together to protest a zoning change in their neighborhood does not constitute a social movement. The temperance movement, however, begun in the early 1800s, spread rapidly throughout much of the world, and 100 years later, was still going strong. As part of the movement, the International Prohibition Federation was formed in 1909, with representatives from practically all European countries, the United States, China, Japan, and the British Commonwealth. Shortly before the turn of the century, another

---

**BOX 13.1
THE CROWD AS AN AGENT OF SOCIAL CHANGE**

Sociologists are particularly interested in the form of collective behavior called the crowd, and in how crowds can respond to or help bring about social change. While it is the active crowd that is intent upon some action or objective, other types of crowds can become active ones. It is useful, therefore, to distinguish among several types of crowds. We can then examine how active crowds develop and how much impact they have on social change.

The sociologist defines crowd as a collection of people who are gathered together for a single purpose or to respond to a single stimulus. Such a definition would include rock concert audiences, church congregations, protest rallies, and riots. A crowd, such as that at a rock concert, is an expressive crowd: the people have gathered to experience the performance and to participate in it by expressing their feelings. Collections of people at a protest or a riot are an active crowd: they have gathered for action, whether violent or symbolic. That is, rioters protest conditions or express their feelings by violating norms while protestors often gather peacefully, in hopes of showing, by their numbers, the force of public opinion behind their position. Frequently, a riot will spring from what is known as a casual crowd—a crowd that gathers spontaneously to witness some incident, such as a traffic accident or an arrest. As long as the crowd is passive, simply watching events unfold, it remains casual; it can disperse without producing any incidents of its own. But, if a precipitating factor appears, the casual crowd may be transformed into an active crowd.

The sociologist Neil Smelser (1963) theorizes six preconditions, each one building on the other, that are conducive to the production of active crowds. The more of the six conditions that exist, the greater the likelihood that collective behavior will take place. Let us take the example of the race riots of the mid-1960s to illustrate these six preconditions.

1. Structural conduciveness. The sheer density of population in large cities makes life in them impersonal and anonymous. Some areas of the city gather different racial and ethnic groups, which can prevent common bonds from developing among people living there. Other areas are segregated according to race, nationality, and the like. Many of these are ghettos, where people share the common experiences of racial discrimination and poverty. The race riots of the 1960s all occurred or began in ghettos.

group expressing the movement was formed: the World Women's Christian Temperance Union. At present, there are branches of this organization in over 50 countries. The temperance movement is thus a good example of all the characteristics of a social movement.

2. <u>Structural strain</u>. The coexistence of wealth and poverty in large cities makes the poor far more conscious of their poverty than if they lived a great distance from the wealthy. It is not difficult to understand why minority groups begin to think of themselves as victims of social injustice. Feelings of relative deprivation and social injustice set the stage for potentially explosive collective behavior.
3. <u>Growth and spread of a generalized belief</u>. After years of quiet acceptance of discrimination and poverty or of trying to bring about social change nonviolently, many blacks felt that they were no better off than they had been years before. They had been deprived for hundreds of years, and they were tired of waiting for the white man to give them their share. Many began to hold the idea that something had to be done—and soon—even if it meant bloodshed.
4. <u>Precipitating factors</u>. Each of the riots of the mid-1960s was triggered by what ghetto dwellers considered police harassment or brutality. Members of a crowd of witnesses, who have become emotionally involved in the events, see their friends or members of their community being "unjustly" treated by police, and they become an active crowd.
5. <u>Mobilization for action</u>. Once a precipitating factor has activated the crowd, many people cease to be controlled by the norms that ordinarily guide their behavior, and they may do many things that they would otherwise never have considered doing, such as hurting or destroying property.
6. <u>Traditional social controls are ineffective</u>. The normal modes of external social control become ineffective as the crowd members' norms. The police are greatly outnumbered and on the defensive. They must either retreat or call for reinforcements. But, the last alternative is usually ineffective if the crowd has already reached the fifth stage. The police then find themselves surrounded by a normless vacuum.

Active crowds can initiate social change or speed up change already underway. A crowd of angry shoppers protesting at a supermarket may spearhead a consumer movement. Many of the civil rights demonstrations in the 1960s made it difficult for communities to continue more blatant forms of discrimination. Primarily, however, crowd activity does not have a direct effect on social change but rather calls attention to some problem in society that is driving people to sudden collective action.

A social movement, as such, is informally organized. Leaders emerge, rather than being formally elected. Strategies of action are developed to meet the situation but are not derived from formal rules or from a constitution. Often, members are those who ally themselves to the movement and support it financially, even though there is no formal act of joining. However, social movements often lead to the organization of formal groups and voluntary associations that are rightly part of the movement. The Congress of Racial Equality (CORE), for example, was an expression of the larger civil rights movement, and the National Organization of Women (NOW) is an expression of the women's movement. Often, these formal groups are the action agencies of the movement and seek to bring about social change by influencing legislation, staging demonstrations or boycotts, and publishing literature.

Types of Social Movements

There are many different ways of categorizing movements. None is entirely satisfactory, partly because social movements are loosely organized, and it is difficult to specify all of their goals, to delineate their membership, and to determine their impact on social change. For example, social movements can be classified in terms of the social institution through which the particular social change is sought; but this is not entirely satisfactory, because some movements cut across and affect several institutions. Social movements can also be classified according to their strategies and means of producing change. Some espouse violence, while others espouse peaceful means; some attempt to work through existing structures, while others insist on working from outside the "establishment." Another way of classifying social movements is to focus on their intended effects on the values and norms of society: does the movement seek to alter the core values of society, to preserve the present values, or to restore the values of an earlier period? Because this method focuses on the relationship between the movement and the social change, we will use it for classification purposes here.

Reform Movements A **reform movement** seeks the type of change that will preserve some existing values but will provide a better means of implementing them. For example, the wave of Protestantism that swept Europe in the sixteenth century was not in any way anti-Christian; rather, the Catholic monk Martin Luther, other leaders, and their many followers were seeking what they defined as better means of allowing the masses to learn basic Christian values and to express them in their everyday lives.

Conservative Movements **Conservative movements** advocate the preservation of existing values and norms. Some can be thought of as countermovements, for their focus is on opposition to changes proposed by other movements. Other conservative movements arise as a response to changes in society that they would like to see stopped. The Total Woman movement, for example, probably would not have arisen were it not for the Women's Liberation movement, and at any rate, its ideology stands in contrast to that of the women's movement. In Total Woman classes all over the country, tens of thousands of women are learning that being a woman means pleasing one's husband, looking up to him, being seductive for him, and letting him make the major family decisions. It is an attempt, in other words, to preserve the value of the patriarchal family and the subservient role of women in it.

The marriage enrichment–marriage encounter movement is still small, but it illustrates another kind of social movement that is working to preserve existing values. Its goal is to help couples achieve a full measure of happiness and growth in egalitarian, companionship, monogamous marriage. The movement is not "fighting" another movement but rather is trying to preserve values that are seen to be threatened in a society marked by a high divorce rate and many unstable marriages.

Progressive Movements A **progressive movement** espouses new social arrangements, new values, and new norms but stops short of a complete revamping of the social order. The civil rights movement has espoused nothing less than complete social, political, and economic equality for all races. The women's movement seeks to remove all injustices, discrimination, and prejudicial attitudes toward women. For either movement to achieve complete success, many profound changes in the social order are necessary. For example, the removal of sexist and racist attitudes requires changes in socialization practices, school textbooks, television programs and advertisements, and so on. The many changes that have been effected and are being sought will reach into the major institutions of society and will affect the lives of all of us. Yet, neither movement espouses the complete overthrow of the political-economic order: each simply wants fair treatment within the existing order.

Some might be tempted to classify the women's movement and the civil rights movement as reform movements, claiming that they seek to preserve basic values guaranteed by our Constitution. However, in actual practice, our society has not endorsed equality and has become both racist and sexist. One should not place too much emphasis on the "correct" classification of social movements. It is enough to recognize that movements vary according to how their goals are related to the basic values of society.

Revolutionary Movements A **revolutionary movement** has as its goal the overthrow of an existing social order and the establishment of a new one. It seeks to completely reorganize the existing power relationships in a society, frequently focusing first on the political-economic institution and moving next to complete reorganization of other institutions, such as education and religion.

Let's take the Russian Revolution of 1917 as an example. It is difficult to establish the origins of the socialist revolution in the Soviet Union. The 1880s saw large-scale labor strikes and poorly organized peasant uprisings in many parts of the country, indicating a growing discontent among workers. Various revolutionary political parties arose to protest the plight of the masses. The most memorable of these was the Social Democratic party, which was formed in 1898, and which drew its doctrines from the writings of Karl Marx. Five years later, a split in the party gave birth to the Menshevik (minority) and Bolshevik (majority) factions. It was the latter faction, of course, that overthrew the government in 1917 and set about to establish a new order.

The Russian Revolution resulted in swift and far-reaching change. Workers became the new elite, rulers became the ruled, and owners found themselves without property. Industrialization began in earnest when the factories were taken over by the government. Collective, government-owned farms were spurred on to produce food. Broad health and welfare services financed by the state were made available to the masses. Illiteracy was reduced. Marriage and divorce were removed from church control. Day nurseries were built and staffed at state expense to encourage women to work outside the home. These are but a few of the ways in which the revolution impinged on the major social institutions and affected the lives of citizens.

Some historians question whether the American Revolution should rightly be called a revolution. They contend that the colonists were not seeking fundamental changes in the social order, but rather, that they were seeking to unify the colonies and to separate this new unit from England. Yet, the constitutional government that was established articulated some profound new ideas, including a basic commitment to egalitarian principles, the consent of the governed through popular vote, and the protection of basic rights of individuals. The American experience was not characterized by complete social upheaval like the Russian Revolution, but the new ideas that grew out of the American movement were truly revolutionary.

The Natural History of Social Movements

The history of any social movement will reveal that it undergoes changes throughout its existence. Thus, sociologists have sought to identify typical or common stages that social movements progress through, even though each movement is unique. According to one approach, social movements go through four major stages (Ryan, 1969).

At the *preliminary stage,* there is a certain amount of discontent, excitement, and unrest in society, which center around a specific issue. There is a readiness to "do something." Frequently, the leaders that emerge at this stage are personally dynamic people who can dramatize the situation and develop a small following of concerned individuals. In some movements they may be thought of as agitators but the main function of such leaders

SOCIAL AND
CULTURAL CHANGE

seems to be to serve as a point about which people can rally. Betty Friedan, with her book *The Feminine Mystique* (1963), served this function in the reawakening women's movement, and Rachel Carson played a similar role in the environmental movement with her book *Silent Spring* (1962). Ralph Nader served as the symbol of the consumer movement at its preliminary stage.

The second or *popular stage* of a social movement is marked by large numbers of people identifying with the movement. Intellectuals begin to emerge as leaders, clarifying the issues and writing and speaking out on what must be done. As the membership grows, leaders are faced with the problem of dealing with the heterogeneous masses. Some members understand the goals of the movement fully and want to get on with the business

As the Women's Movement goes into the formal stage, splinter groups with their more restricted goals continue to arise.

of correcting the situation. Others, who have been called "true believers," are those for whom almost any movement has an appeal, as long as it gives them a chance to fight for something, to hate something, or to otherwise satisfy personal needs for involvement (Hoffer, 1958). These people may shift their loyalties readily from movement to movement and are often overzealous. Still others join social movements primarily to give meaning to their lives. They have vague dissatisfactions with life and are pleased to find a cause that makes sense in a troubled world. Organizing the

---

**BOX 13.2
BIOGRAPHY
OF A SOCIAL
MOVEMENT:
THE ANTIRAPE
MOVEMENT**

In the United States, rape is officially regarded as a serious crime. In ten states it carries the death penalty. Yet, for years, the law seems to have been more concerned with assuring that a man not be falsely convicted of rape than with convicting a rapist. The eighteenth-century English jurist Sir Matthew Hale held that rape is "an accusation easy to be made, hard to be proved, but harder to be defended by the party accused, though innocent." Guided by this concept, for years American judges allowed defense attorneys to probe into the moral character of a rape victim in an effort to discredit her testimony. Judges have instructed juries to examine the testimony of the woman with caution. The result of this has been a veritable toleration of rape in American society (V. N. Rose, 1977). The crime has often gone unreported, because women fear embarrassment, harsh treatment at the hands of law enforcement officers, and a degrading experience in court—if, indeed, the case ever gets that far. In the past, only about ten percent of reported rapes resulted in conviction. It is no wonder that rape victims often conclude that it is futile to try to do anything about the crime. Recently, however, an antirape movement has swept our society, and it is going through the same stages as have other social movements.

The preliminary stage of the antirape movement began in the 1960s as a part of the more general women's movement. Women's groups brought forth evidence challenging the concept of "victim participation" in the crime, drew attention to the existence of the problem, and wrote about the shameful treatment of rape victims in court. Groups were formed to raise the public consciousness about rape and its relation to the sexist nature of our society, with its tolerance of the subjugation of women and its glorification of aggressiveness and power displays among men.

Through the efforts of many women, the antirape movement passed into the popular stage. The communications network of the women's movement allowed the new ideas on rape to be spread quickly across the country. People became more aware of the problem. Rape victims became more willing to report the crime. From 1968 to 1973, the number of reported rapes increased by 62 percent. Most of the rise was due most likely to more frequent reporting, rather than to an increase in the in-

masses at the popular stage of a social movement, and keeping the activities of the diverse membership directed toward goals can be a real problem.

The third stage of a social movement is the *formal stage*. At this stage, goals become better clarified and a number of formally organized groups may be set up, with clearly defined leadership roles and programs for action. For example, the National Organization of Women (NOW) is one of the formal groups that has grown out of the women's movement. There are state and local chapters of NOW, national meetings, and specified programs. At

---

cidence of the crime itself. The conviction rate was still the lowest for any violent crime, however. For 51,000 reported rapes in 1973, 20,288 adults were arrested. Only 15,419 were prosecuted in courts. Of these, 5,551 were found guilty of rape, 2,621 were convicted of a lesser charge, and 7,247 were either acquitted or had their case dismissed.

In July 1972, the Rape Crisis Center in Washington, D.C., opened the first phone line for receiving calls from rape victims. At that point, the antirape movement had reached the formal stage, in which its goals were clarified and its programs for action were developed. Hundreds of cities now have rape crisis centers, and many cities have a rape task force to gather better data on the problem and to help victims. Organized groups continue to spring up to prevent rape, to ease the trauma of the rape experience for the victim, and to help obtain convictions of rapists. Among these organizations are the Women Organized Against Rape and Men Organized Against Rape (both Philadelphia groups), the Women United Against Rape in Indianapolis, and the Seattle Rape Reduction Project.

In about 1974, the antirape movement entered the institutional stage. Its goals began to be integrated into the legal and social structures of society. For example, many cities now use public instead of private funds to maintain rape crisis centers where victims can receive counseling and advice on what to expect in terms of medical, police, and court help following a rape. New York and other cities have developed special rape-analysis units in their police departments and have hired female detectives to investigate rapes. The American Bar Association adopted a resolution dealing with revision of the rules of evidence in court to protect victims from unnecessary invasion of privacy. The federal government is funding research on the causes and prevention of rape. In short, the antirape movement has gained acceptance by "the establishment." Its goals are recognized as legitimate. Informal, privately funded groups fighting rape will continue to exist, but it is likely that, in the immediate future, much of the reform will come from governmental agencies and formal organizations that are a part of community structures.

the formal stage of a social movement, there is also the likelihood that splinter groups will break off from the main movement to pursue more restricted goals. Factions may develop because the movement has become too large to allow some people to remain intimately involved, because it is embracing issues and goals not in keeping with the faction's ideas, or because potential leaders seek new arenas in which to exercise leadership, power, and control.

The formal stage of social movements flows into the final stage, which is called the *institutional stage.* This stage is reached when a successful movement is integrated into the legal and social structure of society. For example, there are branches of the federal government, such as the Environmental Protection Agency, to deal with the problems articulated by the environmental movement. This movement lives on, but it has reached the stage of social acceptance and integration into the social order. Bureaucrats of governmental agencies and elected officers of accepted formal groups play a large part in the leadership of the movement in this final stage.

Outlining the natural history or life cycle of a social movement has many practical applications (see Box 13.2). Perhaps most important, it allows us to identify the common problems faced by movements at a particular stage, so that we know what sorts of problems must be solved if the movement is to succeed.

The Results of Social Movements

Throughout our discussion of the types of social movements and how they evolve, we have referred to a number of movements that have produced significant and fundamental social changes. The socialist revolution affected not just Russia but the entire world. To take another example, for hundreds of years the Jewish people hoped and dreamed of someday returning to Zion, or Palestine, and establishing a publicly recognized national state. The Zionist movement reached the popular stage in the late 1800s and culminated in the formation of the state of Israel in 1947.

Coming closer to home, the temperance movement that began in the United States before the turn of the century resulted in national prohibition, which in turn encouraged gangsterism and organized crime. Social changes already wrought by the civil rights movement and the women's movement have altered the life chances of millions of Americans and have brought millions closer, in their thinking and their actions, to the goals of equality and fairness. In short, social movements continue to have profound effects on social change.

For several reasons, it is likely that in the immediate future social movements will continue to have an important impact on social change. For one thing, there will continue to be social problems that lead to feelings of discontent, frustration, and deprivation. This condition will lead to the con-

Social movements of various sorts will continue to be part of the American scene because we have lots of social problems and because past movements have helped to produce change.

tinued development of social movements because of a second factor: the belief, in democratic societies, that social change can be wrought by people banding and working together. In part, this belief has come about from the success of past social movements. For example, people joining the emerging social movement to remedy the plight of older people know that other movements for the rights of minorities have been effective.

A third condition that suggests that social movements will continue to be a feature of nontotalitarian societies is the existence of rapid, relatively uncontrolled mass communication. Events and ideas can be spread from group to group and from one section of the country to another, as happened with the student movement in the late 1960s. Our society will continue to be marked by social change, and one of the reasons for this will be the continued existence, or even an increase in the number, of social movements.

DEALING WITH SOCIAL CHANGE

Social and cultural change are not mysterious forces that descend on society. Real people initiate change, accept its effects on their lives, or try to stave off its consequences. Social change occurs within a context of values and beliefs, and we must recognize that people's attitudes toward change affect their responses to it. (For an example of how social change has affected one cultural group, see Box 13.3.)

An entire body of social-change research deals with how people learn of new ideas and decide to use them or not to use them. Much of the early research was done by rural sociologists who sought to explain why many farmers were slow to adopt new farming practices. For example, it took 14 years after the development of hybrid-seed corn for its use to be widespread. It could easily be demonstrated that it was a better grade of corn, had a greater yield per acre, and was more profitable for the farmer. Yet farmers

---

BOX 13.3
SOCIAL CHANGE AND THE IRISH TINKERS

For generations, small bands of people have wandered the Irish countryside, living in tents by the side of back roads, performing odd jobs for the farmers, selling wares, and then moving on to look for new markets for their goods and skills. In some ways, they are like the Romany Gypsies who are found in many European countries. But in Ireland they are called Tinkers, or Travellers.

In the old days, the major occupation of the Travellers was tinsmithing, from which the name Tinker originated. The wandering tinsmiths made pots and pans, cups, milk pails, lanterns, and many other useful articles, which they sold to the rural population. As they traveled through the country, they would also do repair work. These were the days when many consumer goods were expected to last a lifetime. So, the Tinkers tightened loose handles, mended holes in pots, and fixed umbrellas. Many also sold or traded draft animals to the farmers. During the harvest season, they would work on a day-to-day basis, pulling beets, digging potatoes, or putting up hay. The women sold household items, such as brushes, needles and thread, and boot polish. Some also told fortunes.

In recent years, modernization has had a major effect on the way of life of the Irish Tinkers, virtually destroying their traditional way of life (Gmelch and Gmelch, 1978). The need for Tinker goods and services has declined severely. Mass-produced plastic wares have all but eliminated the demand for tinware. Items that formerly would have been repaired by a Tinker are now thrown away. People can drive to the city to buy what they need instead of waiting for the Tinker to come around. Mechanized farmers no longer need the workhorses or donkeys provided by the Tinker, nor do they need the Tinker himself at harvest time. Thus, the Tinkers have had to abandon the countryside for the cities and towns. Fewer than 25 Tinker families were camped in Dublin in 1952. In 1976, 359 families—about 2,500 individuals, or over 20 percent of Ireland's Tinker population—were in the cities.

The Tinkers have always occupied the lowest rung on the socioeconomic ladder in Ireland, and their migration to the cities has not changed this status. In the 1960s, the government investigated the "Tinker problem." The original focus was on the litter and squalor in the camps and on the damage caused by wandering horses. But the report also mentioned the Tinkers' extreme poverty, illiteracy, and high infant mortality rate. As a result of widespread publicity on the Tinkers' plight, charities began to

were slow to adopt it. To take another example, it took more than 30 years for farmers in a Colombian village to completely adopt the use of chemical fertilizers, although the need for great crop yields was a desperate one. Why did it take so long for these practices to be adopted? Perhaps some clues to this can be found in the adoption process itself.

---

assist them, and the people were sympathetic to the Tinkers' needs. The Tinker women found that they could make a living by begging. Wearing old clothes and carrying a baby, they would go from house to house asking for money, food, or clothing. For a while, the men tried to collect scrap metal, but they found it increasingly difficult to find and sell enough to make it worthwhile. Furthermore, the man's traditional job of caring for the wagon and horses was lost, because the family no longer moved around.

Despite their move to the city, the Tinkers have tried to maintain their cultural traditions. Nevertheless, they have experienced many changes. For one thing, the traditional roles of husband and wife have been altered. The woman has become the chief income earner, and often, the chief decision maker. This switch in roles has led to excessive drinking among Tinker men. Traditional approaches to marriage have also changed. The Tinkers place a high value on premarital chastity. In the past, teenage girls were closely supervised, and when they were old enough to marry, their father chose a husband from another band that traveled in the same territory. Today, in the large city camps of the Tinkers, parents find it difficult to keep an eye on their teenagers. Their solution is to marry off their daughters at an early age (14 or 15) and to choose the husband from among the girl's first or second cousins. In this way, the girl's virtue is preserved and she marries someone known to the parents.

Some Tinkers have tried to become a part of the settled community. They have carefully tried to erase their social past, so that their new neighbors will not recognize them as Tinkers and thus discriminate against them. They dare not even invite their families to visit them for fear the neighbors will discover they are Tinkers. But, often, these families return to Tinker life, for they miss their families and other close personal ties. Furthermore, the Tinkers value their autonomy and freedom from fixed work schedules and find it difficult to adjust to the regimentation of work in the city.

The once proud, economically independent Tinkers have been reduced to begging and accepting charity. As the forces of social change became stronger, none of them could prevent the collapse of their traditional way of life. In the long run, a settled life in the city may prove a good thing, but for the present, the change has caused many problems and has required many psychological and social adjustments.

424
UNDERSTANDING
CONFLICT AND CHANGE

FIGURE 13.1   Time and Space References of Human Concerns

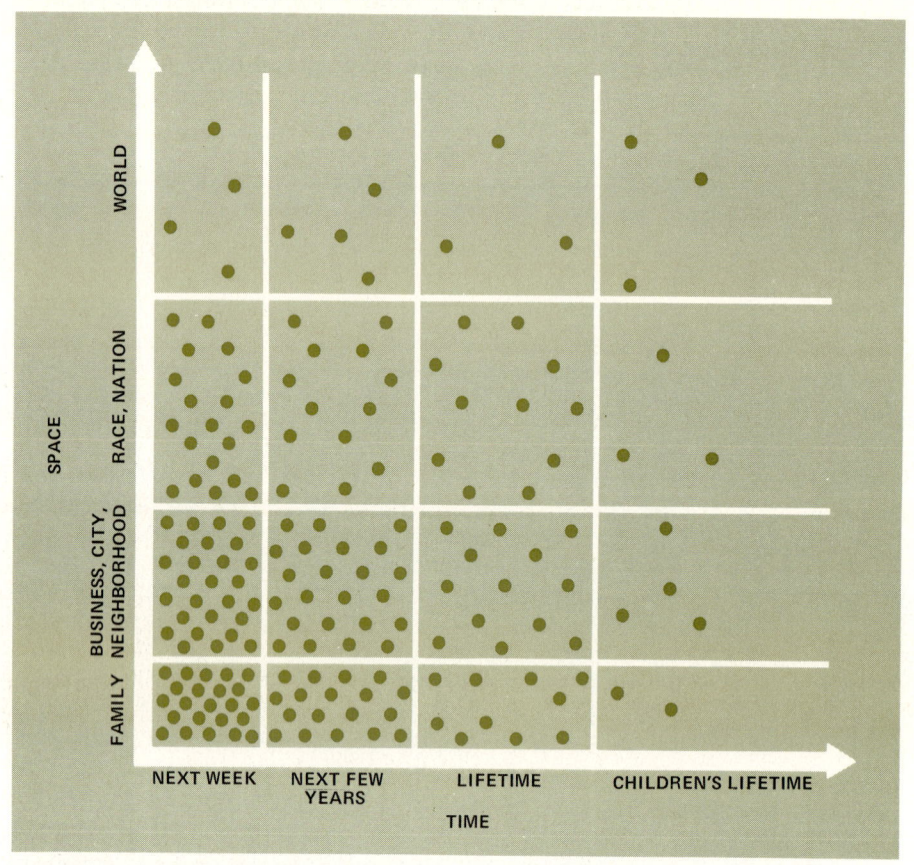

SPACE axis (bottom to top): FAMILY NEIGHBORHOOD; BUSINESS, CITY; RACE, NATION; WORLD
TIME axis (left to right): NEXT WEEK; NEXT FEW YEARS; LIFETIME; CHILDREN'S LIFETIME

The things with which people are concerned fall somewhere on this space-time graph. Some hold that the majority of the world's population is concerned with matters that affect only family and friends over a short period of time. Few are concerned about the world or about the long-term future. The close time-space frame of reference of most people makes it difficult for them to understand social change over the long course of human history and to imagine the tremendous changes that await us.

Source: *The Limits to Growth: A Report for THE CLUB OF ROME'S Projects on the Predicament of Mankind*, by Donella H. Meadows, Dennis L. Meadows, Jorgen Randers, William W. Behrens III. A Potomac Associates book published by Universe Books, New York, 1972. Graphics by Potomac Associates.

Stages in the Adoption Process

An idea is said to be adopted when it results in changed behavior. Believing that it is a good idea to be vaccinated against polio, for example, is not adoption of the idea. Adoption, or full acceptance, comes only when the person receives the vaccine. Research has demonstrated that the adoption process consists of a number of stages (Rogers and Shoemaker, 1971). It is not a matter of learning about something and then adopting it or not adopting it, nor is it a matter of ideas somehow automatically filtering down to the masses from those who first accept them. The stages through which individuals adopt an idea can be described as follows:

1. *Awareness stage.* The individual learns of the existence of a new idea but lacks information about it.

Before this Idaho potato farmer adopted the new farming equipment he had to be aware it was available, to become interested in it, and to decide it was wise to buy it.

2. *Interest stage.* The individual seeks additional information about the new idea.
3. *Evaluation stage.* The individual makes mental application of the new idea to his or her situation and decides whether or not to try it.
4. *Trial stage.* The individual actually applies the new idea, frequently on a small scale, to determine its usefulness in his or her own situation.
5. *Adoption stage.* The individual uses the new idea continuously or on a full scale.

The acceptance of new ideas does not necessarily follow this scheme, however. For example, the trial stage of using polio vaccine really means that one has accepted the idea. Nevertheless, recognition that adoption is a process rather than an instantaneous act has proved of value. Other research has shown that the mass media, such as newspapers and television, are helpful at the awareness stage but that personal contacts are better at the evaluation stage. It has also been found that when it is possible to use it, the trial stage can be very important. Getting families to actually try home canning of vegetables, or getting a peasant community to dig a well or two for drinking water often moves them a step closer to full adoption. For people who have moved to the evaluation stage of mentally weighing the merits of an idea, time and effort can be better spent getting them to try the idea rather than supplying them with more information about it. Research on the adoption process has thus led to strategies for producing social change.

Other research has concentrated on the social and psychological differences between those who are first to try new ideas, those who adopt them later, and those who are the last to try them or who reject them. This research, too, has practical applications. It has been found that the "innovators"—those first to adopt a new practice—are better educated and have higher status in the community. However, such people often have little influence in the community when it comes to the new practice. Perhaps it is felt that because of their wealth and position, innovators can afford to take risks and that just because they try something, it does not mean necessarily that it is a good idea. Someone wishing to bring about change, therefore, would be better off digging a little deeper in the community to discover who the true opinion leaders are. Working with these people can speed up the adoption of a practice.

Knowledge and application of adoption research findings can be used for good or ill. For example, the use of these findings can help speed up adoption of farming practices, home maintenance ideas, nutrition and health practices, and new teaching methods; but this research can also be used to get people to adopt ideas that will hurt them, other people, or the environment. Some of the applications of this research, such as the introduction of family planning practices in places with a serious problem or improving health measures in a society plagued with a high death rate, have had relatively

Change and Social Values

If an idea, invention, or discovery is entirely hostile, or simply irrelevant, to the values and beliefs of a society, it will be rejected or neglected, either temporarily or permanently. In Chapter 3, we saw that, in the eleventh century, the Scandinavians made little use of their discovery of what they called Vinland—the North American continent. Their culture and their values and beliefs simply did not motivate them to attempt any major colonization; it would not have benefited them in any way. That idea may seem shocking to us today, but then, there is a vast difference between the values of our society today and their society then. The Scandinavians were a vigorous, active, inquisitive people (their discovery of Vinland, so far from home, attests to that), yet they made no use of what to us would have been an exciting discovery.

We live in an age created by cultures that have increasingly developed the *value of change.* In both significant and trivial ways, we have come to consider change not merely a fact of life but a value—something to be desired and sought after. The evidence is everywhere around us, although chiefly in the material realm of our culture. Our economy depends, in part, on our acceptance of change. Many people change their present car for a new one as often as they can afford to, and it has been common knowledge for years that car makers introduce cosmetic design changes to encourage rapid turnover.

Curiously enough, while change itself has become one of our values, we

A kind of cultural lag within technology is represented by the use of both traditional and modern farming practices in India.

change the values themselves very slowly and with great reluctance. This paradox seems to relate to another value of ours—one that is more refined in the United States than anywhere else in the world—the value of materialism. Most of us are more receptive to and curious about new *things* than we are about new ideas. This cautiousness seems to be a basic human trait and is the chief cause of **cultural lag**—the disparity between our material culture and our values and beliefs. To cite a familiar example of such lag, consider the generous size and natural abundance of this country in relation to the libertarian social and political values that are the nation's foundation. These elements have produced a complex set of norms and folkways expressing our values of individual freedom and privacy. In the last decade or so, however, it has become clear that we are polluting our environment, destroying its natural beauty, and rapidly exhausting its finite supplies of many resources. But our personal right to be wasteful of resources by perpetuating the "throw-away culture" is being firmly maintained against the facts.

We have long believed that the human mastery of nature is a fact and a right—a value. The disparity between our environmental circumstances and our values, which worsen the crisis by resisting its remedies, is a painful example of cultural lag. Many scientists and ecologists maintain that unless we change our values and norms that relate to the environment voluntarily, the environment will change them for us.

CHANGE AND THE FUTURE

In this chapter we have discussed social change as it relates to technology, mass movements, the adoption of new ideas, and social values. Only passing consideration has been given to the future of these and other influences on change. No one, of course, really knows what the future holds in store for us. But a whole new field of study, called *futurology,* has arisen in an attempt to identify the trends and directions of future change. Issues of just one publication, *The Futurist,* contain fascinating articles by engineers, theologians, business leaders, architects, and scientists, among others. These people are not utopian dreamers but realists who are trying to make sense out of present trends and to determine where these trends are leading us.

Everything points to the conclusion that the *rate* of change, already much more rapid now than it was in the past, will continue to increase. Major and minor changes will follow more quickly on the heels of earlier changes, giving us little time to catch up and to become accustomed to the new. It is easy to recognize the quickening pace of change in the area of technological development. Take, for example, the field of human communication. Prior to 3500 B.C., information was stored in human brains and was transmitted by speech. The first use of external memory banks and retrieval systems

SOCIAL AND CULTURAL CHANGE

came about 5000 years ago, with the Sumerian invention of cuneiform writing on clay tablets. The invention of papyrus and then of paper reduced bulk and facilitated transportation of written messages, but no really significant changes occurred until 500 years ago, when movable type for printing was invented. By 1850, the telegraph was in operation; 25 years after that we had the telephone. By 1920, we had the radio, and 25 years later, television. Now, satellites, lasers, holography, magnetic tape, and electronic computers create a vast mechanism for communication.

Or consider transportation. If we wanted to travel from one place to another in 6000 B.C., about the best we could do would be to hitch a ride on a camel and go six miles per hour. It took more than 4000 years to improve on this mode of transportation. The chariot, invented about 1600 B.C., made travel at up to 20 miles per hour possible. Thirty-five hundred years later, the steam locomotive came along, boosting that top speed to 100 miles per hour. Then, a mere 60 years after that, we invented the airplane, capable of speeds of up to 400 miles per hour. Today, about 50 years since the first working airplane, we have rockets, whose speeds exceed 4000 miles per hour.

What is significant about these changes is the steadily decreasing period of time between each development. The same accelerating growth is evident in virtually all technological fields, in the generation of new information, in the ability to control the environment, and in many other areas. The changing role of women in the family and in society has come about rapidly. Our ideas as to what constitutes a good family size have quickly gone from the three- or four-child family of 25 years ago to the one- or two-child ideal family of today. Civil rights issues that festered for about 100 years after the Civil War are now met with demands that something be done, and of course, much has been done.

Rapid change has become a fact of life in West Germany as well as in the United States. Many of these goods, now readily accepted, did not exist just a couple of decades ago.

Rapid change will become the way of life in the future. Experience has shown, however, that rapid change can produce problems of adjustment and lead to discontent, depending in part, as we saw in the discussion of cultural lag, on what it is that is changing. Should full equality of the sexes come rapidly, as it promises to do, it will be upon us before many have had time to become comfortable with the idea of women in positions of high authority, as business leaders, and in roles requiring the supervision of men. Changes in technological growth, energy consumption, and our impact on the environment are likely to come quickly, or at least they had better, if we are to survive.

One change that many people may find hard to accept is the move toward social organization and cooperation on a global level. This situation is unprecedented in the history of our species. Yet, the nations and peoples of the world are so intricately bound up with one another that, sooner or later, we will be forced to admit that we are faced with species-related problems rather than problems of this or that society. Even today, oil from the same Arabian wells runs tractors in the United States, Japan, Germany, and many other countries. Food production is a specieswide problem, a lot bigger in its dimensions than the problem of our maintaining good relations with the oil-producing countries.

It is interesting that science fiction writers who posit life on other planets, space exploration, and colonization of the stars almost always refer to "Federated Earth" or some other political-economic unit. Such writers seem to simply assume that technologically sophisticated people will come to recognize that they are one people sharing a single planet. But, many will find this a hard lesson to learn.

In this chapter, we have seen that all societies change. Sociologists, whether they subscribe to structural-functional theory, conflict theory, or some other theory, attempt to explain social change. To deal with what is unique in the human experience—the rapidity of change in modern society—we had to investigate how technology has penetrated our lives. Another element of social change is important enough to devote a full chapter to—the population of our society. Social demography, the topic of the next chapter, deals with changes in population size and with how these changes affect and are affected by social interaction.

SUMMARY

1. Many theories have been put forth to account for social change. According to the **cyclical theory,** societies are destined to go through stages of growth followed by stages of decline. The most notable cyclical theorists were Spengler, Toynbee, and Sorokin (who felt that civilizations alternate between an **ideational stage** and a **sensate stage**).

2. According to **evolutionary theory,** societies evolve in stages, with each

stage being better than the previous one. Evolutionary theorists include Spencer, Marx, and Durkheim.

3. According to the **structural-functional model,** social change is a process that leads society toward a state of equilibrium. As change occurs, the various structures of society adjust themselves so that they can continue to perform their functions.

4. According to the **conflict model,** struggles between contending forces in society are the source of social change. The ideas of Marx influenced this approach, and Dahrendorf is its chief contemporary proponent.

5. Social change may be achieved through **collective behavior,** such as the actions of **crowds,** public opinion, and social movements. A **social movement** is a relatively long-lasting collective enterprise formed to bring about or prevent social change. Social movements tend to involve large numbers of people and to be widespread geographically. Although social movements are informally organized, formal groups and voluntary associations may arise from them.

6. Among the types of social movements are **reform movements, conservative movements, progressive movements,** and **revolutionary movements.** Most social movements go through four major stages: (1) a *preliminary stage,* in which a specific issue arises and a leader appears; (2) a *popular stage,* in which large numbers of people identify with the movement; (3) a *formal stage,* in which goals are clarified and organized groups appear; and (4) an *institutional stage,* in which the movement is integrated into the legal and social structure of society.

7. Social movements will continue to exist and to find success as long as: (1) there are important social problems that people have strong ideas about, (2) people feel that group activity can affect social change, and (3) mass communication continues to be rapid and relatively uncontrolled.

8. Adoption of new ideas is said to go through a five-stage process: awareness, interest, evaluation, trial, and adoption. Knowing this process can help societies speed up the adoption of a particular idea.

9. In American society, change has become a value in itself — something to be desired and sought after. However, Americans are slow to change their values. For example, the value of materialism that has long been a part of America is now under criticism. The fact that people hold onto this value, despite potential damage to the environment, is an example of **cultural lag** — a disparity between material culture and values.

10. The rate of change in the world today is much more rapid than in the past, and it is increasing. Such rapid change can produce problems of adjustment and can lead to discontent, unless society prepares people to deal with the constant change.

UNDERSTANDING CONFLICT AND CHANGE

KEY TERMS

collective behavior
conflict model
conservative movement
crowd
cultural lag
cyclical theory of change
evolutionary theory of change
ideational stage
progressive movement
reform movement
revolutionary movement
sensate stage
social movement
structural-functional model

SUGGESTED READINGS

Applebaum, Richard P. *Theories of Social Change.* Chicago: Markham, 1970.
   The author presents and classifies the major theoretical frameworks used to account for social change.

Ash, Robert T. *Social Movements in America.* 2nd ed. Chicago: Markham, 1977.
   The author examines past and recent social movements, including those of the 1960s, and emphasizes the economic factors involved.

Edwards, Lyford. *The Natural History of Revolutions.* Chicago: University of Chicago Press, 1970.
   Edwards explores the relationship between revolution and modernization. An important book on social change.

Etzioni, Amitai. *Studies in Social Change.* New York: Holt, Rinehart and Winston, 1966.
   A short book dealing with strategies and theories of social change. It also includes a number of case studies.

Lauer, Robert H., ed. *Social Movements and Social Change.* Carbondale: Southern Illinois University Press, 1976.
   An interesting collection of articles showing how social movements and social change are interrelated.

McPherson, William, ed. *Ideology and Change.* Palo Alto, Calif.: National Press, 1973.
   A reader on social thought, radicalism, fundamentals, ideology, and propaganda and the effects of these systems of thought on social change.

Moore, Wilbert E. *Order and Change: Essays in Comparative Sociology.* New York: John Wiley & Sons, 1967.
   The author focuses on order and change in various societies and the effects of modernization on these processes.

Schneider, Kenneth R. *Destiny of Change.* New York: Holt, Rinehart and Winston, 1968.
   An analysis of the effect of industrialization, urbanization, and bureaucratization on the personality of the individual.

Smelser, Neil J. *Theory of Collective Behavior.* New York: The Free Press, 1963.
   Smelser develops a paradigm for the analysis of collective behavior, especially such phenomena as the panic, the craze, and the social movement.

Theobald, Robert, ed. *Futures Conditional.* New York: Bobbs-Merrill, 1972.
   A collection of readings, from sociology to science fiction, designed to orient the student to possible futures.

Toffler, Alvin. *Future Shock.* New York: Random House, 1970.
   A fascinating work on social change in modern society. Toffler argues that the lack of permanence of both products and social institutions is psychologically disorienting.

In the last few hundred years, the population of the world has grown tremendously. Only recently, however, have humans been able to study population scientifically and to understand what is now called the "population explosion." The results of human efforts to deal with population problems in the world, as well as in the United States, will affect everyone's lives in one way or another.

The scientific study of population is called social demography. Social demographers do much more than count people. They study the composition of societies: the age, sex, and marital status of the people, for example. They seek to explain how the composition of a population changes and how other factors, such as the interplay of birth and death rates, affect societies' numbers. You will see that there are social explanations for demographic changes within populations and differences between populations. For example, the poor have more children than the rich, and the infant death rate is higher among the poor.

Once you have a basic understanding of how demographers go about studying human populations, you will find it fascinating to learn about the tremendous population growth in the United States and in the world. It is safe to say that, for the rest of your life, newspapers will continue to report on population pressures in underdeveloped countries, on changes in the birth and death rates in our own society, and on the geographic migrations of people. A general understanding of social demography should allow you to make more sense of what you read and to realize the implications of such information for your own life.

14
Social Demography

In November 1970, a giant tidal wave swept the Bay of Bengal and killed 300,000 Pakistanis. But, within 15 days, 300,000 babies were born in Pakistan, bringing the population back to where it had been before the catastrophe. Almost a year later, another tidal wave hit the coast of India and killed an estimated 15,000 persons, slightly fewer people than are born there in six hours. It is tragic and frightening to realize that nature can unleash its fury and instantly destroy huge numbers of people. Yet, when the deaths from these occurrences are related to the births in these countries, we find a dramatic illustration of the population explosion in underdeveloped nations. This, too, is frightening—and even tragic.

World population rose from about 2.5 billion in 1950 to over 4 billion in 1975. With current birth and death rates, there are over 197,000 more people every day than there were the day before. In the United States, there are now 100 million more people than there were in the year in which I was born. Things don't just *seem* more crowded—they really are!

What would happen if our own and the world's rates of growth were to continue as they are? Or, what would happen if somehow we could achieve zero population growth throughout the world? It would be foolish to promise answers to these questions, as important as they are. The best we can promise is to describe how sociologists who specialize in the study of populations seek answers to these and other serious questions.

The subject matter of **social demography**—the analysis of human populations—should be of concern to all of us. One of the crucial problems facing all humanity is how to deal with a surging growth in the population. The population time bomb and the fury it can unleash cannot be ignored, and we consider such concerns later in the chapter. But, demographers do much more than calculate rates of growth and total populations. They seek to explain *how* human populations grow and change, *why* they do so, and what difference it makes. In this chapter, we will be exploring not only how demographers gather data and what the data are, but the implications of these findings, especially for our own society.

THE GOALS OF SOCIAL DEMOGRAPHY

Perhaps the easiest way to begin our many-faceted task is to imagine a hypothetical community and to ask what kind of information the demographer would like to collect about it. Ideally, the demographer would want to know the age, sex, and physical location of each person, and often, the marital status and race of each. Information on these individual characteristics is gathered for two purposes. The first is to develop a description of the social system under study. If the data were complete, we would know how many people live in the community, the proportion of males to females, the number of children and old people, and so forth. Second, we would obtain a fuller description of the community if we examined different combinations of these factors, such as relating age and sex, or age, sex, and marital status. By such analyses we could give a more meaningful statistical description of the community than we would by simply saying that 50,000 people live in it.

A demographic description of a community can be extremely valuable, even without knowing how the community evolved to its present state or where it is heading. For example, if we found that there are more four year olds than six year olds, we would know that more schoolrooms would be needed, not just two years from now but for the next twelve years. Again, knowing how many people will soon become 18 years old tells us how many jobs or places in college will be needed.

Or, suppose that we wanted to know how many young people should be encouraged to leave a given community. We would need to find out how many young people actually leave the community. This can be done by analyzing two time periods and comparing the number of persons between 15 and 19 years old at the first period with the number between 20 and 24 years old five years later. We could further determine whether more males than females left the community or more unmarried than married individuals left. To take another example, a simple count of the number of people over age 65 would indicate what kinds of social services, homes, recreational facilities, and hospitals are needed for senior citizens.

Social demographers thus go well beyond a merely descriptive analysis of a community or nation. In sociological and social psychological studies, basic demographic factors are used in two different ways. On the one hand, they are treated as the **independent variables** (those that produce change), and the social and cultural factors are treated as the **dependent variables** (those that are changed or that show change). The analyst seeks to discover how the demographic factors affect society. For example, will the changing age structure make the community more conservative politically? Will the present growth rate add to problems of pollution and overcrowding? What are the effects of the current death rate? Perhaps the deaths of older people give younger people a feeling that there are ample opportunities to assume leadership roles and to effect changes in the community. Questions such as these clearly suggest that demographic factors have an effect, for good or for ill, on the society.

Social demographers also look at the reverse situation: how various features of a society affect the population structure and demographic processes. In such analyses, the social and cultural characteristics are considered the independent variables, while the demographic factors are the dependent variables. Demographers may examine how the level of industrialization affects the migration rate, or how a group's aspirations for a higher standard of living influence the number of children couples choose to have. One could also study how health knowledge or the availability of medical services affects the death rate for, perhaps, persons in a particular age group or social class.

Although treating demographic factors as either independent or dependent variables is useful for conducting studies, it often oversimplifies the matter. Social and cultural factors and demographics often interact in far more complex ways. Consider the following hypothetical situation. Because a demographic survey reveals that a certain community has a potential labor force of young women, a light industry that usually employs women to assemble small electronic components decides to locate in the community. If the employment opportunities encourage unmarried women to postpone marriage and married ones to postpone having children, the birth rate would be reduced. A continued decline in the birth rate would eventually produce an unbalanced population, with too few people of working age, which in turn would encourage migration into the community, perhaps changing its ethnic, racial, or religious composition. Thus, two or three decades after the original demographic survey, we might find a very changed community, both culturally and demographically, which would have evolved through a complex interplay of demographic and social factors.

GATHERING DEMOGRAPHIC DATA

Basic demographic statistics are gathered in three different ways: by censuses; by registration of events, such as births and deaths, when they occur; and by surveys of a population sample or studies of special groups within a population.

Census Data

A **census** counts the number of individuals in the population of a given area, such as a nation or state, at a certain time. According to the United States Constitution, a census must be taken every ten years, so that seats in the House of Representatives can be apportioned among the states on the basis of population size. But, over the years, the scope of these censuses has been greatly enlarged to gain considerably more information. So important is this information that, beginning in 1985, a census will be taken every five years. A partial list of the kinds of information reported in the census is presented in Table 14.1.

Many informative analyses could be made to describe the population at the time of the census and to indicate how it has changed between censuses. For example, a women's liberation group might study the trend in the number of years of school completed by each sex. They could discover whether relatively more or fewer women earn higher degrees today than they did in the recent past. Furthermore, they could compare the median incomes of fe-

SOCIAL DEMOGRAPHY

TABLE 14.1   Types of Data Reported in Population Census and Special Studies*

Personal Characteristics	Educational Characteristics
Age	Total enrollment in schools
Sex	Highest grade in school
Marital Status	completed
Race	College degrees awarded

Economic Characteristics
  Employment in major industrial groups
  Employment in major occupational groups
  Employment by sex and marital status
  Number of hours worked
  Unemployment
  Family income
  Per capita income
  Characteristics of low income families

Residential Characteristics
  Distribution of population in regions
  Rural-urban distribution
  Population in urbanized areas
  Characteristics of farm population
  In- and out-migration
  Condition of housing
  Plumbing facilities available

Family and Fertility
  Number of families
  Size of family households
  Number of children born

*Listing is incomplete. A better idea of the scope of the reports and studies of the Bureau of the Census can be obtained by consulting a library card catalog under *U.S. Bureau of the Census.*

male and male workers. To cite another example, studies of median family income would reveal whether poverty is decreasing or increasing. If age, geographic location, and other data were included in a study of poverty, we would have a better understanding of it, and we would be better equipped to pinpoint selected groups for social action. As a final example, the number of children born to mothers of specified ages is an important indication of what to expect in continued population growth.

Because census data are gathered by counting people and asking them questions, they are not always as accurate as one might think (Spiegelman, 1968). For example, a recent census in Hungary discovered considerably more married women than married men, an obvious impossibility. Apparently, divorced men reported themselves as divorced. But, in this Roman Catholic country, divorced women, perhaps considering their marriages not truly dissolved because the Church does not grant divorces, reported themselves married.

Other types of errors have been discovered. Entire households may be missed in a census. Frequently, black male adults are undercounted, as many are not permanently attached to a household or live in apartments that have no registered address. Homeless individuals, black or white, are not counted. And since they are likely to be unemployed, a typical census therefore undercounts unemployment and poverty, thus providing a low estimate of the need for social services in a society. Sometimes ages are misstated; very old people tend to exaggerate their ages, and some people round off their ages, saying, for example, that they are 30 when they are in fact 28 or 31. Those who enter the country illegally are not likely to report accurately on their place of birth and may falsify other information as well.

Even totally objective data must be interpreted. The same facts, whether they deal with the number of children under five years of age, housing conditions, per capita income, or whatever, can be used in different ways. They may support one person's satisfacation with the American way of life, another's pessimistic outlook, or still another's ingrained feeling that a total revolution is needed to correct a dismal situation.

Registration Data

Demographic data are also obtained from registrations of important life events: births, marriages, divorces, and deaths. These data are called **vital statistics.** Such data are collected when the event occurs, and so the information differs from what we get from a census. When a marriage is performed, the date of the marriage is recorded, as well as the age and previous marital status of the spouses. We can tabulate all the marriages that occur in a given month or year in a given place, and by comparing this information with records for previous months or years, we can determine whether the marriage rate is going up or down. When a census is taken, we obtain information on everyone who has the status "married" at the time the enumeration is made. But, some people were married the day before the census taker called, some five years before, and so on. Still, the census gives us a record of the proportion of the population that is married, and we can determine whether this proportion changed between censuses. Each source of data—statistics, records, and censuses—is useful for different kinds of studies.

Governments have recorded vital statistics for a long time. Apparently, the Incas of Peru had a system for counting their births and deaths. In the sixteenth century, Henry VIII ordered the clergy throughout England and Wales to record baptisms, marriages, and deaths. In the United States, beginning in 1842, Massachusetts required that births, marriages, and deaths be recorded. Not until 1900 did the federal government annually collect national death statistics, and not until 1915 did it begin to annually collect national birth statistics.

Today, information in addition to the vital event itself is usually obtained and recorded. With births, for example, it is common to record the mother's and father's age and race and whether it is the mother's first, second, third, or later child. Most states record the mother's marital status, allowing for compilations of illegitimate births. These facts can be cross-tabulated and analyzed. We can determine the birth rate for specific racial groups or determine which age group of women contributes most of the illegitimate births.

Despite laws that require the recording and reporting of vital events, the records are not actually complete. Through error or oversight marriages sometimes are not reported. The marital status of mothers can be falsified. In the past, many births went unrecorded, particularly when births took place in the home and without the assistance of a physician. Because the large proportion of births takes place in hospitals today, we now have a far more complete registration of births. It has been estimated that over 99 percent of all white births and about 97 percent of all nonwhite births are currently reported.

Surveys and Special Studies

Each month, the Bureau of the Census conducts a population survey to gather some of the same kinds of information obtained in the regular census. The surveys allow us to keep up with changes in the size and makeup of the population. Results are published under the title *Current Population Reports,* and each report usually deals with a specific topic, such as the number and types of families who have or have not moved within the past year, and the marital status of the population. In these surveys, a sample of the population, up to 50,000 households, is selected for interviewing. The findings thus vary slightly from what is obtained when a full census is made.

In addition to these surveys, the Bureau of the Census conducts many special analyses of demographic data. One such recent study dealt with the probability of marriages, by age and race, and the probability of divorce, by number of years married. Another special study was devoted to the social and economic status of blacks. These special studies are quite valuable. They often use data collected in the special surveys, but because they consist of detailed analyses rather than a mere report of head counts, they sometimes are not issued until several years after the survey was taken.

ANALYZING DEMOGRAPHIC DATA

Demographers use a variety of statistical methods to examine the data they have collected. We will look at only a couple of these methods here: population pyramids and dependency ratios.

Population Pyramids

Demographers have developed a number of ways to display statistical data. One way of visually displaying the age and sex composition of a society is to construct a **population pyramid,** such as those shown in Figure 14.1. Each

FIGURE 14.1 Population Pyramids

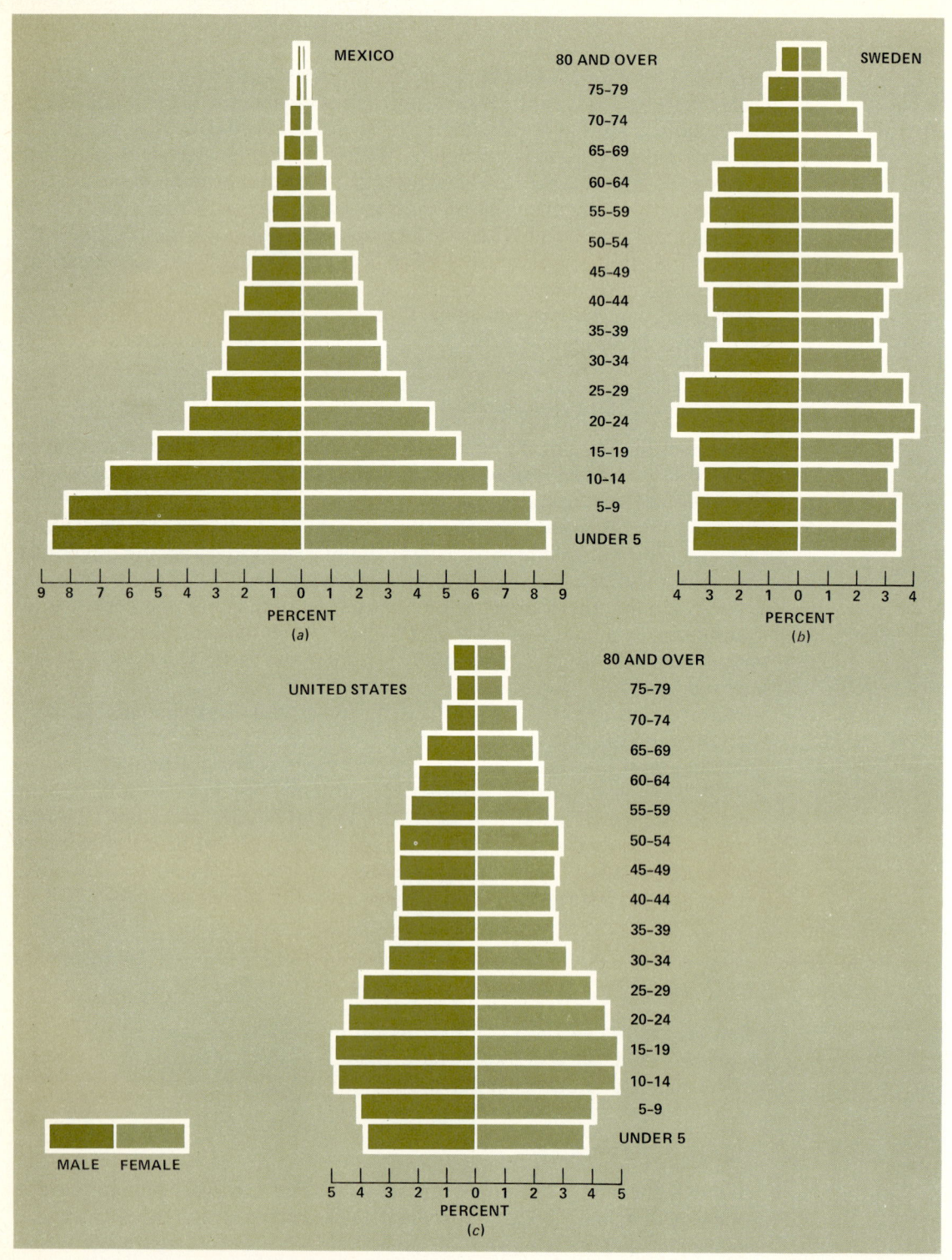

Source: 1972 *Demographic Yearbook* (New York, United Nations, 1972), p. 204.

bar represents the percentage of each age group in the total population; the bars on the left side represent the percentage of males in the age group, and those on the right represent the percentage of females.

Pyramid (a) is typical of societies with high birth rates and high death rates. Note that the longest bar is at the base of the pyramid, suggesting that there were more births in later years than there were in previous years. Moving up the pyramid, the increasingly shorter bars are also due to deaths, which take a larger toll at each older age group.

Pyramid (b) represents the population of Sweden in 1972. Note that the four lowest bars are essentially the same length, indicating that there are the same number of people in each of the lowest age groups. A pyramid like this is typical of countries in which the population is growing very slowly, if at all. The bulge for the age groups 20–24 and 25–29 is caused by the high birth rates following World War II.

Several important things can be noted in pyramid (c), which represents the age and sex composition of the population of the United States in 1975. Beginning at the base, it is clear that the group of young children is smaller than it used to be. The bulge in the 15–19 age group corresponds to the high point of the post-World War II baby boom in 1957. The bars representing the age groups 35–39 and 40–44 are shorter than one would expect, and they are also shorter than those for the next higher age groups. These notches in the pyramid are caused by the extraordinarily low birth rate during the depression decade, 1930–1939. Finally, even without measuring the bars for males and females age 60 and over, it is obvious that there are more females than males. Males of this age do not typically move to another country, so it can be assumed that the death rate is higher for older males than for females.

Dependency Ratios

Another way of analyzing demographic data is to determine a population's **dependency ratio** — a figure representing the ratio of people of working age to the number who are either too young or too old to work. It is usually computed by totalling the number of dependent children (age 14 and younger) and the number of dependent older people (age 65 and older) and dividing by the number of people age 15–64. These age groups are not entirely appropriate for industrial societies, since many youth remain dependent to age eighteen or older. But the age categories have become standardized internationally and allow us to compare countries.

The lower the dependency ratio, the fewer people of nonworking age there are relative to those who are potential workers. At the turn of the century, the dependency ratio in the United States was 63, but it has now dropped to 55, about the same as that found in England, Denmark, and other industrialized countries. In contrast, countries such as the Dominican Republic and Egypt have a dependency ratio close to 100, indicating that for every person of working age there is one dependent old or young person. Developing countries usually have a high dependency ratio because of the large number of children that have to be supported. While the proportion of old people in the United States has increased, our birth rate has declined considerably, leaving us with fewer individuals who have to be supported by those within their productive years.

Thus, we can see that simply by knowing the age and sex composition of populations, we can construct population pyramids, compute dependency ratios, and develop other analyses to tell us a great deal about the history of a society, its present situation, and where it is going in the future. Age and sex are also important influences on three major processes studied by social demographers: fertility, morality, and migration. These processes themselves profoundly influence the characteristics of a population. We will now look into these three processes in detail, explaining common methods used for studying them. We will also be exploring some of the findings in these areas, particularly as they relate to the United States.

FERTILITY

Fertility, the number of births within a group in a given period, has a profound effect on a group's destiny. Without enough births, a group would die out. Today, many fear that there are too many births and that our planet is in as much trouble as it would be if there were too few births. But terms like "too few" and "too many" are vague. For not only can births be counted, it can also be determined how rapidly or slowly the birth rate is changing. Social demographers indicate how fertility affects society—other than its obvious effect on population size—and how social factors affect fertility. First let us see how fertility is measured.

Fertility Statistics

A simple measure of fertility is the number of births that occur within a specific time for a specific group. As you can see in Table 14.2, in recent years, about three million babies were born each year in the United States. We can look back to, say, 1957 and note that the sheer number of births per year has been dropping. Turning to 1976, we could compare 3.1 million births with the number in other countries. During 1976 in India, there were 23 million births; in the People's Republic of China, over 25 million; and in Sweden, about 110,000.

Sheer numbers are both fascinating and full of useful information. They can tell us whether our society will need more or fewer diapers, diphtheria shots, or baby blankets, and they can tell us whether there are more Indians than Americans born each year. The number of births over a period of time can suggest the rate at which a society is growing. We can note, for example, that the over four million babies born in the United States in 1957 reached

TABLE 14.2 Number of Live Births, Birth Rates, and Fertility Rates (United States, 1910–1977)

Year	Number of Births	Crude Birth Rate	Fertility Rate
1910	2,777,000	—	126.8
1920	2,950,000	27.7	117.9
1930	2,618,000	21.3	89.2
1940	2,559,000	19.4	79.9
1950	3,632,000	24.1	106.2
1951	3,823,000	24.9	111.5
1952	3,913,000	25.1	113.9
1953	3,965,000	25.1	115.2
1954	4,078,000	25.3	118.1
1955	4,104,000	25.0	118.5
1956	4,218,000	25.2	121.2
1957	4,308,000	25.3	122.9
1958	4,255,000	24.5	120.2
1959	4,295,000	24.3	118.0
1960	4,257,850	23.7	117.2
1961	4,268,326	23.3	112.2
1962	4,167,362	22.4	108.5
1963	4,098,020	21.7	105.0
1964	4,027,490	21.0	96.6
1965	3,760,358	19.4	91.3
1966	3,606,274	18.4	87.6
1967	3,533,000	17.8	85.1
1968	3,470,000	17.5	85.5
1969	3,539,000	17.7	87.6
1970	3,718,000	18.2	87.6
1971	3,559,000	17.3	82.3
1972	3,256,000	15.6	73.4
1973	3,141,000	15.0	69.3
1974	3,166,000	15.0	68.4
1975	3,149,000	14.8	66.7
1976	3,100,000	14.7	66.2
1977	3,133,000	15.3	67.4

Source: U.S. Department of Health, Education, and Welfare, *Vital Statistics of the United States, 1966,* vol. 1 (Washington, D.C.: U.S. Government Printing Office, 1967); and *Monthly Vital Statistics Report,* various issues.

marriageable age (18–21) between 1975 and 1978 and are beginning to have babies of their own.

The Crude Birth Rate Whether we look at our own society at different times or compare different societies, the sheer number of births does not tell us enough about the fertility pattern of the group. Demographers have other measures as well. The **crude birth rate** measures the number of births at a given time against the number of people in the society at the same time; it is expressed as the number of births per 1,000 persons in the population. The crude birth rate of the United States is available as far back as 1910, and for many other countries it is available at least as far back as 1945.

A look at the United States data makes it clear that, since 1910, the crude birth rate first declined, reaching a low point during the depression years, then began to rise steadily. (Not shown in Table 14.2 is a dip in 1944-1945, when many men were out of the country fighting in World War II.) The rise continued until 1957, when the crude birth rate reached 25.3; thereafter, it began to decline again, with a slight upsurge for a couple of years. The present crude birth rate, 15.3, is nearly the lowest in our history.

The fact that the crude birth rate is calculated from the total population is one of its limitations, for only women between certain ages can have babies. Thus, two societies with identical population sizes could have widely different crude birth rates because of differences in their age and sex compositions. A higher proportion of women at childbearing ages will create a higher crude birth rate, other things being equal. But, alas, other things are seldom equal. What we need, then, is a measure of the actual reproductive performance of women.

The General Fertility Rate

The **general fertility rate** is the number of births in a year per 1,000 women age 15 to 44. Fertility rates also can be computed for narrower age groups, such as women 15 to 19, 20 to 24, and so on. (Fertility rates for such narrower age spans are called specific fertility rates.) In the depression year of 1932, the general fertility rate was 81.7, and it was not much lower in 1940 (79.9); today's rate is about 66. Yet, today there are over half a million more births annually than there were in 1940. The reason is that there are now more women in their reproductive years, so even though they are averaging fewer births per woman, the total number of births is still larger than it was 40 years ago. The high birth rate in the mid-1950s can be attributed, in part, to the fact that there were more women of childbearing age, but it was primarily due to the fact that women were having more children—that is, the fertility rate was higher.

Fertility rates in the United States are highest for women between ages 20 and 29. In 1975, there were 18.2 million women in this age group. By 1980, this number will increase to almost 20 million; and by 1985, to about 20.5 million. Our marriage rate continues to be high, so we can assume that most of these women will marry. Obviously, when 20 million married couples go to bed each night, more conceptions are likely to occur than in a population of two million fewer women. Yet, will there actually be more conceptions and births? Although the general fertility rate has dropped rapidly, there still may be more births in 1980 than in recent years, thus making a larger base of potential mothers in the year 2000 and after. Whether potential mothers, now and in the future, actually bear children, and at what rate they do so, depends, in large part, on the social factors that affect fertility.

Large families are not necessarily contributing to the population problem. A combination of natural and adopted children gave this couple the family size they wanted.

Social Factors Affecting Fertility

Fertility is so obviously biological—intercourse, conception, development of the fetus, birth—that it can be amazing to discover that social factors do influence fertility. For example, the number of births varies with the seasons. According to a study that lasted more than ten years, the peak months for births are August and September, and the low months are in the spring, usually April and May (Pasamanick, Dinitz, and Knobloch, 1959). Folk belief has been that during the cold winter months couples engage in sexual intercourse more frequently, and during the hot, sticky summer months less frequently. This would account for the seasonal pattern of births. However, the widespread use of air conditioning might be expected to have altered this seasonal variation, but so far, it does not seem to have done so.

Because so many couples in the United States use birth control methods, it could be that the seasonal variations in conceptions reflect the fact that more couples decide to attempt conception at one time of the year than at others. If so, we must ask why parents seem to prefer to have their children at certain times of the year rather than at others. Since the seasonal variation in births is not large, and since a high proportion of births are first births, and thus, first conceptions, perhaps the seasonal peak is related to the seasonal peak in marriages. Whatever the answer, we can see that social factors obviously affect the birth rate.

Socioeconomic Status Sociologists have long known that social class and fertility are strongly related. Whether we describe social class by income, educational level, or occupation, the conclusion is the same: the higher the social class, the smaller the family. This relationship existed before widespread birth control information was available, and certainly before Margaret Sanger opened her first birth control clinic in 1916. For example, the New York State Census of 1865 showed that wives of unskilled laborers had the most children, wives of skilled laborers had fewer, and wives of white-collar workers had the fewest (Bash, 1955). Even at this early date, then, higher-class couples somehow were able to control their fertility, and they continued to do so until 1940. Between 1940 and 1952, however, the fertility difference between classes narrowed. As economic conditions improved after the depression years, higher-class couples began to have more children than previously, thus bringing their fertility closer to that of lower-class couples.

Class differences in fertility, while narrowing slowly, are still very much with us. In 1974, among married women age 15 to 44, the college educated had an average of 1.5 children; high school graduates 2.0; and those with less than eight years of school 3.5. Income and occupation showed the same pattern. Wealthier families and those with high-prestige occupations have fewer children than families at lower levels of society. A recent study found that 7.5 percent of young college-graduate wives do not expect to have any children, while this was true of only 2.2 percent of wives who did not graduate from high school. As we look at the future, then, it appears that low socioeconomic status will continue to be associated with high fertility.

Values, Knowledge, and Fertility Such a relationship between socioeconomic status and fertility does not provide its own explanation. The numerous studies that have been done to explain this relationship are roughly of two kinds: (1) those that focus on values, attitudes, and other social-psychological characteristics of people, and (2) those that concentrate on differences in contraceptive knowledge (Kenkel, 1977). Studies of the first type hypothesize that working-class people have their own outlook on family size, either wanting many children or not really caring how many they have. It is also hypothesized that the fertility values of lower-class people are influenced by their having been raised in large families or having migrated from rural areas, where fertility has traditionally been high. But recent studies indicate that attitudes toward desirable family size do not differ as much by social class as was once supposed (Whelpton et al., 1966).

It may be difficult to believe that, despite the efforts of Planned Parenthood, despite the contraceptive advertisements in women's magazines, and despite the contraceptive devices often displayed and always available at the corner drugstore, people of the lower classes still do not know how to control conception. No one seems to be trying to keep contraceptive knowledge from them—quite the contrary. Even so, information and the ability to make choices are not the same thing. Lacking money, the poor are less able to consult private doctors or to become able in other ways to choose knowledgeably among contraceptive alternatives. And, because the less educated communicate less effectively, they are not likely to understand fully what they hear or read about contraception. Furthermore, lower-class husbands and wives generally do not like to talk about sexual matters with each other, so they are less likely to discuss possible ways of limiting family size by a mutually acceptable, effective method. The continued inverse relationship between socioeconomic class and fertility, and the various explanations for it, clearly indicates how social factors can affect fertility.

Our Rural Background Rural families have traditionally been larger than urban families. In the past, the more children that rural parents had, the more help they could expect in the fields and in the home. In addition, because farms were more isolated and family farms were economically important, the young farm boys and girls working for their families were preparing themselves for adult roles on a farm. Today, much of this pattern has changed. With greater mechanization, fewer hands are needed, and those few must be trained adults, not children. Proper management is essential to successful farming, again requiring educated and experienced adults, not children. And, because the farm is no longer isolated from the mainstream of life, farm children have an extensive life away from the home. As the number of farms shrink, many children born on the farm will spend their adult lives living and working in a city.

If it makes little sense for farmers to have more children than city people have, why do they continue to do so? For one thing, many couples seem to have families the same size as their families of orientation. Apparently, the idea of the "right" number of children to have is learned early and dies hard. But it is dying. Rural-urban differences in fertility have been narrowing consistently over the years. In 1940, urban families were about two-thirds as large as farm families. By 1969, nonfarm families were about 72 percent as large as farm families. Today, nonfarm women bear about 84 percent as many children as farm women.

Religion and Fertility Catholics, Mormons, and Southern Baptists have more children than people of other religions. An obvious explanation for Catholics is the official prohibition of any form of "artificial" birth control: mechanical, chemical, or hormonal devices. But what seems obvious is not necessarily true; at least two-thirds of all Catholic couples in the United States practice some form of family limitation (Freedman et al., 1959). Catholic families average about 11 percent more children than Protestant families, not as large a difference as might be expected. Because Southern Baptists number more rural and working-class people than do, say, Episcopalians or Congregationalists, the higher Southern Baptist fertility rate may not be due to religion itself, but to residence and social-class factors. Mormons place great emphasis on strong families, and traditionally, this has meant large families. Thus, Mormon family size is less likely to be a matter of religious prescription than a social value toward family life that encourages high fertility.

Internationally, the relationship between religion and fertility is not clear-cut. Throughout Latin America, we find high fertility and the predominance of Catholicism. Nevertheless, the high fertility regions of Asia and Africa are not predominantly Christian, nor do the native religions expressly forbid birth control practices. Finally, when 11 Roman Catholic countries were compared with 15 non-Catholic countries, the fertility rates were found to be very much the same (*Population Profile*, July 1968). Although in the United States, religion itself, particularly Catholicism, does influence family size, the differences clearly traceable to religion are small.

Race and Fertility For as far back as adequate records go, blacks have had higher birth rates than whites (Grabill et al., 1958). The difference seemed to be directly related to race, because it was found at various class levels, and rural blacks have higher fertility rates than rural whites. But recently, college-educated black women, on the average, are bearing somewhat fewer children than college-educated white women. At the same time, a minority of blacks are suspicious of attempts to get them to reduce their fertility, feeling that family planning programs for blacks are really a form of genocide. A study of 159 black households in New England, for example, found that 20 percent of black females age 30 and younger and 47 percent of males of similar age agreed with the statement, "Encouraging blacks to use birth control is comparable to trying to eliminate this group from society" (Darity, 1971, pp. 5–12). Since most blacks presumably do not feel this way, a reduction in fertility is still expected, particularly as blacks become better educated and achieve higher incomes.

Whatever the factor used for comparison—class, rural-urban residence, religion, or race—differences in family size are narrowing. Nevertheless, for the present, these social factors are related to childbearing performance. Although it is intriguing that social rather than biological factors allow us to predict fertility in different categories of the population, no less intriguing are the social factors that affect deaths, the topic to which we now turn.

MORTALITY

Through the ages, humanity has applied its intelligence and skills to preserving life, to preventing and curing diseases and ailments, and to improving the health of its members. Yet, throughout most of human history, attempts to lower the death rate were not too successful. It has been estimated that in the Early Stone Age, the death rate—the number of deaths per 1,000 people per year—was 49.7, while the birth rate was 50. This difference is about as close to zero population growth as one can get. In some places in the world today, such as in most of Africa, the death rate is still high—in some countries, it is as high as 26 per 1,000 population. In the United States, the **crude death rate** dropped from 17.0 in 1900 to 8.8 in 1977. Our current death rate is one of the lowest in the world (but it's lower for women than for men—see Box 14.1).

Modern medical technology like that being used with this premature baby leads to a low infant mortality rate. But it is expensive and not always available.

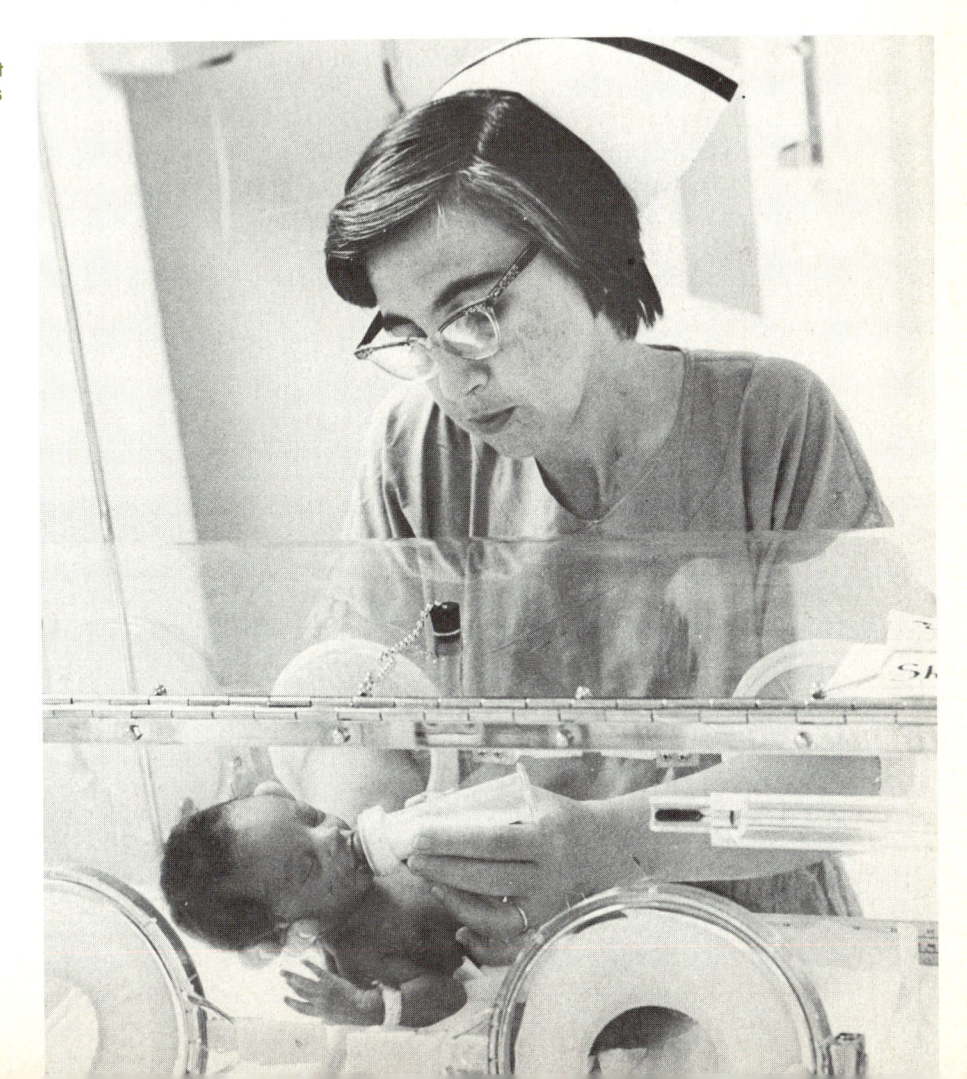

Since all people are mortal, social and cultural factors do not determine *whether* a person will die, but they have a clear influence on *how* and *when*. A society's ability to prevent famine, to control epidemics and communicable diseases, to learn and practice proper nutrition and sanitation, and to avoid wars or minimize their effects all have profound effects on when its members will die and how.

Infant Mortality Rates

The death rate of a society can tell us much about the group, its standard of living, its knowledge, and whether its priorities reflect humanistic or materialistic values. Particularly revealing is the **infant mortality rate:** the number of deaths within the first year of life per 1,000 live births a year. The human infant, weak, helpless, and susceptible to many diseases, has had a very high mortality rate throughout history; had there not also been a high birth rate, the species could not have survived. As recently as about 150 years ago, one-third of European children died in infancy.

In the United States, the infant mortality rate has dropped sharply, from almost 100 in 1915 to about 16 in 1976. To understand the social importance of this change, consider what would have happened had the 1915 infant mortality rate continued: from then until now, 10 million fewer infants would have survived. Or, imagine that today's infant mortality rate had prevailed from 1915 to the present day: close to four million more babies would have survived their first year; a predictable number of them would have lived until adulthood and would have had children of their own, who in turn would have had children, and so on. Our population would be larger by many millions than it is now.

**BOX 14.1
MEN,
WOMEN,
AND DEATH**

The death rate is consistently lower for women than for men. This difference could be due to social factors or it could be a biological indication of the natural superiority of women. It could be argued that because men have traditionally engaged in hazardous occupations, the difference is social. They work in mines where they risk accidents daily and eventually ruin their lungs. They suffer more farm accidents than women, they go off to war, are employed in heavy construction work, and do more occupational traveling than women.

Of course, giving birth is a hazardous occupation, so the role of women has also been fraught with danger. As early as 1900, however, the death rate for females was 16.5, as compared with 17.9 for males. A biological explanation for the lower death rate of females is suggested by the fact that fewer females are miscarried or die in infancy. But the female mortality rate has declined much more rapidly than that of males; in a mere

The infant mortality rate has other, more subtle effects on society. Before medicine demonstrated that something could be done to prevent infant deaths, societies with high infant mortality rates had to accept them as a tragic fact of life and encourage a high birth rate to sustain society's need for new members. This need for a high birth rate became so ingrained in some societies that they have failed to respond to new conditions by adopting family planning. In India, for example, many families fail to realize that they no longer need as many children to ensure that a certain number will survive to adulthood.

The same social factors that affect the death rate in general also affect the infant mortality rate: knowledge of medical and nutritional rules, the availability of doctors and hospitals, and related to these, standards of living and education. One might suppose that the United States, with its affluence, its gleaming hospitals, and funds spent for medical research, would have the lowest infant death rate in the world. But we do not, and according to the best data available, we stand in about twentieth place, behind such countries as Sweden, Finland, the Netherlands, Iceland, Norway, Switzerland, Denmark, New Zealand, Australia, Japan, France, and England.

Although not the lowest, the American infant death rate is low and has been dropping. Perhaps the likeliest reason why it has not been as low as in some other countries is that in our society people receive the medical services they can afford. Again, income and education chiefly determine whether mother and child have the proper nutrition. The cards are stacked against the poor and the blacks. In every state, the infant mortality rate of nonwhites is higher than that of whites. In some states, such as Mississippi and Florida, the nonwhite rate is twice that for whites. The rate varies among regions, with the Southern states generally the highest—sometimes

50 years, from 1900 to 1950, the death rate of women was cut in half, surely too short a time for nature to improve on presumed biological superiority. In the same period, the death rate for males dropped from 17.9 to 11.1. Even today, it is only 10.2, the rate achieved by women 45 years ago. All things considered, it would appear that the female is the more durable of the species, although the biological edge is narrow.

Social factors, such as our ability to deal effectively with a once-common cause of female deaths—deaths of mothers during childbearing—add to the advantage that women already have. As more women are employed outside the home, particularly as they are found in high-pressure and industrial jobs previously held by males, it will be important to note whether their death rate from heart diseases, hypertension, industrial accidents, and the like increases.

These men in the Soviet Union have already lived a total of 600 years. Diet, exercise, and genetic factors are among the reasons that some groups have a long life expectancy.

50 percent higher than the national average. The infant mortality rate among American Indians is also high, second only to that of blacks. There is, thus, ample evidence that social factors affect the infant death rate, and more than this, affect different social groups unequally. It is painfully obvious that the chances of living through the first year of life are not equal.

For perspective, the generally low infant mortality rates in our own and other industrialized societies should be compared with those in some developing countries. In Egypt, the rate is 100.4, in Colombia 98.4, and in the Philippines 58.9. These rates can be reduced considerably, and the populations will increase, just by saving more of the infants that are born. Our own infant death rate cannot be reduced as significantly, so that even if it does decrease, it will not have a tremendous effect on the total population size.

Life Expectancy

Life expectancy is the average number of years that a group of persons born at a given time *will* live under present circumstances, not how long they *can* live. Of all the people born in a given year, a certain predictable number will die in infancy, some will die each year thereafter, and a few will live out the life span of the species. If we knew the number that die at each age, we could calculate the average life expectancy at birth for the group. Life expectancy averages can be computed for groups at any given age, and not just at birth. In such cases, they would refer to the average number of additional years persons of the same age can expect to live.

In many places in the world today, the average life expectancy at birth is exceedingly low. In 20 African nations, including Angola, Ethiopia, Nigeria, and Madagascar, it is less than 40 years; in Bangladesh, it is 36 years; in India, Afghanistan, and Nepal, it is no more than 45 years; while the worldwide average is about 59 years. The world's highest life expectancy for societies that keep accurate records is 77.6 for Norwegian women. There may be some small ethnic groups in the Soviet Union with even higher life expectancies.

In the United States at the turn of the century, life expectancy at birth was 48 years for males and 51 for females. Today, it is 68 and 76, respectively. The sharp increase in life expectancy is due largely to the decline in the death rate of infants and children. It does not mean that, on the average, people live to older ages than their parents or grandparents did. For example, males who reached age 65 in 1900 could expect to live an additional 11.5 years; today, males who reach 65 have a life expectancy of about 13 additional years. Death control, in other words, has so far been much more effective for younger than for older people.

MIGRATION

A part of us seems to yearn for stability — to put down roots and to remain where we are — but another part is restless, seeking to be on the move. As we saw in Chapter 3, two of the four basic human wishes are contradictory in the behavior they demand: the wish for security and the wish for new experience. Of course, individuals, groups, and entire populations have had to move, whether they wanted to or not, fleeing political or religious persecution. Thus, as a result of both curiosity and necessity, millions of people have moved from continent to continent, from nation to nation, from city to city.

Studies of **migration,** the third major demographic process, deal with the number of migrants, their social and personal characteristics, where they came from and where they are going, the reasons for migrating or not migrating, the effects of migration on the community the migrants leave, and the effects of migration on the receiving community.

Immigration

Our nation came into being through **immigration.** What started as a trickle of Europeans to our shores took on larger and larger proportions. From 1820 to 1970, over 45 million people migrated to the United States, about 80 percent from Europe and about 6 percent from Africa. (In the early years, of course, the Africans did not come by their own choice.)

Beginning in 1921, a ceiling was placed on immigration for the first time. The yearly quota for each country was set at three percent of the number of people from that country who were living in the United States in 1910. Northern European countries, by virtue of the large number of people from such countries already in the United States, had the largest quotas. The quota system thus tended to maintain the ethnic mix of our population, and in particular, to keep out people from China, Japan, and other Asiatic countries.

There were changes in the quota system over the years, but a major modification was not made until 1968. This law, still in effect, places a ceiling of 120,000 on immigrants from Western Hemisphere countries, with no limitation on the number from any one country. The ceiling is 170,000 for those from Eastern Hemisphere countries, with a maximum of 20,000 from any one country. Selection procedures favor family reunification and persons with skills and talents needed here. In addition to the combined ceiling of 290,000, there are allowances for nonquota and special immigrants, such as refugees, orphan children, and immediate relatives of citizens.

Since 1968, there have been about 400,000 legal immigrants to our country each year, considerably more than there were before the law went into effect. In addition, there are at least 40,000 illegal entrants, many of whom are the "wetbacks" who cross the border from Mexico. It is difficult to know how many illegal entrants there are, let alone to control their numbers. The total number of people from other countries who come to our shore is small, but it does affect our population growth. In 1960, for example, 94.4 percent of the additions to our population were births, while 5.6 were legal immigrants. In 1974, legal immigrants accounted for 11 percent of the additions to our society. Immigration, of course, helps to keep alive the cultural variety within our social system.

Internal Migration

Internal migration is migration within a society. Demographers who study internal migration are interested in why and how people redistribute themselves and in the results of such movements. People who leave a community are **out-migrants;** people who enter a community are called **in-migrants.** (Clearly, just about every out-migrant becomes an in-migrant somewhere else.) The distinction between in- and out-migrants is useful, for the terms relate the migrating individuals to groups or communities. If the number of people moving into a community equals the number who leave, the community remains stable in size. But if the rates of in- and out-migration are uneven, or if they are even but substantial, the community is likely to be unstable, for its class, age, or ethnic composition could change drastically.

The net migration of a region, state, or community for a given period of time is obtained by determining the population change for the period, then subtracting the births and adding the deaths for the same period. For example, if we found that a population increased by 1,000 people in a year, we would subtract the 500 births for that year and add 300 deaths, arriving at the conclusion that there was a net in-migration of 800 people during the year. (Perhaps there were actually more in-migrants, but the additional ones are offset by the number of out-migrants.)

Internal migration is not random or haphazard. In general, the streams of

This abandoned Iowa farmstead gives silent testimony to the migration stream that runs from rural to urban areas. In recent years there has been a small reverse stream.

migration in the United States run from South to North, from East to West, from areas of poor employment opportunities to those with good opportunities, and from rural to urban areas. Migration figures show that rural areas, the South, and places with poor employment opportunities have lost population. Also, young adults, men, and the better educated are more likely to migrate. Furthermore, people who move once are more likely to move again.

The extent of migration is significant in the United States. In March 1971, for example, about 36 million Americans were not living in the same house in which they had lived in the previous March. About seven million people had crossed state lines in their moves, and another six million crossed county lines. Whether to near or far, between 18 and 20 percent of the population moves each year. (Some of these are repeaters, so the number of different individuals or families who move annually is not quite as large as the percentage indicates.)

When about 13 million migrants cross county or state lines annually, the effects of migration can be staggering. The effects on the counties or regions from which there is a net out-migration can be as devastating. Letcher County, in the Appalachian area of Kentucky, had a total population of about 40,000 in 1950; 30,000 in 1960; and 23,000 in 1970 (Ramsey, 1971). Between 1950 and 1960, the county experienced a net out-migration of over 10,000. The excess of births over deaths between 1960 and 1970 was less than half of what it had been for the previous decade. With fewer children, and fewer still expected in the future because of lowered birth rates, it seemed reasonable to curtail the building of schools and other facilities needed by young people. But, then came the coal boom triggered by the embargo on Arabian oil. Between 1970 and 1975, the population of Letcher County *increased* by 3,435. About half the increase was due to net in-migration, and half of it was due to births. The factors are related, for many of the births were to the young adults who migrated into the county. More or less suddenly, the number of people age 20 to 24 went up by over 89 percent; and the number of children under five increased by 29 percent, indicating that soon the schools would be overcrowded.

To summarize what happened to Letcher County, first economic conditions pushed young adults away, affecting the age composition and birth rate of the remaining population. Then, economic conditions pulled people back into the county, creating a bulge in the young adult and young children population segments. Once again, we see how demographic factors are affected by, and in turn, affect the social characteristics of a community.

WORLD POPULATION GROWTH

In Chapter 3, we saw that the evolution of human societies can be divided into epochs based on the means by which humans utilized the material resources of their environment to satisfy their basic needs. The most basic of these needs was food, and as technology improved, more food was produced and more people lived and were able to help others to live. (You will recall that population growth is one of the fundamental changes in human society that results from significant change in technology.)

At the hunting and gathering stage, much of the daily activity consisted in getting enough food to survive that day and perhaps the next. Sheer survival was precarious. Later, with the cultivation of plants and the invention of the plow, more food could be produced, and it could be produced more easily and more efficiently. The survival of the species seemed secure. Yet, as recently as the fourteenth century, the bubonic plague, or Black Death, was able to sweep through Europe, killing an estimated 40 percent of the population. Today, the struggle for survival and the balance between food and people has taken on new dimensions. The concern is that the best of our technology will not be good enough to provide food for the teeming millions already on the earth and the millions more destined to be born.

Although almost everyone today knows that there is a world population problem, many are confused about it. This confusion arises partly because of the problem's complexity and partly because so many kinds of statistics are cited and so many predictions are made. We should say, immediately, that the future population of the world cannot be *predicted* (that is, foretold with certainty). Any book or tract that claims otherwise should be swiftly and unceremoniously transferred from the science to the fiction section of your library. Yet, population *projections* are both valuable and necessary.

Projections are based on observed facts, such as current population sizes, birth rates, and death rates. These facts are then subjected to the most sophisticated statistical techniques which take many factors into account. Why, then, are population predictions fictions? First, we do not know, with any certainty, how many people there are on earth; second—and the main problem—is that the rates that affect natural increase may change in unexpected ways. Moreover, the "self-defeating prophecy" we discussed in

Chapter 2 might come into play. That is, precisely because some predictions for the future are made, they are bound *not* to come true. If people believe the predictions and take their implications seriously, and if they evaluate such implications negatively and have the proper knowledge, they can take corrective action. The original prophecy will be false, precisely because it could have been true! Note the number of *ifs:* there is no assurance that once the facts are known, people will quickly modify their behavior to relieve the world's population pressure.

Was Malthus Right?

Concern with the impact of population growth can be traced to 1798, when the Reverend Thomas Malthus first published his book *An Essay on the Principle of Population.* In this work, Malthus set forth the theory that human populations increase geometrically (2, 4, 8, 16, 32, ...), while the food supply necessary to sustain life increases arithmetically (2, 3, 4, 5, 6, ...). As Malthus put it, "A slight acquaintance with numbers will show the immensity of the first power in comparison with the second." With low death rates, Malthus posited that human populations could double every 25 years, but even if the doubling time were longer, there would be no way for the food supply to keep up with the growing population.

Malthus described what he called *positive* population checks and *preventive* checks. Among **positive population checks** were the forces that have reduced human populations over much of human history—famines, pestilence, disease, and wars. If humans were not content to allow these forces to keep their numbers from exploding, they could employ the **preventive population checks** of late marriage and celibacy. (Malthus considered artificial birth control to be morally wrong.) Only sexual restraint could help humans avoid the positive checks of premature deaths. Was Malthus right or wrong? Perhaps this is the wrong question, and we should ask, instead, what aspects of his grim theory may yet be applicable. Let us briefly review the history of population in light of Malthus's theory.

Despite a high birth rate, a high death rate throughout most of our past resulted in an extremely slow rate of human population growth. In 6000 B.C. there were no more than a few million people on the entire earth. It took the 6000 years from then to the time of Christ for the population to increase tenfold, to about 250 million—not too many more people than now live in the United States. For the last 2000 years, it is more appropriate to deal with the **doubling time** for the earth's population rather than with tenfold increases. From the time of Christ, it took 1600 years for the population to double, leaving us with about 500 million people by the year 1650. Then, in only 200 years, it doubled again, bringing world population close to an even one billion by 1850. In 80 years, it doubled again to about two billion in 1930. In 1976, the world's population stood at over four billion, representing a doubling time of about 46 years.

Recently, the growth rate of the world's population has slowed down a

FIGURE 14.2   World Population Growth, 1650–1976

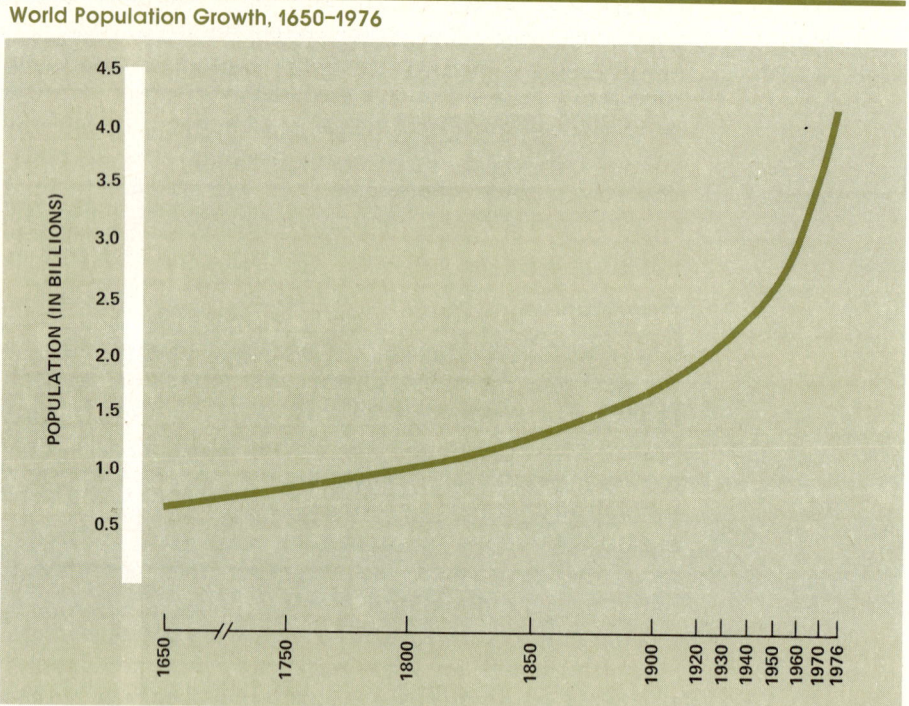

little. Our numbers are nevertheless increasing at 1.7 percent annually, giving a doubling time of about 41 years. The sheer numbers must also be taken into account. While it once took 1600 years for 250 million people to double their population, it now takes 41 years for over four billion people to double their numbers. Because of the enormous number of people, an annual growth rate of two percent, which sounds low, is actually so high that babies born today will see the population of the world double before they are even middle aged, and many will live long enough to see it double *twice* — if all rates (birth, death, and fertility) remain what they are now. We have indeed had a world population explosion, as the slope of the graph in Figure 14.2 shows. We are on a collision course with disaster. Unless we want the positive checks of Malthus — famine, pestilence, and disease — to control our growth for us, our only hope is to get off the collision course. But how? Understanding how we got on the course in the first place should help us to answer the question or at least to appreciate the bewildering complexity of it.

Population Growth in Western Societies

Since 1650, numerous events have combined to transform the Western world from agrarian to urban and industrial societies. The change has had profound effects on the population of these societies. Not only was there a surplus of food that allowed farmers to leave the land, but the new industries desperately needed increasing numbers of workers. Cities began to grow rapidly (as described in detail in Chapter 15). Meanwhile, there was an impressive revolution in the treatment and prevention of disease and in the development of good water and sewage systems.

In the early part of the nineteenth century, as can be seen in Figure 14.3, the population of Western societies began to grow, in keeping with the predictions of Malthus. This was the first stage of what has come to be called the **demographic transition** (Cowgill, 1963). In the second stage, death rates began to drop rapidly, furthering the population growth. The third stage was marked by a decline in birth rates, which was unanticipated by Malthus. From Figure 14.3 it is clear that the drop in birth rates lagged behind the drop in death rates by over 25 years. But, with urban living, first the better educated, and later, others realized that having many children was a liability in the kind of industrialized society that was developing.

The fourth, and so far the final, stage of demographic transition was reached when birth and death rates leveled off at low levels. Today, Western Europe has an annual growth rate of .6 percent, the United States one of 1.1 percent, and Eastern Europe .8 percent, all considerably below the world average of 1.8 percent. While these populations are growing somewhat, the

FIGURE 14.3 Estimated Birth and Death Rates, 1770–1970

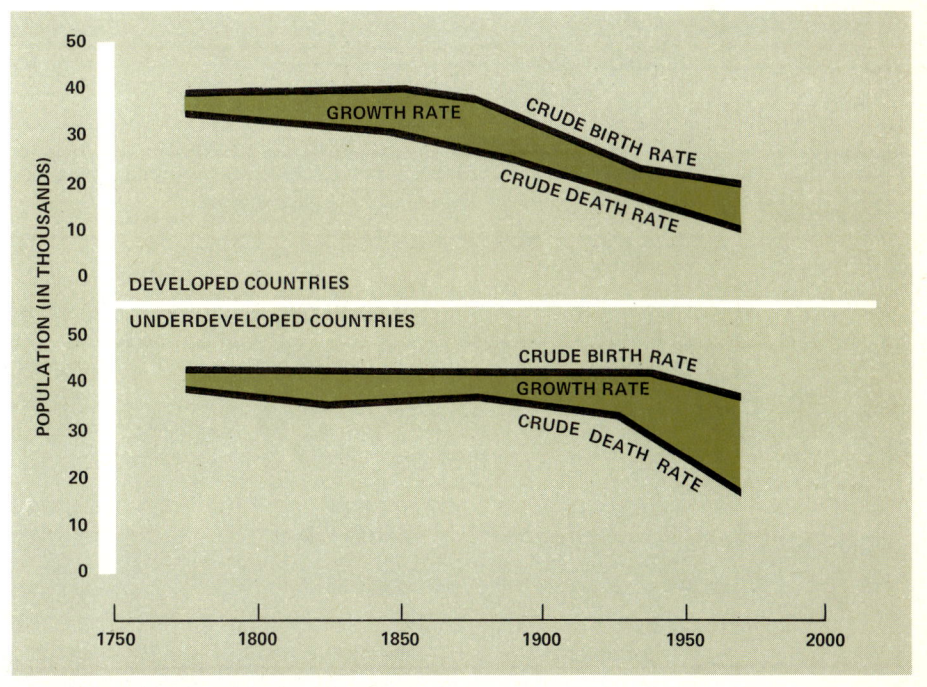

Source: United Nations, *A Concise Summary of the World Population Situation in 1970* (New York: United Nations, 1971), p. 43.

growth has lost its explosive force. What Malthus did not anticipate, then, were the combined effects of urbanization, which gave people the desire to reduce their birth rates, and the development of reliable contraceptives, which gave them the means to do so. (Not all industrialized cultures experienced a decrease in birth rate—see Box 14.2.)

Population Growth in Developing Countries

In developing countries, the population growth picture has been quite different. This situation is dramatically illustrated in Figure 14.3, which shows a sharp reduction in the death rate but only a slight reduction in the birth rate. Unlike the Western countries, these countries are not yet reducing their birth rate as their death rate drops. Timing explains the difference: death control, deliberately introduced into the countries of Africa, Asia, and Latin America, is readily accepted, requires little initiative from the people, and often is relatively inexpensive. For example, DDT sprayed from airplanes greatly reduces malaria, once the scourge of these nations. Birth control has been introduced to the developing countries, but it has not met with similar success. It is not as popular as death control, it requires initiative and cooperation from people, and on a mass basis, it can be expensive.

The developing countries, therefore, have not experienced the demographic transition. Their fertility remains higher than the world average,

---

**BOX 14.2
VALUES AND
FERTILITY:
THE HUTTERITES**

What country has a population with a four percent growth rate, and with a doubling time of less than 18 years—the highest growth rate in the world? In what country will you find that the women of ages 40–44 have a higher fertility rate than French, Swedish, and British women in their maximum fertility years of 20–29? The answer to all these questions is the United States.

To be sure, we are referring not to the entire population of the United States but to a group that makes up only a tiny percentage of it—the Hutterites. Although they are now less than a fraction of one percent of our population, if their growth remains constant and the present overall growth rate of the United States remains constant, then in 100 years the Hutterites will make up about 15 percent of the population.

Who are these superfertile people? The Hutterites are a strongly religious communal farming people found in South Dakota, Montana, and parts of Canada. They emigrated from Russia about 100 years ago—440 persons in all. They now number around 20,000. Why have their numbers grown so rapidly? They are strict followers of the Bible. In Genesis it says, "Be fruitful and multiply." The Hutterites follow this commandment so well that some social scientists suspect them of having actually inbred a superfertility.

Although the Hutterites have many children per family they are prosperous and are thus an exception to the inverse relationship between social class and family size.

even while their death rates approach the world average and probably will continue to decline. And, so, their populations grow and grow. The developing countries have gigantic problems in feeding and housing more and more people.

On an immediate basis, food is the problem. For a time the so-called

Fertility rates not even as high as that of the Hutterites have been among the chief causes of economic and social distress in India, South America, and parts of Africa. But, so far, the Hutterites have been blessed for following the Bible. Because the Hutterites use labor-saving machinery, they have no need for large numbers of workers. Their communities are prosperous, even though members can retire from work at the age of 45. Because they are prosperous, when a "colony" reaches a certain size—say 150 people for 4,000 acres—they buy more land and begin a new colony.

Even so, the Hutterites may be in for hard times. Their neighbors have sought to prevent the sale of land to them. The Hutterites are disliked because they are "communists"; because they shun nearby communities and educate their own children; because they buy their supplies wholesale in cities rather than in nearby towns; and because their large land purchases "disrupt rural patterns of business and livelihood." The Hutterites have maintained tight-knit, stable communities by controlling the size of each. If they become unable to expand, their future may become a grim forecast of what awaits the rest of us. How their values change, or fail to change, in response to conditions that make them dysfunctional will be, perhaps, a rich source of sociological knowledge.

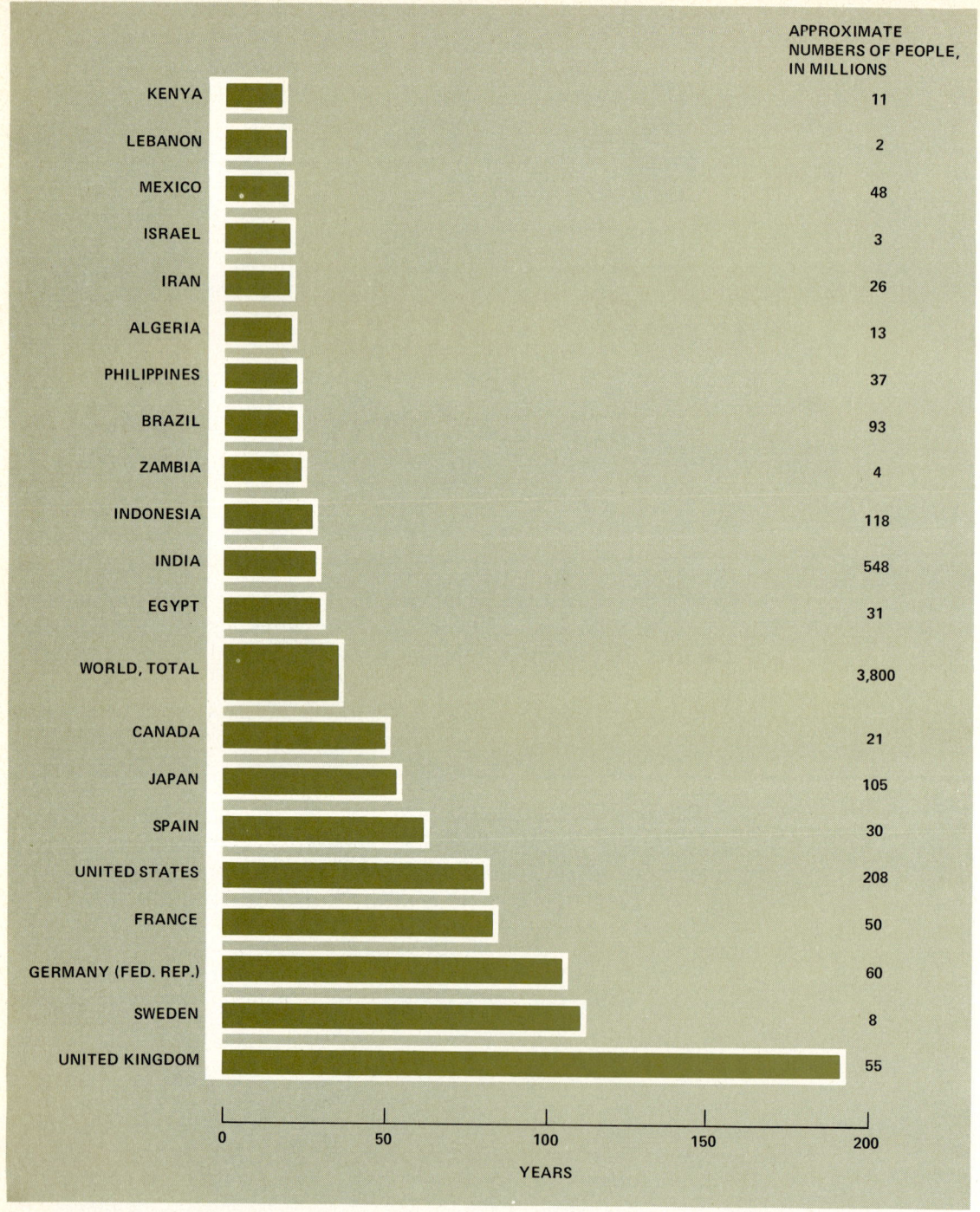

FIGURE 14.4 Years Required to Double Population, Selected Countries, Based on 1970–1974 Average Annual Growth Rate

Country	Years to Double	Approximate Numbers of People, in Millions
KENYA	~20	11
LEBANON	~22	2
MEXICO	~22	48
ISRAEL	~23	3
IRAN	~24	26
ALGERIA	~24	13
PHILIPPINES	~25	37
BRAZIL	~26	93
ZAMBIA	~27	4
INDONESIA	~30	118
INDIA	~31	548
EGYPT	~32	31
WORLD, TOTAL	~37	3,800
CANADA	~50	21
JAPAN	~55	105
SPAIN	~63	30
UNITED STATES	~80	208
FRANCE	~85	50
GERMANY (FED. REP.)	~105	60
SWEDEN	~112	8
UNITED KINGDOM	~195	55

Before the turn of the century, the population of the world is expected to double. It will take even less time for India's population of over 500 million to double. By contrast, Sweden's population of eight million people will not double for over 100 years. Population pressures, now and in the future, are due both to the numbers of people and to how fast the numbers are increasing.

Source: Executive Office of the President: Office of Management and Budget, *Social Indicators, 1976* (Washington, D.C.: U.S. Government Printing Office, 1976), page 19; U.S. Bureau of the Census, *Statistical Abstract of the United States: 1975* (Washington, D.C.: U.S. Government Printing Office, 1975), pp. 826–828.

"Green Revolution"—use of new varieties of high-yielding crops, fertilizers, and the like—seemed to be working. But in 1972, there were sharp declines in food production. The food situation is touch and go, but it is not quite as bad as it was ten years ago. India, for example, produced three times as much wheat in 1975 as in 1965. There is much hunger in the developing countries, but famine is becoming more rare.

For the long run, it will not be sufficient merely to increase the food supply in the developing countries. Somehow, their birth rates must be reduced, if they are to escape the spectre of Malthusian theory. During the years 1965–1974, the countries of Asia, including India, China, Korea, and Pakistan, showed progress in controlling fertility. Birth rates also declined in the Caribbean area. Africa showed a small decline in birth rates, from 48 to 47, and Central and South America also showed slight declines, going from 39 to 38. These declines are encouraging, but obviously, still better fertility control is needed.

POPULATION GROWTH IN THE UNITED STATES

The fertility rate in the United States has now reached **replacement level fertility.** That is, younger women are expected to complete their childbearing years with an average of about 2.1 children, just enough to balance deaths. Even so, we have not reached **zero population growth** (ZPG) and will not do so for some time. This is because of the *echo effect* of fertility pat-

Feeding the teeming millions of India and other developing countries is a problem of gigantic proportions. Starvation is rare, but hunger still abounds.

terns. Because of high birth rates in the past, the number of potential mothers is still increasing. Even if they average two children each, the population will continue to grow. It is extremely difficult to forecast how much the population will grow, when it will reach ZPG, and what the ultimate size of the stationary population will be.

If family size stabilizes at 2.1 children, if there is only a slight improvement in mortality, and if our immigration rates remain stable, the growth rate would be slow by the year 2000, and the population would stabilize by 2050. Under these assumptions, the population would reach 262 million by 2000 and would stabilize at 300–325 million. To cut about 20 million from the total for the year 2000, it would be necessary to reduce fertility to an average of 1.7 children instead of 2.1. On the other hand, if the average family size were to go back up to 3.0, our population would be 320 million by 2000 and would hit 600 million in 2050. Frankly, there are no indications that we will return to an average family size of three children. The most plausible projection is that replacement level fertility will continue and that we will reach ZPG in about 70 years.

Optimum versus Maximum Population Size

A distinction should be made between maximum and optimum population size. The **maximum population size** is the largest number of people who somehow could be fed, clothed, housed, and otherwise cared for at approximately a subsistence level of living by a community, a society, or the planet. The **optimum population size** is the ideal population size, the size that would permit the society to provide a good life for its members. Although neither maximum nor optimum size is precisely measurable, the distinction remains useful. For example, many middle-class families could afford to support a maximum family of, say, ten children. They would have a home, food on the table, and clothing. But, obviously, most middle-class families do not consider this the optimum family size. Housing would be so crowded that there would be little or no privacy or freedom of movement, so tensions and irritations would constantly be high. The time demanded of parents to rear so many children and to manage the home would allow little or no individual attention for each child. With the constant financial drain on such a family, time or money for leisure activities or vacations would be rare or nonexistent. The family could probably not support any of the children beyond high school. Such a family could survive, but most people would agree they would not be living "the good life."

If you extend this example to the scope of a community, a society, a continent, or the entire planet, you can see that maximum and optimum populations make for important differences in living. Although there is room for disagreement, our society probably could support a population of 300 million or more, even if this number were reached within a few decades. There is no danger that, in the immediate future, we will smother ourselves to death with sheer numbers of bodies or take to eating seaweed in order to

Population growth can interfere with the good life. There is a tendency among humans to stake off their personal space or "territory." Note how this is done even on a crowded beach.

survive. But, would such greatly increased numbers be in the best interests of the people?

The signs are that we have enough problems coping with 215 million people. Crowds are everywhere; it takes longer to commute to and from work; supermarket lines are longer; recreation areas are overcrowded; and each year, more and more of the countryside is used for factories and homes. We are polluting our environment and using up our natural resources (and those of many other countries) at an alarming rate. The list, which could go on and on, is not very encouraging, even if we somehow manage to adjust to the conditions. What does it profit us to gain a few years in life expectancy only to spend them commuting to work or driving long distances to "get away from it all"?

Some people, such as Stewart Udall, former Secretary of the Interior, believe that if we judge by the destruction of our environment, we have already passed the optimum population level in this country (Westoff and Westoff, 1971). Others see not the sheer number of people but our high standard of living and our mismanagements as being responsible for pollution, destruction of the environment, and overcrowding. Even people of this persuasion admit that we are unable or unwilling to provide the "good life" for our present 215 million. How, then, could we do so for 300 million? Since there seems to be general agreement that our fertility patterns of recent years have adversely affected society, the optimum population growth would seem to be as near replacement level as possible for the immediate future. The rate would at least give us time to catch up with our various unsolved problems and to plan for the future.

Maintaining Replacement Level Fertility

For the most part, the social factors that affect fertility have not been the result of a deliberate policy. Millions of Americans have nevertheless restricted their childbearing, so that as a nation we have achieved replacement level fertility. Drastic measures to reduce fertility are not needed, unless as a society we want to lower our fertility still further, to achieve zero population growth more quickly, or to reach a stationary population faster than

---

FIGURE 14.5 World Energy Consumption

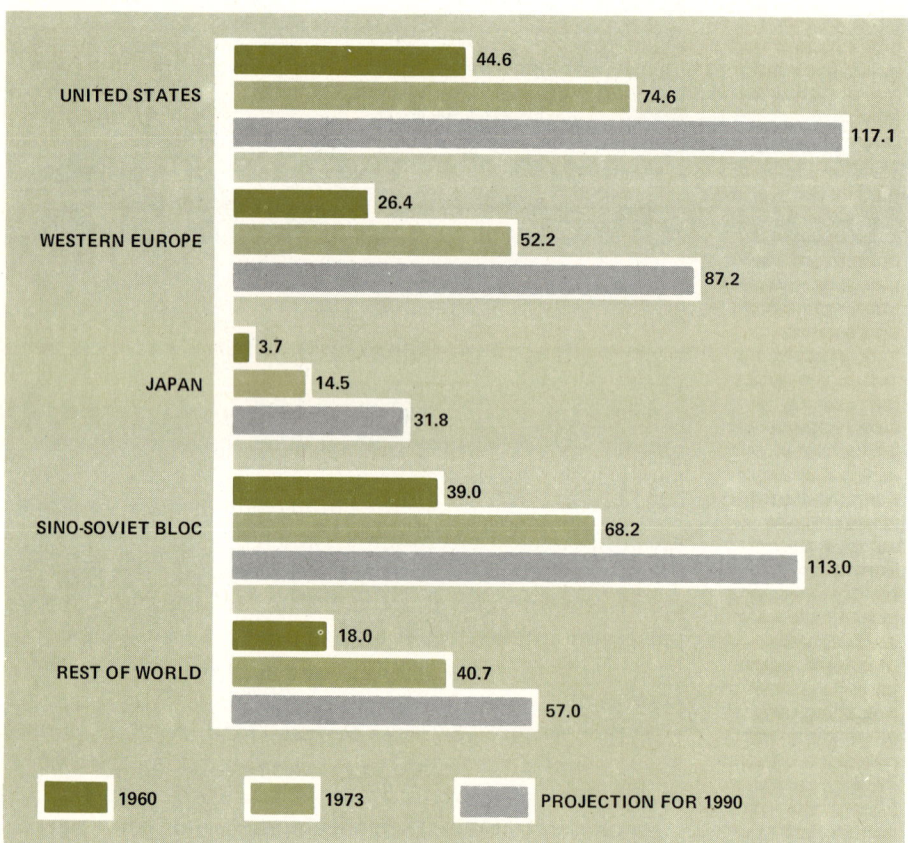

Region	1960	1973	Projection for 1990
UNITED STATES	44.6	74.6	117.1
WESTERN EUROPE	26.4	52.2	87.2
JAPAN	3.7	14.5	31.8
SINO-SOVIET BLOC	39.0	68.2	113.0
REST OF WORLD	18.0	40.7	57.0

The ever-growing population of the world needs more energy for its industries and for personal consumption. Currently, the United States consumes more energy than the countries of Western Europe and Japan combined, but by 1990, those countries are expected to consume more than we do. World energy consumption is computed in quadrillions of a British thermal unit (BTU). One quadrillion BTU is equal to 500,000 barrels of petroleum each day for a year, or its equivalent in coal or natural gas.

Source: U.S. Bureau of the Census, *Statistical Abstract of the United States: 1977* (Washington, D.C.: U.S. Government Printing Office, 1977), p. 595.

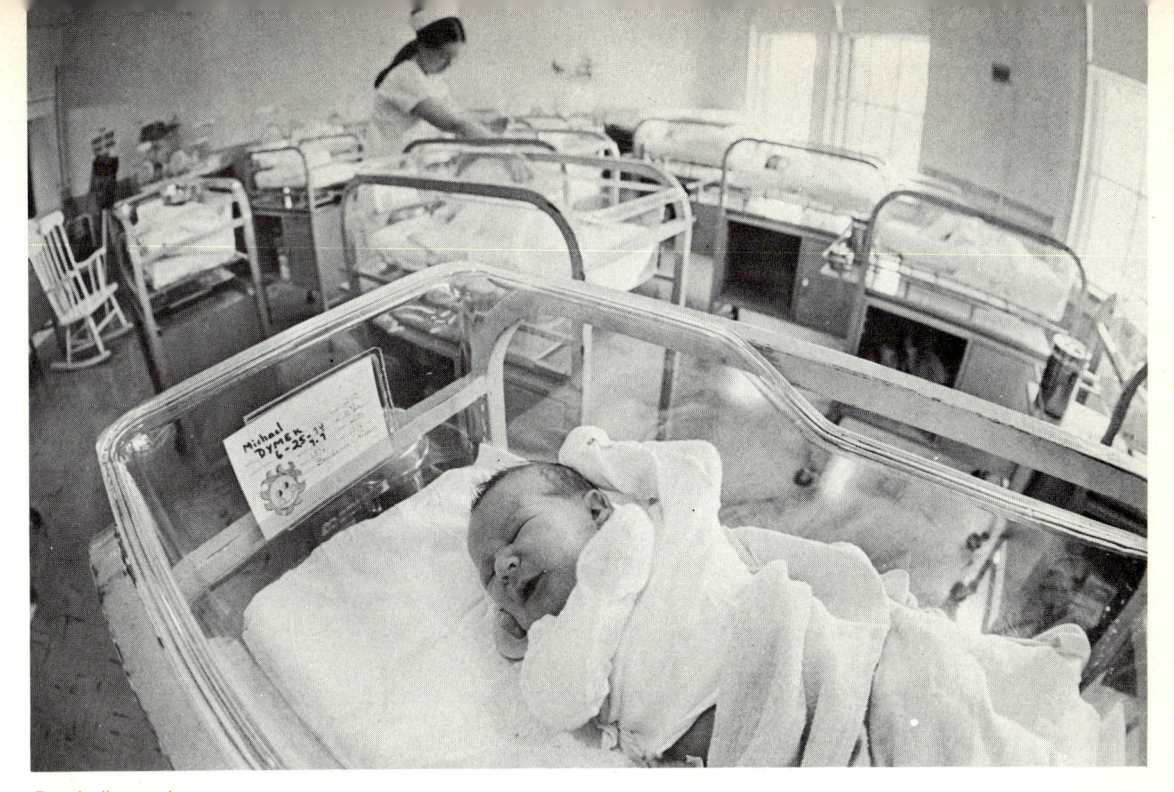

Due to the post World War II baby boom, there were lots of potential mothers the year this baby was born. Even though women are now having fewer children, the echo effect of the earlier high birth rates will not allow us to reach zero population growth for some time.

would occur under present rates. There is some concern over the fact that there is no well-articulated national population policy that would set forth what our national objectives really are.

In the United States, about 80 percent of all births are wanted. Family planning centers and educational programs are still needed for those, particularly the poor, who are having more children than they want. A society that does not want to grow should, it would seem, take measures to reduce the number of unwanted births.

All sorts of measures have been suggested to reduce fertility, including persuasive public service messages in the mass media, bonuses for small or childless families or for voluntary sterilization, the addition of temporary sterilizing agents into drinking water, and even the requiring of licenses for childbearing, coupled with stiff penalties for those who bear children without a license. For the present, there would appear to be no need for such extreme measures. There is always the possibility, however, that as a nation we will relax our efforts at maintaining replacement level fertility and that vigorous measures of some kind will be needed to assure that we will reach a stationary population level in a reasonably short time.

Adjusting to a Stationary Population

Throughout this chapter, we have seen how the social demographer alternately studies the demographic effects on the group and the social effects on the demographic processes. It seems fitting, therefore, to conclude the chapter with a few remarks on the social consequences of a replacement level population growth and the stationary population that would result. We can probably imagine more positive consequences than negative ones. Our numbers and rate of growth are not our only problems, but as Senator Tydings put it, "A growing population makes the solution of nearly all of our problems more difficult and more expensive" (Westoff and Westoff, 1971).

As we approach a stationary population, there will be marked changes in the age composition of our population. About 30 percent of our population today is under 15 years of age, while about 10 percent is 65 and older. With a stationary population, these age categories would be about even, with about 20 percent in each. Some claim that an older age composition would harm us, by slowing down the rate of new ideas and the pressures for social change. On a more mundane level, the Old Age and Survivors Insurance program (Social Security) is already in financial trouble, and more difficulties can be expected as the number and proportion of older people rise.

The low birth rates and generally small families that accompany a stationary population mean that there would be a decreased need for child care. With both husband and wife in the labor force, and with fewer children dependent on them, there should be a higher standard of living. Perhaps men and women would decide that neither needs to work full time. This could be a mixed blessing, unless meaningful leisure activities are available.

It is not certain how much, if at all, the racial, ethnic, religious, and class composition of our population will change as we move toward a stationary population. As noted in our discussion of differential fertility, traditionally, the better educated, white Protestants have had fewer children than the less educated, nonwhite members of society. It is likely that the fertility differentials among groups will eventually decline, but since they will continue for some time, it means that the composition that exists when we reach a stationary population will be different than it is today.

A stationary population will affect our economic system. For a long time, our economic system has been based on the idea of growth. We have needed more food, more houses, more of all sorts of goods and services. A stationary population would require a readjustment in our thinking. It is not just that the demand for some goods and services would slow down, but with a different population composition, more leisure, and a potentially higher per capita income, there would be a demand for new and different goods and services. Again, there should be many positive effects of a stationary population. But we will need all the thought and imagination we can muster to minimize the negative consequences and take full advantage of the positive ones.

We have seen that social demographic studies can tell us much about the people of a society—not only in numbers but in age, sex, racial, and other composition. Such studies reveal how the numbers and characteristics of people are changing, and how these changes affect and are affected by society. Demographic studies show us where people live, and how many move about within a geographic territory, and why they do so. But we need to know more about how people live, particularly how they live together in large cities and the particular problems they face as they become urbanized. These topics are covered in the next chapter.

SUMMARY

1. **Social demography** is the study of human populations. Demographers gather data so that they can both describe a social system and analyze demographic factors to see how they affect and are affected by social and cultural factors.

2. Demographic data are collected in three ways: (1) by census, (2) by registration of major life events (**vital statistics**), and (3) by surveys and special studies. Each method has its own drawbacks.

3. Two methods used for analyzing demographic data are **population pyramids** (graphic presentations of the age and sex composition of a society) and **dependency ratios** (statistics representing the ratio of people of working age to the number who are either too young or too old to work).

4. Besides determining the age and sex of a population, demographers are primarily concerned with three major processes: fertility, mortality, and migration.

5. **Fertility** is the number of births within a group in a given period. Fertility can be studied by looking at the sheer number of births in a society in a given time period, at the **crude birth rate** (the number of births per 1,000 persons in the population during a given time period), or at the **general fertility rate** (the number of births per year per 1,000 women age 15 to 44).

6. Among social factors affecting fertility are socioeconomic status, values and attitudes, contraceptive knowledge, rural versus urban background, religion, and race.

7. **Mortality** refers to the death rate in a society. One measure of mortality is the **crude death rate,** which has been steadily declining in the United States, although it is significantly lower for women than for men.

8. One important death statistic is the **infant mortality rate** — the number of deaths within the first year of life per 1,000 live births a year. The infant mortality rate is affected by knowledge of medicine and nutrition, availability of medical care, and standards of living and education. In turn, the infant mortality rate can have a profound effect on the population of a society.

9. Another measure of mortality is **life expectancy** — the average number of years that a group of persons born at a given time can expect to live under present circumstances. Since the turn of the century, life expectancy at birth has increased dramatically in the United States, but life expectancy for older people has changed very little.

10. Studies of **migration** focus on the characteristics of migrants, their reasons for migrating, and the effects of migration on communities that receive and lose people.

11. **Immigration** has always been a major source of additions to the American population, and currently, it accounts for 11 percent of the population increase each year.

12. **Internal migration** is migration within a society. People who leave a community are *out-migrants;* people who enter a community are *in-migrants.* Internal migration in the United States is extensive.

13. In previous times, the population problem was keeping people alive. Today, the world population problem refers to the fact that there are too many people in comparison to the food supply and other resources.

14. Malthus suggested that human populations increase geometrically, while the food supply increases arithmetically. He described both **positive population checks** (famine, pestilence, disease, wars) and **preventive population checks** (late marriage, celibacy). As Malthus predicted, world population has increased tremendously, with the **doubling time** now at about 41 years. What he did not realize is that technology could improve on food production—although it still lags behind population growth.

15. Western societies have gone through four stages of **demographic transition:** (1) rapid growth in population, (2) a drop in death rates, (3) a decline in birth rates, (4) a leveling off of birth and death rates at low levels.

16. The picture is different in developing countries, where the death rate has declined greatly but the birth rate remains high.

17. In the United States, the fertility rate has reached **replacement level fertility,** although it has not yet reached **zero population growth** (ZPG). At present, it appears that Americans will continue to maintain replacement level fertility.

18. **Maximum population size** is the largest number of people who could be cared for at a subsistence level of living by a community or society. **Optimum population size** is the ideal population size—the size that would permit the society to provide a good life for its members.

19. Replacement level fertility will have major effects on the composition of our society and will result in a stationary population. In turn, a stationary population will affect our economic system and other aspects of society.

KEY TERMS

census
crude birth rate
crude death rate
demographic transition
dependency ratio
dependent variables

doubling time
fertility
general fertility rate
immigration
independent variables
infant mortality rate
in-migration
life expectancy
maximum population size
migration

optimum population size
out-migration
population pyramid
positive population checks
preventive population checks
replacement level fertility
social demography
vital statistics
zero population growth

SUGGESTED READINGS

Borrie, W. D. *The Growth and Control of World Population.* London: Weidenfield and Nicolson, 1970.
A world overview of the major demographic patterns, movements, and policies. The book contains numerous migratory and population maps and statistics.

Brown, Harrison, and Edward Hutchings, Jr., eds. *Are Our Descendants Doomed?* New York: Viking Press, 1972.
A series of essays dealing with the problems that an overpopulated world will face and some of the methods that might be used to alleviate the consequences of projected population growth.

Davis, Kingsley. "The Migration of Human Populations," *Scientific American,* 231 (September 1974), 93–105.
An experienced social demographer deals with the causes of widescale human migrations in prehistoric times and in the present. He investigates why European countries that formerly had high out-migration rates now need to import workers from other societies.

Ehrlich, Paul R., and Ann H. Ehrlich. *Population, Resources, Environment.* 2nd ed. San Francisco: W. H. Freeman, 1972.
A revealing presentation of the interrelationship of population growth, exhaustion of natural resources, and pollution of the environment.

Ford, Thomas R., and Gordon Dejong, eds. *Social Demography.* Englewood Cliffs, N.J.: Prentice-Hall, 1970.
An excellent general treatment of the field of social demography.

Herr, David M. *Society and Population.* 2nd ed. Englewood Cliffs, N.J.: Prentice-Hall, 1975.
The author shows how an understanding of population is important to a proper study of sociology. He also deals with the current population explosion.

Peterson, William. *Population.* 3rd ed. New York: Macmillan, 1975.
A comprehensive book that examines the factors that affect demographic processes in primitive, preindustrial, and modern societies.

Population and the American Future. New York: New American Library, 1972.
Prepared by the President's Commission on Population Growth and the American Future, this report deals with the effects of growth in numbers on social conditions and on the quality of life.

The city is a paradox. Cities are the seat of both the greatest cultural achievements of humankind and its severest problems. In the cities, we find great universities and the largest libraries, as well as the highest school dropout rate and the lowest educational attainment. In them we find magnificent cathedrals and high rates of crime, the beauty of art treasures and the ugliness of slums. Great medical centers are found in the city, but so are organized prostitution and traffic in illegal drugs. People come to the city for excitement, but those who live in the city are said to be bored and unhappy. The contrasts and contradictions of the city make it a fascinating system to study.

About three-fourths of all the people in the United States live in cities, and the trend is toward increasing urbanization. Within cities, patterns develop—interconnections between people, goods, and services—that affect their layouts. These patterns are what sociologists seek to study in what is known as urban ecology.

Of major interest to the sociologist are the slums of the inner city and the suburbs on its fringe. The problems of the slums and ghettoes seem almost to defy solution, despite numerous attempts at urban renewal. Suburbs are part of the problem, since suburb dwellers often use city services without paying city taxes.

Even a slight acquaintance with any American city makes one realize that it could do with better planning, to say the least. Urban planning is a complex matter, involving a lot more than deciding where the streets and parks should go. The basic thing we must determine is what we really want our cities to be like.

15
The City

The inner city is dying. Gracious old mansions, lived in for generations by the city's leading citizens, are being abandoned rapidly. The middle-class families that leave them head for the newer areas outside the old city.... Behind them into the decaying city come the poor families of the rural areas of the south. As each middle-class family leaves, the vacated house is soon divided into tenements, and five to ten rural families jam into it. The process is accelerating, and the inner city is probably on its way to becoming an overcrowded slum where young, jobless men in increasing numbers peddle pot.

The city described above is: (a) New York, (b) Detroit, (c) Chicago, (d) all of the above, (e) none of the above. The correct answer is (e). The city is Fes, Morocco, founded in A.D. 808, the exotic walled city described in the fourteenth century as one of the wonders of its time. Our description was written in 1972 by Richard Holbrooke, who spent two years in Morocco directing the Peace Corps there.

That the description of a deteriorating Moroccan city could be applied to many places in the United States may give us little consolation. Yet, it is good to be reminded that cities have been around for a long time and that urban problems are not uniquely American. A brief overview of the origin of cities and worldwide trends in urbanization should give us insight into what created cities. It will also help us to understand their growth, and at times, their decline. Surely these remarkable changes in the settlement patterns of our species are not haphazard. Once we know something of the origin and growth of cities, we can deal with urbanism in the United States. Although the origins of cities may seem only remotely relevant to the problems of pollution and congestion facing urban America in the 1970s, it is fascinating to explore why and where it all began (see Mumford, 1961).

THE ORIGIN OF CITIES

No one knows for sure, but it can be estimated conservatively that humans have been on this planet for at least 100,000 years. In Chapter 3, when we traced the evolution of human cultures, we noted that for about 65,000 years human culture was at the simple hunting and gathering stage. For at least two-thirds of human history, people lived by gathering wild plants and killing animals with their hands, or perhaps, with a wooden spear. It was not until 10,000 years ago that the idea of deliberately planting roots or seeds was implemented and that simple tools for cultivating plants were developed. Thus began the horticultural stage, and while it provided a more reliable source of food and permitted larger and more permanent human settlements, conditions were not yet ripe for the development of cities.

Essentially, three conditions were needed before cities could come into being. First, the technology had to be drastically improved; second, there had to be a regular and recurring agricultural surplus; and third, a new form of social organization was needed. The first two conditions are closely related. Although improved technology, including the development of the plow (and the use of draft animals for pulling it) and systems of irrigation were necessary to achieve consistent agricultural surpluses, such surpluses did not automatically result from technology. The earliest cities arose about 7000 years ago in the Near East, in the fertile valleys of the Tigris and Euphrates rivers. Here, the improved technology and the natural fertility of the land worked hand in glove to result in an agricultural surplus. Year after year, some people were able to produce more food than they needed for their own families. Thus, some others were freed to engage in nonfarming activities. Technology not only helped to create the food surplus but, in the form of the wheel and domesticated draft animals, it allowed the surplus to be transported from the producers to the consumers. Later, technology also enabled city workers to produce various goods of value, in addition to farm implements, for those in the hinterland.

Technology and farm surpluses were not in themselves enough for the development of cities. A new form of social organization was needed, one that would contain a fairly elaborate system of roles that would permit food and other goods to be traded in an orderly manner. The roles of merchant and shopkeeper needed to be developed, as well as roles for those who were responsible for hauling and storing goods, for making and repairing equipment, for building stalls and booths to display goods, and so on. The roles of scribe and clerk were needed to keep track of the grain that was stored or the amount that had to be produced. It was in this period of human history that writing and counting systems were developed, which were very likely inspired by the need for keeping records.

Later, as commerce became more important, seaport cities grew up in many parts of the world. These early cities were quite small, and even many of the later ones were small by contemporary standards. Ancient Babylon probably had no more than 25,000 people, and Athens, which reached its peak during the fifth century B.C., probably contained only 150,000 people. But thousands of years ago, the die was cast. We, the nomads of the forest, the cave dwellers, the primitive farmers, had begun to live in cities.

World Urbanization Trends

At the birth of Christ, there were about 12 cities in the Mediterranean area, each with no more than 100,000 inhabitants. In Asia, a few cities probably approached that size. By the second century, when Rome was at the peak of its power, its population was somewhere between 250,000 and one million people. At about the same time, there were other cities around the world with populations of up to 20,000. Understandably, records are imprecise, but the best estimate is that, at the time of Christ, there were 250 million people on earth, and a generous estimate would be that one-half of one percent of them were living in cities with populations of 20,000 or more.

Packing many people into a small area creates clutter problems on the roofs as well as in the streets. This picture is of Madrid, Spain, but it is typical of crowded cities around the world.

The collapse of the Roman Empire in A.D. 476 dramatically affected civilization and cities. The decline of the mighty Roman political organization cast an eclipse on the cultural skies of Western Europe. Trade and commerce, no longer centrally controlled, came to a virtual standstill during the Dark Ages. Although historians no longer consider the Dark Ages to have been completely "dark," the distinction that the phrase suggests is still sound. Cities lost their importance as centers of art and intellectual life, and their populations gradually declined (Pirenne, 1925). The population of the once glorious city of Rome was reduced to about 20,000.

The eclipse of the cities lasted for about 800 years, until the beginning of the Renaissance, in the thirteenth century. At about that time, printing with movable type was invented, and interest in the fine arts and scholarship was rekindled. Trade within Europe was restored, and cities were once again centers of cultural and economic happenings.

The real growth of cities was not to come until the Industrial Revolution, in the latter part of the eighteenth century. Once again, we see the importance of technology in the development of human culture. Steam, the newfound source of power, proved to be efficient and relatively cheap, but it had to be used close to where it was produced. The workers were collected into an immense place, and their looms and other machines were fed the magic power of steam. The factory system was born, and with it, the factory town and the factory city. The numerous workers in the city were, at the same time, both producers of huge quantities of goods desired by the rural population and a market for food and fiber. Meanwhile, agricultural techniques were improving. Many farm laborers found themselves out of work and responded to the lure—however illusory it may have seemed later—of better work and better living conditions in the city. Everything thus fit together to produce one of the greatest migrations in human history, the trek of huge numbers of people from rural areas to the cities. This brings us up to the recent past, and the growth of cities in the United States.

Urbanism in the United States

According to the census definition, any place that is incorporated as a city, village, borough, or town and that has at least 2500 inhabitants is considered to be **urban.** Recently, unincorporated areas of this population size have also been designated urban. Some exceptions exist, but if you live in a town or city with at least 2499 other people, you are living in an urban area.

In Table 15.1, we can see the contrast between the year 1800, when a little over 300,000 people (six percent of the population) were living in urban areas, and 1980, when almost 170 million (over three-fourths of the population) are urbanites. It can be noted, also, that in 1920 a simple plurality of the population lived in urban areas. Sixty years later, the urban population is 75 percent. And we can expect still more change in the same direction. By

TABLE 15.1 Growth of Urban Population, 1800–1980

Year	Number of People in Urban Areas	Proportion of Total Population*
1800	322,371	6%
1820	693,255	7
1840	1,845,055	11
1860	6,216,518	20
1880	14,129,735	28
1900	30,214,832	40
1910	42,064,001	46
1920	54,253,282	51
1930	69,160,599	56
1940	74,705,338	57
1950	96,846,817	64
1960	125,268,750	70
1970	149,324,930	74
1980	170,000,000	76

*Rounded to nearest full percentage point.
Source: U.S. Bureau of the Census, *1970 Census of Population, U.S. Summary* (Washington, D.C.: U.S. Government Printing Office, 1970), p. 42. (Data for 1980 are estimates.)

TABLE 15.2   Number and Size of Cities, 1900-1970

Size Classification	1900	1910	1920	1930	1940	1950	1960	1970
1,000,000 or more	3	3	3	5	5	5	5	6
500,000–1,000,000	3	5	9	8	9	13	16	20
100,000–500,000	32	42	56	80	78	88	111	130
50,000–100,000	40	60	77	98	107	126	201	240
25,000–50,000	83	119	143	185	213	252	432	520
Under 25,000	1579	2037	2437	2802	3072	4278	5276	6146
All urban places	1740	2266	2725	3179	3485	4764	6041	7062

Source: U.S. Bureau of the Census, *1970 Census of the Population, U.S. Summary* (Washington, D.C.: U.S. Government Printing Office, 1970), p. 46.

the year 2000, which is not all that far off, the best estimate is that 90 percent of us will be living in urban areas.

Another way to see the rural-to-urban change in our society is to look at how cities in general and large cities in particular have increased in number since the turn of the century. As shown in Table 15.2, 80 years ago there were fewer than 2000 urban places; now there are a little over 7000. In 1900, there were only six cities in the United States with populations of a half million or more; now there are 26. Only 15.6 percent of urban dwellers, as indicated in Table 15.3, live in cities with populations of 500,000 or more. And this proportion has not changed much since 1920; the big increase since the turn of the century is in the proportion of people living in cities with under 100,000 inhabitants.

Another indicator of how highly urbanized our nation has become is the proportion of the population that lives in **standard metropolitan statistical areas** (SMSAs). An **SMSA** usually consists of a city of at least 50,000 inhabitants, the county in which the central city is located, and any adjacent counties that are found to be metropolitan in nature and are socially and economically tied to the central city. In 1970, there were 263 SMSAs in the United States, 148 of them with populations of 200,000 or more. In the same year, over 150 million Americans, or over 70 percent of the population, were living in SMSAs. Thus, the bulk of our population lives in places that are economically and socially integrated with a city.

The emergence of the **megalopolis** is still another indication of how urbanized we have become. A megalopolis consists of several to many large cities within a fairly large geographic area that were once separated by large expanses of forest or farmland but that have now essentially been joined together by the meeting of their suburbs and satellite cities. The Northeast

TABLE 15.3   Urban Population of the United States, 1900–1970

	1900	1910	1920	1930	1940	1950	1960	1970
Percent in cities of 1,000,000 or more	8	9	10	12	12	12	10	9
Percent in cities of 500,000 to 1,000,000	2	3	6	5	5	6	6	6
Percent in cities of 100,000 to 500,000	8	10	10	13	12	12	13	12
Percent in cities of under 100,000	21	24	25	27	28	35	41	46
Percent in cities, all sizes	40	46	51	56	57	64	70	74

*Percents rounded to nearest full point.
Source: U.S. Bureau of the Census, *1970 Census of Population, U.S. Summary* (Washington, D.C.: U.S. Government Printing Office, 1970), p. 46. Prior to 1950 some large and densely settled areas were not classified as urban because they were unincorporated. The data in this table use the current definition of urban for 1950 and beyond. The data prior to 1960 do not include the population of Alaska and Hawaii.

seaboard megalopolis stretches from New Hampshire to Washington, D.C., including its Maryland and Virginia suburbs, and is called BosWash. Almost 40 million people, or nearly 19 percent of our total population, live in BosWash. Millions more live in other emerging megalopolises, such as ChiPitts, which stretches from Chicago to Pittsburgh; JaMi, which reaches from Jacksonville to Miami; and SanSan, which goes from San Francisco to San Diego. The megalopolis is not, of course, a political unit; it can cross state, county, and local governmental unit lines. There is more interdependence within a megalopolis than is usually found within a comparable geographic area. The people of BosWash, for example, are more socially and economically interdependent than would be the people who live in a strip extending westward from Virginia to Ohio.

Americans are often said to be deserting their cities. In recent years this is true to some extent. Each year between 1970 and 1975, for every 100 people who moved into a metropolitan area, 131 moved out. Nearly one in six of all SMSAs had fewer residents in 1975 than they had in 1970. The declining population of SMSAs is particularly noticeable in the larger ones, including New York, Los Angeles-Long Beach, Chicago, Philadelphia, Detroit, St. Louis, and Pittsburgh. Even in the majority of SMSAs that continue to show increases in population, growth is more pronounced in the suburbs than in the central cities. Figure 15.1 clearly shows what has happened over the last 35 years: suburbanites, once the smallest category of the population, have become the largest. This is one reason why suburbs will receive considerable attention later in this chapter.

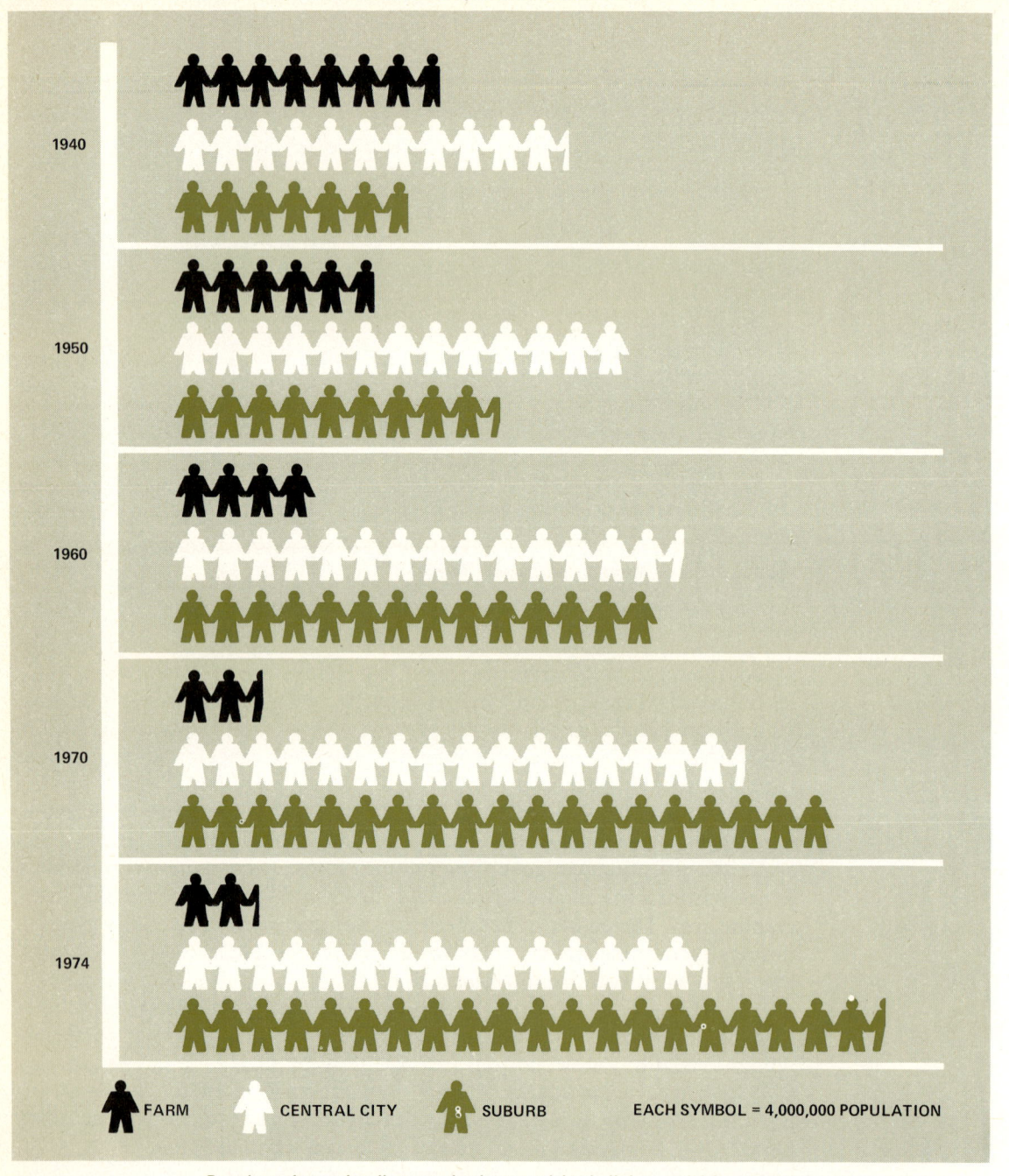

FIGURE 15.1 Farm, City, and Suburban Population, 1940–1974

▟ FARM   ▟ CENTRAL CITY   ▟ SUBURB   EACH SYMBOL = 4,000,000 POPULATION

Rural nonfarm dwellers and urban residents living outside of metropolitan areas are not included in this chart. Some farm dwellers are also included in the suburban category. The definitions of central city and suburb for the years 1940–1960 are according to the 1960 census. The 1970 figures reflect some slight changes in the definitions that were used in the 1970 census.

Source: Reproduced by permission. Carl Behrens, "Where Will the Next 50 Million Americans Live?" *Population Bulletin,* vol. 27, no. 5 (Washington, D.C.: Population Reference Bureau, October 1971), p. 9; data for 1974 from U.S. Bureau of the Census, *Current Population Reports,* series P-23, no. 55 and series P-27, no. 47.

URBAN ECOLOGY: THE CITY AS A SYSTEM

In the 1920s, several sociologists at the University of Chicago, notably Robert E. Park, Ernest W. Burgess, and Roderick D. McKenzie, began studying the American city. They concentrated on the *spatial patterns* of cities, how these patterns got to be the way they are, and how they are likely to change. Through the efforts of these and other pioneers, the subfield of sociology called **human ecology** came into existence.

Today "ecology" is an "in" term. To many, it means little more than not throwing beer cans along the highways, not flushing soapsuds down the drain unless they are biodegradable, and not cutting down too many trees to make newsprint. Beyond these popular notions, there is a broader concept that deals with the interrelationship of organisms. It was Charles Darwin, writing in 1859, who first described this interrelationship of living things as the "web of life," and it was Darwin who recognized the different forms this interrelationship could take—sometimes a struggle for existence among species, sometimes cooperation, and sometimes a process of helping. Darwin also dealt with how these processes affected the geographic distribution of species—that is, how the picture of an area could change through the interaction of species.

Possibly because plants do not run away when you try to study them, plant scientists were the first to recognize the importance of the interdependence of species and to develop a science of interdependence—plant ecology. Animal ecology followed, but not until 1921 was the concept of human ecology used in a sociology text (Park and Burgess, 1921). Now, the term **urban ecology** is often used instead, because so much of human ecology research deals with how humans in and around cities interact and are interdependent and with how these processes affect the spatial patterning of activities in cities.

It is not surprising that urban ecologists, as latecomers to the field of ecology, adapted many of the concepts of plant ecology to human populations. While plant ecologists dealt with the invasion by one species into an area previously dominated by another, urban ecologists used the concept of **invasion** to indicate the intrusion of new types of population units or kinds of activities into an area. Examples include the establishment of a few stores or offices in what was once an area of single-family homes, or the movement of a few black families into an all-white area. If the residential area becomes predominantly commercial, or if the all-white suburb eventually becomes predominantly black, the process is complete, for the time being at least, and we refer to it as **succession**.

Just as an area in which a hardwood forest has succeeded a stand of softwood trees presents a new *configuration*, so does an area where businesses displace homes or one ethnic group displaces another. The competition for space within an urban area is presumably no less orderly than is the competition for space among plants and animals. Urban ecologists thus study the processes that occur among segments of the urban population, the

484
UNDERSTANDING
CONFLICT AND CHANGE

FIGURE 15.2 Burgess' Concentric Zone Theory of Urban Growth

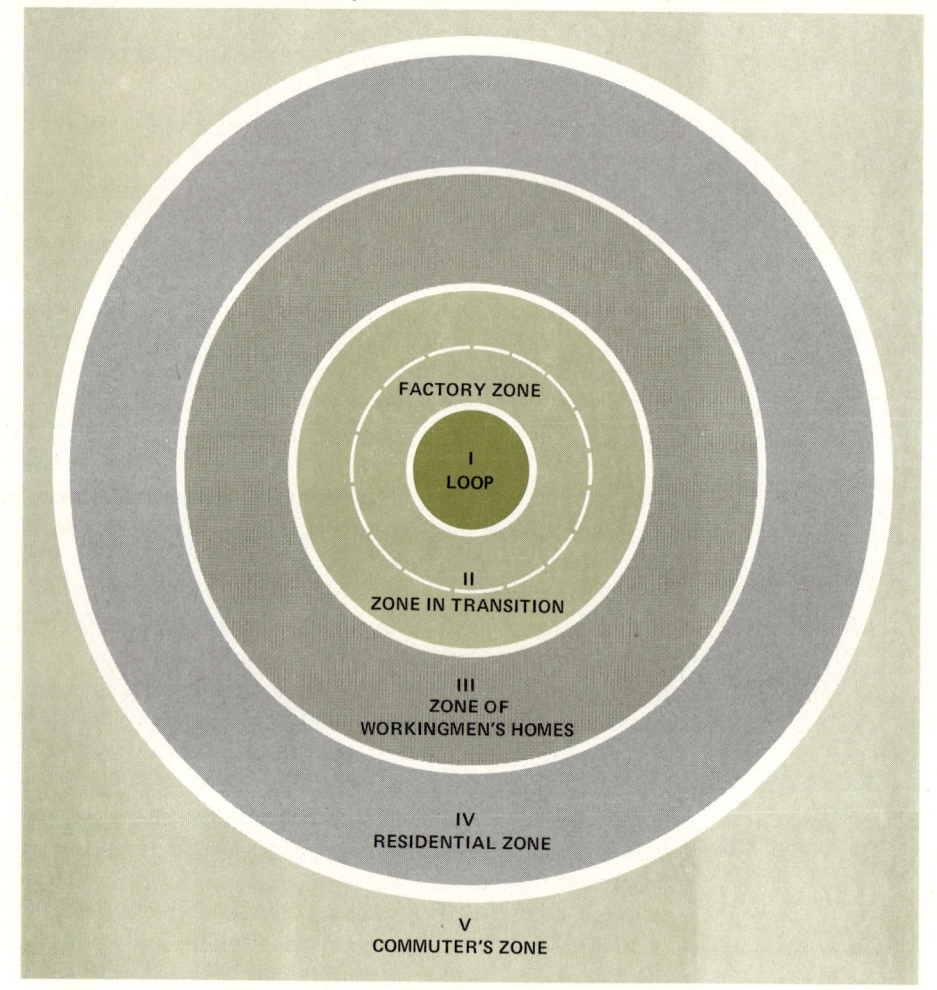

- I LOOP
- FACTORY ZONE
- II ZONE IN TRANSITION
- III ZONE OF WORKINGMEN'S HOMES
- IV RESIDENTIAL ZONE
- V COMMUTER'S ZONE

Source: Reproduced by permission, from Robert E. Park, Ernest W. Burgess, and Robert D. McKenzie, *The City* (Chicago: University of Chicago Press, 1925), p. 51.

processes that affect urban activities, and the ways in which these processes affect the spatial pattern of the city.

From his studies of Chicago, sociologist Ernest Burgess theorized the **concentric zone model,** which posits that American cities could be depicted as a series of concentric zones, as presented in Figure 15.2 (Park, Burgess, and McKenzie, 1925). The central business district (called the Loop in Chicago) is at the center, and each of the other zones was hypothesized to have more or less distinct populations and land use. It is just beyond the central business district that the slums are usually found. Early in the history of American cities, before the advent of the automobile, the better residential areas were close to the center of the city, so that middle- and upper-class workers would have ready access to their places of work. Now, the better homes are, for the most part, beyond the city in what Burgess called the Commuter's Zone.

Other theories of the structure and growth of cities have been advanced. Homer Hoyt (1943), for example, devised a **sector model.** The essential feature of this theory is that beyond the central business district, different land uses expand outward in pie-shaped sectors. Thus, as shown in Figure 15.3, a high-class residential area may spread out basically to the east, while manufacturing districts may develop toward the north and south. The result is that the city would resemble a circle that has been cut into a number of wedge-shaped pieces, with each wedge, or sector, dominated by a particular kind of residential, business, or manufacturing activity. Note, however, that the poorest residential areas basically surround the central business district in the same way as is posited in the concentric zone theory. Richmond, Virginia, fits the sector theory reasonably well.

Understandably, neither of these theories adequately describes all American cities. Rivers or mountains may effectively prevent growth in certain directions. The spatial arrangement of a city may also be affected by the values or traditions of the inhabitants. In Boston, for example, the Common remains a large park in the center of the business district, even though, economically, the land could be put to better use (Firey, 1947).

FIGURE 15.3 Hoyt's Sector Theory of Urban Growth

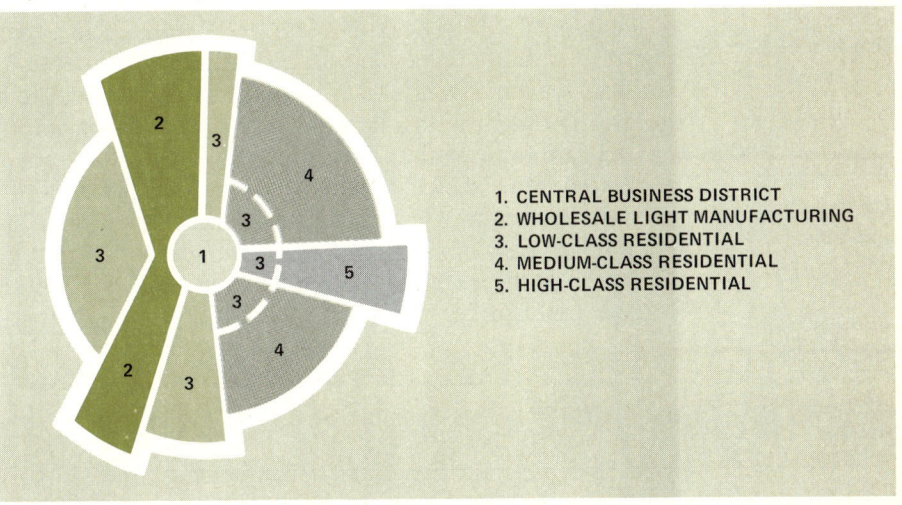

1. CENTRAL BUSINESS DISTRICT
2. WHOLESALE LIGHT MANUFACTURING
3. LOW-CLASS RESIDENTIAL
4. MEDIUM-CLASS RESIDENTIAL
5. HIGH-CLASS RESIDENTIAL

Source: Reprinted from "The Nature of Cities" by Chauncey D. Harris and E. L. Ullman in volume no. 242 of *The Annals* of the American Academy of Political and Social Science. Copyright 1945 by The American Academy of Political and Social Science.

FIGURE 15.4   A Simplified Ecological Diagram of the Urban Region

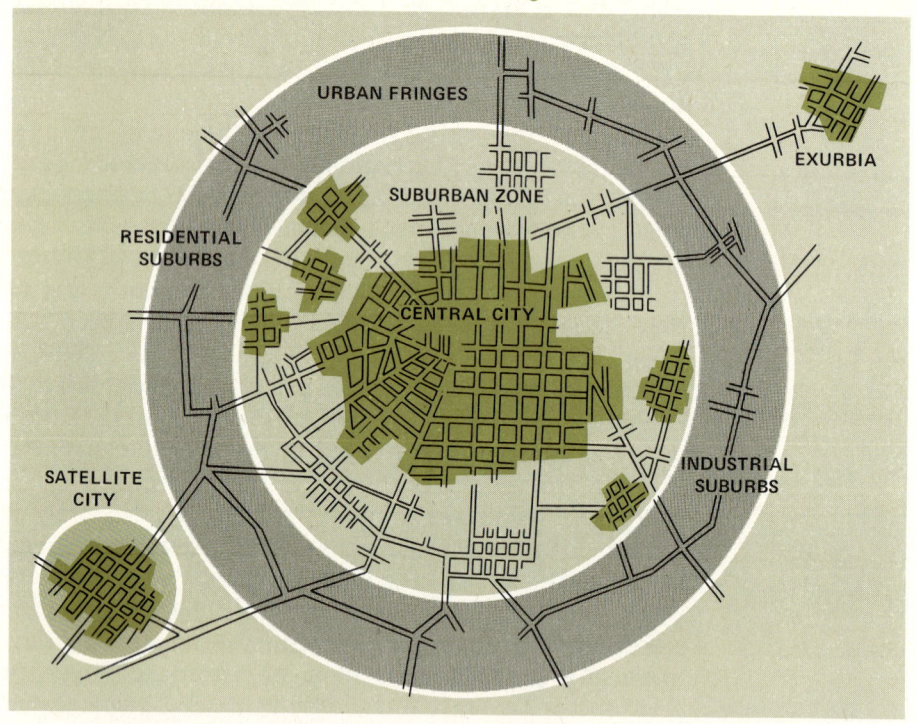

Source: Reproduced by permission from Alvin Boskoff, *The Sociology of Urban Regions,* 2nd ed., © 1970, p. 107. Reprinted by permission of Prentice-Hall, Inc., Englewood Cliffs, N.J.

Sociologist Alvin Boskoff's (1970) diagram of an urban region, shown in Figure 15.4, takes us beyond the city and its immediate surrounding areas to show how even a smaller city, called a **satellite city,** can be socially and economically linked with a large city. Within the scope of this chapter, we cannot give more than an indication of how areas of a city are functionally interrelated, nor can we analyze the various segments of the city and show how they relate to one another. It should suffice for us to say that cities are complex centers of socioeconomic interaction and that every city in history has fitted into a larger network of such interaction, whether on a national or international scale.

SLUMS AND GHETTOS

Within the central city, just beyond the business district, is the area that Burgess called *Zone Two,* or the *Zone in Transition.* Earlier in the history of the city, this zone was usually a residential area, but it is now becoming a part of the business district, with stores, shops, and office buildings. If the business district actually does expand to take over the area, the value of the land will increase. While waiting for the expansion, most landlords do not consider it good economics to keep up or improve residences that they believe will soon be torn down; so they rent out the houses or apartments for the best price they can get and hope that, in time, they can sell the property at an inflated price. Because the growth of central business districts has slowed, however, areas around them really may not be in transition. They could, therefore, be destined to remain slums for a long time.

Slums: Hells with an Escape Hatch

Even though the rats may be as large and the roaches as annoying in one as in the other, it is useful to distinguish between a slum and a ghetto. At its worst, a **slum** may consist of woefully deteriorated buildings with leaky roofs, sagging floors, and hazardous electrical wiring. To produce more rental income, the older homes or apartments may have been cut up into extremely small units, producing severe overcrowding. People from several apartments may have to share toilets and sinks, and sometimes, even these indoor facilities are lacking. Not all slums are this bad, but by definition, none of them is a decent place in which to live.

Socially, slums are no more desirable than they are physically. Knifings, shootings, and crimes of other sorts are all more prevalent in slums than in other sections of the city (see Box 15.1). Divorce, desertion, prostitution, some forms of mental illness, suicide, and drug abuse are also more prevalent. No wonder some people consider the larger society criminal for

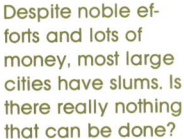

Despite noble efforts and lots of money, most large cities have slums. Is there really nothing that can be done?

allowing the slum dwellers to destroy themselves and one another, either physically or psychologically.

In the past, migrants from foreign countries or from rural areas settled in the slums of the city, usually because they could not afford to live anywhere else. As their economic lot improved, they moved out. True, the Irish, Italians, and other ethnic groups at times had difficulty finding homes in better sections of the city, but the pressures to keep them out of such areas were not extreme. And therein lies the difference between a ghetto and a slum.

Ghettos: Hells with No Way Out

The term "ghetto" was first used to describe the sections of European cities in which Jews were required to live; they could not, by law, live elsewhere. Today, *ghetto* is a tragic but apt description of some sections of American cities. Blacks, the poor, and particularly poor blacks live in these areas, and almost no one else does. Our laws do not require them to do so, but social and economic factors, which have had the force of law, have all but created a wall around our urban ghettos. Despite open-housing laws, blacks find it exceedingly difficult to find housing outside the ghetto. And many simply cannot afford to buy or rent in the suburbs. The term **ghetto** thus implies a forced segregation, and it often implies slum conditions as well. Even a suburb or good apartment complex with a virtually all-black population is

---

**BOX 15.1
WILL THE FOLKS WHO BROUGHT YOU ACUPUNCTURE BRING YOU CRIME-FREE CITIES?**

Between 1949 and 1972, fear of crime in the streets of our central cities rose 550 percent. A sample survey in 1949 found that four percent of respondents considered crime to be the major problem in their cities (of 500,000 or more population); in 1977, crime was named as the major problem by 22 percent. In 1968, 31 percent of city dwellers were fearful of walking in their own neighborhoods at night; in 1977, 45 percent felt that fear. And 15 percent of city dwellers are also fearful of being attacked in their own homes. All of these fears are felt more by blacks than by whites.

One-third of the people living in densely populated areas of the United States have been touched by urban crime in the last 12 months. They have been mugged, robbed, raped or have suffered property loss. Crime is a way of life in the central city, both for the criminals and for those who have been or fear to be victims.

For older people, it is probably difficult to remember the good old days, when the major urban problems were such nuisances as corrupt politicians, traffic congestion, high taxes, and poor housing. For younger people, it is probably hard to believe that most urban crime was confined to smoke-filled rooms in city hall.

technically a ghetto if forced segregation accounts for the lack of racial mixture.

We have had no shortage of rhetoric on what to do about our urban ghettos; nor, to be fair, have we lacked noble plans and efforts. But we still have the ghettos. Attempts to improve the lot of ghetto dwellers fall into two categories: (1) removal of the ghetto by providing decent, integrated housing elsewhere; or (2) rebuilding of the ghetto. There are problems with both approaches, and to make matters worse, both of them may be missing the crux of the problem.

Integrated Housing Outside the Ghetto   That all future housing should be located outside existing ghettos sounds like a reasonable and humane goal, and quite in keeping with our democratic ideals. The big trouble is that, so far, it has not worked, at least not very well. Black ghettos are growing larger; between 1960 and 1970, blacks in the central cities increased by 3.2 million, mostly in the already black ghettos (Halebsky, 1973). By contrast, the number of blacks who live in or have moved to integrated areas outside the central city is scarcely noticeable. Between 1970 and 1975, the number of whites in central cities declined by about seven percent, while the number of blacks increased by about ten percent. This trend has been going on for some time. The result is that blacks, many of them poor, now constitute a large proportion of the people in a number of American cities. Almost three-fourths of the population of Washington, D.C., is now black; in De-

---

Oddly enough, at least one large city in the world has been transformed in the last 25 years from a worldwide symbol of crime to a virtually crime-free city of 10 million people: Shanghai, China. This is a city whose name was even used to denote a certain crime (to shanghai someone was to drug or intoxicate him and kidnap him for involuntary service at sea). But, when the Communists came to power in 1949, Shanghai's days of crime were over. Or so it is claimed.

How was this transformation accomplished? By what sociologists call resocializing, and what Communist spokesmen call ideological education. By 1973, 60,000 criminals and prostitutes had been rounded up, reeducated, and resettled, with jobs. In 1972, foreign visitors on their own unescorted journeys through the city could find no police other than those directing traffic. What could account for the success of such resocializing? Is there something about a classless society that drastically reduces the motivation for antisocial behavior? Or did the authorities use techniques in their resocializing that are contrary to our democratic values? The secret—if we could make use of it without radically altering our political values—would be well worth discovering and studying.

troit, about half the population is black; and the population of Cleveland is over 40 percent black. Some of the black arrivals to our cities can move into homes abandoned by whites, thus extending the size of the black ghetto, but this does not really change the phenomenon of racial segregation. For other blacks who move to the city, there is literally no decent housing available.

Few homes are built within the central city by the private sector at a price that the urban poor of any race can afford. Public housing is usually located near the central cities, partly because people in other sections refuse to allow the poor to live among them. In addition, much public housing is racially segregated; integrated housing outside the ghetto helps only a small number of the more affluent blacks. A good case can be made for not abandoning the struggle to create integrated housing outside the ghetto at prices people can afford to pay. In the immediate future, though, this approach seems unlikely to enable us to tear down the ghetto walls.

Urban Renewal Urban renewal may sound like a viable way to rebuild and renovate the ghettos and slums; but, curiously, rebuilding projects under the Urban Renewal Act of 1954, which is still in effect, have not really cleared the slums. For one thing, the local urban renewal agency has the power to decide what constitutes a slum. Once an area has been labeled a slum, the city can then buy the land, raze the property, and secure low-interest federal loans for rebuilding. Often, the areas being renewed are the best of the slums. Part of the city is beautified, but the worst of the slums remain. The criterion for renewal often seems to be not whether slum dwellers need better housing but whether the area in question has the potential for producing income for the city.

Urban renewal can ignore human needs in still other ways. The act requires the local agency to demonstrate that "decent, safe, and sanitary" housing is available elsewhere in the city, and to help relocate the people who are being evicted by urban renewal. Nevertheless, the new locations may not be any better than the old ones, and the forced relocation can destroy a neighborhood and break up long-established interaction patterns. (The acute anguish of some people who were forced out of an inner-city neighborhood in Boston is vividly described by Marc Fried in his article "Grieving for a Lost Home," 1963.) Middle-class planners seem unaware of the attachment that many of the poor have to their neighborhoods, and particularly, of how they define the streets and alleys as part of their social space. Edward Ryan describes this aspect of life in the slums:

> Social life has an almost uninterrupted flow between apartment and street: children are sent to the street to play, women lean out of windows to watch and take part in street activity, women go "out on the street" to talk with friends, men and boys meet on the corners at night and families sit on the steps and talk with their neighbors at night when the weather is warm (Fried and Gleicher, 1973).

The experience of St. Louis, Missouri, with slum clearance is one worth noting. In the early 1960s, a high rise project, the Pruitt-Igoe Housing Project, was built to replace some of the city's slum dwellings. Within a few years, it had deteriorated dramatically. Crime and drug addiction were rampant. Tenants complained about the broken glass all around, the trash, the mice and roaches, and most of all, the attacks they were experiencing in the halls and laundry rooms. People would urinate in the elevators and halls. Eventually, it was admitted that, despite efforts to bring about order and provide a decent place to live, nothing worked to save the project. Twenty-three buildings were closed, and three were torn down. Basically, what happened was that human values and living styles were ignored or went unrecognized in the designing of the project. There was too much space—halls, elevators, laundry rooms—that belonged to no one and for which no one felt responsible.

The decaying portions of our cities must be saved and revived. But, true renovation of the ghettos requires much more than the rebuilding of dilapidated housing. Parks, playgrounds, libraries, and schools would have to be added or improved to make the ghetto a decent place in which to live. Because ghetto rebuilding would allow racial segregation to continue, some people are opposed to it. But, so far, urban renewal has failed in meeting human needs, chiefly because slum and ghetto inhabitants have little power and can exert little influence over the decisions that affect their lives.

One imaginative approach to urban renewal is *urban homesteading.* Under this plan, the Department of Housing and Urban Development (HUD) sells rundown and abandoned houses to private families for one dollar. Buyers have to pledge that they will rehabilitate the house and live in it for three years. If they do so, they acquire unconditional ownership of it. This plan has been put into practice in at least forty cities. Baltimore has expanded urban homesteading by using city funds in addition to the HUD program. In one section of the city, there were 900 applicants for 90 of these houses. Not all cities have empty houses that can be sold in some kind of homesteading program. Then, too, funds for urban homesteading are not unlimited. Nevertheless, even a modest effort of this kind will result in a few better homes, and more important, a sense of pride among those who choose to live in an area and fix up the homes. (Another approach to urban renewal is described in Box 15.2.)

Reducing Poverty The problem of ghettos and slums cannot be separated from the more general problem of poverty. A massive attack on poverty would make slums and ghettos less oppressive to their inhabitants, and it would give many people greater choice about where and how they are to live. The differences in family incomes between those inside and those outside the central city are a telling sign of the magnitude of the effort that is needed. In 1975, blacks living in the central cities of large metropolitan areas had a median family income of $9,874, while whites living outside the cities of these same metropolitan areas had a median family income of $17,436. In smaller metropolitan areas, white suburbanite families had a median income $7,000 higher than that of black central-city dwellers. More than three million black families live in the central cities of metropolitan areas. Releasing this large group from poverty would be an enormous task; among other things, new jobs would have to be created and better job training programs as well as various welfare measures would be needed. Because inner-city black families have incomes $5,000 lower than those of inner-city whites, and $7,000 lower than those of white suburbanites, they cannot afford to move out of the ghettos, either to better sections of the city or to the suburbs.

**BOX 15.2
YOUNG PROFESSIONALS DISCOVER THE INNER CITY**

For a number of decades, but particularly since World War II, middle- and upper-class Americans have sought the good life in the suburbs. Areas around the central city have been left to the poor and the minorities. Large, old houses in the inner city, once the pride of the rich, were converted into apartment houses for the urban poor. Neighborhoods became more dense; streets, yards, and houses were neglected; and services by the city were reduced. Only those who could afford nothing better remained in or moved into the areas. But, recently, things have changed.

The city has been "rediscovered" by young professionals, who have moved into the areas and have renovated the old homes. The Parkman Center for Urban Affairs (1977) has studied this movement in an effort to discover who is moving into the inner-city, why they are choosing this environment, and what impact the in-migration is likely to have on cities.

The Parkman Center refers to the new migrants as "the young professionals." They are well educated, relatively affluent, and mostly in their twenties or early thirties. Almost all of them are white. Their children, if they have any, are pre-school age. The husband and most frequently, the wife, too, have well-paying, steady employment. Both are usually college graduates and have had a wide variety of experiences. They have many options and could live just about anywhere they wanted to. Why, then, do they choose the inner-city?

Clearly, the young professionals who move into the city are different from their suburban counterparts. Not only are they different, but they like to be different and to do what is not typical of people with their education and income. Many exhibit an anti-suburban bias and feel superior to isolated suburbanites. In addition, they are attracted to the city by the character, quality, and relative low prices of housing. "Interesting" old houses appeal to them. They like racially mixed neighborhoods, and the

SUBURBS

The next time you are at the beach, make a pile of sand and then pour more sand on the center of the pile. Some of it will remain in the center, making the pile higher, but much of it will spread out in a ring around the base. In the same way, while skyscrapers and high-rise apartments have created upward growth in our cities' centers, most city growth has been outward, in an ever-expanding ring of suburbs around the edges.

Those who consider the growth of suburbs to be a recent plot against the central city seem to miss the basic fact that sizable growth of urban populations demands outward growth. There is no plot, and the outward movement has not exactly been recent. New York began to decentralize as early

---

presence of ethnic stores and shops adds to that appeal. The convenience of travel to their jobs is also a factor.

Whatever forces and values bring the young professionals to the inner city, their presence there would seem to be desirable: they clean up and renovate old homes, thus retarding the decay of the neighborhood and conserving energy needed for new housing construction; and living close to their jobs, they relieve the burden on public and private transportation. But, is there a negative side to their presence?

The first middle-class families that move into the deteriorated inner-city neighborhoods are, in the phrase of urban ecologists, the "invaders." Their numbers are few, they are well aware that lower-class culture dominates the neighborhood. They do not try to change the neighborhood, only their own homes. Typically, the invaders are followed by what the Parkman Center calls the "early settlers." They are forced to pay a little more for their homes, for the number of houses is limited. As still more middle-class migrants move into the area, the scarcity of old homes forces the prices up still further. The later wave of migrants seems more inclined to change the neighborhoods and to protect their investment. The later migrants worry about "nonauthentic" renovations, such as awnings and aluminum siding.

As more and more middle-class people move into the inner city, minority groups and the poor find that they can no longer afford to rent in the area. Housing problems of low-income families become intensified, for in most cities, such housing is scarce. When middle-class people, for whatever their reasons, invade a low-income neighborhood, they ultimately displace the poorer people, who do not have many options for other places to live. When the succession is completed, the physical appearance of the area has improved, but in the process, poor people are hurt.

Even less affluent suburbs offer home ownership plus roomier homes and quieter streets than can be found in the city.

as 1850, and some 22 other cities did so around the turn of the century. As the urban historians Charles Glaab and Theodore Brown (1971) point out, the movement of population from the center of Philadelphia to its suburbs was proportionally greater in the years from 1860 to 1910 than it was between 1900 and 1950. Following these early beginnings, the suburbs grew in great spurts in the 1920s, when the automobile allowed commuting to and from the central city. After World War II, the unmet needs for housing that built up during the war, coupled with greater general affluence and government-supported home-loan plans, produced a further growth of suburbs, and this time, it was to unprecedented proportions.

The Myth of Suburbia

Both as part of the growth pattern of urban areas and as settlement groups we have invented to satisfy our needs, the suburbs are fascinating to the sociologist, as they are, also, to novelists and journalists (see, for example, Gordon et al., 1961; Keats, 1956; McPartland, 1957; Spectorsky, 1955; Wyden, 1960). It is amazing how many ways the popular view of the suburbs and of suburbanites differs from the reality of the suburbs discovered by sociologists.

The suburb that intrigues novelists, and presumably their readers, is often a colony of mass-produced houses whose occupants are as indistinguishable from one another as are their homes. The typical suburbanite is described as a status seeker *par excellence*, moving to the suburbs to display and enjoy the material fruits of past efforts. Once there, the suburbanite works at an exhausting pace to keep up with his or her neighbors, by gathering a bewildering display of appliances, gadgets, and furnishings. Meanwhile, the truly successful family moves to a better suburb, where the race continues, but on a higher materialistic plane, with backyard swimming pools, country club memberships, and expensive cars. Suburbanites are described as lonely or as too much caught up in the affairs of their neighbors. If the stereotype is to be believed, suburbanites undergo something approaching a religious conversion. That is, seemingly nice, ordinary people move to the suburbs and are mysteriously transformed into ultraconservative conformists and racists. They fled the city, but now, although bored, alienated, and altogether disenchanted with suburban living, they have lost the will to flee, except, perhaps, to another suburb.

The Facts of Suburbia

It is easy to debunk these extremely critical views of the suburbs. For the suburbs simply have not produced all the pathological people that one would imagine from the stereotype. Most sociologists have recognized the popular description of surburbia for what it is—a myth. But, at least two sociologists have taken the myth seriously enough to conduct research in suburbia. Bennett Berger (1960) studied a suburb of San Jose, California. In his study, he not only applied the general misconceptions about suburbs as hypotheses for proof or disproof, but he also conducted a detailed case study of the way of life of suburban blue-collar families. The findings of his study were quite at odds with the conventional wisdom. The working-class families who had moved to the suburb, Berger found, "had not been profoundly affected in any statistically identifiable or sociologically interesting way." When Herbert Gans (1967) made a participant observation study of Levittown, near Philadelphia, he found that the suburbanites were happy, engaged in many family activities, and continued to visit relatives. They were neither in a status race with the neighbors or unduly concerned about conformity. He, too, found the rule to be contentment without unwanted conformity.

An important reason why the sociological findings differ from the suburban myth is that sociological principles do not allow us to predict dramatic changes in people—the so-called "conversion effect"—as a result of spatial move. You will recall that in our discussion of adult socialization (Chapter 4), we saw that people are required to take on new roles as they move into new and different social situations. But this process is not a "conversion." The adults who are being socialized—or, in suburbia, who are frequently socializing each other—bring with them their basic values and keep as much of their way of life as is considered appropriate.

Therefore, many sociological studies of the suburban movement have focused on the background of people who move to the suburbs and on their motives for doing so. From such studies, there emerges a sociological profile of suburban people, including their age, class, race, and so on. Compared and contrasted with profiles of populations from other parts of the urban area, these profiles show that the suburbs are a functional part of the larger social system.

The Push-Pull of Cities and Suburbs

Sociologists commonly categorize motives for moving to the suburbs into those that *push* people *away* from the central city and those that *pull* them *toward* the outskirts. When the combination of push and pull factors is sufficiently strong, people move. Of course, many people have never lived in a central city; having grown up in one or more suburbs, they settle in another suburb upon marriage. No push factors are involved for them, unless they have mentally weighed the pros and cons of living in an urban environment but have opted for the suburban life. In still other instances, no pushes from the city are involved. A few years ago, for example, several hundred employees were transferred from an IBM plant in Lexington, Kentucky, to one in Austin, Texas. Few, if any, of these families could have settled in the central city of Austin, for adequate middle-income family housing is not being built there or in any of our cities. And, so, these families moved from the suburbs of Lexington to the suburbs of Austin: they did not flee from anything or anybody.

What, then, do people not like about the city, and what draws them to the suburbs? The factors that usually push people out of the city are known to anyone who has lived or thought of living in a central city: old and rundown buildings; air pollution, noise, and traffic congestion; high crime rates; the age and condition of the schools; and the fact that there are crowds everywhere. Central to our cultural heritage is the idea that the good life is to be found in rural areas and small towns (see Box 15.3); and the closest most

---

BOX 15.3 LIVING PATTERNS: DAYDREAMS VERSUS FACTS

Do people live where they want to live? Gallup pollsters asked people, "If you could live anywhere in the United States that you wanted to, would you prefer a city, a suburban area, a small town, or a farm?" Although these categories do not allow an exact comparison with census definitions of cities, SMSAs, or rural areas, we still form some idea of the discrepancies between where people live and where they would like to live.

Rural living appeals to over half of all Americans, as shown in Table 15.4, but only one-quarter of all Americans live in rural areas. Five times as many people say they would like to live on a farm as actually do. Conversely, only 13 percent say they prefer to live in a city, but 54 percent live in cities of over 100,000 population.

Some people could move if they wanted to, just as some people can and do move to Australia or New Zealand. Yet, most people who would like to live in rural areas are prevented from doing so by the scarcity of rural jobs and the difficulties in commuting long distances to work in the city. Then, too, small towns no longer would be small if one-third of our population, roughly 70 million people, moved to them. The Gallup poll

TABLE 15.4   Where Americans Live and Would Like to Live, in Percentages*

Percent Who Actually Live in:		Percent Who Would Like to Live in:	
Central city	32	City	13
Urban fringe	27		
Outside urbanized area	15	Suburbs	31
Rural nonfarm	22	Small town	32
Farm	5	Farm	23

*Rounded to nearest full point.
Source: *Gallup Index*, December, 1972, p. 22; and U.S. Bureau of the Census, *Statistical Abstract of the United States: 1972* (Washington, D.C.: U.S. Government Printing Office, 1972), pp. 16 and 584.

Americans come to this vision is suburbia. Various studies have found that those who move to the suburbs place a high value on family living and on what they consider the good life for all family members (Bell, 1958; Berger, 1960; Gans, 1967). They want roomier homes than the city provides, and they consider owning a home important. Quiet streets, yards with trees and grass, good schools, and convenient shopping centers with ample parking

does show little enchantment with urban living. The proportion preferring the city has gone down considerably over the years the public has been polled on their preferences: 22 percent in 1966, 18 percent in 1970, 17 percent in 1971, and 13 percent in 1972 preferred city living.

The difference between where people live and where they say they would like to live points up a persistent problem in sociological research. We have data on what people do—they live in cities. And we have data on what they say—many want to live on farms and in small towns. How do we interpret what they say? Do the statements reflect strong desires or nostalgic dreams? And, how do we interpret the discrepancy between actual behavior and stated preferences? Are most Americans extremely unhappy about where they live? These would make interesting topics for further research, which might enable us to answer some of these questions. We could ask those people now living in cities but stating a preference for rural living how long they have felt this way, how strongly they feel about it, how frequently (if ever) they have priced or inspected farms, whether they know the commuting time from the nearest small town to their place of work, and so forth.

Do most people living in apartments in the city really want to leave? Where could they possibly go?

are all part of the vision. Suburbanites also expect that they and their children will find friends among neighboring families who share these values.

Millions of Americans invest a great deal of time and money to achieve the values of suburban living, and in general, they are not disappointed. As we noted earlier, studies consistently find that people in the suburbs have a sense of well-being and are content with their lot. There are problems, to be sure, but much of their dream has come true.

Social Characteristics of the Suburbs

Not everyone in our cities has the values that send people to suburbia to seek the good life, nor can everyone afford to go. Thus, the suburbs gather certain kinds of people, mainly people of the working, middle, and upper class, as opposed to those of the lower class. Among the working class, there is an overrepresentation of foremen, craftsmen, and other more highly skilled workers. In our society, the upper class are few in number, so the suburbs are chiefly middle class.

Suburbanites have a higher median family income and a higher level of educational attainment than people in the central city. Home ownership is high. A high proportion of college-age children in the suburbs are enrolled in college, because the middle-class family values education and can afford to pay for it. Divorce and separation rates are low. Less clearly related to social class in the suburbs is the concentration of families with children and the rarity of single people and childless couples.

Racial segregation is quite apparent in the suburbs, but this is not due primarily to economic factors. In their book *Negroes in Cities*, Karl and Alma Taeuber (1965) conclude that economic factors figure little in segregation. One way or another, blacks who could afford to live in white suburbs are kept out. Deep-rooted fears and prejudices keep most American suburbs all white, or nearly so. People continue to fear that property values will tumble if a black family moves into a white neighborhood, despite studies that show that, if anything, prices go up (Laurenti, 1960; Ladd, 1962). Regardless of income increases among blacks, therefore, it is likely that many suburbs will continue to be all white, at least for quite a while.

It would be more accurate to call some of the larger suburbs within metropolitan areas *satellite cities*, as they have their own political, economic, and social base. For example, a study of 129 suburban communities within large metropolitan areas found that almost two out of five workers were employed in the same suburb in which they lived. This means, of course, that the majority of workers were *not* employed in the suburb but commuted to the city to earn a living. Then, too, many suburbanites go into the city for major shopping excursions, entertainment, and the like, and they thus make use of the city's streets, its transit system, and its parks, and they benefit from the police and fire protection provided by the city (and paid for primarily by those who live in the city). Smaller suburbs are, in reality, only dormitories for city workers, with scarcely anyone working in the same suburb in which he or she is living.

It is clear that suburbs are economically and socially linked to the central cities and that boundaries between units are, in some sense, artificial. Yet, the self-segregation of white, primarily middle-class suburban families makes it difficult for the suburbs to be a truly functional part of the larger urban community. The social and sometimes political separation could, in time, lead to real polarization, as blacks and urban poor on the one hand and the more affluent suburbanites on the other view one another with suspicion and distrust. This is not the way to achieve the good life, not to mention orderly growth and change.

The urban community might be integrated functionally by legally annexing the suburbs to the central city. This annexation is not always possible, though, because some suburbs have incorporated as separate entities; and others, such as the suburbs of St. Louis, Washington, New York, and Cincinnati, lie across a state line, thereby making annexation virtually impossible.

One answer to segregation is some form of metropolitan government for the whole urban area, although suburbs and central cities separated by state lines are not open to this solution. Even without the problem of state lines, the polarization between the city and the suburbs can stand in the way of metropolitan government. Suburbanites fear the domination of minorities in the central city, who, in turn, suspect that any changes will reflect the interests of the more powerful white suburbanites. The suburbs need the city, for no small suburban unit can possibly supply jobs for all its workers or organize large-scale projects, such as flood control and public health services. The city needs the suburbs as a place to house many of its workers and as a source of financial support for urban services used by suburbanites.

PLANNING OUR URBAN FUTURE

The suburban movement is likely to continue. During the next 25 years, we will add approximately 50 million people to our population. Most of them will live in urban areas, primarily in suburbs. We can hope that the 90 percent of our future population that will, for the most part, be living, working, buying, selling, worshiping, and playing in and around cities will suffer from fewer of the tensions and frustrations of urban living than are usual today.

Such a change will not happen by itself. We must seek to improve urban living, and we need sound planning to fulfill this commitment. It is difficult to estimate the magnitude of such a commitment, because we have never made one like it before. Its scope and effort would probably have to equal the efforts we have so far devoted to exploring outer space. That is, improving the urban condition would have to be a high-priority national goal. We would need political leadership to guide and direct the commitment with realism and enthusiasm, and we would need planning of the most imaginative and comprehensive sort.

Urban Planning: The Major Challenge

In one sense, urban planning is very old; in another, it has scarcely even been tried. It all depends on what you mean by "planning." In the fifth century B.C., the Greek architect Hippodamus laid out the design for Piraeus, the port of Athens. In the early nineteenth century, the New York state legislature appointed a commission to develop a plan for Manhattan Island. The commission recommended a gridiron layout, and it did not ignore human needs, as it acknowledged that "a city is to be composed of the habitations of men, and that straight sided and right angled houses are the most cheap to build and the most convenient to live in." Our nation's capital, with its gridiron arrangement of streets and diagonal avenues radiating from the Capitol Building and the White House, was laid out by Pierre L'Enfant.

What sociologists mean by **urban planning** is something far more comprehensive than laying out streets, or even locating parks and playgrounds, organizing welfare services, or establishing traffic flow patterns. Ideally, planning should begin with human values, with the question, "What do we want our urban areas to be like?" The sequence of steps needed to create the desired urban condition should be spelled out in enough detail to make their implications clear. Lawrence Haworth (1963), for example, has defined a good city as one "whose institutions are flexible, voluntary, and controllable" (p. 77), and in which there is a sense of community.

Haworth stresses individual freedom: people have a right to accept or reject the activities available in a city and a right to control the destiny of their settlements. It is hard to fault these ideas, as abstract principles, but putting them into practice might be difficult, and even divisive.

Planning versus Other Values: The Inescapable Compromises?

Should people be completely free to settle wherever they wish? Already, some American cities are attempting to curb their growth, or at least to discourage further growth. There is some doubt as to whether population limits can be set by law. Legal or not, the wishes of the people in a given city to halt growth could clearly conflict with the desires of others to move into the area. There is also doubt as to whether restricting growth is practical. In Russia, for example, it was decided in 1931 that both Moscow and Leningrad had reached their ideal sizes and that further growth would be actively discouraged (Ward, 1967). In 1931, each city had a population of between two and three million; by the 1960s, each city had over six million. Of course, deciding on the ideal size of a city or urban area is not the only problem in planning the desirable urban condition. Even so, contemplating the ideal can reveal the difficulty of trying to create an environment that contains all the elements of the good life. It seems that when some elements are planned, such as fixed size, other elements, such as freedom of movement and personal choice of location, sometimes have to be excluded.

Perhaps if city planning had taken human needs into account, a little more space could have been set aside for this playground in New York.

The best contribution urban sociologists can make to urban planning is to stress that planning start with the human values that individuals and groups want incorporated into their settlement patterns. The sociologist is also in a position to recognize two other points: (1) the carrying out of plans requires that many different sorts of activities be carried on simultaneously; and (2) planning should be as broad and comprehensive as possible. Both of these points are illustrated by the creation of "new towns." To a planner, "new town" does not mean simply a town that is new, but rather a community that is planned to be an integrated entity. The new town of Columbia, Maryland, is an example of a city developed with human values and human needs in mind (see Rouse, 1971). Located between Washington, D.C., and Baltimore, Columbia is designed for a population of 100,000. Eventually, it will consist of ten villages, each having five neighborhoods. Elementary schools are located in each neighborhood, so that each child can walk to school. Buses run on their own rights-of-way, forests and streams have been preserved, cultural activities are provided, and a unique system of comprehensive medical services is being developed. The careful, comprehensive plan for Columbia clearly gave full attention to the convenience and freedom of its residents, and so far, it seems to be working well. Yet, as a nation, we cannot devote all of our efforts to the creation of new towns, neglecting the many problems in our existing urban areas.

In our discussion of slums and suburbs, we saw that the sections of an urban area are functionally interrelated and interdependent. The families in residential areas need incomes from the business areas, and the commercial areas need customers from the residential areas. Not only are the problems of one section the problems of all, but the solutions for one area may create problems for another. Planning, therefore, must be as comprehensive as possible, based on the broadest socioeconomic unit possible. Thus, some political changes, such as the creation of a metropolitan government whose power goes beyond the legally defined city, have much to recommend them. But, even a metropolitan government may not deal with a large enough socioeconomic unit. The creation of Columbia, Maryland, is a possible case in point. Surely, when it reaches its population maximum of 100,000, it will have effects on Washington, D.C., Baltimore, and their many suburbs.

A fuller appreciation of the need for comprehensive planning can be gained from the realization of what urbanization is doing to the prime farm and forest lands of the United States. Each year, 1.4 million acres of good agricultural land are destroyed to provide space for homes, shopping centers, streets, parking spaces, and offices. In California in recent years, urbanization has required the withdrawal of 367 acres of prime agricultural land each day. Surely, urban growth requires land, but just as surely, comprehensive planning could minimize the destruction of prime farm and forest lands. Although sociologists do not have the final answer to our nation's urban problems, their perspectives should allow all of us to get a better grasp on the full dimensions of the problem.

When urban sociology got its start in the United States around 1920, scarcely more than half our population lived in cities. Early research, as we have seen in this chapter, was devoted to the ecology of the cities—that is, to how their spatial arrangement arose and then changed. Today, about three-fourths of our population lives in urban areas. Since 1920, both the number of our cities and the number of our urban problems have increased significantly. Basic to our urban problems are the past discrimination and segregation, which created slums and ghettos in the first place, and our present treatment of racial and other minorities, which perpetuates those blighted areas. Of course, minority group relations create other problems, too, as we will see in the next chapter.

SUMMARY

1. Cities arose as a result of three factors: improved technology, regular agricultural surplus, and a form of social organization. At the birth of Christ, there were more than a dozen cities of over 100,000 population, but in the Dark Ages, cities declined and did not really see major growth again until the Renaissance and the Industrial Revolution.

2. Any place that is incorporated as a city, village, borough, or town and that has at least 2500 inhabitants is considered to be **urban.** In the United States, nearly three-fourths of the population live in urban areas.

3. A **standard metropolitan statistical area (SMSA)** usually consists of a city of at least 50,000 inhabitants, plus adjacent areas tied socially and economically to the central city. The bulk of the American population lives in SMSAs.

4. A **megalopolis** consists of several to many large cities within a fairly large geographic area that are essentially joined together by the meeting of their suburbs and satellite cities. There is more interdependence within a megalopolis than is usually found within a comparable geographic area.

5. In the 1920s, sociologists began studying **human ecology**—now called **urban ecology**—the spatial patterning of activities in cities. They used terms borrowed from biological ecology to describe the patterns of **invasion** and **succession** in urban areas, producing new *configurations.*

6. Burgess depicted the American city as a series of concentric zones, while Hoyt described it in terms of pie-shaped sectors. Both were trying to show how the different areas (residential, industrial, and so on) are functionally interrelated. Boskoff extended his city diagram to include surrounding areas, thus showing how **satellite cities** can be linked to the larger city.

7. **Slums** are city areas in which buildings are deteriorated, people are overcrowded, and the crime rate is high. **Ghettos** are areas where blacks and the poor are forced to live, because social and economic factors prevent them from living elsewhere. Ghettos are usually slum areas.

8. It has been suggested that slums and ghettos can be reduced or eliminated by providing decent housing elsewhere or by urban renewal. So far, neither method has proved workable, and in fact, they have made matters worse by breaking up important patterns of human interaction and ignoring other psychological needs. Two approaches to urban renewal that are beginning to have some effect are urban homesteading and the in-migration of young professionals to the inner city.

9. The continuing increase in urban populations can be attributed to the growth of suburban areas. Suburbs have been around for more than 100 years, but the greatest growth occurred in the 1920s and after World War II.

10. The popular description of suburban life is a myth. Berger and Gans both found that people in suburbs are not the ultraconservative conformists in a status race with neighbors portrayed in the popular stereotype.

11. American suburbs tend to consist of white, middle-class homeowners with families. Most suburbanites work in a different city from the one in which they live. Many experts are alarmed at this virtual segregation of white middle-class families and have suggested such approaches as metropolitan governments to try to integrate the suburbs into the overall urban community.

12. Sociologists are presently concerned with **urban planning**—creating urban conditions that stress human values. Comprehensive planning involves not only finding solutions that will be satisfactory to all concerned but realizing that solutions may have ramifications for areas outside the area being affected. One method of urban planning currently being tried is the "new town," one example of which is Columbia, Maryland.

KEY TERMS

concentric zone model
ghetto
human ecology
invasion
megalopolis
satellite city
sector model
slum
standard metropolitan statistical area (SMSA)
succession
urban
urban ecology
urban planning

SUGGESTED READINGS

Banfield, Edward. *The Unheavenly City.* Little, Brown, 1970.
  An unorthodox view of the city and the problems of urban poverty, crime, and riots.

Boskoff, Alvin. *The Sociology of Urban Regions.* New York: Appleton-Century-Crofts, 1970.
  A demographic approach to the city. The author deals with urban problems as essentially regional ecological problems.

Clark, Kenneth B. *Dark Ghetto.* New York: Harper & Row, 1965.
  Clark analyzes the problems of the ghetto dweller in relation to the educational, economic, political, and religious institutions of American society.

Gist, Noel P., and Sylvia F. Fava. *Urban Society.* 6th ed. New York: Crowell, 1974.
  A comprehensive textbook in urban sociology. The authors deal with the history of cities, the growth and organization of cities, and the life of city people. Attention is given to urban life in other societies.

Glaab, Charles, and Theodore Brown. *The History of Urban America.* New York: Macmillan, 1967.
  A survey of the development of the American city from the colonial period to the 1950s, dealing with such issues as immigration, bossism, and reformism.

Haar, Charles M., ed. *The End of Innocence: A Suburban Reader.* Glenview, Ill.: Scott, Foresman, 1972.
  A collection of essays on living in suburbia, the relation of the suburbs to the city, and the future of the suburbs.

Jacobs, Jane. *The Death and Life of Great American Cities.* New York: Random House, 1961.
  An excellent, readable depiction of what cities are like and what they could be like. A classic in the field.

Liebow, Elliot. *Tally's Corner: A Study of Negro Street-Corner Men.* Boston: Little, Brown, 1967.
  Insights into personal reactions and adjustments to urban life can be gained from this classic study of a group of black men who gather on a corner in the inner city of Washington, D.C.

Lottman, Herbert R. *How Cities Are Saved.* New York: Universe Books, 1976.
  Cities can be rebuilt, but first, it is necessary to understand how urban problems arose. A practical book that stresses rebuilding strategies.

Walton, John, and Donald Carns, eds. *Cities in Change: Studies on the Urban Condition.* 2nd ed. Boston: Allyn & Bacon, 1977.
  A collection of articles on the sources of the problems of cities and possible solutions to them.

The interaction of parent and child, supervisor and worker, guard and prisoner is marked by inequality of status. The interactions with which we deal in this chapter are also characterized by inequality, but in these cases, it is entire portions of society that are unequal. Sociologists speak of groups that are set apart and treated unequally as minority groups, and they have devoted a great deal of study to majority-minority interaction.

A minority group is singled out for unequal treatment because of some combination of physical and cultural characteristics. Blacks are a minority group, and so are Jews, Mexican Americans, Puerto Rican Americans, and American Indians. Race relations is one of the most serious American social problems. In this chapter, we look at the origins of races and the differences among races, and then we explore the nature of prejudice and discrimination.

Sociologists have identified a number of majority-minority interaction patterns. Historically, majorities have tried to kill off minorities, to expel them from society, or to segregate them, forcing them to live apart and to be treated differently. But, in some places, groups live side by side, their differences preserved, with no group considered better than any other group. In other societies, minority groups have been absorbed by the majority. Finally, there can be a blending, or amalgamation, of the cultures of two or more groups, so that a new culture, containing elements of several, is formed. It is desirable to understand these possible patterns of majority-minority relations in order to recognize what is going on with ethnic minorities in the United States.

16 Minority Group Relations

> America is God's crucible, the great melting pot where all the races of Europe are melting and re-forming.
> —ZANGWILL, 1908

At one time, Zangwill's sentiments were widely held. It was believed, or hoped, that the people from many nations who were coming to our shores would soon blend or melt together, so that they would all be Americans, and nothing more. Had this happened, there would be no need for this chapter, at least with its focus on our own society.

Sociologists, as you have learned by now, are concerned with the interaction among people and stress the importance of the groups to which people belong. A distinctive type of interaction takes place when groups are considered unequal—when some groups stand in an inferior or subordinate position to others. In this case, there can be no melting and blending of the members of the several groups, and interaction across groups reflects the superior-inferior, dominant-submissive, high-low status of the groups themselves. The results of interaction—whether considered in terms of human happiness, the realization of human potential, or the exploitation of one group by another—are also distinctive when the interaction is one of dominance and submission. The nature, extent, and results of this kind of intergroup interaction in the United States are, understandably, of interest to the sociologist, and they are the subject of this chapter.

MINORITY GROUPS

The term "minority" has several meanings. A "minor," for example, is someone who has not attained full legal age and who has not acquired all civil rights. "Minority" also implies that something is of lesser importance or is lower in rank, as the minor leagues in baseball or the minor suits in bridge, which have a lower value in scoring. "Minority" is also used in a statistical sense to designate a portion of the whole that is less than 50 percent. In society, if there is a minority, there must, of course, be a "majority"—that is, a segment of the society that is larger and more important and in which the people have acquired full legal and civil rights.

The sociological meaning of "minority-majority" contains all of the usual meanings, except that it recognizes that the minority group need not be numerically smaller than the majority group. For example, in South Africa, nonwhites make up over three-fourths of the population but are dominated by the relatively small group of whites. Women in the United States, while constituting about 51 percent of the population, have played in the minor leagues for years, and for a long time, did not have full civil rights, such as the right to vote. On a global basis, Americans are a distinct minority, numbering about six percent of the world's population. Yet, Americans control half of the world's wealth and use many times more electric power, coal, oil, steel, and general equipment than the rest of the peoples of the world. Clearly, small membership does not make a group a minority in the sociological sense, although, of course, subordinate groups, such as the blacks, American Indians, Jews, and Chicanos in the United States, often are numerical minorities.

The sociologist Louis Wirth (1945) defined **minority group** as "a group of people who, because of their physical or cultural characteristics, are singled out from the others in the society in which they live for differential and unequal treatment, and who therefore regard themselves as objects of collective discrimination" (p. 347). Members of minority groups are excluded from having full membership rights, privileges, and responsibilities in their society and so have poorer life chances (see Chapter 8). Accompanying the differential and unequal treatment of minorities is an attitude on the part of the dominant group that it is somehow superior to or better than the minority. Such **ethnocentrism** is widespread and arises whenever a group of humans senses a difference between itself and others—between "us" and "them." It becomes more pronounced, however, when one group is able to dominate another. The feelings of superiority then serve both to justify the domination and to perpetuate it. (We will return to a discussion of the range of majority-minority group relations later in the chapter.)

According to our definition, minority groups may be set apart from the rest of society by virtue of their physical or cultural characteristics. When we think of physical characteristics that are used to differentiate groups, we immediately think of race. In addition to race, there is the **ethnic group,** a broader category that refers to "any group that is defined or set off by race, religion, or natural origin, or some combination of these categories" (Milton Gordon, 1964, p. 28). The term *ethnic* stresses the cultural characteristics of a group: its religion, customs, language, family patterns, and so on. Some ethnic minorities in the United States, such as Italians and Swedes, are not set apart by race; others, such as blacks and Japanese Americans, exhibit both cultural and racial characteristics that differentiate them from the majority. Historically and currently, racial discrimination has been important in American society, and interaction between the majority and the racial minorities has been punctuated by misunderstandings, tension, and sometimes, downright hostility. It is a good idea, therefore, to explore what is known about race and racial differences.

WHAT IS RACE?

Race can be defined as a grouping of human beings that is distinguishable by the possession of similar combinations of anatomical features due to a common heredity (Cuber, Kenkel, and Harper, 1964). Physical anthropologists have experienced great difficulty in determining which anatomical features are acceptable for racial classification, however. Singly and in combination, many standards have been used—shape of head, skin color, color of eyes and hair, shape of nose, and others. Usually, we think of there being three major races: Caucasoid, Mongoloid, and Negroid. Yet, entire groups of people, amounting to millions of individuals, do not fit into any of these three categories. For example, millions of dark-skinned Hindus are visibly different from Caucasians and Mongolians in one respect—skin color—but are visibly different from Negroes with respect to hair texture, shape of nose, and shape of lips. To which race do these millions of people belong? Similarly, the Ainu of northern Japan, the Polynesians, the aborigines of Australia, and many other groups cannot be classified as Negroid, Mongoloid, or Caucasoid. Clearly, the concept of race is far from precise.

The range of physical types within the major races can be quite great. The Mongoloid race includes the Chinese as well as the American Indian; while the Caucasoid race includes Northern Europeans, Greeks, Arabs, and Turks. Among Caucasians, eye color ranges from blue to dark brown, hair from yellow to black, and skin color from from what is usually called "white" to at least a moderate brown. It would seem almost to defy the concept of race to include such different types in the same category. One solution would be to utilize more racial classifications; one anthropologist who used this approach ended up with 32 races (Dobzhansky, 1962).

The Origin of Races

Today, the existence of groups with common, genetically based physical characteristics is largely due to three factors: natural selection, random genetic drift, and geographical isolation. Working in combination, these three factors seem to explain how tens of thousands of years ago, different physical types emerged and gradually resulted in large groups of humans sharing similar anatomical features.

Natural Selection The human species has continually had to adjust to the varied environments in which its members have found themselves. At times, certain gene patterns are more suitable than others to the prevailing environment. **Natural selection** refers to the evolutionary changes that occur whenever the environment favors the survival and reproduction of individuals having one gene or pattern of genes over individuals having another gene or pattern of genes. Let us see how this process works with racial characteristics.

Skin color is determined by two chemicals, carotene (yellow tinge) and melanin (brown tinge). Everyone, except albinos, has both of these chemicals in his or her skin, and the proportion of melanin and carotene determines skin color. Biologically, skin color determines how much sunlight is screened out, which, in turn, affects the body's production of vitamin D. Since both too little and too much vitamin D can cause abnormal bone structure, dark skin is biologically adaptive to the tropics (where there is much sunlight), while light skin is adaptive to the northern European environment (which receives less sunlight). By natural selection over many generations, among people who migrated to areas of less intense sun, those with lighter skins were healthier, lived longer, and were able to reproduce more of their kind than those with darker skins. Similarly, darker-skinned people had a biological advantage in the tropics, and in time, reproduced faster than lighter-skinned people in the area.

Sickle-cell anemia makes an interesting example of biological adaptation and natural selection. This inherited disease, a malformation of the red blood cells, is found only among Africans and their descendants. If both parents carry the gene, the offspring will not survive to adulthood. However, if only one parent passes on the gene, the child will be a carrier of the disease but will be free of the disease itself. It seems that the carriers of sickle-cell anemia are particularly resistant to malaria, a serious killer, and thus will be more likely to reach adulthood and reproduce than those who are free of the sickle-cell gene and are, thus, more likely to succumb to malaria. Apparently, in malaria-infested regions, group survival is less threatened by sickle-cell anemia than by malaria.

Random Genetic Drift   Not all physical traits characteristic of a race are the result of adaptation to the environment. **Random genetic drift** refers to the process by which a particular trait appears in or is lost by one or a few individuals and then is transmitted to their offspring. Unlike natural selection, random genetic drift involves traits that appear by chance, not in response to the environment. Eventually, the chance occurrence of a trait becomes widespread in the group, if the group is small and does not intermarry with groups not possessing the trait. Such racial differences as fingerprint swirls, lip shape, and the ability to taste certain chemicals are thought to be due to random genetic drift.

Geographical Isolation   The third major factor that accounts for racial differences is **geographical isolation,** the tendency, early in history, for human groups to become isolated from one another. As humans spread out around the earth, groups that settled in different regions lost contact with other groups for long periods. The result was that the gene pool of some groups became relatively small. Natural selection and random genetic drift produced differences that were not counteracted by the infusion of different genes from intermarriage with other groups. People within the group became more and more similar with regard to some physical characteristics, and at the same time, more and more different from other groups with whom they had lost contact.

At a later stage in human history, we find an illustration of the effect of geographical isolation in the migration of Mongolian people to North America. The early migrants were probably quite similar physically to those who remained in Mongolia or China, but after many, many generations, the restricted gene pool of the migrants resulted in a somewhat different physical type, the American Indian. On a smaller scale, and more recently, the effects of this factor can be seen in the high incidence of hemophilia, the bleeder's disease, in parts of Appalachia, and in the extraordinary old ages reached by people in some areas of South America and the Soviet Union. In both instances, traits once established tended to become widespread, due to the restricted gene pool of the isolated groups.

Human wanderings have also served to mix groups, so that we find a rather wide range of physical types within any one race. You will recall, for example, that the Caucasoid race has a wide range of eye, hair, and skin color. This is the result of mixtures that became increasingly numerous as migrations and conquests increased. Fewer and fewer groups could remain truly isolated.

The origin and history of racial differences is an extremely complex subject. Put simply, all humans have a common origin. Because of natural selection, random genetic drift, and geographical isolation, physical differences arose and were transmitted to offspring, thus producing differences between groups. Meanwhile, there was also a mingling of groups and a mixing of physical types, resulting in differences within what we call racial groups. Yet, there is only one human species. No matter what our skin color or hair texture, our anatomies are identical. Furthermore, we can interbreed and produce offspring, while, say, a wolf and a fox cannot, because they are not of the same species or same genetic make-up. It thus makes considerable sense to refer to the *human* race rather than to specific races. But, are there important differences between so-called races, aside from skin color and hair texture? For example, it has been suggested that there are important differences in intelligence between races.

Are There Racial Differences in Intelligence?

By **intelligence,** we mean your *capacity* to learn—not how much you have learned. People frequently refer to intelligence as being an innate characteristic, because almost everybody will admit that humans are born with this capacity, regardless of whether or in what way they use it. Intelligence cannot be measured easily or directly. An IQ (intelligence quotient) test results in a score that relates your apparent mental age to your chronological age. IQ scores are an approximate measure of the capacity to learn, but no one knows how close the approximation is. The usual IQ test measures more than just innate intelligence, however. It is also subject to the influence of environmental factors, such as the child's upbringing and exposure to stimulating experiences. Since we cannot measure "only intelligence," we cannot determine whether environmental factors influence the capacity to learn, or whether they just influence test-taking ability.

It is highly unlikely that any human group would find itself in an environment in which biological adaptation would favor lower than average in-

The man on the right is an accountant, the one in the middle is the founder of this Kansas City bank. Knowingly or unknowingly, they also serve as role models for younger blacks.

telligence. On the contrary, throughout the long course of human history, the survival of the species has been a struggle, so that natural selection would favor the more intelligent members of the group over the less intelligent ones. The range of differences in intelligence within any reasonably large human grouping, therefore, would tend to fit the normal curve: the bulk of the members would be within the normal range, with a few people falling at each extreme. From what we know about the capacity to learn and about human societies, it is highly improbable that there would be genetic differences in intelligence among the races.

Nevertheless, in 1969, Arthur Jensen reported on research that found the average IQ scores of blacks to be 15 points lower than the average for whites in the United States. He suggested that genetic factors accounted for about 80 percent of the difference between the races. In a later study, Jensen (1977) examined the IQ scores of children in a poor town in Georgia and those of children in Berkeley, California. The scores of rural black children in Georgia showed a decline of one IQ point each year between the ages of five and eighteen. The scores of black children in Berkeley, however, did not show a decline, nor did those of white children from a less impoverished background than that of the rural blacks. This would indicate that environmental influences do, indeed, affect IQ. This evidence that IQ is not primarily genetic is not conclusive, but it does demonstrate the importance of environmental factors in IQ test scores.

Even if IQ scores do differ by groups, the fact that IQ is not the same as intelligence should be taken into account. People can score lower on tests because of their unfamiliarity with the things included in the tests. It is reasonable to expect that an immigrant will have a lower IQ score when tested in America with American tests than when tested in his or her homeland. IQ tests relate mainly to middle-class values and problems and are thus foreign to those outside the mainstream of American life, such as the poor. Thus racial differences in IQ scores can often be explained by cultural factors. Average score differences do not mean that there are proven genetic differences in intelligence among ethnic groups. What they *do* indicate, however, is still a matter of debate.

The fact that there are no important differences among races, that race itself is an ambiguous idea, and that there are great differences within so-called races does not mean that racial classification is insignificant. Although, biologically, race is insignificant, we have been taught to attach importance to the *social race* into which we classify one another. Our society has developed the need to distinguish among races, has attached significance to differences, such as skin color, and has socialized its young to see these differences and to attach meaning to them.

MAJORITY-MINORITY RELATIONS

Sociologists have studied a variety of aspects of the relationships between majority and minority groups. One focus is on *attitudes*—how the majority group thinks and feels about minority groups and individuals. Another focus is on *behavior*—how the majority acts toward minorities. Still a third approach focuses on the *outcome* of attitudes and behavior on the identity of the minority group. Outcomes can range from inhuman extermination of minorities to complete integration of groups as social equals. Let us examine these attitudes, behaviors, and outcomes in fuller detail.

Prejudice

Literally, **prejudice** means prejudgment. People are prejudiced, therefore, who have preconceived ideas or beliefs that are not based on facts. Prejudiced people hold on to their beliefs, even when exposed to new knowledge that is contrary to their prejudgments. A man is prejudiced against women, for example, if he believes that women are poor credit risks and if he continues to believe so even after he is shown evidence that women meet their financial obligations at least as well as men. When used to refer to attitudes toward minority groups, the term "prejudice" means incorrect and unfavorable opinions about minority groups. That is, undesirable qualities are attributed to all members of the group, regardless of individual differences. Usually included in the concept of prejudice are the hostile emotions, the hate, the desire to maintain social distance, and other such feelings that accompany negative attitudes toward a group. Prejudice thus includes beliefs, opinions, and feelings about a particular group.

Discrimination

In contrast to prejudice, **discrimination** is an action concept. It refers to unequal and unfair treatment and the denial of rights to members of a particular group. If women, otherwise qualified, are denied home mortgage loans because of their sex, they are being discriminated against. Preventing blacks from buying homes in certain areas, barring Jews from country club membership, paying women less than men for the same work, denying anyone the right to vote, and other forms of overt action toward members of a minority group are properly referred to as discrimination.

Prejudice and discrimination are interrelated. If one is prejudiced against a group, one is likely to discriminate against it. For example, the belief that most American Indians are unreliable can result in employers refusing to hire them. On the other hand, denying Indians decent employment reinforces the attitude that they are lazy or unable to hold steady jobs. Thus, the forbidding of discriminatory practices would have the dual effect of better treatment for minorities and reduction of prejudicial thinking. (Giving preferential treatment to minorities has been termed reverse discrimination. See Box 16.1.)

Prejudice and discrimination need not exist together in the same person. A male employer may be prejudiced against women workers but find that it is legally impossible to discriminate against them in terms of wages or promotions. White realtors in a prejudiced community may not themselves be prejudiced but might refuse to show blacks homes in some areas of the city because they feel that it would hurt their business. Often, of course, we find that the same people are both prejudiced and discriminatory with regard to certain minorities.

Racism

The most pronounced form of discrimination in our society is that directed against racial minorities, particularly blacks. This type of discrimination is commonly called **racism,** and whites who discriminate against nonwhites are referred to as white racists. Racists are not merely aware of differences among races; they also believe that the differences are part of the basic inferiority of the other race. In their book *Black Power* (1967), Stokely Carmichael and Charles Hamilton defined racism as "the predication of decisions and politics on considerations of race for the purpose of subordinating a racial group" (p. 3). Most members of the dominant group would probably deny having anything to do with a "purposeful subordination" of a minority group, be it racial, ethnic, sexual, or whatever. If pressed, they might admit to having inherited a system of policies based on the decision of those before them or those in power today.

Racism as a Social Creation   Our society is beginning to realize how deeply within it — in its norms, values, and social institutions — the seeds of white racism are buried. Our thinking, our attitudes, our actions, and even our institutional structures force persons or groups to be systematically subordinated for physically insignificant but culturally quite significant characteristics, such as skin color.

Even preschool children, whether white or black, learn to sort people by skin color and begin to attach value judgments to it. Prejudiced racial attitudes are learned not only in the home or in small face-to-face groups, but also in the community and in broader experiences children have away from home. Once children have begun school, they are exposed to numerous other influences on their behavior and thinking. Even if parents are unprejudiced, the school and the larger community can work against the parents' efforts.

Such a likelihood is compounded by the circumstances we saw in Chapter 11—there is little racial integration in our neighborhoods and schools. In segregated environments, children often learn attitudes toward minorities without any exposure to members of those minorities that could

---

**BOX 16.1
REVERSE DISCRIMINATION: THE BAKKE CASE**

In the early 1970s, Allen Bakke, a 32-year-old engineer, applied for admission to the medical school at the University of California at Davis. The school turned him down twice, even though his admission test scores were higher than those of some of the applicants who were accepted. This was because the university had an affirmative action program that gave special preference to minority students. Of 100 places in the freshman class, 84 places were filled by one set of standards, while the remaining 16 places were filled through special standards for "disadvantaged minority students." Members of minority groups thus had two chances to be admitted, as they could apply to both the regular program and the special one.

Bakke felt that he had been a victim of "reverse discrimination"—that he had been discriminated against for not being a member of a minority group. He took his case to court, and the Supreme Court of California ruled that the University of California had violated the Fourteenth Amendent to the Constitution by refusing his admission. The University of California appealed the case to the Supreme Court of the United States.

After a long legal battle, the Court finally handed down a decision. Four of the justices agreed that Bakke's rights had been violated, under the provisions of the Civil Rights Act of 1964. Four other justices felt that race-conscious programs are justified "if the purpose of such programs is to remove the disparate racial impact its actions might otherwise have and if there is reason to believe that the disparate impact is itself the product of past discrimination." The ninth justice cast the deciding vote in Bakke's favor, although he agreed with the four dissenting justices that some racial bias should be allowed by the government. The Court's decision was, thus, in favor of Bakke, but the ruling contained a disclaimer that "In order to get beyond racism, we must first take account of race. There is no other way. And in order to treat some persons equally, we must treat them differently."

dispel such attitudes. In recent years, legislation has been passed to revise the social structure of our institutions to provide equal opportunities for all groups and individuals. In practice, though, equal opportunity is frequently a myth. The white majority still dominates major social institutions and has the power to implement racially discriminating practices.

Individual and Institutional Racism Racism can be either individual or institutional. *Individual racism* takes the form of acts by one or more individuals against individuals of another race; whereas **institutional racism** is built into our very institutions, and therefore, into the overall relations between the dominate race and the subordinate race or races. Acts of individual racism include such things as lynchings, bombings, and harassment of

---

What is at issue is more than just the admission policies of the University of California. The federal government's affirmative action requirements affect not only schools and universities but also thousands of companies with government contracts. In order to keep these contracts, the companies must demonstrate that they are actively recruiting minorities and women and that these people are being employed at all levels. In many cases, companies have set up affirmative action programs that set strict quotas on the employment and promotion of minorities and women. Such policies have led to the promotion of less-qualified individuals over more-experienced white males and to the hiring of less-qualified individuals.

Many of the white males who have been turned down for such jobs or have been passed over for promotions have taken their complaints of reverse discrimination to court, and they have been winning their cases. Supporters of affirmative action believe that those businesses that have gone too far in their affirmative action programs have created a backlash that is putting the whole idea in jeopardy. For this reason, many civil rights organizations petitioned the Supreme Court not to grant the University of California's appeal.

<u>Affirmative action</u> is an idea that grew out of the Civil Rights Act of 1964. Its supporters feel that such programs are remedies for wrongs done to minorities and women in the past and that they are the only method for bringing minorities and women into the economic mainstream. Those who are being pushed out of jobs and promotions by less-qualified individuals want to know why they should suffer for the wrongs done to minorities in the past. Instead of being rewarded for their past efforts, which qualify them for jobs and promotions, they are being penalized. Does discrimination in the past justify this new kind of discrimination? If you were a justice of the Supreme Court, how would you have ruled in the Bakke case?

minority-group children newly integrated into a dominant-group school. Less violent but more frequent forms of behavior indicate how dominant-group members feel about minority-group members—the names they are called, the tone of voice used toward them, the reactions they often experience when they are in dominant-group neighborhoods, and the like.

Institutional racism, on the other hand, is less open. No specific act can be singled out, for the entire circumstances of a minority-group member's life may be the result of it. Evidence of such racism is revealed in segregated schools, churches, and housing; discriminatory practices in employment and promotion; and mass media and textbooks, which sometimes ignore or distort the role of minority-group members.

Institutional racism usually operates through well-established and respected procedures. For this reason, it is difficult to identify or even bring to public awareness, much less to change. Hence, as we found in Chapter 15, our large cities have ghettos where low-income minorities attempt to survive, in spite of inadequate housing, food, clothing, income, and other physical needs, not to mention unfulfilled social and psychological needs. Moreover, these circumstances are both destructive to the ghetto dwellers and dangerous for the future of all society.

Treatment of Minorities

The attitudes that people hold toward minorities and their day-to-day behavior toward them result in broad patterns that describe majority treatment of minorities. The minority group can cease to exist because its members are exterminated or expelled from society, or because the people and their culture are blended into the majority. Or, the minority can continue to exist on a separate but equal basis or in a subordinate position to the majority.

Extermination A particularly brutal way of dealing with a minority group is to bring about its **extermination.** The dominant group may take what it wants—farming skills, technology, wealth, or whatever—and then, gradually or swiftly, annihilate those minority-group members whom they consider to be of no further use, or possibly, a threat to them. The term **genocide** refers to the systematic killing of a whole nation of people and was first used in reference to the Nazis' extermination of the Jews: six million Jews, about two-thirds of the Jewish population of Europe, were eliminated by the Nazis. More recently, the Nigerians exterminated countless Ibos who were seeking independence for Biafra. The term *genocide* could also be applied to the treatment of the Indians by American pioneers and colonists. In part, the extermination was direct—the Indians were simply slaughtered. But many also died as a result of the whites taking Indian land and killing the buffalo, which deprived the Indians of their livelihood.

MINORITY GROUP RELATIONS

Expulsion Dominant groups have, at times, rid themselves of a minority in their midst by **expulsion,** or forcibly removing them. Indians in various parts of the country were removed from their tribal homelands and forced to settle elsewhere. As late as the 1830s, for example, the Cherokees were forced to walk from their homes in Georgia to a reservation in Oklahoma. At least 4,000 died on the long trek, and the route has since been designated as the Trail of Tears. During World War II, Japanese Americans living on the West Coast were forced out of their homes and into "relocation camps." During the same period, Germany and the Soviet Union deported millions of minorities from their countries. In 1972, Uganda deported East Indians; many of them had been born in Uganda and had no other country to call home. Their businesses, homes, and savings were confiscated by the government.

Segregation-Discrimination Another method of treating minorities is segregation and discrimination. In essence, **segregation** is the forced separation of a minority group from the majority—the construction of social barriers between the groups. The involuntary separation is accompanied by unequal treatment, or discrimination.

South Africa is a modern example of a segregated society. The less than four million whites, a distinct statistical minority, constitute the dominant group. The Bantu, or blacks, number 15 million and make up about 70 percent of the population. The rest are mainly people of mixed ancestry, who are called colored. Blacks and coloreds are strictly segregated. They cannot live in white districts or even be in such districts after dark. Social facilities are segregated, and the Immorality Act forbids whites and nonwhites from interacting socially. South Africa is in troubled times with its segregation

Segregation is forced separation of a minority group from the majority. Not so long ago, signs similar to this one at a South African plant were common in our Southern states.

(which is called *apartheid*), and some of the more extreme barriers are beginning to tumble.

Americans, of course, have had firsthand acquaintance with segregation. Many of you are familiar with segregated schools and neighborhoods, and your parents may remember segregated churches, restaurants, theaters, restrooms, drinking fountains, swimming pools, and parks. Accompanying such dominant-subordinate relations was a set of roles for each group to play in dealing with each other. The subordinate group was required to *act* subordinate, the dominant group to act dominant. Once, such role divisions were much in evidence in our society. A Southern black man was not expected to feel insulted when called "boy," or if he were elderly, "uncle." In the North, such roles were far less obvious and less formalized, but still, a black knew better than to try to rent an apartment in certain areas, to apply for certain jobs, and so on.

Although racial segregation is no longer legal in America, and the civil rights legislation of the late 1960s prohibits discrimination in education, housing, and employment, there is still much segregation and unequal treatment of minorities. As we saw in Chapter 15, blacks are concentrated in the central cities, whites in the suburbs. Thus, in many places, there is no way to have neighborhood schools that are racially integrated, and achieving integration by busing is unpopular and is a sensitive political issue. Racially segregated schools imply that the minority is inferior, and historically, schools for poor blacks have been of poor quality, thus affecting the chances of blacks for attaining good jobs that would enable them to move out of the black ghetto. The pattern of segregation and discrimination continues, with changes at any point in the cycle occurring slowly.

Pluralism Another pattern of relations between and among groups in a society is **pluralism,** in which groups are distinguishable by ethnic cultural background but are treated as equal to one another. Each group maintains its own identity and fits into the larger society, with no group being discriminated against or receiving special privileges. Switzerland is an example of a pluralistic society. Swiss of German, French, and Italian descent retain their own language and customs. Protestantism and Catholicism cross-cut and overlap the ethnic boundaries, producing a society with a number of separate-but-equal groups that have lived in relative harmony for a long time. Canada approaches pluralism, but the French Canadians are somewhat disadvantaged economically, not fully accepted socially, and indeed, from time to time, speak out for political separation.

Some see the United States as moving toward a pluralistic society in terms of its ethnic groups as well as its religious groups. Protests and civil rights legislation of the 1960s began building into the social structure the right and opportunity for minority groups to be different yet equal. Furthermore, American Indians, Chicanos, and blacks are questioning whether they want to give up their cultural identity in order to participate in the larger society. Should pluralism come to prevail, whites would simply become one of many ethnic groups. The culture of the larger society would probably continue to be dominated by white ethnic cultures, with other ethnic groups socializing their young into both their own subculture and that of the larger society.

Assimilation Still another pattern of majority-minority relationships is **assimilation.** If the minority group gives up its previous culture—its language, values, customs, dress, and so on—and adopts the culture of the dominant group, it is said to be assimilated. Assimilation often occurs in steps, with each successive generation becoming more assimilated. Cultural minorities, such as German Americans and Irish Americans, illustrate this pattern. By now, they have almost completely lost their identities as ethnic groups.

Assimilation is a two-way process. The minority has to want and attempt to give up its cultural heritage and adopt the way of life of the majority. But, the dominant group has to allow it to do so, and indeed, must help it. Early German immigrants to the United States, for example, found psychological comfort in living together. They spoke their native language and published newspapers in German. The majority put up no severe barriers to assimilation, so over a few generations, the Germans were able to adopt the culture of the majority and to be admitted to full participation in American society. Blacks, on the other hand, were required to give up their languages, customs, and loyalties and to adopt the language and many of the customs of the dominant group; but barriers to complete assimilation were erected to keep blacks from full participation in the society.

Cultural Amalgamation A final pattern of majority-minority relations is cultural **amalgamation**—the blending of two cultures to produce a new one. The new culture is a more-or-less indiscriminate mixture of the two that are blended. For this to occur, the groups must accept each other as equals. It cannot be a matter of "they" have to learn "our" ways. The term *amalgamation* is also used in a biological sense to describe a situation in which people of different races freely intermarry, producing a blend of their physical types.

Hawaii is a good illustration of the process of amalgamation. Intermarriage between the native Hawaiians (themselves a blend of Polynesians and Tahitians) and Japanese, Americans, Europeans, Chinese, and Filipinos has occurred more or less freely. (Some high-status native Hawaiians are opposed to intermarriage with other groups, but many such intermarriages have already occurred.) English is spoken by almost everybody, but Hawaiian words are freely mixed into everyday speech. In its art forms, dress, food, customs, and other ways, Hawaii evidences a blending of several cultures, as well as a blending of races.

There seems to be little support in the rest of our states for racial amalgamation from either whites or nonwhites. As minority groups struggle to develop pride and their own identities, they show no interest in becoming culturally or racially different from what they are. The change they want is for society to grant them their rights to equality. Yet, integration, even in this pluralist sense, has come far more slowly and with more difficulty for racial minorities than for cultural minorities. This will become apparent as we investigate the current status of several minority groups.

TRENDS AMONG MINORITY GROUPS IN THE UNITED STATES

As a social force, minorities were once all but invisible. When they were noticed, it was only to persuade them to hurry their assimilation into American culture—unless, of course, they were racially undesirable. Some groups, such as blacks, many Mexican Americans, and Puerto Rican Americans, tried, without being invited to do so, and failed. Others, like the American Indian, did not want to become assimilated at first. In recent years, those who once tried but failed have worked energetically to revive their own identities and restore their consciousness of their roots. We will look briefly at how this process works for each minority group, and at how it affects the group's relation to the larger society.

Indian Americans

Few people learn in school exactly how much the Europeans assimilated of American Indian agriculture, both for survival here by the early colonists and for new ideas to use in Europe. Some people jokingly allow that Squanto was the first County Agricultural Agent in the New World. (A county agent is a government worker whose job is to advise the farmers and other growers in a county about agriculture and to pass on new practical knowledge and ideas.)

Few Indian Americans voluntarily converted to Christianity. To make matters worse, they did not believe in ownership of land. For these two reasons, among others, the settlers and pioneers found it easy to justify pushing the Indians aside in pursuit of land. After all, they were savages who refused to see the good and the right, even when it was presented to them by missionaries. We still send missionaries, teachers, government agents, and even soldiers to help "civilize" the Indians. Until recently, we sent their children off to distant boarding schools for long periods of time, so that they would forget their native language, customs, and ceremonies. Now, we just bus them to white schools, where they learn very little that is positive about their own heritage.

As the American Indians say, the government is spending millions of dollars to *change* them, not to help them. They remain the poorest of all mi-

The American Indians are the poorest of our minority groups. Must they become assimilated in order to have a decent level of living?

nority groups. Some Indians have tried to become assimilated into the larger culture, and a few have succeeded. Others have not been completely accepted and live on the fringes of both groups. Some quietly survive, practicing their traditional ways, while others protest loudly and even violently for the right to be both Indian and American.

As a group, the American Indians have assimilated the material culture of our society but still cling to their own nonmaterial culture—their own philosophy of life. They have some special rights that other American citizens do not have, because our government has always treated Indian reservations as parts of an autonomous nation. Many Indians still live in tribal communities and are fighting to maintain them. After all, such communities represent their tradition, their identity. If they were to be assimilated, their tribal communities would disappear into history, and their identity would be lost.

Mexican Americans

The 1970 census counted five million Mexican Americans, but members of this minority group believed that twice that number are living in the Southwest alone. After the Mexican War, about 70,000 people who were a mixture of Indian and Spanish automatically became part of the United States territory. Traditionally, they were farmers or ranchers, having been well-established in these vocations some 200 years before the European settlers arrived in the West. Again, we borrowed from their culture, learning much about ranching and farming, and we adopted their words into our language—words like "rodeo," "corral," and "bronco." Over the years, the Mexican

Ethnic minorities who have not been the objects of intense discrimination have been upwardly mobile and have been able to achieve a good level of living in the United States. But often the process takes several generations.

Americans have farmed and followed the harvests as migrant farm laborers. Those who dropped out of the migrant agricultural force sought employment in such large cities as Chicago, or they settled in Wisconsin, Michigan, Washington, Oregon, and Florida, in addition to their major concentration in the Southwest. The Mexican Americans exchanged their problems as rural migrant laborers for those of an underprivileged, urban minority group. Overall, Americans of Mexican descent have become so fragmented that it is difficult to generalize about them.

The Mexican American minority in Southern California, for instance, has changed with the times from the traditional folk culture to a more urbanized one that is moving toward middle-class status (Penalosa, 1971). In the process, the traditional family structure has been weakened, and juvenile delinquency has become a problem. Mexican Americans lag behind in education, because many clung to Spanish as their first language, in conflict with the educational policy in our society that English is the primary language. (This policy is losing favor in many culturally mixed parts of the country, and many court decisions are helping it on its way to extinction.)

Today, many Mexican immigrants come from the middle class of the more industrialized sections of Mexico. Most of these immigrants, who have settled in the urban neighborhoods of Southern California, fit into blue-collar and white-collar jobs. Along with veterans of World War II and later wars, who attended college on the GI Bill and went on to professional jobs, these new middle-class immigrants are breaking down social barriers. In recent years, more and more well-trained Mexican American professionals have been returning to positions of leadership in the old Mexican American neighborhoods, or *barrios,* where they help to solve the long-standing problems of their people. The picture for this minority group is beginning to brighten somewhat—in Southern California, at least. Only time will tell whether they will become accepted and fully assimilated, or since their motherland is so close by, whether they will retain their own heritage and remain a minority group in a pluralistic America.

Puerto Rican Americans

Puerto Rican Americans suffer many of the same hardships as other minorities. Most live in the ghetto areas of New York City, to which they have been migrating for over a century to escape the hardships of their homeland, a Caribbean island that is partially controlled by the United States. Their heritage is a mixture of Taino Indian, Spanish, and Black African; some have French, Italian, and Irish ancestry from later settlements on the island. Much like Mexican Americans, the Puerto Rican Americans have tried to better themselves through education, hoping to enter medical and other professions, so that they can help their own people better themselves, both in Puerto Rico and on the mainland. But, often, poverty is too great an obstacle, and they, too, suffer from poor education, high unemployment rates, and racial prejudice.

Japanese Americans

This national and racial group suffered much discrimination during World War II, when they were expelled from the Pacific Coast and placed in relocation camps. It was claimed that, because so many of them lived on the coast, they were potential collaborators with the Japanese military, yet no grounds for such suspicions were ever established. Furthermore, many Japanese Americans had been born in this country, and—perhaps bitterest of all ironies—many of the families in the camps had sons who were fighting and dying in the American armed forces. Because no German American or Italian American was ever placed in such a camp, the conclusion is inescapable that this was purely an episode of racist hysteria. Consequently, it was expected that Japanese Americans would face a difficult adjustment period after their release from these camps, as a result of anti-Oriental prejudices on the West Coast. To avoid this difficulty, many Japanese Americans migrated eastward to large metropolitan areas. But, because they were traditionally small farmers, and their culture was considered to be alien to that of the majority, they were again expected to have problems.

Fortunately, the expected problems arose only rarely, partly because the Eastern communities did not have a built-in rejection of the Orientals. In fact, research on Japanese Americans in Chicago indicated they were well accepted by their neighbors, employers, landlords, and most other middle-class Americans with whom they interacted. Most Japanese Americans completed high school, went on to college or vocational training, and held professional or skilled jobs that were respected in the community.

Research shows that while there are marked differences in the American middle class and the Japanese culture, both share many basic values and norms: "politeness, respect for authority and parental wishes, duty to community, diligence, cleanliness and neatness, emphasis on personal achievement of long-range goals, importance of keeping up appearances for others" (Caudill and De Vos, 1971). Not only are Japanese and middle-class Americans similar in their values and goals, but they also share similarities in personality development. Both are highly sensitive to cues from others and adapt their behavior accordingly, by suppressing their real emotions. Thus, even though some factors were working against the Japanese Americans (racial visibility, alien culture, and a general American prejudice against foreigners), the compatibility of the Japanese and the American middle-class

---

FIGURE 16.1 The Higher Education of Minority Groups: Ratios of College Completion Rates to that of Majority Male Population, 1976

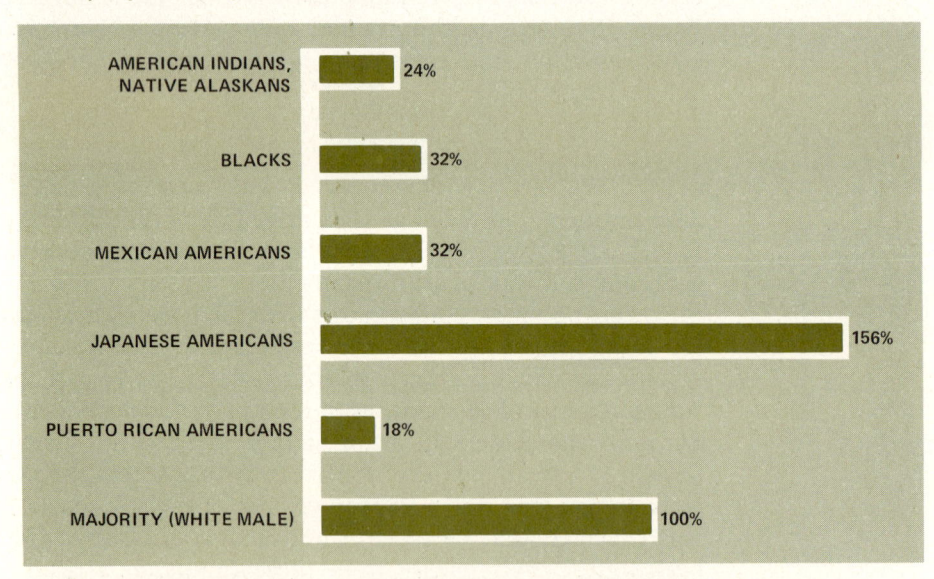

Group	Ratio
AMERICAN INDIANS, NATIVE ALASKANS	24%
BLACKS	32%
MEXICAN AMERICANS	32%
JAPANESE AMERICANS	156%
PUERTO RICAN AMERICANS	18%
MAJORITY (WHITE MALE)	100%

In 1976, the percent of American Indians/Native Alaskans aged 25–29 who completed at least four years of college was 24 percent of the rate for majority (white) males. Note the extremely low rate of college completion among Puerto Rican Americans as compared to that of the majority. Japanese Americans place a high value on education; since they are not living in poverty and are not the objects of severe discrimination, they are able to express this value and have a college completion rate even higher than that of white males.

Source: United States Commission on Civil Rights, *Social Indicators of Equality for Minorities and Women* (Washington, D.C.: U.S. Government Printing Office, 1978), p. 14.

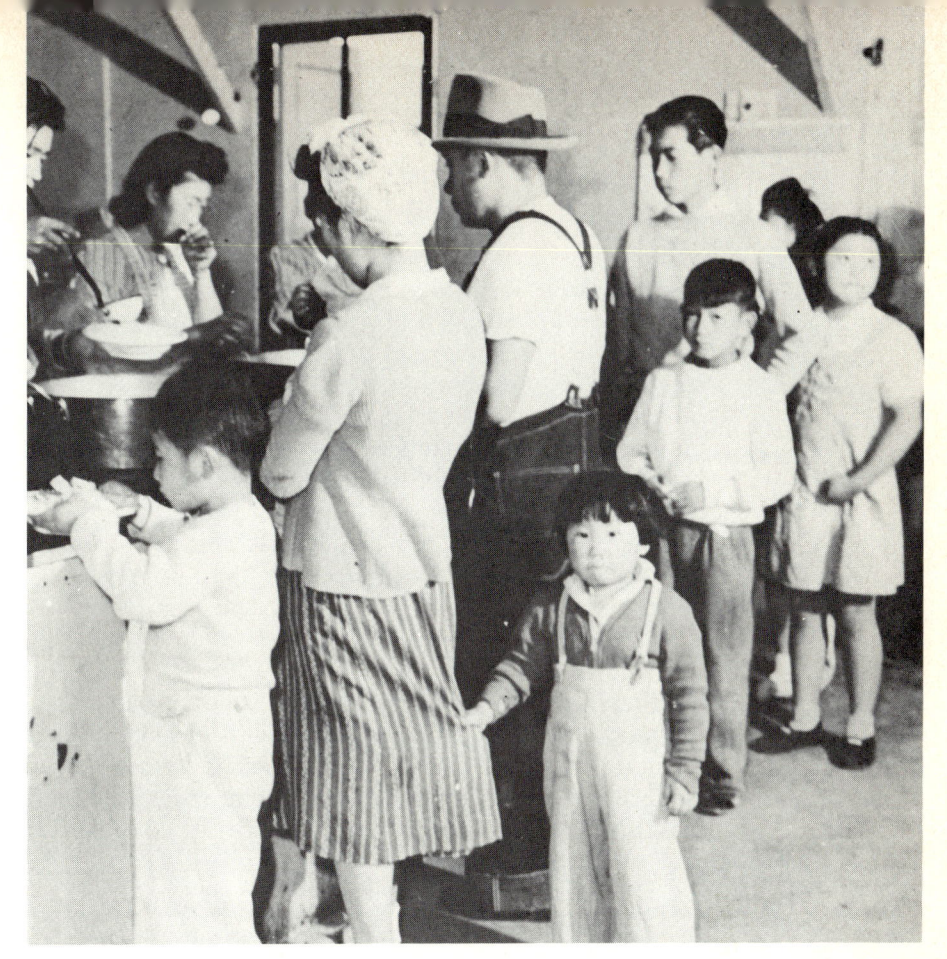

During World War II, Japanese Americans were moved from California to this relocation camp in Colorado. Racial prejudice was largely responsible.

value systems allowed them to find their niche, just as such similarities have helped Chinese, Filipinos, and other Orientals living in America.

American Jews

In an ethnological sense, the Jews have always held a confusing position in the world. They were once considered by many to be a race, and then later, a dispersed nation (which is historically correct). They are, in fact, of many nationalities, and people of every social race include Jews among them. Jews are simply people who adhere to the Jewish religion or to its concomitant cultural traditions. They combine ancient values and norms with the folkways and mores of their countries of birth or adoption.

Discrimination against Jews extends far back into history. For centuries, European Christians maintained a vicious stereotype of them. They were rigidly controlled as to where they could live, how they could earn a living, and with whom they could mingle. Although they settled all over Europe, for centuries they were so carefully isolated that little intermingling took place with the dominant group. For these and other reasons, the Jews developed a separatist urban history and became proficient in managing their own small businesses. They arrived in the United States in large numbers at just the right time to benefit from their specialized background. Many quickly moved into middle- and upper-middle class positions, despite prejudice and discrimination.

In recent decades, Jews have experienced less discrimination in our society, although prejudice and stereotyping have been resistant to complete extinction. The probable cause for their improved status is the greater feeling of ecumenism among religious believers and the overall decline in the importance of religion in our society. Originally, Christians considered Jews to be "unclean" (spiritually), so they were restricted to occupations that were apparently necessary to the economy but perilous to the Christian soul. Thus, from being forced into those trades and occupations, the Jews later acquired the stereotype of greed and obsession with money.

Blacks

Love of money may be the root of all evil, but having an adequate supply of it would help to remedy many problems of blacks, for being black usually means being poor. In 1975, the median family income of whites was $14,268, and that of blacks $8,779. The median income of black families was thus about 60 percent that of white ones. For both races, husband-wife

---

**BOX 16.2
PIOUS RACISM**

Who is most likely to be prejudiced against blacks and to hold more racist attitudes—a churchgoer or a nonchurchgoer? Studies have shown time after time that it is the churchgoers who tend toward prejudice and discrimination, even when age, education, and geographical region are taken into account.

The sociologist Robert C. Brannon (1972) was fascinated with these data and developed a hypothesis regarding this seemingly contradictory situation. After all, Christians are taught of the brotherhood of man—they should be the first to welcome those of other races as equals. Brannon came up with the idea that there are at least two types of church members: those who are religious and who believe in the teachings of Jesus, and those who use churchgoing for purposes other than religious experience. He termed the first group _devotional_ church members and the second group _instrumental_ church members. Whereas devotional members attend church because their religious beliefs are a fundamental part of their lives, instrumental members attend church because it offers status, entertainment, business contacts, fellowship, leadership training, and other personal benefits.

To test his hypothesis, Brannon developed a questionnaire to determine the degree of devotionalism and instrumentalism present in churchgoers. He then found a perfect situation for applying the questionnaire: a small Protestant church in the South that had recently split into two churches

families tend to have incomes double those headed by women. Black families are nearly three times as likely to be headed by a woman, which partly accounts for the low median family income of blacks as a group. About four times the number of blacks than whites live below the poverty level. Finally, black males earn only from two-thirds to three-fourths as much as do white males with comparable education. As we saw in Chapter 11, black males at the same educational level as whites are less likely to hold white-collar jobs and are more likely to be service workers. There is still much discrimination in the United States, which results in blacks being disproportionately poor. (The continued discrimination sometimes comes from unlikely quarters—see Box 16.2.)

Other evidence of gross differences in the well-being of blacks and whites abounds. Blacks have a lower average life expectancy than whites. Their death rate from hypertension is four times that of whites, and they are more likely than whites to die of heart disease and cancer. Death by homicide is almost ten times higher for blacks than whites, and the death rate by accidents is 50 percent higher. But blacks have a significantly lower suicide rate than whites.

The educational level of blacks has improved dramatically over the years. Nevertheless, they are less likely to enroll in college and more likely to be

---

over the racial issue. The parent church favored gradual desegregation, while those who left the congregation to form the new church opposed that measure, and instead, instituted a rule reserving their membership for whites only. Brannon administered his questionnaire to members of both churches, and his findings supported his hypothesis: the degree of instrumentalism was much higher in members of the splinter church than in those of the parent church. Devotional sentiments were much more common among those in the parent church than among those who formed the segregationist church.

In explaining the connection between instrumentalism and racism, Brannon points out that the same basic lifestyle and circumstances that determine the one shape the other. "If a person craves status he can attain it by attending a fashionable church, while prejudice will assure him that there is a whole class of people lower in status than he. Prejudice can enhance the self-esteem of the threatened and insecure, while religion offers him security and promise of heavenly reward. Both prejudice and religion can be crutches for a weak ego" (p. 127).

Other studies seem to support Brannon's conclusions, since it has been found that those who attend church more frequently (more likely to be devotional) are quite low in prejudice, while those who attend church moderately to regularly (more likely to be instrumental) are generally high in prejudice.

school dropouts than whites. The unemployment rate in the United States varies from year to year, and even from season to season; but, over many years, one thing has not varied—the jobless rate for blacks is twice that for whites. If you are a black teenager, the odds of your being unemployed are high; over one-third of black teenagers, but only 14 percent of white teenagers, are unemployed.

In Chapter 15, we referred to the concentration of blacks in urban ghettos. This and other factors result in blacks being more poorly housed than whites. Blacks are less likely than whites to be homeowners. The census of 1970 found that almost half of black dwellers located outside metropolitan areas lacked some or all plumbing facilities, compared with only nine percent of white dwellings. Rent takes a larger share of the family income among blacks than among whites.

Even though enforcement of social legislation in recent years has helped raise the standards of black housing, wages, education, and the like, it is clear that great inequalities still exist. Many whites feel that blacks should be pleased with the overall improvements. But blacks are not pleased, because compared with whites, they are still deprived. This continued deprivation, coupled with historic factors, affects the assimilation of blacks into the general society.

Judith Kramer (1970) summarizes the plight of American blacks with regard to socialization into the larger society in one sentence: "Without a communal ideology to define an independent identity there can only be

Ethnic pride can help promote a personal feeling of worth. Both were hard to achieve under strict segregation and its implied inferiority status.

socialization into the nonidentity of personal invisibility and racial visibility" (p. 214) That is, the black minority group has no identifiable culture or hertiage of its own that is acceptable to its members. Before their ancestry of slavery, they had a "pagan," primitive tribal culture that most American blacks cannot identify with. Aside from that, blacks could no more transport their culture from the past and from the African continent to our society, rural or urban, than could a German American transport the culture of the nomadic hordes that wandered pre-Christian Europe. Thus, parents have no cultural heritage to hold up for their young.

Ironically, before a minority group can become acculturated into the larger society, it must first have a culture of its own. The culture that blacks once had was torn from them traumatically and was systematically broken down during their many generations of slavery. But, when they tried to take on the culture of the larger society, they began to see themselves as inferior beings—for, why else were they slaves? The recent emergence of free African nations, coupled with Black Nationalism, Black Power, and other such movements, has helped many blacks to begin to identify with a living, usable tradition. As Kramer says, this "communal ideology" would lend support and meaning to a person's life, so that he or she might better "define an independent identity."

Without such a "communal ideology," black people are not seen as individuals. They are given a categorical status based upon their skin color ("racial visibility"), and are judged by this minority-group status and stereotype rather than by their own merits. Before long, even people with untapped resources and abilities may begin to hold themselves in the low esteem of their racial stereotypes.

One sign that a positive self-identity is developing among blacks was the popular emergence, a few years ago, of the notion of "soul." Soul idealizes the achievements and superiority of the black way of life: the dignity, strength, courage, and shrewdness required to survive in a ghetto of a racist society, combined with compassion and loyalty for one's "brothers and sisters." Notions, such as "soul" and "black pride," and slogans like "black is beautiful" can be the prelude to the forming of a personal identity. Whatever their limitations as guides for action, they acknowledge the black person's wounds, and the strength that has enabled black people to survive for so long; in short, they help to undo some of the injuries to identity that come from being treated as a "personal invisibility."

We found that one detail in the pattern of human interaction encompassed by a society can be the failure or the refusal to interact, as happens when a dominant racial or ethnic group treats members of other groups as inferiors. If we treat a person as a stereotype of his or her race, religion, nationality, or sex, we are denying that person's individual identity. And, if members of a dominant group treat every member of another group by the stereotype they were socialized to hold, the individual reality of every one of those people is being denied. Until a few decades ago, and then changing only slowly, such was the history of racial and ethnic relations in our society. Although not every society has, at all times, had subordinate minority groups—primitive tribal societies, for example, have usually been quite homogeneous—every known society has had to deal with some form of *deviancy*—behavior that strays too far from the culture's norms to be tolerated. What constitutes deviant behavior differs from society to society, as does how it is handled, but the occurence of deviancy itself seems universal. The next chapter examines this social phenomenon at length.

SUMMARY

1. The term "minority" has many implications—exclusion from full citizenship rights, being of lesser importance, numerically small. A **minority group** has these characteristics, although, numerically, it may be larger than the majority group. In American society, minorities are singled out for differential and unequal treatment and so have poorer life chances.

2. **Ethnocentrism** is a dominant group's belief that it is somehow superior to the minority.

3. Minority groups are set apart from the rest of society by virtue of their physical or cultural characteristics. Race is one such characteristic; **ethnic group** is another.

4. **Race** is a group of human beings possessing similar combinations of anatomical features due to a common heredity. It has been suggested that there are three major races: Caucasoid, Mongoloid, and Negroid. There are so many variations within these races that the concept of race is almost meaningless today.

5. The racial differences that do exist have arisen from three factors working in combination: **natural selection, random genetic drift,** and **geographical isolation.** However, groups have mingled, producing a mixture of physical types.

6. It has been suggested that racial differences occur in such characteristics as intelligence, as well as in physical characteristics. However, this connection is yet to be proven, since the only evidence is from IQ tests, and such tests are subject to bias toward the white middle class.

7. Although there do not appear to be any important differences between races, our society has developed a need to distinguish differences among *social races* and to attach meanings to these differences.

8. Identification of minority groups has led to specific attitudes and behav-

iors toward these groups on the part of the majority. Majority group members may feel **prejudice** toward minorities and may practice **discrimination** against them.

9. The most pronounced form of discrimination in American society is **racism**—the belief that members of another race (usually blacks) are inherently inferior to those of one's own race. *Individual racism* refers to specific acts against individuals of another race; **institutional racism** refers to racist policies built into society's institutions.

10. As a result of their attitudes toward minorities, majorities have treated minorities in a number of different ways. In some societies, minorities have actually been victims of **extermination** or **expulsion**; in others, **segregation** and **discrimination** have been practiced. Today, there is a move toward **pluralism** in the United States—groups retain their ethnic differences but are treated equally in society. **Assimilation** requires a group to give up its previous culture and totally adopt the culture of the dominant group. **Amalgamation** occurs when two cultures blend to produce a new one.

11. American Indians are among the most poorly treated minorities. They have assimilated our material culture but have clung to their own non-material culture.

12. Mexican Americans are a highly fragmented group, so it is difficult to generalize about them. In Southern California, Mexican Americans are breaking down cultural barriers and are moving toward middle-class status.

13. Most Puerto Rican Americans live in the ghetto areas of New York City; they are trying to better their lot in life but are meeting barriers of poverty, poor education, high unemployment, and racial prejudice.

14. Although Japanese Americans were poorly treated during World War II, they have achieved acceptance rather easily in American middle-class culture, because of shared values and norms.

15. Although Jews have a long history of discrimination and stereotyping in American society and elsewhere, their status seems to be improving.

16. There are gross differences in the well-being of blacks and whites in American society. Black families have significantly lower incomes than white families, a higher death rate, and a higher unemployment rate. In addition, blacks are more poorly educated and housed than whites.

17. It has been suggested that blacks cannot become assimilated into the larger society until they have a distinct culture of their own—a communal identity that will increase their self-esteem.

KEY TERMS

- amalgamation
- assimilation
- discrimination
- ethnic group
- ethnocentrism
- expulsion
- extermination
- genocide
- geographic isolation
- institutional racism
- intelligence
- minority group
- natural selection
- pluralism
- prejudice
- race
- racism
- random genetic drift
- segregation

SUGGESTED READINGS

Brown, Claude. *Manchild in the Promised Land.* New York: Macmillian, 1966.
    An autobiography about the author's experiences growing up in Harlem.

Brown, Dee. *Bury My Heart at Wounded Knee.* New York: Bantom Books, 1972.
    The early relationships between white settlers and the American Indian are described from the Indians' point of view.

Fanon, Frantz. *Black Skins, White Masks.* New York: Grove Press, 1967.
    A study of the psychological problems that the black man experiences living in the white world. Fanon draws on literature, dreams, and case histories.

Fitzpatrick, Joseph. *Puerto Rican Americans.* New York: Random House, 1971.
    This book about Puerto Rican Americans in New York City centers on the events and the meaning of migration, both to the migrants and to the neighborhoods they enter.

Glazer, Nathan, and Daniel Patrick Moynihan. *Beyond the Melting Pot.* 2nd ed. Cambridge, Mass.: MIT Press, 1970.
    The authors trace the experiences of blacks, Puerto Ricans, Jews, Italians, and Irish in New York City. They stress survival patterns and the continuing importance of ethnicity.

Levine, Stuart, and Nancy Lurie, eds. *The American Indian Today.* Deland, Fla.: Everett Edwards, 1968.
    Essays on the culture and values of American Indians, the conflict between these values and those of the dominant culture, and the Indians' attempt to preserve their culture.

Lewis, Oscar. *La Vida.* New York: Random House, 1965.
    An intensive study of one Puerto Rican family. Lewis uses this study as a vehicle for understanding the conditions of poverty, both in San Juan and in New York City, and the specific problems encountered by Puerto Ricans.

Myrdal, Gunnar. *An American Dilemma.* 2 vols. New York: Harper & Row, 1944.
    An analysis of the American social structure and the role it gives to blacks. Myrdal points out the contradiction of the ideal of equality and the status of the black.

Peterson, William. *Japanese Americans.* New York: Random House, 1971.
>The author discusses the migration of the Japanese to the United States, the problems they have faced here, and their attempts to become an integrated part of American society.

Simpson, George E., and Milton Yinger. *Racial and Cultural Minorities.* 4th ed. New York: Harper & Row, 1972.
>A good general text on race and ethnic relations that explores the nature of prejudice and discrimination.

Yaffe, James. *The American Jews.* New York: Random House, 1968.
>The author presents an interesting discussion on Jewish culture and values on the operation of Jews within American society. He deals with the various myths about Jews and the problems of survival faced by Judaism.

What do a skid row alcoholic, a catatonic schizophrenic, a bank robber, a heroin addict, and a homosexual have in common in our society? They are all <u>deviants</u>: people whose behavior goes beyond the norms of society and is considered undesirable. All societies try to get people to avoid deviant behavior, but none is completely successful in doing so. Sociologists have developed several theories to explain the various types of deviant behavior.

There are many different forms of deviant behavior, but one classification method identifies three broad types: criminal deviants, the mentally ill, and social dropouts. The role of society in defining deviancy is apparent from this classification. Criminal laws are not the same everywhere, and even in any given society, what is a crime today, such as possession of marijuana, may not be a crime tomorrow. Some of what our society considers mental illness or dropping out may be tolerated in another society.

The sociological explanations for deviant behavior stress social conditions and social characteristics rather than personality traits or personal idiosyncrasies. The <u>anomie theory</u>, for example, sees the roots of deviancy in situations where there is a lack of harmony between the goals established by society and the approved means of reaching the goals. Another theory, the <u>deviant subculture</u> approach, points to the groups within society that have developed a system of values and practices that are at odds with those of the larger society. Finally, the <u>labeling theory</u> shows how society creates deviancy by its reactions to someone discovered to have broken a law or to have otherwise committed a deviant act. Shoplifters who are never caught or punished may give up this behavior without ever thinking of themselves as deviant. But if arrested and punished, and thus labeled criminals, they may come to think of themselves as such.

No one theory adequately explains deviancy. This becomes apparent as we explore three major forms of deviancy in our society: drug abuse, homosexuality, and crime and delinquency. Yet, as we apply the theories to these forms of deviancy, both the theories and the deviancy become more understandable. By studying this chapter, you should gain insights into the nature and extent of deviancy in our society.

17
Deviancy

Sardinia is a small island in the Mediterranean, just west of Italy. Settlements on the island go back to before the time of Christ. The Sardinians are an independent people who fiercely resist change and outside influences. They want to be left alone to live out their lives and work out their own problems. Sheep herding is the principal economic activity there, and many of the villages have changed little in 300 years. The anthropologist Graeme Newman (1976) called Sardinia a "subculture of violence," a label that seems quite appropriate. In one four-year period, for example, one small Sardinian village was the site of 27 homicides of shepherds by other shepherds, and twelve policemen (sent from outside) were killed in ambush.

The vendetta is part of the ancient culture of Sardinia. The relatives of a murdered person must avenge the act by killing the murderer or a member of the murderer's family. This code is considered binding on all those who live in the community. There is also a "rule" of silence that prohibits people from talking to outsiders about homicides and other crimes in their villages. Sardinians passively accept the Italian criminal code as an imposed necessity but readily abandon it if it conflicts with the vendetta.

The Sardinians have not been able to eliminate homicide, even though a potential killer, aware of the vendetta, should realize that he will almost surely be caught and killed. It is likely that their code, which calls for a personal and violent reaction to murder, actually encourages the acceptance of violence. The Sardinians have a code of behavior and react negatively to those who break the rules. In Newman's cross-cultural study, the Sardinians were found to define as seriously wrong such acts as robbery, incest, and even drug use to about the same extent as did people in India, Indonesia, Iran, Yugoslavia, and New York City. But, the Sardinians are not as likely as people in other places to say that such acts should be reported to the authorities. They prefer to deal with them in their families and communities.

The Mbuti Pygmies of the Ituri Forest, Africa, live in small, close-knit tribes. Hunting is their major economic activity. They hunt in groups, which requires cooperation and trust. The anthropologist Colin Turnbull (1965) reports that the Pygmies have a particular abhorrence of stealing and "never" steal from one another. On occasion, however, there are thefts. One reaction is to ignore them, for in this way, the Pygmies do not have to deal with the reprehensible act. They have been socialized to trust one another, to respect each other's right to possess food, and to believe that stealing is the worst of offenses. And, yet, thievery does occur.

All societies attempt, through socialization, to instill in individuals the fact that it is undesirable to break the social rules—to deviate from the norms. People are taught to desire the approval of others and to expect to feel shame and guilt if they behave in ways contrary to group expectations. As a backup for these inner controls, societies may employ external controls, such as physical punishment, banishment from the group, or execution to force people to comply with norms. However, neither the internal nor the external controls are 100 percent effective. Sardinians still murder, and Pygmies still steal.

Murder in Sardinia and thievery among the Pygmies are both forms of **deviancy** — behavior that significantly departs from the standards of conduct of a given group. What is defined as deviant in one group may be considered normal behavior in another. Sociologists are concerned with what is *considered* deviance, why some people stray from the rules of conduct and others do not, and how much deviance there is in a given society.

TYPES OF DEVIANCY

We have referred to homicide among the Sardinians and to thievery among the Pygmies. These acts are considered crimes in the United States. But deviancy consists of more than criminal acts. Any type of unusual behavior that is judged by society to be undesirable is deviant. Because deviancy is as much a form of social behavior as is conforming to norms, it has been much studied by sociologists. One approach has been to classify deviant behavior into broad categories. While there are many types of deviants, and a number of different ways to classify them, one classification system considers three broad types of deviants: criminals, the mentally ill, and social dropouts. (People can be classified in more than one category — see Box 17.1.)

The Deviant as Criminal

Some behavior is deviant because it violates criminal law. By this standard, anyone who commits a criminal act is a deviant, no matter how prevalent this act may be in society. Even if many people cheat on their income taxes or smoke marijuana, these acts are still crimes and are, therefore, considered deviant. Thus, by this definition, even if a given act is statistically "normal" (that is, committed by an overwhelming majority of those in a society), it is still deviant behavior (Lefton et al., 1968).

Some crimes have victims; other crimes do not (Schur, 1965). Crimes against persons or property, or those in which someone is hurt or wronged, have victims. Other acts that are against the law, such as homosexuality, heterosexual prostitution between consenting adults, use or abuse of drugs, and gambling, do not properly have victims. Nevertheless, they are crimes. At times, the designation "victimless crime" is blurred by actions that take place as a result of or in connection with a victimless crime. If a person is beaten for failure to pay a gambling debt, or if venereal disease is spread through prostitution, it is difficult to say that there are no victims.

Although all crimes are deviant, some crimes are considered to be more serious than others. In a sociological study in Baltimore, a sample of 200 adults rated 140 descriptions of crimes according to how serious they considered these acts to be (Rossi et al., 1974). Planned killing, selling heroin, and forcible rape were at the top of the list, while disturbing the peace, refusal to answer a census taker, and being drunk in a public place were at the bottom. The researchers found that the norms defining the seriousness of criminal acts are widely held by blacks and whites, males and females, and people of different social classes.

The Deviant as Mentally Ill

There is nothing illegal about going into a catatonic state, or believing yourself to be Napoleon and acting accordingly, or changing your mood radically from one of great excitement to one of deep depression. These forms of behavior are considered to be symptoms of mental illness and are judged to be socially disruptive or possibly dangerous and, thus, deviant (Dinitz et al., 1969).

Unlike criminal deviants, the mentally ill are not held responsible for

---

BOX 17.1 THE FAT PERSON AS TRIPLE DEVIANT

What does it mean to be overweight in American society? The sociologist Natalie Allon (1973) talked to and observed 1,400 overweight persons (95 percent of them women) in 90 group dieting meetings, and as a result of her studies, she has gained considerable insight into this question. According to Allon, the overweight woman is a triple deviant—she is considered a sinner, a sick person, and in some respects, a criminal.

Obesity is considered a sin by those who view it as a result of immoral self-indulgence. With will power, a fat woman could put herself on the road to salvation. In their weekly meetings, dieters were found to use religious images: sinner, saint, devil, angel, guilt, and transgression. They confessed their overeating sins and the errors of their eating ways. Dieters condemned themselves for their needs for immediate gratification, their inability to handle frustration, and the self-destructiveness of their overeating. Some of the dieters offered testimonies to the Ideal of Thinness as they talked about being born again or really living for the first time in their lives, now that they were on the road to salvation from their sin of fatness. In seeking redemption for their sin, they placed a weekly fee in the collection plate.

Allon found that obese people are also viewed as sick, either physically or emotionally. Doctors see obesity as a pathological condition in its own right, as well as a major contributor to such disorders as heart disease, diabetes, and kidney trouble. Others see overweight people as emotionally ill—as people who have an emotional attachment to food that leads to its misuse. Or, perhaps food symbolizes an insatiable desire for love. In Allon's study, some of the women discussed their feelings of being abnormal or sick with extra fat—they said they felt swollen or puffy or about to burst open. The view of a fat person as a sick deviant implies that, to some extent, the condition is beyond the control of the patient.

their actions: they are considered "sick." Some forms of behavior have remained deviant, but the categories of deviancy into which they are placed have been changed. Homosexuality, for example, is a crime in most states, and it is also seen as a sickness. The dual status of homosexuality is further complicated because many experts do not consider gay people to be sick and in need of treatment. Although some physicians and lay people continue to define homosexuality as pathological, many are changing their views. In 1974, a body of psychiatrists decided to vote that homosexuality no longer be considered a mental illness. However, a poll of 2,500 psychiatrists conducted in 1977 found that 69 percent held that homosexuality is a pathological adaptation, as opposed to a normal variation (*Behavior Today*, December 5, 1977).

The deviant-as-sick model assumes that we can distinguish the mentally ill from the well, but there is some doubt that we always can (Szasz, 1961,

---

In contrast, criminals are held to be responsible or accountable for their norm-breaking behavior. Many consider the fat person responsible for the overeating and underexercising that are presumed to be the cause of obesity. Society is continually issuing warnings about the dangers of becoming fat, so the person who deviates from the norm of thinness has only himself or herself to blame. Often, it is considered a "crime" for a welfare recipient to be obese—he or she is using public funds to support a "habit."

There is more direct evidence of the "obese as criminal" concept. Allon notes that "one New York assemblyman suggested that since obesity is the result of addiction to food, all cases should be reported under the city's drug-addiction laws" (p. 93). She also notes that in the 1920s, Sweden levied a tax on obesity, but the law was declared unconstitutional. Fat people are not put into jail, but they are frequently imprisoned in their stigmatized role as a fat person; and they are often discriminated against in employment because of the stigma.

In some nonliterate societies, fatness is a sign of beauty in women. In the modern United States, fat is considered ugly—an example of how culture determines what is deviant. Is the fat person in America a sinner, a sick person, or a criminal deviant? He or she can be any of these, depending on who is defining the deviancy. We do not leave the fat person alone but label him or her a deviant of some sort. Often, as in accordance with labeling theory (which is discussed later in this chapter), the fat person accepts the deviant label and feels most comfortable in the company of other deviants. Fat deviants, however, band together not to continue their deviant behavior but to change it.

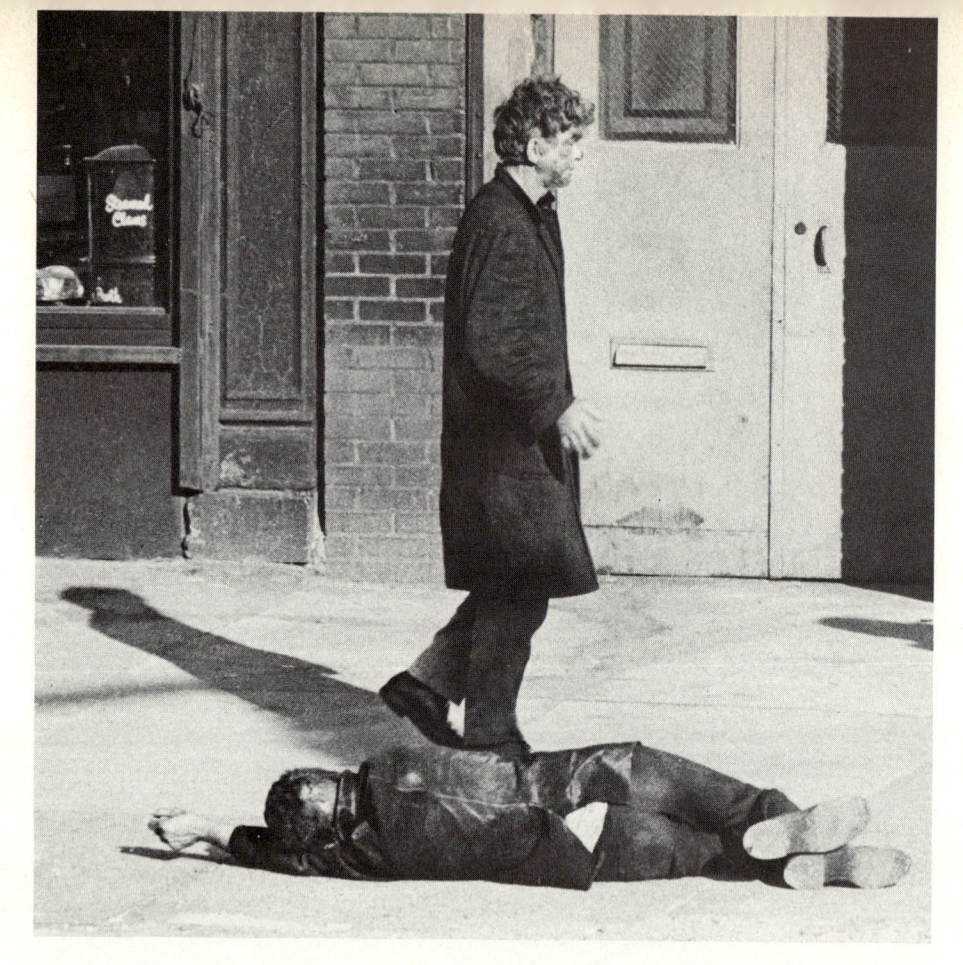

The winos on the Bowery have dropped out of society. Many would consider them sick deviants as well.

1970). Psychiatrists often differ on diagnoses. To cite a bizarre example, psychiatrist David Rosenhan (1973) conducted a participant observation experiment in which eight sane persons had themselves admitted to different mental hospitals by falsely complaining that they had been hearing voices. Seven were diagnosed as schizophrenic, and one as manic-depressive. Once admitted, these persons acted their normal selves while in the wards; their only deception had been in their initial false claims. They spent their time in the wards observing and taking notes. Yet, in not a single case was their deception detected by doctors, nurses, or ward attendants, although 35 of the 118 "real" patients on the ward of one hospital suspected that the pseudopatient was not sick. In fact, one patient came close to the truth by asserting that the pseudopatient was not crazy but was a professor checking up on hospitals. The hospital staff observing the same behavior recorded it as "persistent obsessive note-taking behavior." What the patients considered sane behavior, the staff considered mentally deranged. The so-called sick were pretty good diagnosticians. The discharge records of the incorrectly diagnosed schizophrenics bore the notation "schizophrenia in remission." In other words, these normal people were still considered mentally ill when they left the hospitals.

Are behaviors such as hallucinations, anxiety, depression, and mental anguish sufficiently different from normal behavior to make the diagnosis "mental illness" meaningful? Extreme cases, such as the catatonic who remains in a trancelike condition for months, are clearly distinguishable from normal kinds of behavior, but many other behaviors are not. Yet, people exhibiting less extreme symptoms who are labeled mentally ill are not necessarily much different from other normal people. The sick may not *really* be deviant; that is, such individuals may not exhibit behavior that is very different from behavior of the average person.

The Deviant as Social Dropout

Not all types of deviancy in the United States are classified neatly as either criminal or sick. Some are considered both, such as in the case of the "criminally insane." As we saw, homosexuality is considered both a crime and a sickness by various people, and compulsive gambling can also be considered both a sickness and a crime.

Still other types of behavior are defined as socially undesirable but are neither crimes nor sickness. Alienated people, mostly young, who reject the "straight" life and seek escape in a rural commune are considered by many to be deviants. Their so-called deviancy lies in their basic values and lifestyle, which are at odds with the dominant culture. These differences produce feelings of distrust, suspicion, and sometimes fear in members of the larger society. The behavior of such alienated individuals is considered odd, strange, or wrong, and therefore deviant.

Surely, some people reason, there is something wrong with these people who choose to live simply, to use secondhand clothes and furniture, to grow

Life at the Libra commune in New Mexico is at odds with the dominant culture. Are the people therefore deviant?

much of their own food, and to remain aloof from politics and organized religion—particularly when they have had a chance for a good education, a good job, and a "good" (that is, middle-class) way of life. Many people hold that those who choose alternate lifestyles and values are not deviant—that they are responsible for their own behavior. They feel that the values of the dominant culture were rejected voluntarily by those who could have chosen to accept them. Others sense that such rejections may have roots in some profound difficulties with the society itself. There is no agreement among sociologists on what theory explains why deviancy, in its various forms, occurs.

SOCIAL THEORIES OF DEVIANCY

Sociologists rely most heavily on three theories to explain deviancy: the anomie theory, the deviant subculture theory, and the labeling theory. As we shall discover, no one of the theories fully explains all types of deviancy, and each provides some element of explanation that the others lack.

The Anomie Theory

In his study of different rates of suicide in the late 1890s, the French sociologist Emile Durkheim (1951) used the concept *anomie*—literally translated as "normlessness," the condition of being without norms. Durkheim discovered that *rates* of suicide could be linked to social conditions—to confusion and contradiction in norms and roles, such as during wars or otherwise politically or economically unsettled times. Such suicides he named *anomic* suicides, for they were related to anomie.

Another sociologist, Robert K. Merton (1968), later adapted the concept of anomie to describe a condition in a society or a social system in which the culturally shared goals do not fit together with the institutionalized means for achieving the goals. The disharmony between cultural goals and institutional means has two chief sources: the institutional means for achieving the cultural goals are either confused and ambiguous, or they are inaccessible.

In the first case, the goal becomes so important that the accepted institutional means are abandoned. Recent American history has shown many instances of this form of anomie, from the Watergate scandal, in which electoral victory was sought at the price of democratic norms that elected officials are sworn to uphold, to cases of gigantic stock and insurance frauds on the scale of many millions of dollars.

In the second case, when means to achieving goals are inaccessible to some groups, the lower classes in our society may accept the goal of economic success but find themselves unable to get or keep jobs that will allow them to reach the goal. Early in their working lives, many people learn that they will never be able to consume goods and services at anything close to the rates of successful people.

Thus, the condition of anomie involves confusion about norms. The **anomie theory** holds that the greater the degree of anomie within a society, the more individuals will turn to deviant behavior as a way out of the difficult situation. The deviant behavior could take different, broad forms, depending on the kind of disharmony between means and ends and the social reactions to it (Clinard, 1964; Cloward, 1959).

Merton has described four strategies for meeting anomic conditions. He calls the first strategy **innovation.** Part of the American dream is economic success. Society holds this goal out to all, but it withholds the means for achieving the goal from many. Some people who accept the goal but find the means to achieve it blocked adopt new, culturally disapproved means of achieving it. This is what Merton means by innovation. Some crime and juvenile delinquency can be understood best as a subgroup's reaction to frustration, for the young or the poor want the same things that middle- and upper-class people want—money and what it can buy.

Cheating in college is no doubt motivated by an acceptance of the goal but not the means. Many students accept the ultimate goal of getting a college degree and the intermediate goals of passing grades, "but anything goes" to reach these goals. Perhaps students rationalize their cheating by saying the course is "irrelevant" or a "mere requirement." Or, the instructor may unwittingly encourage cynicism about approved means by stressing the value of independent thinking or the mastery of general principles while suggesting the opposite by the trivia on his or her tests. In this case, the approved means to achieve the approved goal have not been blocked, but a certain ambivalence has been created about them.

If both the goals and the means are rejected, the deviant behavior can take the form of **retreatism,** Merton's second strategy for anomie. People say, in effect, that they do not want the prize and are not going to run the race. In one way or another, they drop out. The wino on Skid Row and the hobo are retreatists. Some forms of mental illness represent retreatism. A more recent form of retreatism is the rural communes set up to allow their members to function usefully outside the materialistic, individualistic values of modern American society and to seek a better way of life.

The third strategy is **rebellion**—active attempts to change society's goals. In pursuing the strategy of rebellion, some may get into trouble with the law. Even if peaceful demonstrators and other rebels avoid legal trouble, they are often distrusted as deviants by the larger society. But, if they were to succeed in changing society, there would be new norms, and the old rebels would no longer be deviant.

The fourth strategy for anomie is **ritualism:** the individual rejects the culturally approved goals but conforms to the means. Such conformity is ritualistic, because it involves going through the motions rather than making actual commitment to the goals, as, for example, the behavior of people who attend church services out of habit or because of social pressure but have no commitment to the basic goals or values of the religion. Ritualists in society can be considered prone to deviant behavior, because they lack commitment to the goals their behavior serves and are thus susceptible to other goals and norms. Their conformity is only an appearance. They are unstable types, needing only a triggering event or idea to reveal themselves as, in fact, anomic.

Innovation, retreatism, rebellion, and ritualism are thus different types of reactions to anomic conditions in society. The behavior accompanying these reactions either is deviant or could easily become so. According to the anomie theory, if confusion or contradictions surround society's means for achieving its basic goals, high rates of deviant behavior will result. Nevertheless, the theory does not explain why some individuals in a society adopt deviant behavior, while most others do not. In Merton's terms, most of us are **conformists;** that is, we seek culturally approved goals by culturally approved means.

Deviant Subculture Theory

Within any given society, subgroups with their own distinct cultures often can be found (Cohen, 1966). These are called *subcultures,* because they contain the elements of a culture but exist *within* the larger society and its dominant culture. Subcultures range from Ukrainian Americans living in a large city to motorcycle gangs, jazz musicians, organized prostitutes, juvenile gangs, and rock groups. If its values and norms contradict or conflict with those of the dominant culture, the subcluture is a *contraculture.* The **deviant subculture theory** holds that deviant subcultures are what transmit and perpetuate deviancy within a society. According to this theory, people who are members of certain subcultures or have sufficient contact with members will come to learn their values and norms in much the same way that any values and norms are learned.

Edwin H. Sutherland, a criminologist, developed the concept of **differential association** to explain how criminal behavior is learned (Sutherland and Cressey, 1966). According to his theory, within a given society, some people have greater opportunity than others to associate with criminals and delinquents and thus learn not only criminal values but even criminal skills and techniques. According to the deviant subculture theory, the very behavior that is condemned by the larger society is supported and rewarded within the subgroup.

The deviant subculture theory is concerned primarily with how deviancy is transmitted. Once a recognizable subgroup and its subculture are at odds with the dominant culture, the deviant behavior of members can find approval and be reinforced. In addition, through differential association, some are attracted to the subgroup and adopt its behavior patterns. But the theory does not explain how deviant behavior or deviant subcultures arose in the first place. Subcultures seem to arise because deviants or potential deviants

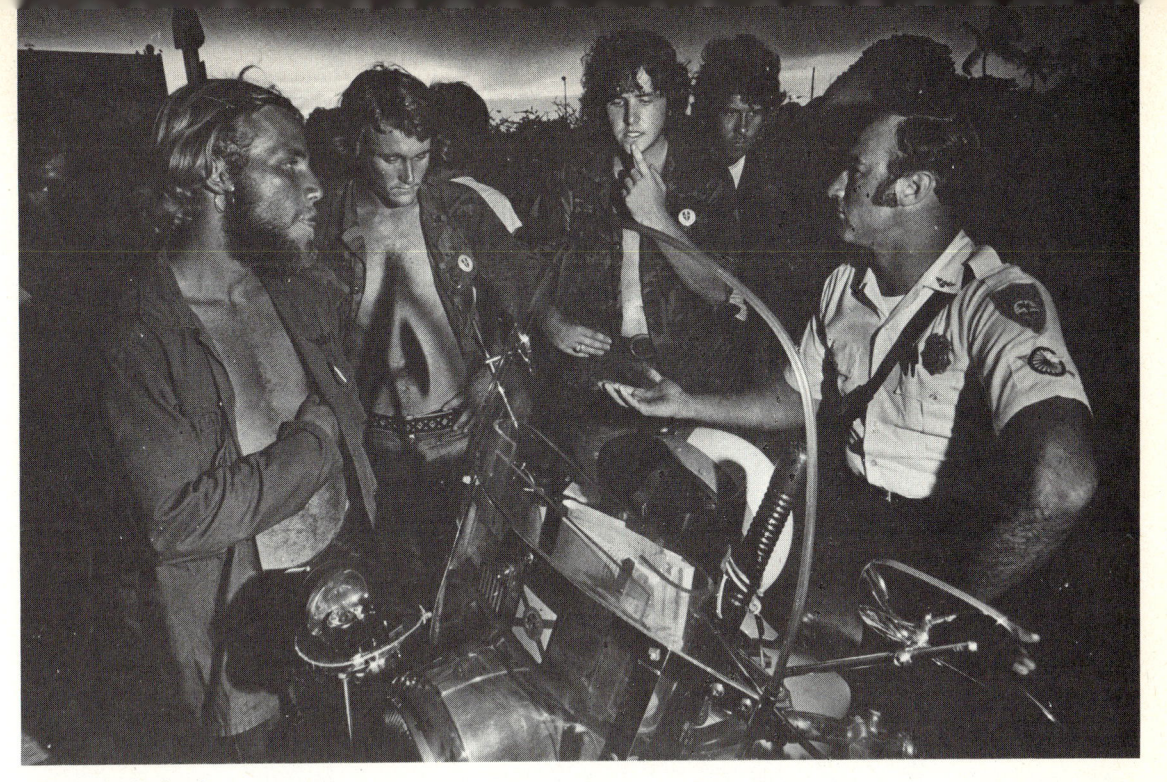

In a deviant subculture new members find acceptance and take on the values and behavior of the group. And so deviancy continues.

keep each other's company. Around college campuses, for example, we find subgroups whose culture includes the use of marijuana and other drugs. About a decade ago, such groups began to emerge as people with common attitudes and a common stance toward the "straight" society banded together. Once formed, such groups reinforce, support, and reward the behavior that brought them together in the first place.

Labeling Theory

Another way of trying to understand deviancy is to focus on how people in the larger society react to norm-violating behavior, what they do about it, and what effects their actions and reactions have on those who perform the behavior (Becker, 1963; Goffman, 1963; Schur, 1972). In **labeling theory,** the act itself is played down, and emphasis is placed on the label—"delinquent," "psychopath," "criminal," "homosexual"—that society gives a person known to have committed the act. Labeling theorists make a fundamental distinction between what they call primary deviancy and secondary deviancy.

Primary deviancy is simply rule breaking or norm violation. At this stage, offenders do not think of themselves as deviants but somehow rationalize their behavior to fit into a socially acceptable role. But, if this behavior becomes known to others, who label it deviant, the self-concepts of offenders are likely to change. As we have seen, our selves are social creations, and our sense of self is always more or less susceptible to the influence of others. No longer will the offenders think of themselves as normal persons who occasionally breaks rules, just like "everybody else" does. They are now deviants. For example, the young man who feels somewhat attracted to

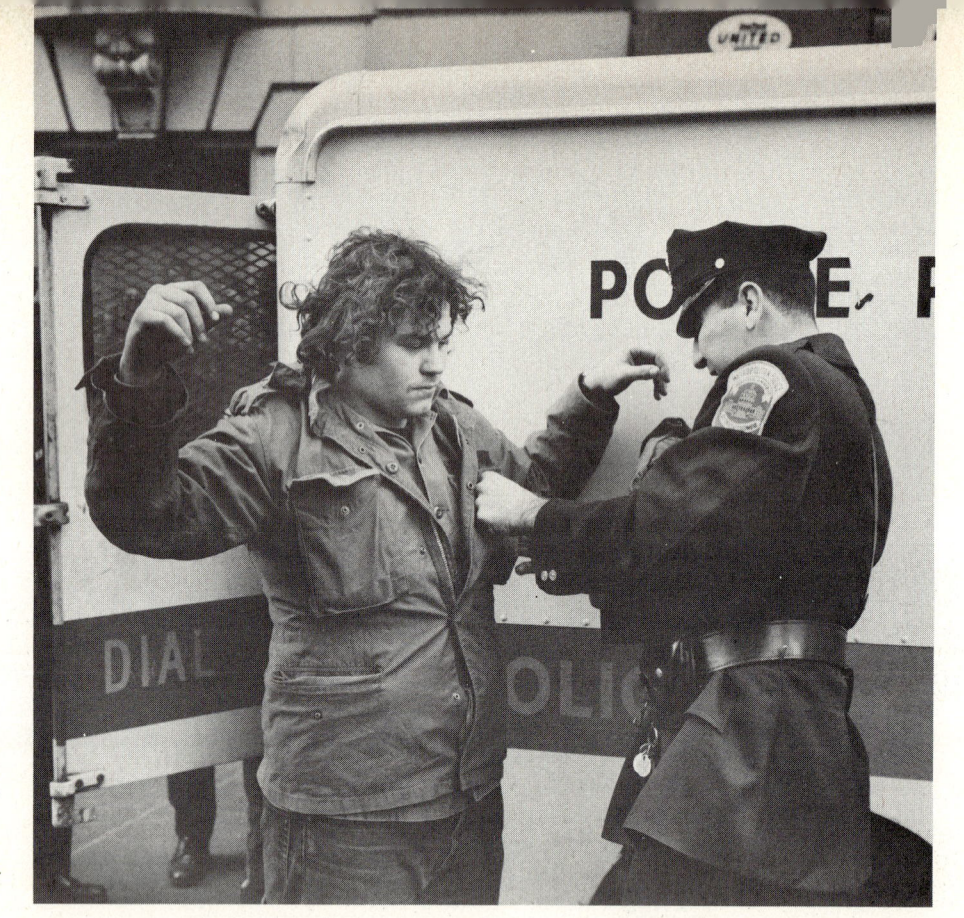

If this man accepts the label "criminal" implied by his arrest, he could progress to secondary deviancy.

other men and has had a few homosexual experiences may have worried about his sexual identity but has still thought of himself as basically heterosexual. What happens if he is caught in a homosexual act and is arrested and charged with homosexuality? He has been officially labeled a homosexual, and his employer, friends of both sexes, parents, and others are likely to think of him as a homosexual and to react to him as one. Perhaps he will now find acceptance only among homosexuals. Thus, a self-fulfilling prophecy may be at work, for having been given the label "homosexual," he is more likely to adopt homosexual behavior than if he had not been so labeled.

The behavior such a man adopts as the result of labeling is his **secondary deviancy.** This is how society creates deviants—by labeling people on the basis of single, discovered acts of primary deviancy. Howard S. Becker (1963), a labeling theorist, contends that:

> Social groups create deviancy by making rules whose infractions constitute deviance, and by applying those rules to particular people and labeling them as outsiders.... The deviant is one to whom the label has successfully been applied (p. 9).

Again, this theory does not explain how some people are moved to the acts of primary deviancy and others are not.

Needed: Integration of the Three Theories

We have seen that although each of the theories purporting to explain deviant behavior has merit, none alone can explain all deviancy. Perhaps further research will link the theories together. For instance, there could be a chain reaction from anomie to labeling to subcultural influences (Reiss, 1970). In a society suffering from considerable anomie, strain on individuals will produce norm-breaking behavior. If this behavior comes to the attention of conformists within the society, the norm-breaking individuals are likely to be labeled deviant. The pool of labeled deviants, in turn, is a potential subgroup of deviants who could support and reward one another's behavior and serve as a recruiting force for more deviants.

Even a linking of the three dominant theories of deviance cannot completely explain the phenomenon; many fundamental variables remain unexplained. Why do some people respond to anomie or deviant subcultures, or practice primary deviancy, while others do not? Why do many persons whose behavior should be explained by these theories violate their predictions, like individuals who do not respond to labeling by acts of secondary deviancy? These questions remain to be pursued by sociological thinkers.

MAJOR FORMS OF DEVIANCY IN THE UNITED STATES

As we have seen throughout this book, and as newspapers, television, and perhaps your own direct experiences have demonstrated, our society is in the midst of change, uncertainty, and great unrest. Not only do we have major social problems, such as energy crises, urban deterioration, and racial discrimination, but we also face major problems of deviancy. We now look at three major areas of deviancy—drug abuse, homosexuality, and crime—and at how well the theories we just examined can explain them.

Drug Abuse

The deviant use of drugs in our society has become well known in recent years—not only in the broadening popularity of marijuana but also in heroin addiction and the growing use of many drugs among high-school students. The various forms of drug abuse simply do not fit within one neat definition. Many people are addicted to drugs, but the drugs themselves, such as barbiturates to induce sleep or amphetamines to help dieters, may be legal when prescribed. Marijuana is illegal, but it is not physiologically or psychologically addicting. And alcohol, which is respectable in most circles as a social lubricant and is legal almost everywhere, is our most abused drug.

Although an estimated nine million people are addicted to alcohol—that is, are alcoholics—alcohol receives almost none of the attention directed to

Alcohol is the most commonly abused drug. Sometimes it is used with other drugs as well.

drug abuse. This lack of attention is probably due to the fact that it has been among us as a respectable form of emotional and social release for so long, whereas we view even the nonaddicting drugs as novel and exotic—as things to be shied away from and kept illegal to discourage their use. For these reasons, we concentrate here on the drugs that many people in our society consider the objects of deviant use—heroin, LSD and other hallucinogens, marijuana, and abused prescription drugs. These are the most common drugs, and most of them are illegal to possess or use.

Prevalence of Drug Abuse No one knows for sure how many drug abusers, or even drug addicts, there are in the United States. In 1976, 244,514 persons were admitted to federally funded drug abuse treatment programs (National Institute on Drug Abuse, 1977). It is estimated that this number represents only about half of all persons treated for drug abuse. The treatment figures, of course, deal only with those who seek help for drug problems and do not include those who do not seek treatment or those who use drugs but do not feel they have a problem.

One of the major problem drugs is heroin, because it has a high potential for physical addiction. A 1976 nationwide survey found that almost 4 percent of young adults had used heroin, while one-half of one percent of youth and older adults had tried it (Response Analysis Corporation, 1976). A study in San Mateo County, California, found that among eleventh graders heroin had been experienced by 1.8 percent of males and .9 percent of females (San

FIGURE 17.1   Drug Use in San Mateo, California, High Schools

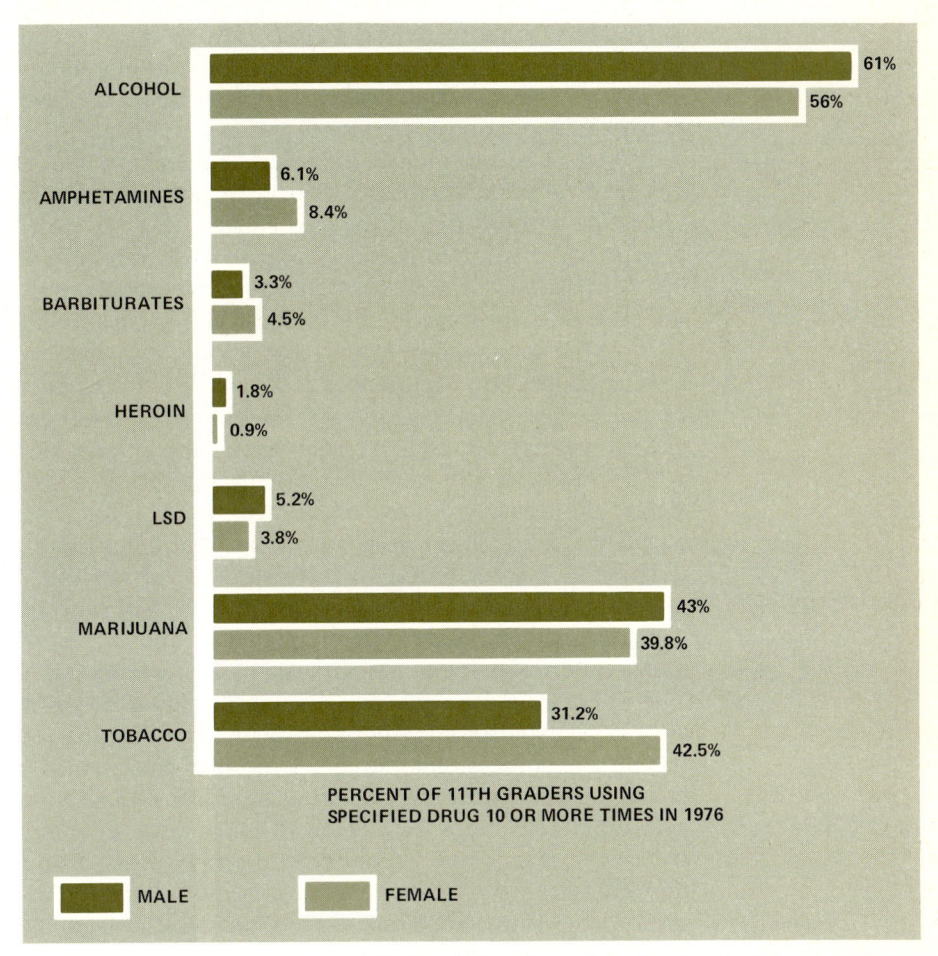

Drug	Male	Female
ALCOHOL	61%	56%
AMPHETAMINES	6.1%	8.4%
BARBITURATES	3.3%	4.5%
HEROIN	1.8%	0.9%
LSD	5.2%	3.8%
MARIJUANA	43%	39.8%
TOBACCO	31.2%	42.5%

PERCENT OF 11TH GRADERS USING SPECIFIED DRUG 10 OR MORE TIMES IN 1976

Since 1968, the Department of Public Health has been keeping track of drug use in San Mateo, California, high schools. Drug use seems to have leveled off, but at a fairly high level. How social factors influence drug use is illustrated by the fact that somewhat more females than males use amphetamines and barbiturates. The reasons for this are not yet clear, but possibly, they are related to the way in which illegal drugs are obtained. Amphetamines and barbiturates are often obtained through forged prescriptions, while heroin and LSD are "street drugs."

Source: Report on Drug Use, San Mateo County Department of Public Health and Welfare (San Mateo, Calif.: 1977), p. 3.

Mateo County Department of Public Health and Welfare Annual Survey). A few years ago, researchers discovered 2,000 heroin users in Harlem between the ages of 7 and 15. The use of heroin has not gone up recently, and it appears to be leveling off. Despite its reputation as a dangerous, addicting drug, and despite efforts to dry up the supply, heroin is still used by at least

300,000 addicts in the United States, many of whom began using it at a very young age.

Heroin's primary effect is to make the user feel mellow, relaxed, and unconcerned about the world. LSD, on the other hand, has been called a "mind-expanding" drug, because the user frequently sees strange sights and beautiful colors and experiences various unusual, intense sensations. The incidence of severe mental disorders and suicide related to the use of LSD has been well-documented. The occurrence of flashbacks—the return to the LSD state without the taking of the drug—has also been verified. Nevertheless, its use continues among young people, even high-school students. The San Mateo study found that among eleventh graders, 5.2 percent of the males and 3.8 percent of the females had used LSD ten or more times in 1976. A national study found that about one percent of all older adults have at some time experienced LSD, while 5.1 percent of all youth age 12-17 and 17.3 percent of adults age 18-25 have experienced it. While the rates of LSD use have leveled off, they have done so at a fairly high level.

The most widely used illegal, mind-altering substance is marijuana. Again, the rates of use are highest for young adults. More than half of all people age 18-25 have used marijuana, and one in four are current users—that is, they were found to have used it within the month prior to the research (Response Analysis Corporation, 1976). Among San Mateo County eleventh graders, 43 percent of the males and almost 40 percent of the females reported using marijuana ten or more times in 1976.

In 1977, the American Medical Association and the American Bar Association issued a joint statement calling for the elimination of criminal penalties for the possession of small amounts of marijuana. President Carter has called for the decriminalization of marijuana possession. As of 1977, however, only ten states had changed their laws so that possessing a small amount of marijuana, generally under one ounce, is punishable by only a fine (these ten states, however, contain one-third of the country's population). Other states are expected to enact similar legislation. Decriminalization does not condone the use of pot, nor is it designed to encourage its use. Pot users are thus still deviant in that they are breaking laws, but the punishment for the offense has, in many places, been greatly reduced.

Second to marijuana in extent of use is the nonmedical use of prescribed drugs, such as stimulants, sedatives, and tranquilizers. About 22 percent of those age 18-25 have used such drugs, as have 7.5 percent of those age 17 and younger. The nonmedical use of prescription drugs is difficult to counteract, for such drugs can be obtained from parents or friends who have them on a doctor's prescription, or they can be obtained readily on the street.

Anomie Theory Two reactions to an anomic social condition, retreatism and rebellion, seem to explain drug abuse. Many heroin addicts exhibit a retreatist reaction when the means of achieving their goals are blocked. Frustrated and disappointed in life, they seek personal escape in drugs and find life intolerable without them. Some LSD users are also retreatists, while other LSD users and many marijuana users are reacting rebelliously to the anomie they perceive. Some of them reject the individualistic, materialistic goals of society and feel that freedom of expression and openness in human relations are higher values.

Deviant Subculture Theory There is clear evidence of a drug subculture in the United States. Of course, a sophisticated social organization is needed to produce and distribute the illegal drugs. But, for many drug users, there is also a common culture of shared values, dress styles, music, and jargon. Although some of these features do not belong exclusively to the drug culture, studies such as Isidor Chein's *The Road to H* (1964) have shown that people are introduced to drug use not by a pusher but through contact with unconventional groups. Bingham Dai's (1970) study of drug users in Chicago revealed that over half of them had personal acquaintances with other users and could identify many more.

Thus, once there is a subgroup of drug users, their way of life can be transmitted to others who themselves fail to find a place in the conventional world. Despite the need to keep their drug use a secret, the drug culture is sufficiently visible to attract new members. Even so, the deviant subculture theory does not fully explain why people ever start to use drugs, for not all those who are aware of the subculture seek to attach themselves to it. One researcher, Harold Firestone (1957), has suggested that those young people whose careers are blocked by dropping out of school or by juvenile delinquency are particularly susceptible to the lures of the drug culture.

Labeling Theory Labeling theory has almost nothing to contribute to an understanding of drug abuse. Like the other two theories, it fails to explain why people start using drugs. In addition, it fails to explain why people become long-term, regular users. Only a tiny fraction of marijuana users, for example, are ever apprehended. For this reason, their prolonged primary deviancy never becomes secondary deviancy. The same is true for most LSD users and quite a few heroin addicts. Marijuana and LSD users consider the laws to be wrong, so their persistent use of their chosen drug or drugs cannot be considered secondary deviancy. And, since heroin is physically addicting, it is useless to speculate as to whether the addict is engaged in primary or secondary deviancy. He or she is simply hooked.

Homosexuality

In most of our states, a homosexual act is a criminal act. Many people think such behavior is deviant not because it violates criminal statutes, but because they feel it is immoral, sinful, or against nature. In one study (Simmons, 1965), for example, 180 people of different ages, sexes, occupations, religions, and races were given the following instructions on a questionnaire: "In the following spaces please list those things or types of persons whom you regard as deviant." They were not furnished with a list of types of deviancy. The most frequent response, given by almost half of the people, was "homosexuality"; 12 percent listed "lesbian," and 11 percent wrote "pervert." These are the things that came into their minds when they saw the word deviant.

Why do so many people in our society think first of homosexuality or lesbianism when they hear the word "deviant"? In some societies, such as ancient Greece and Rome, homosexuality was freely practiced and not considered wrong. Some American Indian tribes created a special role for the homosexual male, who they sometimes referred to as "squaw man." He was considered different from other men and from women, but he was not looked upon with horror or disgust. In 1967, the British Parliament repealed its law that made homosexuality a criminal offense. Prior to the decision, the appointed Wolfenden Commission had made a careful study of homosexuality as a disease and of its effects on the family. The commission concluded that homosexual behavior between consenting adults in private should not be considered a criminal offense.

Perhaps some day far fewer Americans will consider homosexuality to be deviant. Already, as we mentioned, the American Psychiatric Association has moved that homosexuality no longer be classified as a form of mental illness. The 1976 poll of 2,500 psychiatrists, while not constituting an offical action of organized medicine, nevertheless found that almost seven out

Increasingly, homosexuals have become more open and are rejecting the label of deviant. This could lead to more Americans refusing to bestow the label on them.

of ten psychiatrists now feel that homosexuality is not a normal variation of sexual expression but a pathological adaptation. Of this same group of psychiatrists, 40 percent felt that homosexuals could become heterosexual with the proper therapy, whereas 58 percent felt that homosexuals could not be "cured." Apparently, despite the official vote of the American Psychiatric Association, there is disagreement among the experts as to whether or not homosexuality is an illness, and if so, whether or not it can be cured.

This situation among psychiatrists indicates at least two things. First, attitudes toward homosexuality are changing among those closest to the study and treatment of it. Second, the evidence is still ambiguous enough that such a matter has to be decided by vote rather than by the traditional presentation of overwhelming convincing research reports.

This odd occurrence—bestowing mental health by vote—can perhaps give us some insight into the social origins of deviancy. Clearly, murder, rape, and theft are deviant because they assault at least two, if not all three, of the basic social functions of society. They interfere with social order and threaten individuals' physical survival and psychological well-being. Perhaps, as a deviancy, homosexuality has never had such firm grounds for social intolerance. The Bible is interpreted as condemning homosexuality, and interpretation of the Bible was, for many centuries, a source of many mores and folkways. But, we have seen such practices as divorce, abortion, and extramarital sexual relations becoming increasingly acceptable in our society. Is it possible that now, when sex is no longer considered justifiable only as a means of producing offspring—and when the Bible is no longer the source of our secular laws—we lack any reason to consider homosexuality deviant?

To answer this question, sociologists will have to do some delving into the past of our culture and society. Meanwhile, sickness or not, homosexuality is still a crime almost everywhere in our society. And, interestingly enough, there seems to be more reaction to male homosexuality than to female homosexuality. Perhaps this is because our society has been male-dominated, and because male sexuality, or masculinity, is much more rigidly defined as exclusively heterosexual than is female sexuality. Women are permitted to show each other much more affection through many more intimate physical gestures (hugging, kissing, and so on) than are men.

Prevalence of Male Homosexuality Because homosexuality is essentially a private matter, it is almost impossible to estimate the extent of this type of deviancy. In addition, the definition of what is homosexual greatly affects the statistics. About four percent of the adult, white males in Kinsey's (1948) study, for example, were exclusively homosexual throughout their lives. Kinsey also found that about 37 percent of the males in the study had had some homosexual experience, to the point of orgasm, between adolescence and age 45. In addition to practicing homosexuals and those who have experimented with homosexuality, there are those who can be called *latent* *homosexuals*, in that they are aroused by homosexual stimuli or recognize that they have a strong sexual preference for other males but never give active sexual expression to the preference.

How can we develop theories to account for homosexuality, unless we are clear about what behavior—sporadic or lifelong—we are trying to explain? Are we seeking to explain why four percent of American males are exclusively homosexual or why over one-third have had at least one homosexual experience? To date, sociological theories of deviance seem unable to explain the original cause of a person's homosexual behavior. The deviant subculture theory allows us to better understand the life cycle and lifestyle of some homosexuals. The labeling theory is useful for understanding how social influences move individuals from commission of a few deviant acts to accepting the role of deviant.

Deviant Subculture Theory The homosexual subculture is surprisingly visible for one based on a deviant activity. The banding together of those who share a common value has positive effects for the individual homosexual. In the homosexual group, the behavior that society considers wrong meets with approval; homosexuality is normal. In homosexual groups, there is typically much gossip about sex and bragging about sexual encounters. This serves to reaffirm for the participants the subcultural value that homosexuality is acceptable—even good. The emotional support gained from belonging to such a group has a strong psychological value. The individual finds that not only does the group reward his homosexuality but that it will help him find means of expressing it. He learns how to solicit, how to give recognition cues to others, and which are the bars, parks, street corners, or public toilets where sexual contacts can be made (Humphreys, 1970). The homosexual subgroup thus performs a socializing function.

Visible signs of the homosexual subculture include gay bars and restaurants, and in some cities, entire neighborhoods; the many magazines published for homosexuals; their formal organizations; and, of course, the Gay Liberation Front, which fights for the rights of homosexuals as persons. The network of homosexual groups across the nation is less visible, but it exists nonetheless. Although a study of homosexual subcultures reveals how homosexuals live, what values they hold, and the norms and folkways they have developed to assure adherence to their central values, the deviant subculture theory does not explain why people choose the homosexual way of life in the first place.

Labeling Theory According to the labeling theory, the fairly large minority of males who have had only a few homosexual experiences would be described as primary deviants. Despite such encounters, most could continue to think of themselves as basically heterosexual. The entrance into secondary deviancy can take different forms. It is not always caused by public discovery of their primary deviancy by police, family, or friends.

Some sociologists believe that, just as we develop a self through socialization, we can take the role of the generalized other in respect to our primary deviant acts and decide for ourselves that other people would judge us as deviant. From then on, our acts can be secondary deviant acts.

There are some weaknesses in the variant on labeling theory that holds that a person can progress from primary to secondary deviancy by his concept of himself as homosexual rather than by society's labeling him as such. This variant assumes that inside every homosexual, there is a heterosexual male begging to be let out. That is, if only the person practicing the primary homosexual acts hadn't come to think of himself as a homosexual, he eventually would have become heterosexual. There is no evidence that this assumption is correct, however. So this "internal labeling theory" has to be treated with skepticism for now. Whatever the source of homosexual behavior, Kinsey found that of 550 practicing, exclusive homosexuals, three-fourths were not known by society to be homosexuals. The labeling theory, thus, could not apply to them.

In some instances, labeling theory can explain how people become secondary homosexual deviants. A young man who experiments with homosexual behavior and who is apprehended and charged with homosexuality or receives a dishonorable discharge from the armed forces because of the incident might accept the label. Had he not been labeled publicly, he might have given up his homosexual practices, as do most young men who experiment with this type of behavior.

The label of homosexual, when applied to a person by society, frequently can be a terrible cross to bear, despite current efforts to deal with the situation openly and honestly. A person who candidly admits that he is a homosexual may find himself shunned by his friends and almost disowned by his parents. Occupationally he may be hurt, for many employers do not want "that kind" of person around. If his homosexuality is known, it is unlikely that he could obtain a government position involving the handling of confidential or sensitive materials, for there is the fear, justified or not, that he would be subject to blackmail. Groups like the Gay Liberation Front are fighting such discrimination, but counterparts have also been formed to try to prevent homosexuals from holding government positions and from achieving other rights.

Crime and Juvenile Delinquency

In a technical sense, no one is a criminal until he or she has been found guilty of breaking a criminal law. In a sociological sense, though, anyone who has committed an act defined as a crime has engaged in deviant behavior, whether or not the act is discovered or the person is apprehended, arrested, or convicted. Legally, juvenile delinquency includes all deviant acts that, if committed by an adult, would be criminal. It also includes some acts by minors that would not be crimes if committed by adults. Such acts include staying out all night, even with no evidence of specific wrongdoing; truancy from school; curfew violation; and refusal to obey parents. Most Americans are well aware that there is considerable adult crime and juvenile delinquency in our society. Unfortunately, the true extent of either is very difficult to assess.

The Extent of Criminal Deviancy In the United States, on a typical day in 1976, there were 51 homicides, 155 forcible rapes, 1345 aggravated assaults, 1151 robberies, 8465 burglaries, 17,180 larcenies, and 2624 auto thefts. These are only the crimes reported to the police, of course. Many crimes, particularly rapes, but also other, less serious offenses, are simply never reported. Even when a crime is reported, in half or more of the cases, no one is arrested. Nevertheless, the annual number of arrests does give some indication of the extent of criminal deviancy. As indicated by the figures in Table 17.1, the number of arrests is staggering.

Note that males constitute the great bulk of people arrested for all crimes, except prostitution and running away from home. In recent years, there have been increases in arrests of females for such crimes as fraud, embezzlement, and forgery, which is probably due to the fact that more women now hold jobs in which such offenses can be committed. There has also been an increase in the proportion of women arrested for homicide and a slight increase in their arrest for carrying a weapon, arson, robbery, and a few other crimes. Nevertheless, about 90 percent of all persons arrested for violent crimes are males, as are about 80 percent of all those arrested for property crimes.

The data in Table 17.1 also show that a high percentage of those arrested for a number of crimes are under 18 years of age. Since, as we saw in Chapter 14, the birth rate in the United States began dropping in 1958, each year from now on there will be fewer young people than in the previous year. This demographic fact should be reflected in a lower number of crimes and arrests. Indeed, if these numbers do not decline, it would be evidence of an increase in crime. Arrests for some offenses typically committed by youth, such as auto theft and curfew violation, have, indeed, gone down. But arrests of youth under age 18 for vandalism and larceny have actually gone up. This does not necessarily mean that there are more such crimes, however; it could simply be that more offenders are being arrested.

Official records of arrests and convictions reveal that lower-class individuals have a far greater chance of being labeled as criminals or delinquents than those of other classes. But some studies in which young people reported on their own behavior show that the social class differences are not as great as the official records would indicate (Nye et al., 1958; Empey and Erickson, 1966). Crime and delinquency rates for blacks have been estimated to be two to five times higher than the rates for whites. Theories attempting to explain criminal deviancy must take into account what is statistically known about such deviants. That is, they are far more likely to be

TABLE 17.1 Persons Arrested by Major Crimes in the United States, 1976, by Age and Sex

Offense	Number of Persons Arrested	Male	Female	Under 18	Over 18
Criminal homicide					
(a) Murder and nonnegligent manslaughter	14,113	85	15	9	91
(b) Manslaughter by negligence	2,650	90	10	10	90
Forcible rape	21,687	99	1	17	83
Robbery	110,296	93	7	34	67
Aggravated assault	192,753	87	13	17	83
Burglary	406,821	95	5	52	49
Larceny	928,078	69	31	43	57
Auto theft	110,708	93	7	53	47
Other assaults	354,010	86	14	20	80
Arson	14,534	89	11	52	48
Forgery and counterfeiting	55,791	70	30	12	88
Fraud	161,429	63	37	3	97
Embezzlement	8,218	69	31	6	94
Stolen property: buying, receiving, possessing	92,055	90	10	31	69
Vandalism	175,082	92	8	63	37
Weapons: carrying, possessing, etc.	121,721	92	8	16	84
Prostitution and commercialized vice	58,648	29	71	4	96
Sex offenses (except forcible rape and prostitution)	51,776	91	9	19	81
Narcotic drug law violations	500,540	86	14	24	76
Gambling	65,437	90	10	4	96
Offenses against family and children	58,249	89	11	7	93
Driving while intoxicated	837,910	92	8	2	98
Liquor laws	302,943	86	14	36	64
Drunkenness	1,071,131	93	7	4	96
Disorderly conduct	545,639	84	16	21	80
Vagrancy	32,731	78	22	18	82
All other offenses (except traffic)	1,330,969	85	15	22	78
Suspicion	31,298	86	14	26	74
Curfew and loitering violations	88,601	80	20	100	
Runaways	166,529	43	57	100	

*Percentages have been rounded off.

Source: Federal Bureau of Investigation, Crime in the United States, Uniform Crime Reports, 1976 (Washington, D.C.: U.S. Government Printing Office, 1975).

male than female, to be young than old, and to be black than white. (We know a few things about who is most likely to be the victim of a crime, too — see Box 17.2.)

Anomie Theory If it is assumed that the success goals of American society are shared by all or most people, regardless of class background, then anomie theory could explain much of criminal deviancy. As we noted in Chapter 8, lower-class youth, for example, often find little real acceptance in the schools, which usually reflect middle-class values and norms. Teachers are likely to expect "trouble" from lower-class students, and they frequently get it. The curriculum and extracurricular activities are geared to the presumed needs of the middle class. The educational route to success is not exactly

---

**BOX 17.2
FEAR
OF CRIME**

Some sociologists believe that the fear of crime in the United States has become a problem as serious as crime itself. Fear of crime has resulted in economic costs, a reduction in the quality of life, and a lack of psychological well-being among millions of Americans.

The crime most feared is personal violence. Americans have spent a great deal of money installing alarms and security locks in their homes, and many have bought firearms to protect themselves. Some have bought watchdogs that have to be cared for and fed. Fear of crime has other economic ramifications as well. Some people will not accept good jobs that require night work, will not take jobs in certain cities, or will give up a job in order to leave a high-crime area. People who cannot afford to do so will take taxis, because they are afraid to walk on the street.

Fear of crime also takes its toll in social costs and in personal unhappiness and anxiety. People stay home rather than walk around their neighborhood or visit friends. They avoid parks for fear of being mugged. Evening community meetings are poorly attended and recreational facilities and libraries are underutilized, because people do not want to be on the streets after dark.

As the sociologist Jennie McIntyre (1967) pointed out, reduced social interaction and fear of crime make people afraid of strangers in general. People who are afraid of each other may show a lack of concern for each other. This may be one reason why people hearing cries for help refuse to respond. The costs of the fear of crime are staggering. The most difficult to measure is the price paid by individuals who spend life's precious moments guarding themselves against criminal attack, worrying about being victims of crime, and avoiding other people or social activities for fear of violence. Surely, fear of crime in our society has affected the quality of life.

It is not unreasonable for even brave people to fear fearful things. But, to some extent, the fear of being the victim of a violent crime is inconsistent with the real risk involved. McIntyre notes that the risk of ac-

blocked to lower-class youth, but it is certainly strewn with obstacles. Those who drop out of school either cannot find decent jobs or must work in low-paying, menial positions. Illegal activities, then, become one means of achieving material success.

As a general explanation of criminal deviancy, anomie theory presents several difficulties. First, sociologists are in disagreement as to the extent to which lower-class people accept the success goals of American society. If they do not accept the goals, then it can hardly be said that lower-class deviants are choosing illegal means to reach prescribed goals. The higher rate of criminal activity among blacks would fit the anomie theory, since by any reasonable perspectve, the opportunities for success are fewer for blacks than for whites. This explanation, however, rests on the assumption that

---

cidential injury calling for medical attention is far greater than the risk of being the victim of violence. What is more, the chances of being attacked by a stranger are about half as great as they are of being attacked by a person well known to the victim.

The sociologists Clemente and Kleinman (1977) have shown that groups with statistically greater risks of being victims of criminal violence are not necessarily the ones that express the greatest fear. Males are twice as likely as females to be victimized, but women are three times as likely as men to fear criminal violence. Many old people are afraid of violent crime, but the rate of crimes against persons is 25 per 1,000 for those age 20 to 34 and 4.4 per 1,000 for those age 65 and over. Blacks are somewhat less fearful of being victimized than the statistics would warrant, while whites, based on their actual chances of being a victim, are slightly more fearful than they should be. However, higher income people both fear violent crime the least and are the least likely to be victims of such crime.

Regardless of the fact that much fear of crime is out of proportion to the actual risks of being a victim, the fear is "real" to the people who express it. As the early sociologist W. I. Thomas pointed out, what people define as real is real in its consequences. When 60 percent of women are afraid to walk alone in their own neighborhoods at night, what they define as real has serious consequences.

Should society try to reduce fear of crime in order to improve the quality of life for its members? If so, how can fear of crime be reduced? In the short run, reducing crime itself may not reduce fear of crime, for, as we have seen, some of the most likely victims (males and young people) are less fearful than those who already have low victimization rates. Enormous sums of money are spent on reducing crime, apparently with only limited success. Perhaps we should divert some of these funds into research on fear of crime to find out how it can be reduced.

the criminally delinquent blacks accept the cultural success goals—which may or may not be true.

In addition, why should males be so much more likely than females to perceive society as anomic? Traditionally, of course, many women did not aspire to an occupational role: their economic success was tied to the activities of their husbands. Should not lower-class women be extremely frustrated, then, to know that they could never have the good things of life because legitimate means of achieving them are unavailable to their husbands? If they experience such frustrations, why is there so much less criminal deviancy among women?

Finally, some types of crimes do not fit in well with the anomie theory of deviancy. Vandalism, malicious mischief, sex crimes, and gang violence, for example, bring no financial reward to the perpetrators. All of these crimes may be related to frustrations inherent in society, but they do not fit the scheme of reaction to unattainable material success goals.

Deviant Subculture Theory In some ways, the deviant subculture theory is in contradiction to the anomie theory. That is, some authorities believe that a fairly well-developed criminal subculture perpetuates the criminal way of life. Furthermore, some feel that there is a close connection between lower-class culture and crime. Such authorities do not subscribe to the notion that the success goal cuts across all classes and groups. Walter Miller (1958), for example, believes that the culture of the lower class is relatively distinct from that of the middle class. Lower-class culture is said to contain such primary concerns as toughness, trouble, excitement, and "fate." These concerns can easily be translated into delinquent or criminal behavior. The deviant subculture, then, is seen almost as an offshoot of the lower-class culture. The toughness and courage required for delinquency or crime are also necessary for some lower-class jobs.

Whether or not one ties criminal deviancy to the lower-class culture, it is apparent that in practically all communities, groups of delinquents and criminals have developed something akin to a distinct way of life. As with other deviants, the criminal subculture consists of a set of values, attitudes, and beliefs that guide the behavior of participants. The culture defines appropriate role models—that is, successful criminals and delinquents. An individual who wants to be accepted into the criminal subculture can imitate the role models' behavior, and through association with others, can learn the values and behavior rewarded by the subgroup. The more involved he or she becomes with the subculture, the more he or she rejects and is rejected by the noncriminal world. It is difficult to tell how much recruitment to the ranks of criminals and delinquents is done by the criminal subculture.

Labeling Theory As with other types of deviancy, labeling theory works better for explaining criminal careers than it does for isolating the original cause of the deviancy. It is well known that many young males break criminal laws and thus are primary deviants. Many are never caught, however, and of those who are caught, many never receive formal punishment for their behavior. The majority give up their sporadic acts of delinquency and go on to live law-abiding lives. But if society officially labels the person a delinquent, the result is likely to be quite different. Thrown in with delinquents in a detention facility, he or she is likely to think of him or herself as one of them. He or she makes new friends who praise and reward his or her behavior, and more than likely, can teach him or her to be a better delinquent. As his or her delinquency continues, the social stamp becomes firmer, in the sense of sterner punishments, more rejection by nondelinquents, and greater stigmatization. The label "delinquent" was first earned by the person's behavior, but once the process was started, the label itself pushed him or her in the deviant direction more and more.

White-Collar Crime: Crime by "Noncriminals"

Edwin H. Sutherland has defined **white-collar crime** as "crime committed by a person of respectability and high social status in the course of his occupation" (Dinitz et al., 1969, p. 100). The concept now includes various nonviolent crimes usually committed by middle- and upper-class people, often but not always in connection with their occupation. Crimes that fall in this category include false advertising, antitrust violations, price fixing, income tax evasion, embezzlement, bribery, and so on. (Street crimes, such as muggings, robbery, and rape are not considered white-collar crimes, even if committed by a high-status offender.)

The person who commits a white-collar crime usually does not think of him or herself as a criminal and is not so stigmatized by society. Many Americans probably thought of Billy Sol Estes, who was convicted of a $30 million fertilizer swindle, as a "wheeler-dealer" who happened to get caught. Price fixing is another crime that is often rationalized as being part of the "business game." Even those who go to prison for income tax evasion manage to escape the label "criminal." Several of those sentenced to brief prison terms for their roles in the Watergate affair complained that in prison they were "treated like common criminals." Nevertheless, in spite of having committed crimes, they generally can resume their respectable lives after release from prison. It is unlikely that conviction for a white-collar crime results in a life of crime. The white-collar criminal, in other words, rarely becomes a secondary deviant. Is this perhaps because the middle class does not consider such crimes to be deviant?

There is some evidence that Americans are beginning to judge white-collar crime more harshly, and in particular, to question the lenient treatment of white-collar criminals. As Benjamin R. Civiletti of the Department of Justice put it, "When the public sees a ghetto youth incarcerated for stealing a used car while a prominent securities adviser who misapplies millions of dollars in trust funds is placed on probation, it cannot be faulted for wondering whether a dual system of justice is operative in this land; one for the affluent and the influential, another for the weak and disadvantaged"

(*Behavior Today,* September 1977, p. 5). Our changing attitude toward white-collar crime is a reminder that we are socialized to consider certain behavior deviant, and to feel more sternly about some forms of deviancy than about others. A comparison of our society at two different periods would reveal not only different frequencies of certain kinds of deviant behavior but also different attitudes toward such behaviors. Although it is likely that deviancy will always be with us in one form or another, it, too, like everything else in our society, has undergone change.

The study of deviancy is a fitting way to conclude this text. First, it illustrates the sociological approach to the study of human interaction. The anomie, deviant subculture, and labeling theories represent efforts to seek explanations for deviant behavior, not in the individual but in human groups. Indeed, the very definition of deviancy — forms of unusual behavior considered undesirable by society — is social. The study of deviant behavior also illustrates how sociologists work to further their understanding of human interaction. Theories, even though logical, are not merely accepted but are tested with the hard facts of observed behavior. If white-collar crime, for example, cannot be adequately explained by the labeling theory of deviancy, the theory needs to be modified or reformulated. The study of deviancy shows, too, the necessity for understanding basic sociological concepts before working in applied areas. An understanding of how, through socialization, the culture of a society enters the individual and shapes his or her personality is at the root of the deviant subculture theory. Finally, the study of deviant behavior illustrates the excitement of sociology. Working in an area of clear benefit to society, we can recognize the validity of the sociological approach, even if we must admit that final answers are not possible and that there is much work yet to be done.

SUMMARY

1. **Deviancy** is behavior that significantly departs from the standards of conduct of a group. According to one classification, deviants can be seen as belonging to one of three groups: criminals, the mentally ill, or social dropouts. Some forms of behavior, such as homosexuality, fall into more than one category.

2. Three major theories have been used to explain deviancy: the **anomie theory,** the **deviant subculture theory,** and **labeling theory.**

3. *Anomie* refers to a condition in society in which the culturally shared goals do not fit together with the means for achieving these goals. According to the anomie theory, people who find themselves in anomic situations will turn to deviant behavior as a way out of their difficulty.

4. Merton has described four strategies for dealing with anomic conditions: **innovation, retreatism, rebellion,** and **ritualism.**

5. According to the deviant subculture theory, deviant subcultures are

what transmit and perpetuate deviancy within a society. Sutherland has suggested that deviant behavior is learned by **differential association** with a subculture.

6. According to labeling theory, there are two kinds of deviancy: **primary deviancy,** which is breaking rules or violating norms, and **secondary deviancy**—the deviant behavior one adopts after accepting a deviant label.

7. None of the three theories explains why some people become deviants and others do not. Perhaps some combination of the theories will help to better explain deviancy.

8. One major form of deviancy in the United States is drug abuse. Among the most widely used drugs are heroin, marijuana, and prescription drugs. Anomie theorists say that drug abuse is an example of retreatism or rebellion. Deviant subculture theorists point to a drug subculture. Labeling theory has little to contribute to understanding this form of deviancy.

9. Homosexuality is considered to be deviant by a majority of people in American society, although attitudes appear to be changing. It is difficult to analyze homosexuality, because it is not clearly defined. Deviant subculture theory emphasizes the emotional support that the gay community offers the individual. Labeling theory suggests that many men consider themselves to be homosexuals because society has labeled them as such and not because they are actually inclined in that direction.

10. Crime is the major form of deviant behavior in American society. The crime rate is highest among males, youth, blacks, and the lower classes. The anomie theory rests on the idea that most criminals accept the cultural goals of middle-class America. According to deviant subculture theory, there is a well-developed criminal subculture that perpetuates the criminal way of life. According to labeling theory, primary deviants who are caught in their criminal acts are those most likely to consider themselves criminals and to continue with criminal behavior.

11. Those who commit a **white-collar crime** usually do not think of themselves as criminals and are not so stigmatized by society. However, attitudes toward white-collar crime appear to be changing.

KEY TERMS

anomie theory
conformity
deviancy
deviant subculture theory
differential association
innovation
labeling theory

primary deviancy
rebellion
retreatism
ritualism
secondary deviancy
white-collar crime

SUGGESTED READINGS

Becker, Howard, ed. *The Other Side: Perspectives on Deviance.* New York: The Free Press, 1964.
A good basic collection of articles on deviancy.

Buckner, H. Taylor, ed. *Deviance, Reality, and Change.* New York: Random House, 1971.
Readings on a variety of deviant forms of behavior and the social control of such behavior.

Clinard, Marshall B. *Sociology of Deviant Behavior.* Englewood Cliffs, N.J.: Prentice-Hall, 1974
A basic authoritative text on deviancy.

Cloward, Richard, and Lloyd E. Ohlin. *Delinquency and Opportunity.* New York: The Free Press, 1960.
The authors deal with delinquency subcultures, particularly the gang.

Cressey, Donald R., and David A. Ward, eds. *Delinquency, Crime, and Social Processes.* New York: Harper & Row, 1969.
A book of readings centered on the criminal from a subcultural perspective.

Dinitz, Simon, Rusell R. Dynes, and Alfred C. Clark, eds. *Deviance.* New York: Oxford University Press, 1969.
A reader covering a wide variety of topics, including crime, riots, alcoholism, drug addiction, homosexuality, and victimless crimes.

Lofland, John. *Deviance and Identity.* Englewood Cliffs, N.J.: Prentice-Hall, 1969.
The author deals with the effects of being labeled a deviant on the individual's identity, self-concept, and relationships.

Merton, Robert K. *Social Theory and Social Structure.* New York: The Free Press, 1968.
Chapters 6 and 7 present Merton's anomie theory and deal with types of reaction to anomie.

Mitford, Jessica. *Kind and Usual Punishment.* New York: Alfred A. Knopf, 1973.
A study of the criminal justice system in the United States. The approach is critical and provides many examples of flaws in the system.

Schofield, Michael. *Sociological Aspects of Homosexuality.* Boston: Little, Brown, 1965.
A thorough research study on homosexuality, presenting factors that are associated with homosexuality and describing how society deals with homosexuals.

Sutherland, Edwin H. *White Collar Crime.* New York: Holt, Rinehart and Winston, 1961.
A study of corporate and other forms of white-collar crime and a presentation of the theory of differential association as an explanation for some types of crime.

Szasz, Thomas. *The Manufacture of Madness.* New York: Harper & Row, 1970.
The noted psychiatrist Thomas Szasz argues that mental illness is a myth—a label imposed by society to control certain types of deviants.

Glossary

adult socialization The learning process through which adults adapt to a new phase of life, take on new jobs, or join new groups.

agents of socialization The persons or groups who are responsible for socializing the young.

agrarian stage A stage of human societies in which the distinguishing technology is the plow and agriculture is the primary means of subsistence.

alienation Feelings of meaninglessness, isolation, and depersonalization within a society.

amalgamation A blending of the culture of a minority group with that of a majority, so that the new culture becomes a mixture of the two.

anarchism A political system based on the principle that formal government in society is unnecessary and undesirable.

anomie theory As a theory of deviancy, anomie refers to a disharmony between the goals of a society and the means for achieving them, which may be confused, ambiguous, or inaccessible.

assimilation The pattern in which a minority group gives up its previous culture and takes on completely the culture of the majority.

authority Power that is vested in a position and considered legitimate by those over whom it is exercised.

beliefs In religious terms, an idea or statement about reality that is accepted as true.

bourgeoisie Karl Marx's term for the class of people in society who own or control the means of production, such as factories and shops.

bureaucracy A type of formal organization characterized by a division of responsibility, a chain of command, governance by formal rules, and a mechanism for coordination.

capitalism An economic system in which the means of production are privately owned, and government control over such property is minimal.

caste A layer or portion of a rigid stratification system in which the classes (castes) are clearly set apart, and movement from one to another is practically impossible.

census A counting of the number of individuals in the population of a given area at a certain time.

chromosome The matter in a cell that carries the determinants of hereditary characteristics.

coercive power Power derived from the use of force.

collective behavior Relatively unstructured behavior of people responding to a common influence, as in crowds, panics, and social movements.

communism An economic system in which the government owns and controls the major means of production, such as factories and farms, and most lesser means of production as well. Under pure communism, the government would be synonymous with the people.

concentric zone model Burgess' theory of the

spatial organization and growth of cities, depicted as a series of concentric circles or zones, with the business district in the center and each of the other zones having distinct populations and land use.

concept A way of summarizing a large number of experiences we have had with an object or idea by use of a label or a name.

conflict model A sociological approach that views society as being held together by unequal distribution of power among groups, with group struggling against group and constant clashes of interest.

conformity Merton's designation for the pattern practiced by members of society who use culturally approved means to seek culturally approved goals.

conservative social movement A social movement that advocates the preservation of existing values and norms.

constitutional democracy A form of government characterized by the existence of a formal statement of essential laws and of what can be expected of the government, a specification of the rights of citizens, and a mechanism for voting by the people to assure the consent of the governed.

correlation An association between two variables, which is usually expressed in statistical terms.

counter role A role played in a group that is opposite to another role played in the same group. The roles of parent and child or teacher and student are examples of counter roles.

crowd A collection of people who are gathered together for a single purpose or to respond to a single stimulus.

crude birth rate The number of births in a society per thousand people in the total population occurring in a given year.

crude death rate The number of deaths per thousand people per year.

cultural diffusion The process by which new cultural elements are spread from one society to another.

cultural lag A situation in which the material culture changes faster than the attitudes, beliefs, and values associated with it.

cultural universals Patterns of behavior found in all cultures that relate to the survival and well-being of the group.

custodial function A function served by the schools whose purpose is to keep children and young people out of the home and out of the work force.

cyclical theory of change A theory of social change that sees societies as going through a growth-maturity-decline sequence.

deduction The process of reasoning from the general to the specific, such as reasoning from a general theory to a hypothesis that would apply in a specific situation.

democracy *See* constitutional democracy.

demographic transition The change in population growth pattern from high birth and death rates, through a high birth-low death rate, to a leveling off of birth and death rates at low levels.

demography *See* social demography.

dependency ratio The ratio of the number of children age 14 and younger plus the number of people age 65 and over to the number of people age 15 to 64 in a given society.

dependent variable In a sociological study, a factor that shows change that has resulted from changes in other variables.

deviancy Behavior that significantly departs from the standards of conduct of a given group.

deviant subculture theory An approach holding that deviant subcultures transmit and perpetuate deviancy within a society by providing a way that deviant norms and values can be learned.

differential association A theory of deviancy that holds that criminal values, skills, and techniques are learned through the association with criminals and delinquents.

discontinuity in socialization A condition in society in which the progression from one role to the next is not orderly but requires the unlearning of attitudes or behaviors associated with prior roles.

discovery Describes the situation in which an entirely new material or nonmaterial element is added to a culture.

discrimination The unequal and unfair treatment of and the denial of rights to members of a particular group.
doubling time The number of years it will take for the population of a given society to double in number, at current birth and death rates.
dyad A two-person group.

eclecticism The selection of elements from various sociological models in order to study different aspects of human societies, rather than strict adherence to a single model.
economics The science that deals with the production, distribution, and consumption of goods and services; also, the institution concerned with these functions.
ecumenism A movement with the goal of universal integration and unity of all Christian groups.
educational outputs The output of the school system, in quality and quantity of education, which pupils are receiving.
egalitarian marriage A type of marriage in which power, authority, and prestige are afforded equally to husband and wife.
emigration Movement from one's country of birth to establish permanent residency in another country.
endogamous rule The requirement that in choosing a mate a person must select someone from within a certain group such as a tribe or race.
estrogen One of the female sex hormones.
ethnic group Any group that is set off in society by race, religion, or national origin, or some combination of these categories.
ethnocentrism The tendency for people in a society to view their own customs and way of life as better, more natural, or superior to corresponding practices in other societies.
evolutionary theory of change Any social change theory that views societies as progressing or moving from one stage to another because of natural or inherent laws.
exchange theory The idea that, when given a choice between two relationships, a person is likely to choose the one that promises to yield greater rewards or satisfactions.

exogamous rule A requirement that in choosing a mate a person must select someone outside a designated group.
expulsion The forcible removal from a society of a minority group by the dominant group.
extended family Two or more nuclear families joined by the extension of the parent-child relationship.
extermination The killing off of a minority group by the dominant group.
extragroup linkage The network of relationships and the interlocking of groups, due to the fact that members of any one group also belong to various other groups.
extramarital sexual intercourse Sexual intercourse between a married person and someone other than his or her spouse.
extrapolation Extending an observed trend, such as a rate of growth, by simple arithmetic means that assume that past changes will continue indefinitely.

family See extended family; nuclear family.
family of orientation The family in which one was born and reared.
family of procreation The family that a married pair begins with the birth of their first child.
fertility The number of births within a group in a given period.

game stage A stage in the development of children at which they are able to imagine the roles of several people simultaneously—an ability that is necessary for playing even a simple, organized game.
Gemeinschaft Tönnie's designation for a group, usually translated as "community," which is characterized by a sense of unity, solidarity, and shared values.
general fertility rate The number of births in a year per 1,000 women age 15 to 44.
generalization A method of learning a new role that involves applying what one has learned in a similar, previous role or roles.
generalized other A concept developed by George Mead to describe how, after the game stage in child development, a person learns to regulate his or her behavior according to how

it would appear to society or the generalized other.
genes The units of heredity, which are carried on the chromosomes.
genocide The systematic killing of a whole nation or race of people.
geographic isolation A factor that accounts for racial differences, due to the separation of a group of humans from other groups and the resulting small gene pool that increases their inherited similarities.
Gesellschaft Tönnies's designation for a group, usually translated as "society," which is characterized by rationality, secondary group relationships, and commitment by members to group objectives, rather than to one another as persons.
ghetto An inner-city area where the poor and minorities are forced to live, for lack of access to other areas.
group Two or more people who are mutually aware of and interact with one another, who think of themselves and are thought of by others as a unit, and who accept roles as members of the unit.

heredity The transmission of certain characteristics through the genes from parents to children.
hidden curriculm The rules and regulations of a school, ways of obtaining the teacher's praise without alienating oneself from peers, and the like, which must be learned if one is to survive psychologically and socially in the schools.
horizontal mobility A movement from one position to another in society that does not involve a change in prestige.
hormones Chemical substances, produced by endocrine glands, that effect changes in the body.
horticultural stage A stage of human societies starting about 10,000 years ago characterized by deliberate planting of roots and seeds and use of the wooden hoe and the digging stick.
human ecology The study of spatial patterns that result from the distribution of people, groups, and services in a given area.
hunting and gathering stage The earliest stage of human societies, at which human energy alone is used to obtain food and provide for other subsistence needs.
hypothesis An element in the scientific research process that states a relationship expected to exist between two variables or facts.

ideational stage Sorokin's term describing a phase in social change during which society is characterized by dependence on authority, a belief that truth lies beyond the human senses, and faith.
immigration The movement of people into a country for permanent settlement.
incest taboo A rule that forbids sexual intercourse between parent and child, between brother and sister, and between other relatives specified by the society.
incumbent The person who fills a position.
independent variable In a sociological study, any factor that produces change.
industrial stage The stage of human societies, which began in the eighteenth century, characterized by large-scale use of mineral energy and reliance on industrial activities as the chief means of subsistence.
infant mortality rate The number of deaths of those within the first year of life per thousand live births per year.
in-migrant A person who moves into a community, state, or section of a country.
innovation Merton's designation for the pattern used by members of society who seek culturally approved goals by culturally disapproved means.
institution A set of interwoven folkways, mores, and laws built around one or more functions. The major social institutions are the family, education, economics, government, and religion.
institutional racism Discrimination against a racial group that is built into the institutions of a society and expressed through such systems as housing, employment, and schools.
intelligence The capacity to learn, which I.Q. tests attempt to measure.
intergenerational mobility Evidence of vertical mobility when the social class of parents and their children are compared.
intragenerational mobility Movement up or

down the status hierarchy by persons within their own lifetimes.

invasion An urban ecological term to describe the intrusion of new types of population units or kinds of activities into an area of the city.

invention The making of a new combination of existing material and nonmaterial elements of a culture to produce something distinctive.

kibbutz A communal society in Israel characterized by group ownership of the means of production and most other property, economic support furnished by the group, and frequently, the collective rearing of children in separate children's houses.

labeling theory An explanation for deviancy that focuses on the reaction of society to people who have violated a norm. A distinction is made between primary deviancy, or norm violation, and secondary deviancy, or acceptance of the deviant label.

language A system of symbols that allows for the transmission and storage of information.

latent functions Those group functions that are neither intended nor recognized.

life chances The odds of receiving an advantage or suffering a disadvantage in some important aspect of our lives on the basis of a social characteristic, such as social class.

life expectancy The average number of years a group of persons born at a given time can expect to live.

lifestyle The way of life of a category of people within a society, including their material possessions, attitudes, and behavior that is associated with a social characteristic, such as social class.

looking-glass self The process, described by Charles Cooley, of developing self-feelings as a result of imagining how others view us. The three steps are: (1) what I think you see, (2) what I think you think, and (3) how I, therefore, feel about myself.

magic A system of belief that assumes the existence of supernatural forces that humans can learn to control to achieve some goal.

manifest functions Those functions of a group that are intended and recognized and otherwise refer to the group's objectives.

marriage A socially approved relationship between two adults that permits sexual intercourse and that is sufficiently enduring to provide for the procreation and rearing of children.

mass movement *See* social movement.

mass society A recent type of social organization characterized by impersonal and contractual relations, specialization and division of labor, mass production and mass consumption, large-scale organizations, and preference for change.

material culture Physical objects made by humans that are shared by a group and passed on to the next generation.

matriarchal family A social type of family in which power and authority are vested chiefly in the wife-mother, who also has superior privilege.

maximum population size The theoretically largest number of people that could subsist in a given social or geographic area.

mean The average, computed by adding the figures or scores in a series and dividing by the number of figures.

measures of central tendency Any statistical technique for describing the middle of a series of numbers or scores; the mean, median, and mode are measures of central tendency.

mechanical solidarity Durkheim's concept of the social organization characteristic of small communities in which there is little division of labor and people are held together by the strong bonds of their personal, intimate groups.

median The middle score in a series of scores that have been arranged from high to low.

megalopolis Several to many large cities that have essentially joined together by the meeting of their suburbs and satellite cities and that form a functioning unit.

migration A general term referring to movement of people from one community to another.

minority group A group of people who, because of their physical or cultural characteristics, are singled out from others in society for differential and unequal treatment and who, therefore, regard themselves as objects of discrimination.

mobility *See* social mobility.

mode The score that occurs most frequently in a series of scores.

model A set of integrated assumptions about some system we wish to understand.

monogamy A form of marriage with one man married to one woman.

mortality *See* crude death rate; infant mortality rate.

natural selection Evolutionary changes that occur whenever the environment favors the survival and reproduction of individuals having a certain gene or pattern of genes over individuals not having the gene or genes.

nonmaterial culture Intangible cultural traits, such as ideas, beliefs, and knowledge, which are shared by a group and transmitted to the next generation.

nonparticipant observation A research method in which the researcher witnesses interaction from outside the group, and not as a group member.

norms Rules or standards of behavior.

nuclear family A married pair and their immature offspring.

observation Gaining information necessary to test a hypothesis; observation methods include watching, counting, and asking questions.

open class A stratification system characterized by the absence of barriers against moving up or down the status hierarchy or moving from one class to another.

operational definition The defining of a concept in terms of how it will be measured, and a clear statement of what measure will be used.

optimum population size The ideal population size for a given social or geographical area, in terms of the quality of life for the area's members.

organic solidarity Durkheim's concept of the social organization characteristic of large societies in which there is much division of labor and in which people are held together by formal contracts and common interests.

out-migrant A person who moves from a community, state, or section of a country.

participant observation A research method in which the researcher is or becomes a member of the group and takes part in the group interaction, while also observing it.

patriarchal family A social type of family in which power and authority are vested chiefly in the husband-father, who also has superior privilege.

peer group A group of persons of roughly equal status and of similar age.

personality The sum total of the traits and characteristics that are unique to an individual.

persuasive power The use of arguments and reasoning to control the behavior of others.

placement A function of the educational system that consists of sorting and steering students toward jobs or further education, largely on the basis of tests and grades.

planned obsolescence The producing of items designed to wear out or go out of style in a short time.

play stage According to George Mead, a stage in the development of the self at which children act out a particular role they have observed.

pluralism A pattern of group relations in a society in which there are distinguishable ethnic, religious, or other groups, each with its own identity, but in which there are no discrimination or special privileges.

political socialization The process through which the young in any society learn about the political system, its beliefs, and the expected participatory role of the individual in it.

political systems Organizational approaches to the fulfilling of the functions of government.

polyandry A form of marriage in which one woman is married to two or more husbands at the same time.

polygamy A form of marriage in which one spouse of either sex has two or more spouses of the other sex at the same time.

polygny A form of marriage in which one man is married to more than one woman at the same time.

population pyramid A graphic method for

showing the age and sex composition of a society.

positions The elements or parts of a social system.

positive population checks According to Malthus, such factors as famine, disease, and war.

positivism Comte's system of thinking, which stresses invariable laws and the need for observation, experimentation, and comparison to discover the cause of events.

power The ability to control the behavior of others, even without their consent.

power elite A small group who occupy the key posts in the military, the government, and industry and who, thus, have the greatest influence on the direction society will take.

power pluralism A division of power among diverse groups, such as the government, labor unions, and political parties, rather than its concentration in a single elite group.

power structure The power figures in a social unit, what they control, and how they relate to one another.

prejudice Beliefs, opinions, and feelings about a particular group, which are not based on fact and are usually unfavorable.

premarital sexual intercourse Sexual intercourse between two unmarried persons.

prestige The recognition and respect afforded a person who occupies a given position.

preventive population checks According to Malthus, such factors as celibacy and late marriage.

primary deviancy Rule breaking or norm violation that does not result in the person considering himself or herself deviant.

primary group A relatively enduring group characterized by close, intimate, usually face-to-face interaction in which the total personalities of members are exhibted.

profane A religious term designating that which is secular or is not holy.

progesterone One of the female sex hormones.

progressive social movement A social movement that seeks major change within the existing social order.

proletariat Karl Marx's term for the class in society that consists of those who do not own any means of production but must sell their skills to those who do.

race A grouping of human beings distinguishable by the possession of similar combinations of anatomical features due to a common heredity.

racism Prejudice and discrimination on the basis of race.

random genetic drift The process by which a particular trait appears in or is lost by one or a few individuals, by chance, and then is transmitted to their offspring.

rebellion Merton's term for the pattern used by those members of society who actively attempt to change society's goals or means.

reciprocal role *See* counter role.

reform movement A social movement that seeks to improve existing values.

reification The tendency to think of the ideas that we create as real objects.

religion A system of beliefs and practices by means of which a group of people struggle with the ultimate problems of human life.

religiosity A concept describing how religious people are, and in what different ways they are religious.

remunerative power The use of material goods as rewards and punishments to control the behavior of others.

replacement level fertility A birth rate situation, such that births balance deaths and the society neither increases nor decreases in population.

retreatism Merton's designation for the pattern used by members of a society who reject culturally approved goals and the means for achieving them.

revolutionary movement A social movement that seeks a whole new social order.

rite of passage A ceremony used in some societies to symbolize the role change from child to adult.

ritual In religious terms, behavior and practices prescribed by a religion, because they relate to the religious beliefs.

ritualism Merton's term for the pattern used by

society's members who reject culturally approved goals but go through the motions associated with the approved means.

role The sum of the culturally prescribed duties, characteristics, and rights expected of and granted to the incumbent of a particular position.

role behavior The actual behavior of persons exhibited in the course of performing a role.

role conflict A disharmony between the demands or expectations of one role a person enacts and those of one or more of the other roles enacted by the same person.

role discrepancy The difference in the interpretation of a role between a role incumbent and a person enacting the counter role.

role failure Difficulties associated with the performance of roles, including role discrepancy, role conflict, and role strain.

role incumbent The person enacting a role attached to a certain position.

role strain A condition in which one has negative feelings about how well one is performing a role.

sacred A religious term applied to objects, entities in the natural or supernatural world, and beliefs that are holy or set apart from the secular or profane.

sampling Taking for study a portion or representative part of a population rather than the entire population.

satellite city A city near a larger city but only somewhat socially and economically dependent upon it.

school inputs The total amount of money and dollar value of other resources used for schools.

secondary deviancy When a deviant act is discovered and punished, the person is labeled a deviant and may accept the label and thus continue deviant behavior.

secondary group A group in which relationships are impersonal, superficial, and businesslike, and in which participants exhibit only one aspect of their personalities.

sector model Hoyt's theory of the structure and growth of cities, according to which a city resembles a circle cut into a number of wedge-shaped pieces, with each wedge or sector having a particular population and land use.

segregation The forced separation of a minority group from the majority, usually accompanied by discrimination.

self The attitudes and beliefs one has about himself or herself.

self-defeating prophecy A prediction that does not come true precisely because it was made.

self-fulfilling prophecy An originally false prediction that can come true simply because it was made.

sensate stage Sorokin's term describing a phase in social change during which society is characterized by a philosophy stressing that which can be studied objectively and empirically.

sex chromosomes The chromosomes that determine whether an individual will be male or female.

sex role A role designated as appropriate for either males or females, but not both, and assigned to members of society on the basis of sex.

sex-role socialization The process throughout which an individual learns appropriate behaviors for his or her sex in a particular society.

sex-role stereotyping *See* stereotype.

sexism A system of beliefs and attitudes concerning the differences between the sexes, which holds that women and their roles are inferior to men and their roles and that, therefore, discrimination against women is justified.

slum An inner-city area characterized by run-down buildings and poor social conditions.

social characteristics Traits that, while applied to an individual, are defined by society, such as marital status, social class, and minority group.

social class A broad portion of the status hierarchy that is distinguished from other portions by the rank of its members.

social demography The study and analysis of human populations.

social-emotional leader A person in a group, not usually designated as the official leader, who relieves tensions, eases conflicts, and otherwise keeps the group running smoothly.

socialism An economic system in which some of the major means of production, such as railroads and major industries, are owned by the government, but in which other means of production are privately owned.

socialization The process through which an individual learns the rules of behavior of a society.

social mobility Movement from one position to another in society; usually refers to vertical mobility—movement up or down the status hierarchy.

social movement A relatively long-lasting, collective enterprise formed to bring about or prevent social change.

social stratification A system in which the members of society are assigned to different categories, and the categories themselves are ranked one above the other, according to the amount of society's rewards and privileges they receive.

social system The interaction that exists or could exist whenever two or more people interact.

society A group of people who share a culture, occupy a distinguishable territory, and regard themselves as a unit.

sociology The study of interaction among people and of the way this interaction affects human behavior.

sovereignty The concept that a nation-state has supreme and exclusive authority within the geographic area it occupies.

spurious relationships The possibility that when two variables are statistically associated the relationship found between them is false or accidental.

standard metropolitan statistical area (SMSA) An area consisting of at least one city of 50,000 inhabitants, the county in which the central city is located, and any adjacent counties that are found to be metropolitan in nature and are socially and economically tied to the central city.

statistics Any mathematical techniques that are used to summarize or describe a characteristic of a sample. Measures of central tendency and of correlation are examples of statistics.

status A term often used interchangeably with position to refer to an element or part of a social system.

status consistency The similarity of a person's ranks on different dimensions of social class, such as on education and income.

status symbol A material good or thing that signifies that the possessor has attained a certain economic or social rank.

stereotype A set of biased generalizations about a group or category of people that is unfavorable, exaggerated, and oversimplified.

stratification *See* social stratification.

structural-functional model An approach that views society as a harmonious whole, with the various systems contributing to the well-being of the whole.

succession An urban ecological process involving the replacement of one type of population unit or kind of activity in a section of a city by another type or kind.

survey research A method of collecting data that relies on the administering of a set of questions, through interviews or mailed questionnaires, to a group of people.

symbol Something that stands for or represents another thing. Words are symbols that represent objects or ideas.

symbolic interaction model A sociological model that stresses the human bonds and linkages that are created by the interaction of individuals through the use of words, gestures, and other symbols that have a shared meaning.

task leader The task, or instrumental, leader of a group restricts his or her behavior to helping the group solve the group's problems or reach the group's goals.

technology Information, techniques, and tools with which humans utilize the material resources of their environment to satisfy their needs and desires.

testosterone The male sex hormone.

theory A systematic statement of propositions or ideas that are logically related and give general descriptions of phenomena and relations among phenomena.

totalitarianism A political system characterized by near total control of the lives of citizens, a single political party, an official ideology permitting no deviations, and state ownership or rigid control of the economy.

triad A three-person group.

ultimate meanings That aspect of religion concerned with a reality beyond experience, reasons for human existence, the purpose of humans, and their eventual fate.

urban In the United States, any place that is incorporated as a city, village, borough, or town and has at least 2,500 inhabitants.

urban ecology The study of the interaction and interdependence of humans in and around cities and how these processes affect the spatial patterning of activities in cities.

urban planning An attempt at creating urban conditions that stress human values.

variables See dependent variable; independent variable.

vertical mobility Movement up or down the status hierarchy of a society; movement from one class to another, or change in privilege, prestige, or power.

vital statistics The official registration of important life events, including births, deaths, marriages, and divorces.

voluntary association A group deliberately formed to bring together people with similar interests, so that they can achieve certain goals.

voucher system A proposed alteration of the school system, in which parents would be able to "shop" for schools for their children.

welfare state A society in which it is considered that the government has responsibility for ensuring that all citizens have such necessities as food, housing, health care, and education.

white-collar crime Nonviolent crimes, such as false advertising, embezzlement, and bribery, committed by middle- and upper-class people, usually in connection with their occupation.

zero population growth A situation in a society such that births balance deaths, and the society neither increases nor decreases in population.

Bibliography

Allon, Natalie. "The Stigma of Overweight in Everyday Life." *Health Services,* 2 (October 1973), 83–102.

Arkin, William, and Dobrofsky, Lynne R. "Military Socialization and Masculinity." *Journal of Social Issues,* 24 (1978), 151–168.

Athens, Lonnie H. "Violent Crime: A Symbolic Interactionist Study." *Symbolic Interaction,* 1 (Fall 1977), 56–70.

Baker, Luther G., Jr. "The Rising Furor Over Sex Education." *The Family Coordinator,* 18 (July 1968), 210–217.

Bales, Robert F. *Interaction Process Analysis.* Cambridge, Mass.: Addison-Wesley, 1951.

Bardwick, Judith. *Psychology of Women.* New York: Harper & Row, 1971.

Barr, Thomas C., Jr. "Cave Ecology and the Evolution of Troglodytes." In Theodosius Dobzhansky, M. K. Hecht, and William C. Steere, eds., *Evolutionary Biology,* vol. 2. New York: Appleton-Century-Crofts, 1968.

Barrett, Nancy Smith. "Women in Industrial Society." In Jane Chapman, ed., *Economic Independence in Women.* Beverly Hills, Calif.: Sage Publications, 1976.

Bash, Wendell H. "Differential Fertility in Madison County, New York, 1865." *Milbank Memorial Fund Quarterly,* 33 (April 1955), 161–186.

Bates, Frederick. "Position, Role, and Status; A Reformulation of Concepts." *Social Forces,* 34 (May 1956), 313–321.

Becker, Howard. *Through Values to Social Interpretation.* Durham, N.C.: Duke University Press, 1950.

Becker, Howard S. *Outsiders: Studies in the Sociology of Deviance.* New York: The Free Press, 1963.

———. "Whose Side Are We On?" *Social Problems,* 14 (Winter 1967), 239–247.

Bell, Wendell. "Social Choice, Life Styles, and Suburban Residence." In William M. Dobriner, ed., *The Suburban Community.* New York: G. P. Putnam's Sons, 1958.

Bellah, Robert N. "Religious Evolution." *American Sociological Review,* 29 (June 1964), 358–374.

Benedict, Ruth, "Continuities and Discontinuities in Cultural Conditioning." *Psychiatry,* 1 (May 1939), 161–167.

Berger, Bennett M. *Working Class Suburb.* Berkeley: University of California Press, 1960.

Biddle, Bruce J., and Thomas, Edwin J., eds. *Role Theory: Concepts and Research.* New York: John Wiley & Sons, 1966.

Birch, Lloyd. "A Comparison of Observational Data: A Validity Study." Unpublished Ph.D. dissertation. Lexington, Kentucky: University of Kentucky Graduate School, 1971.

Blumer, Herbert. *Symbolic Interactionism: Perspective and Method.* Englewood Cliffs, N. J.: Prentice-Hall, 1969.

Borofsky, Gerald L.; Stollak, Gary E.; and Meese, Lawrence A. "Sex Differences in Bystander Reactions to Physical Assault." *Journal of Experimental Social Psychology* 7 (May 1971), 313–318.

Bossard, James H. S., and Boll, Eleanor Stoker. *The Sociology of Child Development.* New York: Harper & Row, 1966.

Bowerman, Charles E. "Prediction Studies," in Harold Christensen, ed., *Handbook of Marriage and the Family.* Chicago: Rand McNally, 1964.

Bradley, Jeff. "Women Make Gains Worldwide, But Problems Remain," *Louisville Courier-Journal* (November 26, 1978), 9.

Brannon, Robert C. "Gimme That Old Time Racism." In *Change: Readings in Society and Human Behavior.* Del Mar, Calif.: CRM Books, 1972.

Briffault, Robert. *The Mothers.* New York: The Macmillian Co., 1931.

Brim, Orville G., Jr. "Socialization Through the Life Cycle." In Orville G. Brim, Jr. and Stanton Wheeler, *Socialization After Childhood: Two Essays.* New York: John Wiley & Sons, 1966.

Bronfenbrenner, Urie. "Split-Level American Family." *Saturday Review* (October 7, 1967), 60–66.

———. *Two Worlds of Childhood: U.S. and U.S.S.R.* New York: Russell Sage Foundation, 1970.

Brown, Donald R., ed. *Women in the Soviet Union.* New York: Teachers College Press, 1968.

Bryan, James H. "Apprenticeships in Prostitution." *Social Problems*, 12 (Winter 1965), 287–296.

Calderone, Mary S. "Special Report: SIECUS in 1969." *Journal of Marriage and the Family*, 31 (November 1969), 674–676.

Campbell, Ernest Q., and Pettigrew, Thomas F. "Racial and Moral Crisis: The Role of Little Rock Ministers." *American Journal of Sociology*, 64 (March 1959), 509–516.

Carmichael, Stokely, and Hamilton, Charles. *Black Power.* New York: Vintage Books, 1967.

Carnegie Quarterly, 26 (Summer 1978), 4.

Carson, Rachel. *Silent Spring.* Greenwich, Conn.: Crest, 1962.

Caudill, William, and De Vos, George. "Achievement, Culture and Personality: The Case of the Japanese Americans." In Norman R. Yetman and C. Hoy Steele, eds., *Majority and Minority.* Boston: Allyn & Bacon, 1971.

Centers, Richard. *The Psychology of Social Classes.* Princeton, N.J.: Princeton University Press, 1949.

Chafetz, Janet S. *Masculine, Feminine or Human?* Itasca, Ill.: Peacock, 1978.

Chein, Isidor. *The Road to H: Narcotics, Delinquency and Public Policy.* New York: Basic Books, 1964.

Chirot, Daniel. *Social Change in the Twentieth Century.* New York: Harcourt Brace Jovanovich, 1977.

Clark, Burton R. "The 'Cooling-Out' Function in Higher Education." *American Journal of Sociology*, 65 (May 1960), 569–576.

Clemente, F., and Kleinman, M. B. "Fear of Crime in the United States." *Social Forces*, 56 (1977), 519–531.

Clinard, Marshall B., ed. *Anomie and Deviant Behavior.* New York: The Free Press, 1964.

Cloward, Richard A. "Illegitimate Means, Anomie and Deviant Behavior." *American Sociological Review*, 24 (April 1959), 164–176.

Cohen, Albert K. *Deviance and Control.* Englewood Cliffs, N.J.: Prentice-Hall, 1966.

Cohen, Morris. *Reason and Nature: An Essay on the Meaning of Scientific Method.* New York: Harcourt, Brace and World, 1931.

Coleman, James S. *The Adolescent Society.* New York: The Free Press, 1961.

———, et al. *Equality of Educational Opportunity*, Washington, D.C.: U.S. Government Printing Office, 1966.

Comas, Juan. *Racial Myths: The Race Question in Modern Science.* Westport, Conn.: 1976.

Comte, Auguste. *The Positive Philosophy*, vol. 1. New York: D. Appleton, 1853.

Cooley, Charles Horton. *Human Nature and the Social Order.* New York: Charles Scribner's Sons, 1902.

———. *Social Organization.* Glencoe, Ill.: The Free Press, 1956. (Originally published 1907.)

Coser, Lewis. *The Functions of Social Conflict.* New York: The Free Press, 1956.

Cowgill, Donald O. "Transition Theory as General Population Theory." *Social Forces*, 41 (March 1963), 270–274.

Crowley, James W., and Ballweg, John A. "Religious Preference and Worldly Success: An Empirical Test in a Midwestern City,"

Sociological Analysis, 32 (Summer 1971), 71–80.

Cuber, John F., and Kenkel, William F. *Social Stratification in the United States.* New York: Appleton-Century-Crofts, 1954.

———; ———; and Harper, Robert A. *Problems of American Society,* 4th ed. New York: Holt, Rinehart and Winston, 1964.

Dager, Edward Z. "Socialization and Personality Development in the Child." In Harold T. Christensen, ed., *Handbook of Marriage and the Family.* Chicago: Rand McNally, 1964.

Dahrendorf, Ralf. *Class and Class Conflict in Industrial Society.* Stanford, Calif.: Stanford University Press, 1959.

———. "Toward a Theory of Social Conflict," in Eva Etizioni-Halevy and Amitai Etizioni (eds.), *Social Change.* New York: Basic Books, 1973.

Dai, Bingham. *Opium Addiction in Chicago.* Montclair, N.J.: Patterson Smith, 1970.

Darity, William A., Turner, Castalleno B., and Thiebaux, "Race Consciousness and Fears of Black Genocide as Barriers to Family Planning." In *Perspective from the Black Community.* Washington, D.C.: Population Reference Bureau, June, 1971.

Darwin, Charles. *Origin of Species.* Cambridge, Mass,: Harvard University Press, 1964.

Davis, Kingsley. "Final Note on a Case of Extreme Isolation." *American Journal of Sociology,* 52 (March 1947), 232–247.

———. *Human Society.* New York: Macmillan, 1949.

———, and Moore, Wilbert E. "Some Principles of Stratification." *American Sociological Review,* 10 (April 1945), 242–249.

Dawson, Richard E., and Prewitt, Kenneth. *Political Socialization.* Boston: Little, Brown, 1969.

Dinitz, Simon, et al., eds. *Deviance: Studies in the Process of Stigmatization and Societal Reaction.* New York: Oxford University Press, 1969.

Divoky, Diane. "New York's Mini-Schools: Small Miracles, Big Troubles." *Saturday Review* (December 19, 1971), 60–68.

Dobzhansky, Theodosius. *Mankind Evolving.* New Haven, Conn.: Yale University Press, 1962.

Domhoff, G. William. *Who Rules America?* Englewood Cliffs, N.J.: Prentice-Hall, 1967.

Doress, Marvin, and Porter, Jack Nusan. "Kids in Cults." *Society* (May/June, 1978), 69–71.

Durkheim, Emile. *Elementary Forms of Religious Life.* New York: Macmillan, 1926.

———. *Suicide: A Study in Sociology.* Edited by George Simpson. New York: The Free Press, 1951.

———. *The Division of Labor in Society.* Translated by George Simpson. New York: The Free Press, 1949.

Edelstein, Barbara. *The Women Doctor's Diet for Women.* Englewood Cliffs, N.J.: Prentice-Hall, 1977.

Edgerton, Robert B. *Deviance: A Cross-Cultural Perspective.* Menlo Park, Calif.: Cummings Publishing Company, 1976.

Empey, Lamart, and Erickson, Maynard L. "Hidden Delinquency and Social Status." *Social Forces,* 44 (June 1966), 546–554.

Farrell, Warren. *The Liberated Man.* New York: Bantom Books, 1974.

Fast, Julius. *Body Language.* New York: Simon & Schuster, 1971.

Fediaevsky, Vera. *Nursery School and Parent Education in Soviet Russia.* New York: E. P. Dutton & Co., 1936.

Firestone, Harold. "Cats, Kicks, and Colors." *Social Problems,* 15 (July 1957), 3–13.

Firey, Walter. *Land Use in Central Boston.* Cambridge, Mass.: Harvard University Press, 1947.

Frazer, Sir James G. *The New Golden Bough.* Edited by Theodor H. Gaster. New York: Criterion Books, 1959.

Freedman, Ronald, et al. *Family Planning, Sterility and Population Growth.* New York: McGraw-Hill, 1959.

Fried, Marc. "Grieving for a Lost Home." In Leonard L. Duhl, ed., *The Urban Condition.* New York: Basic Books, 1963.

———, and Gleicher, Peggy. "Some Sources of Residential Satisfaction in an Urban Slum." In Sandor Halebsky, ed., *The Sociology of the City.* New York: Charles Scribner's Sons, 1973.

Friedan, Betty. *The Feminine Mystique.* New York: Dell, 1963.

Friedl, Ernestine. *Woman and Men.* New York: Holt, Rinehart and Winston, 1975.

Friedrichs, Robert W. "Choice and Commitment in Social Research." *American Sociologist,* 3 (February 1968), 3–7.

Frieze, Irene H., et al. *Women and Sex Roles.* New York: Norton, 1978.

Gallup, George, Jr., and Davies, John O., III. *The Gallup Opinion Index.* Princeton, N.J.: Gallup International, 1971.

Gans, Herbert J. *The Levittowners.* New York: Pantheon Books, 1967.

Gergen, Mary K.; Gergen, Kenneth; and Morse, Stanley J. "Correlates of Marijuana Use Among College Students." *Journal of Applied Social Psychology,* 2 (January–March 1972), 7–8.

Gist, Noel P. "Caste Differentials in South India." *American Sociological Review,* 19 (April 1954), 126–137.

Glaab, Charles N., and Brown, Theodore A. "The Emergence of Metropolis." In Victor E. Ficker and Herbert S. Graves, eds., *Social Science and Urban Crisis.* New York: Macmillan, 1971.

Glock, Charles Y., and Stark, Rodney. *Religion and Society in Tension.* Chicago: Rand McNally, 1965.

Gmelch, George, and Gmelch, Sharon Bohn. "The Irish Tinkers." *Human Nature* (March 1978), 66–74.

Goffman, Erving. "On Cooling the Mark Out." *Psychiatry,* 15 (November 1952), 462–463.

———. *Stigma.* Englewood Cliffs, N.J.: Prentice-Hall, 1963.

Goldberg, Philip. "Are Women Prejudiced Against Women?" *Transaction,* 5 (April 1968), 28–30.

Goldschmidt, Walter. *Man's Ways: A Preface to the Understanding of Human Society.* New York: Holt, Rinehart and Winston, 1959.

Goode, William J.; Hopkins, Elizabeth; and McClure, Helen M. *Social Systems and Family Patterns.* New York: Bobbs-Merrill, 1971.

Gordon, Milton M. *Assimilation in American Life.* New York: Oxford University Press, 1964.

Gordon, Richard E., et al. *The Split Level Trap.* New York: Bernard Geis Associates, 1961.

Gouldner, Alvin W. "Anti-Minotaur: The Myth of Value-Free Sociology." *Social Problems,* 9 (Winter 1962), 199–213.

———. *The Coming Crisis of Western Sociology.* New York: Basic Books, 1970.

Grabill, Wilson H., et al. *The Fertility of American Women.* New York: John Wiley & Sons, 1958.

Gross, Ronald, and Gross, Beatrice, eds. *Radical School Reform.* Hinsdale, Ill.: Dryden Press, 1970.

Gurin, Gerald; Veroff, Joseph; and Feld, Sheila. *Americans View Their Mental Health.* New York: Basic Books, 1960.

Halebsky, Sandor, ed. *The Sociology of the City.* New York: Charles Scribner's Sons, 1973.

Haney, Craig, and Zimbardo, Philip G. "It's Tough to Tell a High School from a Prison." *Psychology Today* (June 1975), 26–30.

Harris, Marvin. "India's Sacred Cow." *Human Nature* (February 1978), 28–36.

Harrison, James. "Warning: The Male Sex Role May Be Dangerous to Your Health." *Journal of Social Issues,* 34 (Spring 1978), 65–86.

Haworth, Lawrence. *The Good City.* Bloomington, Ind.: Indiana University Press, 1963.

Hechinger, Fred M. "Murder in Academe: The Demise of Education." *Saturday Review* (March 20, 1976), 11.

Henderson, A. M., and Parsons, Talcott. *Max Weber: The Theory of Social and Economic Organization.* New York: Oxford University Press, 1947.

Herskovits, Melville J. *Cultural Anthropology.* New York: Alfred A. Knopf, 1955.

Hockett, Charles F., and Anscher, Robert. "The Human Revolution." *Current Anthropology,* 5 (June 1964), 135–147.

Hodge, Robert W.; Siegel, Paul M.; and Rossi, Peter H. "Occupational Prestige in the United States: 1935–1963." *American Journal of Sociology,* 70 (November 1964), 286–302.

———; Treiman, Donald J.; and Rossi, Peter H. "A Comparative Study of Occupational Prestige." In Reinhard Bendix and Seymour Martin Lipset, eds., *Class, Status, and Power,* 2nd ed. New York: The Free Press, 1966.

Hoffer, Eric. *The True Believer.* New York: New American Library, 1958.

Holbrooke, Richard. "An Extraordinary City

Fights for Its Life." *The Washington Post*, (April 24, 1972), A-20.

Hollingshead, August B., and Redlich, Fredrick C. *Social Class and Mental Illness.* New York: John Wiley & Sons, 1958.

Horowitz, Irving L., ed. *The New Sociology.* New York: Oxford University Press, 1964.

Howe, Florence. "Sex Role Stereotypes Start Early." *Saturday Review*, 54 (Oct. 16, 1971), 76-82.

Hoyt, Homer. "The Structure of American Cities in the Post-War Era." *American Journal of Sociology*, 48 (January 1943), 475-492.

Humphreys, Laud. *Tearoom Trade: Impersonal Sex in Public Places.* Chicago: Aldine, 1970.

Hunt, Morton. *Sexual Behavior in the 1970s.* New York: Playboy Press, 1974.

———. "Women and Their Work." *Redbook Magazine* (April 1978), 69-73.

Hutton, John H. *Caste in India: Its Nature, Function and Origins.* Cambridge, Mass.: The University Press, 1946.

Inkeles, Alex, and Rossi, Peter H. "National Comparisons of Occupational Prestige." *American Journal of Sociology*, 61 (January 1965), 329-339.

Jackson, Philip W. *Life in Classrooms.* New York: Holt, Rinehart and Winston, 1968.

Jencks, Christopher, et al. *Inequality: A Reassessment of the Effect of Family and Schooling in America.* New York: Basic Books, 1972.

Jensen, Arthur R. "How Much Can We Boost IQ and Scholastic Achievement?" *Harvard Educational Review*, 39 (Winter-Summer 1969), 1-123.

———. "Cumulative Deficit in IQ of Blacks—the Rural South." *Developmental Psychology*, 13 (May 1977), 184-191.

Kagan, Jerome. "Acquisition and Significance of Sex Typing and Sex Role Identity." In Martin L. Hoffman and Lois W. Hoffman, eds., *Review of Child Development Research*, vol. 1. New York: Russell Sage Foundation, 1964, pp. 137-196.

Kahl, Joseph A. *The American Class Structure.* New York: Holt, Rinehart and Winston, 1957.

Kahn, Robert L., ed. "Stress, From 9 to 5." In *Change: Readings in Society and Human Behavior.* Del Mar, Calif.: CRM Books, 1972.

Kanter, Rosabeth Moss. *Work and Family in the United States.* New York: Russell Sage Foundation, 1976.

Kantner, John F., and Zelnick, Melvin. "Sexual Experiences of Young Unmarried Women in the United States." *Family Planning Perspective*, (October 1972), 1-25.

Keats, John. *The Crack in the Picture Window.* Boston: Houghton Mifflin, 1956.

Kelly, K. Dennis, and Chambliss, William J. "Status Consistency and Political Attitudes." *American Sociological Review*, 31 (June 1966), 375-382.

Kenkel, William F. "Influence Differentiation in Family Decision Making." *Sociology and Social Research*, 42 (September-October 1957), 18-25.

———. *The Family in Perspective*, 4th ed. Santa Monica, Ca.: Goodyear, 1977.

———, and Hoffman, Dean K. "Real and Conceived Roles in Family Decision Making." *Marriage and Family Living*, 18 (November 1956), 311-316.

Kesey, Ken. *One Flew Over the Cuckoo's Nest.* New York: The Viking Press, 1962.

Kinsey, Alfred C.; Pomeroy, Wardell B.; and Martin, Clyde E. *Sexual Behavior in the Human Male.* Philadelphia: W. B. Saunders, 1948.

———; ———; ———; and Gebhard, Paul H. *Sexual Behavior in the Human Female.* Philadelphia: W. B. Saunders, 1953.

Kluckhohn, Clyde. *Mirror of Man.* New York: Fawcett Books, 1957.

Kramer, Judith R. *The American Minority Community.* New York: Thomas Y. Crowell, 1970.

Kreuz, Leo, and Rose, Robert. "Assessment of Aggressive Behavior in a Young Animal Population." *Psychiatric Spectator*, 7 (August 1971), 15-16.

Ladd, William F. "Effect of Integration on Property Values." *American Economic Review*, 52, (September 1962), 801-808.

Lake, Alice. "Are We Born into Our Sex Roles or Programmed into Them?" *Women's Day* (January 1975), 24-25.

Langton, Kenneth. *Political Socialization.* New York: Oxford University Press, 1969.

Lapidus, Gail Warshofsky. "Political Mobilization, Participation, and Leadership." *Comparative Politics*, 8 (October 1975), 90–118.

Laurenti, Luigi M. *Property Values and Race.* Berkeley: University of California Press, 1960.

Lee, Alfred McClung. *Toward Humanistic Sociology.* Englewood Cliffs, N.J.: Prentice-Hall, 1973.

Lefton, Mark, et al., eds. *Approaches to Deviancy.* New York: Appleton-Century-Crofts, 1968.

Leiner, Marvin. *Children Are the Revolution.* New York: Penguin, 1978.

Lenski, Gerhard. *Power and Privilege.* New York: McGraw-Hill, 1966.

———. *The Religious Factor*, rev. ed. Garden City, N.Y.: Doubleday & Co., 1963.

Lenski, Gerhard, and Lenski, Jean. *Human Societies*, 3rd ed. New York: McGraw-Hill, 1978.

Leonard, George B. *The Man and Woman Thing.* New York: Dell, 1964.

Levin, Robert J., and Levin, Amy. "Sexual Pleasure: The Surprising Preferences of 100,000 Women." *Redbook Magazine* (September 1975), 51–58.

Levy, Leon H. "Self-Help Groups: Types and Psychological Processes." *Journal of Applied Behavioral Science*, 12 (1976), 310–322.

Linton, Ralph. *The Study of Man.* New York: Appleton-Century-Crofts, 1936.

———. *The Tree of Culture.* New York: Alfred A. Knopf, 1955.

Lipset, Seymour M. "Democracy and the Working Class Authoritarianism." *American Sociological Review*, 24 (August 1959), 486.

Lofland, John. *Doomsday Cult.* Englewood Cliffs, N.J.: Prentice-Hall, 1966.

Lundberg, George A. *Can Science Save Us?* New York: Longmans Green, 1947.

Lynd, Robert S. *Knowledge For What?* Princeton, N.J.: Princeton University Press, 1939.

Lyness, Judith L.; Lipetz, Milton E.; and Davis, Keith. "Living Together: An Alternative to Marriage." *Journal of Marriage and The Family*, 34 (May 1972), 305–311.

Mace, David, and Mace, Vera. *Marriage East and West.* New York: Doubleday & Co., 1960.

Mack, Raymond, et al. "The Protestant Ethic, Level of Aspiration, and Social Mobility." *American Sociological Review*, 21 (June 1956), 295–300.

Malewski, Andrzej. "The Degree of Status Incongruence and Its Effects." In Reinhard Bendix and Seymour Martin Lipset, eds., *Class Status and Power*, 2nd ed. New York: The Free Press, 1966.

Malcom, Andrew H. "Police in Osaka Develop a New Anticrime Method." *New York Times.* (March 17, 1977), A-8.

Marx, Karl. *Capital.* Edited by Friedrich Engels. New York: International Publishers, 1967.

———, and Engels, Friedrich. *The Communist Manifesto.* Edited by Samuel H. Beer. New York: Appleton-Century-Crofts, 1955.

McIntyre, Jennie. "Public Attitudes Toward Crime and Law Enforcement." *The Annals*, 374 (November 1967), 34–46.

McPartland, John. *No Down Payment.* New York: Simon and Schuster, 1957.

Mead, George Herbert. *Mind, Self, and Society.* Chicago: University of Chicago Press, 1967.

Mead, Margaret. *Sex and Temperament in Three Primitive Societies.* New York: Dell, 1969. (Originally published in 1935)

Merton, Robert K. *Social Theory and Social Structure.* New York: The Free Press, 1957.

Miller, Delbert C. *Handbook of Research Design and Social Measurement.* New York: David McKay, 1970.

Miller, James G. "Living Systems: Basic Concepts." *Behavioral Science*, 10 (July 1965), 193–237.

Miller, Walter B. "Lower-Class Culture as a Generating Milieu of Gang Delinquency." *Journal of Social Issues*, 14, no. 3 (1958), 5–19.

Mills, C. Wright. *The Power Elite.* New York: Oxford University Press, 1956.

———. *The Sociological Imagination.* New York: Oxford University Press, 1959.

Money, John, and Ehrhardt, Anke. *Man and Woman, Boy and Girl.* Baltimore: Johns Hopkins Press, 1972.

Montagu, Ashley. *The Natural Superiority of Women*, rev. ed. New York: Collier Books, 1975. (Originally published in 1952)

———. *Race, Science and Humanity.* Princeton, N.J.: D. Van Nostrand Co., 1963.

Moody, Raymond. *Life After Life.* Harrisburg, Pa.: Stackpole Books, 1976.

Morgan, Robin, ed. *Sisterhood is Powerful.* New York: Vintage, 1970.

Mumford, Lewis. *The City in History.* New York: Harcourt Brace Jovanovich, 1961.

Murdock, George P. *Social Structure.* New York: The Macmillan Co., 1949.

Newman, Graeme. *Comparative Deviance.* New York: Elsevier, 1976.

Nye, F. Ivan. *Role Structure and Analysis of the Family.* Beverly Hills, Ca.: Sage Publications, 1976.

———, et al. "Socio-Economic Status and Delinquent Behavior." *American Journal of Sociology,* 63 (January 1958), 381–389.

O'Dea, Thomas F. *Sociology and the Study of Religion.* New York: Basic Books, 1970.

Orwell, George. *1984.* New York: New American Library, 1949.

Park, Robert E., and Burgess, Ernest W. *An Introduction to the Science of Sociology.* Chicago: University of Chicago Press, 1921.

———; ———; and McKenzie, Robert D. *The City.* Chicago: University of Chicago Press, 1925.

Parkman Center for Urban Affairs. "Young Professionals and City Neighborhoods." Boston: Parkman Center, 1977.

Parsons, Talcott. *The Social System.* New York: The Free Press, 1951.

———. *The Structure of Social Action.* New York: The Free Press, 1949.

Pasamanick, Benjamin; Dinitz, Simon; and Knobloch, Hilda. "Geographic and Seasonal Variations in Births." *Public Health Reports,* 74 (April 1959), 285–286.

Peddiwell, J. Abner. *The Sabre-Tooth Curriculum.* New York: McGraw-Hill, 1939.

Penalosa, Fernando. "The Changing Mexican-American in Southern California." In Norman R. Yetman and C. Hoy Steele, eds. *Majority and Minority.* Boston: Allyn & Bacon, 1971.

Pirenne, Henri. *Medieval Cities.* Princeton, N.J.: Princeton University Press, 1925.

Pleck, Joseph H., and Sawyer, Jack. *Men and Masculinity.* Englewood Cliffs, N.J.: Prentice-Hall, 1974.

Pocs, O., and Godow, A. G. "Can Students View Parents as Sexual Beings?" *The Family Coordinator,* 26 (January 1977), 31–36.

Preiss, Jack J.; and Ehrlich, Howard J. *An Examination of Role Theory: The Case of the State Police.* Lincoln, Neb.: University of Nebraska Press, 1966.

Rabkin, Leslie. "The Institution of the Family Is Alive and Well." *Psychology Today* (February 1976), 66–73.

Ramsey, Ralph. *Population Change in Kentucky Counties: 1950, 1960 and 1970.* Lexington, Kentucky, 1971.

Redfield, Robert. *The Folk Culture of Yucatan.* Chicago: University of Chicago Press, 1941.

Reiss, Ira L. "Premarital Sex as Deviant Behavior: An Application of Current Approaches to Deviance." *American Sociological Review,* 35 (February 1970), 78–87.

Reys, Roger E. "Consumer Math: Just How Knowledgeable are U.S. Young Adults?" *Phi Delta Kappan,* 58 (November 1976), 258–260.

Ribble, Margaret A. *The Rights of Infants.* New York: Columbia University Press, 1943.

Rogers, Everett M., and Shoemaker, F. Floyd. *Communication of Innovations.* New York: The Free Press, 1971.

Rose, Arnold M. *The Power Structure.* New York: Oxford University Press, 1967.

Rose, V. N. "The Rise of the Rape Problem." In A. L. Mauss and J. C. Wolfe, eds., *This Land of Promise.* Philadelphia: Lippincott, 1977.

Rosenham, David L. "On Being Sane in Insane Places." *Science,* 179 (January 19, 1973), 250–258.

Ross, Ralph. *Symbols and Civilization.* New York: Harcourt Brace Jovanovich, 1957.

Rossi, Peter H.; Waite, Emily; Bose, Christine E.; and Beck, Richard E. "The Seriousness of Crimes: Normative Structure and Individual Differences." *American Sociological Review,* 39 (April 1974), 224–237.

Rouse, James W. "The City of Columbia." In Victor E. Ficker and Herbert S. Graves, eds., *Social Science and Urban Crisis.* New York: Macmillan, 1971.

Ryan, Bryce F. *Social and Cultural Change.* New York: Ronald Press, 1969.

Schur, Edwin M. *Crimes Without Victims.* Englewood Cliffs, N.J.: Prentice-Hall, 1965.
———. *Labeling Deviant Behavior.* New York: Harper & Row, 1972.
Simmel, Georg. *The Sociology of Georg Simmel.* Translated by Kurt H. Wolff. New York: The Free Press, 1950.
Simmons, J. L. "Public Stereotypes of Deviants." *Social Problems,* 13 (Fall 1965), 224.
Simon, Julian L. *Basic Research Methods in Social Science.* New York: Random House, 1969.
Simpson, Richard L. "A Modification of the Functional Theory of Social Stratification." In Joseph Lapreato and Lionel S. Lewis, eds., *Social Stratification: A Reader.* New York: Harper & Row, 1974.
Singh, J. A. L., and Zingg, R. M. *Wolf-Children and Feral Man.* New York: Harper, 1939.
Smelser, N. *Theory of Collective Behavior.* New York: The Free Press, 1963.
Smigel, Erwin O., and Seiden, Rita. "The Decline and Fall of the Double Standard," *The Annals,* 376 (June 1968), 6–17.
Sorokin, Pitirim. *Social and Cultural Dynamics.* New York: American Book Co., 1941.
Spectorsky, A. C. *The Exurbanites.* Philadelphia: Lippincott, 1955.
Spencer, Herbert. *The Principles of Sociology,* 3rd ed. New York: D. Appleton, 1910.
———. *The Study of Sociology.* New York: D. Appleton, 1873.
Spengler, Oswald. *The Decline of the West.* New York: Knopf, 1926.
Spiegelman, Mortimer. *Introduction to Demography,* rev ed. Cambridge, Mass.: Harvard University Press, 1968.
Spiro, Melford E. *Kibbutz: Venture in Utopia.* Cambridge, Mass.: Harvard University Press, 1956.
Spitz, René A. "Hospitalism." In *The Psychoanalytic Study of the Child,* vol. 1. New York: International University Press, 1945.
Steffensmeier, Darrell J., and Steffensmeier, Renée H., "Who Reports Shoplifters? Research Continuities and Further Developments." *International Journal of Criminology and Penology,* 5 (1977), 79–95.
Steinmetz, Suzanne K. *The Cycle of Violence.* New York: Praeger, 1977.
Stinchcombe, Arthur L. *Rebellion in a High School.* Chicago: Quadrangle Books, 1969.
Sutherland, Edwin H., and Cressey, Donald R. *Principles of Criminology.* New York: J. B. Lippincott, 1966.
Szasz, Thomas. *The Manufacture of Madness.* New York: Dell, 1970.
———. *The Myth of Mental Illness.* New York: Harper & Row, 1961.
Taeuber, Karl, and Taeuber, Alma. *Negroes in Cities.* Chicago: Aldine, 1965.
Theodorson, George A., and Theodorson, Achilles G. *Modern Dictionary of Sociology.* New York: Crowell, 1969.
Thomas, William I., and Znaniecki, Florian. *The Polish Peasant in Europe and America,* vol. 2. New York: Alfred A. Knopf, 1927.
Thorman, George. "Cohabitation: A Report on Couples Living Together." *The Futurist,* 7 (December 1973), 250–254.
Tiger, Lionel, and Shepher, Joseph. *Women in the Kibbutz.* New York: Harcourt Brace Jovanovich, 1975.
Tocqueville, Alexis de. *Democracy in America,* Translated by Henry Reeve. New York: Schocken Books, 1961.
Tönnies, Ferdinand. *Community and Society.* East Lansing: Michigan State University, 1957. (Originally published in 1887)
Toynbee, Arnold. *A Study of History.* New York: Oxford University Press, 1946.
Tracy, Phil. "The Making of a Madman." *New West* (December 18, 1978).
Tumin, Melvin. "Some Principles of Stratification: A Critical Analysis." *The American Sociolgical Review,* 18 (August 1953), 387–393.
Turnbull, Colin. *The Wayward Servants: Two Worlds of the African Pygmies.* Garden City, N.Y.: Natural History Press, 1965.
Twain. Mark. *Life on the Mississippi.* Boston: J.R. Osgood, 1883.
United States Commission on Civil Rights. *Social Indicators of Equality for Minorities and Women.* Washington, D.C.: U.S. Commission on Civil Rights, 1978.
U.S. Bureau of the Census. *Statistical Abstract of the United States: 1975.* Washington, D.C., U.S. Government Printing Office, 1975.
U'Ren, Marjorie B. "The Image of Women in

Textbooks." In Vivian Gornick and Barbara K. Moran, eds., *Women in Sexist Society.* New York: Basic Books, 1971, pp. 218-225.

U.S. News and World Report. "The Drive to Open Up More Careers for Women." *U.S. News and World Report,* 76 (January 1974), 69-70.

Vallier, Ivan. "Church, Society, and Labor Resources." *Amercian Journal of Sociology,* 68 (July 1962), 21-33.

———. "Religious Elites in Latin America: Catholicism, Leadership and Social Change." Unpublished manuscript, 1965.

Vonnegut, Kurt, Jr. "Harrison Bergeron." In Kurt Vonnegut, Jr., *Welcome to the Monkeyhouse.* New York, Delacorte Press, 1968, pp. 7-13.

von Frisch, Karl. "Dialectics in the Language of Bees." *Scientific American,* 207 (August 1962), 78-87.

Walker, Kathryn E., and Ganger, William H. "The Dollar Value of Household Work." *Information Bulletin No. 60.* Ithaca, N.Y.: New York College of Human Ecology, 1973.

Wallace, Walter L. *The Logic of Science in Sociology.* Chicago: Aldine, 1971.

Ward, Barbara. "Cities for 3,000 Million People." *The Economist,* 245 (July 8, 1967), 116.

Watson, John B. *The Ways of Behaviorism.* New York: Harper & Row, 1928.

Weber, Max. *Max Weber: Essays in Sociology.* Edited and translated by Hans H. Gerth and C. Wright Mills. New York: Oxford University Press, 1946.

———. *The Protestant Ethic and the Spirit of Capitalism.* Translated by Talcott Parsons. New York: Charles Scribner's Sons, 1958.

———. *The Theory of Social and Economic Organization,* Translated by A. M. Henderson and Talcott Parsons. New York: Oxford University Press, 1947.

Westermarck, Edward. *The History of Human Marriage,* 5th ed. London: Macmillian & Co., 1921.

Westoff, Charles F., and Rindfuss, Ronald R. "Sex Preselection in the United States: Some Implications." *Science,* 184 (May 1974), 633-636.

Westoff, Leslie A., and Westoff, Charles F. *From Now to Zero.* Boston: Little, Brown, 1971.

Whelpton, Pascal K., et al. *Fertility and Family Planning in the United States.* Princeton, N.J.: Princeton University Press, 1966.

Whiting, Beatrice B., ed. *Six Cultures: Studies in Childbearing.* New York: John Wiley & Sons 1963.

Wilson, Record. "Black Studies Movement in Higher Education." *American Sociologist,* 7 (May 1972), 10-11.

Wirth, Louis. "The Problems of Minority Groups." In Ralph Linton, ed., *The Science of Man in the World Crisis.* New York: Columbia University Press, 1945.

Wiseman, Jacqueline P. *Stations of the Lost.* Englewood Cliffs, N.J.: Prentice-Hall, 1970.

———, and Aron, Marcia S. *Field Projects for Sociology Students.* Cambridge, Mass.: Schenkman Publishing Co., 1970.

Wispé, Lauren G. "A Sociometric Analysis of Conflicting Role-Expectations." *American Journal of Sociology,* 61 (September 1955), 134-137.

Wyden, Peter. *Suburbia's Coddled Kids.* Garden City, N.Y.: Doubleday, 1960.

Yinger, J. Milton. *Religion, Society and the Individual.* New York: Macmillan, 1957.

Yorburg, Betty. *The Changing Family.* New York: Columbia University Press, 1973.

Zangwill, Israel. "The Melting Pot." In Israel Zangwill, *Works.* New York: AMS Press, 1969.

Zimbardo, Philip G. "Pathology of Imprisonment." *Society,* 9 (April 1972), 4-8.

Indexes

Name Index

Allon, Natalie, 540–541
Arkin, William, 124
Athens, Lonnie H., 24–25

Baker, Luther G., 346
Bakke, Allen, 516–517
Bales, Robert F., 166–167
Ballweg, John A., 18
Balzac, 156
Bardwick, Judith, 189
Barr, Thomas C., Jr., 35
Barrett, Nancy Smith, 208
Bash, Wendell H., 448
Becker, Howard, 16
Becker, Howard S., 58, 547, 548
Bell, Wendell, 497
Bellah, Robert, 297, 298
Benedict, Ruth, 149
Berger, Bennett, 495, 497
Biddle, Bruce J., 135
Birch, Lloyd, 46–47
Borofsky, Gerald, 8
Boskoff, Alvina, 486
Bowerman, Charles E., 54
Bradley, Jeff, 188
Brannon, Robert C., 528–529
Briffault, Robert, 264
Brim, Orville G., Jr., 122
Bronfenbrenner, Urie, 114, 161, 273
Brown, Donald R., 197
Brown, Theodore, 494
Burgess, Ernest W., 483, 484
Bryan, James, 140

Calderone, Mary S., 346

Campbell, Ernest Q., 144
Carmichael, Stokely, 515
Carson, Rachel, 417
Castro, Fidel, 110
Caudill, William, 526
Celemente, Frank, 561
Centers, Richard, 247
Chafetz, Janet, 213
Chein, Isidor, 553
Chambliss, William J., 229
Chirot, Daniel, 392
Civiletti, Benjamin R., 563
Clark, Burton R., 338
Clinard, Marshall B., 545
Cloward, Richard A., 545
Cohen, Albert K., 546
Cohen, Morris, 23
Coleman, James S., 57, 358
Comas, Juan, 83
Comte, Auguste, 14, 17, 87, 297, 408
Cooley, Charles Horton, 119, 157, 162
Coser, Lewis, 21
Cowgill, Donald O., 461
Cressey, Donard R., 546
Crowley, James W., 18
Cuber, John F., 228, 509

Dager, Edward Z., 103
Dahrendorf, Ralf, 21, 410
Dai, Bingham, 553
Darity, William A., 450
Darwin, Charles, 15, 35, 36, 302, 483

Davies, John O., III, 313, 324, 326
Davis, Keith, 26
Davis, Kingsley, 6, 36, 182, 264, 309
Dawson, Richard E., 394
de Tocqueville, Alexis, 156, 168–169
DeVos, George, 526
Dinitz, Simon, 447, 563
Divoky, Diane, 362
Dobrofsky, Lynne, 124
Dobzhansky, Theodosius, 510
Domhoff, G. William, 392
Doress, Marvin, 162
Durkheim, Emile, 16, 305, 316, 409, 544

Edelstein, Barbara, 189
Ehrhardt, Anke, 190
Ehrlich, Howard J., 144
Einstein, Albert, 36
Empey, Lamar T., 558
Erickson, Maynard L., 558

Farrell, Warren, 218–219
Feld, Shiela, 313
Firestone, Harold, 553
Firey, Walter, 485
Frazer, James George, 298–299
Freedman, Ronald, 450
Fried, Marc, 490
Friedan, Betty, 417
Friedrichs, Robert W., 58
Frieze, Irene H., 192

589

Galileo, 56, 302
Gallup, George, Jr., 313, 324, 326
Ganger, William H., 207
Gans, Herbert, 495, 497
Gebhard, Paul H., 279
Gergen, Kenneth, 51
Gergen, Mary K., 51
Gist, Noel P., 230
Glaab, Charles, 494
Gleicher, Peggy, 490
Glock, Charles, 303, 323
Gmelch, George, 422
Gmelch, Sharon Bohn, 422
Godow, Anette G., 276-277
Goffman, Erving, 547
Goldberg, Philip, 209
Goldschmidt, Walter, 88
Goode, William, 37
Gordon, Milton, 509
Gordon, Richard E., 494
Gouldner, Alvin W., 21, 58
Grabill, Wilson H., 450
Gross, Beatrice, 362
Gross, Ronald, 362
Gurin, Gerald, 313

Hale, Sir Matthew, 418
Halebsky, Sandor, 489
Hamilton, Charles, 515
Hammurabi, 13
Haney, Craig, 340-341
Harper, Robert A., 509
Harris, Marvin, 306-307
Harrison, James, 216
Haworth, Lawrence, 500-501
Hechinger, Fred M., 363
Henderson, A. M., 229
Herskovitz, Melville J., 81
Hodge, Robert W., 235
Hoffer, Eric, 418
Hoffman, Dean K., 167
Holbrooke, Richard, 476
Hollingshead, August B., 240, 242
Hopkins, Elizabeth, 37
Horowitz, Irving L., 21
Hoyt, Homer, 485
Humphreys, Laud, 44-45, 556
Hunt, Morton, 207, 279, 280
Hutton, John H., 230

Inkeles, Alex, 235

Jackson, Philip, 359-360
Jencks, Christopher, 337
Jensen, Arthur R., 57, 336, 513
Jones, James (Rev.), 314-315

Kagan, Jerome, 211
Kahl, Joseph A., 248
Kahn, Robert L., 147
Kantner, John F., 279
Keats, John, 494
Kelly, K. Dennis, 229
Kenkel, Scottie, 204
Kenkel, William F., 46, 67, 228, 243, 271, 272, 448, 509
Kennedy, John F., 71
Kesey, Ken, 122
Khrushchev, Nikita, 71
King, Martin Luther, Jr., 311
Kinsey, Alfred C., 276-277, 279, 280, 555
Kleinman, M. B., 561
Kluckhohn, Clyde, 72
Knobloch, Hilda, 447
Kramer, Judith, 530, 531
Kreuz, Leo, 189

Ladd, William F., 499
Lake, Alice, 211
Langton, Kenneth, 394
Lapidus, Gail Warshofsky, 198
Laurenti, Luigi M., 499
Lefton, Mark, 539
Leiner, Marvin, 110-111
L'Enfant, Pierre, 500
Lenski, Gerhard, 88, 231-232, 297, 298, 310-311, 323, 324-325
Leonard, George, 351
Leonardo da Vinci, 93
Levin, Amy, 290, 313
Levin, Robert I., 290, 313
Levy, Leon H., 170-171
Linton, Ralph, 75, 151
Lipetz, Milton E., 26
Lipset, Seymour M., 247
Locke, John, 380
Lofland, John, 314
Lowell, Percival, 35, 36
Lundberg, George A., 58
Lynd, Robert S., 58
Lyness, Judith L., 26

McClure, Helen M., 37
Mace, David, 268

Mace, Vera, 268
McIntyre, Jennie, 560
Mack, Raymond, 325
McKenzie, Roderick D., 483, 484
McPartland, John, 494
Malewski, Andrzej, 229
Malthus, Thomas, 459
Martin, Clyde E., 279
Marx, Karl, 15-16, 17, 21, 87, 254, 310, 408-409, 410-411
Mead, George Herbert, 119, 120-122
Mead, Margaret, 191, 192
Meese, Lawrence A., 8
Merton, Robert K., 18, 54, 172, 544-546
Michelson, Albert, 36
Miller, Delbert C., 33
Miller, James G., 133
Miller, Walter, 562
Mills, C. Wright, 6, 58, 391-392
Money, John, 190
Montagu, Ashley, 83, 190
Moore, Wilbert, 36
Morgan, Robin, 79
Moreley, Edward, 36
Morse, Stanley J., 51
Moses, 13
Mumford, Lewis, 476
Murdock, George P., 86, 265, 277, 278

Nader, Ralph, 417
Nye, F. Ivan, 148, 558

O'Dea, Thomas F., 317
Orwell, George, 226

Park, Robert E., 483, 489
Parsons, Talcott, 18, 133, 229, 410
Pasamanick, Benjamin, 447
Peddiwell, J. Abner, 350
Penalosa, Fernando, 524
Pirenne, Henri, 478
Pettigrew, Thomas F., 144
Plato, 387
Pleck, Joseph H., 217
Pocs, Ollie, 276-277
Pomeroy, Wardell, B., 279
Porter, Jack N., 162
Preiss, Jack J., 144

NAME INDEX

Prewitt, Kenneth, 394

Rabkin, Leslie, 201
Ramsey, Ralph, 457
Record, Wilson, 57
Redfield, Robert, 16, 182
Redlich, Frederick C., 240, 242
Reiss, Ira L., 549
Reys, Roger E., 347
Ribble, Margaret A., 281
Rindfuss, Ronald R., 209
Rogers, Everett M., 425
Rose, Arnold, 392
Rose, Robert, 189
Rose, V. N., 418
Rosenhan, David, 542
Rossi, Peter H., 235, 539
Rouse, James W., 502
Ryan, Bryce F., 416
Ryan, Edward, 490
Ryan, Leo J., 314

Saretsky, Gary, 364
Sawyer, Jack, 217
Schur, Edwin M., 547
Scopes, John, 302
Shoemaker, F. Floyd, 425
Seiden, Rita, 280
Shepher, Joseph, 200
Siegel, Paul M., 235
Simmel, Georg, 163-164
Simmons, J. L., 553

Simon, Julian L., 42
Simpson, Richard, 253
Smelser, Neil, 412–413
Smigel, Erwin O., 280
Sorokin, Pitirim, 408
Spectorsky, A. C., 494
Spencer, Herber, 14–15, 17, 87, 408
Spengler, Oswald, 407
Spiegelman, Mortimer, 439
Spiro, Melford E., 252
Spitz, René A., 281
Stark, Rodney, 303, 323
Steffensmeier, Darrell J., 40
Steffensmeier, Renée H., 40
Steinmetz, Suzanne, 9
Stinchcombe, Arthur L., 358
Stollack, Gary E., 8
Sutherland, Edwin H., 546, 563
Szasz, Thomas, 541–542

Taeuber, Alma, 499
Taeuber, Karl, 499
Thomas, Edwin J., 135
Thomas, William I., 78, 561
Thomsen, Christian, 87
Thorman, George, 26
Tiger, Lionel, 200
Tönnies, Ferdinand, 180, 182
Toynbee, Arnold, 407–408
Tracy, Phil, 315
Treiman, Donald J., 235

Tumin, Melvin, 253
Twain, Mark, 52

Udall, Stewart, 467
U'Ren, Marjorie, 211

Veroff, Joseph, 313
von Frisch, Karl, 120
Vonnegut, Kurt, Jr., 252–253

Walker, Kathryn E., 207
Wallace, Walter L., 33
Ward, Barbara, 501
Watson, John B., 105
Weber, Max, 17, 177–178, 229
Westermarck, Edward, 265
Westoff, Charles, 209, 467, 470
Westoff, Leslie A., 467, 470
Whelpton, Pascal K., 449
Wirth, Louis, 509
Wiseman, Jacqueline, 46
Wispé, Lauren G., 146
Wyden, Peter, 494

Yinger, J. Milton, 303
Yorburg, Betty, 268, 291

Zangwill, Israel, 508
Zelnick, Melvin, 279
Zimbardo, Philip, 136–137, 340–341
Znaniecki, Florian, 78

Subject Index

Achievement, and education, 354–358
Adoption process, of social change, 421–426
Adultery. *See* Extramarital sex
Affirmative action programs, 516–517
Agents of socialization, 109–116
Aggression, sex roles and, 189, 190–191, 191–192
Aggressive behavior
   heredity and, 190–191
   hormones and, 189
Agrarian stage, 91
   family in, 285–286
   inequality in, 227
   political-economic institution in, 373
   religion in, 298
   sex-role differentiation in, 195–196, 209
Alcohol abuse, 549–550
Alienation, 376–377
Amalgamation, cultural, 521–522
American Psychiatric Association, 554–555
American Sociological Association, 52
American Sociological Review, 52
Americans View Their Mental Health (Gurin, Veroff, and Feld), 313
Amniocentesis, 58
Anarchism, 387
Anomie theory, 544–546
   of crime, 560–562
   of drug abuse, 552–553
Apartheid, 519–520
Artifacts, 74
Assimilation, cultural, 521

Beliefs, religious, 305–306
Berkeley Men's Center, 217
Birth control, fertility and, 449, 450

Birth statistics, 11, 444–450
   seasonal variations in, 447–448
Black Power (Carmichael and Hamilton), 515
Blacks, 528–531. *See also* Minorities; Race
   criminal deviancy and, 558
   education and, 352–358
   fertility and, 450
   income and, 232–233
   infant mortality, 239, 453
   unemployment among, 378
   urban ghettos and, 488–492
Bourgeoisie, 254
Brown v. *Board of Education of Topeka*, 365
Bureaucracy, 166
   characteristics of, 174–178
   problems with, 178–180
   in schools, 340
   of the U.S. government, 387

Calvinism, 17
Capitalism, 15, 17, 384, 386
Carnegie Quarterly, 211
Caste system, 230, 231, 311
Catholicism, 18. *See also* Religion
   fertility and, 450
Census data, 438–440, 441
Chain of command, bureaucratic, 177
Change. *See* Social change
Child-rearing practices, 108–109
Children, socialization of, 109–118, 270, 272–275
Chromosomes, sex, 190
Church. *See* Religion
Churchgoing, 322–323, 528–529
Cities. *See also* Urbanization
   layout of, 483–486

Cities (continued)
  origins of, 476–481
  slums and ghettos, 486–492
  urban planning, 500–502
City-state, 373
Civil Rights Act of 1964, 214, 217
Civil rights movement, 415
Class. See Social class
Coal mining, women in, 204–205
Cohabitation, 26, 290
Collective behavior, 411. See also Social movements
College degrees, 344
Columbia, Maryland, 502
Communes, 543–544
Communication
  development of self and, 120
  nonverbal, 71, 192–193
  in primary groups, 158–159
  sex-role stereotyping and, 192–193
Communism, 110–111, 198, 384
Community, 180, 181
Concentric zone model, 484
Concepts, sociological, 38–39
Conflict model, 21–22, 24
  of education, 364–366
  of social change, 410–411
  of stratification, 254–255
Conformity, 546
Copernican theory, 56, 302
Constitutional democracy, 389–390
Contracultures, 546
Correlations, 48–50
Counter roles, 141–142
Crime, 25, 246, 539–540, 557–563
  fear of, 560–561
  in inner cities, 488–489
Crowds, 411, 412–413
Crude birth rate, 445–446
Crude death rate, 451
Cuba, childhood socialization in, 110–111
Cults, 162–163, 314–315
Cultural change, 91–97. See also Social change
Cultural diffusion, 93–94
Cultural lag, 428
Cultural universals, 75, 372
Culture, 68–71
  in animals, 82–83
  changes in, 91–96
  diversity in, 80–86
  evolution of, 87–91
  functions of, 75–80
  meaning of, 72–75
  sex roles and, 191–194
  socialization and, 107–109

Current Population Reports, 441
Custodial function, of schools, 339, 358–360
Cyclical theory of social change, 407

Decision making, family, 46
Decline of the West, The (Spengler), 407
Deduction, 33, 34
Defense, as government function, 382–383
Democracy, 389–390
Democracy in America (de Tocqueville), 168
Demographic transition, 461–462
Demography, social
  analyzing data, 441–444
  defined, 436
  fertility data, 444–450
  gathering data, 438–441
  goals of, 436–438
  mortality data, 451–455
  migration data, 455–458
  population data, 458–470
Dependency ratios, 443–444
Developing nations, population growth in, 462
Deviancy, 538–539
  theories of, 544–549
  types of, 539–544
  in the United States, 549–564
Deviant subculture theory, 546–547
  of crime, 546, 562
  of drug abuse, 553
  of homosexuality, 556
Dieting, 540–541
Differential association, 546
Differential rewards, 231–238. See also Inequalities, social
Discovery, culture and, 92–93
Discrimination, 514–515, 519–520
  reverse, 516–517
Division of labor, 88, 287, 409. See also Specialization
  inequalities and, 227–228
  in kibbutzim, 200
Divorce, 289–290
Doubling time, 459, 464
Dropouts
  school, 355, 356
  social, 543–544
Drug abuse, 549–553
Dyads, 164–165

Eclecticism, 23
Ecology. See Urban ecology
Economic consumption, 279–280, 376–377
Economic determinism, 15–16
Economic institution, 182, 372, 375–380
  evolution of, 373–375
  government and, 383–387

population and, 470
Economic production, 375-379
Ecumenism, 319, 320-321
Education, 182, 334
   blacks and, 352-358, 529-530
   fertility and, 448
   functions of, 334-341
   goals of, 345-351
   income and, 356
   issues in, 345-364
   of minorities, 352-358, 526
   occupation and, 356
   sex differences in, 201-202
   sociological models of, 364-366
   in the United States, 341-345
Egalitarian marriage, 268
Elementary Forms of Religious Life (Durkheim), 305
Endogamous rules, 268
Energy consumption, world, 468
Enrollments, in U.S. schools, 342-343
Environment, population and, 467
Equal Rights Amendment, 188, 208, 217
Equality of opportunity
   education and, 336-337, 351-358
   income and, 380
Essay on the Principle of Population (Malthus), 459
Estrogen, 190
Ethnic groups, 509. *See also* Minorities
Ethnocentrism, 73-74, 220, 509
Ethnology, 297
Evolutionary model, 18
   of social change, 408-409
Evolution of culture, 15, 87-91
Evolution, theory of, 35, 302
Exchange theory, 37
Exogamous rules, 268
Expulsion, 519
Extended family, 265-267
Extermination, 518
Extragroup linkage, 168
Extramarital sex, 278, 279-280
Extrapolation, 52

Family, 182
   as agent of socialization, 109-113
   biological basis of, 264-265
   forms of, 265-267, 267-269
   functions of, 269-288
   future of, 288-291
   as primary group, 161
   sex roles in, 207-208, 217-218
Family of orientation, 265
Family of procreation, 265

Family size, 270-272, 449
Feminine Mystique, The (Friedan), 417
Feral children, 102-103
Fertility, 444
   among Hutterites, 462-463
   U.S. population and, 465-466, 468-469
   world population and, 461, 462
Fertility rates, 444-450
Feudal system, 230
Food, culture and, 84-85
Food supply, population and, 463-465
Formal groups, 166
Free schools, 364
Futurist, The, 428
Futurology, 428

Game stage, of self development, 120-121
Gay Liberation Front, 556-557
Gemeinschaft, 180-181
General fertility rate, 446
Generalization, role learning through, 142-143
Generalized other, 121-122
Genes, 190
Genetic drift, 511
Genocide, 518
Geographic environment, culture and, 80-82
Geographic isolation, 511-512
Gesellschaft, 180, 181-182
Ghettos, 488-492
Golden Bough, The (Frazer), 298
Government, 182-183, 372, 380-387
   evolution of, 373-375
Green Revolution, 465
Group marriage, 86, 267
Groups
   as agents of socialization, 114, 115
   bureaucratic, 174-180
   defined, 156-157
   leadership in, 166-168
   primary, 157-162
   secondary, 162-168
   social characteristics of, 10-11
   voluntary, 168-174
Group size, 163-166
Group stability, roles and, 136-138

Happiness, income and, 245
"Harrison Bergeron" (Vonnegut), 252-253
Heredity, sex differences and, 190-191
Heredity vs. environment, 104-105
Heroin, 550-552
Hidden curriculum, 360
High schools, as prisons, 340-341
Hinduism, 306-307, 311
Homosexuality, 45-46, 541, 547-548, 553-557

Horizontal mobility, 248
Hormones, 189–190
Horticultural stage, 90
    cities in, 476
    family in, 285
    inequalities in, 227
    religion in, 298
Housework, 212
Housing, blacks and, 530
Human ecology, 483
Humanistic model, 23
Hunting and gathering stage, 89–90, 132
    education in, 334
    family in, 284–285
    inequalities in, 227
    political-economic institution in, 373
    population growth and, 458
    religion in, 297–298
    sex role differentiation in, 194–195
    social change and, 406
Hutterites, 462–463
Hypothesis, 33, 34, 39

Ideational culture, 408
Identity, religion and, 316
Illegitimacy, 272, 440–441
Imagination, role learning through, 143
Imitation, as method of socialization, 116–118
Immigration, 455–456
Incest taboo, 268, 277–278
Income. *See also* Social class
    distribution, in U.S., 232, 234
    education and, 233, 356
    equal opportunity and, 380
    fertility and, 448
    happiness and, 245
    inequalities in, 232–234
    infant mortality and, 453
    of inner city blacks, 492
    race and, 232–233, 528–529
    sex differences in, 206–207, 233–234
Incumbent, 135
Index of Social Position, 240–241
India, 230, 231, 305, 306–307, 311
Indian Americans, 522–523
    infant mortality, 454
Industrial societies, 91
    family in, 286–287
    inequalities in, 227–228
    political-economic institution in, 374–375
    sex roles in, 196, 209
    social change in, 406
    social mobility in, 249
Inequalities

    in education, 352–358
    sexual, 201–210
    social, 226, 227–238, 251–255
Infant mortality rate, 452–454
Informal groups, 166
Inherited characteristics, socialization and, 103–105
In-migration, 456–458
Inner city
    renovation of, 492–493
    slums and ghettos, 486–492
Input-output model of schools, 352–356
Instinct, 68–69
Institute for Social Research (University of Michigan), 146–147
Institutional racism, 517–518
Institutions, 182–183
Instruction
    learning by, 139–140
    as method of socialization, 116
Instrumental leader, 167
Integrated housing, 489–490
Intelligence
    defined, 512
    education and, 336–337
    race and, 512–514
    testing for, 105
Interest group theory of social classes, 247
Interpretation, of research findings, 50–51
Invasion, ecological, 483
Invention, culture and, 92
IQ tests, 105
    race and, 512–514
Irish tinkers, 422–423

Japan, gangsterism in, 158–159
Japanese Americans, 525–526
Jews, American, 527–528
Journal of Marriage and the Family, 52
Juvenile delinquency, 557–563

Kibbutzim, 36, 198–201, 252–253, 272–275
Knowledge for What? (Lynd), 58
!Kung Bushmen, 132, 227, 373

Labeling theory, 40, 541, 547–548
    of crime, 562–563
    of drug abuse, 553
    of homosexuality, 556–557
Labor unions, 378–379
Language
    culture and, 69, 70–71
    development of self and, 120
    sex-role stereotyping and, 192–193

SUBJECT INDEX

Latent functions, 172-173
Laws, 13
Leadership, 166-168
League of Women Voters, 169-170, 204
Learned behavior, 68-69
Lesbianism. *See* Homosexuality
Letcher County, Kentucky, 457-458
Liberated Man, The (Farrell), 218
Life chances, 239, 240-244
Life expectancy, 454-455
   race and, 529
Lifestyles, 239
   social class and, 244-248
Looking-glass self, 118-119
Los Angeles City School Board, 349
Love, need for, 281-284
LSD, 552

Magic, 299-301
Manifest functions, 172
Marijuana, 552
Marriage, 85-86, 440. *See also* Family
   forms of, 267-269
Marxism, 196
Mass media
   as agent of socialization, 114-115
   sex-role stereotyping and, 213
Mass movement, 392-393
Mass society, 374
Material culture, 74-75
Materialism, 428
Matriarchal family, 268
Maximum population size, 466
Mean, arithmetic, 47
Measures of central tendency, 47-48
Mechanical solidarity, 16
Median, 47
Megalopolis, 480-481
Men, sex roles and, 216-217
Men's liberation, 217, 218-219
Mental illness, 540-543
Mexican Americans, 523-525
Migration, 455-458
Military socialization, 124-125
Minorities, 508-509. *See also* Blacks; Indian Americans
   control of schools and, 362
   education and, 352-358
   majority-minority relations, 56-57, 514-522
   unemployment among, 378
   in the United States, 522-531
Mode, 47
Models, sociological, 18-23
Monogamy, 85, 267

Mormons, fertility and, 450
Mortality rates, 451-455
Moynihan Report of 1965, 57
Myth, 317

National Institute for Occupational Safety and Health, 204
National Opinion Research Center, 235
National Organization of Women (NOW), 419
Nation-state, 374
Natural selection, 510-511
Nazi Germany, 388
Neutrality, scientific, 55-59
"New towns," 502
New York Times, 158, 159
1984 (Orwell), 226
Nonmaterial culture, 74-75
Nonparticipant observation, 43, 46
Nonverbal communication, 71, 192-193
Norms, 78
Nuclear family, 265

Obesity, 540-541
Observation
   learning by, 140-141
   scientific, 33-34
   sociological, 41, 43-45, 45-47
Occupations
   changing nature of, in U.S., 375-376
   education and, 356, 357
   fertility and, 448
   mobility in, 250-251
   prestige of, 235-238
   sexual inequalities in, 202-205
Old age, socialization for, 123-124
One Flew Over the Cuckoo's Nest (Kesey), 122
Open class system, 230-231
Optimum population size, 466-467
Organic solidarity, 16
Out-migration, 456-458
Overcrowding, population and, 467

Parenthood, 123
Parkman Center for Urban Affairs, 492
Participant observation, 43-45, 46
Patriarchal family, 268
Pearson Product Moment Correlation Coefficient, 49
Peer group, as agent of socialization, 114
People's Temple, 313, 314-315
Personality, 118. *See also* Self
Personal space, 192-193
Placement, 335, 338-339

Planned obsolescence, 376–377
Play stage, of self development, 120
Pluralism
   ethnic, 520–521
   political, 392
   religious, 319–320
Political institution, 372
   evolution of, 373–375
   functions of, 380–387
   power and, 390–396
   systems of, 387–390
Political participation, 394–395
Political parties, 393–394
Political socialization, 394
Political systems, 387–390
Pollution, and population, 467
Polyandry, 85–86, 267
Polygamy, 267
Polygyny, 85, 267
Population growth, 54–55, 88
   United States, 465–470
   of urban areas, 479–481
   world, 458–465
Population pyramids, 441–443
Positions, social, 78, 133–135
Positive population checks, 459
Positivism, 14
Poverty, 491–492. *See also* Income
   education and, 352–353
Power, 196, 229, 372, 390–396
   inequalities in, 21–22, 207, 231–232
   over schools, 360–363
Power elite, 391–392
Predictions, 54–55
Prejudice, 514. *See also* discrimination
Premarital sex, 278, 279, 280
Prestige, 196, 231–232
   inequalities in, 235–238
Preventive population checks, 459
Primary deviancy, 547–548, 557
Primary groups, 16, 152–162
Privilege, social, 196
Progesterone, 190
Progressive movements, 415
Proletariat, 254
Property, 195, 196
Protestant Ethic and the Spirit of Capitalism, The (Weber), 17
Protestantism, 17. *See also* Religion
Protestant reformation, 297
Pruitt-Igoe Housing Project, 491
Psychological needs, culture and, 78–80
Ptolemic theory, 56

Puerto Rican Americans, 525
Punishment, as method of socialization, 116

Race, 509–510. *See also* Blacks
   culture and, 82–83
   fertility and, 450
   intelligence and, 105, 512–514
   origins of, 510–512
Racial segregation, 353–354, 499, 519–520
Racism, 515–518
Random genetic drift, 511
Random sampling, 42–43
Rank. *See* Social class
Rape, 418–419
Reciprocal roles, 141–142
Redbook Magazine, 290, 313
Reform movements, 414
Religion, 183, 296
   evolution of, 297–298
   fertility and, 450
   functions of, 309–317
   magic and, 298, 299–301
   nature of, 303–308
   prejudice and, 528–529
   science and, 298, 301–303
   in the United States, 317–328
Religiosity, 323
Replacement level fertility, 465, 468–470
Republic, The (Plato), 13
Research, sociological, 33–34
   analyzing data, 47–52
   collecting data, 40–47
   ethics of, 55–59
   reporting of, 52–54
Reverse discrimination, 516–517
Revolutionary movements, 415–416
Rewards, as method of socialization, 116
Riots, 412–413
Rites of passage, 150
Rituals, 301, 307–308
Road to H, The (Chein), 553
Role analysis, 135
Role behavior, 137
Role conflict, 144–148
Role discrepancy, 143–144
Role failure, 143–149
Role preparation, 148–149
Roles, 78, 132–133
   changes in, 138–139
   defined, 135
   evolution of, 132
   failure in, 143–151
   in groups, 136–138

SUBJECT INDEX

    learning of, 139–143
    positions and, 133–135
Role strain, 148
Role Structure and Analysis of the Family (Nye), 148
Rural residence
    appeal of, 496–497
    family size and, 449
    out-migration from, 457
Russian Revolution, 416

Sabre-Tooth Curriculum, The (Peddiwell), 350
Sampling, 41, 42–43
San Diego school system, 350–351
San Francisco Unified School District, 364–365
Satellite cities, 486, 499
Scholastic Aptitude Test (SAT), 346–347
School boards, 361
Schools, 334–366
    socialization in, 113–114, 211–213, 218–219
Science, religion and, 301–303
Scientific method, 14
Scientific research, 33–34
Secondary deviancy, 548, 557
Secondary groups, 16, 162–168
Sector model of urban growth, 485
Segregation, racial, 519–520
    in schools, 353–354
    in suburbs, 499
Self, 118–122
Self-defeating prophecy, 54, 458–459
Self-fulfilling prophecy, 54
Self-help groups, 170–171
Sensate culture, 408
Sex differences, 189–191
    in mortality rates, 452–453
Sexism, 201
Sex roles
    biological basis of, 188–191
    changes in, 217–220
    culture and, 191–194
    evolution of, 194–196, 208–209
    in kibbutzim, 198–201
    socialization for, 211–214
    in the Soviet Union, 196–198
    in the United States, 201–210, 214–217
Sex-role stereotyping, 200
    consequences of, 214–217
    in marriage, 283
    nonverbal behavior and, 192–193
    social inequalities and, 201–210
Sexual behavior, family and, 276–281
Sexual Behavior in the 1970s (Hunt), 279

Sexual variability, culture and, 85–86
Shanghai, China, 488–489
Shoplifting, 39, 40–41
Sickle-cell anemia, 511
Silent Spring (Carson), 417
Skin color, natural selection and, 510–511
Slums, 486–488, 490–491
Social change, 14, 406, 421–430
Social characteristics, study of, 10–11
Social class, 226, 228–229
    crime and, 558, 562
    determining, 240–241
    effects of, 239–248
    evolution of, 227–228
    fertility and, 448
    inequalities and, 231–238
    life chances and, 240–244
    lifestyle and, 244–248
Social demography. *See* Demography
Social-emotional leader, 167
Socialism, 384
Socialization
    adult, 122–126
    agents of, 109–116
    childhood, 103–122
    discontinuity in, 149–151
    family and, 272–275
    political, 394–395
    in schools, 339–340, 350
    sex role, 211–214
Social mobility, 226, 230, 248–251
Social movements, 411–421
Social Problems, 52
Social rigidity, 230–231
Social Security, 470
Social statics, 14
Social stratification. *See* Stratification
Social system, 133–135
Society, 73, 180, 181–182
Sociograms, 179
Sociology, 6–13, 23–26
    defined, 13, 18
    models in, 18–23
    origins of, 13–18
    as science, 32–59
Sovereignty, 374, 380, 381–383
Soviet Union, 388
    family in, 270–271
    sex roles in, 196–198
    urban planning in, 501
South Africa, 519–520
Specialization, 16, 132. *See also* Division of labor
Spurious relationships, 51

Standard deviation, 48
Standard Metropolitan Statistical Areas (SMSAs), 480
Statistical methods, 47–50
Statistics, demographic, 438–444
    fertility rates, 444–446
    mortality rates, 452–455
Status ascription, in the family, 275–276
Status consistency, 229
Strata, social, 228. See also Social class
Stratification, 36, 226, 228–231. See also Social class
    inequalities caused by, 231–238
    origins of, 227–228
    social mobility and, 230–231, 248–251
    theories of, 251–255
Structural-functional model, 18–21, 24
    of education, 364–366
    of social change, 410
    of stratification, 251–254
Study of History, A (Toynbee), 407
Subcultures, 546
Suburbs, 493–500
Succession, ecological, 483
Suicide, 16
Suicide (Durkheim), 316
Survey research, 40–41
Symbolic interaction model, 23, 24–25
Symbols, 24, 70

Tasaday culture, 88–89
Task leader, 167
Technology, 375. See also Industrial societies
    origins of cities and, 476–477, 478–479
    social change and, 87–89, 428–429
    social mobility and, 249
    specialization and, 249
Television, as agent of socialization, 114–115
Temperance movement, 411–413
Territoriality, 45–46
Testing, 338–339
Testosterone, 189, 190
Theory
    scientific, 33, 34, 35–38
    sociological, 36–38
Totalitarianism, 387–388
Total Woman movement, 415
Transcendental Meditation, 70
True believers, 418

Underemployment, 234
Unemployment, 378
U.S. Bureau of the Census, 247, 438–440, 441
U.S. Commission on Civil Rights, 202, 203, 206
U.S. Department of Health, Education, and Welfare, 56, 272
U.S. News and World Report, 203
University of Heidelberg, 17
University of Michigan, 147
University of Wisconsin, 346
Urban ecology, 483–486
Urban homesteading, 491
Urbanization, 286
    of early civilizations, 477–478
    population growth and, 460–462
    United States, 479–481
Urban life. See also Cities
    fertility and, 449
Urban planning, 500–502
Urban renewal, 490–491

Value judgments, in sociology, 55–56
Vandalism, in schools, 359
Variables
    dependent, 437
    independent, 437
Vertical mobility, 248–250
Victimless crimes, 539
Violence, 25. See also Crime
    in schools, 359
    wife abuse, 8–9
Vital statistics, 440–441
Voluntary associations, 168–174
Voting behavior, 394–396
Voucher system, 361–362

Welfare spending, 385
Welfare state, 386
White-collar crime, 563–564
Wife abuse, 8–9
Women. See also Sex roles
    church and, 326–328
    employment and, 378
Women's liberation movement, 188, 218–219, 284, 415, 418, 420. See also Social movements
Work, 132, 375–379
    role conflict and, 146–147
World Council of Churches, 321
Writing, 71

XYY chromosome pattern, 190

Zero Population Growth (ZPG), 12, 54–55, 465–466

80 81 82 83 84 9 8 7 6 5 4 3 2 1